INTERNATIONAL RELATIONS
AND
WORLD POLITICS
SECURITY, ECONOMY, IDENTITY

Second Edition

Paul R. Viotti
UNIVERSITY OF DENVER

Mark V. Kauppi
DEPARTMENT OF DEFENSE

Prentice
Hall

Upper Saddle River, New Jersey 07458

Library of Congress Cataloging-in-Publication Data

Viotti, Paul R.
    International relations and world politics: security, economy, identity / Paul R. Viotti,
Mark V. Kauppi.—2nd ed.
      p. cm.
    Includes bibliographical references and index.
    ISBN 0-13-017277-4
    1. World politics—1989- 2. International relations. 3. Security, International. 4.
International trade. 5. Nationalism. I. Kauppi, Mark V. II. Title.

D860.V56 2001
327—dc21

00-058482

*The views expressed in this book are those of the authors and
do not necessarily reflect those of any part of the U.S. government.*

VP, Editorial Director: *Laura Pearson*
Assistant Editor: *Brian Prybella*
Editorial Assistant: *Jessica Drew*
AVP, Director of Manufacturing
  and Production: *Barbara Kittle*
Executive Managing Editor: *Ann Marie McCarthy*
Production Liaison: *Fran Russello*
Project Manager: *Linda B. Pawelchak*
Prepress and Manufacturing Manager: *Nick Sklitsis*
Prepress and Manufacturing Buyer: *Ben Smith*
Cover Director: *Jayne Conte*
Cover Design: *Bruce Kenselaar*

Cover Art: *Rob Day/Stock Illustration Source, Inc.*
Director of Marketing: *Beth Gillett Mejia*
Creative Design Director: *Leslie Osher*
Interior Art Director and Designer: *Kathryn Foot*
Dirctor, Image Resource Center: *Melinda Reo*
Interior Image Specialist: *Beth Boyd*
Photo Researcher: *Kathy Ringrose*
Manager, Rights and Permissions: *Kay Dellosa*
Electronic Art Creation: *Mirella Signoretto*
Manager, Production/Formatting and Art: *Guy Ruggiero*
Copy Editing: *Julie Hotchkiss*

This book was set in 10/12 Janson Text by TSI Graphics
and was printed and bound by Courier Companies, Inc.
The cover was printed by Phoenix Color Corp.

Photo credits begin on page 514, which constitutes
a continuation of this copyright page.

©2001, 1997 by Prentice-Hall, Inc.
A Division of Pearson Education
Upper Saddle River, New Jersey 07458

Printed in the United States of America
10 9 8 7 6 5 4 3 2 1

ISBN 0-13-017277-4

Prentice-Hall International (UK) Limited, *London*
Prentice-Hall of Australia Pty. Limited, *Sydney*
Prentice-Hall Canada Inc., *Toronto*
Prentice-Hall Hispanoamericana, S.A., *Mexico*
Prentice-Hall of India Private Limited, *New Delhi*
Prentice-Hall of Japan, Inc., *Tokyo*
Pearson Education Asia Pte., *Singapore*
Editora Prentice-Hall do Brasil, Ltda., *Rio de Janeiro*

To three scholars—

Ernst B. Haas,
James N. Rosenau, and
Kenneth N. Waltz—

whose diverse perspectives
on international relations
and world politics have so
profoundly influenced the
writing of this volume

CONTENTS ⪜

PART II   STATE SECURITY AND STATECRAFT

CHAPTER 3   **Interests, Objectives, and Power of States   72**

CHAPTER 4   **Diplomacy: Managing Relations Among States   102**

CHAPTER 5   **Military Force: War, Just Wars, and Armed Intervention   140**

PART III   INTERNATIONAL SECURITY

CHAPTER 8   **International Terrorism and Transnational Crime   248**

PART IV   CIVIL SOCIETY AND THE GLOBAL ECONOMY

CHAPTER 9   **An Emerging Global Civil Society: International Law,**
International Organization, and Globalization   278

BOX FEATURES

APPLYING THEORY

OTHER BOXES

PREFACE

This book is designed for use in courses on international relations or world politics. Unlike a number of such textbooks, we believe it is necessary and possible to introduce students to the literature on international relations (IR) theory. It is necessary because theory takes us beyond mere description of current events and into the realm of explanation and prediction of important trends. Theory helps us to focus on what is critical in making sense of the world around us. It is also possible, we believe, to introduce the student to IR works in such a manner that the literature is accessible and understandable yet does justice to the complexity and sophistication of the original works.

Further structure for this book is provided by emphasizing

- *Two trends*—interdependence and crises of authority—that characterize the international system

- *Key concepts*—in particular, security, economy, and identity

- *Key actors*—states, international organizations, and transnational organizations and movements (such as nongovernmental organizations, multinational corporations, and terrorist groups)

- *Two basic images or perspectives* on world politics—realism and pluralism (or liberalism, as pluralist thinking is frequently called). These images are reflected in the title of this volume—realism focusing primarily (though not exclusively) on security in international (or interstate) relations and pluralism tending to take the broader view that goes well beyond the state and relations among states to encompass a wide array of nonstate actors interacting transnationally on a greater diversity of issues

Our goal, therefore, is to provide the basic theoretical and conceptual tools required to make some sense out of the often confusing realm of world politics.

In discussing contemporary international relations and world politics, however, we agree with P. G. Wodehouse's character Bertie Wooster that in telling a tangled story it is fatal to assume the reader knows how matters got to where they are. Hence, compared to many other textbooks, we devote a significant amount of space to the historical development of various international systems and some of the great thinkers associated with world politics. We operate under the assumption that it is difficult to determine what is new about the current world system unless we know what it has in common with the past. We also believe that in order to understand the functioning and future development of the international system, a basic understanding of economics and international political economy is an imperative.

We are grateful to our colleagues for their careful reading of the manuscript and for their insightful suggestions: Charles Bukowski (Bradley University), William O. Chittick (University of Georgia), Larry Elowitz (Georgia College), Harvey Nelsen (University of South Florida), John F. L. Ross (Northeastern University), David E. Schmitt (Northeastern University), Stafford T. Thomas (California State Universitry, Chico), Richard R. Weiner (Rhode Island College), George DeMartino, David Goldfischer, and Micheline Ishay (all of the Graduate School of International Studies, University of Denver), Pauletta Otis (University of Southern Colorado), and Christopher Carr (Air University). Warren Miller's inputs on the globalization and economics chapters were particularly helpful. We wish to thank the following reviewers for their suggestions: Roxanne L. Doty, Arizona State University; Dr. Larry Elowitz, Georgia College and State University; Steven W. Hook, Kent State University; Larry F. Martinez, California State University, Long Beach; and Dr. Bob Switky, SUNY Brockport.

We would also like to thank our friends at Prentice Hall for their support throughout the writing and production process, especially Beth Gillett Mejia, Brian Prybella, and Linda Pawelchak for this edition and Jennie Katsaros, Barbara Reilly, Karen Horton, and Tom Kubiak for the first edition.

Finally, we wish to thank our immediate families for the many animated discussions of world politics down through the years, whether the venue be Europe, Asia, the dining room table, or more recently Internet e-mail. Beyond moral support, we are also indebted to them for substantive contributions, in particular Kathleen's insights on diplomacy, Linda's comments on the flow and pace of the manuscript, Michelle's and Paul's inputs on economics, and David's perspectives on just war and questions of international law.

Market Size by Gross Domestic Product, 1996

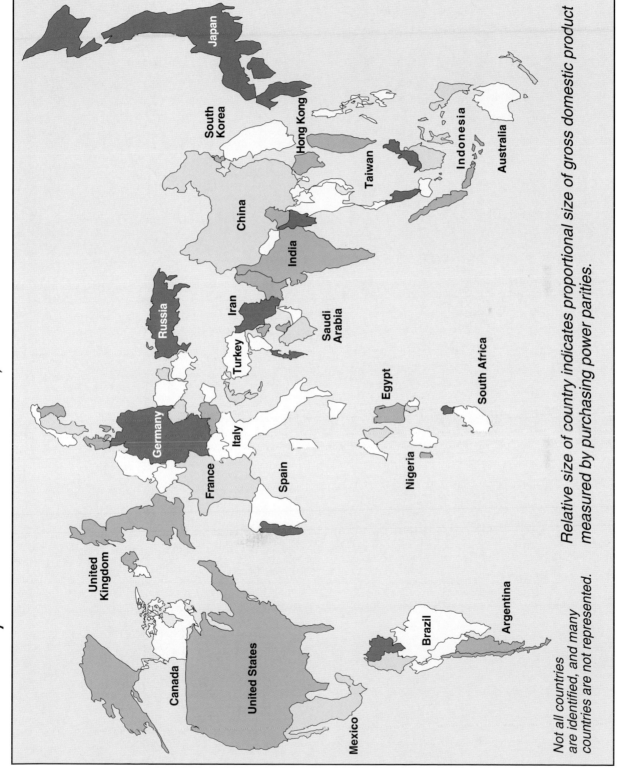

Relative size of country indicates proportional size of gross domestic product measured by purchasing power parities.

Not all countries are identified, and many countries are not represented.

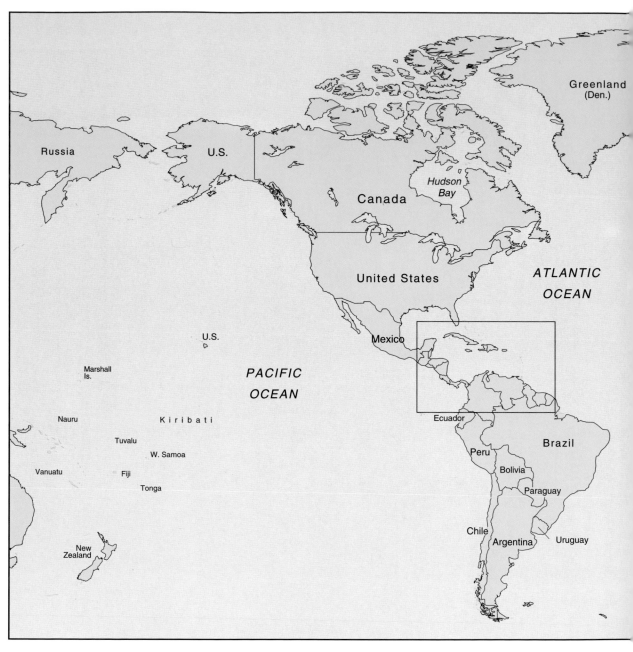

Greenland
(Den.)

Russia

U.S.

Canada

Hudson
Bay

ATLANTIC
OCEAN

United States

U.S.

Mexico

Marshall
Is.

PACIFIC
OCEAN

Ecuador

Nauru

K i r i b a t i

Brazil

Tuvalu

Peru

W. Samoa

Bolivia

Vanuatu

Fiji

Paraguay

Tonga

Chile

Uruguay

New
Zealand

Argentina

Bahamas

Cuba

Dom.
Rep.

St. Kitts and
Nevis

Guatemala

Haiti

Antigua and
Barbuda

Belize

Jamaica

Puerto Rico
(u.s.)

Guadeloupe (Fr.)

Honduras

Dominica

Martinique (Fr.)

El
Salvador

Nicaragua

St. Vincent And
The Grenadines

St. Lucia

Barbados

Grenada

Panama

Trinidad and
Tobago

Costa
Rica

Venezuela

French
Guiana

Guyana

Colombia

Suriname

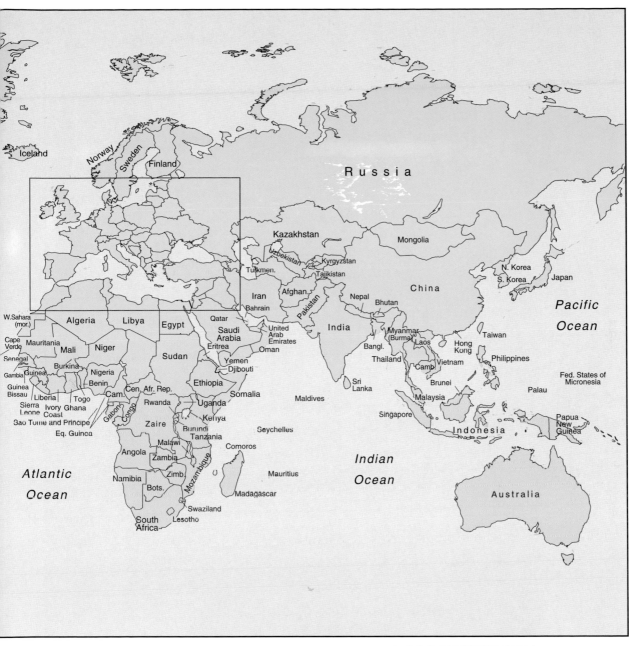

Iceland
Norway
Sweden
Finland
Russia
Kazakhstan
Mongolia
Uzbekistan
Kyrgyzstan
Turkmen.
Tajikistan
N. Korea
S. Korea
Japan
Iran
Afghan.
China
Pacific
Ocean
Bahrain
Pakistan
Nepal
Bhutan
W.Sahara
(mor.)
Algeria
Libya
Egypt
Qatar
India
Taiwan
Cape
Verde
Mauritania
Mali
Niger
United
Arab
Emirates
Saudi
Arabia
Eritrea
Oman
Myanmar
(Burma)
Laos
Hong
Kong
Senegal
Sudan
Yemen
Djibouti
Bangl.
Thailand
Vietnam
Philippines
Gambia
Guinea
Burkina
Nigeria
Benin
Camb.
Guinea
Bissau
Liberia
Togo
Cen. Afr. Rep.
Ethiopia
Somalia
Sri
Lanka
Brunei
Fed. States of
Micronesia
Sierra
Leone
Ivory
Coast
Ghana
Cam.
Congo
Rwanda
Uganda
Maldives
Malaysia
Palau
Sao Tome and Principe
Eq. Guinea
Gabon
Zaire
Kenya
Burundi
Tanzania
Seychelles
Singapore
Indonesia
Papua
New
Guinea
Malawi
Angola
Zambia
Comoros
Indian
Ocean
Atlantic
Ocean
Namibia
Zimb.
Mozambique
Mauritius
Australia
Bots.
Madagascar
Swaziland
South
Africa
Lesotho

Norway
Sweden
Estonia
Russia
DENMARK
Latvia
Ireland
Lithuania
(Russia)
Great
Britain
Neth.
Belarus
Poland
Germany
Belgium
Czech
Rep.
Moldova
Lux.
Liech.
Slovakia
Ukraine
France
Switz.
Austria
Hungary
Romania
Slovenia
Croatia
Andorra
Monaco
San
Marino
Bosnia
& Herz.
Yugo.
Bulgaria
Georgia
Portugal
Spain
Italy
Albania
Macedonia
Turkey
Armenia
Azerbaijan
Gibraltar
Malta
Greece
Cyprus
Syria
Iran
Morocco
Tunisia
Lebanon
West
Bank
Iraq
Israel
Kuwait
Algeria

Europe

Atlantic Ocean

★ Reykjavik
Iceland

Sweden

Norway

Finland

Russian Federation

• Helsinki

• Oslo

Belfast

Scotland

• Edinburgh

North Sea

• Stockholm

Baltic Sea

• Tallinn
Estonia

• Moscow

DENMARK

• Riga
Latvia

Russian Federation

Lithuania

• Vilnius

Rep. of Ireland

• Dublin

England

Netherlands

• London

• Copenhagen

• Amsterdam

• Berlin

Belgium
• Brussels

• Bonn

Germany

• Luxembourg

• Warsaw

Poland

Belarus

• Minsk

• Kiev

Paris

France

• Prague

Czech Republic

• Vienna

Slovakia

• Bratislava

Ukraine

Moldova

• Berne
SWITZERLAND

• Liechtenstein

Austria

• Budapest

Hungary

Romania

• Bucharest

Black Sea

• Ljubljana

1

• Zagreb

4a

Italy

2

3 • Sarajevo

Belgrade

4

Bulgaria

• Sofia

• Istanbul

• Rome

5

4b

Andorra

6 • Skopje

Portugal

• Madrid

Spain

• Tirane

Lisbon

Gibraltar

Albania

Greece

Turkey

Ceuta(Sp)

Melilla(Sp.)

Mediterranean Sea

• Athens

1. Slovenia
2. Croatia
3. Bosnia–Herzegovina
4. Serbia
4a. Vojvodina
4b. Kosovo
5. Montenegro
6. Macedonia

Africa

kilometres
0   1000
0   miles   500

Middle East and Asia

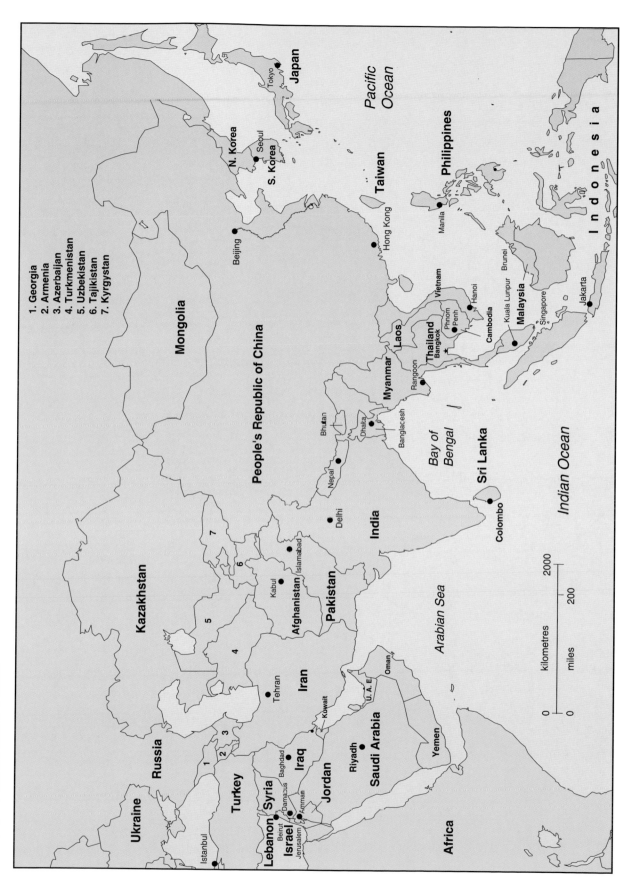

South America

Panama

Caracas
Venezuela

Trinidad and Tobago

Bogota

Georgetown
Guyana
Paramaribo
Cayenne
Suriname
French Guiana

Colombia

North Atlantic Ocean

Quito
Ecuador

Peru

Brazil

Lima

Bolivia

Brasilia

La Paz

Pacific Ocean

PARAGUAY

Asuncion

CHILE

South Atlantic Ocean

Uruguay

Santiago

Buenos Aires
Montevideo

Argentlna

0   miles   500

0   kilometres   1000

Falkland
Islands
(UK)

Africa: Dates of Independence Since 1945

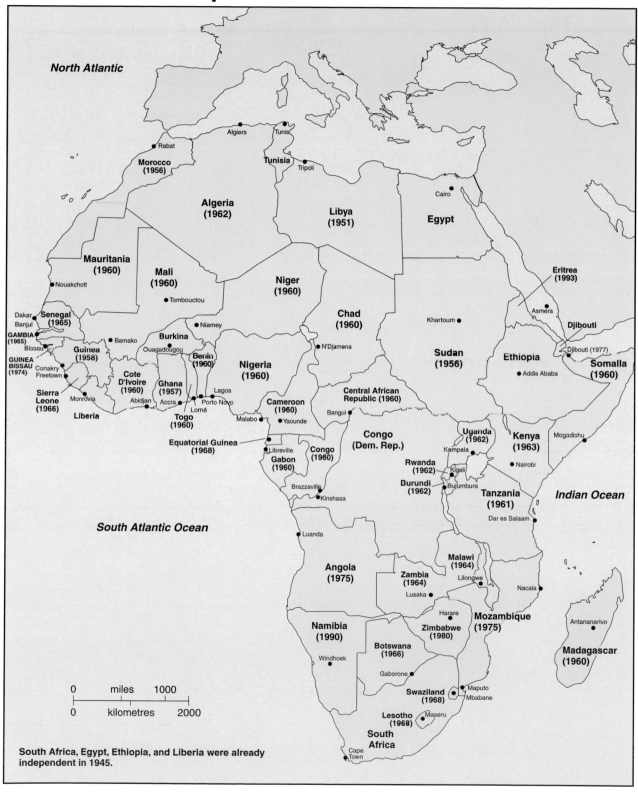

North Atlantic

Algiers
Tunis
Rabat
**Morocco
(1956)**
Tunisia
Tripoli

**Algeria
(1962)**
**Libya
(1951)**
Egypt
Cairo

**Mauritania
(1960)**
**Mali
(1960)**
Nouakchott
Tombouctou
**Niger
(1960)**
**Chad
(1960)**
Khartoum
**Eritrea
(1993)**
Asmera
Djibouti

Dakar
**Senegal
(1965)**
Banjul
**GAMBIA
(1965)**
Bissau
**GUINEA
BISSAU
(1974)**
**Guinea
(1958)**
Bamako
Niamey
Burkina
Ouagadougou
**Benin
(1960)**
**Nigeria
(1960)**
N'Djamena
**Sudan
(1956)**
Ethiopia
Addis Ababa
Djibouti (1977)
**Somalia
(1960)**

Conakry
Freetown
**Cote
D'Ivoire
(1960)**
**Ghana
(1957)**
Abidjan
Accra
Lomé
Lagos
Porto Novo
**Sierra
Leone
(1966)**
Monrovia
Liberia
**Togo
(1960)**
**Cameroon
(1960)**
Malabo
Yaounde
**Central African
Republic (1960)**
Bangui

**Equatorial Guinea
(1968)**
Libreville
**Gabon
(1960)**
**Congo
(1960)**
Brazzaville
Kinshasa
**Congo
(Dem. Rep.)**
**Uganda
(1962)**
Kampala
**Rwanda
(1962)**
Kigali
**Burundi
(1962)**
Bujumbura
**Kenya
(1963)**
Nairobi
Mogadishu
**Tanzania
(1961)**
Indian Ocean
Dar es Salaam

South Atlantic Ocean

Luanda
**Angola
(1975)**
**Zambia
(1964)**
Lusaka
**Malawi
(1964)**
Lilongwe
Nacala

Harare
**Mozambique
(1975)**
Antananarivo

**Namibia
(1990)**
**Botswana
(1966)**
Windhoek
**Zimbabwe
(1980)**
Gaborone
Maputo
Mbabane
**Swaziland
(1968)**
**Madagascar
(1960)**

**Lesotho
(1968)**
Maseru
**South
Africa**
Cape Town

0   miles   1000
0   kilometres   2000

South Africa, Egypt, Ethiopia, and Liberia were already
independent in 1945.

The World in 1945

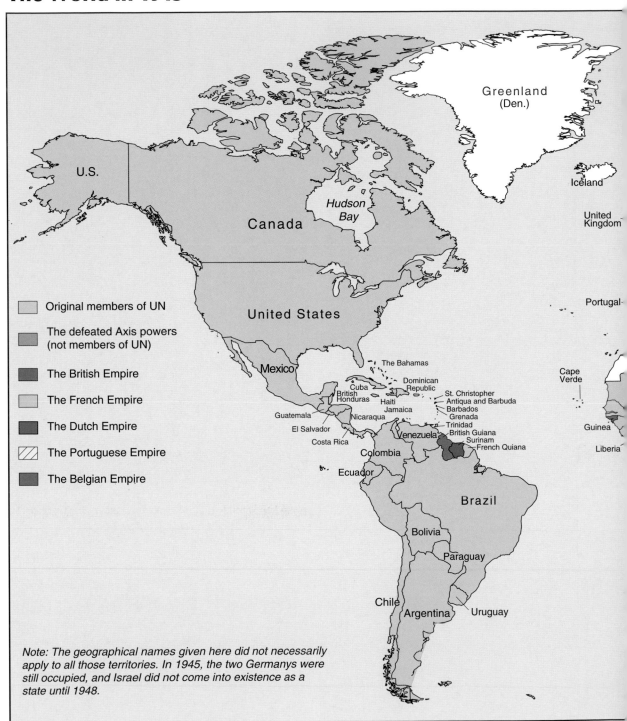

Greenland
(Den.)

Iceland

United
Kingdom

Portugal

U.S.

Canada

Hudson
Bay

United States

Mexico

The Bahamas

Cuba
Dominican
Republic

British
Honduras

Haiti

Jamaica

St. Christopher
Antiqua and Barbuda
Barbados
Grenada
Trinidad

Guatemala

Nicaraqua

El Salvador

Costa Rica

Venezuela

British Guiana
Surinam
French Quiana

Colombia

Ecuador

Brazil

Bolivia

Paraguay

Chile

Argentina

Uruguay

Cape
Verde

Guinea

Liberia

☐ Original members of UN

▨ The defeated Axis powers
(not members of UN)

■ The British Empire

☐ The French Empire

■ The Dutch Empire

▨ The Portuguese Empire

■ The Belgian Empire

*Note: The geographical names given here did not necessarily
apply to all those territories. In 1945, the two Germanys were
still occupied, and Israel did not come into existence as a
state until 1948.*

The Islamic World

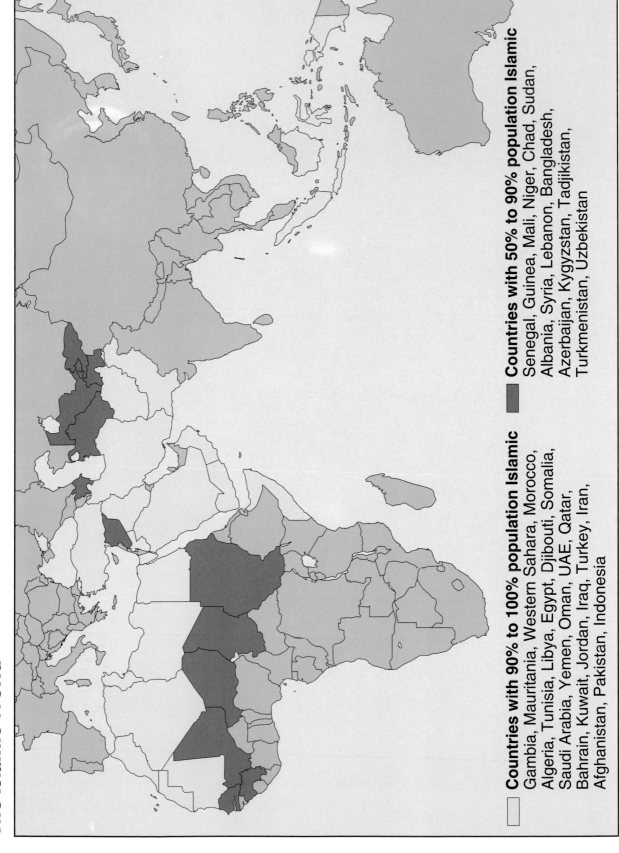

Countries with 90% to 100% population Islamic
Gambia, Mauritania, Western Sahara, Morocco, Algeria, Tunisia, Libya, Egypt, Djibouti, Somalia, Saudi Arabia, Yemen, Oman, UAE, Qatar, Bahrain, Kuwait, Jordan, Iraq, Turkey, Iran, Afghanistan, Pakistan, Indonesia

Countries with 50% to 90% population Islamic
Senegal, Guinea, Mali, Niger, Chad, Sudan, Albania, Syria, Lebanon, Bangladesh, Azerbaijan, Kygyzstan, Tadjikistan, Turkmenistan, Uzbekistan

INTERNATIONAL RELATIONS
AND
WORLD POLITICS

INTRODUCTION: TRENDS, CONCEPTS, ACTORS, AND PERSPECTIVES

"The obscurest epoch is today."

ROBERT LOUIS STEVENSON, AUTHOR OF *TREASURE ISLAND*

"We playwrights, who have to cram a whole human life or an entire historical era in a two-hour play, can scarcely understand this rapidity [of change in Europe] ourselves. And if it gives us trouble, think of the trouble it must give to political scientists who spend their whole life studying the realm of the probable and have less experience with the realm of the improbable than us, the playwrights."

VACLAV HAVEL, PRESIDENT OF CZECHOSLOVAKIA

"Developments in science and social organization are altering the world profoundly—too profoundly for conventional habits of thinking to grasp. History suggests that mankind rarely understands revolutionary change at the time it is coming about."

FORMER U.S. SECRETARY OF STATE GEORGE P. SHULTZ

CHAPTER 1

In the summer of 1967, Jim McCool, a recent college graduate and survivor of Marine Corps boot camp, arrived at Danang, Vietnam, for his first tour in that war-torn country. The cold war was a hot war in this corner of the world: "One of the things I remember most of all is traveling on the highway from Chu Lai to Danang. The fields were deserted, and we were always on a high level of alert. We never went up or down that road without armored personnel carriers, tanks, and air cover. It was unnerving, to say the least." He's handed a magazine with a full-page advertisement for Thai Airlines. It shows a picture of an ancient temple and the accompanying words: "Ancient Danang. Another first in time travel from THAI. How would you like to travel back two hundred years in only ninety minutes? Beginning October 31st, THAI flies three times a week to Danang—the gateway to Central Vietnam." McCool shakes his head and smiles ruefully. "Yeh, times sure have changed."

Wang Qishan, age 36, is a successful businessman in China. Once a sheet-metal worker in a state-owned factory, he exemplifies a new value system that is taking hold and rejects the ideals of the communist state. His first business venture was a four-table restaurant in Shenyang. "It was the early '80s," Wang said, "people looked down on us private guys. They thought we were bandits. While everyone else was going to work without a care, I was out there pushing a tricycle piled high with vegetables, sweating, trying to make a few bucks. It was the worst thing you could be in China at the time. I was outside the system." But Wang continued to work hard, and today he owns a drive-in movie theater and runs a private school, and China's state-run television has done a documentary on his business.[1]

Such vignettes illustrate how much has changed politically and economically over recent years. The fall of the Berlin Wall in November 1989 symbolically marked the beginning of the end of the cold war, setting the stage for the reunification of Germany and the collapse of the Soviet empire. When on December 25, 1991, the communist hammer and sickle flag was lowered for the last time from the Kremlin palace in Moscow, the cold war was definitely over. There was no formal declaration, no surrender, no peace conference or fireworks.

During the late 1940s and 1950s, the cold war label was first used to describe crises in such diverse locations as Germany, Cuba, and the Middle East, as well as "hot" wars in Korea and Vietnam. During this period a series of related concepts developed. Much of the world, for example, was conveniently divided into East versus West or capitalist versus communist. The Soviet Union and the United States had the largest industrial economies and were termed *superpowers* in that no other states could come close to the magnitude or size of their economic or military—particularly nuclear—capabilities. When the American president met with the leader of the Soviet Union, it was called a summit and was guaranteed worldwide media coverage. The major military alliances were the North Atlantic Treaty Organization (NATO) in the West and the Warsaw Pact in the East.

The world's political, military, ideological, and even economic fault lines were captured by these cold war dualities. Even developing or poverty-stricken countries—despite their diversity—came to identify themselves as the **Third World** in contrast to the **First World** of the capitalist West and the **Second World** of the communist East.

Such concepts allowed observers to orient themselves, make sense of the world around them, and impose a certain degree of order. Without such simplifying road maps, the world appeared unintelligible and chaotic, if not frightening.

[1]"Chinese Search for New Values," *Washington Post*, September 26, 1999, p. A28.

Despite such fears as a superpower conflict escalating into a nuclear holocaust, political leaders were nevertheless at least able to devise relatively coherent policies and gain support around the world from states and societies sharing either Marxist-Leninist or anticommunist orientations.

For many people—politicians as well as publics—the current state of the world lacks any such coherence. It is revealing that the most common description of today is the "post-cold war era." Note that this concept essentially describes the world in terms of what it is not—it is not the cold war. But then what is it? The *New York Times* asked its readers to submit suggestions, and the responses ranged from the serious to the whimsical—Millenni-end, the Muddle Ages, the Internetcine Era, the Centrifugal Age, the Citizen's Century, the Transnational Era, and the Age That Even Historians From Harvard Can't Name.[2]

The range of responses reflects the uncertainty and, we would suggest, the uneasiness that pervades seasoned observers as well as common citizens when they contemplate the state of the world today. There continues to be a real sense of drift and disorientation. The end of the cold war stimulated debates and creative thinking about where the world is headed and how best to analyze it. Would the end of the cold war mean the end of NATO and the United States–Japanese alliance? Would Japan and Germany reassert themselves? Would the United States become more isolationist? Would the West in particular now spend less money on defense and more on foreign aid and ameliorating the political, social, and economic problems of the developing world? Would global economic and welfare issues come to predominate over political-military concerns? Would the United Nations play a more significant role on the global stage?

The fall of the Berlin Wall at the end of 1989 has come to represent symbolically the end of the cold war.

[2]"No Time Like the Present to Leave Something for Posterity," *New York Times*, April 2, 1995, sec. 4, p. 7. See also "Naming an Era," *Foreign Policy*, No. 119 (Summer 2000): 29–69.

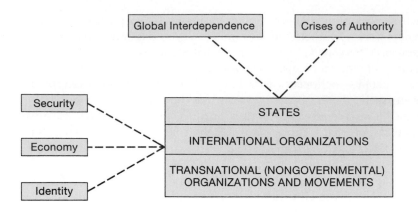

FIGURE 1.1   CONCEPTS

Particular events seemed to clarify the situation temporarily. Iraq's invasion of Kuwait in 1991 and Iraq's subsequent defeat in the Gulf War by a U.S.-led coalition buoyed the hopes of many that we were entering a "new world order" in which aggression anywhere would be met by a multilateral response. Events in the former Yugoslavia, however, have proven to be a particularly trying series of tests for the United Nations and NATO in particular. The NATO effort to end Serb aggression in Kosovo in 1999 actually raised more questions than it answered in terms of international relations. For example, Kosovo is a province of Serb-dominated Yugoslavia and the NATO military campaign was launched against Yugoslavia despite the fact that Yugoslavia committed no acts of aggression against any NATO state. Does this mean that states are now more likely to intervene under the banner of humanitarian intervention and violate a state's **sovereignty** in the name of human rights? If so, is this a good or bad thing?

Defining the current era is a task that can be deferred, but there is another task that cannot. The purpose of this textbook is to help the reader gain a better understanding of the shape of the emergent world order. This requires making some basic judgment calls about current and emergent key trends, concepts, and actors. Because it is impossible to discuss every aspect of world politics, we must be selective. The fulfillment of this task depends on the development of a game plan, road map, theory, or conceptual framework that provides guidance concerning what to look at and what to discard. Such a framework also influences how we interpret what it is we have chosen to examine. The game plan we have devised is depicted in Figure 1.1.

TRENDS

interdependence A situation in which actions and events in one state, society, or part of the world affect peoples elsewhere. There is some degree of mutual dependence or reciprocal ties and effects among the parties involved.

Global Interdependence

The two key trends we wish to emphasize are *increasing globalization and global interdependence* on the one hand and *crises of authority* on the other. *Interdependence* refers to a situation in which actions and events in one part of the world affect people elsewhere. For interdependence to exist, there must be some degree of mutual dependence or reciprocal effects in relations between or among states or other actors. In most cases the relationship is asymmetric, meaning one party is more affected than the other. As we will see in Chapter Two, interdependence is not new, but *global* interdependence is a relatively recent phenomenon.

Global interdependence is exemplified in the *economic realm* by the formation and accelerated growth of a global capitalist economy that increasingly disregards state boundaries and makes economic **autarky** (self-sufficiency) virtually impossible. Multinational corporations (MNCs), for example, are more beholden to stockholders and other interested parties—whatever their nationality—than to any one state. Trade integration—the share of trade volume in **gross domestic product**—has continued to increase steadily over the last two decades from 30 percent or less to more than 40 or 50 percent.[3]

Similarly, global financial linkages continue to grow rapidly:

- Daily foreign exchange trading was about $10 to $20 billion in the early 1980s, but by the 1990s the figure was $800 billion, and today it is more than a trillion dollars a day!

- The combination of world stock and bond markets plus markets in financial futures, options, and swaps accounts for an additional trading volume of some $10 to $20 trillion annually.

- International bank lending grew from $40 billion in 1975 to more than $300 billion by 1990, an upward trend that continues in the twenty-first century.

- Major foreign stock exchanges operate in London, Tokyo, Paris, and Frankfurt. Their interdependence is exemplified by the fact that when the New York Stock Exchange fell 508 points in October 1987, equity value fell by an average of 30 percent worldwide.[4] Upward or downward shifts in one market frequently have ripple effects with comparable swings in other markets.

Perhaps a more easily grasped example comes from the television commercials of credit card companies: Whether cruising in the Mediterranean, exploring a Middle Eastern bazaar, or wandering the back roads of Latin America, one seemingly can always obtain ready cash.

The communications revolution has been particularly important in the growth of economic interdependence. As noted, it has encouraged the globalization of financial markets, which can be influenced instantly by electronically communicated buy and sell orders. An investor no longer even has to utilize a broker but can engage in financial transactions via the Internet from the comfort of home.

Communications networks also allow work to be parceled out anywhere in the world, rendering geographical distances irrelevant. In the Philippines, for example, a company specializing in data entry keys in such diverse information as patient hospital records from Pomona, California, and Greensboro, North Carolina; the names and addresses of U.S. purchasers of Stride Rite Shoes; articles from *Playboy* and the *Christian Science Monitor*; and presidential speeches, French novels, and the card catalogue of the National Library of Helsinki, Finland. Or consider the fire department of Malmo, Sweden: Its database of street routes is managed by computers at General Electric in Cleveland, Ohio.[5]

---

[3]Erik R. Peterson, "Surrendering to Markets," *Washington Quarterly*, v. 18, no. 4 (1995): 104. The developed states are members of the Organization for Economic Cooperation and Development.

[4]Roy C. Smith, "Risk and Volatility," *Washington Quarterly*, v. 18, no. 4 (Autumn 1995): 117; Ethan B. Kapstein, "Governing Global Finance," *Washington Quarterly*, v. 17, no. 2 (Spring 1994): 77.

[5]John Maxwell Hamilton, *Entangling Alliances: How the Third World Shapes Our Lives* (Cabin John, Md.: Seven Locks Press, 1990), pp. 27–28.

Global interdependence is also evident in the *social realm*. Satellites facilitate virtually instantaneous Cable News Network (CNN) coverage of famines, civil wars, and airplane hijackings from heretofore remote spots on the globe, altering our perception of distances. Satellites and cable also bring programs from different countries and cultures into student union buildings and homes around the world, often to the distress of parents and governments worried about "cultural pollution" or the allegedly pernicious effects of foreign values. Global communications webs—exemplified by the Internet—allow people to communicate easily with one another, in a manner that few experts ten years ago even imagined being possible. For governments there is a difficult trade-off: While such media as the Internet help transmit scientific information essential to economic development, such networks also allow political dissidents to communicate with the outside world or encourage global dissemination of potentially dangerous information, such as how to build a powerful explosive device.

GLOBAL SPORTS

The globalization of sports is largely the result of the transportation and communications revolutions. Just as a U.S. national sports market did not exist until radio and later television reached into homes across America (and jets made transcontinental travel feasible), it is only in recent years that American and other countries' sports have become of global interest. It is estimated, for example, that more than 400 million households (100 million of which were in China) watched the National Basketball Association title game in 1992, setting a milestone in the globalization of sports. ESPN and other networks have continued to expand into foreign television markets, not only broadcasting games from North America, but also from around the world. Thanks to satellites, Michael Jordan, the former basketball superstar, became a celebrity in China, Germany, and South Africa. Soccer games, popular throughout the world, now draw global audiences.

Globalization is also evident in the ethnic makeup of many American sports teams. In 1996, more than 100 non–North Americans played in the National Hockey League. Latin Americans—for years key players on many baseball teams—are even more prevalent in baseball today and have been joined by a handful of Asians. The 1996 Dodgers pitching staff, for example, on opening day included a player from Japan, two from Mexico, two from the Dominican Republic, and one from Korea. The pitching ace of the 1999 world champion New York Yankees was from Cuba, and another member of the staff was from Japan. Furthermore major league baseball is investigating the feasibility of adding teams in such countries as Mexico and Japan.

Point: In addition to sports already popular in many countries, even the American pastime, baseball, has taken on an increasingly global character.

Source: Adapted from "The (Multi)National Pastime," *Los Angeles Times*, March 31, 1996, PM1.

Increasing global interdependence is also evident in the military *strategic realm*. Modern technology has led to the development of powerful weapons that have the potential to put all countries at risk. Strategic interdependence was demonstrated in cold war relations between the United States and the Soviet Union, whose respective nuclear forces could obliterate each other's countries. Elaborate monitoring and communications systems were designed to minimize this possibility. In the modern world, however, the existence of weapons of mass destruction (nuclear, chemical, biological) as well as powerful conventional weapons has increased, to varying degrees, the vulnerability of all states. Nor will such weapons always necessarily be limited to states: Terrorist groups or other organizations with a political or religious agenda could conceivably turn to such weapons.

Finally we would note that the world's growing interdependence is also evident in the way global issues are interlinked. It is increasingly difficult to view any one issue in isolation. For example world population growth has both socioeconomic and political dimensions. If population growth outstrips the ability of a society and its economy to feed and clothe its burgeoning masses, political unrest may result, which then spills over into neighboring states and societies.

Crises of Authority

Growing global interdependence is one obvious trend in world politics. But there is another trend that seems at first to be running in the opposite direction—***crises of authority***. Where authority exists, individuals and groups follow because they believe that those in authority have the legitimate right to lead. Parents, teachers, religious leaders, and business executives all may be authority figures, but in the realm of world politics the concept is most closely associated with states and their governing officials. Consequently, the crisis of authority has been most evident in the disintegration of states and state authority, exemplified by the demise of the former Soviet Union and Yugoslavia. Ethnic conflicts in many other states threaten to rip them apart. It is manifested around the world, however, in a number of other ways—terrorist movements in Egypt and Algeria attempting to overthrow regimes; the power of drug organizations in Colombia and Mexico; and the collapse of public order in cities in West Africa that are virtually controlled at night by armed burglars, carjackers, and muggers. Ironically, the erosion of state authority in part is due to the actions of states themselves: Foreign humanitarian intervention in the name of human rights undercuts state authority. Similarly the strengthening of the powers of the European Union (EU) sometimes comes at the expense of its constituent states' ability to make unilateral decisions.

The crisis of authority also stems from a growing cynicism among citizens about their political leaders and institutions, resulting in the public's withdrawal from politics. It is also bred from a sense of personal, not national, insecurity arising from government's inability to protect citizens from such events as gas attacks on subways (Tokyo, February 1995) or truck bombs placed in public areas (World Trade Center, February 1993 and Oklahoma City, March 1995). For some, the response has been not withdrawal but rather a shift of loyalty from the state or society to some smaller entity, perhaps an ethnic group or geographic locality. Conversely, one may transfer loyalty to an entity, movement, or ideal that transcends the state. Examples include support for world government, transnational religious identification, or a cosmopolitan belief that one is a citizen of the world.

Connections and Cautions

It can be argued that global interdependence and crises of authority are interconnected. For example, with the growth of the global economy, states increasingly believe they are unable to exert influence—let alone control—over their domestic economies. Global competition leads to the collapse of certain industries as cheaper

authority A legitimate right to direct or command and to make, decide, and enforce rules. Authority has a moral or legal quality to it in contrast to brute force or coercion.

Not everyone loves globalization. Protestors in Seattle, Washington, in November 1999 representing trade unions, environmentalists, and human rights groups hold the World Trade Organization responsible for many of the excesses and failures of global capitalism.

labor is available elsewhere or as companies simply move their production facilities to lower-cost countries. The American steel industry lost much of its market to Japan, which in turn lost much of it to South Korea. The resultant anger or discontent of displaced workers is often directed at not only business executives but also at government leaders, who are judged to have failed to protect domestic jobs from foreign competition. A good example are the riots and demonstrations that occurred in Seattle, Washington, in November 1999 in protest of the meeting of the World Trade Organization.

Particularly in Third World countries, where the source of foreign income is often limited to a few basic commodities, the power of the global economy can have a devastating effect. If there is a drop in copper, tin, or rubber prices, for example, the resultant unemployment is not cushioned by such state support programs as exist, for instance, in many advanced-industrial, high-income countries. The problem is compounded in those less-developed countries with high birth rates and a limited capacity to absorb young persons into the workforce.

 CASE & oint

GLOBAL INTERDEPENDENCE:
A CAUTIONARY TALE

The global financial tremors caused by the downturn of the U.S. stock market in 1987 are often cited as evidence of increasing global economic interdependence. The integration of world financial markets means a major downturn in any one market can have a substantial effect on all markets. But is the global role of the American economy and stock market perhaps unique? Consider the case of Asia. Asian markets collapsed in 1997, and many analysts and brokers recommended that investors get out of the stock market at least temporarily until the global impact of Asia's downturn had played itself out. But the American stock market actually proceeded to move to new heights, with the Dow Jones Industrial Average eventually crossing the 10,000 threshold. Similar fears about Russia's economic problems in 1998 also seemed to have little impact on the U.S. stock market.

Point: *Global* interdependence does not equate to *mutual* dependence; not all states are equally affected by various crises or trends.

Such conditions are ripe for political and social discontent and a loss of governmental authority.

In all nations, there is a real sense that the world is rapidly growing smaller, and we are only now considering what this implies. It must be emphasized, however, that all people do not experience the impact of interdependence equally over the globe. Interdependence is neither a uniform nor a homogeneous condition. There is no doubt that advanced industrial states in Europe, North America, and Japan are much more economically and politically interdependent with one another than they are with the countries of sub-Saharan Africa. Although commercials for computer firms would have us believe that the communications revolution is already well entrenched in Tibetan monasteries and Brazilian rain forests, this is simply not the case. Similarly, areas of the euphemistically termed *developing world* are not equal players in the global economy. In fact, they are dependent on, and sometimes see themselves as exploited by, better-off countries.

The severity of crises of authority also varies. In the United States, a crisis of authority is seen by many to be reflected in low voter turnouts for elections and hence is really a matter of political disillusionment. In other countries, by contrast, crises of authority are serious and are reflected in street riots, military coups, insurgencies, and revolutions.

Finally we want to note that the concepts of interdependence and crises of authority are not limited in their applicability to the contemporary era. As we will see in the next chapter, interdependence characterizes a number of historical international systems over the past two thousand years, just as crises of authority help to explain the American Revolution in 1776, the French Revolution in 1789, and the Russian Revolution in 1917. What is different today, however, is the extent and depth of interdependence and its global character. Two hundred years ago, letters took weeks if not months to make their way from one end of Europe to another, just as cultural and political influences and trends took time to affect distant societies. Today all that has changed.

GLOBALIZATION: HOW NEW?

Globalization or internationalization has been depicted, for much of the past twenty years, as a condition of the present and the future—a phenomenon without a past. For both its admirers and its opponents, it is associated with new and unprecedented technologies: the Internet, international capital markets, supersonic travel, cable news, and just-in-time deliveries across very large distances. But there is indeed a history of globalization. There have been several such periods over the past 250 years: The export and investment booms of the 1860s and the early twentieth century are just two of the more dramatic examples.

Yet international history must be far more than the history of the relations between nations in terms of their diplomacy, or their wars, or their conquests and empires. It is more than the history of exports and imports. It is more, too, than a comparative history; it must be a history of relations between individuals and cultures, including individuals who belong to several different cultures at the same time or who move between different identities, languages, countries of residence, and even nationalities.

Source: Emma Rothschild, "Globalization and the Return of History," *Foreign Affairs* (Summer 1999): 187–188.

IT'S BEEN SAID...

CONCEPTS

Global interdependence and crises of authority have been presented as trends in world politics, but they are also **concepts**. You have already been introduced to a number of concepts (highlighted in boldface type) in this chapter. A concept is a construct or idea of a general or abstract nature that refers to a particular phenomenon such as war or peace. Concepts are important because they are the building blocks for theories that attempt to explain or predict international trends and events.

We have found that a significant number of students are suspicious or intimidated by the challenge of thinking conceptually or theoretically. How, it is justifiably asked, does thinking conceptually help me understand the "real world"? An example may help make this clear.

Ask yourself and attempt to answer the following question: Why did the Yugoslav regime in Belgrade decide to engage in "ethnic cleansing" of Muslims in the province of Kosovo, precipitating NATO's air war in 1999? You might have pointed to the role of Yugoslavian president Slobodan Milosevic who has the dubious distinction of being the first sitting leader of a country to be indicted for war crimes. Numerous analysts have noted that his personality is marked by an apparently insatiable desire for power and control. You might also have noted that Yugoslavia was a multiethnic state created in 1918 and consisted of such major groups as Slovenes, Croats, Muslims, and Serbs, the latter two with a particularly long history of confrontation. Hence it may have been conflicting ethnic identities that led to the numerous internal wars in the former Yugoslavia. Or perhaps the war resulted from a group of Serbian political and military leaders deciding that having already lost Slovenia and Croatia to independence and failing to achieve its aims in Bosnia, Kosovo would not be allowed to follow the same path. Perhaps the seeds of the war in Kosovo, however, are to be found in the virtual global collapse of communism as an ideology and the actual disintegration of the Soviet empire. With the independence of many former Soviet republics and Eastern European states and calls for national self-determination, the international environment encouraged similar calls in the Yugoslav federation and sparked a Serbian backlash in an effort to keep the country together under Serbian dominance.

All of these explanations can be found in the outpouring of books, magazine and journal articles, and media punditry dealing with Kosovo in recent years. Whatever explanation or combination of explanations proves to be correct or most persuasive is not our concern here. Rather it is to use this example to introduce the utility of the concept *levels of analysis*. Using levels of analysis is a popular way to organize systematic thinking about various aspects of world politics. Figure 1.2 illustrates one version.

Note how the levels proceed from the individual to larger and larger aggregations. In our example, the individual level of analysis would focus on the personality of Slobodan Milosevic. The group level would examine Milosevic in the broader context of other Serbian military and civilian officials. The state and societal level

levels of analysis A means to organize systematic thinking about world politics. In examining a phenomenon such as war, for example, one may identify possible causes as characteristics of the international system, states and their societies, groups, or individuals.

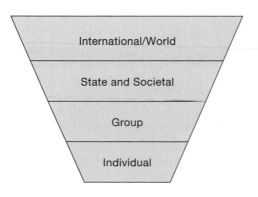

FIGURE 1.2   LEVELS OF ANALYSIS

LEVELS OF ANALYSIS: A MORE DETAILED LOOK

INTERNATIONAL/WORLD (OR GLOBAL) LEVEL
Anarchic quality of the international system
Number of major powers or poles
Distribution of power/capabilities among states
Level and diffusion of technology
Patterns of military alliances
Patterns of international trade and finance
International organizations and regimes
Transnational organizations and networks

STATE AND SOCIETAL (OR NATIONAL) LEVEL
Governmental
    Structure and nature of political system
    Policymaking process
Societal
    Structure of economic system
    Public opinion

Nationalism and ethnicity
Political culture
Ideology

GROUP LEVEL
Government bureaucracies
Interest groups
Other nongovernmental organizations

INDIVIDUAL LEVEL
Human nature and psychology
Leaders and beliefs systems
Personality of leaders
Cognition/perception or misperception

---

draws our attention to the role of ethnic group identity and nationalism. The international or global level of analysis emphasizes the impact of developments beyond Yugoslavia's borders that affect the country.

The levels of analysis framework is a useful starting point for answering various questions about international relations and world politics. For example, we could just as easily have asked you to apply it to the question of why the United States decided to force Serbia to withdraw from Kosovo by leading the NATO air campaign. How much emphasis should be given to the role then played by President Clinton or U.S. Secretary of State Madeleine Albright? What were the bureaucratic politics within the Washington foreign policy and national security establishment that led to the decision? What, if any, was the role of public opinion throughout the broader U.S. society? Does the fact that the United States as a democratic country proclaims the importance of individual rights have anything to do with the decision to go to war against Serbia? To what extent did the opinions of NATO allies and Russia affect U.S. decision making? Did the apparent increased global emphasis on the legitimacy of humanitarian intervention in recent years play a role? If the answer is "all of the above," then the next question is what is the relative weight of each possible explanation found at the different levels of analysis?

The levels of analysis, therefore, provide a framework for classifying **independent variables**—factors that account for either a state's foreign policy behavior or international outcomes (such as war among states). Variables at all levels may be involved in the explanation. What one is trying to explain—a state's foreign policy or international outcomes—is known as the **dependent variable**. Aside from explaining a state's foreign policy or such international outcomes as interstate war, factors at other levels of analysis could also be treated as dependent variables. For example, one might be interested in explaining the decisions made by an individual leader. This may require one to look for variables that affect or influence decision making at the organizational, national, and international/global levels of analysis.

The bottom line is that thinking conceptually is important, necessary, and very satisfying when it comes to attempting to understand world politics. Furthermore, to think conceptually and to use these concepts to think theoretically—seeking explanations or predictions for what we observe in the world around us—can be done by any of us. To think conceptually and theoretically is not something mysterious or impossible to achieve for the uninitiated.

Security, Economy, Identity

Three other key concepts that we use to organize much of the material in this book are **security**, **economy**, and **identity**. In discussions of world politics, all three terms are generally associated with the state and relations among states. *Security*, for example, is viewed in terms of the basic survival, welfare, and protection of the state (a topic we discuss at some length in Chapter Three), and **international security** is seen as common security concerns among states. An *economy* deals with the production, distribution, and consumption of goods and services. Discussions of the international economy generally revolve around which states are rising or declining in comparison to one's own state. The value of currencies are stated in terms of U.S. dollars, Swiss francs, and Japanese yen, and corporate balance sheets are followed closely. *Identity* involves the answer to the question, "Who am I, and with whom do I identify?" In terms of international relations and world politics, identity is most often associated with the state and nation or society and the values or culture and people who fall within that state's borders: People may view themselves, for example, as Bolivian, American, French, Ghanaian, Chinese, or Italian.

These three concepts thus apply not only to states but to groups and individuals as well. For many unfortunate souls, security is defined as sheer physical survival from the ravages of civil strife and war. In fact, the state may be seen not as the ultimate protector of one's security, but rather as the source of the threat. For others, economic concerns boil down to feeding one's family, which dominates every waking moment—global economic trends, balance of payments problems, and exchange rates are irrelevant abstractions for them. Achieving minimum economic subsistence is the goal of the vast majority of humanity. Similarly, one can identify with more than the state and society within which one lives. Particularly for educated women in the Third World, overcoming traditional, limited roles and establishing an individual identity may well lead them to identify more closely with other such women in other countries than with those in their own state and society. For others, an identification with a particular religion such as Islam is more important than association with any one state. Finally some people may identify strongly with an international movement concerned with such goals as protection of the global environment. These people see themselves more as citizens of the world rather than as citizens of any single country.

These three concepts—*security*, *economy*, and *identity*—provide the principal themes of the three major parts of this book. In our opinion, the struggle over these three issues defines much of what is important and interesting today about

A P P L Y I N G   T H E O R Y

WHAT IS A THEORY AND WHY SHOULD YOU CARE?

The word **theory** means different things to different people. In common parlance, for example, something may be true *in theory* but not in fact. In this rather loose usage, in theory equates to in principle or in the abstract, and hence theory is viewed by some as irrelevant to the real world.

Another meaning, consistent with usage in this book, views theory as a way of making the world or some part of it more intelligible or better understood. Theories dealing with international relations and world politics aspire to achieve this goal. Making things more intelligible, of course, may amount to nothing more than better or more precise *descriptions* of the things we observe. Although accurate description is essential, theory is something more.

For many people, theory is *explanation* or *prediction*. One goes beyond mere description of phenomena observed. Theory building may involve starting with a few concepts and assumptions and making an educated guess about some aspect of international behavior. This educated guess is termed a *proposition* or *hypothesis*. The task is to engage in **causal** explanation or prediction based on certain prior occurrences, patterns, or conditions. Thus whenever *A* is present, then *B* can be expected to follow. "If *A*, then *B*" as **hypothesis** may be subject to **empirical** testing—that is, the rigorous, systematic testing of the hypothesis with evidence or data from the real world. An example of a hypothesis is the following: "If states engage in arms races, then the likelihood of war increases." Indeed, formal statement and testing of hypotheses through the use of statistical methods is seen by many scholars as central to the theory-building process. Others prefer to rely on nonquantitative case and comparative case studies, historical methods, and reasoned arguments— the so-called traditional methods of theory building. It is the testing of theory with data that gives meaning to the "facts" about the world. It is a fact, for exam-

ple, that the Soviet empire collapsed in the early 1990s; good theory would help us understand *why* this occurred—an *explanation* for what happened.

Whatever differences international relations scholars might have among themselves, they all agree on one thing—theory is necessary and unavoidable when it comes to explaining and attempting to foresee the future of international relations. Theory is *unavoidable* in that all people approach their subject matter from what has been called variously different perspectives, paradigms, or images. An analyst hence needs to be theoretically self-conscious, meaning being aware of the perspective or even bias one might bring to a problem. Theory is also *necessary* in that it tells us what to focus on and what to ignore in making sense of the world around us. Without theory we would be overwhelmed and immobilized by an avalanche of mere facts. The sense we make of what we observe is informed by the concepts, theories, and perspectives that we hold.

A theory, therefore, is an intellectual construct that helps us to select facts and interpret them in such a way as to facilitate explanation and prediction concerning regularities and recurrences or repetitions of observed phenomena. Fitting pieces into a larger whole makes theory building analogous to puzzle solving. We can certainly think theoretically when it comes to explaining foreign policy processes in general or the foreign policy of a particular state. But international relations theorists tend to be interested in patterns of behavior *among* various international actors. In identifying patterns, the stage is set for making modest predictions about the possible nature and direction of change. To think theoretically, however, is not to engage in point predictions—"*A* will attack *B* the first week of the year"—however much we may want the answers to such questions. Predictive theory usually takes the more general form that given certain specified conditions, certain outcomes are likely or can be expected to follow.

world politics. As noted, all three concepts can be related to the desires of individuals. But issues concerning security, economy, and identity are also relevant to the *collective* aspirations of individuals that compose larger groupings such as states and societies. *The challenge of world politics is to satisfy and to attempt to reconcile common aspirations for security, economic welfare, and identity. World politics, therefore, involves goal-seeking behavior and the processes of deciding who gets what, when, and how.*[6]

In sum, these three themes represent three universal concerns. In this book we examine the *means* by which groups of people have attempted to achieve security, economic welfare, and identity—however defined—and the *obstacles* to this achievement. As we will argue, the means for one person to achieve these goals can be an obstacle to their achievement for someone else. Similarly, while some states at a minimum may seek to be left alone, other states have a more expansive definition of security or the pursuit of other opportunities abroad, the fulfillment of which might come at the expense of their neighbors. One must, therefore, beware of thinking that such common concerns are a force for universal harmony. In fact, the manner in which these concerns for security, economic welfare, and identity are specifically defined and pursued can vary widely. As a result they can just as easily divide people as unite them and be a source of domestic, regional, or global conflict.

ACTORS

Collective efforts are the primary means by which people achieve security, economic welfare, or identity. Individuals certainly make a difference, whether it is a Mahatma Gandhi in India or a Nelson Mandela in South Africa. But even those illustrious leaders found that a cause must be associated with an *organization* if the former is to be achieved. Throughout history humanity has recognized that a pooling of resources and energy is generally the most efficient way for individuals or groups to fulfill their wants and needs. In other words, the weak *I* becomes the strong *we*. The expression of this collective effort—whether at the local, tribal, state, or international level—will vary depending on the importance of the issue and the time available for its resolution. In this book we emphasize three basic organizations by which collective efforts have been expressed:

- States,
- International organizations, and
- Transnational nongovernmental organizations

As is evident from the table of contents, much of our discussion revolves around **states**. A geographical entity governed by a central authority, whose leaders claim to represent all persons within its territory, the state is traditionally viewed as the most important of the three basic organizations. States take the lead in defending the physical security of the population, attempting to ensure the economic welfare of its citizens, and providing a focus for loyalty and identity.

When it comes to world politics, states dominate conventional discourse. Nongovernmental movements such as insurgencies and terrorist groups may attack particular states, but very often their goal is either to take over the reins of power in an existing state or to create a new state. Even if broad-based political-cultural-religious movements transcend state borders, a political-military entity is needed to carry out the agenda. Finally, in those areas of the world burdened by overpopulation, environmental degradation, and mass migration, states are

---

[6]Harold D. Lasswell, *Politics: Who Gets What, When, How* (Cleveland, Ohio: World Publishing Co., 1958).

expected to take the lead in developing and implementing policies to deal with these problems.

States, however, can be viewed as obstacles to the achievement of security, economy, and identity when they persecute their own citizens, pursue counter-productive economic policies, and demand complete and undivided loyalty to the point where no dissent is allowed. In addition, in their pursuit of security, states clash with one another, leading to international tension and perhaps war. A key domestic role of states—to adjudicate domestic disagreements—is difficult to per-form in the international system. There is no world government, international courts are weak, and states often resort to the use of force.

States are not the only prism through which to view world politics, particularly in the current era of global interdependence in which it is apparent that no single state can hope to be the sole agent of collective action to solve global problems. **International organizations (IOs)** (also known as *intergovernmental organizations* or *IGOs*) also play a role. International organizations are multilateral institutions created by states in order to pursue common objectives that cannot be achieved unilaterally. IOs are termed *multilateral* because two or more states are members. Examples would include organizations with limited membership, such as NATO, the European Union (EU), the Organization of American States (OAS), and the Organization of African Unity (OAU). The best-known universal IO is the United Nations. Membership is open to all states. Nongovernmental organizations (NGOs) and even individuals try to influence the UN and other international orga-nizations by lobbying or persuading national and international decision makers and their staffs, holding conferences of their own, and publicizing their views.

There was a dramatic expansion of IOs/IGOs in the twentieth century, rang-ing from military alliances in the security realm to United Nations–related orga-nizations concerned with economic and social issues. Organizations such as the Food and Agricultural Organization (FAO), the International Monetary Fund (IMF), the World Health Organization (WHO), the World Bank (known more formally as the IBRD, the International Bank for Reconstruction and Develop-ment), and the United Nations International Children's Emergency Fund (UNICEF) barely begin to cover the veritable "alphabet soup" of UN-related agencies and other international organizations pursuing specific objectives. The growth in numbers and activities of IOs has also been accompanied by a prolifer-ation of NGOs actively pursuing their own objectives or agendas.

While IOs were created by and for states, it is interesting to consider the extent to which they have come to be significant actors in their own right. Do IOs simply reflect states' interests and at best provide a forum for debate? Do they become a source of financial aid or other assistance when economic or other problems arise? Do they offer an international diplomat when states come into conflict with one another? Or have IOs over time come to the point at which they now actually influence states' interests, preferences, and objectives? Whatever influence IOs may have in particular functional areas such as financial loans or mediation efforts, their key role may come to be purveyors of global **norms**—basic values that over time states come to take seriously. For example, while many states around the world continue to violate human rights, over the years norms have evolved that allow outsiders to make this issue a matter of international and foreign policy discussion and even punishment or sanction. For example, despite vigorous protest from the Chinese government, many states and human rights groups continue to condemn Beijing for its harsh treatment of political dissidents.

The United Nations complex in New York City.

The best example involves NATO military action against Yugoslavia, a sovereign state that did not invade another country but whose officials committed or allowed violations referred to as ethnic cleansing against their own citizens. Such action was a key reason that NATO launched the air war, not such traditional state goals as seizing territory or repulsing an invader.

Finally, as noted earlier, in recent years there has been a veritable explosion in the number of transnational **nongovernmental organizations (NGOs)**. As the term suggests, NGOs are composed of private, nonstate international actors that cut across national boundaries. In this regard, we identify four categories of NGOs of interest and importance to us in the study of international relations and world politics. First are private sector economic organizations. Although some writers reserve the term *NGO* for nonprofit organizations, we apply it to all nongovernmental organizations including multinational corporations (MNCs), most of which are private-sector and thus nongovernmental organizations. Multinational business corporations are understandably primarily motivated by enhancing the economic well-being of their stock- and stakeholders, not the economic well-being of any one particular state. Interest in MNCs is not new. Indeed, the United Fruit Company played a role in the overthrow of the Arbenz regime in Guatemala in 1954 just as British Petroleum was implicated in the overthrow of the Mossadegh government in Iran in 1953. Of particular interest to many observers of world politics, however, is the influence major corporations and banking institutions can have on the economies of states, particularly those in the Third World dependent upon foreign investment.

Second are NGOs with explicit political, economic, or social agendas, such as Amnesty International, Greenpeace, and religious organizations whose diverse memberships and global perspectives make it difficult to associate them with any one particular state. Transnational NGOs claim to have a broader constituency than MNCs or international banks. In their attempt to help define the international agenda, they often act as pressure groups to influence state behavior or international organizations, or, more generally, to increase global awareness of such diverse topics as ozone-layer depletion, deforestation, religious persecution, and human rights in general and advance agendas for dealing with such problems.

While such organizations do attempt to influence world politics by lobbying states and influencing state-sponsored meetings (such as those held during the early-to-mid-1990s in Rio de Janeiro, Cairo, and Beijing on economic development and environment, population, and the role and rights of women), their influence is actually much more pervasive and their goals much more sweeping. Activists aim at nothing less than shaping public affairs and how people perceive national and global problems. As a result, the term **global civil society** is increasingly prevalent in discussions of world politics. Global civil society consists of individuals and organizations that aggregate individual interests usually below the level of the state but operate beyond the border of any single state.[7] That is, certain organizations may originate in a particular country, but their global agenda makes them, in effect, stateless. Their members also tend to be multinational.

Third are nongovernmental organizations that attempt to avoid overtly political roles. The best examples are humanitarian relief organizations such as Doctors Without Borders. Engaging in politics usually means taking sides in civil and international conflicts and hence being denied access to combat zones. This and the previous category are what many people think of when the term *NGO* is used. In recent years there has been a phenomenal explosion in the number of such NGOs, from approximately 6,000 in 1990 to more than 26,000 in the year 2000. NGOs have existed for years—the British and Foreign Anti-Slavery Society existed in the early 1800s. But the process of globalization—spurred by the end of the cold war and subsequent efforts to spread democratic and market-oriented values and structures, technological change, and economic integration—has also encouraged the growth of NGOs. Globalization has exacerbated a number of worries to include the environment, workers' rights, human rights, and consumer rights. When combined, democratization and technological progress have revolutionized the way citizens can unite through NGOs to present their demands to states and international organizations.[8]

Finally, we must take note of nonstate actors such as terrorist organizations and criminal networks. Terrorists often claim to represent a broader constituency, whereas transnational criminal organizations (TCOs) prefer to focus on their narrow economic agenda, becoming involved in politics only when the pursuit of their ill-gotten gains is threatened. Although they usually have limited agendas and relatively small constituencies, we include terrorist and criminal organizations as NGOs that challenge the rule of law and, as such, represent the down (or dark) side of the emerging global civil society.

In sum, these three groups of actors—states, international organizations/IGOs, and transnational, nongovernmental organizations (NGOs)—can be viewed as means by which people strive to attain their individual and collective goals of security, economic well-being, and identity. As already noted, states are not the only means by which *security* can be attained. In fact, where authoritarian governments are in power it may be the state that poses the greatest threat to one's physical security. In such cases, IOs and NGOs might be called upon to help protect human

---

[7]Ronnie D. Lipschutz, "Restructuring World Politics: The Emergence of Global Civil Society," *Millennium*, v. 21, no. 3 (Winter 1992): 389–420.

[8]"The Non-Governmental Order," *Economist*, December 11, 1999, p. 20.

rights, or individuals may turn to organizations or revolutionary movements dedicated to the overthrow of the existing regime.

Similarly, even if one accepts the argument that the state should work to enhance the *economic* well-being of its citizenry, the globalization of the economy has made this a much more difficult task. Indeed, the governments of some countries lacking financial reserves have turned to such international organizations as the International Monetary Fund for financial relief and in the process have had to swallow the subsequent bitter economic "medicine" imposed by the IMF as a condition for loans. Such conditions typically require promises to cut government spending, increase taxes, allow interest rates to rise, or follow other tight, restrictive fiscal and monetary policies.

Finally, just as states have traditionally been the focal point of citizen *identity* and loyalty, at least in the Western world, other entities such as the United Nations or the European Union (EU) hold the potential to be foci of loyalty beyond the state. On the other hand, in some parts of the world where state political authority is tenuous, religious or ethnic identification may be a more important bond among people than any sense of loyalty or identification with a particular state.

Individuals and World Politics

If the focus in this book is on the three broad categories of organizations in world politics, what happens to the average human being? We wish to emphasize that while states, international organizations, and nongovernmental organizations are viewed as the primary actors in world politics, such entities are made up of flesh-and-blood human beings. *States* do not make the decision to go to war; people in their governments or societies do. *States* do not decide to provide famine relief to parts of Africa; people in their governments or societies do. So it is with the people who make up IOs and NGOs.

But the fact of the matter is that while individuals can have a tremendous impact on the short-term course of world events—witness Mikhail Gorbachev, the former president of the former Soviet Union whose actions contributed to the end of the cold war—it is extremely difficult to identify such individuals until after their impact has been felt. For example in 1985 experts initially saw Gorbachev as merely the latest in a long line of Soviet officials or communist party *apparatchiks*. Most people who want to influence world politics must do so in an indirect manner through collective actors such as states, IOs, or NGOs. Gorbachev had at his disposal the communist party and the bureaucratic machinery of the Soviet state. Even Nelson Mandela of South Africa found it useful to be supported by the African National Congress in the presidential election campaign following his release from prison. Although individuals can act on their own, they usually are more effective when they operate from an organizational base.

PERSPECTIVES ON INTERNATIONAL RELATIONS AND WORLD POLITICS

Having provided an overview of basic trends, concepts, and actors in world politics, we turn to a discussion of two basic perspectives or images of world politics today. In this book, an *image* refers to a general perspective on or set of assumptions about

Practicing World Politics

Research and Writing Tools on the Internet

Using search engines such as www.altavista.com is an excellent way to find sites on international relations and world politics. For library resources, check out the Internet Public Library Reference Center [www.ipl.org]. Many classics and other online books and archives can be found on the University of Pennsylvania's site [http://digital.library.upenn.edu/books].

Here are some sites offering dictionaries and translation services. Be sure to visit www.itools.com. For an online Merriam-Webster dictionary, visit www.m-w.com. Several dictionary entries are compiled on www.onelook.com. For rough translations of English, French, German, Italian, Portuguese, or Spanish text you type in, visit www.babelfish.com or http://babelfish.altavista.digital.com.

international relations or world politics that influences what types of questions are asked and how one answers them. As such, images help to orient our reading and research by highlighting certain concepts and ignoring others, as well as influencing the interpretation of particular international trends. Images are perhaps best seen as a pair of glasses through which one views the world. The two images we are about to discuss are not the only ones that can be used to view the world, but they have many adherents among students of international relations and world politics.[9]

The tradition of political thought known as *realism* has dominated thinking about international politics over the millennia. As the term suggests, writers and political theorists associated with realism claim to view the world as it is, not as it ought to be. In terms of domestic politics, the primary concern for any ruler is stability. Without internal stability, it is difficult to pursue other political, economic, or social objectives. Hence the challenge of establishing authority has drawn the attention of many realist writers. In terms of international politics, realists emphasize the struggle for power and influence among states, empires, and principalities. At a minimum, all such political entities seek security. Some, however, may have a more extensive agenda of opportunities to pursue and may even aspire to world conquest.

Realists see a world filled with conflict and struggle. For them, competition among political units such as states—seen as the key actors—is the hallmark of international politics. While realists may have a personal preference for international peace, harmony, and justice, for them the sad reality is that all too often this is simply not achievable. Their advice for political leaders is that to construct their policies around their hopes rather than the eternal realities of international politics is to risk disaster. More than any other image of world politics, realism most closely approximates the perspective of political leaders down through the ages. For purposes of analysis, realists tend to see the ideal state as a rational, unitary actor facing the outside world. Whatever internal disagreements there may be, ultimately the state must speak with one voice.

Realists recognize the existence of international and transnational nongovernmental organizations but view the former as essentially instruments of states and the latter as entities whose influence on world politics is marginal at

realism An image of international relations that can be traced back two thousand years. Realists tend to hold pessimistic views on the likelihood of the transformation of the current world into a more peaceful one, emphasizing the struggle for power among political units each acting in a rational, unitary manner to advance its interests.

[9]For a discussion of other images, see Paul R. Viotti and Mark V. Kauppi, *International Relations Theory: Realism, Pluralism, and Globalism and Beyond*, 3rd ed. (Boston: Allyn and Bacon/Prentice Hall, 1999).

JOURNALS ON INTERNATIONAL RELATIONS AND WORLD POLITICS

The International Studies Association (ISA) mails its members the *International Studies Quarterly* (ISQ) and the *International Studies Review* (ISR); the American Political Science Association (APSA) sends its members the *American Political Science Review* (APSR) and *Political Science Notes* (PS). In both organizations, student members pay substantially reduced annual dues. The APSR does publish book reviews, but it allocates relatively few articles to international relations compared to ISQ and ISR.

Many journals have Web sites, but primary access is still in journal form. Among the many other journals on international relations and world politics that publish articles with a more theoretical or academic orientation are *World Politics, International Organization, International Security, Millennium, International Affairs, Review of International Studies, Journal of Conflict Resolution, International Studies Review,* and the *American Journal of International Law.* Policy-related journals include *Foreign Affairs* (which also publishes book reviews), *Foreign Policy, World Policy,* and *Orbis.* This is hardly an exhaustive or complete list, but it is a start. Consult your library's complete list of journal subscriptions and consider subscribing to one or more yourself.

best. Some realists, however, argue that at certain times in history we can speak of a **society of states**, meaning the basic rules, norms, and international law are agreed upon among states to govern their competition. The Concert of Europe, which we discuss in the next chapter, is one such example.

How do realists explain the eternal competition and conflict among states and empires? The answer varies depending on the writer. For some realists, as we shall see, the explanation is to be found in humanity's supposed innate aggressiveness. Human beings, by nature, are competitive and selfish. Hence, such characteristics are simply carried over to the international arena. Other realists argue that the idea of innate human aggressiveness is overstated and instead note that certain types of states or societies tend to bring out the worst in people. This, they claim, helps to account for international conflict.

All realists agree, however, that the mere existence of independent states, empires, or principalities—all of which reject the notion of being subject to the authority of any other political unit—creates a dynamic that encourages competition and violence. In other words, international politics is conducted in a condition of international **anarchy**, or, as the seventeenth-century writer Thomas Hobbes termed it, a world in which there is "no common power." There is no central, global power to enforce peace among the various political units, whether they are city-states, empires, principalities, or modern states. As a result a political leader's primary concern is to protect the national security of the country. At a minimum this means defending the physical and territorial integrity of the state. We will return to a more extended discussion of the causes of war, but at this point we simply wish to note that for many realists, the competitive and often warlike condition of world politics is essentially the result of some combination of factors to be found at three levels of analysis—human nature or the psychology of individuals and dynamics of small groups; the nature of certain types of states or societies; and the structure of the international system and interactions among units (typically states and alliances) operating at the system level.

An alternative image of world politics is termed *pluralism*. The pluralist image is derived from various related strands of political thought that can be traced back to such thinkers as the ancient Greek Stoics, nineteenth-century liberals, and, more recently, academic writing on interest groups and organizational behavior. As the term suggests, pluralists view world politics in terms of a multiplicity of actors. States are recognized as key actors in world politics, but they are not the only important ones. International organizations such as the United Nations and

pluralism   An image of world politics that emphasizes the multiplicity of international actors, challenging the realist preoccupation with the state as a unitary, rational actor.

Practicing World Politics

Checking Out Some Web Sites on the Media

Mass communication print, radio, and television media in the United States provide a wide diversity of sources for current information and analysis on international relations and world politics. Many of these sources also maintain Web sites that post and update content frequently. If you want to read the weekly news magazine with the broadest (and most balanced) coverage of international events, the choice likely would be the *Economist* [www.economist.com]. Seeing itself as the newspaper of record, the *New York Times* [www.nytimes.com] prints the full length (or at least excerpts) of speeches and other documents of the day. Adding a Washingtonian perspective is the *Washington Post* [www.washingtonpost.com]; for a more right-of-center view, see the *Washington Times* [www.washtimes.com].

In its relatively few pages, the *International Herald Tribune* [www.iht.com] provides a greater breadth of coverage of international events than most domestic papers. Another good alternative is the *Christian Science Monitor* [www.csmonitor.com]. Except for its religious page, it is an otherwise secular newspaper. For stories, analysis, and commentary on international economic, commercial, and political matters, see the New York–based *Wall Street Journal* [www.wsj.com] and the London-based *Financial Times* [www.ft.com]. Among major newspapers reflecting regional views, see the *Boston Globe* [www.globe.com/globe], the *Chicago Tribune* [www.chicago.tribune.com], the *Denver Post* [www.denverpost.com], the *San Francisco Chronicle* [www.sfgate.com/chronicle], and the *Los Angeles Times* [www.latimes.com]. Find the site for your major city or local newspaper listed on its own pages or through a search engine (for example, www.altavista.com).

Though not as widely available in the United States as other networks, one of the best sources for international news from a Canadian perspective available on some satellite systems is the Canadian Broadcasting Corporation's (CBC) Newsworld International [www.nwitv.com]. This also includes news broadcasts from countries such as Japan, Russia, Germany, and other countries either in English or in the original foreign language version. More widely available television networks covering international events include CNN [www.cnn.com], particularly the international versions available on some cable and satellite systems; such public television programs as *The News Hour* [www.pbs.org]; certain programming on C-Span channels [www.c-span.org]; the traditional major networks—ABC News [www.abcnews.com], CBS News [www.cbs.com], and NBC News [www.nbc.com]; and such specialty networks as MSNBC [www.msnbc.com] and CNBC [www.cnbc.com].

Among the major news-related programs on National Public Radio [www.npr.org] are *Morning Edition*, *Fresh Air*, and *All Things Considered*. ABC [www.abcradio.com] and CBS [www.cbsradio.com] are among the major radio networks with affiliates throughout the country. With origins in the cold war and reflecting a pro-U.S. perspective to overseas audiences are Radio Free Europe and Radio Liberty [www.rferl.org] as well as Radio America [www.radioamerica.org].

the European Union (EU) are not simply arenas within which states compete for influence, but often independent actors in their own right that increasingly set the international issue agenda. This trend has accelerated since the end of World War II particularly since the early 1970s. Megacities are an example of governmental actors below the state level. The economic and political clout of cities both within their states and across their borders makes such urban conglomerates as Los Angeles, New York, and Tokyo significant players. In the Third World, underemployed urban populations suffering in sordid living conditions provide the breeding ground for unrest and demands for political change.

A growing number of pluralists, therefore, debate the privileged position in which realists put the state as if it were *the* key international or global actor. Increasing global interdependence is an important factor. They note that emergence of the modern state is a relatively recent phenomenon, going back to perhaps the fifteenth century. Other forms of political and social relations develop and are carried on across state borders in the form of transnational organizations. Indeed, far from seeing the state as a unitary, rational actor, pluralists see the state as a battleground for conflicting bureaucratic interests, subject to the pressures of both domestic and transnational interest groups.

The term *global civil society* describes the multitude of institutions, voluntary organizations, and networks ranging from women's groups and human rights organizations to environmental activists and chambers of commerce that have multiplied rapidly since the beginning of the twentieth century. Whereas most originated and confined their interests to the industrial countries of the West, this is no longer the case. Today such organizations are found in developing countries and in the former communist countries of Eastern Europe and Russia. Pluralists note that such organizations are more than special interest groups attempting to influence state policies. These groups play an important role in forming an international consciousness among peoples around the globe on such diverse issues as the environment, human rights, and weapons proliferation. Indeed, it allows one to speak, at least in terms that originated in the Western world, of a growing liberal-capitalist civic identity.

The realist and pluralist views of the possibilities of peaceful international change are also at odds. Realists are pessimists who tend to view international relations as "more of the same old thing"—conflict and competition in a world constantly threatened with instability and threats to peace. Pluralists, however, tend to be much more optimistic, especially in terms of their underlying view of human nature, which sees the possibility of cooperation and accommodation on a person-to-person level, and in their view that the spread of democratic ideals will have a pacifying effect on peoples and states. According to the eighteenth-century German writer Immanuel Kant in his essay "Perpetual Peace," a world of good, morally responsible states would be less likely to engage in wars. Thus many pluralists argue that the realist emphasis on international anarchy is excessive; there are no intractable obstacles to international cooperation. Pluralists tend to be optimists who rely on the ability of political leaders and nations to learn from mistakes—the past is not necessarily prologue. State interests can be redefined and new identities—not restricted to loyalty to the state—can be created.

The comparison of realist and pluralist images of international relations and world politics in Table 1.1 represents a distillation of a wide body of work. Within each image, one finds a number of different approaches to world politics that vary in terms of methods of analysis. What is lost to simplification, however, is offset by the virtue of clarity. We suggest each reader consider which image of world politics most closely matches his or her own view of the world.

TABLE 1.1 REALISM AND PLURALISM	
Realism	**Pluralism**
VIEW OF INTERNATIONAL SYSTEM	
At best can speak of society of states	Global civil society encompasses or operates parallel to—and influences—the interstate system
TRENDS	
GLOBALIZATION	
Impact overstated	Impact cannot be overstated; extent historically unprecedented
CRISES OF AUTHORITY	
Pronouncements on death of state premature	States losing authority to IOs, subnational groups, NGOs
ACTORS	
STATES	
Key actor	Key actor, but nonstate actors as important
INTERNATIONAL ORGANIZATIONS	
Reflect state interests	Increasingly independent role
TRANSNATIONAL, NONGOVERNMENTAL ORGANIZATIONS (NGOs)	
Secondary importance	Increasingly important and growing in number
SECURITY	
NATIONAL SECURITY	
Analytic focus: states as unified rational actors; interests a given	Analytic focus: states consist of many actors
Security of state and territory key concern	Security of groups and individuals key concern
DIPLOMACY	
Conducted primarily by states, which are also key actors in international organizations and alliances	Conducted by states, IOs, increasingly NGOs in the field

(table continues)

TABLE 1.1   (CONTINUED)

Realism	Pluralism
FORCE	
Necessary and seemingly inevitable instrument of state policy	May well be used, but not inevitable instrument of state policy
INTERNATIONAL SECURITY	
Balances of power, alliances, collective security provide order	International regimes and other socially constructed institutions and values provide order
ECONOMY	
Key source of state power	Key indicator of globalization
IDENTITY	
State, nation-state	State, nation-state, ethnic group; global civil society
TRANSFORMATIVE POTENTIAL OF INTERNATIONAL RELATIONS AND WORLD POLITICS	
Pessimistic about transforming IR into a fundamentally better world	Cautiously optimistic about transforming world politics

INTERNATIONAL RELATIONS AND WORLD POLITICS

Finally a few comments concerning the title of this book. To be precise, the term **international relations** should refer to relations among nations—people with a common identity such as the French or Japanese "nation." However, over the years conventional discourse has come to equate the term with *interstate* relations. When we use the term *international relations*, we are principally referring to relations among states, as we believe it is necessary to emphasize that states continue to be the primary actors on the world stage. Furthermore, various types of states have historically dominated international politics. Realists tend to feel most comfortable with this use of the term *international relations*. As we have noted, however, states are not the only actors. We believe the terms **global** or **world politics**—which we use interchangeably—capture today's reality of a wide range of transnational actors and trends such as economic and social interdependence.

One must be wary, however, as to the assumed connotations of global or world politics. Although a case can be made that the trends we discuss in this book are indeed global or at least have global ramifications, not every one we address is equally salient or important to all peoples or regions of the globe. Sweeping generalizations about the condition of the entire world should be viewed with suspicion. Environmental degradation, for example, may be a global concern, but its manifestations are certainly much worse in some areas of the world than in others. The same is true of population and refugee issues. Similarly, economic

Practicing World Politics

Checking Out Some Web Sites on Membership Organizations

United States-based academic organizations one can join include the International Studies Association (ISA) [www.isanet.org] and the American Political Science Association [www.apsanet.org]. Membership is also available in APSA's organized sections: International Security and Arms Control, Conflict Processes, Domestic Sources of Foreign Policy, Comparative Politics, Politics and Society in Western Europe, Political Economy, Science, Technology & Environmental Politics, and Ecological and Transformational Politics. ISA also has organized sections.

On international and foreign policy issues, World Affairs Councils in various cities are open to the general public. Study groups on foreign policy decisions—the *Great Decisions* program of the Foreign Policy Association [www.fpa.org]—are held in some World Affairs Council or other group settings. Groups with membership limited to professionals in a diversity of fields include the Washington-based American Committees on Foreign Relations [www.acfr.org] with grass-roots committees in more than thirty U.S. cities; the New York- and Washington-based Council on Foreign Relations [www.foreignrelations.org]; the Los Angeles-based Pacific Council on International Policy [www.pcip.org]; and the London-based International Institute for Strategic Studies [www.isn.ethz.ch/iiss].

Practicing World Politics

Using the Internet to Find International Careers and Jobs

A number of Web sites contain information about both private-sector (profit and nonprofit NGOs) and public-sector (governmental and international organization) jobs and positions. Be sure to check out Web sites of international and nongovernmental organizations, many of which are listed in the **Practicing World Politics** boxes throughout the chapters of this book. Here are some sites to begin your search; be sure to check their international listings and links to other sites.

- www.employmentoffice.net
- www.europages.com
- www.globalcareers.com
- www.idealist.org
- www.jobsite.co.uk
- www.monster.com
- www.nonprofits.org

For academic teaching and research positions, visit the American Political Science Association [www.apsanet.org] and explore the international relations and world politics fields. Visit the Web sites of other professional associations, as well as the Chronicle of Higher Education [www.chronicle.com]; the latter contains both academic and administrative position listings in colleges and universities.

Job and position information can also be found on search engines such as www.altavista.com and www.yahoo.com, as well as other general career and job information sites such as www.careermosaic.com and www.careermag.com.

conditions vary widely across the globe. One could, in fact, simply divide the world into two spheres. In North America, Western Europe, and Japan, high or increasing standards of living prevail. Much of the rest of the world, home to the mass of humanity, suffers from varying degrees of poverty, economic development constrained by population growth, and environmental pollution and many countries are plagued by collapsing social and political orders.

A useful metaphor that captures our approach to the study of global politics is a chessboard. Just as chess consists of different actors—kings, queens, rooks, bishops, pawns—so too does world politics—states, IOs, and NGOs. And just as various chess pieces are more important than others, so too is this the case in global politics. In fact, global politics is a three-level game of chess, with at least three games in progress at once—political, economic, and social. Within and between each game various levels of interdependencies exist. But to make it even more of an analytical challenge, the actual size and boundaries of the chessboards are unclear. The constituent elements and complex, multidimensional nature of contemporary global politics are continually evolving. Most observers would agree that the state continues to be the preeminent actor in world politics, but because of globalization and increasing global interdependence and crises of authority, this may or may not be the case at the end of the twenty-first century.

OVERVIEW

At this point we provide an overview of the book—a game plan, if you will. In the next chapter we discuss the *historical development* of international relations and world politics. A key goal is to provide the reader with an appreciation for the continuity as well as the changes in world politics over the centuries. In order to understand what is unique about the current world, one has to know what it has in common with the past. We also discuss writers who have contributed to the realist and pluralist images of world politics.

Part II focuses on *state security and statecraft*. As noted, for good or ill, states are the key actors in world politics. Useful generalizations can be made concerning states' basic interests and objectives, as well instruments used to achieve them, such as military force and diplomacy.

Part III moves from a discussion of state security to an examination of *international security*—global dynamics and trends that are of concern to many, perhaps most, peoples. This includes an analysis of the global spread of armaments, international terrorism, and criminal organizations. Alliances, international law, international regimes, and international organizations—strategies to deal with such common concerns—are also discussed.

Part IV focuses on *global civil society and the global economy*. A discussion of the historical development of a global civil society is followed by an overview of the attributes and development of the capitalist global economy. Topics include international trade, global finance, the divide between the rich and poor, and development. Challenges posed by resource depletion, population growth, and the environment round out this section. Each topic is a source of current or potential international conflict, and each has led to calls for regional or international responses to the dangers they pose. Hence all of these issues can also be viewed as aspects of international security.

In Part V we examine issues concerning basic *human identity* in the context of world politics and civil society—religion, nationalism, and regionalism, and then humanitarianism as reflected in a concern for refugees, justice, human rights, and the issue of humanitarian intervention. We conclude by making some observations—pessimistic and optimistic—on the future of world politics.

The post–cold war world is in a state of flux, exhibiting a number of disturbing trends. Some of these trends certainly existed during the cold war, but the forty-five-year-long confrontation between the democratic capitalist and communist world overshadowed them. Observers of international politics through the centuries have made similar observations about their unique and troubling times. In this book our task as authors is to present an objective and balanced presentation of the key issues of world politics today. Of equal importance is our goal to provide the conceptual tools to make sense of global politics in the new millennium. Readers should examine critically what we present. After all, for most readers of this volume, it is *your* generation, more than ours, that will have to deal with the problems that face us in the twenty-first century.

KEY TERMS

interdependence   *p. 6*   levels of analysis   *p. 12*   pluralism   *p. 23*
crises of authority   *p. 9*   realism   *p. 21*

OTHER CONCEPTS

Third World   *p. 4*   causal   *p. 15*   norms   *p. 17*
First World   *p. 4*   hypothesis   *p. 15*   (transnational) nongovern-
Second World   *p. 4*   empirical   *p. 15*   mental organizations
sovereignty   *p. 6*   security   *p. 15*   (NGOs)   *p. 18*
autarky   *p. 7*   economy   *p. 15*   global civil society   *p. 19*
gross domestic product   *p. 7*   identity   *p. 15*   society of states   *p. 22*
concepts   *p. 11*   international security   *p. 15*   anarchy   *p. 22*
independent variable   *p. 13*   state   *p. 16*   international relations   *p. 26*
dependent variable   *p. 13*   international organizations   global or world politics
theory   *p. 15*   (IOs)   *p. 17*   *p. 26*

ADDITIONAL READINGS

For the reader who wishes to better understand events prior to the 1990s, we recommend the excellent, brief, and eminently readable overview by William Hyland, *The Cold War: Fifty Years of Conflict* (New York: Random House, 1991). For an anthology containing a wide variety of views, see Michael J. Hogan, ed., *The End of the Cold War: Its Meaning and Implications* (Cambridge, England: Cambridge University Press, 1992). For a look back as well as forward, we recommend Sean M. Lynn-Jones and Steven E. Miller, eds., *The Cold War and After: Prospects for Peace* (Cambridge, Mass.: The MIT Press, 1993). The articles first appeared in the prestigious journal *International Security*.

We strongly recommend Michael Kidron and Ronald Segal, *The State of the World Atlas*, 5th ed. (London: Penguin Books, 1995). This book is a unique visual survey of political, economic, and social trends that is superior to the usual charts and tables.

For excellent discussions of significant long-term international trends and transformations, see Eugene B. Skolnikoff, *The Elusive Transformation: Science, Technology, and the Evolution of International Politics* (Princeton, N.J.: Princeton University Press, 1993) and James N. Rosenau, *Turbulence in World Politics* (Princeton, N.J.: Princeton University Press, 1990).

INTERNATIONAL RELATIONS AND WORLD POLITICS IN HISTORICAL PERSPECTIVE

"One age cannot be completely understood if all the others are not understood. The song of history can only be sung as a whole."

JOSE ORTEGA Y GASSET, PHILOSOPHER AND HISTORIAN

CHAPTER 2

Ferdinand III (1608–57), Holy Roman emperor, king of Hungary, and king of Bohemia, had no idea that his actions were partially responsible for the eventual institution of the modern state. Born in Graz, Austria, he was educated by Jesuits and was a noted scholar and musician. But the assassination of the Austrian general Albrecht von Wallenstein led Ferdinand to become the nominal commander of the imperial armies fighting the Thirty Years' War, which involved a long, drawn-out conflict between Catholic and Protestant rulers. Upon his father's death in 1637, Ferdinand became Holy Roman emperor. In 1640 he refused to accept a proposal that called for a general amnesty for Protestants. In 1648, however, he agreed to the Peace of Westphalia, which decreed that the prevailing religion in each part of the empire was to be determined by the local ruler. By recognizing the independence of individual states, Ferdinand and his fellow rulers of the day departed from the idea of unity within the Holy Roman Empire and set into motion the rise of the modern state.

Imagine that in front of you there is a globe completely devoid of any features except continents, islands, and bodies of water. If you were to depict the major actors of world politics or international relations, what would you sketch in?

The first task for most people would be to add lines showing territorial boundaries among states. Indeed, most maps of the world emphasize **states,** showing the globe as a colorful patchwork quilt of populated territories (recognized by each other as legitimate) and over which central governments claim the right to rule, a monopoly on the legitimate use of force, and some degree of influence on the economy and society. You might then add a small star to each state, illustrating the physical location and name of the capital city. Look at the map of the world at the beginning of this book for an example of a map that emphasizes state boundaries.

Political science, economics, history, geography, or international studies majors might feel most comfortable with this depiction, but we are all conditioned to think of international politics as relations among states. You do not have to be a realist to adopt this perspective. Examine any newspaper that covers foreign affairs and the point is easily illustrated. Invariably the reporter's dateline is from some capital city somewhere in the world, and much of what is written refers to government activity, whether it is an announcement of war or an announcement of new social programs. States—or at least the people or government officials who claim to act in the name of the state—are usually viewed as the key actors in world politics if for no other reason than that they control territory and the world's greatest arsenals of weapons. They also have the ability to wreak tremendous havoc and destruction upon their own peoples, neighbors, and the planet as a whole.

How does one think about world politics in a conceptual and historical perspective? The terms *global* or *world* assume, at a minimum, some degree of interdependence among actors. As we have argued in the previous chapter, the contemporary era is the only one that is truly global. Historically, however, most peoples' lives—economic, social, and political—revolved around an isolated

◇ THE STATE ◇

The state as a legal concept includes the following:

- A territory with defined boundaries
- A population (with or without a national or common identity)
- A **government** or administration
- Recognition as a sovereign state by other sovereign states

village, clan, or tribe. Identity derived from these small communities, not some larger entity. Similarly the local economy was usually insulated, particularly in subsistence economies, with little trade among villages, clans, or tribes. Hence political and economic—indeed, any—interdependence outside of one's own community was minimal or nonexistent.

The same is true of relations among different civilizations. When the Spanish and Portuguese explorers set forth in the fifteenth and sixteenth centuries, they had little idea what other cultures and civilizations they would encounter. Similarly, it was not until such adventurers and traders as Marco Polo trekked to China that economic exchanges occurred between West and East. Therefore it makes little sense to begin speaking of global politics until after the rise of the modern state that encouraged and sponsored the outward expansion of capitalism through both trade and an exploitative **colonialism.** The concepts of global interdependence and **globalization,** however, did not take hold until the worldwide expansion of markets, transportation, and communications, especially during the last half of the twentieth century.

INTERNATIONAL SYSTEMS: DEFINITION AND SCOPE

From an historical perspective, therefore, it makes more sense to speak of ***international systems***—systems that were limited in geographic scope and hence cannot accurately be described as global or world systems. The concept of *system* used in this work is defined as an aggregation of diverse entities linked by regular interaction that sets them apart from other systems.[1] The idea of *diverse entities* is useful in that it allows not only for different types of state actors, such as **city-states, empires,** and modern states, but also international organizations and such nonstate actors as corporations and humanitarian relief organizations. The definition of *regular interaction* varies depending on the nature and intensity of the interactions. For example the nature of the interaction could be war, with such conflict of greater or lesser intensity. Or the interaction could be trade, ranging from minimal to intense. Finally the nature of the system's units and their relative capabilities or positions in relation to each other give the system ***structure*** and set the system apart from other systems. This also allows us to speak of a system having *boundaries.* For example we can speak of relations in the contemporary European Union (EU) as a political-economic system or view commercial interactions in the North American Free Trade Area (NAFTA) among firms and consumers in Canada, Mexico, and the United States as a separate North American economic system.

In this regard it can be said that today a world or global system also exists, as the distinct boundaries between separate international systems of earlier historical periods are lacking. Furthermore the current global system—although dominated by states—is also characterized by extensive economic and technological interdependence and a diverse set of international and transnational actors. From

international system
An aggregation of similar or diverse entities linked by regular interaction that sets them apart from other systems, for example, the interstate or international system of states, or world politics understood as a system composed of both state and nonstate actors.

structure (systemic)
In realist usage, structure usually refers to the distribution of power among states. Thus a world subject to the influence of one great power is unipolar, to two principal powers is bipolar, and to three or more is multipolar.

[1]This definition is modified from that provided by Robert A. Mundell and Alexander K. Swoboda, eds., *Monetary Problems of the International Economy* (Chicago: University of Chicago Press, 1969), p. 343, as cited by Robert Gilpin, *War and Change in World Politics* (Cambridge, England: Cambridge University Press, 1981), p. 26. The original definition is "A system is an aggregation of diverse entities united by regular interaction according to a form of control."

this perspective the EU and NAFTA examples could be termed *subsystems* of the larger global system.

It should be remembered, of course, that a system is simply an analytic device to allow an observer to deal with an aspect of international relations that is of interest. It is not meant to be a precise description of reality. For example we could focus on a "Peloponnesian system" limited, for the most part, to interactions of the fifth-century B.C. Greek city-states. This, in effect, was the approach used by the historian Thucydides in his discussion of the ancient conflict between Athens and Sparta. Conversely we could enlarge the system being analyzed to include the neighboring Persian empire, which played an intermittent but crucial role. Whether to view the Peloponnesian city-states and the Persian empire as separate systems with distinct boundaries or as subsystems within a larger international system is really up to the analyst.

To summarize, while we characterize the world today as a global system, we can also focus on various subsystems. Such subsystems may be geographically oriented—for example, relations among members of the EU, NAFTA, or ASEAN (the Association of Southeast Asian Nations). Or the subsystems may be defined in functional terms—a telecommunications subsystem, a trading subsystem, a transportation subsystem, a financial transaction subsystem. These latter types of subsystems could be depicted visually, with lines crisscrossing the globe, illustrating the density of transactions. Instead of the globe being divided into geographic entities—the image with which we began this chapter—it would look more like a cobweb or lattice work. We note that some writers avoid the terms *system* and *subsystem* entirely, preferring instead to see these transactions among diverse actors as part of an increasingly complex and global *society*.

When did the global system come about? It is difficult to determine a precise date, as the globalization process occurred incrementally over many years. We would suggest, however, that the globalization of the state as the key political unit began in the nineteenth century at the same time that global economic interdependence began to accelerate. It has only been since 1945 or the end of World War II that the technological and communications revolutions in transportation, communications, and information transfer, and other technologies have gathered speed and had a global impact.

Up until the nineteenth century, however, it makes more sense to speak of various regional or international systems, meaning they were not global in scope. In historical references we prefer, however, the term *international* to *regional*. In ancient times people had no idea that other civilizations existed in other parts of the world. As far as they knew, they *were* the world if not the center of the universe. This was as true in Europe as it was in the Americas, Africa, China, or elsewhere in Asia and the Pacific.

In this chapter we examine four different types of international systems, reserving more extensive discussions of the current global system for the remainder of the book.[2] There are three purposes in this discussion. First history contributes to our understanding of international politics. After all it is difficult to understand what is unique about the current global system unless we know what it has in common with earlier international systems. Second a discussion of historical

---

[2]The first three systems we discuss follow the categorization of Adam Watson, *The Evolution of International Society* (London: Routledge, 1992).

international systems allows us to mention some of the political theorists who have influenced contemporary thinking about world politics and influenced the realist and pluralist images. Finally our discussion will expose the reader to a conceptual and theoretical understanding of international relations and world politics beyond historical facts and figures.

FOUR TYPES OF INTERNATIONAL SYSTEMS: AN OVERVIEW

First an **independent state system** or *sovereignty* consists of political entities that each claim the right to make both foreign policy and domestic decisions. No superior power is acknowledged and other states recognize these claims. Simply by interacting with other units (the *system*), some interdependence exists, resulting in a certain degree of constraint on any one state's actions. For example an ambitious and rising power may be viewed as a threat to the independence of other states, resulting in the formation of a counterweight or countervailing coalition or alliance. The rising power is constrained by the actions of the others, just as the members of the alliance will witness some degree of limitation on their freedom of maneuver by agreeing to work together to deter or defeat the ambitious state and maintain a ***balance of power***.

States also accept other voluntary restraints such as rules of war. Some rules may be promulgated simply to ease the operation of the system, such as diplomatic practices. One historical example of an independent state system is drawn from what we know about the ancient Greek city-state system prior to the fifth-century B.C. wars against Persia. Independent state systems occasionally arose in later historical periods that were relatively free of hegemonic influences.

Second there is a **hegemonic state system.** By *hegemony* we mean one or more states dominate the system, set the "rules of the game," and have some degree of direct influence on the external affairs of member states. Many writers refer in structural terms to what we call hegemony as having three variants:

- *Unipolarity:* "one pole," or a single dominant state such as the United States in the immediate aftermath of the collapse of the Soviet Union.

- *Bipolarity* or *dual hegemony:* two dominant states such as Athens and Sparta in the second half of the fifth century B.C. or the United States and the Soviet Union during the cold war.

- *Multipolarity* or *collective hegemony:* three or more dominant states such as the five great European powers after 1815 (Great Britain, France, Russia, Austria, and Prussia).

In hegemonic systems the less powerful members may interact with one another but they take their cues from the hegemonic authorities. They may even derive important benefits such as security by aligning with the more powerful states. The domestic affairs of states, however, are generally left untouched by the hegemonic powers. While political leaders are not installed by the hegemonic powers, they have little room for maneuver in their state's foreign policy.

The third type of international system is evident in the ancient empires of Assyria, Persia, Macedonia, and Rome. These are examples of the **imperial** or **suzerain system.** An empire consists of separate societal units associated by

sovereignty A claim to political authority to make policy or take actions domestically or abroad; based on territory and autonomy, historically associated with the modern state.

balance of power A key realist concept generally referring to a condition of or tendency toward equilibrium (or "balance") among states.

BALANCE OF POWER

The concept of balance of power is very important to realists, particularly those who emphasize the critical role of the systemic level of analysis to explain patterns of state behavior in the international system. Three questions of considerable debate among scholars are (1) How is the term defined? (2) Do balances of power automatically occur or are they created by political leaders? (3) Which balance of power—bipolar or multipolar—is more likely to maintain international stability?

Considering the first question Hans Morgenthau, a realist, admitted to at least four different usages or meanings of the balance of power. These were (1) a policy aimed at a certain state of affairs; (2) an objective or actual state of affairs; (3) an approximately equal distribution of power among states; (4) any distribution of power among states, including a preponderance of power by one over the others. One critic of realism, Ernst Haas, found eight meanings for the term. Sometimes it is used by leaders and diplomats simply to justify policies. At other times it is used to describe a tendency in international politics toward systemic equilibrium. Balance of power policies have also been criticized for leading to war as opposed to preventing it, serving as a poor guide to political leaders, and functioning as a propaganda tool to justify defense spending and foreign adventures. Given these diverse usages and meanings, we may ask if the balance of power means so many different things, then does it really mean anything? Despite these constant attacks and continual reformulations of the meaning of the term, balance of power remains a central part of the realist vocabulary. This is true not just with academic theorists, but also of policy makers and practitioners.

Former U.S. Secretary of State Henry Kissinger emphasizes a **voluntarist** perspective to the second question, concerning whether balances of power are automatic or created. The balance of power is a foreign policy creation or construction of political leaders; it doesn't just occur automatically. Makers of foreign policy do not act as automatons, prisoners of the balance of power and severely constrained by it. Rather they are its creators and those charged with maintaining it.

In contrast to this voluntarist conception is that of Kenneth Waltz, who sees the balance of power as an attribute of the system of states that will occur whether it is willed or not. Given the realist assumptions that the state is a rational and unitary actor that will use its capabilities to accomplish objectives, states inevitably interact and conflict in the competitive environment of international politics. The outcome of state actions and interactions is a tendency toward equilibrium or balance of power. From this point of view balance of power is a systemic tendency that occurs whether or not states seek to establish it.

Considering the third question some authors argue that in a multipolar system, war is less likely to occur because as the number of major actors increases, decision makers have to deal with a greater quantity of information and hence more uncertainty. They believe that uncertainty breeds caution in the making of policy and therefore a multipolar world is more conducive to stability. Other authors, however, believe that greater uncertainty makes it *more* likely a decision maker will misjudge the intentions and actions of a potential foe. Hence a multipolar system, given its association with higher levels of uncertainty, is less desirable than a bipolar system because uncertainty is at a low level when each state can focus its attention on only one rival.

Question: Is the emerging multipolar world going to be fraught with greater conflict than the bipolar world of the cold war era? Will national-ethnic conflicts overshadow ideological clashes?

regular interaction, but *one* among them asserts political supremacy and the others formally or tacitly accept this claim.[3] The difference between this and the hegemonic system, however, is that in an empire the dominant state is more likely to manage subject states' affairs, appointing local political officials, collecting taxes, drafting recruits into the imperial military, and creating and maintaining a system of roads and other transportation networks to enhance economic, military, and political interdependence.

These three systems can be depicted along a continuum as shown here:

Independent	*Hegemonic*	*Imperial*
(no superior power)	(dominance typically by one or more states)	(supremacy by one, as in an empire)

Historically there has been a tendency for one or more states to attempt to move from an independent system to a hegemonic state system or to an empire, with other states attempting to prevent this from happening. Military conquest historically has been the principal means by which this has been achieved. But authority crises within a particular political system can make it weak and vulnerable to foreign pressure. Within any particular geographic area, any of these three types of systems can ebb and flow, rise and then decline, evolve from one into another and back again.

The Western European medieval era, from roughly the fifth to the fourteenth century, is perhaps the most interesting period we will examine as we consider different international systems. Particular emphasis is placed upon the **feudal system** from about the ninth to the fourteenth centuries. What makes the medieval system so unusual is the diversity of the entities that composed it and the manner in which the relations among these units were structured. Power was claimed by a diverse group of governmental units, only some of which evolved into modern states. Other actors included trading associations, the great houses of merchant bankers, and local feudal barons. The feudal system comes closest to a historical example of a **pluralist** era.

In the secular realm the Holy Roman Empire, which came to be based in the Germanic area of northern Europe, claimed universal jurisdiction. While the papacy in Rome claimed universal jurisdiction in the spiritual realm, it claimed temporal authority, too, exercising great political power through its international bureaucracy. The Church understood society as *Christendom*—a single, undivided Christian society emphasizing unity among the disparate political entities of medieval Europe. The feudal system reminds us that the key actors of international politics have not always been (and in the future may not necessarily be) states.[4]

All four categories of international systems are **ideal** or **pure types,** meaning actual historical examples placed within any single category will not line up exactly but will have their variations. Furthermore, it is possible for such systems to coexist and overlap, as was the case during the period of Spartan-Athenian hegemony and their relations with the Persian empire to the east. Such systems remained important even as the globalization process was beginning to emerge in the eighteenth and nineteenth centuries. Roughly the first half of the

---

[3]Martin Wight, *Systems of States* (Leicester, England: Leicester University Press, 1977), p. 16.

[4]Mark V. Kauppi and Paul R. Viotti, *The Global Philosophers: World Politics in Western Thought* (New York: Lexington Books, 1992), p. 18.

twentieth century, for example, most closely resembled collective hegemony (or a multipolar system), but the cold war had many of the hallmarks of a dual hegemonic (or bipolar) state system because of the dominance of the United States and the Soviet Union.

How do such international systems develop, evolve, and decay over time? Why do such systems come to be viewed as legitimate, meaning their particular distribution of authority is accepted (decentralized in an independent state system, centralized in an empire)? To what extent do crises of authority account for their collapse? These questions should be kept in mind as we discuss the emergent global system in subsequent chapters.

We do not wish to leave the impression that the development of world politics followed a predetermined course, with various types of international systems leading inevitably to a world marked by global interdependence. The demise of empires and the rise of the state system did not necessarily have to happen. It is possible, for example, that the Roman empire could have lasted for several more centuries. Similarly, if Charles Martel had not defeated the Arabs at Tours in 733 or if the Turks had successfully breached the walls of Vienna in 1683, it is conceivable that a substantial part of Europe could have come under the sway of a Middle East civilization. More recently, what if Nazi Germany (1933–45) had succeeded in its imperial ambitions?[5] Conceivably even today's world, marked by global economic interdependence, could give way to regional trading blocs with limited interactions among them.

Just as we must be wary of assuming that the past was somehow predetermined, we must also realize that the future is not inevitably a mere continuation of present trends. It is extremely difficult to judge how various political, economic, social, and technological forces may come together to influence the evolution of the global system. History is full of surprising twists and turns that few could have foreseen: The collapse of the Soviet Union and end of the cold war are simply the latest examples.

A related point we wish to make is that some of the most critical concepts and ideas that have shaped contemporary thinking about the nature of world politics have deep historical roots. One should not underestimate the power of ideas in influencing the course of history. Human beings do not just passively react to their environment, whether ecological, economic, social, or political; they also shape it. For example, political movements designed to redress the grievances of working **class** people do not spring simply out of economic deprivation; they are also inspired by notions of justice and a sense of what is right or fair that is held by both leaders and their followers.

Ideas about world politics are sometimes used to justify the status quo in any era. But ideas can also help to overturn that status quo by providing inspiration and guidance to those who seek an alternative world future. Consider, for example, how the concept of "democracy" has gripped the imagination of many people all over the world. It has motivated them to take up a struggle against authoritarianism even though in many countries the quest for democracy would appear to be nearly hopeless. Ideas about democracy, political economy, social justice, and other concerns *do* matter, sometimes succeeding against enormous odds. In this

---

[5]For a novel that takes this scenario as its starting premise, see Robert Harris, *Fatherland* (New York: HarperCollins, 1993).

chapter we will refer to writers who have given such questions serious thought, highlighting their contribution to thinking about world politics.

We now turn to a discussion of historical international systems. Our purpose is to illustrate the diversity of systems, actors, and processes of international relations. We also hope to provide a backdrop or context for the evolving global system of today.

The Persian Empire

Persia is one of the best examples of imperial organization in the ancient world. Centered in present-day Iran, Persia was founded on the ruins of the Assyrian empire (about 1100–600 B.C.), but was much larger, extending from the eastern Mediterranean south to Egypt and all the way to the western borders of India. The Persians were particularly adept at assimilating those local customs that eased the expansion and efficient control of their empire. The Assyrian network of roads, for example, was extended, and Egyptian advances in administration and science were also adopted. In order to communicate more effectively with locals, they used Aramaic as the common language.[6]

The best way to visualize the political aspect of the Persian empire is as a series of concentric circles. The inner core was directly administered, but as one moved further away from the capital of Persepolis (in present-day Iran), control was more decentralized. In outlying areas the client states were quasi-autonomous. The threat of imperial military forces was always there—garrisons were established at key locations and local troops were trained and armed. But the Persian overlords preferred to rely on persuasion to maintain control. Indeed, historians note the relative moderation of Persian rule over other peoples. Local governors, termed *satraps*, were either Persians brought in from outside or members of the local royalty. Aided by advisory councils the jurisdiction of political rulers was separate from that of the local garrison commander and the representative of the imperial intelligence service. To accommodate regional and cultural differences across the far-flung empire, local administrative customs were generally adopted without substantial change. Administrators below the imperial level ranged from priests and kings to landowning aristocrats or merchant families, depending on the custom of the area.

The Persian rulers were successful in avoiding conflict among the diverse members of their empire. After failing to conquer the Greeks directly, the Persians astutely supplied money and ships to whatever Greek coalition was formed to counter the strongest Greek city-state. During the reigns of Cyrus and Darius, the Persians extended their authority over the Greek and Phoenician cities located along the Mediterranean shore. These trading cities brought the Persians considerable economic benefits, so the Greeks and Phoenicians retained almost complete control over their internal affairs. Special rules also were devised for the government of Egypt, which by some estimates accounted for one-fifth of the population of the Persian empire.

In sum, the Persian approach to empire—providing internal autonomy to constituent states as a means to lower military, administrative, and financial costs—established a practical precedent adopted subsequently by leaders of the Macedonian and Roman empires.

---

[6]This section is drawn from Watson, *Evolution of International Society*, pp. 40–46.

Acropolis of Athens: Porch of the Caryatids. The costly Peloponnesian War constrained but did repress the artistic and intellectual brilliance of ancient Athens.

Classical Greece: Independent State and Hegemonic Systems

The Greek world of the sixth to the first century B.C. was composed of a variety of political entities that today we call city-states. Their small populations, limited control of territory beyond city walls, and their proximity to each other are similar to the Italian Renaissance city-state system, not to modern states, which consist of comparatively large populations and often vast territorial expanses. The political forms of Greek city-states, as discussed by Plato and Aristotle, included monarchies that often degenerated into despotism (both of which involved dominance by a powerful individual) and other forms of rule. These ranged from leadership by enlightened aristocracies to exploitative oligarchies (rule by the few) and in some cases democracy, although participation was limited to those deemed worthy of the title "citizen."[7]

However they were organized, all of the city-states worked assiduously to maintain their independence. Some city-states were naturally more powerful than others, dominating weaker city-states and sometimes extracting tribute in return for military protection. Diplomatic practices were rudimentary, generally consisting of delegations that travelled to other city-states in order to present demands, resolve disputes, or negotiate trade agreements. Aside from its cultural and artistic

---

[7]Kauppi and Viotti, *Global Philosophers*, p. 36.

impact, the classical Greek period also served as a model of interstate relations for European and American diplomats in the eighteenth and nineteenth centuries.

Although all city-states desired to be independent, during the fifth century B.C. the rise of two city-states—Sparta and Athens—turned the Greek independent state system into a dual hegemony. In the middle of the sixth century B.C., the city-state of Sparta was ruled by an aristocracy, considered by them to be an excellent form of government, compared to the many tyrannies and oligarchies that ruled elsewhere. The expansion of Spartan power was confined principally to the Greek peninsula south of Athens known as the Peloponnese, and its purpose was to prevent neighboring states from stirring up trouble among the lower class, known as *helots*. This concern for domestic security limited the extent of Spartan ambitions beyond the Peloponnesian peninsula: The Spartan leadership did not wish to have its military forces distant, in case of a *helot* revolt. City-states allied with Sparta were allowed to conduct their own affairs and were assured Spartan military protection but were pledged to support Sparta in time of need.

The Spartans played a minor role in repelling the Persian invasion of northern Greece in 490 B.C., which ended with the spectacular Greek victory at the battle of Marathon. Ten years later, however, the Spartans reluctantly agreed to accept command of combined Greek forces to repel the second Persian invasion led by King Xerxes in 480 B.C. Spartan forces were unable to hold back the Persians at Thermopylae. The city-state of Athens, known for its navy as well as its democratic form of government, argued for a naval confrontation and at the battle of Salamis, the Persian fleet was defeated. The following year the Spartan army routed the Persians at the battle of Plataea, and Xerxes' forces retreated.

With the repulse of the Persians, Sparta returned to its traditional concerns and more limited sphere of influence on the Peloponnese. At this point Athens came to the fore and, hoping to prevent the Persians from launching another invasion of Greece, proposed the creation of the Delian League. This was comprised principally of the city-states most vulnerable to Persian pressure, including those along the west coast of Asia Minor (present-day Turkey) and islands in the Aegean. In order to protect these city-states and sweep the Persians out of northern Greece, Athens continued to expand the size of its navy and other military forces. In the process it became a major military power.

After a series of victories against Persian forces, the Delian League of city-states totalled some 200 members. But as so often happens in alliances, once the foreign threat has been neutralized, problems among the member city-states soon began to appear. This was in part due to resentment and fear of Athenian domination. These states, although formally autonomous political units or *polities*, were forced to pay tribute to Athens, which determined not only their foreign policies but also important domestic policies.

A deterioration in relations between Athens and Sparta led to the outbreak of war in 457 B.C. The two hegemonic states derived their power from different sources. Athens dominated central Greece and was easily the supreme sea power, whereas Sparta controlled the Peloponnesian peninsula and was the dominant land power. By 454 B.C. direct conflict died down, and a truce finally was achieved in 451 B.C.

Following a peace treaty between the Greeks and Persians in 449 B.C., the Athenians and Spartans eventually negotiated a peace treaty that in effect recognized spheres of influence and a balance of power between the two city-states. The ensuing peace allowed the two hegemonic rivals to consolidate control in their respective spheres. It is at this point, in 435 B.C., that the historian Thucydides takes up the story in detail and discusses the specific events that led to the outbreak of the second Peloponnesian War. The Greek international system was essentially an Athenian-Spartan dual hegemony, but other states such as Corcyra, Thebes, Argos, and Corinth also had significant capabilities that distinguished them from the vast majority of city-states.[8]

The final defeat of Athens in 404 B.C. at first seemed to usher in a return to the independent state system. But Sparta soon began to assert hegemony over the rest of Greece, interfering in the internal affairs of other city-states and losing the support of its former allies. The Corinthians, who had earlier encouraged the Spartans to lead an antihegemonic alliance against Athens, now joined with Athens, Thebes, and others against Sparta.

The Persian empire, alarmed by Sparta's attempts to extend its rule to city-states in Asia Minor, joined in this new alliance. Unable to control Greece directly, they realized that the next best thing was to support whatever antihegemonic coalition was formed as a way to be sure no single Greek city-state could threaten Persia itself. But their primary concern was stability on the western border of their empire. Hence they pushed for a negotiated peace with Sparta and later a general peace conference among all the belligerents. The resultant settlement has been compared to the Peace of Westphalia of 1648 as both were based on the idea of an international system composed of independent states and a balance of power among them. The difference is that the Persians were financially willing to underwrite the settlement.

The peace, however, was fragile. The Spartans, Athenians, and Thebans maintained their respective hegemonic ambitions. Thebes defeated Sparta in 371 B.C., after which Theban hegemonic ambitions became evident. As a result, the Corinthians resumed their role as creator of an antihegemonic coalition, supporting the defeated Spartans against Thebes. Over time more congresses were held that allowed city-states of any strength to participate. The basic principle of independence was reiterated, although it was recognized that Sparta, Athens, and Thebes were "first among equals." This international system, therefore, can be characterized as one with several states vying for hegemonic control but thwarted in their effort by shifting state coalitions or balances of power. A common Greek identity did not prevent war among them. It is no wonder that later European political leaders found many parallels between their condition and the classical Greek international system.

With the rise to power of Philip of Macedon to the north and then his son Alexander the Great (356–323 B.C.), both the Persian empire and the Greek system ultimately came under Macedonian imperial rule.[9]

India: Independent State and Imperial Systems

Prior to the sixth century B.C., ancient India drew much of its common identity from geographic isolation and the impact of Hinduism. More than a religion, Hindu ideas represent a broad-based set of values that became deeply embedded

Statue of Alexander the Great (356–323 B.C.), king of Macedonia.

---

[8]Mark V. Kauppi, "Contemporary International Relations Theory and the Peloponnesian War," in *Hegemonic Rivalry: From Thucydides to the Nuclear Age*, in Richard Ned Lebow and Barry S. Strauss, eds. (Boulder, Colo.: Westview Press, 1991), pp. 101–24.
[9]Watson, *Evolution of International Society*, pp. 63–68.

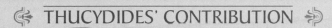

⟪ THUCYDIDES' CONTRIBUTION ⟫

The Greek historian Thucydides' (ca. 460–406 B.C.) untitled history of the Peloponnesian War is an account of the first twenty years of the fifth-century struggle. Filled with tales of heroism and tragedy, it illustrates the nature of war in all of its brutality, intertwining moral issues with political analysis. His is the foremost ancient work on international relations, for Thucydides was interested in examining current events in order to shed light on underlying patterns of politics that transcend any particular age. Indeed, he states at the outset that his work was designed to last forever and undoubtedly he hoped it would be instructive for political leaders through the ages.

For Thucydides, as for other observers of international politics known as *realists*, the underlying cause of the war could be traced to the nature of the Greek international system. He claimed that war was inevitable, given the increase in Athenian military power and the fear this caused in Sparta. His explanation, therefore, focused on the changing distribution of power in the Greek system of city-states and how this shift generated suspicion and distrust among Sparta and its allies.

Thucydides is credited with being the father of what has come to be known as **power transition theory.** Like balance of power theory, which we have already mentioned, power transition theory is a systems level theory. Realist adherents to both theories claim that the distribution of power among states is the key to understanding international relations. Power transition theorists, however, see the international system as hierarchically ordered, with the most powerful state dominating the rest, which are classified as satisfied or dissatisfied with the ordering of the system. But whereas balance of power theorists argue that the equality of power (balance) leads to peace, power transition theorists claim war is most likely when leading states are relatively equal, particularly when the differential growth in two states' economies brings a challenger close to becoming the dominant or hegemonic power. When this transition occurs, war is more likely.

Question: What does the increasing economic and military power of China mean for the stability of the international system?

This focus on the implications of changing balances of power has been generalized to explain the rise and fall of great powers through the centuries. **Long-cycle theory** claims the global system goes through distinct and identifiable cycles or patterns of behavior. According to one proponent of this theory, George Modelski, since A.D. 1500, four states have played dominant or system-leading roles, each one corresponding to a *long cycle:* Portugal (the sixteenth century), the Netherlands (the seventeenth century), Great Britain (early eighteenth century to the Napoleonic Wars and a second cycle from 1815 to 1945), and the United States (1945 to the present). War tends to mark the end of one cycle and the beginning of another. Modelski notes that as with long-term business cycles, world order is also subject to decay. The dominant power is inevitably faced with the growth of rival power centers, and attempts to maintain territorial control around the globe prove to be costly. This is what the historian Paul Kennedy refers to as "imperial overstretch," a policy that ultimately drains the vitality and energy of the country. Each cycle, therefore, exhibits a particular ascending and then a descending phase. With the end of the cold war, power transition and long-cycle theories have been of particular interest to many observers of global affairs for obvious reasons.

Question: If one accepts the long-cycle theory, is it therefore likely (or even inevitable) that U.S. global dominance will decay eventually?

in Indian culture. As such Hinduism influenced social and economic life in one of the world's great civilizations. Despite a common civilization, however, the Indian subcontinent was divided into a number of independent political units. Some were more powerful than others, and warfare and expansionism were common. But aided by Hinduism, there was a degree of common cultural identity and interdependence that encouraged the development of common rules and customs to guide relations among the various states. Although some were ruled by elected leaders and a few were republics, most were governed by kings belonging to the second-highest *kshatriya* caste, who believed their primary role in life was to govern and to fight.[10]

To enhance one's power and glory does not seem to be an unusual objective for kings and warriors. But over time it came to be accepted in India that it was not legitimate to destroy a conquered kingdom's social and economic way of life. Such forbearance was unusual in the ancient world. This is probably due in part to the Hindu tradition that would treat all of nature with great respect, whether vegetation, animals, or humans.

As is so often the case, however, it was Hindu contact with the outside world that led to fundamental changes in the Indian international system of independent states. As the Persian empire expanded eastward, it eventually conquered what is present-day Pakistan. It was at this point that the concept of empire began to circulate among Indian rulers and the educated castes. The Persians showed how a vast territory could be governed from an imperial center and how an extensive road network could facilitate interdependence through commerce and the movement of people. Some two centuries of Persian influence (from 520–327 B.C.) were followed by the invasion of Alexander's armies. With them they brought new Greek ideas (Alexander, after all, was one of Aristotle's students). This influx of foreign ideas followed hard on the heels of the spread of Buddhism, which also had a major impact on Hindu life.

Out of this intellectual, social, and economic turmoil arose Chandragupta Maurya, who managed to transform an independent state system into an empire. Although it was similar in scope to Persia, day-to-day rule of the Indian empire was heavily infused with indigenous values and customs. This man of action was accompanied in his rise to power by a man of intellect who worked to provide Maurya an extensive treatise on the ways and means of governing. That man was Kautilya.

With the death of Alexander, Chandragupta and Kautilya seized the opportunity to put their plans and ideas into motion and eventually established the Mauryan empire. Although not all of India was brought under Chandragupta's control, most of it was. An attempt to reconquer what had been the Persian part of India was turned back in 305 B.C. Domestic security and the neutralization of foreign threats encouraged the expansion of trade. But against Kautilya's advice Chandragupta's rule became heavy handed, and not surprisingly he made enemies. He became isolated and withdrawn, surrounding himself with a large personal bodyguard of armed women for protection.

Empire building continued under his son and grandson. The grandson Asoka (272–231 B.C.) initially expanded the empire by brutal methods, but once he became a devout Buddhist he was known for his concern over the welfare of his subjects. Upon his death, however, the bonds of the empire began to loosen. The

---

[10]This section is drawn from ibid., pp. 77–84.

KAUTILYA

Kautilya was the author of a work entitled the Arthashastra *or* Book of the State. *Rightly compared to Machiavelli, who also wrote a book for a ruler, Kautilya had the advantage of actually having the confidence of a man in power. The* Arthashastra *essentially describes the nature of the Indian independent state system and the relations among the various rulers and then proceeds to provide advice on how to exploit the system in order to create an empire similar to the Persian model.*

Kautilya's work is conceptually and empirically brilliant. He attempted to lay out precise formulas to aid the aspiring conqueror and is also given credit for such pithy bits of advice as "the enemy of my enemy is my friend." In contrast to the ancient Greeks or today's conventional thinking, Kautilya did not believe that an independent state system was necessarily the best. Rather Kautilya believed that benevolent imperial rule was most likely to achieve the ultimate objective of happiness for its subjects.

desire for independence was reasserted by elements throughout the empire, a crisis of authority ensued, and the empire eventually collapsed. India reverted to a series of independent warring states, the very condition Chandragupta had surmounted over a hundred years before.

The Roman Empire

At least to those educated in the West, Rome represents the ultimate historical expression of the imperial international system. Rome started out, however, as a city-state, indistinguishable from its neighbors on the Italian peninsula. Over several centuries it gradually expanded its control to all points of the compass, as seen in Map 2.1: north and west to present-day Germany, Britain, Spain, and France; south to North Africa and Egypt; and east to Iran. The importance of the Roman empire, however, lies not in its size, but in the fact that it came to be viewed as the legitimate authority by the vast majority of its diverse communities. For two centuries beginning with Augustus (63 B.C.–A.D. 14), the Roman empire provided internal stability, two common languages (Latin and Greek), and a conduit for the dissemination of Greek and Eastern culture that helped to establish the foundations of European civilization. In terms of world politics, Rome shaped current thought and practice about the state, international law, and international society.

In its early years Rome was ruled by kings, but with the development of aristocratic rule came the rise of the Senate with executive authority residing in two consuls. The lower class or plebeians also elected tribunes to keep watch over their interests. Internal strife assuredly occurred, but as Roman rule expanded outward so did Rome's wealth. Increased wealth combined with able rulers strengthened the power of the Senate.[11]

To conquer territory is a difficult feat, but to retain it is perhaps even harder. The senators were shrewd enough to realize that their long-term interests would suffer if they abused the newly subjected communities. Instead they bestowed upon these populations the advantages of Roman order and law, co-opting certain individuals via the extension of Roman citizenship. As with such earlier empires as

---

[11]The rest of this section is drawn from ibid., pp. 94–106.

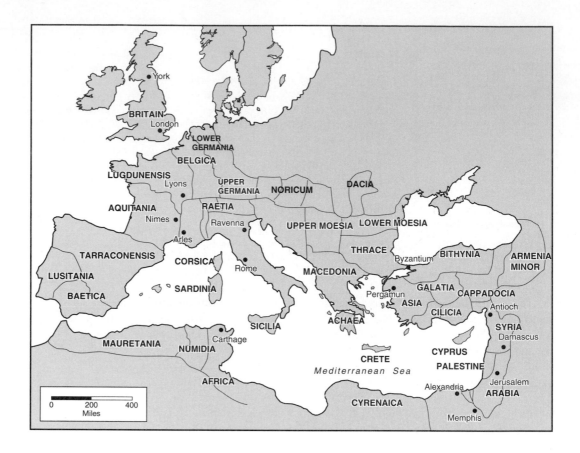

MAP 2.1   THE ROMAN EMPIRE, SECOND CENTURY A.D.

Persia, the degree of direct rule lessened with increased distance from the imperial capital, allowing more distant communities substantial self-rule.

Rome's interest in Sicily brought it into contact with the Phoenician trading city of Carthage, now the capital city of Tunis located on the Mediterranean coast of present-day Tunisia. From approximately 250 to 200 B.C., Rome and Carthage vied for supremacy in the western Mediterranean. With ultimate victory in the Punic wars, Rome absorbed the Carthaginian empire. As this struggle concluded, Rome looked to the east toward Greece and the Macedonian kingdoms. With the Greeks and Macedons unable to form an antihegemonic coalition, Rome soon gained control of the region. At this point the Roman imperial lands were divided into provinces, ruled and taxed by Roman governors. As long as they pledged loyalty, these kingdoms were granted local autonomy and indigenous customs were generally respected. In fact it was due to Roman occupation that the values and culture of these Eastern civilizations made their way back to Rome.

The rapid expansion of the empire, however, made it difficult to control territories effectively, particularly as the central government was constrained by a weak executive authority and a small bureaucracy. Attempts to fill this executive vacuum were made by various military leaders who promised stability but generally brought unrest and near civil war to Rome. The military dictator Sulla returned power to

Hannibal's troops are depicted during the Second Punic War, 218–201 B.C., which was one of the titanic struggles in history. The war was marked by Hannibal's invasion of Italy and his initial victory there, but his ultimate failure came at the battle of Zama (202 B.C.) in Africa.

the Senate and then retired. But ten years later Pompey, another military hero, came into conflict with the Senate over a number of issues including administrative rules in the provinces and the payment of his war veterans. With the aid of Julius Caesar, Pompey restored civil order to Rome and then coopted the Senate, agreeing to act as its protector. Caesar, however, had his own ambitions and following his conquest of Gaul (present-day France), defeated Pompey's armies in various campaigns throughout the empire. With victory Caesar imposed imperial authority and strengthened Rome's administrative power. Following his assassination civil war wracked the empire, ending when his adopted son Octavian—later known as Augustus—emerged as the ultimate victor.

Ruthless in battle, as a ruler Augustus was a moderate who brilliantly reorganized the empire and provided it with a respite from internal strife. Although he retained ultimate power, Augustus helped to legitimate his authority by allowing for the restoration of the Senate and some of its privileges and responsibilities. His successors helped to consolidate his basic achievement, which was to improve dramatically the governance of the empire. Periods of instability spurred the further growth of a centralized bureaucracy that encouraged the development of Roman law and in turn helped to streamline and rationalize the legal and administrative systems throughout the empire.

As with the case of Persian and Macedonian rulers before them, Roman emperors in the first and second centuries A.D. preferred indirect rule, relying on loyal local rulers to carry out their bidding. Local customs were maintained and identity was usually derived from one's ethnic group. But aside from Roman law, a web of other interdependencies was created thanks to the standardization of currency, weights, and measures. Commerce throughout the empire thrived as the Roman navy kept Mediterranean pirates in check. The quality of city life—housing, cleanliness, food, and personal security—attained standards that Europe would not see again until the eighteenth century. Educational opportunities became more widespread, which encouraged at least the educated classes to view themselves as part of a cosmopolitan empire. This was consistent with the Greco-Roman Stoic philosophy that recognized the universality of a common, human identity.

Problems began to arise in the third century, however. Armies of the Persian Sassanid empire invaded Roman territory; when Roman troops in Germany were called back, the northern frontier of the empire became open to attack. Not surprisingly a series of Roman generals came to power, vowing to restore order. Imperial authority became even more concentrated in the hands of the emperor at the expense of the Senate. To those parts of the empire under threat from foreign armies, such a development was welcome. But gradually, following the death of the emperor Constantine in A.D. 337, the western half of the empire began to crumble. The stronger eastern half of the empire, based in Constantinople (present-day Istanbul, Turkey) remained politically, economically, and culturally vibrant for several more centuries. But in the West, the Roman empire came to a formal end in A.D. 476 as Germanic invaders swept south. Although the new rulers adopted many of the Roman administrative forms and functions, communities missed the stability the empire had provided.

The beginning of the Islamic era in the seventh century led to dramatic changes in the East. Muhammad (A.D. 570–632), the founder of Islam, was inspired by Christianity, Judaism, and an abhorrence of the moral decadence of Mecca. Islam offered a comprehensive system of law and precepts for good government that have influenced millions of people around the globe down to this day. While Europe wallowed in backwardness and superstition, Muslim scholarship drew on the philosophical and scientific heritage of Persia, ancient Greece, India, and China, and expressed little interest in the "barbarians" to the north.

Medieval Europe and the Feudal System

The decline and fall of the Roman empire and the resulting decentralization of authority produced a high degree of diversity in Western Europe. The final collapse of Rome in the fifth century A.D. was followed by some thousand years that came to be known by later scholars as the Middle Ages or the medieval period. Its end point is generally marked by the Renaissance and the Reformation of the fifteenth and sixteenth centuries. This period is of particular interest to students of international relations because it encompasses the period immediately prior to the onset of the current state system. As we will see, the organization of the world into territorially based states was not an inevitable outcome of the Middle Ages; other possibilities existed.[12]

During the Middle Ages the major purveyor of the notion of the unity of humankind was the Christian church, the teachings of which became the religion of the Roman empire after Constantine's conversion in A.D. 312 or 313. As Rome's empire collapsed, Christian leaders realized that they would need to develop their own sources of worldly power to support their evangelical mission. Thus the Church became an increasingly wealthy and privileged organization with much to lose from invasions and general chaos. Even later, as more and more "barbarians" came under the influence of Christianity, the Church continued in self-defense to strengthen its organization and centralized authority through the papacy. Despite the sometimes corrupt and hypocritical behavior of many members of the Church

---

[12]This section is drawn from Kauppi and Viotti, *Global Philosophers*, pp. 124–29.

A P P L Y I N G   T H E O R Y

THE STOICS

Realism emphasizes what separates political entities and people. **Idealism** is another tradition of political thought that emphasizes what unites people. Idealism has had great influence on contemporary pluralist thinking. Idealism can be traced back to a philosophical school of thought known as *Stoicism,* which arose around 300 B.C. in Greece. Today the term *stoicism* is generally associated with the idea that one should bravely face life's adversities and persevere despite all odds. But the Stoics also argued that we are all part of a larger community of humankind regardless of our different political communities and cultures. Stoic ideas were very influential in republican and imperial Rome, and they anticipated the world views of the seventeenth-century Dutch legal writer Hugo Grotius and the nineteenth-century German scholar Immanuel Kant.

For the Stoics, the ability to reason is a quality shared by all humans. Reason is a divine spark, a reflection of the God within us. Many followers of Stoicism thought of the divine as the source of the laws of nature. Humanity's universal ability to reason and the universal applicability of these laws of nature led the Stoics to emphasize the equality of people and the factors that unite them as opposed to what divides them, whether those divisions are geographic, cultural, or political.

Roman authors continued to write in the Greek Stoic tradition and attempted to put Stoic ideas into practice. Cicero, Seneca, Marcus Aurelius, and others supported the organizing principle by which Rome managed imperial affairs—a universal image of humanity that transcended the boundaries of a city-state or other small political units. The idea of natural law (**jus naturale**) as well as laws of nations binding on all peoples everywhere (**jus gentium**) are important Roman contributions to Western political thought that have had profound influence on the succeeding centuries.

The Stoic emphasis on the unity and equality of humankind has obvious political implications: *What does it mean if the world is held together by laws of nature that transcend the laws of any particular king or emperor?* Furthermore the Stoics raised an issue that is debated to this day: *If everyone is part of humanity, to what extent do we have obligations to humanity as a whole as opposed to the more narrowly defined political community in which we live?* Such a question is of relevance today when satellite communications bring into our homes pictures of victims of starvation and civil war. What are we to do?

Question: What is your response to the Stoic question of the extent of obligations to humanity?

hierarchy, Christianity was the framework within which medieval life, private as well as public, was conducted.

Although the Church in Western Europe proclaimed the universality of its message in the sacred realm, political power in the secular or temporal realm was greatly fragmented with a wide variety of different types of actors claiming legitimacy. The Holy Roman Empire, founded by Charlemagne in the early ninth century, was centered in Germany and as the philosopher Voltaire wryly noted, was not very holy, Roman, or much of an empire, compared to that of the Caesars or

Nürnberg was typical of many medieval cities, relying on castle walls for defense and rivers for transportation and economic exchange.

even that of Byzantium (in present-day Turkey) to the east. Yet Charlemagne's successors provided a limited secular counterweight to the growing power of the Church. Indeed, Christian doctrine initially allowed for two separate but essentially equal papal and imperial powers.

The Holy Roman Empire effectively collapsed, however, because of internal weaknesses and invasions by the Saracens, Magyars, and Norsemen. Constituent kingdoms still existed, but administratively they lacked efficient bureaucracies and permanent military forces. As a result kings often had little power over local barons. Thus there developed a contradiction between the actual diversity of medieval institutions and the religious and philosophical emphasis on greater unity as provided by emperor or pope.

The power of local barons was reflected in feudalism, the preeminent form of authority that emerged earlier and became prominent by the tenth century. A defining characteristic of feudalism is public authority placed in private hands. As a result of the chaos of late ninth-century Europe—a time in which the stability provided by Roman law and legions was fast fading from memory—public authority came to be treated as the private possession of local lords who controlled territory known as *fiefs*. The lords held their authority at the expense of kings who were often distant and weak. For example, courts of justice were viewed as a private possession of individual lords who passed judgment as they saw fit. Similarly a vassal's loyalty and obligation to a lord was of a personal nature; it was not owed to some distant and abstract entity called "the state." In sum, this privatization of public authority in the hands of local nobles was a cause and consequence of the predominance of local government over the claims of kings and the general fragmentation of political authority throughout Europe.

Political authority during feudal times was therefore claimed by a diverse collection of institutions and individuals, including local barons, bishops, kings, and popes. Furthermore, it was also a time in which the middle-class merchants or **bourgeoisie** of the towns became a political force, often lending their support to religious or secular leaders in return for charters allowing them to establish free "communes" and over time, commercial leagues. For students of international politics, it is interesting to note that, depending on their status, any one of these entities could be granted or denied the diplomatic status or right of embassy. This medieval system, which seems in certain respects so alien to the modern mind, has been characterized by historians as "a patchwork of overlapping and incomplete rights of government" that were "inextricably superimposed and tangled" and in which "different juridical instances were geographically interwoven and stratified, and plural allegiances, asymmetrical suzerainties and anomalous enclaves abounded."[13]

Can we speak of this motley collection of polities during the latter half of the Middle Ages as an international system? Definitely so, even though it does not have the elegant simplicity of an international system composed of sovereign states. The present-day distinction between *internal* and *external* political realms with rigid territorial demarcations, a centralized bureaucratic structure claiming to exercise public authority, and the claim to a right to act independently in the world would have seemed odd to the medieval mind.[14]

But during the Middle Ages, diplomacy still existed. The papacy adopted certain Roman principles and established new ones that have become part of international law: the safe conduct of ambassadors, secrecy in diplomatic negotiations, and condemnation of treaty violations. In terms of secular contributions, personal relationships were a key to diplomacy. Marriages were particularly important. Territorial borders were fluid and relations between kingdoms were a function of dynastic marital connections. One did not speak of the "national interest" but rather the interest of particular rulers or dynasties. The high Middle Ages were a much more cosmopolitan era for the **elites** of the time than anything we have seen since: Political courtships and marriages could result in a prince of Hungary becoming heir to the throne in Naples or an English prince legitimately claiming the throne of Castile in present-day Spain. This web of dynastic interdependencies characterized by royal mobility and sense of common identity was paralleled in the rising merchant or bourgeois classes whose interest in commerce also made for a more cosmopolitan view of the world.

THE RISE OF THE EUROPEAN INDEPENDENT STATE SYSTEM

By the twelfth century, there was some reconcentration of political power in the hands of kings. Invasions around Europe's periphery ceased, allowing kings and nobles to devote more attention and resources to internal affairs and expand the size of their bureaucracies. Peace on the periphery also helped to account for the dramatic increase in the size of the European population. A larger population helped to revive towns, increase the size of the artisan class, and encourage greater trade. With expanded economic activity, taxation reappeared and was

---

[13]John Gerard Ruggie, "Continuity and Transformation in the World Polity," in Robert O. Keohane, ed., *Neorealism and Its Critics* (New York: Columbia University Press, 1986), p. 142, citing, respectively, J. R. Strayer and D. C. Munro, *The Middle Ages*, 4th ed. (New York: Appleton-Century-Crofts, 1959), p. 115 and Perry Anderson, *Lineages of the Absolutist State* (London: New Left Books, 1974), pp. 37–38.
[14]Ruggie, "Continuity and Transformation," pp. 142–43.

levied against churches, towns, and nobles. This required the establishment of a salaried officialdom. Greater royal income encouraged the payment of troops as opposed to relying on the vassalic contract based on mutual obligation. Kings, therefore, began to acquire two of the key elements associated with effective rule—financial resources and coercive power.

The twelfth and thirteenth centuries were also an era in which major strides were made in education. It is impossible to underestimate the importance of the growth of literacy to the rise of the state. As literacy expanded, the idea of written contracts gained currency, and ideals, norms of behavior, and laws could more easily be passed from one generation to another. Aquinas drew inspiration from the ancient Greek writers, universities were established (Paris, Padua, Bologna, Naples, Oxford, Cambridge), Roger Bacon engaged in experimental science, Dante wrote in the language of the common person, and Giotto raised art to a higher level. With the rise of educated bureaucrats, states formed archives that were essential to the continuity of government.[15]

This was also an era, however, in which there were major clashes between the sacred and secular or temporal realms over learning, commerce, and politics. In terms of learning, the clash between scholars with their emphasis on reason and the Church with its claims to authority based on the revealed word of God would continue through the centuries.

In the realm of commerce, the growth of capitalism led to a clash between the Church's emphasis on religious man and the emerging capitalist view of economic man. The medieval Christian attitude toward commerce was that those engaged in business should expect only a fair return for their labor efforts; earning interest on the loan of money (usury) and even making profits on sales were considered sinful. Gradually the feudal notion that the ownership of property was conditional on explicit social obligations was replaced by the modern notion that property is private, to be disposed of as the individual sees fit.

Politically the clash between the sacred and secular realms resulted in a breakdown in the balance of power between the pope and the emperor. This contributed to the breakup of the unity of Christendom, weakened the empire and the papacy, and hence assisted the rise of national states.

The fourteenth century, however, was particularly difficult for several reasons. The Black Death swept through Europe between the years of 1348 and 1352. It was also a time of popular insurrections and the first concrete evidence of the rise of national identity or consciousness. In the following century Henry V could count on the passionate support of the English in wars against France, just as Joan of Arc appealed to the patriotism of the French. The fifteenth century was also a time of decay in parliamentary institutions. Over time the power of the monarch and the royal court increased under the reigns of Louis XI in France, Edward IV and Henry VII in England, Ferdinand in Aragon, Isabella in Castile, and their successors.

During the sixteenth century there was much conflict and resistance to monarchical state building on the part of ordinary people coerced into surrendering their crops, labor, money, and sometimes land to the emerging states. In England, for example, rebellions were put down in 1497, 1536, 1547, 1549, and 1553. Lesser nobles and other authorities, often members of local assemblies, also

---

[15]Marc Bloch, *Feudal Society*, v. 2 (Chicago: University of Chicago Press, 1964), pp. 421–22.

NICCOLÒ MACHIAVELLI

Niccolò Machiavelli (1469–1527) is considered by many to be the first truly modern political theorist because of his emphasis on "what is" as opposed to "what should be," a hallmark of all realist writers. To Machiavelli—as opposed to many earlier Greek and Roman writers—the purpose of politics is not to make people virtuous, nor is the purpose of the state to pursue some ethical or religious end. Rather politics is the means to pursue and enhance the internal and external security of the state. His concern over state security is understandable: During his lifetime he witnessed domestic turmoil and the devastation of his native Italy by French, Spanish, and northern invasions. His most famous work, The Prince, was designed to be a handbook for Italian princes who sought to expel foreign invaders and bring unity to a divided Italian peninsula. Hence Machiavelli was the earliest writer to espouse the benefits of achieving national unity.

Unless security is achieved, Machiavelli claims, the pursuit of all other goals is pointless. The prince "must not flinch from being blamed for vices that are necessary for safeguarding the state." The two major dangers are internal subversion and external aggression by foreign powers. Domestic turmoil is avoided by keeping the people satisfied. As for invasion by foreign powers, "princes should do their utmost to escape being at the mercy of others." The best defense is being well armed and having good allies. Machiavelli agrees with other realists that a permanent or perpetual peace is a dangerous illusion. Any leader who succumbs to such illusions risks losing his country's liberty. Machiavelli did not favor war for war's sake but believed it was justified when the security of the state was at issue.

resisted this usurpation of their powers. The religious wars in France in the sixteenth century were in part a function of a contest between royal prerogatives and regional liberties. A common thread running through all types of resistance to the emerging state was the issue of taxation. Increased taxes provided monarchs with revenues to support larger armies that in turn were used to defend and expand frontiers and overcome internal resistance to their authority.[16]

Two immensely important developments during the one hundred years commencing with the mid-fifteenth century were the Renaissance and the Reformation. Taken together, they have been viewed by historians as the twin cradles of modernity.[17] The Renaissance, generally associated with western Europe's cultural rebirth, was an ethical and humanistic movement that also elevated the individual and individual accomplishments. The Reformation, closely associated with the German religious leader Martin Luther (1483–1546) and his personal struggle for a right relationship with God, was a religious movement that eventually undercut papal authority and any hope for a unified Christendom. Luther and fellow Protestant John Calvin (1509–64), a native Frenchman who emigrated to Geneva to escape religious persecution, believed that secular and religious authority should be separate. As the Protestant movement spawned greater religious pluralism, national monarchies grew in strength, and religious differences among the ruling houses exacerbated political problems.

Conflict over religion and the power of the Holy Roman Empire touched off civil war in Bohemia in 1618, eventually expanding throughout Europe into what

---

[16]Charles Tilly, "Reflections on the History of European State-Making," in Tilly, ed., *The Formation of National States in Western Europe* (Princeton, N.J.: Princeton University Press, 1975), pp. 22–23.

[17]Lewis W. Spitz, *The Protestant Reformation, 1517–1559* (New York: Harper and Row Publishers, 1985), p. 5.

has come to be known as the Thirty Years' War. Although religion was an important factor, the underlying cause of war was arguably the shifting balance of power among the major states, harkening back to Thucydides' description of the origins of the Peloponnesian War—the rise of Athenian power and the fear this inspired in Sparta.

The Thirty Years' War had a number of important results. First the Peace of Prague in 1635 addressed the religious problem in the Empire, providing a basis for dealing with the issue in the Peace of Westphalia, which ended the war in 1648. As a result, secular leaders of Catholic countries could ignore the papacy's call for a militant counter-reformation policy. Second a new balance of power emerged that led to the rise of Brandenburg-Prussia, Sweden, and France as the most powerful states in Europe. The chance, therefore, of a secularly or temporally based empire was now as distant as the pope's hope for the unity of Christendom under papal guidance. The writings of the Englishman Thomas Hobbes captured the essence of the new international system of independent states.

By 1660 the territorial state was the primary political unit in Europe, so we can begin to speak of an independent state system. The peace agreement at Westphalia in 1648 helped to solidify the trend of increasing power to the modern state at the expense of the other political forms. Not only were rulers put in the position of determining the religion of the inhabitants of their states, but the virtually complete authority of these princes in matters of state was recognized. With the realignment of territorial borders, the notion of the sovereignty of the state also came to the fore. *Sovereignty* involves political authority based on territory and autonomy. *Territoriality* means that there is a right to exclusive political authority over a defined geographic space—sometimes referred to as the *internal* dimension of sovereignty. *Autonomy* means that no external actor—such as another state—enjoys authority within the borders of the state.[18] For example, by agreeing to recognize each ruler as the final and absolute authority within his kingdom, rulers also essentially agreed not to support internal subversion in neighboring states or stir up religious discontent.

Notwithstanding claims by princes to a right to be independent or autonomous in their foreign relations—the *external* dimension of sovereignty—the Peace of Westphalia established a system that did little to curtail the drive for territorial conquests. In fact the relative military equality of the major states seems to have stimulated war, as many rulers thought they might be able to turn a system of independent states into an imperial system. As a result antihegemonic coalitions arose whenever a would-be emperor such as Louis XIV or Napoleon Bonaparte tried to conquer Europe. The balance of power, in other words, became a key aspect of the European independent state system, a system severely lacking in collective governing principles or conflict resolution norms or procedures.

Another equally important trend occurred along with the rise of the independent state system. Over time people began to identify with a particular state to the point that the nation and the state merged into the concept of **nation-state.** Leaders could draw on their public's *nationalism* to gain popular support for national defense and wars fought against foreign enemies. Wars no longer would be fought by mercenaries. Instead citizens provided the troops for imperial conquest or national defense. This trend further restricted movement toward the

nationalism A mindset glorifying the national identity, usually to the exclusion of other possible identities, infused with a political content.

---

[18]Stephen D. Krasner, "Compromising Westphalia," *International Security*, v. 20, no. 3 (Winter 1995/96): 115–16.

THOMAS HOBBES

Along with Thucydides and Machiavelli, Thomas Hobbes (1588–1679) is renowned for his contribution to the realist perspective on international relations. Just as Thucydides wrote his masterpiece during the Peloponnesian War and Machiavelli put pen to paper during a time of political upheaval on the Italian peninsula, Hobbes wrote his most famous work, Leviathan (1650), while in exile following the overthrow of King Charles I during the English civil war in the 1640s.

Hobbes's principal concern was with the establishment of domestic authority, such as determining the relationship between the ruler and the ruled. But his discussion of the **state of nature** has had an important impact on realist thinking about international relations. Although there is some dispute among them, scholars of international relations have come to see his arresting image of the state of nature as analogous to the **anarchy** of the international system—a world without central authority.

Hobbes did not claim that the state of nature he describes—a time prior to the creation of civil society—actually existed. Rather, Hobbes's state of nature was his attempt to imagine what the world or a particular society would be like without governmental authority. His starting point was to describe basic human nature. How one defines this has an obvious impact on the type of government required to ensure a stable political order. If human nature is essentially benign, little coercive power is required. If, however, as Hobbes believed, people are ruled by passions, a strong central authority would be required. If governments did not exist, we would have to create them.

In Hobbes's state of nature, people are roughly equal, as each has the ability to kill another, either by brute strength, cleverness, or in confederacy with others. Out of this basic equality comes the hope of attaining desired ends, but as two people cannot enjoy the same thing equally, conflict results. In one of the most famous passages from Leviathan, Hobbes notes that "during the time men live without a common power to keep them all in awe, they are in that condition which is called war; and such a war, as is of every man, against every man."

Hobbes's description of the state of nature has been viewed as analogous to the international system. Just as in the state of nature in which individuals stand alone, so too in the international system are states driven to maintain their independence. As in the state of nature, the international system is marked by constant tension and the possibility of conflict.

---

effective regulation of relations among states. The pursuit of narrow national interests was the order of the day.

The rise of the state and the independent state system was seen not only in the political, diplomatic, and military spheres, but also in the economic realm. Indeed, economic developments were critical in contributing to the ultimate victory of the state system over other contenders. For example the seventeenth century was the heyday of large trading companies. But while in earlier years these companies were associated with families, now the companies were chartered by monarchs in the name of the state: the East India Company in England (1600), the Dutch East India Company (1602), the Hamburg Company in north Germany (1611). As these state-backed firms increased in power, private city-based firms and trading associations declined. By 1629, for example, only the cities of Lubeck, Hamburg, and Bremen (members of the earlier Baltic commercial association known as the Hanseatic League) maintained their importance. Similarly leaders of the large territorial states such as England and France worked to free themselves from their dependence on the foreign Florentine and other Italian and German banking houses. In part this was because such family firms were unable to provide the amount of capital monarchs required in order to carry out their wars. Commercial and industrial firms also came to prefer more secure domestic capital sources, leading to the rise of national banks.

The development of state trading companies and banks was part of the dominant economic doctrine of the seventeenth century known as **mercantilism.** Proponents of mercantilism preached that the state should play a major role in the economy, seeking to accumulate domestic capital or treasure by running continual trade surpluses in relation to other states. This was not in pursuit of some lofty moral aim or simply for the benefit of private entrepreneurs; the ultimate objective was to provide resources that could be used for war or conquest. In the name of regulating and protecting commerce, authoritarian state bureaucracies emerged, contrasting dramatically with the primary economic units of the late Middle Ages, the autonomous and self-regulating guilds. These national bureaucracies viewed competition in zero-sum terms: Whatever one state gained came at the expense of another.

In retrospect, all of these developments may seem to have led inexorably to the rise of a system of independent, belligerent states. This was certainly the view of such realists as Niccolò Machiavelli and Thomas Hobbes. But there were also developments working to counteract or at least mitigate this trend. They included developments of a transnational character: the impetus to commerce resulting

WORLD ACTORS

GROTIUS

One of the most important writers on international law was the Dutch legal theorist Hugo Grotius (1583–1645). On the one hand Grotius is a realist in that he accepted the state as the key political unit and the fact that competition and war are inescapable aspects of world politics. On the other hand he exhibits aspects of the idealist tradition by claiming there is a basis upon which one can view the state system as a community or **society of states** that is not simply Hobbes's "war of all against all."

Grotius believed that laws created by human beings and natural laws could contribute to tempering the conflict among states. According to natural law, people in the state of nature are equal and free, with no superior power able to tell them what to do. Following this same logic, states are also equal and free. But just as individuals cannot live in isolation, so too must states associate with their neighbors. This requires creation of laws of nations—international law—based on custom, consent, or contract. Hence Grotius has no single term for international law, but discusses jus naturale and jus gentium—the

laws of nature and laws of nations or people. He therefore differed from writers such as Hobbes in that he believed states are subject to the laws of nations, and that the observance of these laws was actually in the self-interest of states.

Writing at the time of the devastating Thirty Years' War, Grotius's work gained even greater prominence after the Peace of Westphalia in 1648. As we have noted, the war and its settlement completed the transformation of an international system based on the tenuous unity provided by the papacy and the Holy Roman Empire to a system of sovereign independent states. In order to regulate relations among these newly legitimized entities, a system of law was required. Grotius provided the intellectual foundation for this evolving state system. He also served as an inspiration for later writers such as Emmerich de Vattel (1714–67), who argued that a recognition of moral obligations among states could coexist with balance of power policies. Taken together, power and international legal **norms** of behavior could aid in the stability and independence of states. For that reason, Grotius can be claimed by realists as well as idealists as one of their own.

WORLD ACTORS

IMMANUEL KANT

Perhaps the most famous work dealing with international cooperation and peace was by the German scholar Immanuel Kant (1724–1804), whose writings have influenced some contemporary pluralists. While influenced by Rousseau, the Stoic roots of Kant's thoughts on world politics are quite clear—as evidenced by his universalism, his concept of world citizenship, and his advocacy of a **federation** *among states as a means to peace. Kant's vision is of a diverse world in which human beings can live freely and without war.*

Kant, however, was no head-in-the-clouds idealist, and he realized the transformation of world politics was neither imminent nor easy to achieve. The sovereign state was a reality, and any plan to deal with international anarchy had to take states into account. Even if it were possible to eliminate states and create an empire, this would not solve the problem of war because warring groups could still arise within any such empire.

Kant proposed instead something less than an empire—a league or federation of nations that would leave sovereign states intact. How did Kant reach this conclusion? On the one hand he agreed that the natural human state might well be war, or at least the continuous threat of war due to the condition of anarchy. On the other hand Kant disagreed with Hobbes in that he believed that the gradual transformation of human beings and international society was possible. Over time, Kant maintained, discord among human beings will lead them to learn ways to avoid future wars. As reasoning beings concerned with self-preservation and self-improvement, people will learn that states are necessary to secure internal peace. This emphasis on learning is also shared by many present-day pluralists.

The best way to ensure progress toward peace is to encourage the growth of republics the constitutional arrangements of which check or balance competing interests. In a statement echoed by many political leaders to this day, Kant argued that a federation of republics would be inclined toward peace and more likely to take international law seriously than would monarchies or empires. As the number of republics gradually increased, the world would move ever closer toward a "perpetual peace." By transforming the state, the violent manifestations of international anarchy can eventually be overcome.

from the discovery of America and new routes to the Indies; a common intellectual background resulting from the flowering of the Renaissance; a sympathy bond between coreligionists in different states that transcended national borders; and a common revulsion toward armed conflicts due to the horrifying cost of earlier religious wars. As one author argues, such "causes co-operated to make it certain that the separate state could never be accepted as the final and perfect form of human association, and that in the modern world as in the medieval world it would be necessary to recognize the existence of a wider unity."[19]

Such recognition was evident in the development of *international law.* Grotius and other writers abandoned the medieval ideal of a world-state and accepted the existence of the modern, secular, sovereign state. But they denied the absolute separateness of these states and the extreme version of international anarchy as propounded by Thomas Hobbes. However limited it might be, the idea of *community* or international society of states could be applied, they argued, to the modern European independent state system. Even the recognition of sovereignty's external aspects—the claimed right of all states to be independent or autonomous in their international relations—expressed a certain degree of community.

international law Laws that transcend borders and apply to states and in some cases individuals and corporations.

---

[19]J. L. Brierly, *The Law of Nations: An Introduction to the International Law of Peace,* 6th ed. (New York and London: Oxford University Press, 1963), pp. 6–7.

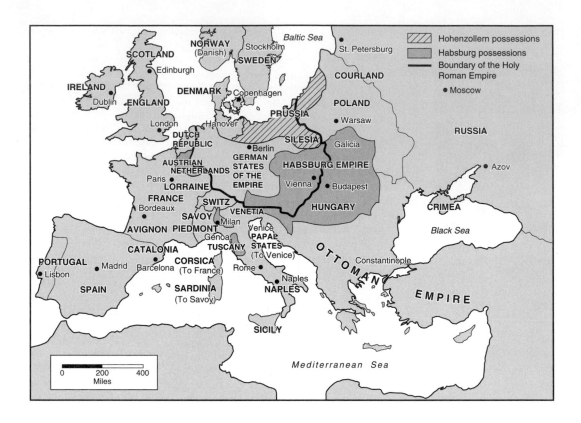

MAP 2.2   EUROPE IN 1789

The Emergence of Collective Hegemony

It was in the seventeenth century that we find the beginnings of what could be termed a society of European states. Despite political differences, all of the major European powers from the time of the Peace of Westphalia in 1648 to the start of the twentieth century worked gradually to regulate, delegitimize, and eventually eliminate the practices of such nonstate actors as mercenaries and pirates. If force were to be used, armies organized by states and *only* states would carry it out.[20]

The rise of Napoleon after the French Revolution that began in 1789 upset the European order as France moved eastward beyond the borders shown on Map 2.2, invading other countries and establishing a French empire. The subsequent defeat of Napoleon was followed by the Congress of Vienna (1814–15), which created a collective hegemonic (or multipolar) system. Certain rules, values, and expectations developed by the major powers influenced not only relations among these states but also among the lesser powers as well.

Leaders of the major powers had their various reasons for attempting to institute an international order that promised stability in Europe. Britain, with its global

---

[20]Janice E. Thomson, *Mercenaries, Pirates, and Sovereigns: State-Building and Extraterritorial Violence in Early Modern Europe* (Princeton, N.J.: Princeton University Press, 1994).

Napoleon Bonaparte.

economic and political commitments, hoped to expand its foreign dominance, but to do so required peace in Europe. Russia also desired a quiet Europe so it would be better able to attempt expansion south into the Ottoman empire. Both countries realized that to attain a stable Europe, Austria would have to regain its independence from France. Political leaders also perceptively recognized that to achieve long-term stability, France would have to be brought back into the European system. Along with Prussia, therefore, these major powers formed the core membership of what has been termed the **Concert of Europe.** This was an attempt to devise international rules of conduct that would prevent situations that had arisen in the past, such as Napoleonic France attempting to turn an independent state system into an empire. Conflicts of interest would continue, but it was hoped that disagreements also could be worked out in a pragmatic fashion.[21]

Furthermore the five major players realized that nationalist and democratic sentiments could conceivably threaten all of them, and in this sense their interests were broadly compatible. Europe, therefore, was viewed as a unique international society—not merely an international system. Such a vision was at odds with Hobbes's view of an anarchic world of states and more in line with that of Grotius.

Pragmatism was evident in European diplomatic practices. Between 1830 and 1884, twenty-five meetings were held among the representatives of the major powers. Though not formally promulgated, the underlying practices and norms that served in practice as the bases for these meetings included the following:

---

[21]Watson, *Evolution of International Society*, pp. 238–39.

1. The Concert powers have a common responsibility for maintaining the Vienna settlement.
2. No unilateral changes to the settlement are allowed.
3. No changes should be made that significantly disadvantage any one power or upset the balance of power in general.
4. Changes are to be made by consent.
5. Consent means consensus, but formal voting does not occur.[22]

Despite revolutionary outbursts in a number of countries in 1848, the Crimean War of 1853–56, and the Franco-Prussian war of 1870–71, during the rest of the nineteenth century Europe experienced its longest period of stability since the rise of the modern state system. It is important to note that no single crisis or conflict in this period ever threatened to erupt into a continental war.

The collective hegemony of the great powers was demonstrated in the way they decided the fate of the smaller powers. The Concert sanctioned the independence of Belgium, Romania, Serbia, and Montenegro, and prevented war between Luxemburg and Belgium and between Holland and Belgium. Aside from a common interest in European stability, the Concert powers were also able to make the system work because of their generally flexible approach to the balance of power politics. Permanent coalitions or alliances did not develop. This situation was also encouraged by the British desire to keep continental Europe divided.[23]

The Globalization of the European System

The European system of independent states did not confine territorial and economic competition to Europe. Over the centuries, the European system spread over the world. Following Europe's stunning realization in 1492 that a much larger world existed than was previously thought, the Spanish and Portuguese agreed to spheres of influence. They treated the Americas as they treated the lands that fell under their dominion in the Iberian peninsula—as integral parts of their kingdoms bound by their laws, administration, and Catholicism. Indigenous civilizations such as the Inca in Peru and the Aztec in Mexico were destroyed as attempts were made to replicate the authority of the kings in Spain and Portugal.[24]

The Dutch, French, and English, however, believed the riches of the Americas and Asia were fair game for all. Few inroads were made initially in the Muslim-dominated areas of the Middle East and North Africa. In fact the Ottoman empire controlled approximately a quarter of Europe until the end of the seventeenth century. In Asia direct colonial rule was initially not possible as indigenous authorities proved to be formidable representatives of advanced civilizations. The Europeans were allowed to establish trading posts at the behest of local rulers, but in this sense they were no different than Arab and Chinese traders who sailed through the same waters. The Portuguese, for example, established a trading post in China in 1516 and another in Japan in the 1540s. The British and French trading companies concentrated on India; although the initial amount of trade was minimal, the prospect for future gain was great. Such activities marked the

---

[22]Kalevi J. Holsti, *Peace and War: Armed Conflicts and International Order, 1648–1989* (Cambridge, England: Cambridge University Press, 1991), p. 167.
[23]*Ibid*, pp. 167–68.
[24]Watson, *Evolution of International Society*, p. 219.

SELECTED WARS AND PEACE SETTLEMENTS IN MODERN EUROPEAN HISTORY

As historians and political scientists have observed, peace settlements at the end of wars often go beyond cessation of hostilities to establish major principles or alterations in the structure of power relations:

- Peace of Westphalia (1648) ended the Thirty Years' War and established more formally the sovereignty or right of princes to exercise authority over the people in territories within their jurisdictions and to be autonomous in the conduct of foreign relations. The prince or sovereign authority could even determine the religion of the inhabitants of a state. This had even broader application to a wide range of other matters subject to state authorities.
- Peace of Utrecht (1713) provided for an end to the War of the Spanish Succession (1701–14), curbing French expansionism and Spanish power in Europe and the new world to the advantage of Britain. (Claims to the French crown by Bourbon King Philip V of Spain, grandson of French King Louis XIV, were renounced.)
- Congress of Vienna (1815) ended the Napoleonic Wars that followed in the aftermath of the French Revolution that began in 1789. These negotiations established a new balance of power and provided for diplomatic arrangements known as the Concert of Europe among Britain, Austria, Prussia, Russia, France, and other European states. Although the Bourbons were restored to the French throne and the territorial boundaries of France were drawn comparable to those that had existed in 1789, French power was again constrained by these formal agreements.
- Crimean War (1853–56) and the Treaty of Paris ended a relatively minor armed conflict (although one with substantial casualties), curtailing Russian power in southeastern Europe. The dispute nominally began over contrary Russian and French claims to guardianship of Christian holy places in Palestine. Subsequent movement of Russian forces into Ottoman-Turkish areas of Moldavia and Walachia in present-day Romania were met by the forceful opposition of Britain, France,

Sardinia, and the Ottoman Turks. The war was fought primarily to prevent the Russians from establishing military positions in the Crimea on the Black Sea.

- Franco-Prussian War (1870–71) once again curbed French power but was followed by a Prussian-led unification of German states into a newly formed German empire or *Reich*. The dispute began with protests by France over efforts to assume the Spanish crown by a branch of the ruling Hohenzollern dynasty in Prussia. Although in the popular view the French military under Napoleon III were favored to win, in fact the Prussians prevailed.
- World War I (1914–18) set a unified German empire allied with the Austro-Hungarian and Turkish empires as "central powers" against British, French, Russian, and by 1917 American allies. The war contributed substantially to undermining the Romanov dynasty in Russia, leading to its overthrow by Bolshevik revolutionaries in 1917. The new regime in Russia under Vladimir Lenin quickly made peace with Germany in the Peace of Brest-Litovsk (1918); however, the western allies continued to fight until they defeated Germany in 1918. The Peace of Versailles (1919) established a League of Nations (and World Court) for a new postwar order but also imposed harsh terms on Germany. Most historians believe these terms contributed to the failure of democracy in Germany and the subsequent rise in the 1930s of nationalist **revanchism** that led to World War II.
- World War II (1939–45) set a German-Austrian and Italian "Axis," joined later by Japan, against the same World War I Allies—the United Kingdom, France, Russia (which had become the communist Soviet Union), and by 1942 the United States. The defeat of Axis powers by the Allies was followed by three peace conferences in 1945 at Yalta in the Crimea, Potsdam just outside of Berlin, and San Francisco, where the United Nations Charter was signed, laying a basis for a postwar world order.

beginning of European involvement with the advanced civilizations of Asia as well as the beginning of conflict among European states for commercial advantage in Asia.[25]

The pattern of dependent states in the Americas and mutually beneficial commercial operations in Asia continued until the end of the 1700s. Toward the end of the century, Britain lost North American colonies, but European leaders continued to believe that colonies and their commodities were important sources of state power. The eighteenth century, therefore, witnessed an increase in the ultimate expression of economic exploitation—the capture or purchase of African slaves destined to provide backbreaking labor in the colonies of the Caribbean and North and South America.

European rule continued to be established where indigenous authority was weak or divided. The advance of British rule in India was initially aided by the collapse of the Mogul imperial system into numerous warring states, just as the Dutch managed to spread their influence gradually throughout the East Indies (present-day Indonesia). But in the nineteenth century Britain worked hard for the independence of Latin America colonies. A primary reason was that, following the Napoleonic war, Great Britain aggressively pursued international trade. By opening up heretofore closed markets, British industry rapidly expanded, leading to dramatic gains in economic growth and wealth that could be translated into state power. The British navy, in conjunction with the Monroe Doctrine of the United States, discouraged the European powers from attempting to reassert control over the newly independent states of Latin America.

European imperial expansion in the nineteenth century therefore was directed toward the Middle East, Africa, and Asia. As the Ottoman empire—which included the Balkans and Greece—began to weaken, both Russia and Austria saw an opportunity for imperial expansion. But with both Britain and France concerned about the implications of a slow disintegration of the Ottoman empire, diplomatic compromises kept the Concert powers from military confrontation except during the Crimean War (1853–56). A similar process of compromise was evident in the Congress of Berlin in 1884, during which the major powers carved up the remaining territory of Africa, the slave trade having long since ended. In Asia, great-power cooperation was also evident during the collapse of the Manchu dynasty. With the outbreak of the Boxer Rebellion in 1900 and the attacks against foreign traders and diplomatic legations, the European powers, along with the United States and Japan, worked together in joint policing and military operations.[26]

By the early part of the twentieth century, the areas of the world outside Europe and North America consisted of a variety of states with differing degrees of political, economic, and cultural dependence. None, however, could avoid the influence of the emerging global capitalist system and all took on at least some of the formal trappings of the modern state as defined by the European experience. This meant, at a minimum, acceptance of Western economic practices, commercial standards, and international law. Especially in colonial situations, locals who were hired to assist in administrative matters also were influenced by Western values. This was especially true for those few who studied in France and Britain and then returned to their native lands.

Karl Marx.

---

[25]*Ibid.*, pp. 220–24.
[26]*Ibid.*, p. 272.

A P P L Y I N G   T H E O R Y

 ## LIBERALISM, TRADE, AND PEACE VERSUS CLASS STRUGGLE

Kant's belief in the potential for harmony among states and peoples, joined with the faith that unrestricted economic activity would enhance the possibility of international harmony, came together in the works of nineteenth-century **liberals** who distrusted the concentration of power in the hands of the state (as opposed to many modern-day liberals) and argued for the expansion of individual rights and guarantees.

Richard Cobden (1804–65) was the foremost exponent of this perspective. He made three ambitious claims concerning the impact of free trade on peace. First he asserted that most wars were fought by states to achieve their mercantilist goals. Free trade would show leaders a much more effective—and peaceful—means to achieve national wealth. Second, even in the case of wars not arising from commercial rivalry, domestic interests that would suffer from the interruption of free trade caused by war would resort to hostilities. Finally Cobden argued that with an expansion of free trade, contact and communication among peoples would expand. This in turn would encourage international friendship and understanding. This posited relation between international trade and international peace has been a recurrent proposition, and indeed it is found in some present-day works that claim that interdependence and international trade can have pacifying effects on the behavior of states.

Question: If Cobden is right in his analysis, then shouldn't globalization make for an increasingly peaceful world? Does this appear to be happening?

Very different conclusions were reached by Karl Marx (1818–83) and his followers. Although hostile to the capitalism of his day, Marx was heavily influenced by certain of Adam Smith's ideas, especially Smith's presentation of history as a series of stages progressing from one form of political economy to another. For Marx the focus of analysis was economic class structure, not the state. He viewed much of history as a tale of increasing human productivity and **class struggle,** with the rich against the poor, the haves against the have-nots.

Marx actually had a grudging admiration for early capitalists because they were critical in sweeping away the feudal order. For him the world as a whole was divided by materially based class conflict. These horizontal, transnational class divisions cut across state boundaries and were a prime source of conflict, an analysis in contrast to the realist emphasis on conflict arising from interstate competition. Hence Marx began his famous *Communist Manifesto* in 1848 with the words "Workers of the world unite! You have nothing to lose but your chains!" Marx predicted that the growth of class consciousness—the realization on the part of workers that their situation was intolerable and that that would lead them to the point at which they would act together—would result in a **proletarian** or workers' revolution. This would happen first in the most highly developed, industrial countries, as their working classes were largest and had suffered oppression the longest, particularly in the later stages of capitalism beset by declining rates of profits. Over an unspecified period of time, the state—and consequently world politics as we know it—would fade away as a stateless world society was created.

Building on Marx's emphasis on class conflict and applying it to world politics were followers such as Vladimir Ilyich Lenin (1870–1924), the Bolshevik leader of the Russian Revolution of 1917. **Marxist-Leninists** saw conflict not as the result of anarchy and the **security dilemma,** but rather as the result of capitalist states competing economically against one another. Drawing on the work of non-Marxist English economist John Hobson and German socialist Rosa Luxemburg, Lenin argued that capitalism had reached its highest stage of development—**imperialism.** Since there were no more new areas of the world to exploit—each piece of real estate had been claimed or colonized by a European power—the capitalist states would begin to covet one another's territory, resulting in imperialist wars. The world would be divided and redivided. This struggle among capitalist states was intensified by the continual yet uneven growth of capitalism that would witness the rise of some states and the relative decline of others.

Question: Can you make the case that Lenin was at least partially correct—that the uneven growth of capitalism is a source of conflict and tension among advanced capitalist states?

TWENTIETH-CENTURY HEGEMONIC SYSTEMS
IN A GLOBAL CONTEXT

At the same time European values and economic practices were creating a web of global interdependencies, increasing political separatism was occurring among the major powers in Europe. Perhaps the single most important factor accounting for the collapse of the Concert of Europe was the inability of Europe to adjust to the political, military, and economic rise of Germany (a favorite case study for the application of power transition theory). When World War I finally broke out in August 1914, its viciousness and degree of devastation were shocking. Partly this was due to the Industrial Revolution, which had helped to produce weapons of tremendous destructiveness. The other important factor was inflamed nationalism, which spurred the development of mass armies and a political-ethnic consciousness coterminous with state boundaries. Karl Marx's hope that workers of the industrial world would unite to overthrow existing governments and institute an international system of peaceful socialist states was not to be.

At the end of World War I in 1918, an attempt was made to create an international organization that would prevent the outbreak of future wars. The key legal concept underlying the League of Nations was faith in **collective security,** the idea that if one state behaved aggressively, other states had a legal right to enforce international law against aggression by taking collective action to stop it. In other words, the League of Nations hoped to institutionalize legally the historical phenomenon of antihegemonic coalitions. The League, however, failed to keep the peace, as evidenced by its inability to halt German, Italian, and Japanese aggression, which resulted in the outbreak of World War II (1939–45).

A second attempt to institutionalize global collective security was the United Nations, created at the end of World War II. But with rare exceptions—Korea in 1950, the Congo in 1960, and peacekeeping missions in places as diverse as the Mediterranean island of Cyprus and the Sinai desert—cold war politics and ideology prevented the United Nations from playing the major collective-security or law-enforcement role originally intended for it in 1945. On the other hand, the UN Charter did permit the formation of alliances as states pursued individual and **collective defense.**

While East and West were locked into a conflictual situation of strategic interdependence—particularly because of the development of nuclear weapons capable of devastating much of the globe—economic, ideological, and political independence between the blocs was the norm. Within the blocs economic, social, and political interdependence dramatically expanded. A political disjuncture, however, was occurring between the so-called First World of the West and the newly emerging states and developing societies of the Third World. The victorious allies had fought Germany, Japan, and Italy in the name of freedom and independence. Now the leaders of the independence movements asked the embarrassing question: Why did the West not apply the same logic to its colonies? In some cases, such as the British in India, Palestine, and Yemen, the colonial power grudgingly disengaged. In other cases, particularly the French in Vietnam and Algeria, insurgencies came to power violently and eliminated direct foreign rule. This process continued through the 1970s as the Portuguese disengaged from Angola and Mozambique in Africa and reached its logical conclusion in South Africa in 1990 when the indigenous white elite finally recognized the impossibility of maintaining a monopoly on political power in the face of the political and economic demands of the black majority.

DUAL HEGEMONY DURING THE COLD WAR: A CLOSER LOOK

Given the fact that we continue to sort out the implications of the end of the cold war on present-day international relations, it is worthwhile to examine this era more closely. When did the cold war actually begin? It could be argued it began in 1939 when two dictators, Joseph Stalin of the Soviet Union and Adolph Hitler of Germany, agreed to divide Poland. Stalin's broader European goals were consistent with his Kremlin predecessors: dominate the states bordering the Soviet Union and gain control over the Turkish Straits and Baltic region. Beyond that Stalin hoped to influence strongly events in Eastern Europe and Germany.

With the German invasion of the Soviet Union in 1941, the Soviets joined the western alliance in the battle against fascist Germany, Italy, and Japan. Moscow's ultimate goals, however, remained the same. This was apparent at the Yalta Conference (in Soviet Crimea) where Stalin, President Franklin Roosevelt, and Prime Minister Winston Churchill of the United Kingdom met to discuss the postwar future of Europe. The Soviet Union had suffered twenty million dead and vast destruction. It was not surprising, therefore, that Stalin argued Eastern Europe should fall within Moscow's sphere of influence. With defeated Germany under four-power control (United States, United Kingdom, France, and Soviet Union), Berlin became a symbol of the cold war as relations between Moscow and the West rapidly deteriorated.

The U.S.-sponsored Marshall Plan, designed to revive economically war-torn Europe, was viewed with suspicion by Stalin. An ominous sign was the creation of the Communist Information Bureau (Cominform) in September 1947. At its inaugural meeting, a close aide to Stalin announced to the assembled delegates that

Much of Berlin remained devastated in 1949, four years after the end of the war.

Europe and the world in general was divided into two hostile camps, capitalist and communist. Then in February 1948 the Czech government was overthrown and soon after the Soviets began harassment of western trains into Berlin. By mid-June the blockade of the three western sectors of Berlin had begun and was only broken by a dramatic eleven-month airlift resupply effort. The West, believing it could not work out a deal with the Soviets on a unified Germany, proceeded in its preparations for a West German government and the creation of the North Atlantic Treaty Organization (NATO) in 1949.

Events in Asia also alarmed the West. In 1948 in China, communist forces led by Mao Zedong came to power. Then in June 1950 the North Korean communist regime invaded South Korea. The invasion galvanized the United States and led to a dramatic increase in the defense budget, a decision also influenced by the Soviet Union's successful test of an atomic bomb in 1949. In September 1950 the administration of Harry Truman adopted a new national security document, NSC 68, that essentially laid out the U.S. view of its Soviet adversary throughout the cold war. The Soviet Union, it was stated, aimed at nothing less than the destruction of the free world. The U.S. response was to be a policy of global **containment** of the Soviet Union specifically and communism in general. The Chinese intervention in the Korean War in November 1950 only reinforced this view, and officials in Western capitals discussed the danger of a major East-West war.

With the death of Stalin in 1953, there was cautious hope that a new Soviet leadership would be more accommodating in trying to settle East-West differences. A summit meeting in Geneva in 1955 left political leaders and outsiders with the feeling that although the cold war would continue in Europe and Asia, it would not turn into a "hot" or shooting war. But even as the summit was taking place, a Soviet ship was unloading Czech weapons in Egypt, marking the expansion of the cold war into other areas of the Third World.

Throughout the 1950s and 1960s a number of crises occurred: the defeat of the French in Vietnam in 1954, the Taiwan Straits crises of 1955, the Warsaw Pact invasion of Hungary in 1956, and the second Berlin crisis of 1960 during which the Berlin Wall was constructed by the Soviet Union, dividing the occupied city into separate eastern and western sectors and restricting movement of people across the barrier. Soviet support for national liberation movements in the Third World was matched by U.S. support for pro-Western regimes and attempts to overthrow a number of nationalist and pro-Soviet leaders in these countries.

The most dangerous crisis, however, focused on Cuba and thirteen days in October 1962. It was then that President Kennedy learned the Soviets were constructing sites for intermediate-range ballistic missiles in Fidel Castro's Cuba. The president and his key advisors at the time saw Soviet leader Nikita Khrushchev's actions as an intolerable provocation. Kennedy, therefore, in his view had no choice but to compel the Soviets to withdraw the missiles to defend the balance of power, preserve NATO, and illustrate the United States' resolve to Moscow. The key political-military decision was to establish a naval blockade of Cuba as opposed to an air strike to take out the missile batteries. Although the tactic was successful, the president later stated that the probability of a nuclear disaster had been "between one out of three and even." A second major crisis occurred in 1973 during the Arab-Israeli war when Moscow made noises about armed intervention in the conflict. The United States responded by putting its nuclear forces on alert, signaling its resolve to oppose any such action.

APPLYING THEORY

THE COLD WAR

Question: Despite a political and ideological chasm and conflicting interests, why did the cold war not develop into a hot war? In fact this period has also been characterized as the "long peace." The cold war witnessed a series of protracted and devastating limited wars fueled by revolutionary, religious, and ethnic competition. But there was no Third World War involving the Soviet Union and the United States. Explanations for this nonevent include the following:

- *Nuclear weapons:* Once nuclear weapons were available to both the Soviet Union and the United States, neither side was willing to run the risks required to achieve its objectives by force as major states had routinely done throughout history. The consequences of a nuclear war could easily be imagined by leaders on both sides, hence these leaders were "self-deterred" from using their nuclear arsenals.
- *Bipolarity:* Some theorists argue that the replacement of a multipolar world with a bipolar structure of power after World War II contributed to international system stability. As noted earlier the supposed

advantage of a bipolar distribution of power over multipolarity is that the responsibility for maintaining the system is concentrated, not dispersed. A superpower can even tolerate an occasional defection from an alliance because the overall distribution of power would not be dramatically affected.

- *Obsolescence of major war:* This view argues that the two previous explanations are essentially irrelevant to explaining the long peace. Recognition of the escalating costs of war for advanced industrial societies is the key and this was evident to all in World War I. It took the evil genius of Hitler, the bumbling of Mussolini, and a handful of Japanese militarists to start World War II. This war simply confirmed the catastrophic results of war in the industrial age, hence from this perspective the long peace after 1945 would have ensued even if nuclear weapons had never existed.

For further discussion and other arguments, see Sean M. Lynn-Jones and Steven E. Miller, *The Cold War and After: Prospects for Peace* (Cambridge, Mass.: MIT Press, 1993).

After the Cuban missile crisis the Soviet leadership embarked on a sustained buildup of strategic nuclear weapons that further strained East-West relations. Armed intervention by the United States in Vietnam and support for the South Vietnamese government were also countered by Soviet aid to North Vietnam and its communist (Viet Cong) allies in the South, actions that added to tensions between the superpowers.

Another major development was the Chinese-Soviet split leading to a clash along the Sino-Soviet border in 1969. This opened the way for the United States to play the so-called China card, epitomized by national security advisor Henry Kissinger's secret trip to Beijing in July 1971. President Nixon made a formal visit in February 1972. The Sino-U.S. summit and other factors also persuaded Leonid Brezhnev and the Soviet leadership that a relaxation of tensions (or *détente*) with the

Cuban Premier Fidel Castro (left) applauds Soviet Premier Nikita Khrushchev at a Moscow Stadium athletic display in May 1963, less than a year after the dangerous Cuban missile crisis.

West was a viable option and, in any event, better than strategic isolation. Hence Nixon was invited to Moscow and the first set of Strategic Arms Limitation Talks (SALT) resulted in an arms control agreement that was signed by Nixon and Brezhnev in May 1972. Further progress in arms control was made by the subsequent U.S. administrations of Gerald Ford and Jimmy Carter and their Soviet counterparts.

Détente suffered a major setback with the Soviet invasion of Afghanistan in early 1980. This event and the inability of the United States to do very much about it aided the election of Ronald Reagan, who continued and expanded substantially the massive U.S. military buildup begun under his predecessor. The imposition of martial law in Poland (December 1981), designed to squash a reformist labor movement (and thought to be due at least in part to Soviet pressure), further soured East-West relations. The Soviet experience in Afghanistan resulted over several years in enormous human and material losses, proving to be a disaster. This was one reason Mikhail Gorbachev (who termed Afghanistan "a bleeding wound") came to power in the Kremlin in March 1985 at a time when it was obvious to all that the Soviet economy was failing. Gorbachev revived the policy of *détente* with the United States and the West with an eye to providing some relief from ruinous spending on the arms race. Under his economic policy of *perestroika* (restructuring), the goal was to introduce limited economic incentives into the socialist economy. Gorbachev neither desired nor expected that his shifts in domestic and foreign policy would set in motion events that ultimately led to the collapse of the Soviet empire and the end of the cold war.

For those who grew up during the cold war, concern over a cataclysmic nuclear war between East and West was the dominant international anxiety. Other issues tended to be overshadowed. Given the proliferation of modern weaponry and the persistence of still unresolved national conflicts, concern over interstate wars remains. But with the obvious exception of the coalition war against Iraq in 1991, civil strife and internal (or intrastate) wars have dominated the headlines, in large part due to the national, ethnic, and humanitarian issues at stake. As the bipolar world faded, scholars attempted to discern the implications of increasing multipolarity and the higher profile of such transnational issues as refugees, pollution, and arms proliferation.

CONCLUSION

As noted, there are three reasons for devoting this chapter to a discussion of historical international systems. First it is hard to discern what may be unique about the current global system unless we know what it has in common with (or how it differs from) earlier international systems. The history of constant competition and conflict among diverse political entities should make us cautious about expecting global peace and harmony to break out any time soon. War or the threat of war has been constant down through the centuries no matter the time period, the region, the civilization, or the types of political units (city-states, empires, or modern states). On the other hand, we have noted how international systems come and go, and it is shortsighted to assume the planet's future must necessarily replay the past. A look into the past also teaches us that other peoples have experienced dramatic changes in the international systems of their day. They too no doubt looked to the future with a mixture of consternation and hope.

Second our brief overview of writers who have influenced contemporary thinking about world politics through the centuries helps to explain the development of the realist and pluralist images of international relations and world politics. Such writers as Thucydides, Machiavelli, and Hobbes have been particularly important in terms of realism. As we have noted, for realists world politics essentially refers to politics among states, which realists often refer to as interstate or international politics. At times they use the term *international state system*, noting that there is a hierarchy of states due to their disparate economic, technological, and military capabilities. When it comes to power, states are inherently unequal. Similarly while realists recognize global economic interdependence, they tend to believe that its influence on international relations is overemphasized: More powerful states, at least, can take steps to reduce the influence of outside factors. But no matter the relative power or degree of interdependence, for realists states dominate global politics.

For some realist scholars, however, defining global politics as merely a Hobbesian system of competitive states is too restricting and historically misleading. As exemplified by the Concert of Europe, one can also view world politics as a society of states. From this view, states compete for power and influence, but they also have common interests that are reflected in basic rules of behavior and international norms. The world is not always a Hobbesian "war of all against all": Cooperation is evident, particularly in the economic realm for advanced industrial states. States also create international organizations, such as the European Union and United Nations, in order to facilitate limited common objectives, but in so doing they may alter the international environment within which they operate.

Third one can speak of an emerging global civil society. Without some knowledge of the history of thinking about world politics, one would fail to appreciate the contribution of such writers as the Stoics, Immanuel Kant, and the nineteenth-century liberals. From this more pluralist perspective, the importance of the state is acknowledged, but its primacy is questioned. As noted in Chapter One, global civil society consists of a series of networks of economic, social, and cultural relations created by individuals and organizations in order to pursue political goals consistent with the rule of law.

Although such organizations as Greenpeace or Amnesty International may attempt to influence the actions and policies of states, they have a broader agenda that consists of influencing the perceptions and actions of individuals around the globe. Much of their activity takes place outside the framework of the state system. Furthermore such transnational activity broadens the concept of identity—commitment and loyalty is not exclusively associated with a particular state. In this pluralist view, the terms *global* or *world politics* are much preferred to the realist terminology of interstate or international relations and politics that puts so much emphasis on states as if they were the only actors of consequence.

Finally placing our historical overview in the framework of the rise, fall, and evolution of various types of international systems encourages the reader to think conceptually. In the following chapters we continue to introduce different concepts associated with globalization and global politics. We begin with the realist perspective and its emphasis on the key conceptual building blocks for understanding global politics in this or any age—interests, power, and security.

KEY TERMS

international systems *p. 33*	sovereignty *p. 35*	nationalism *p. 54*
structure *p. 33*	balance of power *p. 35*	international law *p. 57*

OTHER CONCEPTS

states *p. 32*	ideal or pure type *p. 37*	society of states *p. 56*
government *p. 32*	class *p. 38*	norms *p. 56*
colonialism *p. 33*	power transition theory	federation *p. 57*
globalization *p. 33*	*p. 43*	Concert of Europe *p. 59*
city-states *p. 33*	long-cycle theory *p. 43*	revanchism *p. 61*
empires *p. 33*	idealism *p. 49*	liberals *p. 63*
independent state system	*jus naturale* *p. 49*	class struggle *p. 63*
p. 35	*jus gentium* *p. 49*	proletarian *p. 63*
hegemonic state system	bourgeosie *p. 50*	Marxist-Leninist *p. 63*
p. 35	elites *p. 51*	security dilemma *p. 63*
imperial (suzerain) system	nation-state *p. 54*	imperialism *p. 63*
p. 35	state of nature *p. 55*	collective security *p. 64*
voluntarist *p. 36*	anarchy *p. 55*	collective defense *p. 64*
feudal system *p. 37*	mercantilism *p. 56*	containment *p. 66*
pluralist *p. 37*		

ADDITIONAL READINGS

If we were to recommend a single book on historical international systems, it would be Adam Watson, *The Evolution of International Society* (London: Routledge, 1992). Our debt to this superb work is evident throughout this chapter. We would also suggest S. N. Eisenstadt, *Political Systems of Empires* (New York: The Free Press, 1963); Martin Wight, *Systems of States* (Leicester, England: Leicester University Press, 1977); and Michael W. Doyle, *Empires* (Ithaca, N.Y.: Cornell University Press, 1986). Kenneth Waltz deals with modern state systems (since 1970) in Chapter Eight and considers the concept of international systems more generally throughout his *Theory of International Politics* (Reading, Mass.: Addison-Wesley Publishing Co., 1979). K. J. Holsti deals with historic and contemporary state systems (including the ancient Chinese Chou dynasty not discussed here) in Part Two of his *International Politics* (Englewood Cliffs, N.J.: Prentice-Hall, 1967 and all subsequent editions). For more ideas about world politics from early theorists and others not mentioned here, we would immodestly suggest the reader examine Mark V. Kauppi and Paul R. Viotti, *The Global Philosophers: World Politics in Western Thought* (New York: Lexington Books, 1992).

For an elaboration of power transition theory, see Robert Gilpin, *War and Change in World Politics* (New York: Cambridge University Press, 1981). On long cycles, see George Modelski, *Exploring Long Cycles* (Boulder, Colo.: Lynne Rienner, 1987) and Joshua S. Goldstein, *Long Cycles: Prosperity and War in the Modern Age* (New Haven, Conn.: Yale University Press, 1988). See also Paul Kennedy, *The Rise and Fall of the Great Powers* (New York: Random House, 1987).

INTERESTS, OBJECTIVES, AND POWER OF STATES

International politics, like all politics, is a struggle for power. Whatever the ultimate aim of international politics, power is always the immediate aim.

HANS J. MORGENTHAU, REALIST SCHOLAR

In June 1944 one of the greatest concentrations of conventional military capabilities in the history of the world was ready to be deployed in the invasion of continental Europe by the United States and its allies. Dwight D. Eisenhower was supreme commander of the Allies in Europe. Invasion day—or D-Day—was set for June 5. On the fourth, however, a storm swept into the English Channel. In the early morning hours of June 5, Eisenhower met with his officers. The heavy rain and wind were expected to end that afternoon, but the seas would be rough for the flotilla poised to cross the channel and land on the French beaches at Normandy. Eisenhower asked his colleagues and subordinates what they recommended. The army generals wanted to proceed. The air force generals and navy admirals preferred to delay the invasion until the weather improved. Eisenhower paced for a few moments, stopped, and said, "O.K., let's go!" Beginning shortly after midnight on June 6, airborne troops began parachuting into the French countryside.

At first light infantry came ashore at Normandy under brutal fire from the Germans dug in along the coast. The greatest invasion in the history of warfare had begun and with it the eventual liberation of Europe.

This chapter discusses the types of resources or capabilities a state—and secondarily nonstate actors—may have in order to serve their interests and achieve their objectives. As we noted in Chapter One, a wide range of nonstate actors are important—international organizations and transnational actors such as multinational corporations (MNCs) and banks, environmental movements, labor and human rights organizations, and churches. Indeed, some of the larger MNCs and banks have greater financial clout than most states, which have relatively low national incomes. Our emphasis, however, is on states, on these matters still the most important global actors or *units of analysis,* with more in-depth discussion of international organizations and transnational actors reserved for later in the book. As a result much of the discussion in this chapter is influenced by the realist image of international relations.

FRAMEWORK: INTERESTS, OBJECTIVES, THREATS, AND OPPORTUNITIES

A basic framework or game plan is useful to provide some degree of order and logic to our discussion. We can summarize the chapter using our framework.

Constructing the Framework

From the realist perspective states are actors in global politics with separate **national interests** in a world without a central authority to regulate their activities. In such a world states are often assumed to be rational or "purposive" actors, pursuing various **objectives** understood to be consistent with their separate interests. Within the global system, *opportunities* present themselves that, if handled properly, can help to achieve specific objectives. Similarly *threats* emanating from the global system have to be dealt with if they interfere with the achievement of basic objectives. But to exploit these opportunities and to handle these threats, states are required to mobilize the various **capabilities** they have at their disposal in order to exert *power* constructively to achieve those objectives and protect those interests. A key responsibility of leaders is to make sure that objectives are in line with available capabilities. A country such as the United States, for example, has many more capabilities than Kenya. Hence, Kenya's ability to exert power on the global stage is severely limited compared to the United States, which can seek much more ambitious objectives due to much greater capabilities.

Figure 3.1 depicts this framework. Although the emphasis is on states, it will become apparent that the framework can also be useful in analyzing the behavior of international and transnational organizations and movements. In this chapter

unit of analysis   What is being studied; for example, a state or a decision-making unit.

power   The actual or potential influence or coercion a state (or other actor) can assert relative to other states or nonstate actors because of the political, geographic, economic and financial, technological, military, social, cultural, or other capabilities it possesses.

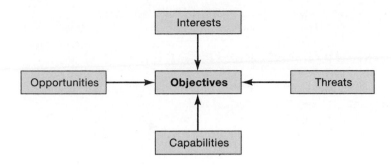

FIGURE 3.1   UNDERSTANDING STATE BEHAVIOR

we discuss each of the highlighted terms, setting the stage for our discussion in subsequent chapters of two important means states use to achieve their objectives—diplomacy and force.

Interests   A critic would claim that the national interest of any state is simply what political leaders say it is—a mere rhetorical device designed to justify the pursuit of a controversial policy. There is certainly an element of truth to this—all leaders claim they act in the selfless pursuit of the national interest whether dictator, democrat, or demagogue. It is fair to say, however, that there are a few basic national interests that transcend any single type of political leader. First there is no disagreement among policy makers that *national survival* as a state is the minimum objective—sometimes referred to as a core or vital interest common to all states. Survival as a state implies maintenance of its sovereign status. As noted in the previous chapter, the exercise of sovereignty is a right claimed by a state to exercise complete jurisdiction, power, or authority internally or within its territory and externally to act independently or autonomously in the conduct of its foreign affairs.

Second a core interest for states is *economic vitality and prosperity.* Economic prosperity is not only sought on behalf of citizens of a society, but it can also be an important source of power in international affairs. Granted there are despots who assiduously work to plunder their own societies and have little concern for their subjects, but such instances are exceptions to the rule. Even those dictators bent on expansionism realize that without the engine of economic growth their dreams of imperial glory are unlikely to be realized.

Finally the preservation of a society's *core values* can also be a vital interest. In many Western states, for example, democratic values and democracy are key elements of national identity. They are not only reflected in the structure and functioning of the political system but also help answer the question "Who are we and what do we stand for?" Similarly some Islamic states and societies view European and American commercial culture and its emphasis on materialism and overt sexuality as a threat to basic religious and moral values.

Objectives   Interests are so general that they are an inadequate guide for actual policy making. They do, however, inform more specific goals or objectives. The core interest of survival for a landlocked state, for example, could be more specifically defined as defense against invasion by neighboring states. Similarly a state

APPLYING THEORY

JOHN H. HERZ, POLITICAL REALISM AND POLITICAL IDEALISM

John Herz and Hans Morgenthau left Germany after the Nazis came to power, settling in the United States. Both found themselves in the center of a great realist-idealist academic debate. Morgenthau recognized the importance of values but underscored the centrality of power and interest as the basis for understanding international politics. Herz put greater emphasis on ideas and values along with these power and interest considerations. He provided a synthesis he called "realist liberalism" that understood the importance of power but found a critical place for values and norms as also affecting the choices political actors make: "While Realist Liberalism accepts the inevitability of power and, consequently, of 'power politics' in interrelations of 'powers,' it looks for ways and means of bringing such policies into a workable system wherein power is applied in the interest of some order, in particular for the balancing of strength and the prevention of hegemony" as in a "collective security system."

In his *Political Realism and Political Idealism* (1951), Herz found fault with extremes in both camps. He saw "political realism" as too narrowly focused on "security and power factors" and on "the struggle for power and power positions" while "political idealism" emphasized "harmonious cooperation," largely ignoring "the problems arising from the security and power dilemma." At the same time Herz observed how political realists often forget or overlook how "political rationalism or idealism" as a motivator for ideologies underlying political movements (such as "individualism, humanism, liberalism, even anarchism, and beyond these, pacifism and internationalism") have "played a role in influencing the actual course of history and in shaping actual politics." To Herz "ethical considerations intervene" (even universal "values and desirabilities, in principle, for all human beings"), and as a result, we come to see "human relations built, not [so much] on the 'egoistic' instincts and the ensuing 'power policies' of individuals and groups, but on considerations beyond mere self-preservation and self-interest."

Herz made a major conceptual contribution in addressing the **security dilemma** facing states in "anarchic society" within which states interact. This security problem stems from a world in which there is no world government or central authority above sovereign states (much less one with the power or means) to maintain order or assure the prerogatives and territorial integrity of states. In a 1950 article in the journal *World Politics,* Herz wrote that human beings "striving to attain security . . . are driven to acquire more and more power in order to escape the impact of the power of others," but "this, in turn, renders the others more insecure and compels them to" do likewise and "prepare for the worst." As a result, "since none can ever feel secure in such a world of competing units, power competition ensues, and the vicious circle of security and power accumulation is on." Thus in such competitive environments as arms races, increased expenditures on armaments may not enhance but actually undermine security by triggering similar expenditures by adversaries. This problem has become particularly acute in the nuclear age when security failures threaten mass destruction.

Question: How would a pluralist who places importance on the international pacifying effects of globalization respond to Herz's analysis?

with long coastlines that is dependent on foreign trade might see the protection of sea lanes as an important national objective in order to maintain economic prosperity.

The eighteenth-century framers of the U.S. Constitution, for example, were well aware of the security dangers the new country would face. One reason offered by Alexander Hamilton in the *Federalist Papers* in favor of uniting the thirteen states was a belief in greater safety in numbers. Going it alone as thirteen separate states was risky, particularly given the potential for invasion by Britain or Spain.

Achieving the objective of political union such as the United States permitted the pooling of defense resources into a single entity while still maintaining state and local defenses. Spanish power waned, but the United States did in fact go to war with Britain in 1812. The United States survived, although the White House was set on fire by British forces bent on settling old scores in the New World. Of course this was only a sideshow in the larger British campaign against Napoleon's extension of French power in Europe, but it was a major assault on American national security with survival of the still-young country at stake.

Beyond defensive concerns, policy makers may also opt for a broad range of other objectives. Some states may wish to conquer others or take territory by force, as occurred, for example, in both of the twentieth century's world wars, the Korean Conflict in 1950, the Vietnam War in the 1960s and 1970s, and Iraq's invasion of Kuwait in 1990.

As a practical matter, however, most national objectives are usually more modest than conquest or defense against invasion. The scope of these other objectives, however, is really quite broad, covering a wide range of political, social, and economic issues. For example the United States, Canada, or some European state may seek to advance human rights, put a cap on the arms race and reduce the likelihood of war, improve the country's trade and balance-of-payments positions, reduce poverty and increase agricultural and industrial productivity in Third World countries, and slow environmental degradation by putting limits on deforestation and pollution of the oceans and the atmosphere.

Some foreign policy objectives may be more immediate—*short-term* or *short-range*—such as when the United States sought in 1970 (and again in 1973) to achieve a cease-fire between the Egyptians and Israelis, leaving establishment of a more durable peace as a follow-on, longer-term objective to be achieved incrementally over a period of decades. Achieving a lasting peace in the Middle East thus qualifies as a *long-range* objective with various *middle-range* objectives defined along the way.

The Camp David Accords in 1978 between Israel and Egypt were an important step toward this end. The way has been slow with many starts and fits, but progress nevertheless has been made. Partial reconciliation was finally achieved in the 1990s between Israel and the Palestinians, who took back control of some of the territories taken by Israel in 1967. American foreign policy makers have supported a continuing process of negotiations, with the Israelis trading land taken by conquest in return for the apparent security to be drawn from Arab recognition and acceptance of the Israeli state and society.

Objectives to be attained over the longer term often tend to be less urgent but more sweeping than those to be achieved in shorter periods of time. A distinction can thus be drawn between the urgency or importance of various national objectives. The importance to the state of different short-term, middle-range, and long-term objectives varies considerably. Some short-term objectives may have a certain urgency about them (such as a particular negotiating position or objective to be sought in tomorrow's trade or arms control session) but are of relatively small importance in the larger scheme of things. A long-term objective of achieving a lasting peace in the Middle East is far more important but of much less urgency.

The continuing efforts to establish a political and economic union in Europe are another example of a long-term objective driven by attainment of various short-term and middle-range objectives over several decades. Europeans began modestly in the early 1950s to integrate coal and steel markets, later expanding over the next four decades to a full-blown economic community and common market as successive steps toward economic (and at least some degree of greater political) union.

Of course, short- and middle-range objectives sought by states and international organizations may not always be tied to overarching, long-term goals such as European union or lasting peace in the Middle East. Consider, for example, the following short-term or middle-range objectives:

- Achieving a more competitive position for farmers and agribusiness in grain or corn exports
- Establishing a corner on some part of the global microelectronics market by a country's multinational corporations or other firms

Both may well stand on their own, quite apart from any larger purposes to be served. Table 3.1 provides other examples of objectives in the context of our three themes of security, economy, and identity.

Threats   Specific objectives states decide to pursue are not decided upon in a vacuum. Objectives are also influenced by threats emanating from the global system. Up until 1992, for example, Western European states paid relatively less

TABLE 3.1	CATEGORIZING THE FOREIGN POLICY OBJECTIVES OF STATES		
EXAMPLES OF ISSUES	**OBJECTIVES**		
	SHORT-TERM (VARYING IMPORTANCE, OFTEN HIGH URGENCY)	MIDDLE-RANGE (NOT URGENT, BUT OF SOME DEGREE OF IMPORTANCE)	LONG-TERM (NOT URGENT, BUT USUALLY OF GREATER IMPORTANCE)
(A) warfare (security)	Negotiate a cease-fire; separate the warring parties	Maintain effective peacekeeping; manage unresolved conflicts, keeping them from escalating to warfare	Achieve a durable or lasting peace; resolve conflicts and reconcile the parties
(B) commerce (economy)	Persuade the other party to make a trade concession such as lowering a tariff or other trade barrier	Establish a good climate conducive to expanding trade relations	Assure an open trading order will flourish on a global scale
(C) human rights (identity)	Secure the release of particular political prisoners; halt a human rights abuse in another country	Establish and foster greater legitimacy for human rights in as many countries as possible	Achieve the societal and political elements essential to durable or lasting democratic regimes in other states

attention to events in Yugoslavia than they would subsequently. With the breakup of the country and eruption of wars among the Croats, Serbs, and Bosnians, a prime European objective became preventing the spread of the conflict beyond the borders of the former Yugoslavia. More generally states attempt to plan for contingencies that might arise that would require the use of military capabilities in different circumstances.

Opportunities   The global system presents states not only with threats to national interests but also with opportunities that may influence the formulation of foreign policy objectives. The decision by former Soviet leader Mikhail Gorbachev to lift the heavy hand of repression from Eastern European client states in the late 1980s created an opportunity for the Federal Republic of Germany (West Germany) to reunite with the German Democratic Republic (formerly communist East Germany). Communist China's decision to create foreign trade zones in the eastern coastal provinces in the 1980s provided an opportunity for other states to pursue the objective of expanded trade and economic investment with the world's most populous country.

A P P L Y I N G   T H E O R Y

⟨⟨ HANS J. MORGENTHAU AND POLITICAL REALISM ⟩⟩

For more than a quarter century following its initial publication in 1948, University of Chicago Professor Hans J. Morgenthau's *Politics Among Nations*, his *In Defense of the National Interest* (1951), and other writings captured the attention not just of students and their professors, but also of both international relations theorists and foreign policy practitioners. Although he was a lightning rod for much criticism directed against the realist propositions he was advancing, especially the primacy given to state power and state interests, Morgenthau nevertheless had an enormous impact on thinking about international relations, particularly among realists in the United States.

Calling for a science of international politics that went beyond mere description, Morgenthau posited six principles of political realism: (1) "that politics, like society in general, is governed by objective laws that have their roots in human nature"; (2) that "in international politics" realists empha-size "interest defined in terms of power"; (3) that "interest defined in terms of power is an objective category that is universally valid"—applicable to states throughout the world; (4) that there is "tension between the moral command and the requirements of successful political action," but that as a practical matter "universal moral principles . . . must be filtered through the concrete circumstances of time and place"; (5) that "political realism refuses to identify the moral aspirations of a particular nation [such as the United States] with the moral laws that govern the universe"; and (6) that "interest defined as power" is an understanding that gives international politics a separate standing and thus "emancipates" it from other fields of study.

Question: What do you think of Morgenthau's assumption that the essence of international politics has changed little over the centuries due to the constancy of human nature?

APPLYING THEORY

THEORY: THE RATIONALITY ASSUMPTION

If you take a moment to think about it, the discussion of the framework at this point almost seems too neat and straightforward; certainly the calculation of a state's interests and objectives is not so simple. This is a good point at which to elaborate on the important realist theoretical concept of the *unified, rational actor*. From the standpoint of **methodology,** this image is an *assumption,* not a description of the actual world. Theoretical assumptions should be viewed not in terms of descriptive accuracy but rather in terms of how fruitful they are in generating insights and hypotheses about international politics. Assumptions, therefore, are neither true nor false; they are more or less *useful* in helping the theorist derive testable propositions and hypotheses about international relations. As noted earlier, once hypotheses are developed, they are tested with **empirical** evidence. The image of the unified, rational state is, therefore, the *starting* point for realist analysis, not a concluding statement. Hans J. Morgenthau has explained the utility of the rational, unitary actor assumption as follows:

> We put ourselves in the position of a statesman who must meet a certain problem of foreign policy under certain circumstances, and we ask ourselves what the rational alternatives are from which a statesman may choose . . . and which of these rational alternatives this

particular statesman, acting under these circumstances, is likely to choose. It is the testing of this rational hypothesis against the actual facts and their consequences that gives meaning to the facts of international politics and makes a theory of politics possible.*

In other words, even if we were not physically present when a decision was made, the rationality assumption gives us a baseline in attempting to explain what actually happened. Similarly such simplifying assumptions aid the development of hypotheses and theories about the causes of various international phenomena including war, arms races, the formation and maintenance of international organizations, and so on. Many works involving **game theory** and **deterrence,** as we will see in Chapters Four and Five, use the rational, unitary actor assumption.

Question: When we read about foreign policy or international events in the newspaper, don't we usually apply the rationality assumption in an attempt to make sense of them? For example, in trying to figure out why a foreign leader acted as he or she did, don't we in effect put ourselves in his or her place and ask, "Would I respond in a similar manner in similar circumstances?"

*Hans J. Morgenthau, *Politics Among Nations,* (New York: Knopf, 1948, 1973), p. 5.

Policy-Making Conflicts over Interests and Objectives

The previous discussion may leave the impression that the formulation of a state's national security or foreign policy objectives is a straightforward task that can be reduced to a formula:

$$interests + threats + opportunities = objectives$$

An obvious difficulty, of course, is that even if policy makers can agree on basic interests, they may disagree on what constitutes a threat, an opportunity, or a worthwhile foreign policy objective. For example in the mid-1980s Western political leaders across the board viewed Gorbachev as simply the latest in a long line of Soviet leaders hostile to the West. Hence he was viewed as a threat. A few years later German Chancellor Helmut Kohl and then British Prime Minister Margaret Thatcher came to view Gorbachev as an opportunity to be seized to

methodology The approach one takes to an academic study; modes of research and analysis such as historical case studies, comparing cases, or the use of statistics to test hypotheses; and statistical applications as in developing causal or game-theoretic models.

empirical Factual, or known through observation.

achieve a dramatic improvement in East-West relations, a position only belatedly accepted by the Reagan administration. Even so some members of the U.S. government continued to treat Gorbachev as a threat, believing that his reassuring words concerning East-West *rapprochement* and nuclear disarmament were little more than a sophisticated deception campaign.

Even if a state comes to realize that there is an opportunity that can be seized, there can be disagreement as how best to take advantage of the situation. Consider, for example, the collapse of communism in the former Soviet Union and the end of Soviet rule over Eastern Europe. What should be the objective of the United States and its allies? Extend the membership of the North Atlantic Treaty Organization (NATO) to all of the former East bloc? Limit membership to those countries such as Poland, Hungary, and the new Czech Republic that initially made the greatest headway toward democratic rule? Deny membership but extend NATO security guarantees to some or all of the Eastern European countries? Or develop a new consultative security organization and defer the issue of NATO membership for the foreseeable future? All of these ideas were suggested and bitterly debated within Western capitals and among NATO allies. Indecisiveness may result from the absence of consensus on foreign policy and national security objectives both within a state and among allies.

Moreover these controversies are not always confined to government officials. If we shift the level of analysis to the societal level (especially in analyzing democracies), interest groups and the general public may hold quite different points of view. Notwithstanding these difficulties, governmental authorities often use the national interest to legitimize their more specific foreign policy objectives. Indeed, they customarily speak and act as if they were serving precisely defined state objectives or goals deemed to be in the national interest.

Defining objectives would seem to be easier in dictatorships and other authoritarian regimes than in democracies—not many officials dared to disagree with Adolph Hitler of Nazi Germany (1933–45) or Joseph Stalin of the Soviet Union (1930–53) while they were in power. Although democracies are constituted to take popular views or **public opinion** into account, the distinction between democracies and authoritarian regimes in terms of popular influences is often overdrawn. Authoritarian regimes can also be influenced by popular sentiments.

For example Soviet political leaders came to understand domestic misgivings about the 1979 intervention in Afghanistan, particularly when loss of life and other costs became more widely known to the general public. Of course popularly supported, authoritarian regimes may derive considerable strength from their mandates in both domestic and foreign policy objectives. This was the case in China after Mao's successful revolution in 1949 and in Vietnam under Ho Chi Minh during and after the wars against France (which ended in 1954) and later against the United States and its allies (which ended in 1975). Unpopular authoritarian regimes, by contrast, may face resistance to their domestic and foreign policy objectives. The Shah of Iran, for example, was an important U.S. and Western ally, but was overthrown in 1979. Similarly, East European communist regimes, once they lost the Soviet security guarantee, soon found they could not deal with public demands from the emerging civil societies and beginning in 1989 they collapsed, one after the other.

Resolving controversies on interests and objectives by governmental decision is common enough in democracies as well, particularly those with a strong cultural tradition in their politics of deference to authorities in such matters of state as foreign policy. By contrast, mandates of this kind are difficult to sustain in the United States without public support, given the strong American political tradition that allows for challenges to all policies, domestic or foreign. Moreover, although the executive branch has the lead in foreign policy matters, **separation of powers** (or **presidential government**) in the United States also gives substantial authority for the formulation of American foreign policy to the legislature, particularly the Senate.

Indeed, the U.S. president and members of the congress are often at loggerheads in determining interests, objectives, and appropriate actions. By contrast, in the more common **parliamentary government,** the head of government is also the leader of the majority party or coalition in the legislature, which somewhat simplifies the consensus-building task. Difficult as it still may be, parliamentary regimes such as those in the United Kingdom, Germany, and Japan only need to reach consensus within the majority party or governing coalition, not across separate, independent branches of government. Still their foreign policies will encounter opposition if there is not sufficient support from or deference by the general public.

Prioritization of Objectives

Let us assume the leaders of a state have agreed on the objectives they wish to pursue. The next problem they face is that the foreign policy objectives of any given state (or international and transnational organization, for that matter) may conflict with each other and thus not be entirely compatible. For example a state's objective of promoting human rights may well conflict with the objective of maintaining good relations or reduced tensions with countries thought to be in violation of human rights. A corporation may want to get early returns on investments in various countries but not be so aggressive or exploitative as to expose itself to foreign complaints that would put its longer-term business position in jeopardy.

Needless to say such rank ordering is often extremely difficult to accomplish. For example, the Carter administration ranked human rights higher as a foreign policy objective than did the Reagan administration. But both administrations effectively put human rights ahead of some other objectives during the late 1970s and 1980s in a publicly celebrated policy conflict about Soviet emigration restrictions. The U.S. government pressed a liberalization of Moscow's policy to allow those Soviet Jews wanting to emigrate to do so more readily. But U.S.-Soviet relations had deteriorated for other reasons, including U.S. and other Western-bloc disapproval of Soviet intervention in Afghanistan in 1979. Not unexpectedly in this already bad climate of relations, the Soviet Union rejected arguments made by the United States and other countries that the Soviets were guilty of human rights violations by not allowing Jewish citizens to leave the country.

These accusations, which no doubt were intended to embarrass and put pressure on the Soviets, contributed to a further souring of relations between Washington and Moscow with predictably negative impact in a variety of other areas. Beyond scoring propaganda points against the Soviets—an objective in itself—there was considerable debate on how much it actually helped Soviet Jews to emigrate or whether quieter diplomacy would have been more effective. What is important here, however, is that policy makers made a clear choice when they decided to make Soviet emigration policy an issue, putting the objective of publicly exposing Soviet human rights violations ahead of other objectives on their agendas. A contemporary example involves China. To what extent should Western states criticize China's human rights abuses, given the objective of wishing to maintain good commercial and other relations with an economic dynamo and growing military power?

Competing Domestic and Foreign Policy Objectives

Now let us assume that policy makers have decided upon basic foreign policy objectives and their priority. The next problem to consider is the possibility that foreign policy objectives may be consistent with some but conflict with other objectives also sought by policy makers. One set of domestic economic objectives common to most governments is to increase employment (or reduce unemployment) of their country's workers while keeping inflation under control. Thus most countries try to create or maintain existing jobs by promoting exports of the goods and services they produce to other countries. One way for a country to do this is to allow (or even take steps to encourage) the value of its currency to decline relative to other currencies. Why? Because doing so makes the price of Country A's exports to foreigners less expensive and thus more likely to be purchased by them. More sales mean more jobs for the exporting country.

The importing Country B, however, may object to such a policy, perhaps because a relative decline of Country A's currency not only will allow imports from that country to be more competitive with locally produced goods and services but also will tend to make Country B's own exports to that country more expensive and thus less competitive. In other words the employment gains in Country A due to the depreciation of its currency may produce employment losses in other countries. Such policies produce an external, adverse impact on other states—what economists refer to as a negative **externality.** Hence Country A, although pleased with the policy's economic impact on domestic objectives, might regret the policy's impact in terms of foreign policy objectives, particularly if Country B is an important ally.

A real-world example involves the United States and its important relations with Japan since the end of World War II. By allowing U.S. military bases on its soil, Japan has aided in the projection of U.S. military capabilities into the Far East, was a source of inexpensive imports until the 1960s, and has been welcomed as a member of the club of democratic states. The United States, being a major trading nation itself, also has been a leading proponent of an open international trading system, which has made the reduction of tariffs on imports a key foreign policy objective. Over the years, however, U.S.-Japanese relations have had their ups and downs, principally due to Japan's tremendous economic success. The U.S.-Japanese trade imbalance—heavily favoring Japan—has been a U.S. domestic political issue as presidents, Congress, and the public worry about Japanese imports putting U.S. manufacturers out of business. How do policy makers balance the domestic objective to save American jobs, the commitment to an open international trading system, and the foreign policy objective of maintaining good relations with a valued ally such as Japan? It is not an easy task.

Even if senior policy makers are able to sort out conflicting foreign and domestic objectives and prioritize them, there is usually considerable disagreement among individuals, interest groups, corporate leaders, and agency officials as to what foreign policy objectives should be, not to mention in what rank order or priority they should be placed. For example, the U.S. Department of Agriculture and privately owned agribusinesses may favor increasing grain exports because increased sales are beneficial to American farmers. The State Department may agree, but for a different reason: They want to maintain or improve relations with countries wanting to import American wheat. For their parts, the Department of Commerce and the Treasury Department may both be inclined to favor such sales because of the favorable impact increased exports will have on the American trade and payments balances.

On the other hand consumer groups may fear that grain exports will reduce the domestic supplies of wheat, driving up prices of bread and other products made from grain. During the cold war years, some interest groups and government officials in the United States saw increased agricultural (and technological) exports to the Soviet Union as helping the other side in a global, competitive struggle with significant security implications for the United States. Private interests, members of Congress, and various executive branch departments and agencies thus weigh in on the different sides of what may have seemed to be a relatively simple issue.

In short, selecting and rank ordering foreign policy objectives is not as easy as it might first seem when domestic goals are taken into account. Determining foreign policy objectives is a rather complex matter when one understands that a country's foreign and domestic objectives often conflict.

In the final analysis, of course, these conflicting interests and competing objectives are usually resolved either through some form of compromise, concession by one or more interested parties, or decision by the president or other authority. In some cases, however, there may be no clear resolution of policy conflicts. When this occurs separate bureaucratic agencies of government, each purporting to act in the name of the state, may simultaneously carry out conflicting policies designed to achieve their diverse objectives. In such circumstances corporations and other private actors will also be more prone to act independently, perhaps circumventing or trying to go around various government authorities. This last point is worthy of further discussion.

States versus Other Actors

Multinational corporations, banks, interest groups of various kinds, international organizations, and other nonstate actors also pursue interests, objectives, and alternative courses of action that may or may not be consistent with the demands of the states in which they conduct their activities. Consideration of the preferences not only of other states but also of nonstate actors are thus included in formulating and implementing a state's foreign policy.

To illustrate such conflicts we will focus on the relations between one type of transnational actor—the multinational corporation (MNC)—and the state. The primary objective of a multinational corporation is to maximize profits for its stockholders or other stakeholders. To achieve such an objective, the corporation may need to move money into and out of countries with little concern for the effects these financial transactions may have on different countries. Similarly these MNCs may look for legal ways to maximize profits and avoid or shelter themselves from taxes.

Governments may try as a matter of policy to attract foreign capital investment by keeping taxes on corporate profits low, allowing for earnings to be taken out of the country or **repatriated** with few if any **capital controls** or other obstacles. Other governments may be less permissive on such matters, charging higher taxes, demanding that foreign investments be in the form of joint ventures with the host government or other local nationals, imposing environmental or other conditions under which foreign investments are allowed, and placing formal or informal restraints on capital outflow.

Whether corporations operate in a permissive environment or a more restrictive one, their interests and objectives may be at odds with the host government. When this occurs the corporation may try to find ways around restrictions. Given the rapid transfer of assets in capital markets that instantaneous global communications have made possible, it has become increasingly difficult in practice for governments to monitor corporate conduct very effectively.

In sum, for a state, international organization, or a transnational actor, deciding upon and implementing a set of objectives is a complex and difficult process. From the perspective of a state, as we have seen, policy makers may disagree among themselves about what are appropriate objectives to pursue and what their relative priority should be. There also may be conflicts between foreign policy and domestic objectives. Finally states must contend with other international actors who have their own set of objectives that might conflict with those of any particular state. What most likely will decide the outcome of such a confrontation, however, is the relative power of the actors involved.

CAPABILITIES AND POWER: TRANSLATING OBJECTIVES INTO REALITIES

Policy makers can talk all they want about the need to formulate and rank order specific foreign policy objectives based upon fundamental national interests and threats and opportunities emanating from the international system. But such an exercise is academic unless a state has the capabilities and power to pursue those objectives. The relation between capabilities and power is difficult to specify because little consensus on the precise meanings of the terms exists in the social sciences, let alone the literature on international relations.

First of all, for some people *power* is equated with *capabilities;* the terms are used interchangeably. They see a country, for example, with a large military and great economic wealth and pronounce "Country X is a great power." But a "large military" and "great economic wealth" only mean something if one asks, "Large or great compared to what?" France has a large military compared to Switzerland but a small one compared to the United States.

Hence a second view is that the power of a state is evident only when compared to other states and nonstate actors. This concept of power as the relative distribution of capabilities can be viewed from a global perspective. The emphasis is on the importance of the *overall* distribution of capabilities in the international system—unipolar (one state dominates), bipolar (two states dominate), multipolar (three or more major states dominate). Proponents of this theory believe that simply knowing the distribution of capabilities allows us to predict basic patterns of behavior in the international system. For example, in a bipolar system, alliances will coalesce around the two major states; such alliances tend to be stable (or in **equilibrium**) with few defections. Conversely, in a multipolar system, coalitions tend to be much less stable and different combinations of states can ally at different times.

The overall distribution of capabilities will also influence other states that are not major players. Even if a major state is not directly attempting to exert influence on such states, the mere existence of their large, imposing capabilities will influence how states with modest capabilities will act. For example, the cold war era was a bipolar system—the United States and the Soviet Union were termed the *superpowers*. Even if less powerful states were ignored by Moscow and Washington, the former did not have the luxury of similar indifference—the political fallout of Soviet-American competition could affect them directly. As an African proverb notes: "When two elephants fight the grass gets trampled."

Power as a relation can also be looked at from the perspective not of the overall global distribution of capabilities but rather from that of any two states. States accumulate capabilities that at some point can be brought to bear on other states or actors. Power is a potential means of influence, not an end in itself. Although all actors may not be so motivated, it may be that a state will seek as a national objective to increase its power position relative to other countries or other actors. The typical reason for taking such measures, however, is the knowledge that power is necessary in an anarchic world without central authority if a state is to achieve its ends.

People, however, are puzzled when a state with superior capabilities cannot influence an obviously much weaker state. Even the most powerful states are constrained by limits to what their capabilities can accomplish. Moreover the power of a state or other actor depends not just on the reality of having certain capabilities but also on the perception held by other actors of the state's willingness to employ its capabilities for various purposes. Unless a state can make others believe in its willingness to use its capabilities, its actual influence will tend to diminish. In short, **credibility** is an important element in power calculations.

This leads us to the final perspective: Power can be viewed as an **effect,** meaning that influence is actually achieved in a particular situation. Consider, for example, two mechanisms through which military capabilities are transformed into effective or actualized military power—victory in war and a change in state behavior due to threats. Victory in war involves taking one's capabilities and actually applying them in a coercive manner, so that a rival is physically defeated or punished to the point at which it surrenders. But an effective *threat* of force may also be sufficient to change the behavior of another state. In either case power has been achieved over a rival—the net effect is to the advantage of one party over the other.

For our purposes, *power* is defined as *the actual or potential* **influence** *or coercion a state or other actor can assert relative to other states and nonstate actors because of the political, geographic, economic and financial, technological, military, social, cultural, or other capabilities it possesses.* This definition views capabilities as the underpinning of power. Once capabilities are mobilized, their utilization is expressed in the attempt or actual ability to influence (such as by diplomacy) or to coerce (such as by the use of force) the behavior of another state or actor. We will now discuss key capabilities that a state may wish to create or enhance. The particular mix of capabilities will vary depending on the state.

Political Capabilities

When we discuss political capabilities as a contribution to (or constraint on) national power, our focus is on states and their societies. At least four factors are involved in defining a country's political capabilities: human resources, reputation, technology, and the nature of its political system and political culture.

ROUSSEAU'S FABLE ABOUT DEER HUNTING AND THE INTERESTS OF STATES: AN APPLICATION OF GAME THEORY

How are states to act in an anarchical, self-help system without any world government or other central authority to provide order? Is it inevitable that they will be self-seeking, attempting to maximize their short-term individual objectives or self-interest? Or is it possible that states can upgrade their common (perhaps enlightened) self-interest over both the short and long term? What is the rational thing to do?

We can find insights in the Geneva-born, eighteenth-century philosopher Jean Jacques Rousseau's allegory or fable about five primitive human beings in a state of nature engaged in a stag hunt. In this presumed or hypothetical state of nature there is no government, no organizations of any kind, no towns or communities, no family unit, no language of communication, nor any form of social structure. In this environment each hunter has to decide (1) whether to collaborate in the hunting of a stag necessary to meet the hunger needs of all five or (2) to defect from the group to capture a hare or rabbit if one appears. To choose the latter course of action would be to serve one's own interest at the expense of the group.

If the individual prefers to serve the common interest (go after the stag), can he or she trust the others to do so? And if the individual cannot trust the others, is it not rational to go for the hare and defect from the group before any of the others do? Or is it possible to develop the basis for collaboration on a continuing basis by all five?

Scholars who deal with game theory attempt to answer such questions. Game theory is an approach to determining rational choice or optimum strategy under conditions of uncertainty. As such, game theory has direct relevance to the study of foreign policy choice, serving national interests, and achieving national objectives.

How one understands Rousseau's stag hunt fable has a great deal to do with how one sees states interacting in world politics. Some tend to see the state as serving only narrow self-interest. Pessimists point to the number, duration, and intensity of wars. Those of a more optimistic bent note that in many cases states live in peace and harmony for years, and great potential does exist for collaboration among states.

What is the rational thing for any of these hunters (or states) to do? The answer depends in part on whether they only want to serve narrowly construed individual interests or whether there is enough trust and confidence among the parties to pursue a cooperative or collaborative venture as in collective hunting of a stag. The answer also depends on whether any of the parties wants to think beyond achieving here-and-now, short-term interests, instead focusing on attainment of longer-term interests and objectives. These alternative choices are arrayed in the matrix shown in Figure 3.A. In short, if the hunters (and states) learn to communicate regularly, building trust and confidence among them, it is at least possible to achieve mutually satisfying outcomes. Pluralists tend to be more optimistic than realists about the achievement of such outcomes.

Question: Do you think it is easier for states to cooperate in an era of increasing globalization, undermining the pessimistic realist implications of living in a world characterized by anarchy? If so, why? If not, why not?

	Individual Interests: Pursue the Hare	Group/Collective Interests: Pursue the Stag
Short Run	Serve immediate self-interest	May provide basis for possible future collaboration
Long Run	No apparent basis for collaborative behavior	Serve long-term common interest

FIGURE 3.A   THE STAG HUNT FABLE: A DILEMMA OF RATIONAL CHOICE

The Human Factor   First human resources are extremely important. Because of their larger population size and higher education levels, some states have great diplomatic and bureaucratic resources that contribute to their political capabilities. Experienced diplomats and other representatives of the state, backed up by competent bureaucratic staffs at home and abroad, certainly enhance the capacity of the state to exercise influence in international affairs.

Some states, by contrast, are unable to find, recruit, train, and assign enough people competent to carry out diplomatic, bureaucratic, and other governmental tasks effectively. Of course this is often the case with lower-income, developing countries where bureaucracies are often bloated and staffed with individuals whose loyalty is to the current ruler. Third World states, therefore, often have to conduct their foreign policies with diminished political capabilities compared to those states and societies having a larger pool of talent and adequate money to train them.

Technology   Second one should not ignore technology's contribution to political capabilities, particularly communications technology. Not all states can afford the advantages provided by advanced telecommunications and related technologies that can be used to coordinate and direct the efforts of diplomats and other representatives around the world. These resources also facilitate the communication of a country's point of view and justification for its policies to the public at home and abroad. Most countries have propaganda ministries or information services, but some are more effective than others in targeting and reaching their intended audience.

Policy makers' access to intelligence also varies considerably. Some states have better technology at their disposal in addition to their human resources. Although all states engage in intelligence collection, only a few have the necessary means to collect and analyze such information adequately on even a regional much less a global scale. Even if technologies are available, widespread use of aircraft, ships, electronic ground stations, satellites, and other technical devices is prohibitively expensive for most countries. Diplomats with access to top-notch intelligence that can be disseminated to them rapidly have an obvious advantage when engaging or negotiating with their counterparts.

Reputation   Third the reputation and prestige of a state should not be underestimated as a capability. If a state, for example, has a reputation of meeting its security commitments in terms of its allies, other states may hesitate to engage in any action that may be viewed as a threat to those allies. Similarly a state's reputation might convince another state to join with it in an alliance, knowing security guarantees made to it will be met. Conversely a state with a reputation for failing to meet its commitments will find its promises and proposals viewed with skepticism. Particularly in the minds of policy makers, reputation is seen as vital to an effective foreign policy.

Democratic and Authoritarian Regimes   The political capabilities of a state are also related to the nature of its political culture, how its political system is structured, and how it functions.

Power is becoming less fungible (that is, less transferable from one issue to another), less coercive, and less tangible. Modern trends and changes in political issues are having significant effects on the nature of power and the resources that produce it. Co-optive behavioral power—getting others to want what you want—and soft power resources—cultural attraction, ideology, and international institutions—are not new. Yet various trends today are making cooptive behavior and soft power resources more important.

Joseph S. Nye Jr.
Bound to Lead: The Changing Nature of American Power (New York: Basic Books, 1990), p. 188.

IT'S BEEN SAID...

The processes of politics—how domestic and foreign policies are made and how well they serve or respond to national interests or objectives—are influenced or constrained by both cultural and structural aspects of a given political system. The ability to reach decisions that can be implemented effectively in a timely fashion thus varies from country to country.

Machiavelli's argument that the power of the state rests in part on popular consent holds as true today as it did in his time. When governing officials or the regime lose *legitimacy*—their "right to rule" in the eyes of the citizenry based on custom or consent—the ability of these policy makers to carry out either domestic or foreign policy is markedly weakened.

In this respect democracies by their very nature sometimes enjoy greater popular support than authoritarian regimes. Democracies may also be more responsive to public opposition to certain policies, changing course or modifying them consistent with public opinion. This is often frustrating to policy makers and other "experts" who have their own views on what are usually very complex issues, not always well understood by the general public. Nevertheless treating public opinion as an important consideration, which democracies are more likely to do than authoritarian regimes, may pay off in the longer run. Political capabilities are enhanced when policies, domestic or foreign, enjoy widespread support.

Building a broad consensus through public discussion of issues can be a source of enormous strength in democracies. Speed and relative efficiency of decision making are sacrificed in exchange for policies informed by a greater number of alternative views and accompanied by greater prospects for forging a consensus. Foreign policies are easier to carry out when people support them in the first place. Of course maintaining a public-support base for policies over time is a continuing challenge for political leaders in democracies as it is in authoritarian regimes as well.

> ## SOME DOUBTS ABOUT DEMOCRACIES AND EFFECTIVE FOREIGN POLICY
>
> Foreign policy demands scarcely any of those qualities which are peculiar to a democracy; on the contrary it calls for the perfect use of almost all those qualities in which a democracy is deficient. Democracy is favorable to the increase of the internal resources of a state, it diffuses wealth and comfort, fortifies the respect for law in all classes of society, but it can only with great difficulty regulate the details of an important undertaking, persevere in a fixed design, and work out its execution in spite of serious obstacles. It cannot combine its measures with secrecy or await their consequences with patience. These are qualities which are more characteristic of an individual or an aristocracy.
>
> **Alexis de Tocqueville**
> *Early nineteenth century*
> *French observer of America from his*
> Democracy in America
>
> IT'S BEEN SAID...

Regime Type Democracies such as Japan and most European countries have a parliamentary government in a **unitary state.** Political authority is more concentrated than in the United States, which has separation of powers between legislative and executive branches within a **federal state** (see Tables 3.2 and 3.3). Thus in the United Kingdom the executives—prime minister, foreign secretary, defense secretary, chancellor of the exchequer (treasury), and other cabinet ministers—are themselves members of parliament. In the United Kingdom and other countries with parliamentary governments, executive and legislative authority is effectively fused instead of being separated into distinct legislative and executive branches, each with its different bases for authority and power, as in the American form of presidential government. Moreover there is only one government in a unitary state, not the separate state and local governments that may compete with each other and the central government in a federal state such as the United States, Germany, Switzerland, and Canada. In the British case we note there has been some devolution or transfer of authority to component units, as in establishing a Scottish legislature for dealing primarily with issues of local concern; however,

legitimacy In terms of domestic politics, the right to rule or be obeyed based on legal or other authoritative grounds or more commonly in the eyes of the citizenry based on custom or consent.

TABLE 3.2	STRUCTURAL TYPES OF STATES AND DEMOCRATIC GOVERNMENTS	

TYPES OF STATES	CHARACTERISTICS	EXAMPLES
unitary states	Those that *concentrate* all political authority or power in one government in its capital city; most states are of this kind.	Japan, the United Kingdom, France, Italy, Argentina
federal states	Those that *divide* all political authority or power between a central government and additional state or provincial governments; although less common than unitary states, many are of this kind.	United States, Canada, Germany, Russia

TYPES OF DEMOCRATIC GOVERNMENTS	CHARACTERISTICS	EXAMPLES
parliamentary governments	Those that *fuse* in particular the executive and legislative functions into a single branch of government; this is the most common form of democratic governance.	Japan, Germany, the United Kingdom, Italy
	The judiciary is usually independent, in some cases with authority to exercise judicial review to assure the constitutionality of governmental acts.	Germany
	In some there is no political authority higher than an act of parliament.	United Kingdom
presidential governments	Those that *separate* the executive, legislative, and judicial functions into separate branches of government; the relative strength of branches varies, with the executive clearly stronger in some countries.	France
	In others there may be more of a contest between the legislature and the executive. In some countries authority for judicial review to interpret and assure constitutionality of laws and executive acts is common.	United States

TABLE 3.3	CATEGORIZING STATES WITH DEMOCRATIC GOVERNMENTS: SOME EXAMPLES	
	TYPES OF DEMOCRATIC GOVERNMENTS	
TYPES OF STATES	**PARLIAMENTARY**	**PRESIDENTIAL**
unitary	United Kingdom, Italy, Japan (greatest concentration of political authority; most common combination)	France
federal	Germany	United States (greatest fragmentation of political authority; least common combination)

authority on foreign policy, national security, and most other issues remains under British parliamentary authority in London.

Considerable debate and compromise still remain both within and outside the majority party or coalition in states with parliamentary governments but not usually to the same degree as in states with presidential governments, in which political power and authority are dispersed or more fragmented. Compromises on foreign policy as in other political matters in parliamentary governments need only be made among legislators within the majority party or coalition of governing parties. Although concurrence by opposition parties can be helpful by providing a broader base of support for a parliamentary government's foreign policy, there is no formal requirement for such a consensus.

Moreover there is no need to compromise in the consensus-building process across branches of government since the executive is in fact part of the legislature in parliamentary regimes. As a result states with parliamentary governments tend to be somewhat more decisive and often have more comprehensive and coherent foreign policies than those with presidential governments. When parliamentary governments exist in unitary states—the most common form of democracy—there are even fewer governmental obstacles to overcome once a decision has been made within the central government. No separate state governments are empowered to challenge the decisions of national authorities in a purely unitary state. Of course efficiency in policy making says nothing about the quality of the actual policy—it could be a failure if not disastrous to the interests of the state.

By contrast, compared to most other countries, there are many more potentially influential voices on foreign policy matters and many more points of access for the exercise of such influence in the United States. Given a federal **division of powers** between central and state and local governments and the aforementioned separation of powers between executive and legislature in all of these governments, there is a fragmentation of authority and a proliferation of points of access for individuals and interest groups. With so many incremental compromises required before decisions are taken, these governments tend to be slower in reaching decisions. When decisions are made they tend to be step-by-step, incremental choices in which short-term factors often dominate. Although not impossible—given the fragmentation of power and authority under *both* federalism and separation of powers—it is much more difficult in the United States to develop comprehensive, logically coherent policies that take mid-range and long-term considerations seriously into account. Again, however, this does not necessarily mean U.S. policy is less effective in defending its interests and achieving its objectives compared to a parliamentary system.

Political Cultures   Political capabilities are also affected by **political culture**—those norms, values, and orientations of a society's culture that are politically relevant. Many societies have a tradition of deferring, for the most part, to political authorities in such matters of state as foreign policy. In some societies, by contrast, there is a greater tendency for people to become involved. Although government officials in the United States often may have greater latitude in foreign policy matters than on domestic issues, Americans are not prone to defer entirely to political authorities on either domestic or foreign policy and readily let their views be known whether the issue is U.S. involvement in Bosnia, Kosovo, Haiti, or some other country.

In some democracies with consensus-oriented political cultures such as Japan, Switzerland, or Sweden, there may be a greater tendency to seek a broader basis of support for policies than is constitutionally or legally required. In other democracies such as the United Kingdom, Germany, or the United States, where conflict-oriented politics prevail as part of their political cultures, a narrow, simple majority of 50 percent plus one vote will do. Wider margins may be desirable but are by no means required in such countries either by law or by expectation within the prevailing political culture.

Social and Cultural Capabilities

The social cohesion of a society has a direct impact on its power position. States suffering from crises of authority and torn apart by economic, ideological, religious, ethnic, racial, language, or other cultural differences can hardly act effectively in the international arena. The states that comprise the former Yugoslavia illustrate this point. Their bloody civil wars undermined their capabilities. Culturally and socially homogeneous states, by contrast, are usually more effective international actors.

The concept of a **nation-state** refers to the nineteenth- and twentieth-century idea that a common national identity can be achieved among the people living within a given state. In fact some states such as Nigeria, Lebanon, Switzerland, the Russian Federation, Belgium, and Canada can be said to contain two or more nations. Unless such sociocultural diversity can be contained, through toleration and compromise, establishment of linkages that effectively connect different communal groups, or assimilation of diverse elements into one national whole, the power of the state as an international actor can become markedly weakened.

Another important aspect of cultural capabilities is the extent to which countries are able to maintain influence over other countries through common language, religion, ethnic or racial identity, or legal and political tradition. The French and the British, for example, have maintained fairly close ties with the elites of many of their former colonies. In spite of political differences, elites in these former colonies typically speak the language and often adopt many of the ways of the former colonial power. In some instances, these cultural ties have been buttressed or reinforced by continuing military, trade, financial, and other commercial relations. Critics refer to such ties as a manifestation of **neocolonialism**—a new form of long-established patterns of dominance by former colonial powers.

The education levels, distribution of skills, and value systems that characterize different societies often have substantial impact on the roles countries play in world politics. Economic strength, for example, depends directly on such factors. Market-oriented cultures in which entrepreneurial skills are valued provide an environment within which individuals and businesses can thrive. A highly skilled and educated population oriented toward productivity makes economic success possible. Societies lacking sufficient numbers of such human resources are hard-pressed to compete successfully in global markets, however committed the country's leadership may be to achieving economic gains and sustaining development.

Geographic, Economic, and Technological Capabilities

Geographic location can affect the capabilities of states. That the United Kingdom and Japan are island states, for example, historically has provided some protection against invasion by continental or other states. Similarly the separation of the United States from Europe enabled the United States early in its history to pursue an isolationist foreign policy, avoiding what George Washington called the "entangling alliances" of European politics. The United States was able, in fact, to delay its entry into both World War I and World War II due to the remoteness of its geographic location from the combat area. Oceans provided valuable insulation from European affairs. Of course this geopolitical advantage has been reduced considerably by technology, in particular the development of intercontinental ballistic missiles (ICBMs) and other weapons systems that have increased the vulnerability of the United States to military attack.

Geography, defined in terms of natural resources, obviously has an important impact on state capabilities. Whatever power the petroleum-producing countries may have stems in large part from the fact that most industrial countries remain so dependent on them for oil and natural gas supplies. Although the United States is somewhat less dependent than Japan and most European countries, more than half of American consumption is from foreign sources. The United States also has vast supplies of lumber, coal, iron, and other raw materials, but the country imports the bulk of its tin, bauxite, chromium, cobalt, manganese, nickel, and zinc. Compared to most countries, however, the United States is still very rich in natural resources. By contrast Japan is at the other extreme and remains dependent on foreign sources for most of its raw

THE INFLUENCE OF FOREIGN VALUES

Until 1960, the University College of Fort Hare was the only residential center of higher education for blacks in South Africa. Fort Hare was more than that: it was a beacon for African scholars from all over Southern Central and Eastern Africa. For young black South Africans like myself, it was Oxford and Cambridge, Harvard and Yale, all rolled into one.

Fort Hare was a missionary college. We were exhorted to obey God, respect the political authorities, and be grateful for the educational opportunities afforded us by the church and the government. These schools have often been criticized for being colonialist in attitudes and practice. Yet, even with such attitudes, I believe their benefits outweighed their disadvantages. The missionaries built and ran schools when the government was unwilling or unable to do so. The learning environment of missionary schools, while often morally rigid, was far more open than the racist principles underlying government schools. Fort Hare was both home and incubator of some of the greatest African scholars the continent has ever known.

Nelson Mandela
Long Walk to Freedom (Boston: Little, Brown, 1994), pp. 37–38.

IT'S BEEN SAID...

materials. Putting this into perspective, however, the comparative advantage of the resource-rich United States is reduced somewhat by the fact that the country is also the world's largest consumer of natural resources.

The United States also has the world's largest economy as measured by its **gross national product (GNP)** or **gross domestic product (GDP).** These are measures of the total dollar value of all goods and services produced in a given year. Economic productivity stems from the efficient use of human and natural resources. Second only to the United States in national economic output is natural resource–poor Japan, which nevertheless has demonstrated its capability to organize its economy into one of the most productive in the world. Beyond the industriousness of Japan's labor force, considerable capital investment in new and advanced technologies has made possible that phenomenal economic growth over the more than half century since the end of World War II.

The leading industrial countries with the largest economies in terms of sheer size include the United States, Japan, Germany, France, Italy, the United Kingdom, Russia, and Canada (see Table 3.4). A number of other advanced industrial countries have smaller economies but often higher standards or levels of living than some of the countries with larger economies (see Table 3.5). Switzerland immediately comes to mind. Taiwan, Singapore, South Korea, and other **newly industrializing countries (NICs)** have made impressive economic gains in recent decades; these countries have educated and skilled populations with market orientations, but economic capabilities in all of these countries are a function more directly of such factors as labor productivity, the effectiveness of management, the extent and quality of capital investment, the degree of technological innovation, and condition of the **economic infrastructure**—such production-support factors as roads, sea- and airports, public transportation, and telecommunications.

By contrast, agrarian societies with less-developed industrial economies are heavily dependent on agricultural production both for their own domestic consumption and in some cases for export. Because these countries rely more heavily on labor to sustain their economies, they are usually less efficient even in agricultural production than advanced industrial countries such as the United States. Advanced industrial countries that are also endowed with good soil and a favorable climate have made very heavy capital investments in machinery used by the large agribusinesses and smaller, cooperative farm arrangements. Technology-intensive agriculture in the United States, for example, has made it the world's largest exporter of food products.

Vulnerability to price fluctuations in the international market is most severe for those countries that are dependent on export of one or a few crops, minerals, or other raw materials. With the notable exception of the oil-exporting countries, attempts to form producer cartels for other minerals and for agricultural products have not been very successful. In part this is because consumers of these products can more easily substitute other minerals or agricultural products or increase their own domestic production of these products. By contrast large-scale substitution of other energy sources for oil in the oil-dependent industrial countries is not easily accomplished, at least not in the short run. The economic disparities between the haves and have-nots are evident in Table 3.5. Note the bottom-line figures comparing industrialized and developing countries.

| TABLE 3.4 | GNP AS INDICATOR OF RELATIVE CAPABILITIES OR POWER POSITION: COMPARING THE SIZE OF SELECTED ECONOMIES[a] | | |

COUNTRY	GROSS NATIONAL PRODUCT (U.S. $ BILLIONS)	COUNTRY	GROSS NATIONAL PRODUCT (U.S. $ BILLIONS)
Group of Seven (World's Major Economies)		*Other Asia and Pacific*	
United States	7,783.1	China	1,055.4
Japan	4,812.1	S. Korea	485.2
Germany	2,321.0	Australia	382.7
France	1,541.6	India	357.4
Italy	1,160.4	Indonesia	221.5
United Kingdom	1,231.3	Thailand	165.8
Canada	595.0	Philippines	88.4
Other Europe		*Latin America*	
Spain	569.6	Brazil	784.0
Russian Federation	394.9	Mexico	348.6
Netherlands	403.1	Argentina	319.3
Switzerland	305.2	*Africa*	
Sweden	231.9	South Africa	130.2
Belgium	272.4		
Austria	225.4		
Denmark	184.3		
Turkey	199.3		
Norway	159.0		
Ukraine	52.6		

[a]Aggregate economic production of goods and services can be used as an indicator of overall capabilities or power. Criterion for selection was economies of about $100 billion ($100,000 million) or more, thus depicting the geographic distribution of great and middle powers. Many smaller economies (less than $100 billion GNP) nevertheless enjoy higher levels of living as measured by per capita incomes (see Table 3.5) than a number of the larger economies included in this table. Ukraine is also included here.

Source: United Nations Development Programme, *Human Development Report* (New York: Oxford University Press, 1999), pp. 180–83.

	LEVEL OF LIVING: PER CAPITA INCOME	
TABLE 3.5	OF SELECTED COUNTRIES	

COUNTRY	REAL GDP PER CAPITA (PPP$)[a]	GNP PER CAPITA (US$)
USA	$29,010	$29,080
Switzerland	28,240	43,060
Japan	24,070	38,160
Canada	22,480	19,640
France	22,030	26,300
Singapore	28,460	32,810
Australia	20,210	20,650
U.K.	20,730	20,870
Iran	5,817	1,780
Mauritius	9,310	3,870
Malaysia	8,140	4,530
Mexico	8,370	3,700
Russia	4,370	2,680
Turkey	6,350	3,130
Botswana	7,690	3,310
Peru	4,680	2,610
Guatemala	4,100	1,580

Military Capabilities

The military is another important capability or component of a state's power. In some countries the military performs a domestic order maintenance function similar to that performed by police forces. Indeed, in some authoritarian regimes the military's primary function is not to protect the country but to protect the regime from its own citizens. Although the ability to maintain stability or order within the state has an important impact on the state's relative power position, the external capacity of its military forces is perhaps even more important. As we will see in Chapter Five, states use force (or threaten to use it) to secure various objectives, the most important of which is their own defense or survival.

The continued development of nuclear weapons since World War II added a new dimension to military capabilities, but conventional or nonnuclear military forces remain a vital part of the calculus of a state's military capabilities. What size and kinds of force a state can deploy, where, and for how long are variables that

TABLE 3.5   (CONTINUED)

COUNTRY	REAL GDP PER CAPITA (PPP$)[a]	GNP PER CAPITA (US$)
Romania	4,310	1,410
Philippines	3,520	0
Zimbabwe	2,350	720
China	3,130	860
Kenya	1,190	340
India	1,670	370
Uganda	1,160	330
Rwanda	660	210
Mali	740	260
All developing countries (average)	3,240	1,314
All industrial countries (average)	23,741	27,174
World (average)	6,332	5,257

[a]PPP$ = Purchasing power parity in U.S. dollars is a measure that takes exchange rates and other factors into account on determining capacity to purchase goods and services on a common standard for comparative purposes.

Source: United Nations Development Programme, *Human Development Report 1995* (New York: Oxford University Press, 1999), pp. 134–37, 180–83.

have a significant impact on a state's relative power position. The United States is clearly the world's biggest military spender.

Paradoxically the rapid advancement of military technology, particularly in nuclear weaponry, has served to constrain those states possessing such capabilities. Indeed, use of such weapons can invite retaliation by one's adversary with unacceptable destructive consequences. Often states not possessing such weapons have been able to assert far more leverage than one would expect, given their apparently inferior military capabilities. As a practical matter, since the end of World War II, the world's nuclear powers have been reluctant to use such weapons to achieve objectives at the expense of nonnuclear states. Nevertheless states tend to believe that the possession of nuclear weapons enhances the state's international reputation and prestige.

It is easy to overstate the importance of the military component of national power relative to other factors. Certainly prudent decision makers will take seriously any existing or potential military capability that could be threatening in order to assure that they have enough military capability of their own to offset it. On the

USS Louisiana, nuclear Trident submarine commissioned in 1997.

other hand military capabilities do depend on the strength of the underlying economy as a source of personnel and for procurement of military equipment and supplies. In this regard economic capabilities may define the limits of the military capabilities a country may choose to develop.

Measuring Power

Given these diverse capabilities, it is exceedingly difficult to produce a single measure capturing all of these capabilities that would enable the political analyst to rank states in order of their power positions. Most would agree that the United States is currently the world's sole superpower or strongest great power, but who comes next: Japan? Germany? France? Great Britain? Russia? China? Not only is there no agreement on the weighting or relative importance of these capabilities, but it is also next to impossible to quantify such factors as cultural and social capabilities in any meaningful fashion.

Moreover some realists as well as scholars working in the pluralist tradition claim that to talk of power as an integrated concept is not particularly useful. They argue that in different *issue areas* different capabilities have different degrees of importance. From this point of view, military capabilities have considerable salience in strategic issues but do not have great weight in trade, investment, and other economic issues. How useful, for example, are American military capabilities when it comes to trade disputes with Japan?

On the other hand most realists argue that one cannot talk of such economic issues as trade and investment relations among the countries belonging to (or associated with) the European Union (EU) strictly in terms of economic capabilities. From this perspective, especially during the cold war, the European states benefited from the security umbrella provided by the United States. Thus, one can argue that military capabilities are at least as important as economic capabilities in determining the power of states in economic issue areas. Certainly the United States derives some **economic leverage** in its relations with EU members and other European states that depend to some degree on America's contribution to the NATO alliance and overall European security.

Similarly realists note that in the 1970s a great deal of attention was given to OPEC, the Organization of Petroleum Exporting Countries. With headquarters in Vienna, this international organization is composed of both Arab and non-Arab oil exporting countries. The members of OPEC had considerable success in the 1970s raising the world price of petroleum, thus markedly improving their collective power position. The oil exporting countries were, in effect, displacing the multinational oil companies from the price-setting role, a task the MNCs had previously performed. OPEC assumed this price-setting function by regulating the supply of oil to world markets. For the first time these industrially less-developed countries were able to assert very real financial leverage on the industrialized countries. Almost overnight, some observers proclaimed, the OPEC member nations had become major international players.

The price-increase "oil shocks" of the 1970s, however, led industrialized countries to take domestic measures in an attempt to reduce their dependence on oil and natural gas. Beyond conservation measures designed to reduce energy waste, these countries also sought to substitute other energy sources such as coal or nuclear power and have invested in longer-term research and development projects in nuclear, solar, wind, geothermal, and other energy sources.

Divisions within the OPEC cartel and decisions by Saudi Arabia and other major producers to maintain an adequate supply of petroleum to world markets have precluded major price increases comparable to those in the 1970s. In particular the United States took measures designed to assure the security of the principal oil supplier, Saudi Arabia, in exchange for at least a tacit assurance of continuing flow of oil to the global market. From a realist perspective Saudi Arabia has proven to be a one-dimensional power as evidenced by its reliance on the military prowess of the United States and other powers such as France and the United Kingdom to deter Iraqi aggression following the 1990 invasion of Kuwait.

In short, little or no consensus exists among analysts as to whether one should treat power as a single, integrated concept or whether one should disaggregate the concept into its separate component capabilities. Contemporary practitioners associated with the realist perspective on international relations seek to enhance the military, economic, and other components of state power. They may do this through domestic or *internal* measures such as taking actions designed to strengthen the national economy or to improve the capabilities of the armed forces. *External* measures designed to increase state power include forming alliances, influencing members of already existing alliances to increase their contributions, and directly arming allies, thus improving their capabilities.

CONCLUSION

Realists argue that there are a few core or vital interests for all states. Interests in conjunction with threats and opportunities in the global system help to define foreign policy objectives. Such a formula for determining a state's foreign policy objectives is more easily stated than actually achieved. Policy makers may disagree among themselves about what is an opportunity or a threat and about the prioritization of foreign policy objectives once they agree to specific objectives. To complicate matters, foreign policy objectives may conflict with domestic objectives. Furthermore merely possessing capabilities or power potential does not make a state effective in world politics unless it has the will to use these capabilities in pursuing its objectives. Even so it may face opposition from both states and non-state actors with which it may have to contend. A country's sensitivity to public opinion, international legal considerations, domestic politics, perceptions of its resolve, and its reputation and degree of international prestige also may constrain the use of its capabilities.

Beginning in the following chapter we turn to statecraft—putting power or capabilities to work through diplomacy, the use of force, and other mechanisms available to achieve objectives and serve interests. While the objectives, capabilities, and power of international and transnational organizations remain important, we continue our focus on states in this section of the book.

KEY TERMS

unit of analysis *p. 74*	methodology *p. 80*	legitimacy *p. 89*
power *p. 74*	empirical *p. 80*	

OTHER CONCEPTS

national interests *p. 74*	externality *p. 83*	nation-state *p. 92*
objectives *p. 74*	repatriated *p. 84*	neocolonialism *p. 93*
capabilities *p. 74*	capital controls *p. 84*	gross national product
security dilemma *p. 76*	equilibrium *p. 85*	(GNP) *p. 94*
game theory *p. 80*	credibility *p. 86*	gross domestic product
deterrence *p. 80*	effect *p. 86*	(GDP) *p. 94*
public opinion *p. 81*	influence *p. 86*	newly industrializing
separation of powers *p. 82*	unitary state *p. 89*	country (NIC) *p. 94*
presidential government	federal state *p. 89*	economic infrastructure
p. 82	division of powers *p. 91*	*p. 94*
parliamentary government	political culture *p. 92*	economic leverage *p. 99*
p. 82		

ADDITIONAL READINGS

Any student who intends to pursue the study of international relations beyond the introductory level would do well to examine the all-time classic realist textbook by Hans J. Morgenthau, *Politics Among Nations* (New York: Knopf), first published in 1948 and reprinted or revised in many subsequent editions. An influential work by two scholars who attempted to draw on the strengths of both realism and pluralism is Robert O. Keohane and Joseph S. Nye, *Power and Interdependence: World Politics in Transition* (Boston: Little, Brown, 1977). For an excellent discussion of the elements of power from a realist perspective, see Klaus Knorr, *The Power of*

Nations: The Political Economy of International Relations (New York: Basic Books, 1975). On power and the balance of power, see also Kenneth N. Waltz, *Theory of International Politics* (Reading, Mass.: Addison-Wesley, 1979) and his earlier *Man, the State and War* (New York: Columbia University Press, 1954, 1959), especially Chapters VI and VII. For a pluralist view of power focusing on cognitive dimensions, see Ernst B. Haas, *When Knowledge Is Power* (Berkeley: University of California Press, 1990).

DIPLOMACY: MANAGING RELATIONS AMONG STATES

"[A diplomat is] a person who can tell you to go to hell in such a way that you actually look forward to the trip."

CASKIE STINNET

"A Foreign Secretary is always faced with this cruel dilemma. Nothing he can say can do very much good, and almost anything he may say may do a great deal of harm. Anything he says that is not obvious is dangerous; whatever is not trite is risky. He is forever poised between the cliché and the indiscretion."

HAROLD MACMILLAN, SECRETARY OF STATE FOR FOREIGN AFFAIRS AND LATER PRIME MINISTER OF THE UNITED KINGDOM, 1955

CHAPTER 4

Napoleon had lost the war and France had good reason to fear the results of the peace conference held in Vienna beginning in 1814. The French **emissary**, Count Talleyrand, faced a seemingly impossible task—to rescue his country from the vengeance of its wartime adversaries. During Napoleon's wars French armies had moved deliberately across Europe, forcibly conscripting troops along the way, overthrowing uncooperative princes, and leaving a trail of devastation in their wake. The anger and bitterness they left behind them promised little chance for a charitable outcome now that the tables were turned.

As a bishop of the Catholic Church, Talleyrand had been part of the **ancien regime**, the old order under the Bourbon dynasty that had been overthrown in the revolution that began in 1789. Always a political survivor, Talleyrand was extraordinarily flexible, jettisoning his clerical identity and navigating through the revolutionary turmoil virtually unscathed. He emerged in 1815 as part of a restoration movement designed to reestablish the prerevolutionary order in Europe as a whole and France in particular.

Talleyrand had to face France's now-formidable adversaries without any military or economic leverage to support his negotiating position. The victims of French aggression now had the opportunity to carve up France, dividing it among them or at least separating the country into such small pieces that it could no longer be a threat.

The most important delegations at Vienna were those representing the interests of the four great powers that prevailed following the defeat of France. Prince Metternich of Austria was the leading figure, known historically for his intelligence, cleverness, and diplomatic acumen—a man extremely adept at serving Austria's imperial interests. Playing lesser but still very important roles in constructing the settlement at Vienna were Tsar Alexander of Russia, Viscount Castlereagh of Britain, and Prince von Hardenberg of Prussia.

In the final analysis Talleyrand was able to save France, but not through any charity felt by its erstwhile enemies. Instead France was restored (territorially even slightly larger than it had been in 1789!) only because it was in the interest of all of the great powers to do so. The French Revolution not only had transformed politics in France; it had also threatened the institution of monarchy in European countries that had never previously experienced such challenges. From this perspective, strengthening European monarchies as legitimate institutions in the post-Napoleonic period meant returning the Bourbons to their "rightful" positions in France as well.

Beyond these considerations, a restored France contributed substantially to maintaining what the British had long favored as a centerpiece of foreign policy—a balance of power on the European continent to keep any one country from becoming too strong. For Austria a restored France kept growing Prussian power at bay. Finally the settlement also served Russian interests by maintaining a balance to its west, not just between Prussia and Austria but also between both of them and France.

For France it was a badly needed diplomatic triumph. Even though he lacked the military and other tangible resources to strengthen his negotiating position, Talleyrand accomplished his short-term goal. He restored France to legitimate standing in Europe as a great power, much as it had been for centuries preceding the defeat of Napoleon's empire. He was able to accomplish this because in the course of negotiations a restored France came to be understood as being in the interest of all of the great powers. More important for Europe as a whole, however, was the lasting influence of the Vienna settlement. It was the basis for a long peace that (with a few interruptions) would last for some 99 years.

In the previous chapter we laid out the basic elements of state interests, objectives, and power. You will recall that power was defined as the actual or potential influence or coercion a state (or other actor) can assert relative to others and non-state actors because of the political, geographic, economic and financial, technological, military, social, cultural, or other capabilities it possesses.

In this chapter we examine a primary means by which states attempt to exert influence over other states—***diplomacy***. Diplomatic activity is one of the most visible aspects of international relations. Almost every day of the week newspapers and news broadcasts report the work of diplomats. If there is a war to be averted, a crisis to be resolved, or a peace settlement to be negotiated, diplomats are on the scene. Lower-profile activity includes the daily work conducted at embassies and consulates: issuing tourist and immigrant visas, providing citizen services for overseas travelers, encouraging commercial activity among nations, and regular meetings with host foreign ministry personnel.

Diplomacy among states includes a wide range of both positive and negative approaches—both incentives and disincentives including the use of force (see Table 4.1). In the following chapter we focus more specifically on the actual use of force in international politics. Diplomacy can be viewed as a basic means by which states attempt to harness their power for the purpose of achieving their objectives and securing their interests.

Generally speaking in those situations in which states' preferences or interests are close enough to be reconciled and the parties involved desire to achieve a mutually beneficial accommodation, noncoercive diplomacy will play a major role

diplomacy The management of international relations by communications to include negotiations leading to a bargain or agreement.

in achieving such an outcome. Examples include the creation of the North Atlantic Treaty Organization (NATO) in 1949, the development of the European Union (EU) over recent decades, and the North American Free Trade Agreement (NAFTA) between the United States, Mexico, and Canada. Although on a number of indices the capabilities will differ among the states involved, all governments believe they have a common interest in seeing an agreement reached.

In those situations in which states' preferences or interests sharply diverge or are viewed as incompatible, policy makers and diplomats may resort to more forceful measures. The active use of physical force is the most basic means to assert power. This characterized the situation involving the major European states in the late 1930s and Japan and the United States commencing with the attack on Pearl Harbor in December 1941. At the risk of oversimplifying, diplomats are in the forefront of negotiations to prevent war. If they fail the military takes over and does what it is trained to do—fight wars. Once force has defeated or demoralized one of the participants, diplomacy plays an important role in any peace negotiations or settlement. This was the case in 1998–99 during the crisis in the Balkans and subsequent NATO war against Serbia over the issue of Kosovo.

Threatening to use force is a prevalent aspect of diplomacy. Some threats are designed to get another state or states to do what they would not otherwise do—to compel them to take particular actions. This is often referred to as *coercive diplomacy* (or *compellence*) and may include the selective application of actual military force to get a foe to accede to one's wishes. Alternatively threats of force can be an aspect of *deterrence*—a way to persuade states from doing what they intend or might like to do. This demonstrates a more passive use of force.

compellence   Threat or use of force aimed at coercing another actor to change course or take an action it would not otherwise do; often called **coercive diplomacy**.

deterrence   Threat or use of force aimed at persuading another actor not to do what it intends or may like to do; a psychological effect on an opponent.

TABLE 4.1	DIPLOMACY AS A RANGE OF ALTERNATIVES	
ALTERNATIVE	**DEGREE OF COERCIVENESS**	**EXAMPLES**
Coercive diplomacy and deterrence	Most coercive; negative approaches and disincentives	Threat or actual use of military force
Economic and other sanctions	Moderately coercive; negative approaches	Threat or actual breaking of diplomatic relations; cutting trade or foreign aid; imposing an embargo
Economic and other positive incentives	Noncoercive; positive approaches and incentives	Promising aid and most-favored-nation trade status; normalizing diplomatic relations; signing cooperative or collaborative agreements; forming alliances
Compromise or finding common ground	Noncoercive; attempt to satisfy separate and common interests of parties	Finding mutual gains as bases for agreements

Not all negative diplomatic approaches use the threat or application of military force. Economic threats or sanctions represent another set of options or disincentives that can be used for the same purposes. For example United Nations economic sanctions were imposed on Libya in an effort to coerce that country into turning over two Libyan intelligence agents charged with the bombing of Pan Am Flight 103 in December 1988. International economic sanctions were also imposed for many years against South Africa in an attempt to change its racial **apartheid** policies.

Interstate relations can be played out anywhere along this continuum, moving back and forth depending on the countries involved, the issues in dispute, and the time period. The United States, for example, utilized more positive diplomatic measures in early 1990 to try to persuade Saddam Hussein of Iraq to resolve his grievances with neighboring Kuwait peacefully. Following Iraq's invasion of Kuwait in June 1990, Iraq was threatened not only with economic sanctions but also with military action unless it withdrew its forces—a prime example of the use of coercive diplomacy. Threat of force was also used to *deter* Iraq from invading Saudi Arabia. When threats failed to coerce Iraq to withdraw from Kuwait, the United States used skillful diplomacy to organize an international coalition. The combined military force physically destroyed much of the Iraqi military capability, liberating Kuwait and safeguarding Saudi Arabia.

In the next sections we define and provide a brief overview of what is meant by diplomacy. Second we discuss the historical development of diplomacy, drawing on examples from the international systems outlined in Chapter Two. Finally we examine in some detail diplomatic structure and process—the nuts and bolts of how states actually use diplomacy to further their interests and objectives. We also discuss how in recent years nongovernmental organizations (NGOs) have come to play diplomatic roles.

DEFINITION AND SCOPE

One of the foremost writers and practitioners of diplomacy believed that the most useful definition of the term was to be found in the Oxford English Dictionary: "Diplomacy is the management of international relations by negotiation; the method by which these relations are adjusted and managed by ambassadors and envoys; the business or art of the diplomatist."[1] The emphasis on negotiation is viewed by most people as the essence of diplomacy—negotiating a *treaty*, reaching an **executive agreement**, or bargaining with another state over the terms of a proposed agreement. The emphasis on the state as key diplomatic actor is consistent with a realist perspective on diplomacy.

In ordinary conversation the words *diplomacy* and *diplomat* usually have a positive connotation. To say someone was "very diplomatic in dealing with the problem" is a compliment that implies that the person is a good communicator—one who possesses understanding, sensitivity, and effective interpersonal skills. Professional diplomats who have developed this ability to communicate effectively often become respected members of their foreign policy establishments. They are able to represent their governments or international organizations quite well even when the messages they convey are not always positive.

treaty   A written agreement or contract between two or more states pledging adherence to any number of commitments.

---

[1] Sir Harold Nicholson, *Diplomacy*, 3d ed. (London: Oxford University Press, 1963), pp. 4–5.

As diplomats they are the advocates of national or international organizational interests and positions on any number of issues. Diplomats may craft a **démarche**, for example, that is a statement to a foreign government, usually making a formal proposal in the expectation of a formal response. Proposals to foreign governments can be expressed in positive, cooperative language or on other occasions in more forceful language. Even when a country wishes to make an **ultimatum**—do this or else—it normally uses language that customarily conforms to diplomatic standards for such communications.

Whether the diplomat personally agrees with or opposes a particular foreign policy position, it is the diplomat's task to represent it as well as he or she can. Lawyers for plaintiff and defense in a civil court case are by necessity in opposition to one another but each can at the same time respect the competency and honesty of the other. So it is with diplomats, who develop international reputations for the degree of competency or trustworthiness they exhibit in representing their countries or international organizations.

Such work is not restricted to a state's *ambassador* assigned and accredited to a foreign country or an international organization such as the United Nations. Diplomacy may be done by heads of state during a summit meeting, foreign ministers and other government officials, or by a specially designated diplomat as in one who seeks to secure peace between warring parties. Examples of summit diplomacy include negotiations between President Nixon and Leonid Brezhnev at U.S.-Soviet summits in the early 1970s, negotiations hosted by President Carter in the late 1970s between Egyptian President Sadat and Israeli Prime Minister Begin that resulted in the Camp David peace accords, meetings on arms control and other subjects by President Reagan and Mikhail Gorbachev at the Reykjavik summit in 1986, as well as by their successors throughout the post–cold war period. An example of interstate diplomacy below the head-of-government level is the effort by former U.S. Secretary of State Henry Kissinger who, in the aftermath of the 1973 Arab-Israeli war, engaged in what has come to be known as *shuttle diplomacy* between various capitals in the Middle East. Effective diplomacy often requires great patience and persistence as exhibited by Ambassador Dennis Ross and other diplomats working between Israeli and Palestinian governments and their representatives. Ambassador Richard Holbrook of the United States assiduously worked throughout 1995 to bring Bosnia's warring parties to the bargaining table. He subsequently persisted in trying to keep the Dayton Accord on track and to prevent the Yugoslavian conflict from drawing in neighboring states.

Diplomacy can involve formal or informal negotiations. These negotiations can be conducted with the full knowledge of the world or in secret. Negotiations can be conducted on a bilateral basis, between two states, or on a multilateral basis, involving three or more states. The secretary general and other diplomats of the United Nations and other international organizations are often in a position to play a constructive role in managing conflicts and assisting parties in the negotiations process.

Diplomacy has traditionally been the almost exclusive domain of official representatives of states and international organizations composed of states. Indeed, the term *diplomacy* has traditionally referred to authoritative communications in international relations. Modern diplomacy, by contrast, is often less restrictive, sometimes including private citizens and nongovernmental organizations. Individuals acting in their private capacities have certainly made a difference, particularly when their diplomatic initiatives were sanctioned by a government. During the 1962 Cuban missile crisis, for example, President Kennedy sent former Secre-

ambassador   A state's highest-ranking representative assigned to an embassy in a foreign country.

tary of State Dean Acheson (then a private citizen) to represent American policy to the president of France, Charles de Gaulle. He was selected in large part because of his positive reputation as a former secretary of state and diplomat. As a result he was more likely than most others to be able to convey the rationale for American policy to the French, thus securing their support.

Similarly former President Jimmy Carter has been asked as a private citizen to perform diplomatic functions among contending parties in the Middle East, Africa, and Latin America. On some of these occasions he engaged in diplomatic activities as a formal representative of the United States. For example with President Clinton's approval in 1994, Carter sought a peaceful transition from military to nonmilitary government in Haiti and led a delegation that included a U.S. senator (Sam Nunn, Chair of the Armed Services Committee) and a retired general (Colin Powell, the former chairman of the Joint Chiefs of Staff).

At other times individuals have entered the diplomatic world without invitation. Much to the dismay of state officials, these private actors sometimes have worked at cross-purposes with policies advocated even by their own governments. Sometimes they have performed supportive (though still independent) roles. Although as a practical matter most diplomacy is conducted by government-employed diplomats, the roles that individuals as private citizens play from time to time can be significant.

International conferences addressing economic and social issues are often accompanied by parallel discussions among interested nongovernmental actors who try to influence the process during the months or years of the planning phase and in the international conference itself. Building a consensus for agreements that goes beyond governments is an increasingly important diplomatic function performed by nongovernmental organizations and key individuals. In the 1995 conference held in China on the global state of women, for example, the official delegations were joined by unofficial delegations that came to influence the conference as well as public debate.

THE HISTORICAL DEVELOPMENT OF DIPLOMACY

In a world of increasing complexity, diplomacy in all of its manifestations will continue to play an important role. The formalization of diplomatic practices, however, has taken centuries.[2] Before recorded history, warring clans and tribes must have found it useful to negotiate with one another, even if this was simply to recover one's dead after a battle. Such envoys were undoubtedly granted different treatment than warriors and hence had a special status that allowed them to return unharmed to their own people to convey the demands or requests of the enemy.

In ancient Greece each city chose a herald to communicate with foreigners. Heralds required a good memory and a strong voice so they could accurately repeat the views of their leaders. The heralds were placed under the tutelage of the god Hermes—perhaps an unfortunate choice from the point of view of future diplomats as Hermes symbolized charm, cunning, and trickery. Beginning in the sixth century B.C., however, the Greek independent state system experienced increased commercial interdependence and political relations became more complex. As a result the city-states chose their finest orators to plead their city's case before foreign assemblies.

---

[2]This section is drawn from ibid., pp. 7–14.

PERCEPTIONS AND IDEAS IN FOREIGN POLICY AND DIPLOMATIC DECISION MAKING

The official positions taken by diplomats are the result of a state's foreign policy decision-making process. Scholars engaged in studying foreign policy decision-making processes from a pluralist or liberal perspective emphasize that entities known as the "United States" or "Canada" do not make decisions; decisions are made by individuals. Similarly, a particular bureaucratic entity termed the "State Department" or "Foreign Office" is composed of individuals. It is, therefore, not surprising that the study of individuals and small groups has been a primary focus of analysis for a number of scholars.

The study of individuals and their role in international relations, foreign policy, or diplomacy has drawn heavily on the disciplines of psychology and social psychology. Some of the work can be termed psychohistory and has focused on how life experiences influence an individual's approach to diplomacy and foreign policy. Other work has attempted to discern an individual's belief system or operational code—preconceptions and particular ways of interpreting and understanding what he or she observes directly influences the actions taken by him or her as decision maker.

A number of research efforts have drawn on the psychology literature in an attempt to generalize about the circumstances under which certain psychological processes occur. What these approaches have in common is an emphasis on how **cognition** and cognitive distortions undermine the realist view of decision making as a rational process. Many of these scholars have also studied political science and history in addition to psychology and social psychology. As a result their insights into the role that perception plays in diplomacy and the foreign policy process or during crisis situations is deserving of further comment.

The work of Robert Jervis, to take one example, focuses on individuals and individual perceptions. Jervis is concerned less with how emotions as such affect foreign policy decision making and more with how cognitive factors and a confusing international environment can result in a poor decision even if the individual is

cognition The process by which human beings acquire knowledge through perception, reasoning, and (some would say) intuition.

relatively unemotional and as intelligent as he or she can be in evaluating alternatives. Furthermore Jervis takes into account how the anarchic nature of international politics contributes to this confusing environment by encouraging cognitive processes that make decision making more difficult. Jervis accepts the realist argument that the anarchic nature of the international system breeds suspicion and distrust. The lack of a single sovereign or authority makes it a self-help system, and it is not necessarily irrational or a sign of paranoia to be preoccupied with real, potential, or imagined threats.

Jervis devotes a great deal of time to applying psychological concepts to historical events and key diplomatic exchanges. His propositions are generalizations about how decision makers perceive others' behavior and form judgments about their intentions. These patterns are explained by the general ways in which people draw inferences from ambiguous evidence and in turn help explain seemingly incomprehensible policies. They show how, why, and when highly intelligent and conscientious political leaders and diplomats misperceive their environments in specified ways and sometimes reach inappropriate decisions.

Jervis is interested in discerning how a decision maker comprehends a complex world filled with uncertainty. Each decision maker has a particular image of the world that has been shaped by his or her interpretations of historical events. Very often these events (such as wars and revolutions) occurred when the individual was young and impressionable. Lessons learned from history, when combined with personal experiences, contribute to the development of particular expectations and beliefs concerning how the world operates that will have a major impact on the decisions made by policy makers. Once formed, these images of reality are difficult to change. Cognitive consistency is the norm. Information that conflicts with the decision maker's image tends either to be dismissed, ignored, or interpreted in such a manner as to buttress a particular policy preference or course of action.

Jervis emphasizes how the striving for cognitive consistency can have a negative effect on decision-making processes, and other scholars focus on how psychological stress arising out of difficult, emotion-laden situa-

A P P L Y I N G   T H E O R Y

tions affects rational calculations. One example of this perspective is the work of Irving L. Janis. Janis has examined the tendency for social pressure to enforce conformity and consensus in cohesive decision-making groups. He calls this tendency *groupthink*, a mode of thinking that people engage in when they are deeply involved in a cohesive in-group, when the members' strivings for unanimity override their motivation to appraise alternative courses of action realistically. Indicators of groupthink include limiting discussions to only a few alternative courses of action, failing to reexamine initial decisions and possible courses of action initially rejected, and making little attempt to seek information from outside experts who may challenge a preferred policy. To make his case for the persuasiveness of concurrence seeking within a group and the resultant impact, Janis examines several foreign policy fiascos, such as the Bay of Pigs invasion in 1961, the military unpreparedness of the United States at Pearl Harbor in 1941, and the American decisions to escalate the Korean and Vietnam wars. He argues that in each case the pressure to conform to group norms interfered with critical, rational thinking.

A number of international relations scholars have been particularly interested in how psychological processes influence decision making during times of *crisis*—a situation between peace and war. The tendency for individuals to strive for cognitive consistency and for groups to enforce consensus among their members is particularly evident in crisis situations characterized by high stress, surprise, exhausting around-the-clock work schedules, and complex and ambiguous environments. As a result there is a general erosion of cognitive capabilities. Tolerance for ambiguity is reduced, policy options are restricted, opposing actors and their motives are stereotyped. Compared to noncrisis situations, decisions are based even more on policy makers' predispositions, expectations, biases, and emotional states. In sum, scholarly work suggests that misperception can play a major role in crisis situations, perhaps contributing to the outbreak of war. Furthermore it has been argued that not all decision makers operate with the same kind of rationality, making it difficult for leaders to judge what actions may deter an enemy. The cumulative effect of such studies is to undermine the image of decision making as a purely rational process. Nevertheless scholars persist at the

same time in exhorting decision makers "to be more rational." See, for example, Alexander George, "The Operational Code: A Neglected Approach to the Study of Political Leaders and Decision-Making," *International Studies Quarterly*, v. 13, no. 2 (June 1969): 190–220 and Ole Holsti, "The Operational Code Approach to the Study of Political Leaders," *Canadian Journal of Political Science*, v. 3, no. 1 (March 1970): 123–57. Jervis's and Janis's ideas are presented, respectively, in Robert Jervis, *Perception and Misperception in International Politics* (Princeton, N.J.: Princeton University Press, 1976) and Irving L. Janis, *Victims of Groupthink* (Boston: Houghton-Mifflin, 1972).

By the mid-1980s there was an evident decline in the amount of literature devoted to the role of cognition in international relations. Indeed, it was not fashionable at the time to study the broader role of ideas in international relations.

The late 1980s, however, witnessed a revival of interest in the role and causative importance of *ideas*, a focus that continued throughout the 1990s and into the present period. On the importance of ideas on policy, Judith Goldstein argues that in order to understand U.S. trade policies over the years, considering only system-level factors or domestic economic interests is insufficient. Rather one must also take into account actors' causal beliefs as to which economic policies can best achieve preferred interests. She and Robert Keohane see world views, principled beliefs, and causal understandings as ideas that become imbedded in institutions and impact diplomacy and the making of foreign policy by acting as cognitive road maps.

Similarly Ernst B. Haas underscores the emphasis he places "on the role of ideas in the heads of actors" and John Ruggie notes how some ideas such as "multilateralism" can become institutionalized regionally and globally as the way to conduct diplomatic relations effectively among states and in both international and nongovernmental organizations. To these writers ideas people carry in their heads are not, as some would contend, merely ideological rationalizations of interests but play an important role as independent variables influencing diplomacy and foreign policy decisions.

No one would deny that the study of individuals is important if we wish to improve our understanding of international relations. *The important question, however,*

(continued)

A P P L Y I N G   T H E O R Y

ever, is how much emphasis should be placed on the individual level of analysis as opposed to other levels? We have noted realist Hans Morgenthau's observation that in order to understand how a political leader reached a particular decision, we speculate how we would respond in similar circumstances. In other words by keeping the decision-making environment constant, we could hypothesize that any rational individual would have acted in the same manner. Despite a diversity of backgrounds or temperaments, the structure of the situation encourages diplomats and decision makers to respond in a similar fashion. On the other hand what if beliefs and perceptions do make a difference and individuals respond to common stimuli or the environment in divergent ways? If so, the individual as a focus of analysis is obviously more important than Morgenthau and other realists have assumed.

This debate over the relative importance of the individual as opposed to the environment in explaining behavior is common to all the social sciences. If the international system is the key to understanding international relations, then other levels of analysis—individual, organizational, societal, or state—are by definition of less importance. If one accepts a more pluralistic view of international relations, however, then greater consideration and weight are given to the constructivist role of the individual. Individuals matter (as do groups and institutions) simply because their choices significantly affect the functioning of day-to-day decision making and diplomacy in world politics.

Question: Do you think these insights are equally applicable to a wide variety of cultures?

To read more about the role of ideas in policy making, see Judith Goldstein and Robert O. Keohane, eds., *Ideas and Foreign Policy: Beliefs, Institutions, and Political Change* (Ithaca, N.Y.: Cornell University Press, 1993) and Ernst B. Haas, *Nationalism, Liberalism, and Progress* (Ithaca, N.Y.: Cornell University Press, 1997). Compare this with his earlier work, *When Knowledge Is Power* (Berkeley: University of California Press, 1990). See also John Gerard Ruggie, *Multilateralism Matters: The Theory and Practice of an Evolutionary Form* (New York: Columbia University Press, 1993) and compare with his *Constructing the World Polity* (London and New York: Routledge, 1998).

We see this most clearly in Thucydides' history of the Peloponnesian War. Thucydides attended a number of the political debates he recorded, and the power of the orators is evident to any reader. Prior to the outbreak of the war, for example, the Spartans summoned their allies to a conference to discuss recent events and to decide on a course of action. The case of the Megarians and Corinthians for declaring war on Athens appears quite persuasive until one reads the subsequent Athenian rebuttal. This event also illustrates how far diplomatic practice had been institutionalized at the time of the Spartan-Athenian hegemony. The Athenians who are allowed to speak were a delegation who happened to be in Sparta on other business. Having heard what their future enemies argued, they presented their rebuttal of the charges that Athens had violated its treaties. They were then allowed to return to Athens to communicate the Spartan assembly's vote for war.

The Romans acquired the Greek diplomatic traditions, but an expanding empire has scant need for negotiating talents when it is crushing all those before it. Roman contribution to international law, however, certainly had diplomatic implications. The Roman emphasis on the fulfillment of contracts, for example, applied to their view of treaties. Their work on **jus gentium** (law applied not just to Romans, but to all peoples whether citizens and foreigners) and **jus naturale** (law whose principles are discovered by reason and thus common to all humanity no matter one's race, creed, or color) had foreign policy implications that extended beyond administrative law for an empire; that is, that certain universal principles should govern relations among political units. Finally the Romans developed trained archivists who became specialists in diplomatic procedures.

During the latter years of the Roman empire, however, a need arose for trained negotiators. The Eastern Byzantine hub of the empire in Constantinople realized force alone could not keep the barbarians at bay. Diplomats, therefore, were critical players in a three-part diplomatic strategy to foster rivalry among the barbarians, secure the friendship of frontier tribes and peoples by flattery and money, and convert as many of the "heathen" to Christianity as possible. Such a strategy helps to account for the emperor Justinian's ability to extend Byzantine influence as far south as Sudan and keep at arm's length the warrior tribes of the Black Sea and Caucasus. In order to implement the strategy, however, the emperor's diplomats had to be more than heralds or orators; they also needed to be perceptive political observers who could accurately assess the strengths and weaknesses of neighboring despots and warriors. This emphasis on astute observations and sound judgment have become hallmarks of the best professional diplomats down through history.

As we have noted, the collapse of the western half of the Roman empire led in the Middle Ages to an end of the political and administrative rationality imposed by Rome. Political authority was fragmented among a wide variety of local and regional rulers and the Church in Rome, which claimed universal moral authority. As communication and civil authority broke down, commerce suffered, as did contact throughout feudal Europe. Indeed, it was often extremely dangerous to pass from town to town or castle to castle. As a result no established system of international contacts existed, resulting in little advancement in diplomatic practices and conventions.

Modern diplomacy arose in the thirteenth and fourteenth century in Italy. Essentially standing outside the rest of feudal Europe, the Italian city-states resembled the Greek independent state system—common cultural and commercial interests racked by intense political and military competition. It is not surprising that out of this turmoil came such ambassador-scholars as Dante, Petrach, and Machiavelli.

The first recorded diplomatic mission was established in Genoa in 1455 by the Duke of Milan. Five years later the Duke of Savoy sent a representative to Rome, site of the Holy See. Then in 1496 Venice—a commercial power of the day—appointed two Venetian merchants living in London to represent the republic's interests. Soon after permanent embassies of the Italian states were established in Paris and London, with other states following suit. It came to be accepted that the ambassador was viewed as the personal representative of his head of state, with the status of the ambassador more a reflection of the power of his ruler and thus his ability to engage in lavish displays of wealth.

The Congress of Vienna (1814–15), however, is of greatest historical importance. Three reasons stand out. First, as noted in Chapter Two, the era of the Concert of Europe could be characterized as a collective hegemonic state system. It is not an exaggeration to observe that ministers, political leaders, and diplomats of the day deserved credit for establishing an international system that successfully mitigated the worst aspects of anarchy among states. Periodic international conferences were held in succeeding decades to make necessary adjustments to the European order—the balance of interests and power supportive of stability that also contributed to the avoidance of general war. Small wars occurred over the next half century, but each was contained and none posed a substantial challenge to the overall order that had been established. Although the Concert of Europe as a formal diplomatic mechanism fell apart after several decades, the underlying order and expectations established by diplomacy at Vienna in 1815 contributed to preserving Europe from another outbreak of general war until 1914. Indeed, one may speak of a society of states in Europe through much of the nineteenth century.

Second, it was not until the Congress of Vienna that a truly organized system of diplomatic practices and norms emerged. The follow-on Congress of Aix-la-Chapelle, for example, agreed on a hierarchy of diplomatic representation: First were ambassadors, papal legates, and papal nuncios; next were envoys extraordinary and ministers plenipotentiary; then came ministers resident; and finally there were those in the position of **chargé d'affaires**. Furthermore within each category diplomatic precedence and status were not a function of who represented the most powerful country, but rather who had held the diplomatic post the longest. Also by 1815 diplomatic services came to be viewed as distinct branches of each government. Diplomacy was increasingly professionalized, with common rules, norms, and expectations.

A certain etiquette, for example, is maintained even between enemies preparing for war. After the Japanese bombed Pearl Harbor on December 7, 1941, the United States declared war on Japan and diplomatic relations were terminated. Consistent with international law, diplomats were quickly given safe passage out of both countries. The rules of diplomatic immunity long established in customary international law were formally codified in the Vienna Conventions on Diplomatic and Consular Relations in the 1960s.

Finally the Congress of Vienna is worth studying because it is a classic example of successful **multilateral diplomacy**—a number of countries communicating and negotiating, often over the most contentious of issues. Successful multilateral diplomacy depends on accommodating the interests and specific objectives of not only two states (as in **bilateral diplomacy**) but rather a number of participants. International organizations and settlements or agreements that prove to be durable over time derive from a broad consensus and can be modified or adapted as conditions and objectives change. Bureaucratic rigidity or an inability to adapt to changing circumstances will reduce the utility or functionality of international institutions in multilateral diplomacy, leading perhaps to their ultimate collapse.

The Versailles Treaty and other multilateral settlements following World War I pale in comparison to the successes of the Congress of Vienna. The Versailles peace lasted only two decades. World War II repeated the mass destruction of lives and property of World War I but at even higher levels made possible by technological advances in military weaponry. Consistent with the obliteration of urban areas through bombing that had become the norm, dropping atomic bombs on two Japanese cities was the cataclysmic finale of World War II.

Perhaps as a result of learning from earlier experiences, multilateral diplomacy following World War II did prove to be somewhat more successful, although the succeeding half century was also marked by periods of high tension that threatened mass destruction on a truly global scale, thanks to East-West competition during the cold war. Nevertheless multilateral diplomacy in international conferences and within international organizations has assumed an increasingly important role in world politics since 1945. More recent examples of multilateral diplomacy dealing with demographic, environmental, economic development, and humanitarian issues are discussed later in the book.

DIPLOMATIC MACHINERY AND PROCESSES

Recognition of States and Governments

A sovereign state comes into existence under international law when a population living in a defined territory that is administered by a government is recognized by other sovereign states. As noted earlier, recognition of a state's sovereignty amounts to an acceptance of its present and future claims to two rights—one *internal* and the other *external*. The internal claim is to a right as a sovereign state to exercise complete jurisdiction over its own territory free of interference by other states in its *domestic affairs*. At the same time there is an external claim to a right to be independent or autonomous in its *foreign affairs*, not subordinated to any other state in the conduct of its international relations.

As a practical matter, of course, states do not always respect the sovereign claims of other states. When they choose to interfere in the domestic affairs of another state, the response may well be a diplomatic protest note or public declaration to the same effect. Thus during the cold war the United States privately and on occasion publicly condemned Soviet policies that violated the human rights of its citizens, particularly Jews, who were not permitted to leave the country. The typical Soviet response at the time was to condemn the United States for unlawful interference in its domestic affairs: Soviet emigration policy in Moscow's view was a domestic matter and not the business of the United States. The American position was that the Soviet Union had obligations under international law to respect the human rights of all peoples (including its own citizens) and should not try to exempt itself from international scrutiny just because it was a sovereign state.

More serious, of course, is when a state commits aggression against another state. For example Germany's invasion of neutral Holland in World War II and neutral Belgium in both world wars clearly violated the sovereignty of these states. They claimed rights to their **neutrality** in foreign policy and to their continued administration of their own countries. As a factual matter, of course, the European states that were successfully invaded ceased exercising their sovereignty over their territories for several years; nevertheless, violation of sovereignty did not extinguish their legal claims to sovereignty. Indeed, invaded states maintained **governments in exile** located in other friendly countries (such as the United Kingdom) that were willing to recognize them as the legitimate governments of their invaded countries then under foreign occupation. These governments in exile maintained their claims to sovereignty throughout the war. Upon liberation of their territories, they were able to reestablish actual control.

Iraq's invasion of Kuwait in 1990 was considered an act of aggression by most outside states, which refused to recognize the legitimacy of Iraqi claims to Kuwaiti territory. The government in Baghdad asserted that Kuwait was not legitimately a state in the first place, since it was created as an artifact of British colonialism. Quite apart from the fact that control of Kuwaiti oil fields was also at stake, Iraq maintained that Kuwait was really Iraqi property that it had rightfully retaken by force. Other states rejected Iraq's efforts to extinguish Kuwait as a sovereign state. They formed a coalition under United Nations auspices to force Iraq to withdraw from Kuwait and restore control to the Kuwaiti government then in exile. When diplomatic efforts failed, military forces of a broad coalition of states drove the Iraqi armed forces out of Kuwait in 1991.

When the invading power establishes a **puppet government**, diplomatic recognition is sometimes withheld. A good example involves the Vichy regime installed in France following the German invasion in 1940. International recognition went to the French government in exile based in London. Even if no government in exile exists, recognition of a regime perceived as illegitimate might still be withheld. This was the case with the former German Democratic Republic (communist East Germany), which was isolated by other states for many years as well as being denied seats in such international organizations as the United Nations and its affiliated agencies.

In some cases decades may pass before diplomatic recognition is granted. The United States and many other states, for example, did not recognize the Soviet annexation in 1940 of the Baltic republics. Estonian, Latvian, and Lithuanian claims to sovereignty were kept alive for half a century through governments in exile that maintained diplomatic ties with foreign governments. At the end of the cold war, when for political reasons Moscow was willing to relinquish control of the Baltic republics, they reemerged on the world stage as independent and sovereign states.

States continue to be recognized as legitimate entities even when governments change. After the communist takeover in China in 1949, the United States and other like-minded countries chose to deny recognition to the new government in Beijing under Mao Zedong even though, as a factual matter, it had control of all of mainland China. Instead these countries continued to recognize the nationalist, non-communist government under Chiang Kai-Shek on the island of Taiwan. Chiang's government maintained that it would one day regain control of all of China.

Neither the Beijing nor the Taiwan governments accepted the two-China solution proposed by some as a settlement to these conflicting claims for legitimacy. Beijing and Taiwan agreed on one thing—that there was just one China, a state that included both Taiwan and the mainland. The dispute was only over which of the two governments had the legitimate claim to political authority. Because they saw it in their interest to do so, United States and other foreign governments friendly to Taiwan and opposed to communism continued the legal fiction of Taiwanese legitimacy as government of all of China for more than two decades.

U.S. President Richard Nixon shakes hands with Chinese Leader Mao Zedong during Nixon's historic visit to China in 1972.

In 1971 and 1972 the United States finally reversed its long-standing policy and recognized the Beijing government as the legitimate government of China. Consistent with the new policy, U.S. diplomats were withdrawn from Taiwan and diplomatic relations were established between Beijing and Washington. Diplomats from Beijing replaced those from Taiwan in the Chinese embassy in Washington. Commercial, cultural, and other nongovernmental ties with Taiwan were maintained as Taiwan remained formally part of the same Chinese state. Government recognition changed, but all the territories recognized as part of China were the same. As a practical matter the government on Taiwan remained in control there, although without much of the international recognition it had depended upon for its legitimacy.

Recognition is at times a function of how outside powers view a particular conflict—as a war between states or a civil war. Consider the United States and the Vietnam War in the early 1960s. The United States government argued that it was aiding the Republic of Vietnam (South Vietnam) in its defense against aggression from the communist Democratic Republic of Vietnam (North Vietnam). Coming to the aid of a state victimized by aggression (by request of the legitimate government) is allowable under international law, and the United States presented itself merely as helping a victimized state against communist aggression, as it had been asked to do.

Critics of the American policy in Vietnam, however, claimed that there were *not* two Vietnamese states, one committing aggression against the other. Rather, these critics argued, the Vietnam War was a civil war between contending governments in the same state. If so, then no outside state had a right to intervene militarily or otherwise in what was really a domestic matter within Vietnam.

Because the U.S. government under Presidents Eisenhower, Kennedy, Johnson, Nixon, and Ford recognized the government in Saigon as the legitimate government of a South Vietnamese state under attack by North Vietnam and its Vietcong insurgents, it rejected the notion that the conflict was a civil war. Pressed on the issue, Henry Kissinger (national security advisor and later secretary of state in the Nixon and Ford administrations) admitted that the Vietnam War really had aspects of both a war between states and a civil war; however, the United States used the former understanding to justify its intervention policy.

A similar problem occurred during the American Civil War (1861–65). British cotton importers and other commercial interests were encouraging London to intervene diplomatically on behalf of the South. They sought recognition for the Confederate States of America as a separate country with the administration under President Jefferson Davis as its legitimate government. Aided by its military victories, however, the United States government under President Abraham Lincoln was successful diplomatically in keeping the British from taking this step.

Had Britain intervened, given its financial and military resources, this would have benefited the South substantially, hurting the North's war effort. As part of its effort to encourage British intervention, the South claimed that the conflict was a war between states and *not* a civil war. To this day historians sympathetic to the South's cause refer to the conflict not as the American Civil War but rather as the War Between the States—that is, the United States *and* the Confederate States of America.

Gaining acceptance in the international community through recognition of state and government is an important prize to those seeking such status. Recognition of Israel as a new state was granted in 1948 by many countries including the Soviet Union, but to this day many Middle Eastern states continue to withhold recognition. Conversely Palestinians seek the same recognition of a territorial state of their own, many having been dispossessed of their homes and property in the newly created Israeli state. Although progress toward a peaceful solution was made in the 1990s, for more than four decades Palestinians have been confronted by Israeli security forces, particularly in territories occupied by Israel since 1967. By contrast no such progress has been made by the Kurds. In a treaty signed after World War I, Kurdish peoples in the mountainous areas of Turkey, Syria, Iraq, Iran, and the Transcaucasus region of the Soviet Union (now parts of the Russian Federation, Azerbaijan, Georgia, and Armenia) were promised status as a separate Kurdish territorial state, but the great powers making that commitment never delivered.

Aspirations of Palestinians, Kurds, and many other national groups for creation of new nation-states remain unfulfilled. Suppression of these nationalist movements by existing state authorities is common. Kurds have faced continued and forceful opposition, particularly by Turkish and Iraqi governments over many years. Similarly, in the same region historical claims to a separate national identity by Chechens has been resisted by Russian authorities. A Chechen secessionist uprising in the Russian Federation has faced confrontation by the military since the mid-1990s with large numbers of casualties on both sides. Significantly outside states accepted Russian claims to sovereignty in the region, effectively treating the Chechen uprising as an internal matter within the Russian Federation.

In the final analysis recognition of governments and states is a political choice left to other sovereign states and their governments. Some favor a policy that bases recognition of a particular government, for example, on the facts of the case as sole criterion: Does a particular government actually have control over the territory over which it claims jurisdiction? If it does, then it warrants recognition. Another approach is to grant recognition based on a second criterion, which is the perceived desirability of a particular state or government. Thus the United States denied recognition for the Soviet Union and its government from 1917 until 1934 when diplomatic relations finally were established.

Diplomatic Immunities and Protections

While living and doing business in the host country, all diplomats on the diplomatic list are immune from arrest or prosecution by local authorities. Diplomats cannot even be prosecuted for traffic and parking violations, which is very frustrating to national or local governments. Nevertheless **diplomatic immunity** is a reciprocal privilege that extends to all diplomats in all of their activities. Private citizens traveling abroad do not have this privilege of immunity from local laws and law-enforcement measures.

The **reciprocity** that assures the mutual safety of diplomats is absolutely essential if countries are to maintain contact and conduct business with one another. Not only would it be unseemly to arrest the diplomats of other countries, it could lead to reprisals against one's own diplomats. The only legal remedies for the host country for unacceptable conduct on the part of a foreign diplomat are to ignore or overlook such transgressions, to protest these activities to the host government, or to declare the diplomat unwelcome (**persona non grata** or PNG for short), forcing his or her removal from the country.

Depending on the circumstances, misconduct can ruin a diplomatic career when it causes one to be declared *persona non grata*. On the other hand some diplomats may face expulsion for reasons unrelated to their personal behavior. If relations sour between the diplomat's country and the host country, he or she may be subject to recall by his or her own country or alternatively to expulsion through the *persona non grata* declaration. Recalling one's own diplomats or expelling the diplomats of foreign countries is one way of signaling displeasure with the policies of those countries and may have nothing to do with the actual conduct of individual diplomats.

Diplomatic conventions, although legally binding as treaties, do not always assure in practice that diplomats will be treated correctly. In 1979, for example, Iranian revolutionaries held American diplomats as hostages. The revolutionaries' takeover of the American embassy and confiscation of its files also violated the same Vienna diplomatic convention as well as customary international law that protects embassy property even in wartime.

When countries break diplomatic relations, the embassy and its grounds are placed in caretaker status, sometimes under the daily control of a third country mutually acceptable to both disputing countries. This is because of the legal fiction of **extraterritoriality**, which assumes that an embassy and the ground it stands on are part of the sovereign territory and property of the foreign country. Because states are required under international law to respect the sovereignty of other states, embassies and their diplomats are given privileged, protected status.

Even though these rules were violated in Iran, this did not give the United States or any other country a right to do the same thing to Iranian diplomats or the Iranian embassy and grounds in Washington. The urge to take reprisals in kind is understandable, but any such action was avoided.

Because embassies are viewed as the property of the foreign country and thus not legally subject to host-country intrusion, they provide for their own security. The U.S. Marine Corps has traditionally been assigned the task of guarding American embassies in conjunction with State Department security officers. Host-country police or other security personnel also have the responsibility of protecting embassies by supplementing efforts of the embassy itself.

Embassies sometimes serve as places of **asylum** for host-country citizens or others seeking protection. The political decision to grant asylum is up to embassy officials and usually is limited or reserved as a humanitarian gesture to those whose political or other rights have been (or likely will be) violated. For example, Roman Catholic Cardinal Mindzenty, an opponent of the communist takeover in Hungary after World War II, was one of the more celebrated recipients of American asylum at the U.S. embassy in Budapest. The host country may protest the granting of asylum or even try to prevent individuals from entering embassy grounds, but once asylum has been granted host-country officials may not legally force entry to the embassy or its grounds to remove those who have found shelter there.

The Organization of Diplomatic Missions

Emissaries of states bear different titles. *Ambassador* is the highest-ranking position in any given **mission**. A *mission* is a term that refers to an **embassy** including a consular section in the same embassy, **consulates** located elsewhere in a foreign country, a diplomatic mission to an international organization, or a **delegation** to

NGOS AND FIELD DIPLOMACY

With the end of the cold war, the increase in ethnic conflict within states, and the often resultant humanitarian crises, NGOs and international organizations are playing a new and increasingly important role. Operational NGOs serve in the field, working directly with the recipients of humanitarian aid and economic development projects. Traditionally humanitarian-relief NGOs have worked assiduously to maintain a strict policy of neutrality and leave the diplomacy and conflict resolution functions to government diplomats. This policy is changing and has caused a great deal of discussion and debate. The following comments from an article by Pamela Aall summarize the findings of a conference sponsored by the U.S. Institute of Peace:

> While NGOs are fast becoming powerful new actors in complex emergencies, managing conflict and taking on certain functions of imperiled governments, several questions arise: Should NGOs be involved in conflict prevention and resolution? If so, how extensive should their involvement be? Effective responses to post–cold war humanitarian crises often mean that many NGOs must go beyond their traditional mission of providing food, water, and medical assistance, entering the realm of ensuring political stability and fulfilling governmental functions in failed states. Are such expanded roles appropriate for NGOs?

John Paul Lederbach, director of the International Conciliation Service of the Mennonite Central Committee, believes that NGOs could effectively manage conflict, noting that they bring several special qualities to peace building, especially through their particular insights into different cultures, their relationships with local partners, and their understanding of the links between crisis management and long-term sustainable development.

In response to the question of roles, there are certain conditions that must be met before NGOs engage in conflict management activities:

- The NGO knows the country and the regional institutions involved in the conflict resolution effort.
- The NGO has indigenous partners.
- The NGO staff has a good knowledge of conflict mediation skills.
- The NGO's field staff members fully understand the personal risks they are assuming.

Equally important is the development of further coordination among the different types of operational NGOs and between the NGO community and other actors involved in complex emergency interventions.

It is more than apparent that NGOs of all varieties are seriously grappling with issues raised by working in situations of conflict. There is widespread recognition that NGOs might unwittingly become a party to conflict in the course of their humanitarian relief work; that their actions could be part of a concerted, coordinated effort involving governments, international and regional organizations, and private groups to avert or resolve conflict; that they have the ability both to provide early warning and to shore up the political will of governments to act; and that they could give guidance to policy makers in their own countries and encourage community building and the development of civil societies in countries decimated by war. In short, the work of NGOs forms an important part of the entire repertoire of intervention strategies for dealing with conflict in the post–cold war era.

Point: Whether due to circumstances or design, NGOs are playing increasingly important diplomatic roles.

Source: Pamela Aall, "Nongovernmental Organizations and Peacemaking," in Chester A. Crocker and Fen Osler Hampson, with Pamela Aall, eds., *Managing Global Chaos* (Washington, D.C.: United States Institute of Peace, 1996), pp. 442–43.

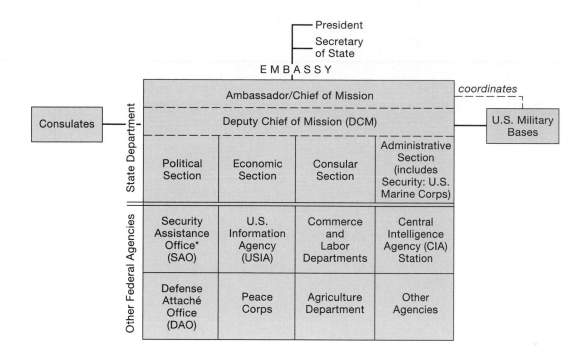

President
Secretary
of State

E M B A S S Y

Ambassador/Chief of Mission   *coordinates*

Consulates

Deputy Chief of Mission (DCM)

U.S. Military
Bases

State Department

| Political Section | Economic Section | Consular Section | Administrative Section (includes Security: U.S. Marine Corps) |

Other Federal Agencies

| Security Assistance Office* (SAO) | U.S. Information Agency (USIA) | Commerce and Labor Departments | Central Intelligence Agency (CIA) Station |
| Defense Attaché Office (DAO) | Peace Corps | Agriculture Department | Other Agencies |

FIGURE 4.1   ORGANIZATION OF A U.S. DIPLOMATIC MISSION

*Also known as Office of Defense Cooperation (ODC), Office of Military Cooperation (OMC), or Military Assistance and Advisory Group (MAAG).

an international conference. In the absence of an ambassador as **chief of mission**, the mission may be left under another person in charge—a *chargé d'affaires* or, more simply, a chargé. The chargé is often the second-ranking person, also known as the **deputy chief of mission** or DCM. Figure 4.1 illustrates the typical organization of a U.S. diplomatic mission.

Consul or **consul general** is usually the title of the official in charge of a consulate in the capital and in one or another of the major cities outside of the host country's capital. These consuls or consuls general work directly for the ambassador, whose residence is in the capital city near or on the embassy grounds. A consulate (or consular section in an embassy) coordinates the issue of passports to its own citizens, issues visas to citizens in the local country, and performs related administrative tasks. Consulates are also a focal point for promoting trade and cultural exchange in areas of the host country outside of the capital city. They also report to the embassy or home country directly on political, economic, and other developments they observe.

The level of representation that a state sends to a host country is politically significant. When relations are fully developed or "normal," countries typically are represented at the ambassadorial level. When conflict has resulted in a breach of diplomatic relations between two countries, restoration of these relations is sometimes implemented in a gradual normalization process. The first step in normalizing relations often entails establishing an **interest section** in a mutually friendly country's embassy. Later the embassy may be reopened with a lower-ranking diplomat serving as chargé d'affaires. Eventually a full embassy with a

Practicing World Politics

U.S. Foreign Service Web Site

The U.S. Department of State has a Web site [www.state.gov] that should be of particular interest to students of international relations and world politics. Information is available on summer internships at the main State Department building in Washington, D.C., as well as embassies overseas. Unfortunately 95 percent of the approximately 800 internships do not offer a salary. If you are interested in working at State as a foreign service officer, information about the written exam, how to order a study guide, an exam bibliography, and suggested courses to take in college to prepare for a foreign service career are provided. Opportunities are available in the U.S. Information Agency, as well as civil service positions in the United States, related agencies, and diplomatic missions abroad. The competition, not surprisingly, is stiff. There are also links to Web sites maintained by U.S. embassies and consulates. So if you are interested in seeing what has been happening in Beijing or Addis Ababa from the point of view of officers serving there, it is only a click away. You can also download literally hundreds of publications from the various bureaus if you are writing a term paper on terrorism, weapons proliferation, refugees, population issues, environmental concerns, human rights, or numerous other topics.

serving ambassador is established, perhaps with consulates in other important cities.

A typical embassy, headed by an ambassador as chief-of-mission and a DCM as second in charge, is divided into a number of functional sections. Most countries staff their embassies to perform various political, economic and commercial, consular, administrative, military, and intelligence functions. Missions to international organizations or international negotiations usually have specific tasks to perform and are staffed accordingly. The precise way in which an embassy or other mission is organized varies from country to country and sometimes from place to place depending in part on the functions to be performed. Not surprisingly embassies and other missions usually mirror the structural and cultural approaches to policy of their home countries.

The United States is no exception. Bureaucratic divisions in Washington are clearly reflected in the typical American embassy or other mission. Serving under the ambassador are the State Department's political, economic, consular, administrative, and embassy security sections composed primarily of career State Department foreign service officers and staff. These sections maintain constant contact with offices in the State Department as well as those in the local foreign ministry and other local agencies. Embassies are often the link between foreign ministries, heads of government, and other senior officials in different countries.

Not to be outdone, the Department of Defense (DoD) often maintains two important diplomatic offices. The Defense Attaché Office (DAO) is staffed mostly by members of the military who may be charged with coordinating policy matters with the host-country defense ministry, collecting information on the host country's armed forces (usually an overt, nonclandestine, intelligence-collection function), and performing protocol functions in relation to host-country armed forces. Within the DoD, defense attachés come under the Defense Intelligence Agency and the armed services—army, navy, and air force. Often of even greater importance to the host country, however, is a separate security assistance office administered by DoD and charged with coordinating and overseeing the transfer of armaments and military training to host-country militaries.

Attachés from the Justice, Commerce, Agriculture, and Labor departments are also often posted to missions. As carriers of American policy, attachés from these agencies establish ties and channels for influencing businesses, unions, and government agencies in the host country. Export promotion in the industrial, agricultural, and service sectors of the American economy is a central concern, for example, of attachés from these departments. Increased exports, after all, mean more profits for business and farm interests and more jobs for American workers. Their views may clash, however, with State, Defense, or other agencies of the U.S. government. Export of supercomputers, for example, may be favored by the Department of Commerce but opposed by the Department of Defense because of their military value.

Finally embassies and other missions also frequently are used for covert **intelligence collection** or **espionage**, defined as clandestine actions sometimes adverse to the host country. The Central Intelligence Agency (CIA) has a station chief who oversees the agency's intelligence program in the host country. This is not unique to the United States. Virtually all countries allocate a portion of the embassy or other mission to intelligence work. This includes human-source intelligence as well as such technical means that enable specialists to intercept signals—communications or other electronic emissions that can be analyzed or evaluated by the appropriate intelligence agencies.

Intelligence officers in an embassy usually enjoy the same diplomatic status and protections of other embassy employees on the host country's diplomatic list. Some intelligence officers in an embassy, usually listed as first or second secretaries or as holding principal offices, are under "deep cover." Others have the same diplomatic titles but have come to be known to the host country as intelligence agents and thus are watched more closely by host-country security services than other embassy personnel. When intelligence operatives have crossed the line of acceptable behavior or otherwise have been uncovered, the host country may force their expulsion. This can, of course, be followed by retaliation of the same kind directed against the host country's own intelligence agents stationed abroad.

Coordinating the diverse work of an American embassy is no easy task for any chief of mission. The **country team** concept is one approach to integrating these efforts. Members of the country team—usually the chiefs or deputies of the different sections within the embassy—meet as a group at least once a week to review the embassy's collective work. Sometimes, particularly in smaller missions, personalities can be brought together under an effective ambassador or DCM to make a country team that can work together well, ironing out differences as they arise. In many cases, however, disputes go well beyond embassy personalities, reflecting conflicts among agencies in the national government that are not easily resolved.

American embassy officials thus are often as divided among themselves as are their respective agencies and agency heads in Washington. The reality is that, just as any president of the United States has difficulty controlling government agencies, whether engaged in domestic or foreign policy, an ambassador and the DCM face comparable challenges on a much smaller scale. Countries with a less-fragmented political structure and less pluralism in political processes domestically than the United States no doubt have embassies that are far less fragmented and more deferential to the central authority of the ambassador and DCM.

Practicing World Politics

The Internet: Checking Out Some Web Sites on Diplomacy

International and nongovernmental organization sites often contain documents, public statements and other useful information on diplomatic activity. In addition to using search engines, links to Web sites for various countries can be found in sites for international organizations of which they are members. For example the United Nations [www.un.org] has links to Web pages and sites of diplomatic missions maintained by member states. One can find similar links on Web sites of such regional organizations as the Organization for Security and Cooperation in Europe [www.osce.org], the European Union [www.europa.eu.int], the North Atlantic Treaty Organization [www.nato.org], the Organization of African Unity [www.oau-oua.org], and the Organization of American States [www.oas.org].

Although in the United States a number of departments and agencies engage in international affairs, it is the Department of State [www.state.gov] that is the senior cabinet office directly tasked with diplomatic representation of the United States. Related agencies of the Department of State are the Agency for International Development [www.info.usaid.gov], the former Arms Control and Disarmament Agency [www.acda.gov], and the United States Information Agency [www.usia.gov].

Other U.S. government executive branch sites at least partly related to international affairs include the departments of Defense [www.defenselink.mil]; Commerce [www.doc.gov], especially its International Trade Administration [www.ita.doc.gov] and its Bureau of Export Administration [www.bxa.doc.gov]; Agriculture [www.usda.gov], including its Farm and Foreign Agriculture Service pages; Labor [www.dol.gov] and its Bureau of International Labor Affairs pages; and the Treasury [www.treas.gov] and its Customs Service and Comptroller of the Currency Pages.

The National Security Council is part of the Executive Office of the President [www.whitehouse.gov/WH/EOP/NSC]. An independent agency, the Federal Reserve Board [www.bog.frb.fed.us] also has links to foreign central banks and the Bank for International Settlements [www.bis.org] in Basel, Switzerland. On intelligence, the Central Intelligence Agency [www.odci.gov/cia] has links to some thirteen related intelligence and other agencies that are part of the U.S. intelligence community, including the Defense Intelligence Agency, State Department and military service intelligence offices, the National Security Agency, the National Reconnaissance Office, and the Federal Bureau of Investigation.

U.S. Congressional committees dealing with foreign affairs in the Senate [www.senate.gov] include Foreign Relations, Armed Services, and the Select Committee on Intelligence. For the House of Representatives [www.house.gov], see pages for the Committees on International Relations and Armed Services.

The Washington-based American Committees on Foreign Relations [www.acfr.org], a grass-roots nongovernmental organization with committees in more than thirty U.S. cities, provides a list of American links to daily news sources, foreign affairs journals and magazines, think tanks, C-Span programs, Congressional links, columnists, and opinion leaders. The government-funded U.S. Institute of Peace [www.usip.gov] sponsors academic research as do such nongovernmental organizations as the New York- and Washington-based Council on Foreign Relations [www.foreignrelations.org], which publishes the journal *Foreign Affairs* and various studies. The Chicago Council on Foreign Relations [www.ccfr.org] also provides a useful set of links to universities and institutes, international organizations, U.S. government and media links. For additional links, see the New York-based Foreign Policy Association [www.fpa.org] and the Institute of International Education [www.ile.org].

Diplomatic Incentives and Disincentives

Carrots   Whether in bilateral or multilateral settings, diplomats depend on the leverage they can bring to their negotiations and less-formal discussions and interactions. Depending on the issue involved, economic or military resources may play an important role. **Foreign aid** may take the form of grants for social, economic, or military purposes; loans, particularly at concessionary interest rates (reduced below market levels by the donor country as a form of assistance); trade preferences (as in reducing tariffs on imports from a foreign country or guaranteeing purchase at a favorable price of one or another of the exporting country's products); or military assistance (the transfer of weapons free of charge or at reduced prices or the provision of military training). Such incentives may be very helpful, but one should always understand them for what they are—incentives. The firmer foundation on which lasting agreements are based is one in which the mutual interests and objectives of the parties are also accommodated.

An example of the use of diplomatic "carrots" is the 1978 accord reached at Camp David, Maryland, between Egyptian President Anwar Sadat and Israeli Prime Minister Menachem Begin that normalized relations between Israel and Egypt. The Sinai desert land taken forcibly from Egypt by Israel in 1967 was returned in exchange for recognition by Egypt of Israel's sovereignty or right to exist as a state. In addition to the positive influence he was able to assert because of personal skills and the high stature of his office, President Carter was able to cement the agreement with promises of substantial military and economic aid to both negotiating parties. (The Camp David Accords and the Arab-Israeli peace process are discussed subsequently in greater detail.)

Effective diplomacy is markedly easier to achieve when the parties have an established record of positive accomplishments over decades or longer. Mutual trust is a very important asset in diplomatic exchanges of any kind. Lack of trust, by contrast—perhaps due to a record of broken obligations or other conflicts—poses a significant obstacle or challenge to diplomats. The Camp David Accords proved to be only the first major step in a continuing peace process.

Sticks   Diplomacy, of course, is not simply about such positive inducements as economic and military aid. Diplomacy, as we have noted, can also be *coercive*—forcing another country to do what it would not otherwise do. In adversarial relations veiled or explicit threats of economic sanctions or military action can influence or coerce diplomats and policy makers in other states.

One country can punish or exercise economic leverage over another by threatening or actually imposing **economic sanctions**. Actually imposing sanctions amounts to economic warfare. If the punishing state has been giving aid or other assistance, it can be reduced or cut off entirely. A **boycott** against the other country's exports or an **embargo** or prohibition against selling or engaging in other commercial transactions can be imposed. These are legal restrictions preventing the sale or purchase of any goods or services to or from that country. The aim is to get the embargoed state to change its policy or comply with the wishes of the state imposing the embargo.

Economic sanctions are not always very effective in achieving their purposes. When a state's exports are boycotted by one country, it may simply find other markets for its goods. Notwithstanding legal prohibitions, it may also find other states willing to avoid or evade an embargo, which will continue to sell their products to the embargoed state or engage in other commercial activities. A multilateral boycott or embargo imposed by a coalition of states may be more effective by bringing greater collective pressure. Even so, ways are often found to circumvent these restrictions. The multilateral embargo against South Africa, for example, took many years to have noticeable effect. But eventually, in the early 1990s, the *apartheid* policy that had segregated the races was abandoned and a regime led by Nelson Mandela finally was put into place.

A more serious "stick" is a **blockade**, a more intense form of economic warfare, in which warships or ground forces are used physically to prevent commerce going into or coming out of a country. Imposition of a blockade is an act of war that can escalate into an armed conflict.

Carrots, Sticks, and Crisis   If two states have a perceived conflict of interest and neither backs down, events can produce a **crisis**. In October 1973, for example, President Nixon and Secretary of State Henry Kissinger decided they could not ignore Soviet leader Leonid Brezhnev's threat to intervene militarily in the Arab-Israeli war. The United States placed its strategic forces on alert, resulting in a possibly dangerous confrontation. Once a crisis begins there is a basic policy dilemma: Each side feels it must do whatever is needed to advance or protect its interests, but at the same time recognizes that it must avoid taking actions that could escalate the crisis to the point that it gets out of control.[3]

Crisis diplomacy usually entails objectives that are both urgent and extremely important. It requires the greatest care in finding common ground as well as the appropriate combination of carrots and sticks. The Cuban missile crisis of 1962 is one such case. When American intelligence sources discovered in October 1962 that Soviet offensive missiles with nuclear warheads had been deployed to Cuba, American decision makers sought to have the missiles removed while, at the same time, attempting to avoid an escalation of the conflict into a major war. A keen awareness of the importance and urgency of accomplishing both of these short-term objectives clearly influenced deliberations on the various policy options open to the United States.

How the Soviets would respond to U.S. military actions was a matter of grave concern to President Kennedy and his advisors. Although American decision makers did not know it then, Soviet commanders in Cuba already had authority from Moscow to use battlefield nuclear weapons in the event of an American invasion. Had the American response been any more provocative than it was, nuclear war might well have occurred.

Fortunately President Kennedy and his advisors decided upon a naval blockade of Cuba rather than a ground invasion or air strikes, while continuing to exercise diplomatic and other channels of communication with the Soviets. Trying to soften somewhat the diplomatic impact of the blockade, some officials in the U.S. administration preferred to call it a quarantine of Cuba, which seemed to them a less-provocative term. Using the metaphor *quarantine* cast the blockade less as an act of war and more as a temporary measure that would be lifted as soon as "health" was restored. Choosing a less-provocative term was a war-avoidance measure, one calculated to allow an adversary to seek a peaceful resolution of the dispute.

Although even this course of action was highly risky, it proved to be successful in getting the Soviets to withdraw the missiles without armed conflict between the two states. But Kennedy wisely provided a carrot to the Soviet Premier Nikita Khrushchev, which was to promise to remove U.S. Jupiter missiles based in Turkey and aimed at the Soviet Union. Significantly the security interests of both

---

[3]Alexander L. George, "A Provisional Theory of Crisis Management," in Alexander L. George, ed., *Avoiding War: Problems of Crisis Management* (Boulder, Colo.: Westview Press, 1991), pp. 22–23.

CRISIS DIPLOMACY AND FOREIGN POLICY DECISIONS

Graham Allison and his colleagues in the late 1960s engaged in a now-classic study of U.S.-Soviet crisis diplomacy when the two countries came to the brink of nuclear war in 1962 over Soviet missiles secretly deployed in Cuba. Both the unitary and rational assumptions associated with realism are relaxed from the *organizational process* and *bureaucratic politics* perspectives adopted by Allison.

The organizational-process model of foreign policy decision making views organizational routines and procedures as determining some and influencing other foreign policy decisions and outcomes. Organizational ethos and world view are also relevant considerations. In an often-cited statement, Allison notes that where a given bureaucratic actor or diplomat stands on a given issue is often determined by where he or she sits; that is, one's view of alternative courses of action is highly colored by the perspective of the organization to which one belongs or role one plays. Perceptions of what is the optimal or best course of action often vary from one bureaucratic actor to another, reflecting organizational biases that raise serious doubts concerning the rationality of the process as a whole. What assurance is there that optimal choices for the state as a whole will be made? Or is optimality, when achieved, purely accidental?

Allison's bureaucratic politics model of foreign policy decision making involves forming coalitions and counter-coalitions among diverse bureaucratic actors in a competitive environment. The focus is on specific individuals in positions at the top of organizations and on the pulling and hauling among them. This is in contrast to the more routine, preprogrammed activity of the organizational-process model. Hence foreign policy decisions at times may be the result of which individual, or which coalition of individuals, can muster the most political power. What may be best for an individual or his or her bureaucracy in terms of increased prestige and relative standing within the government may lead to less than the best foreign policy for the state as a whole. Parochial, personal, and bureaucratic interests may reign over any expressed concern for the national interest.

Allison's work does not pose as direct a challenge to the unitary assumption about state behavior as does some of the other literature on decision making (the

unitary assumption being that the state, whatever its domestic political differences, comes to speak with one voice in its diplomacy and foreign policy). Although multiple actors influenced by diverse organizational and individual interests compete to influence policy choices, in the final analysis these decisions are still made by certain authoritative individuals. Notwithstanding all the competition and airing of alternative views, the state still ultimately speaks with one voice. At the same time, however, the Allison study did at least raise some questions concerning the unitary character of the state in its *implementation* of policy. Decisions made were not always carried out as quickly as anticipated or in precisely the way they were intended. After all, policy involves both decisions and actions. Even if the decisions are unitary and the state speaks with one voice (which may not always be the case), if consequent actions are fragmented or otherwise inconsistent, then how unitary is the state after all?

The bottom line is that Allison's organizational process and bureaucratic politics models do challenge the more traditional (and realist) rational model of decision making, raising serious questions concerning the appropriateness of relying on the rational-actor model to explain foreign policy and diplomatic choices. In other studies of crisis diplomacy (the Cuban missile crisis and events leading up to World War I in 1914), Ole Holsti and his associates also challenge the more simplistic rational-actor model that overlooks cognitive rigidity, time pressures, and stress—factors that can have a decisive (and even devastating) impact if not managed carefully.

Robert Keohane, Joseph Nye, and others have taken the pluralist image of foreign policy a major step forward, arguing that the state may not be able to confine bureaucratic actors operating in its name. Organizations, whether private or governmental, may transcend the boundaries of states, forming coalitions with their foreign counterparts. Such transnational actors even may be working at cross-purposes with government leaders in their home states who possess the formal authority to make binding decisions. For example the British Foreign Office may see a given issue similarly to its American State Department counterpart. On the other hand the British Defence Ministry

(continued)

and U.S. Defense Department may share a common view contrary to that of both diplomatic organizations. Moreover nongovernmental interest groups in both countries may form coalitions supportive of one or another transgovernmental coalition.

To what extent, then, do coalitions of bureaucratic actors, multinational corporations, and other transnational actors circumvent the authoritative decision makers and diplomats of states through formation of such coalitions? An interesting example of a transgovernmental coalition that had a significant, though unpublicized, impact during the October 1962 Cuban missile crisis involved redeployment of Canadian naval units for an "exercise" in the North Atlantic. This decision effectively relieved the U.S. Navy of at least a part of its patrolling responsibilities there, allowing American ships to be deployed to the Caribbean as part of the naval blockade of Cuba. All of this was apparently established between American and Canadian military officers while the Diefenbaker government in Ottawa was still debating the question of what Canadian policy in the crisis would be! Was this apparent circumvention by the Canadian

Navy an exception, or is it commonplace for bureaucratic actors to form coalitions across national borders that in effect make policy? Pluralists would argue that it is more commonplace than most realists would suppose.

If it is typically the way foreign policy is made, then focus by realists on the state as principal actor would seem to be misdirected. From the pluralist perspective more attention should be given to the entire range of transnational actors and their interactions. On the other hand if the example used here is indeed an exception, then it is an exception that makes the rule. From the realist perspective the state in most cases retains its prerogatives, precluding circumvention by transnational, bureaucratic actors.

For more details about these two views of foreign policy, see Allison's *Essence of Decision* (Boston: Little, Brown, 1971); Holsti's article in Paul Gordon Lauren, ed., *Diplomacy: New Approaches in History, Theory and Policy* (New York: 1979); and Robert O. Keohane and Joseph Nye, eds., *Transnational Relations and World Politics* (Cambridge, Mass.: Harvard University Press, 1972).

U.S. President John Kennedy confers with his advisors during the Cuban missle crisis of 1962.

This American U-2 spy plane photo revealed a medium-range ballistic missile launch site on San Cristobal, Cuba. Such intelligence imagery set in motion the events of the Cuban missile crisis.

sides were accommodated. Recognition of how close the United States and the Soviet Union had come to the brink of nuclear war led, however, to setting an arms control agenda aimed at reducing tensions and building a foundation for better communications between the two, particularly in times of crisis.

Perceptions concerning the **credibility** of threats matter a great deal. If threats are not credible, a threatened state may choose to ignore them. Alternatively the other state may make threats of its own: Saber rattling is common enough in diplomacy. States on a collision course may well wind up in armed conflict, particularly in a crisis in which high stakes and time pressure may undercut a reasoned, rational discussion of policy options. Paradoxically, when communications are most necessary, traditional practice is to sever diplomatic relations entirely. As the nineteenth-century Prussian writer Clausewitz observed, war is merely state policy conducted by other means. Inevitably if ceasefires are to be arranged and peaceful settlements made, diplomacy must play a primary role.

There is also a place for diplomatic communications in wartime, sometimes facilitated by the **good offices** of third parties who assist in getting the parties to communicate and cease hostilities. This is the diplomatic peacemaking role as in the Middle East and elsewhere that aims toward a settlement through direct or indirect negotiations, mediation or arbitration, judicial settlement, or other means. In most cases the conflicts that led parties to war in the first place are extraordinarily difficult to resolve. Divisions deepen as each party suffers the scourge that is the human cost of war.

Of course if one side wins or prevails on the battlefield, it may be in a position to dictate the terms of the settlement. The losing party in such circumstances can take some solace in the outcome of the Congress of Vienna. Even without military or economic leverage, a losing party—France—was able to contribute to constructing a settlement that accommodated the diverse and often conflicting interests of the parties. Unfortunately diplomatic miracles of this sort are usually few and far between, with vindictive and punishing terms for the loser of a war—such as Germany after World War I—a distinct possibility.

The Ways and Means of Diplomatic Communications

Diplomacy as a means of communications between or among governments has many sides. In the extreme one can play hard ball, issuing threats or an ultimatum to one's adversary. Such communications are designed to force an outcome desired by the party sending such provocative messages either in writing or orally—such as when an ambassador representing a foreign country tells a foreign minister or head of government in the host country that unless certain steps are taken, economic or military sanctions of one kind or another will be imposed.

Ultimata of this sort are not the usual, day-to-day stuff of diplomacy. We will discuss three other kinds of diplomatic communications: informational transfers, symbolic messages, and negotiations.

First some communications are merely *informational transfers* not designed to produce any particular outcome. Such governmental agencies as departments (or ministries) of foreign affairs, defense, commerce, or their diplomatic representatives in embassies throughout the world let local governments and interested individuals and groups know about newsworthy events or other happenings. For example the U.S. National Aeronautics and Space Administration (NASA), its Jet Propulsion Laboratory (JPL), or its other centers inform governmental counterparts, scientists, and the general public about shuttle launches into space, photographs of space retrieved from the orbiting Hubbel telescope, and missions to Mars or past other planets.

DIPLOMACY AMONG ALLIES

Sometimes the most difficult diplomacy is not between two adversaries but among allies who disagree on how to approach a common adversary. One example from the mid-1990s is about how NATO member states should deal with Serbia and its president, Slobodan Milosevic, concerning Serbian actions in Bosnia. The following account comes from the memoir of former U.S. Secretary of State Warren Christopher.

By the summer of 1995, the crisis in Bosnia had reached its culminating stage. The British and the French, whose troops were the backbone of the United Nations force there, began to signal that they would leave the region by the end of the year. Moreover, in response to 'pinprick' NATO airstrikes in May 1995, the Bosnian Serb Army had taken some UN personnel hostage and chained them to possible air targets. Many of us feared that these acts would be the last straw, and the UN would decide to withdraw. If this happened, the United States was committed to contributing ground troops to a NATO force that would help ensure a safe withdrawal. I felt that this would be an embarrassing as well as perilous use of American forces, but, on the other hand, failure to keep our commitment would undermine our credibility as the leader of the Alliance.

As we debated our diplomatic options, the military situation deteriorated. In July, the Bosnian Serb Army overran two UN safe areas, Srebrenica and Zepa. The massacre in Srebrenica was devastating, and we realized that something had to be done. The UN safe area at Gorazde, the last Muslim enclave in eastern Bosnia, appeared to be the next target.

To determine the international response to these attacks, Prime Minister John Major of the United Kingdom called an emergency meeting of Allied and other interested Foreign Ministers in London on July 20. I led the U.S. delegation, which included Secretary of Defense William Perry and General John Shalikashvili, Chairman of the Joint Chiefs of Staff. At the meeting we decided that there could be no more half measures; we could not permit the loss of the beleaguered town of Gorazde. NATO had to present the Bosnian Serbs with a clear and unambiguous warning to leave Gorazde alone. During a day of tough negotiations in the sweltering heat of London's Lancaster House, and with a major assist from the new British Foreign Secretary, Malcolm Rifkind, we persuaded the Allies to agree that an attack on Gorazde would be met with "substantial and decisive" use of air power. For this reason, the meeting was a vital turning point in our approach toward Bosnia: we finally committed to put some real muscle behind our rhetoric.

Point: Before one can bargain with an adversary, tough negotiations among allies are often required.

Warren Christopher, *In the Stream of History* (Stanford: Stanford University Press, 1998), p. 348.

Other informational communications may have a purpose that goes beyond merely transmitting facts. Government agencies may communicate directly to foreign publics or work through centralized agencies or ministries of information. For example the U.S. Information Agency (USIA), a component of the State Department, wants to convey to foreign publics the rationale for U.S. policies and explain U.S. understanding of and approaches to world events. Most countries have similar information ministries with established press contacts for access to radio, television, and print media. Mailing lists and government sites on the World Wide Web (or Internet) are also used to present a country's point of view—information with a decided purpose. Because such communications are expected by design to be one-sided advocacy of a country's policy positions (not necessarily balanced presentations with all sides of an argument considered), information ministries in democratic countries may well be restricted (as the USIA is) from disseminating their communications to citizens residing within their own countries. Lest they be accused of propagandizing their own citizens, the target audience of information ministries in democratic countries is foreign publics.

Other communications are *symbolic*, usually designed to reinforce positive aspects of relations between two countries. Thus French foreign ministry and other government officials attend a Fourth of July celebration hosted by the U.S. embassy in Paris. Naturally U.S. officials reciprocate by attending a similar Bastille Day (July 14) celebration hosted by the French embassy in the Georgetown section of Washington. On such occasions symbolic references are often made to eighteenth-century French help in the American Revolution, the fact that neither country has ever gone to war with the other, and that both countries share long-established commitments to democratic values.

Another example of symbolic communications is to demonstrate respect by presidents and senior government officials or their representatives, ambassadors, and other diplomats attending important state events such as coronation of a monarch, inauguration of a president, royal family or other state weddings or funerals, and other state events. The level of representation at such events is carefully considered, usually to avoid any insult to the host country. Thus the funerals following the deaths of U.S. President Kennedy in 1963, Egyptian President Sadat in 1981, and Jordanian King Hussein in 1999 brought presidents and prime ministers from all over the world.

Annual events such as Luxemburg's commemoration of U.S. General Patton's role in liberating the country from occupation by Germany during World War II typically draw delegations of American diplomats, generals, and military personnel headed by the U.S. ambassador. Who and what level of position or rank are to be in attendance at such state events are by no means left to chance but are usually carefully coordinated between the two countries beforehand to assure a successful "symbolic" event that contributes to continued good relations between the two countries.

Diplomacy includes not just these and similar kinds of positive exchanges, but (as noted earlier) also has to deal with conflicts in interests and objectives. A third form of diplomatic communications is *negotiations*; however, one or another of the parties may choose not to negotiate.

Avoiding or Sidestepping Conflicts   Indeed, one approach to a conflict is to sidestep, avoid, or ignore it, not confronting it directly. Sometimes the issues dividing the parties are inconsequential or relatively unimportant and thus not worth any bother, particularly when raising such issues may worsen relations without accomplishing much, if anything. At other times, however, there may be important issues at stake that one or more of the parties may wish to defer to a later time, perhaps realizing that the issues are not likely to be resolved satisfactorily any time soon. This may require some fancy diplomatic footwork, leaving matters rest as they are, unresolved, and without yielding anything in principle to the other side.

A good example during the cold war was the preference by the United States, Britain, and France not to renegotiate with the Soviet Union the set of rules that had emerged after previous conflicts concerning air and land access to all sectors of Berlin, then still under post–World War II occupation by these four countries. It was feared that any such renegotiation likely would be used by the Soviets to erode access rights claimed by the three Western allies. In 1948, for example, the Soviets had tried to deny air and land access to Berlin across East Germany, but the United States responded by ignoring the Soviet prohibition, airlifting needed supplies to the beleaguered city. In the process the Western allies established their rights in practice and eventually the Soviet Union lifted its prohibitions on air and land access. The Soviets still claimed rights to regulate land and air access to the city but chose not to exercise them.

For their part the Western allies denied that the Soviet Union had any such right to deny them access because wartime agreements had established these rights, which from the Western perspective remained nonnegotiable. This conflict on rights of access thus remained unresolved throughout the cold war. As a practical matter, however, the Soviets chose not to provoke the Western allies again by forcefully denying them access as they had done in 1948. Importantly, neither side yielded anything in principle on the rights-of-access matter under dispute even as regular flights, railroad trains, cars, and trucks moving across East Germany to and from Berlin were allowed to proceed.

Negotiating Without Expectation of Reaching Agreement   Indeed, the real challenges in diplomatic negotiations occur when the parties are deeply in conflict. Sometimes one or both parties do not really want to reach agreement at all but see some value in the negotiating process, at least appearing to negotiate. The objective may be merely to delay taking any action on the conflict at issue. In this mode one or both sides may set forth a maximum position which neither expects the other side to accept.

For example, in the late 1970s, the United States and its NATO allies responded with a two-track strategy to Soviet deployments in the western Soviet Union of nuclear-armed SS-20 INF ballistic missiles. These intermediate-range nuclear force missiles had a range of 500 to 5500 kilometers (or 300 to 3300 miles) aimed at Western Europe. On one track the United States prepared to deploy the intermediate-range Pershing II ballistic missiles in West Germany as a

Europeans demonstrating against deployment of missiles to Greenham Common, England, in the early 1980s.

counter to the SS-20. The United States also prepared to deploy additional cruise (remotely guided, "airbreathing") missiles in West Germany, the United Kingdom, Italy, the Netherlands, and Belgium.

The second (or negotiations) track favored by many of the U.S. allies in NATO was also initiated. The "zero-zero option" negotiating proposal offered by the United States in 1981 was not expected to be accepted by the Soviet Union. A bold stroke by the West (and particularly by the United States), the zero-zero option called for Soviet disarmament of its INF missiles (reducing them to zero) in exchange for NATO commitment not to counter with Pershing II and cruise missiles, leaving both sides with zero INF missiles in their arsenals.

It was a stretch to believe at the time that the Soviet Union would ever dismantle what it had already deployed in exchange merely for a promise by NATO not to match the existing Soviet deployment. Critics of the zero-zero option in NATO countries doubted the sincerity of the U.S.-NATO proposal, seeing it as a ploy merely to appear committed to the diplomatic negotiating track while fully expecting to go forward with counter-deployments of Pershing II and cruise missiles. Whatever the truth of this allegation, all Western parties were pleasantly surprised when, counter to their expectations, the new Soviet regime under Gorbachev decided in 1987 to accept the zero-zero option and proposed dismantling all INF missiles. The final outcome, by no means anticipated in 1981, was elimination of an entire category of weaponry: intermediate-range nuclear missiles.

Another example of negotiations not expected to succeed in their apparent purpose is the NATO-Warsaw Pact force reduction talks held in Vienna between 1973 and 1989. The negotiations dragged on throughout the 1970s and 1980s until the end of the cold war with very little to show for all the time and effort expended. From time to time each side accused the other of not negotiating in good faith. Some observers joked that the negotiators enjoyed Vienna so much that they did not want to reach an agreement lest they have to leave this beautiful city! These pundits jokingly claimed the way to force agreement was to choose a less desirable city in which to negotiate—an incentive to speeding up the process so the diplomats could go home.

The reality, of course, was that neither side was under any particular time pressure that would force an early conclusion. As recognized leader of the NATO side, the United States entered the negotiations at a time when the Nixon administration wanted to forestall Congressional efforts in the early 1970s to reduce the U.S. troop presence in Europe. The fact was that NATO already had fewer forces deployed in and around Germany in the "central front" between East and West—a numerical disadvantage compared to the Warsaw Pact. Accordingly neither the Nixon administration nor America's NATO allies really wanted a substantial reduction in American or other NATO forces unless there were also substantial reductions in Warsaw Pact forces. For their part the Soviet Union and its Eastern European Warsaw Pact allies already enjoyed numerical superiority and saw little to gain by reducing their numbers and sacrificing their quantitative advantage over NATO. At the same time the Warsaw Pact side found value in negotiating, particularly if domestic political pressures forced the United States or other NATO countries to reduce their forces to even lower levels.

Given its numerical superiority, the Warsaw Pact side indicated willingness to reduce forces equally—these were to be mutual force reductions (MFR) talks. The NATO side countered that the reductions needed to be proportional or balanced—mutual and balanced force reductions (MBFR) talks. For example a 10 percent reduction on both sides would mean a larger number of troops for the

Warsaw Pact to reduce because it had more troops in the area. Thus because the Warsaw Pact had about a million troops and NATO only about 800,000 in central Europe, a balanced or proportional reduction of 10 percent would mean the Warsaw Pact withdrawing 100,000 troops and NATO just 80,000.

Other difficult issues included whether troops in the Soviet Union in striking distance of Western Europe should be counted, particularly since the United States (and Canada) did not want troops counted in their home countries or the other side of the Atlantic. Added to these issues was the so-called "data problem," given differences in composition and size of military units (a division, brigade, or regiment on one side was not the same as a division, brigade, or regiment on the other side either in terms of numbers of combat or support troops or equipment). Indeed, neither side could agree on how many troops the other actually had under arms in central Europe.

Arguably both sides could have resolved such matters if they really had wanted to reach agreement on lower force levels. Although frustrating to many arms control advocates, delaying any outcome appeared to be the real objective (or at least the default position of both sides). Viewed in this light MBFR talks were successful in avoiding any agreement disadvantageous to either side or, in the U.S. case, keeping Congressional pressures from forcing unilateral U.S. force reductions in Europe. Most importantly, perhaps, the MBFR talks had provided a useful opportunity for two opposing military alliances to be in direct and regular communications for some seventeen years, providing a diplomatic forum for registering complaints, coming to understand (if not accept) opposing sides, and contributing to building relations that would bear fruit in other forums at the end of the cold war.

Getting-to-Yes Negotiations as Zero- and Positive-Sum Games   The mentality in negotiations is often what one side gains, the other loses. Game theorists refer to this as **zero-sum**—the pluses one side gains come at the expense of the minuses the other side loses. As discussed earlier, incentives ("carrots") and disincentives or threats ("sticks") may be used by the parties, although such methods are rather blunt instruments. Give and take, pulling and hauling by opposing parties, and formation of coalitions and counter-coalitions in multilateral negotiations are tactics often employed to forge compromise agreements when interests and related objectives are in conflict. Sometimes this is the best that can be achieved—a compromise in which typically each side gains something but also gives up something. Each side achieves some points of satisfaction but is also left with some disappointments—points it may have had to give up in order to get some concessions from the other side or perhaps to get any agreement at all.

A potentially far more productive approach to durable agreements is to use negotiations as a means to search for common ground among the parties, forging a positive-sum outcome based on mutual gains. Such agreements may involve some compromises but rest more fundamentally on satisfying the parties' interests, particularly those they have in common. The Harvard negotiation project has identified several principles or guidelines for "getting to yes"—an essentially positive-sum approach to use when parties are in conflict.[4] The methodology was developed for diverse negotiation settings, but for our purposes it has direct application to diplomatic communications aimed at achieving win-win outcomes.

---

[4]Roger Fisher and William Ury (with Bruce Patton, ed.), *Getting to Yes: Negotiating Agreement Without Giving In* (London and New York: Penguin Books, 1981, 1991).

Although personalities and orientations matter in how negotiators relate to one another, negotiations are about issues, not personalities. In focusing on issues the parties avoid digging in their heels and taking hard-and-fast positions. Instead they pay attention to the interests of all of the parties in a search for common ground. Interests are of two kinds: those related to the substance of what is being negotiated and those related to preserving and improving relationships in the negotiations among the parties and the countries they represent. There also needs to be room for creative approaches to finding common ground—at times inventing options for mutual gain. Finally, not to be content to rest agreements merely on the will of the parties, objective criteria or standards for measuring what has been agreed, accompanied by fair procedures, are essential to effective implementation of any agreement. In point-by-point summary form, the getting-to-yes method is (1) don't bargain over positions; (2) separate the people from the problem; (3) focus on interests, not positions; (4) invent options for mutual gain; and (5) insist on using objective criteria.[5]

Extended three-way negotiations among Canada, the United States, and Mexico in the late 1980s and early 1990s "got to yes" on establishment of a free trade area judged by negotiators and national leaders at the time to satisfy interests of all three parties. This was by no means an easy task. The United States and Canada, with highly developed advanced industrial (or postindustrial) economies, were both relatively rich in capital but markedly different from each other in aggregate size of their economies. In this regard Canadians were concerned that more open trade and commercial relations might make them one of the principal objects of U.S. economic dominance. For their part Mexicans were concerned that their less-developed economy (a per capita income about 10 percent of that in their two northern neighbors) might suffer disadvantage at the hands of both the United States and Canada. Labor unions in the United States objected that jobs in labor-intensive industries would be lost to Mexico where wages were low. The unions were joined by environmental groups concerned that American corporations would continue moving to Mexico where environmental law and law enforcement was less stringent, allowing them to foul or degrade the environment in ways that would be prohibited in the United States.

The North American Free Trade Agreement (NAFTA) that finally emerged addressed trade product by product in difficult negotiations that also took environmental matters and estimates of jobs to be gained or lost into account. Negotiators searched creatively for options in a positive-sum approach to realizing mutual gains (and minimizing losses), even though these gains (and losses) would be asymmetric—not all evenly shared. Numerous compromises were reached. Difficult issues were sometimes settled by agreeing on scheduled but delayed implementation of some provisions. Objective criteria were specified in the details of a final agreement that numbered more than 2000 pages!

Although one could try to add up all the gains and losses (and both advocates and opponents did just that), in the final analysis NAFTA rested on the view that the overall economic interest of each party and North America as a whole would be better served by reducing trade barriers. Whether one agreed with them or not, this was the view held at the time by both U.S. President Bush and his successor President Clinton as well as by their head-of-government counterparts in

---

[5]For details, see ibid., pp. 3–94.

Canada and Mexico. As President Clinton put it, one can add up the pluses and minuses if one wants to, but what NAFTA is really about is a big (and important) idea. Liberalizing trade and commerce was a positive-sum vision he, his predecessor, and his counterparts saw as realizing gains, on balance, for all parties.

The decades-long peace process in the Middle East is another example of the getting-to-yes approach at work. Four major Arab-Israeli wars (1948, 1956, 1967, and 1973), repeated terrorist acts, and civil strife have marked the region and divided Arab states from Israel, at times into separate, hostile, seemingly irreconcilable camps. Enormous patience has been required as well as help from third parties (the United States, other countries, and international organizations) to bring the parties together and to facilitate efforts to find common ground satisfactory to their mutual interests.

In the 1970s, for example, both Egypt and Israel had an interest in avoiding the human and material cost of yet another war. Israel's interest in its security and its related desire for diplomatic recognition as a state, coupled with Egypt's interest in regaining and securing territory lost in wars, ultimately led the parties to the 1979 Camp David Accords mentioned in the previous section. Although the agreement contained compromises, its more solid basis was its grounding in mutual interests: Israel gave land back to Egypt in exchange for Egypt's recognition of Israel as a state (the first Arab state to do so), embassies were established in each other's capital, ambassadors were exchanged, and diplomatic relations were normalized. U.S. President Carter was particularly instrumental in bringing Israeli Prime Minister Begin and Egyptian President Sadat together at Camp David, Maryland, using his good offices to keep them engaged in the negotiations process. Creative approaches to finding common ground were employed in the bargaining process. The agreement was also secured with grants of military and economic aid as incentives offered by the United States to both sides. An agreed timetable and procedures for implementing the agreement in accordance with objective criteria were finally reached.

Significantly the Camp David Accords not only found a substantive common ground based on mutual interest in the peace and security between Egypt and Israel; the accords also served mutual interest in building and maintaining better relationships at both high-level leadership and midlevel or "working" levels among officials on both sides. These relationships were essential both to reaching and effectively implementing the agreement.

Since then the peace process has continued with fits and starts as attention turned to Israel's conflicts with other Arab states (security and territory being the same interests typically at issue) and to the interest of Palestinians as a people in eventually securing a state to call their own. Different American presidents, secretaries of state, and other emissaries from the United States, other countries, and international organizations have continued to use their good offices to try to keep the peace process on track in a patient, although frequently frustrating, search for common ground. Apparent progress has often amounted to small, slow steps, only to be reversed in subse-

BACK-CHANNEL DIPLOMACY

*D*uring my first meeting with President Nixon, I was surprised when he said to me: "Ambassador, I've checked with my predecessor and found out you are a person who never gives leaks to the press or to others. So I believe we could organize a confidential channel. And I have a good man—Mr. Kissinger. He will report directly to me without telling anyone else." Finally [Kissinger] said "We meet so often—let's have a telephone." So White House communications people put a telephone line in the room next to my office at the embassy. It was a regular phone—it wasn't red—but it had no dial or numbers. When I picked it up, only Henry answered.

Source: Former Soviet Ambassador Anatoly Dobrynin, *quoted in* U.S. News and World Report, November 13, 1995, p. 70.

IT'S BEEN SAID...

quent weeks and months. Getting to yes has been anything but easy, requiring enormous reserves of patience—a commitment to continuing the process in spite of major differences, assassinations, and terrorist incidents intended by opponents of the peace process to push it off track, disrupting further negotiations if at all possible.

CONCLUSION

Contemporary diplomatic practices have not escaped the global trends of interdependence and crises of authority. First there has been an erosion of diplomatic norms. Consider, for example, the sanctity of diplomatic missions. Over the years missions certainly have been attacked by mobs, but the takeover of the American embassy in Tehran in November 1979 by radical students established a dangerous precedent because the revolutionary Islamic regime sanctioned the action. In the 1980 Venice Declaration, the seven participating heads of state from Europe, North America, and Japan noted they were "gravely concerned by recent incidents of terrorism involving the taking of hostages and attacks on diplomatic and consular premises and personnel." They had good reason to be, because by 1980 diplomats had become the major targets for terrorism, accounting for 54 percent of all international terrorist attacks. American diplomats were the favored targets.[6] Furthermore the Iranian and Libyan regimes used their overseas missions to plan and support terrorist acts on foreign soil. Add to this the rise in crime in urban areas throughout the world, significant health risks, and increasing social anarchy in a number of developing countries, and it is clear that life for diplomats and their families is a long way from the popular image of champagne-and-caviar embassy parties.

Second the nature of diplomatic communication between governments has evolved. Historically the resident ambassador has been the key communication link with the host government, presenting his state's views and reporting back those of the host government. Now regular summits among leaders, back-channel contacts that skirt the embassy, and direct, secure telephone lines between political leaders all reduce the relevancy of the ambassador. Even in those situations in which the ambassador has direct access to top host government officials, the result can be to go over the head of the professional diplomatic circuit.

Third, the end of the cold war has reduced the importance of Western embassies in the former East bloc as sources of information for policy makers. Particularly during the cold war, Western journalists had little access to Eastern bloc countries, so official political reporting from embassies was critical. As East-West tensions eased, however, journalists were granted entry to previously remote parts of the Soviet Union and Eastern Europe and also found it easier to cultivate their own sources of information in various foreign policy bureaucracies. It is not unusual for policy makers to find important insights in the *New York Times, Washington Post, Le Monde, Times* of London, *Christian Science Monitor, Wall Street Journal,* or other quality newspapers.

---

[6]Geoffrey M. Levitt, *Democracies Against Terror* (New York: Praeger, 1988), pp. 36–37.

Fourth the worldwide communication revolution has also reduced the importance of diplomatic reporting. Thanks to satellites, television networks, the Internet, and radio reports are often the first sources of information on breaking events, with diplomatic and intelligence reporting lagging behind. Indeed, key offices throughout the State Department feature television sets that are tuned to news channels throughout the day. CNN and other networks are also a staple for twenty-four hour operations centers located in various government agencies that deal with foreign policy and national security issues. Satellite transmissions allow government intelligence analysts as well as regular citizens to watch live news broadcasts from foreign television stations covering local events.

One drawback to relying on live broadcasts is that the information viewers receive does not provide the broader, interpretive context that characterizes diplomatic and intelligence reporting. Furthermore the live broadcast of events to millions of people may force the pace of events or sensationalize issues, putting pressure on policy makers to make a decision before diplomats can meet to negotiate a mutually acceptable solution.

Fifth, in an increasingly interdependent world, the diplomatic corps of today and tomorrow have to be more than familiar with complex technological and environmental trends. These are increasingly the subject of international concern— for example, the impact of ozone depletion and the cutting down of the Amazon rain forests, the social and environmental impact of exploding birthrates in the developing world, or the resolution of disputes between states based on conflicting claims to natural resources such as water. It is highly debatable whether the diplomatic corps of most countries are adequately recruiting, training, and retaining persons with expertise in such areas. Yet without such personnel (who must also be skilled in negotiating), it is unlikely that a state will be able to resolve the sorts of challenges and conflicts that are discussed later in this book.

Finally, particularly in the case of humanitarian disasters and civil wars, "field diplomacy" on the part of nongovernmental relief and aid organizations may become increasingly the norm. Often attuned to local politics and knowledge of key players, these nonstate actors may play a key or supporting role in conflict mitigation or even conflict resolution.

KEY TERMS

diplomacy *p. 105*	deterrence *p. 106*	cognition *p. 110*
compellence *p. 106*	treaty *p. 107*	
coercive diplomacy *p. 106*	ambassador *p. 108*	

OTHER CONCEPTS ⌒

emissary *p. 103*
ancien regime *p. 103*
apartheid *p. 107*
executive agreement
 p. 107
démarche *p. 108*
ultimatum *p. 108*
jus gentium *p. 112*
jus naturale *p. 112*
chargé d'affaires *p. 114*
multilateral diplomacy
 p. 114
bilateral diplomacy *p. 114*
neutrality *p. 115*
government in exile *p. 115*
puppet government
 p. 116

diplomatic immunity
 p. 118
reciprocity *p. 118*
persona non grata *p. 118*
extraterritoriality *p. 119*
asylum *p. 119*
mission *p. 119*
embassy *p. 119*
consulate *p. 119*
delegation *p. 119*
chief of mission *p. 121*
deputy chief of mission
 p. 121
consul *p. 121*
consul general *p. 121*
interest section *p. 121*

intelligence collection
 p. 123
espionage *p. 123*
country team *p. 123*
foreign aid *p. 125*
economic sanctions *p. 125*
boycott *p. 125*
embargo *p. 125*
blockade *p. 126*
crisis *p. 126*
crisis diplomacy *p. 126*
credibility *p. 129*
good offices *p. 129*
zero-sum *p. 134*

ADDITIONAL READINGS ⌒

In the preparation of this chapter we found quite helpful Harold Nicholson's short classic *Diplomacy*, 3d ed. (London: University Press, 1963). To get a feel for diplomacy as actually conducted, many university libraries contain the memoirs of diplomats. The U.S. secretaries of state Dean Acheson, Henry Kissinger, Cyrus Vance, Alexander Haig, George Shultz, James Baker, and Warren Christopher have all published lengthy tomes. See also Henry Kissinger, *Diplomacy* (New York: Simon & Schuster, 1994) and on the Congress of Vienna his *A World Restored* (New York: Grosset & Dunlap, 1964). For a classic analysis of the diplomacy that set the foundation of the post–World War II era, see Dean Acheson, *Present at the Creation* (New York: W.W. Norton, 1969). Covering the first half of the twentieth century is George Kennan's *American Diplomacy* (New York: New American Library/Mentor Books, 1951). On the modalities of diplomacy, see Fred C. Iklé, *How Nations Negotiate* (New York: Harper & Row, 1964). Touching on diplomacy over the half millennium since 1500 is Paul Kennedy's *The Rise and Fall of the Great Powers* (New York: Random House, 1987).

MILITARY FORCE: WAR, JUST WARS, AND ARMED INTERVENTION

"War is a matter of vital importance to the state; the province of life or death; the road to survival or ruin. It is mandatory that it be thoroughly studied."

SUN TZU, *THE ART OF WAR*, CA. 500 B.C.

"War is the last of all things to go according to plan."

THUCYDIDES, *THE PELOPONNESIAN WAR*, CA. 404 B.C

"And above all, while defending our own vital interests, nuclear powers must avert those confrontations which bring an adversary to a choice of either a humiliating retreat or a nuclear war. To adopt that kind of course in the nuclear age would be evidence only of the bankruptcy of our policy—or of a collective death-wish for the world."

PRESIDENT JOHN F. KENNEDY, JUNE 1963

CHAPTER

5

 t age thirty Mary Louise Roberts enlisted in the U.S. Army following the attack on Pearl Harbor. She was assigned as the operating room supervisor with the Army's 56th Evacuation Unit and went ashore at Casablanca, North Africa. The fighting in North Africa was intense but only a preview of what lay ahead: Anzio, Italy, which marked the beginning of the Allied invasion of Europe in the southern theater. Robert's medical unit landed five days after the invasion. Situated in the middle of the combat zone with German artillery shells ripping through the operating tent on the Anzio beachhead, she remembers, "At one point our commanding officer got the nurses together and asked whether we wanted to be evacuated. It was pretty bad, but we decided we were going to stay." One male officer was eager to leave, "But he said there was no way he was going to leave until at least one nurse agreed to go—so he stayed, too." One of Robert's colleagues, June Wandrey, wrote home, "We're working twelve to fifteen hours a day now, never sitting

down except to eat. . . . Such young soldiers. They're so patient and never complain. I won't be able to write often and here are the reasons why: Bed 6, penetrating wound of the left flank, penetrating wound face, fractured mandible [jaw], penetrating wound left forearm; Bed 5, amputation right leg, penetrating wound left leg, lacerating wound of chest, lacerating wound right hand."[1]

We begin by posing a simple question: What do you think is the first image that comes to mind for most people when they hear the concepts "world politics" or "international relations"?

A good bet is that war is generally the first thought that comes to mind. All too often **armed conflicts** dominate the newspaper headlines and hence our consciousness when we think of international relations or world politics. This is understandable, because wars are the most destructive of human activities. It has been estimated that 2 million people lost their lives on the battlefields during the Thirty Years' War (1618–48), 2.5 million during the French Revolution and Napoleonic wars (1792–1815), 7.7 million in World War I (1914–18), and 13 million in World War II (1939–45).[2] Such estimates do not even include the death and injury of civilian populations, nor do they adequately reflect the devastation caused by civil wars. Indeed, for countries such as the United States, the great Civil War of 1861–65 resulted in more American deaths—600,000—than all other wars fought by Americans from 1776 to the present combined.

It is not surprising, therefore, that over the centuries observers of international relations have been primarily interested in understanding patterns of conflict and cooperation among various types of political units. These units, as we have seen in Chapter Two, have included ancient Greek city-states of the fifth century B.C., Persian, Roman, and Carthaginian empires, and modern nation-states. The question of "Why do wars occur?" is not all that different from the question of "What factors account for peace?" Indeed, war and peace can be viewed as opposite sides of the same coin.

THE RATIONALITIES AND IRRATIONALITIES OF INTERSTATE WAR

In this chapter we examine the use of *force* in world politics. In the previous chapter we discussed the threat of force and its limited application for coercive and deterrent purposes as part of a diplomatic arsenal available to policy makers. Force also refers to the use of military capabilities in **interstate wars**, **civil wars**, or **armed interventions**. *Interstate wars* are defined as wars by one or more states

force   The use of military capabilities to coerce other states (or actors) against their will.

---

[1]Tom Brokaw, *The Greatest Generation* (New York: Random House, 1998), pp. 174–76.
[2]Jack Levy, "Theories of General War," *World Politics* v. 37, no. 2 (April 1985): 344.

against another state or states. *Civil wars* involve fighting among two or more factions within a state. *Armed interventions* involve the deployment of military personnel to a foreign country in order to tip the balance in a civil war, restore order, maintain peace, or physically coerce a state to change its policies. Whereas the use of military force is the defining characteristic of war, it should be noted that use of propaganda, coercive diplomacy, and economic and other sanctions also usually occur during warfare.

The enormous human costs of war have not prevented countless repetitions of the phenomenon throughout human history in all parts of the world. A propensity to engage in **warfare**—an organized use of force of one group of people against another—is one of the things human beings have in common, however tragic the consequences. Tribes in the rain forests of New Guinea and Amazonia, clans and tribes in Africa and the mountainous or other more remote regions in Eurasia and Latin America, and nations and states throughout the world count war among the experiences they hold in common.

The apparent irrationalities of warfare notwithstanding, the **decision** itself to go to war is often the result, paradoxically, of *rational choice*. Although interstate wars may not occur as frequently today as they have in the past, they have proven difficult to eliminate precisely because rationally motivated decision makers may see war (or other uses of force resulting in war) as serving their national objectives or purposes. The devastation caused by interstate wars and the very real human and economic costs involved may well be viewed as irrational by outside observers, but the decisions to use force or go to war rarely are—at least not in the minds of those who make them. In fact they are usually made based upon *maximizing expected gains* or *minimizing expected losses* consistent with the *objectives* and the *interests* of the parties making the decision. This perspective on war as rational choice is most closely associated with realists.

A country's desire to defend territory and the people who live on it is to be expected. When a people or their leaders see the use of force as worth the expected costs, we understand them as rational. Certain cultures (or individuals) may range from peaceful or pacific to bellicose or warlike, but we know from experience that decision makers in all societies or cultures are quite capable of choosing force or going to war if the circumstances—threats and opportunities—and interests so warrant.

Sometimes, when faced by the overwhelming force of an aggressor with virtually no chance of success, the rational choice may well be to surrender as opposed to going to war. The Belgians, having been overrun by the Germans in 1914 at the beginning of World War I, understood only too well that they could not stop the German armed forces in 1939 at the outset of World War II. Why would a people rationally choose to endure the very high human costs of war when the situation could only be made worse by doing so? Surrender, while still pursuing resistance by other means, seemed to be the rational choice. Belgium had no good choices; it would lose whether it fought or surrendered, but surrendering minimized these losses.

In practice rationality is highly subjective. Deciding which objectives (or expected gains) to pursue and which losses (or expected costs) are acceptable may vary depending on who is making the decision. A disinterested observer may estimate costs and benefits but cannot be sure that those actually making the decisions will see them this way. The value or weight they place on various criteria may be influenced by past experiences and highly subjective perspectives or points of view.

rational choice   A choice that requires a rank ordering of preferences or goals, consideration of alternatives to attain one's goals in light of capabilities, and consideration of costs and benefits typically either to minimize the former or maximize the latter.

Moreover decisions may have to be made without complete information under conditions of uncertainty or under time and other pressures. Misperceptions and miscalculations, coupled with formation of coalitions, counter-coalitions, and other political factors further complicate the decision making process. As a result decisions in practice may be **suboptimal**—less than the best.

THE CAUSES OF WAR

While the decision to go to war may be viewed as rational from a decision maker's perspective, various factors may influence the calculation. In this section we examine some of the most important causes of war, which shape the ultimate decision to resort to the use of force.

Legions of books have been written on the causes of war. For our purposes these causes can be categorized according to our four basic levels of analysis outlined in Chapter One—the international system, state and society, group, and the individual.

International System Level of Analysis

It has been argued that interstate wars start because there is nothing to stop them.[3] In an anarchic world there is no world government or central authority, much less one with the necessary power to constrain states or other organized groups from using force or engaging in warfare. In such a world some states may choose to use force to achieve their objectives. When these actions confront other states, armed conflict may be the result.

There was no central authority, for example, among city-states in ancient Greece. In these uncertain circumstances, according to the writer Thucydides, it was fear in Sparta about the rising power of Athens that was the underlying cause of the Peloponnesian War. The Spartan's perception of a change in the distribution of power upset existing security calculations, making them more fearful. Sparta took measures to counter Athenian power before it became too strong; these steps contributed to the onset of war. Above all there was no authority higher than these city-states to intervene, assure both sides of their security, and preclude them from going to war.

It is this anarchy or absence of any central authority or government in the ancient world (or in the present one, for that matter) that is the underlying or "permissive" cause of war. It is a self-help system in which states seek to attain their objectives or serve their own interests. International relations have a permissive quality, posing no governmental or other authoritative obstacles to countries wishing to use force to achieve their objectives by such means.

Similarly the lack of effective governing authorities with power or capability to keep a society together is an underlying cause of *civil wars*—armed conflicts within a given state and society. Even when a central government exists, a civil war may break out if the regime lacks legitimacy, which is acceptance by its population as a whole that it has the right to exercise political authority. In any event the government also lacks the necessary coercive power (military and police capabilities) to maintain domestic law and order.

---

[3] The analysis in this section draws from Kenneth N. Waltz, *Man, the State and War* (New York: Columbia University Press, 1959).

Competing governments in the same state and society may emerge, perhaps identified with different national, ethnic, or other identities. In such circumstances outside states may intervene to support one side or another, creating the possibility of a civil war turning into an interstate war. Intervention can take a number of forms: diplomatic action, aid to one or another of the parties, or other forms of interference including the use of armed force or *armed intervention*.

Even though outside intervention in civil wars is contrary to international law, states in service of their own interests have often chosen to overlook this legal restraint, taking actions on behalf of one party or another. Partition into separate communities (or even separate states) or reintegration of competing parties as one side defeats the other are typical outcomes of a civil war that could affect the interests of outside states. In some cases the outcome may have territorial, natural resource, or other strategic implications. An outside state may also be concerned about the welfare of a particular party with which it shares a common national or ethnic identity. Thus in the Bosnian civil war Serbia focused on the fate of ethnic Serbs living in Bosnia, just as it was concerned with the fate of Serbs living in Kosovo.

It is often difficult to contain civil wars within the borders of the affected state. Quite apart from outside interference, civil wars can spill beyond their borders and become interstate wars. Again there is no central authority or world government to stop their spread. The effects of intertribal fighting in central Africa between Hutus and Tutsis in Rwanda in the 1990s, for example, quickly involved neighboring Zaire (or Congo) and Burundi. France, the United States, and other outside states also entered the fray under United Nations auspices for humanitarian purposes and to restore peace and security to the region.

Other systemic-level hypotheses or explanations of war involve such phenomena as conflicts between **alliances** or global security competitions that produce arms races. Alliances and counter-alliances were said to have caused World War I. Secret treaties and war clauses committing states to defend one another if injured or attacked resulted in a chain reaction; as one party mobilized for war, others followed suit. The 1914 assassination in Sarajevo of the Austrian Archduke Franz Ferdinand by a Serbian anarchist was merely the spark or catalyst that set into motion a series of actions and reactions among alliance members that resulted in world war.

Many of those who accepted this explanation for World War I argued strenuously for a world in which the use of force for aggressive purposes was outlawed. Rather than the power and balance-of-power politics of alliances, a collective security system of law-abiding states was finally established after the war in the League of Nations. President Woodrow Wilson was a principal advocate of such a League and also argued for a world of open (rather than secret) covenants among states.

If alliances were the cause of World War I, paradoxically it was the absence of alliances, posing no obstacle to a resurgent Germany, that may have contributed to World War II. As a legal system of obligations, collective security within the League of Nations failed to stop aggression or eliminate the use of force by states acting unilaterally.

That arms races contribute to the onset of war is another systemic-level hypothesis. Richardson's equations (see following box) are sometimes used to explain arms race behaviors that can lead to war. Was it the late nineteenth– and early twentieth–century naval and ground-force competition between Britain and

RICHARDSON'S ARMS-RACE EQUATIONS

Arms races and militarized disputes between and among states have been the subject of extensive research using mathematics and statistical analysis. One of the earlier practitioners of this approach was Lewis F. Richardson, who developed differential equations to express formally the relations among variables affecting arms races. The propensity of two countries to engage in arms races is interactive, with the action of one country having causal impact on the other. Equilibrium in an arms race is defined as the point of intersection of lines (or curves) for each equation.

Both Country X and Country Y establish a rate (dx/dt and dy/dt, respectively) by which they increase (a positive number) or decrease (a negative number) the military armaments in their inventories. The opponent's strength (x or y) is an important factor, as is one's own strength (x or y), and the overall climate of relations between the countries (q or r)—a measure of hostility or long-standing grievances between the two.

Richardson subtracts the estimate of one's own strength from that of the arms race opponent. If the difference or gap is increasing, a higher propensity to acquire arms to match a rival is understandable. For Country X this is

$$ay - cx$$

and for Country Y it is

$$bx - dy$$

where **a** and **b** are proportionality constants representing a positive orientation or readiness to acquire arms and **c** and **d** are proportionality constants representing a disinclination to continue acquiring arms due to fatigue or other costs.

Adding the grievance, hostility, or climate-of-relations factor, full equations for both countries are for Country X

$$dx/dt = ay - cx + q$$

and for Country Y

$$dy/dt = bx - dy + r$$

Given these relations, one is able to draw inferences about the stability of arms races—their tendency to remain in equilibrium or to break out of it—as changes in the force posture of one party affect changes in the force posture of the other.

Note: For Richardson's treatment see his *Statistics of Deadly Quarrels* (New York: Quadrangle, 1960) and *Arms and Insecurity* (New York: Quadrangle, 1960). For an excellent discussion and critique, see Anatol Rapoport, *The Origins of Violence* (Brunswick, N.J.: Transaction Publishers, 1995), pp. 366–77. A highly readable account of Richardson's work and other action-reaction models is Greg Cashman, *What Causes War?* (New York: Lexington Books, 1993), pp. 172–76.

France against Germany that was one cause of World War I? If so, could the U.S.-Soviet cold war arms competition have resulted in the same outcome? What kept the peace? Quantitative and other studies have tried to answer such questions, determining how militarized disputes contribute to the occurrence of war.

Individual and Group Levels of Analysis

If anarchy—the absence of effective central authority—is an underlying or permissive cause of all wars, then a particular war may be influenced by perceptions or misperceptions in a leadership group (if not in the society as a whole) of the intentions and capabilities of an adversary. Psychological and social-psychological factors of individuals or small groups may affect such calculations.

In addition to focusing on perception or misperception, explanations at the individual or small-group levels examine individual psychologies and group dynamics. Thus some argue that human beings are by nature aggressive, or the personality of an individual leader such as Adolf Hitler or Josef Stalin is a critical factor in a country's decision to go to war. Others argue that the frustration of groups or individuals in group settings can lead to aggressive behavior which, in turn, can lead to war. Particularly in cohesive small groups, there is the danger of members reinforcing each other's mutual biases, leading to a phenomenon known as *groupthink*. The result is that information that contradicts the group's devoutly held beliefs and prejudices is ignored.

State and Societal Levels of Analysis

Finally it has been argued that the nature of a state or society is critical in explaining the outbreak of war and the propensity of a country to use force. President Woodrow Wilson and others who shared his views argued that dictators and those within their ruling elite are more prone to choose war than those democratically elected to office and held responsible to the people. In his war address to the U.S. Congress on April 3, 1917, Wilson blamed the war on those who "provoked and waged" it "in the interest of dynasties or of little groups of ambitious men."

Wilson saw the 1914–18 world war as "the war to end all wars," defeating dictatorship in Germany and the other central European powers and making the world "safe for democracy." In short the Wilsonian hypothesis was that dictatorships (like "the Prussian autocracy" in Germany) produce war but democracies produce peace.

The Russian revolutionary leader Vladimir Ilyich Lenin, who came to power in 1917, expressed a different view on what type of state or society was more likely to encourage international peace. Socialist states, representing the interests of the working classes traditionally forced to do the fighting and dying in wars, would be inclined to avoid war. In leading the revolution that overthrew the Tsarist regime in Russia, Lenin argued that capitalist states and societies tend to become imperialist as they compete with each other for markets throughout the world. Lenin viewed World War I as a war among imperial powers, and the new socialist workers regime he headed would have no part of it. Peace was made soon after he and the communist party came to power; Russia pulled out of the war.

Or was the economist Joseph Schumpeter right when he argued, contrary to Lenin, that capitalism would be more conducive to peace?[4] Although arms sellers might register some short-term gains, the net effect of war is to destroy capital—the productive capacity of economies. Because it is the capitalists who own this productive capacity, their real interest is in protecting and expanding capital, not destroying it. According to this reasoning peace is served by the spread of capitalism and commercial values that displace heroism, gallantry, glory, and other obsolete, war-oriented values of an earlier precapitalist or feudal period.

Although Wilson, Lenin, and Schumpeter differ respectively over whether democracy, socialism, or capitalism is more conducive to peace, all of these arguments have one thing in common: It is the nature of state and society or the

groupthink   A mode of thinking involving a cohesive group in which the members' striving for unanimity overrides their motivation to appraise realistically alternative courses of action.

---

[4]See his *Capitalism, Socialism and Democracy* (New York: Harper and Row, 1942, 1962).

THE DEMOCRATIC PEACE

As noted in Chapter Two, Immanuel Kant, the eighteenth-century philosopher, argued that the best way to ensure progress toward peace is to encourage the growth of republics whose constitutional arrangements check or balance competing domestic interests. Particularly with the end of the cold war, scholars have attempted to answer empirically the question: Are democracies more peaceful in their foreign relations? This literature, known as the democratic peace, concludes that democracies are quite capable of using force or going to war, perhaps as much as authoritarian regimes. The related question, however, is whether democracies go to war against each other. The answer is that this rarely if ever happens. The virtual absence of war among democracies has led one scholar to conclude that this is "as close as anything we have to an empirical law in international relations."*

The answer to the question of whether democracies are more peaceful is not merely of academic interest; it has potential foreign policy implications. On the one hand state support of democratic movements around the world can be justified on the grounds of enhancing the prospects of peaceful relations among states. On the other hand, however, the literature on the democratic peace could be used (or misused) to justify interventions in the domestic affairs of other states or as an excuse to dismiss past acts of aggression by democracies.

Question: How would you respond to these two observations?

---

*Jack Levy, "The Causes of War: A Review of Theories and Evidence," in Philip E. Tetlock et al., eds., *Behavior, Society, and Nuclear War*, vol. 1 (New York: Oxford University Press), p. 270.

political and economic regime that is responsible for increasing or decreasing the likelihood of war. We can apply the observations of Wilson, Lenin, or Schumpeter in broader terms than merely describing the relative likelihood of one or another kind of state or society to engage in war. Worldwide democracy (as in a universal concert or partnership of democratic regimes), worldwide socialism, or worldwide capitalism are alternative, international system-level outcomes that, if achieved, might affect the likelihood of war.

A combination of causes at the individual and small group, state and society, and international system levels undoubtedly accounts for the outbreak of any particular war. The difficult challenge is to determine which ones are salient in any given case. Realist observers of world politics and war, however, would claim that it is the underlying anarchy of the system that allows wars to happen regardless of the specific cause or set of causes of a particular war. Other observers agree.

Consistent with this logic, those who want to eliminate war need to change the underlying world order. The most ambitious world federalists, for example, would replace international anarchy with some form of world government. They would vest a central authority with enough power (including armed forces and police units) to keep component states and societies from going to war.

Responding to plans to end war in Europe by constructing a confederation of states, Jean-Jacques Rousseau did not fault the logic of such schemes (eliminating the anarchy of international relations through world governance) so much as their impracticality. World federalists are quick to respond that the very act of defining world government as an impossibility makes it so. It is a self-fulfilling prophecy. We are not likely to achieve (or even try to achieve) what we have defined as an impossibility.

Even if world government were the solution to interstate war, many would find it undesirable. Different peoples in different societies value their independence in a world of sovereign states and prefer to hold on to a national identity. For those with this view, implementing world government as a remedy for war would be worse than continuing to live with armed conflicts and the use of force.

NATIONAL STRATEGY AND THE USE OF FORCE

The Prussian general and writer Carl von Clausewitz (1780–1831) worked for years on a theory of war and the use of force. He had practical experience, serving both Russia and his native Prussia in wars against the French that ended with the defeat of Napoleon in 1815. Clausewitz accepted an important position in 1818 as director of the German War School, which allowed him time to think, research, and write. His incomplete work *On War* was published a year after his death in 1832.

The book has had an enormous influence on how states use force to achieve their purposes. To Clausewitz war was merely one means states might employ to achieve objectives set by political authorities. As such, wars (and the armed forces called upon to fight them) were merely *means* to accomplish objectives, not *ends* in themselves. War was not glorified as something good in itself. The only legitimate purpose of war, according to Clausewitz, was to serve political objectives; it is diplomacy by other means:

> War is an instrument of policy; it must necessarily bear its character, it must measure with its scale: the conduct of War, in its great features, is therefore policy itself, which takes up the sword in place of the pen, but does not on that account cease to think according to its own laws.[5]

On War presents chapters on the nature and theory of war, **strategy** and plans for fighting a war, and leadership and **tactics** or methods of combat operations.[6] After establishing that war is an instrument of state policy and as such the armed forces are subordinated to the political authorities of the state, Clausewitz specifies the way in which any battle or war is won. He elaborates what constitutes **military necessity** in war.

The military aim is always the same—*to destroy or substantially weaken an enemy's warfighting or warmaking capability.* Clausewitz observes that "if War is an act of violence to compel the enemy to fulfil our will, then in every case all depends on our

Prussian general, Carl Von Clausewitz (1780–1831). Noted for his book *Vom Kriege* (*On War*), which advocated the total destruction of an enemy's forces as one of the strategic targets of warfare and seeing war as an extension of political policy and not as an end in itself.

---

[5]Carl von Clausewitz, *On War*, Book V, Ch. 6 (B). Originally published as *Vom Kriege* (Berlin: Ferdinand Duemmler, 1832). Readily available English editions include one edited by Anatol Rapoport (New York: Penguin Books, 1968) and one edited and translated by Michael Howard and Peter Paret (Princeton, N.J.: Princeton University Press, 1976). Citations in this chapter are taken from the Penguin edition.

[6]Clausewitz defines tactics as "*the theory of the use of military forces in combat*" and strategy as "*the theory of the use of combats for the object of the War.*" He elaborates that "Strategy forms the plan of the War" and "is the employment of the battle to gain the end [or objective] of the War." Strategy has its "moral, physical, mathematical, geographical, and statistical elements." See *Ibid.*, Book I, Ch. 1 and Book III, Chs. 1 and 2.

overthrowing the enemy, that is, disarming him, and on that alone." More to the point he asserts: "The *military power* [of an enemy] must be destroyed, that is, reduced to such a state as not to be able to prosecute the War."[7] Actions taken in war for this purpose, and this purpose alone, constitute military necessity.

In order "to defeat the enemy" it is necessary to direct and "proportion our efforts to his powers of resistance." Clausewitz identifies a physical factor—military *capabilities* (C)—and a moral factor—*will* to use these means (W)—as two critical and related variables responsible for battlefield effectiveness (E). E is expressed as a "product of two factors which cannot be separated, namely, *the sum of available means* [or capabilities] and *the strength of the Will*."[8] Expressed symbolically this is

$$E = C \times W$$

If either factor C or W declines or approaches zero, so does E. One can lose a battle or an entire war if either military capabilities or will to fight decline, particularly if the enemy has kept up its capabilities and will.

Although Clausewitz does not develop or use the concept of **deterrence**, there is a suggestion of it in his observation that if there is a balance or equilibrium in conflict relations between two states, we can expect peace to be maintained for the time being, at least until one side gains an advantage over the other, thus upsetting the balance. Capabilities and will (or strength of motive to fight) are again key variables: "the equation is made up by the product of the motive and the power."[9]

In its modern formulation, which owes much to Clausewitz, deterrence is a psychological concept. One state makes a credible threat to use military capabilities if another state commits aggression or undertakes some other action the deterring state considers undesirable. The deterred state perceives the deterring state's military capabilities and will to use them in armed conflict and is dissuaded from committing aggression or other offense. Expressed symbolically, deterrence (D) is similar in form to battlefield effectiveness (E). It is the product of perceived capabilities (C) and credibility or will (W) to use them:

$$D = C \times W$$

It is, as Clausewitz had it, a multiplicative function: the product of power and motive or will, expressed nowadays more commonly as military capabilities times credibility. If either of these two factors weakens, deterrence becomes unstable or tends to break down. In the extreme cases when either capabilities or credibility approach zero, deterrence also goes to zero—it fails.

Among the **principles of war** Clausewitz identifies are **mass** (other things aside, the "superiority of numbers" as when "the greatest possible number of troops" is "brought into action at the decisive point"), **surprise** (achieving military successes through "secrecy and rapidity"), **concentration of forces** (maximizing their collective strength or impact "at the decisive point"), and **economy of forces** (a conservative approach that avoids "waste of forces, which is even worse than their employment to no purpose").[10]

[7] *Ibid.*, Book I, Ch. 2.

[8] *Ibid.*, Book I, Ch. 1, Section 5.

[9] *Ibid.*, Book I, Ch. 1, Section 13.

[10] *Ibid.*, Book III, Chs. 8, 9, 11, and 14.

THE FUTURE OF WAR: HIGH TECH OR LOW TECH?

The Revolution in Military Affairs (RMA) is part of the revolutionary shift from an industrial- to an information-based society. The information revolution is a result of advances in computerized information and telecommunications technologies but also innovations in organizational theory. Not surprisingly the United States has been the leader in developing theoretical and operational concepts related to RMA. The RMA is perhaps best illustrated by the use of high technology weapons in the 1991 coalition war against Iraq and in the 1999 NATO air war against Serbia. Cockpit video footage of laser-guided smart bombs finding their way uncannily to their target was a staple of nightly news broadcasts. When the air war against Serbia was over, NATO could claim a victory in which there were no allied casualties. This was certainly an unprecedented event in the history of warfare.

Martin van Creveld has argued that a fundamental change in how war is waged is not new. He identifies four eras of military history. In the "Age of Tools" (lasting to about A.D. 1500), most technology was driven by the strength of the muscles of men and animals. Bronze and iron weapons, the stirrup, and wheeled vehicles are examples. The hallmark of the "Age of the Machine" was the organization and institutionalization of a society's natural resources for conducting war utilizing a mass army. Napoleon's army epitomizes the trend of using manpower mass in wars across great distances. The "Age of Systems" involved the integration of technology into complex networks. The culmination was in World War II with the innovative application of mechanization, aviation, and communications technology. The German development and employment of the *blitzkrieg* is one example. Van Creveld terms the period since World War II the "Age of Automation" due to the vast amounts of information needed to wage wars. Information is required to run a military unit on the ground, conduct air campaigns, or wars in general. To digest all of this information requires the use of computers. This revolutionary change in the conduct of war, however, requires more than advanced technologies; it also requires complementary organizations that can adapt and change their structure to maximize the value of the technology.[*]

Advanced industrial states may be investing in the latest high-tech weaponry, but van Creveld and other military historians have noted another trend in terms of the nature of war—the expansion and intensification of low-intensity conflicts. According to Ralph Peters, crises of state authority in countries around the world have opened the floodgates to civil disorder with important implications in terms of wars and warfighting:

> Future wars and violent conflicts will be shaped by the inabilities of governments to function as effective systems of resource distribution and control, and by the failure of entire cultures to compete in the postmodern age. The worldwide polarization of wealth, afflicting continents and countries, as well as individuals in all countries, will prove insurmountable, and social divisions will spark various forms of class warfare more brutal than anything imagined by Karl Marx. Poststate organizations, from criminal empires to the internationalizing media, will rupture the integrity of the nation-state. . . . The enemies we are likely to face will not be 'soldiers,' with the disciplined modernity that term conveys in Euro-America, but 'warriors'—erratic primitives of shifting allegiance, habituated to violence, with no stake in civil order. Unlike soldiers, warriors do obey orders they do not like. Warriors have always been around, but with the rise of the professional soldiery, their importance was eclipsed. Now, thanks to a unique confluence of breaking empire, overcultivated Western consciences, and a worldwide cultural crisis, the warrior is back, as brutal and distinctly better armed.[**]

A study of armed conflict in the post–cold war world appears to lend credence to the warrior thesis. As noted in Figure 5.A, the number of armed conflicts active in any given year rose steadily from 1946 to 1992. The number peaked at 51 in 1992. In part due to the resolution of

---

[*]Norman C. Davis, "An Information-Based Revolution in Military Affairs," in John Arquilla and David Ronfeldt, eds., *In Athena's Camp: Preparing for Conflict in the Information Age* (Santa Monica, Calif.: RAND, 1997), pp. 81–83.

[**]Ralph Peters, *Fighting for the Future* (Mechanicsburg, Penn.: Stockpole Books, 1999), p. 2.

(box continues)

THE FUTURE OF WAR (CONTINUED)

several long-standing wars in Central America and southern Africa, the trend reversed and the number of armed conflicts declined to 37 in 1995. But only 6 out of 101 conflicts in the period 1989–96 were international, meaning involving the forces or territory of more than one state. Combatants were not only typically uniformed soldiers, but also guerrilla groups, paramilitary forces, drug and organized criminal bands, warlords, and vigilante hit squads.

The key empirical point is that few of these were *high-intensity* conflicts, but rather what researchers term *low-intensity* or intermediate. This means fewer than 1,000 persons were killed in a single year and most deaths were caused by small arms. During the first half of the 1990s, some 3.2 million persons died of war-related causes. The cumulative total from 1945 to 1995 was at least 25 million deaths, and probably more (see Figure 5.B). Civilians accounted for about 70 percent of all war victims since World War II but more than 90 percent in the 1990s. And these figures do not even account for most of the deaths in the Bosnian and Kosovo wars.

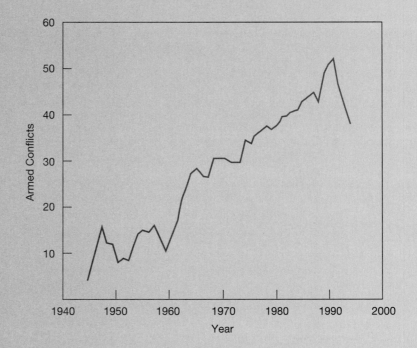

FIGURE 5.A   Number of Armed Conflicts, 1946–95

Source: Lester Brown et al., *State of the World 1998* (New York: W.W. Norton, 1998), p. 133.

Success in war also depends on military leadership with strong mental and organizational capabilities. He calls for officers with strong mental "power of discrimination" and "good judgment."[11] This is particularly important because of the complexities and uncertainties commanders face in war. Things in war often do not go according to even the best laid plans. Clausewitz refers to this as **friction.**

---

[11]*Ibid.*, Book I, Ch. 6.

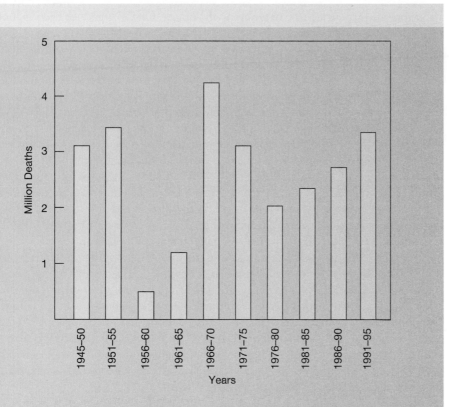

FIGURE 5.B   Deaths in Armed Conflicts, by Five-Year Period, 1946–95

Source: Lester Brown et al., *State of the World 1998* (New York: W.W. Norton, 1998), p. 134.

Questions: Are countries such as the United States, which devotes billions of dollars to field large armies, air forces, and navies, preparing for the wrong type of war? How useful is technology in fighting low-intensity conflicts?

Point: Throughout history changes in technology have affected how warfare is conducted.

To learn more about the changes in warfare through the centuries, see Martin van Creveld, *Technology and War: From 2000 B.C. to the Present* (New York: Free Press, 1989) and Ralph Peters, *Fighting for the Future* (Mechanicsburg, Penn.: Stackpole Books, 1999), pp. 2, 32. See also Michael Howard, *War in European History* (Oxford: Oxford University Press, 1976) and John Keegan, *A History of Warfare* (New York: Knopf, 1993).

In physics or mechanics we calculate on paper or chalkboard the forces we expect will operate on an object in an ideal situation. We try to predict its motion—its velocity or speed and direction—perhaps drawing a diagram specifying the forces with vectors or arrows. As a practical matter, of course, we learn that in the real world the motion of objects is impeded or slowed by friction, which is often difficult to measure in advance. We can get a sense of how much friction is involved through experimental trials and we may decide to take corrective measures to reduce friction by lubricating the surface or streamlining the object. One may reduce friction, but it cannot be eliminated entirely.

So it is with plans for war drawn up in peacetime or in an office setting. According to Clausewitz, a great gap exists between the "conception" of war and its "execution." As he puts it: "Everything is very simple in War, but the simplest thing is difficult. These difficulties accumulate and produce a friction which no one can imagine exactly who has not seen War." He adds that "incidents take place" in war, change in weather for example, that are virtually "impossible to calculate, their chief origin being chance." At best one can conduct military exercises or experimental trials to try to identify and correct major sources of friction.[12]

Through such measures one may be able to reduce the friction that comes from taking war plans off the shelf and putting them into practice, but one cannot eliminate the effect entirely. Compounding the effects of friction and contributing to it is what Clausewitz called the **fog of war**—the sum of all uncertainties and unpredictable occurrences that can happen so rapidly in war.

Clausewitz understood war as a **zero-sum** phenomenon: One side's gain is the other's loss: "In a battle both sides strive to conquer. . . . The victory of one side destroys that of the other."[13] But Clausewitz was never an advocate of war for war's own sake. Given his own participation in the wars against Napoleon's armies, Clausewitz had observed the awful consequences of armed conflict and worried about "its character" as it "approaches the form of absolute War." More than a century before the nuclear age, Clausewitz expressed his concerns about circumstances when general or total war is the expected outcome. He counseled how necessary it is "not to take the first step" into such a war "without thinking what may be the last."[14]

RESTRAINING WAR: MORAL AND LEGAL PRINCIPLES AND THE USE OF FORCE

Pacifism and Bellicism

Pacifism is a philosophical position that in its purest sense rejects all forms of war and any use of force as legitimate means for attaining objectives, resolving conflicts, or any other purpose. Its opposite—a bellicose orientation or **bellicism**[15]— either sees value in war itself or at least understands war as so essential a part of world politics that it cannot be avoided.[16]

Bellicists tend to discount the human costs of armed conflict, observing that war also produces people willing to make sacrifices, who exhibit courage and outright bravery in the face of danger, industriousness, loyalty, obedience, and other martial values a society may wish to cultivate. Taken to the absurd extreme, war is seen to be a "purifying bath of blood and iron"[17] presumedly with therapeutic effects for society as a whole.

---

[12]*Ibid.*, Clausewitz, Book I, Chs. 6–8.

[13]*Ibid.*, Clausewitz, Book I, Ch. 1, Section 15.

[14]*Ibid.*, Clausewitz, Book V, ch. 3 (A).

[15]The term is used by James E. Dougherty and Robert L. Pfaltzgraff, Jr., *Contending Theories of International Relations* (New York: Lippincott, 1971), p. 164.

[16]For example, see Niccolo Machiavelli, *The Prince*, Ch. xiv.

[17]The quote is sometimes attributed to Georg Hegel, although the attribution may be apocryphal.

◇ THE WAR PRAYER ◇

by Mark Twain

It was a time of great and exalting excitement. The country was up in arms, the war was on, in every breast burned the holy fire of patriotism; the drums were beating, the bands playing, the toy pistols popping, the bunched firecrackers hissing and spluttering; on every hand and far down the receding and fading spread of roofs and balconies a fluttering wilderness of flags flashed in the sun; daily the young volunteers marched down the wide avenue gay and fine in their new uniforms, the proud fathers and mothers and sisters and sweethearts cheering them with voices choked with happy emotion as they swung by; nightly the packed mass meetings listened, panting, to patriot oratory which stirred the deepest deeps of their hearts and which they interrupted at briefest intervals with cyclones of applause, the tears running down their cheeks the while; in the churches the pastors preached devotion to flag and country and invoked the God of Battles, beseeching, His aid in our good cause in outpouring of fervid eloquence which moved every listener. It was indeed a glad and gracious time, and the half-dozen rash spirits that ventured to disapprove of the war and cast a doubt upon its righteousness straightway got such a stern and angry warning that for their personal safety's sake they quickly shrank out of sight and offended no more in that way.

 Sunday morning came—next day the battalions would leave for the front; the church was filled; the volunteers were there, their young faces alight with martial dreams—visions of the stern advance, the gathering momentum, the rushing charge, the flashing sabers, the flight of the foe, the tumult, the enveloping smoke, the fierce pursuit, the surrender!—then home from the war, bronzed heroes, welcomed, adored, submerged in golden seas of glory! With the volunteers sat their dear ones, proud, happy, and envied by the neighbors and friends who had no sons and brothers to send forth to the field of honor, there to win for the flag or, failing, die the noblest of noble deaths. The service proceeded; a war chapter from the Old Testament was read; the first prayer was said; it was followed by an organ burst that shook the building, and with one impulse the house rose, with glowing eyes and beating hearts, and poured out that tremendous invocation—

"God the all-terrible! Thou who ordainest,
Thunder thy clarion and lightning thy sword!"

Then came the "long" prayer. None could remember the like of it for passionate pleading and moving and beautiful language. The burden of its supplication was that an ever-merciful and benignant Father of us all would watch over our noble young soldiers and aid, comfort, and encourage them in their patriotic work; bless them, shield them in the day of battle and the hour of peril, bear them in His mighty hand, make them strong and confident, invincible in the bloody onset; help them to crush the foe, grant to them and to their flag and country imperishable honor and glory—

An aged stranger entered and moved with slow and noiseless step up the main aisle, his eyes fixed upon the minister, his long body clothed in a robe that reached his feet, his head bare, his white hair descending in a frothy cataract to his shoulders, his seamy face unnaturally pale, pale even to ghastliness. With all eyes following him and wondering, he made his silent way; without pausing, he ascended to the preacher's side and stood there, waiting. With shut lids the preacher, unconscious of his presence, continued his moving prayer, and at last finished it with the words, uttered in fervent appeal, "Bless our arms, grant us the victory, O Lord our God, Father and Protector of our land and flag!"

The stranger touched his arm, motioned him to step aside—which the startled minister did—and took his place. During some moments he surveyed the spellbound audience with solemn eyes in which burned an uncanny light; then in a deep voice he said:

"I come from the Throne—bearing a message from Almighty God!" The words smote the house with a shock; if the stranger perceived it he gave no attention. "He has heard the prayer of His servant your shepherd and will grant it if such shall be your desire after I, His messenger, shall have explained to you its import—that is to say, its full import. For it is like unto many of the prayers of men, in that it asks for more than he who utters it is aware of—except he pause and think.

(box continues)

"God's servant and yours has prayed his prayer. Has he paused and taken thought? Is it one prayer? No, it is two—one uttered, the other not. Both have reached the ear of Him Who heareth all supplications, the spoken and the unspoken. Ponder this—keep it in mind. If you would beseech a blessing upon yourself, beware! lest without intent you invoke a curse upon a neighbor at the same time. If you pray for the blessing of rain upon your crop which needs it, by that act you are possibly praying for a curse upon some neighbor's crop which may not need rain and can be injured by it.

"You have heard your servant's prayer—the uttered part of it. I am commissioned of God to put into words the other part of it—that part which the pastor, and also you in your hearts, fervently prayed silently. And ignorantly and unthinkingly? God grant that it was so! You heard these words: 'Grant us the victory, O Lord our God!' That is sufficient. The *whole* of the uttered prayer is compact into those pregnant words. Elaborations were not necessary. When you have prayed for victory you have prayed for many unmentioned results which follow victory—*must* follow it, cannot help but follow it. Upon the listening spirit of God the Father fell also the unspoken part of the prayer. He commandeth me to put it into words. Listen!

"O Lord our Father, our young patriots, idols of our hearts, go forth to battle—be Thou near them! With them, in spirit, we also go forth from the sweet peace of our beloved firesides to smite the foe. O Lord our God, help up to tear their soldiers to bloody shreds with our shells; help us to cover their smiling fields with the pale forms of their patriot dead; help us to drown the thunder of the guns with the shrieks of their wounded, writhing in pain; help us to lay waste their humble homes with a hurricane of fire; help us to wring the hearts of their unoffending widows with unavailing grief; help us to turn them out roofless with their little children to wander unfriended the wastes of their desolated land in rags and hunger and thirst, sports of the sun flames of summer and the icy winds of winter, broken in spirit, worn with travail, imploring Thee for the refuge of the grave and denied it—for our sakes who adore Thee, Lord, blast their hopes, blight their lives, protract their bitter pilgrimage, make heavy their steps, water their way with their tears, stain the white snow with the blood of their wounded feet! We ask it, in the spirit of love, of Him Who is the Source of Love, and Who is the ever-faithful refuge and friend of all that are sore beset and seek His aid with humble and contrite hearts. Amen.

(After a pause) "Ye have prayed it; if ye still desire it, speak! The messenger of the Most High waits."

It was believed afterward that the man was a lunatic, because there was no sense in what he said.

Source: Mark Twain, *Europe and Elsewhere.* Copyright 1923, 1951 by The Mark Twain Company.

Pacifism or commitment to nonviolence is a perfectly defensible philosophical or moral position. The same cannot be said for bellicism, which sees positive value in violence and the use of force. Just because we live in a world prone to violence does not mean that violence is morally right or good in itself, particularly not in an age when war can lead to mass destruction on an unprecedented scale. The principal challenge to pacifism, of course, is also the question of its practicality in an anarchic world, in which states and even nonstate actors may use force to attain their objectives.

Just-War Theory

Just-war theory (sometimes called just-war doctrine) is an example of ***normative theory*** that prescribes right conduct—how states and their agents *ought* to act. International law concerning war—the law of armed conflicts—rests on treaty obligations, customary practice, the writings of jurists, and general principles closely linked to just-war theory. This theory adopts a position between the pacifist and bellicist positions but is somewhat closer to the pacifist pole because it

normative theory   A value-oriented or philosophical theory that focuses on what ought to be.

seeks to avoid war or, failing that, to limit its destructive consequences. Every effort is made to avoid armed conflict in the first place.

Pacifism——————Just-War Theory——————Bellicism

Just-war theory encompassing both **jus ad bellum** (the right to go to war) and **jus in bello** (right conduct in war), comes from a long tradition in Western thought that can be traced to Plato (427–347 B.C.). The first explicit reference to the just-war concept is from Plato's Roman follower Cicero (106–43 B.C.), who stated that "just wars should be fought justly."[18] The ideas elaborated by Cicero in a non-Judaic, pre-Christian context were developed further by St. Augustine, who presented it as an alternative to pacifism that had been dominant in the early Christian Church. Aquinas (1225–74), Vitoria (1480–1546), Suarez (1548–1617), Gentili (1552–1608), and other writers contributed further to establishing just-war concepts as a more formal philosophical or moral foundation upon which *international law* concerning war would come to rest.

Building on the work of Suarez and Gentili, who had dealt with legal aspects of just-war theory, the Dutchman Hugo Grotius (1583–1645) incorporated much of just-war thinking in his writings on international law. His *Law of War and Peace* (first published in Latin in 1625 as *De Bellum ac Pacis*) took just-war theory from its moral or theological base to develop what would become legally binding principles. As with other international law, the **law of war** has been drawn from general principles, customary practice, formal treaties, court cases, and the writings of jurists. The Hague Conventions and Regulations (1899 and 1907) and Geneva Conventions and Protocols (1949 and 1977) represent a formalization or codification of the modern-day law of war.

The *jus ad bellum* or right to go to war depends upon having a *just cause*, such as when a country comes under attack by an aggressor state. The decision to go to war cannot be made by anyone; it must be made by the legitimate authority within the state. Determining which is the legitimate authority is not always an easy matter, of course, particularly not in civil wars within a state when each side contends that it is *the* legitimate authority.

Because war usually causes so much death and destruction, it is not a decision to be taken lightly. Accordingly just-war theory dictates that resort to armed force as an option must be proportionate to the provocation, not a disproportionate response to a relatively minor cause. There also must be some chance of success or resort to war would be a futile enterprise wasting lives and property unnecessarily. Finally war is the *last* resort. The decision to use armed force should be delayed whenever possible until peaceful means for settling the dispute have been exhausted.

These conditions for a just war are very demanding. They clearly are skewed in the direction of avoiding war if at all possible. As such they stand much closer to the pacifist than to the bellicist pole. War is not to be sought. Every reasonable means must be taken to avert armed conflict and its awful human consequences if one is to have a *jus ad bellum*, a right to go to war.

Satisfying all of these criteria does depend heavily on *right intention*. If decision makers are not committed to doing the right thing, no set of moral or legal

---

[18]See Cicero, *The Republic*, II: xxvii, III: xxiii, xxiv, and xxix and *The Laws*, II: ix, xiv, and III: iii, xviii.

principles can be effective. Clever political leaders and diplomats can always find ways to skirt any set of rules, perhaps even manipulating them in an elaborate rationalization of their conduct.

Critics of just-war theory make precisely this point. The historical record suggests to them that more often than not the practitioners of statecraft have manipulated just-war principles to justify some rather unjust causes. Even if this is so, of course, it is more a criticism of the orientation and conduct of many leaders and diplomats than it is an effective assault on the logic of the just-war position. Defenders of just-war theory use this same evidence to underscore the need for greater compliance with a practical mechanism for avoiding war, especially in an age when the mass-destructive consequences of war are so great.

Conduct During War

Just-war theory does not confine itself merely to whether one has a right to use armed force or resort to war in international relations. It goes beyond the *jus ad bellum* to raise questions of right conduct *in* war once armed conflict breaks out. Another set of principles governs right conduct in war (*jus in bello*), whether or not the decision to go to war was just. Very real limits are set in an effort to limit or confine the death and destruction of warfare to what is militarily necessary.

The principle of *military necessity* can be construed so broadly as to allow almost any conduct in war, if political authorities or military commanders do not approach the use of force with a spirit consistent with the human-cost reduction purpose of just-war theory. It is a narrow construction of military necessity that is prescribed by just-war theory. Consistent with the earlier discussion of Clausewitz's theory of war, armed force is used only to destroy or substantially weaken an enemy's war-making capability.

Destroying an enemy's war-making capability focuses destructive efforts on an adversary's armed forces and *only* those parts of the society's infrastructure that directly contribute to its war-making effort. It is not a call to destroy an entire society, its population, or anything else of material or cultural value. People will still be killed and property destroyed, but probably far less damage will be sustained when the principle of military necessity is narrowly interpreted to limit the destructiveness of war to what is absolutely necessary for military purposes.

Obliteration bombing of cities or other population centers was widely practiced by both sides in World War II. At the time many defenders of this strategy saw these raids as undermining societal morale in enemy countries, thus weakening an enemy's will to resist. But postwar evaluation of strategic bombing and other uses of air power raised a serious challenge to this rationale. Rage among survivors contributed in many cases to an increased will to resist rather than to submit. If so, then obliteration bombing proved to be counterproductive or dysfunctional, even militarily speaking.

With the benefit of hindsight, obliteration bombing of population centers has been discredited both militarily and morally in the years since World War II. Put another way, there can be no moral justification under just-war doctrine for such mass death and destruction, particularly since these military actions did not serve legitimate military purposes. Just because military purposes are served, of course, is not enough to justify *any* conduct in war. Additional conditions need to be met to satisfy *jus in bello* obligations.

The human cost of war: A wounded soldier in World War I.

Noncombatants

An effort must be made to spare noncombatants and other defenseless persons. Guilty or not, noncombatants—civilian populations—are not the proper object of warfare. Even captured enemy soldiers, though combatants, are now defenseless persons who may be taken prisoner but may not be executed just because they are prisoners. Prisoners of war (sometimes called PWs or POWs) have rights and these have been made part of international law.

A distinction is often drawn between **counterforce** and **countervalue** targets. *Counterforce* targets include military headquarters, troop or tank formations, combat aircraft, ships, maintenance facilities, and other military installations the destruction of which would *directly* weaken an enemy's war-making capability. *Countervalue* targets are factories, rail junctions, civilian airports, and power plants in or near cities that contribute to an enemy's war-making capability or overall war effort. Even if people are not the intended victims, the bombing of countervalue targets usually produces more civilian, noncombatant casualties than counterforce targeting.

Moreover the means used to accomplish military purposes need to be proportional to the goal. If a 300-pound bomb can be used to destroy a particular military target, a 10,000-pound ought not to be used, particularly if doing so increases the **collateral destruction** of lives and property. In the same spirit, navy warships may choose to avoid sinking an enemy merchant ship by disabling the propeller, so they can board and search the cargo instead. Just-war theory aims to reduce unnecessary death or other damage.

Some just-war theorists invoke the **dual** or **double-effect principle** in dealing with the moral problem of killing noncombatants and producing collateral damage in warfare. Any action may have two or more effects or consequences. If the *intent* is to destroy a legitimate target that contributes to an enemy's war-making capability or overall war effort, then every reasonable effort must be made to avoid unnecessary casualties or other destruction. The "good effect" is destroying the legitimate military target. Dropping bombs, sending missiles, landing artillery shells, or firing on such a target may also have unintended human and material consequences—the "bad effect."

Following double-effect logic and assuming proportionality—that the target is worth destroying in light of its military value when weighed against the expected consequences—just-war theorists argue that killing noncombatants or destroying civilian property may be morally justifiable *when both effects occur simultaneously or the good effect precedes the bad*. For example in targeting an armaments factory at night when most workers were expected to be at home, it is accepted that a few workers may still be killed when the factory is destroyed. Or a bomb may go astray and kill some people in a residential area next to the factory even though efforts were made to avoid this unfortunate outcome. That is the misfortune of war. Bad things happen in war, which is why just-war theory puts so much emphasis on avoiding war in the first place. Principles by which wars need to be examined in order to be deemed just are outlined in Table 5.1.

If warriors *intend* the bad effect or if it precedes the good, such conduct does not satisfy the principle of double effect and is therefore morally wrong. Bombing workers at their homes next to the armaments factory (the bad effect) will likely reduce or eliminate the production capacity of the factory (the good effect, militarily speaking). The problem is that this good effect depends upon achieving the bad effect first. However good one's objectives or purposes may be, just-war theorists

TABLE 5.1 JUST-WAR PRINCIPLES	
JUS AD BELLUM	**JUS IN BELLO**
1. Just cause	1. Military necessity
2. Legitimate authority	2. Spare noncombatants and other defenseless persons
3. Proportionality of war	3. Proportional means
4. Chance of success	4. Means not immoral *per se*: not indiscriminate or cause needless suffering
5. War as last resort; exhaust peaceful means to resolve dispute	

Note: Application of all principles assumes *right intention.*

argue that good ends cannot justify evil means: *The ends do not justify the means.* It would be wrong to bomb the village. If factory production must be halted, then the factory itself should be targeted, preferably at a time when as many workers as possible can be spared.

Any weapon can be used immorally, but some could not be used morally even if one intended to do so. Immoral weapons are those that are indiscriminate or cause needless suffering. A rifle is not immoral in itself; if used properly it can be used with discrimination, sparing noncombatants. If used improperly to murder noncombatants, for example, it is the action and not the weapon that is immoral.

The same is true for most conventional bombs delivered accurately by airplanes or missiles. They can be used morally or immorally, depending for the most part on the target selected and how it is to be destroyed. The more accurate the better is true from both a military and a moral position. Indeed, destruction of a legitimate military target is more likely and collateral or unnecessary death and destruction, if not eliminated, can at least be minimized if accurate weapons are employed.

Chemical and Biological Weapons   By contrast wildly inaccurate weapons—including chemical or biological agents as in gas or germ warfare—by their very nature eliminate the distinction between combatant and noncombatant. Such weapons usually are not useful militarily as winds disperse chemical agents indiscriminately, and diseases can spread to both sides of the battlefield. Such weapons are immoral in themselves and have been declared illegal.

Treaties prohibit use of chemical and biological weapons. The international consensus that led to these chemical and biological conventions rests on this moral argument. Not only are these weapons indiscriminate; they fail another moral test by causing needless suffering. Rifle bullets or other antipersonnel weapons designed to prolong or otherwise increase agony also fail this moral test. Killing in war is supposed to be as humane as possible. Most categories of weapons that are intended to enhance rather than reduce human suffering have also been defined in treaties as illegal.

Nuclear Weapons   Nuclear weapons are a more controversial case. The two atomic bombs that the United States dropped on the Japanese cities of Hiroshima and Nagasaki in 1945 were justified by many on the **utilitarian** grounds that the bombings would shorten the war. Those who made this argument saw the loss of life at Hiroshima and Nagasaki as precluding an even greater loss of life that would have resulted from an Allied invasion of the Japanese home islands. The Japanese had fought tenaciously to defend islands in the Pacific such as Iwo Jima and Guam; it was believed they would fight with even greater determination to defend their homeland. Others questioned the morality of bombing people even for this purpose, suggesting that if the bombs were to be used at all they should have been directed toward strictly military targets, not population centers interspersed with military targets. Decision makers responded that the Japanese leaders could take the blame, as they made the decision to locate military-related plants where they did.

Each of the weapons dropped on Japan were under 20 kilotons (20,000 tons) in yield. Many nuclear weapons today have a much larger megaton (million tons) yield, with such heat, blast, and radiation effects, that they cannot be used with discrimination, so these weapons fail on human-suffering grounds as well. On the other hand some have argued that lower-yield, tactical nuclear weapons (perhaps as small as one kiloton or less, with reduced-radiation effects) can be used with discrimination and need not cause unnecessary suffering.

Critics are skeptical of this claim. They also counter that using any nuclear weapons at all "opens Pandora's box," legitimating this category of weaponry and increasing the likelihood that even larger nuclear weapons will be employed by one or another of the parties. Indicative of the lack of consensus on these issues, and unlike chemical and biological agents, nuclear weapons have not yet been declared illegal, however ill advised or immoral their use might be.

LAW, ARMED INTERVENTION, AND WORLD POLITICS

The 1928 Pact of Paris (or Kellogg-Briand Pact) was an unsuccessful attempt to eliminate the use of force in international relations, outlawing "recourse to war for the solution of international controversies." Hope was placed in world peace through law in a system of collective security under the League of Nations. As such, *collective security* is different from **collective defense**—alliances or coalitions that rely ultimately on *armed* defense or military power rather than law.

The League of Nations tried to substitute law-abiding behavior for individual and collective-defense relations based on power, balance of power, and military might. Law-abiding states under collective-security arrangements enforce international law against law-breaking states. But the League of Nations seemed powerless to counter such aggressive actions as French intervention in Germany and the Italian capture of the Mediterranean island of Corfu (1923), the outbreak of the China-Japan war (1931), the Bolivia-Paraguay Chaco war (1932–35), Italy's invasion of Ethiopia (1935), Germany's annexation of Austria and part of Czechoslovakia (1938), and finally the outbreak of World War II in 1939.

In an attempt to put the lessons of the interwar period to practical effect, the United Nations Charter (1945) does specify conditions under which force may legally be used:

1. *Unilaterally* in self-defense,
2. *Multilaterally* when authorized by the UN Security Council "to maintain or restore international peace and security," or
3. *Multilaterally* by regional collective defense action.[19]

Armed interventions occur frequently enough, sometimes justified by the participants as serving humanitarian purposes or as a measure to maintain or restore international peace and security—a broad grant of legal authority for UN-sponsored actions. In a world of sovereign states, intervention, especially armed intervention, in the domestic affairs of another state is normally prohibited under international law. Article 2 of the UN Charter establishes the United Nations "on the principle of sovereign equality of all its Members." Members pledge themselves to "settle

---

[19]See the UN Charter, Articles 39–54.

their international disputes by peaceful means" and to "refrain in their international relations from the threat or use of force against the territorial integrity or political independence of any state."

States that have suffered violation of their legal rights may choose arbitration, mediation, or a judicial remedy as offered by the International Court of Justice or an appropriate regional or national court. The critical weakness, however, is that these tribunals do not have enforcement powers.

As a practical matter, therefore, force remains very much a part of international relations. In an anarchic world that lacks a central government or other governing authority with the power to enforce international law, sovereign states do not always comply with such legal authorizations and restrictions. States sometimes choose to violate or ignore their obligations under international law. At other times political leaders and diplomats have proven to be quite capable of interpreting or manipulating legal principles to justify what they already have done or plan to do in any event.

Intervention and Civil Wars

If applying international law is difficult in the case of interstate wars, it is even more complicated when the conflict is internal to a particular state and society—a civil war. Given the crises of authority faced by so many states today, it is not surprising that internal wars, not interstate wars, are the most likely threat to international peace and security.

Even when motives are legitimate and not contrived, intervention in the domestic affairs of sovereign states conflicts with a long-established principle of international law that prohibits them. Consider the American Civil War (1861–65) and the debate in Great Britain as to whether or not Britain should support the South. The southern states claimed sovereignty as the Confederate States of America and sought outside assistance in their struggle against the United States of America, from whom they claimed to be separate.

The Lincoln administration in Washington denied the South's claim, arguing that the southern states had no right to secede from the Union in the first place. Thus to Lincoln it was not a war between sovereign states but rather a civil war fought between loyal U.S. armed forces and those loyal to the rebellious states. Through careful diplomacy Washington made its interpretation of events clear to the British, stressing that outside intervention was illegal. Whether they accepted the Lincoln administration's rationale or not, London chose not to intervene either diplomatically or militarily.

Determining the difference between an interstate war and a civil war is often difficult. American armed intervention in Vietnam, for example, was justified by the United States as coming to the defense of South Vietnam (the Republic of Vietnam) against aggression from North Vietnam (the Democratic Republic of Vietnam). If this were factually correct, then going to the aid of a victim of aggression was legitimate under international law. On the other hand, if the situation in Vietnam were understood as a civil war, with a single state torn between two rival governments and an insurgent movement tied to one of the parties, then outside intervention in such an internal matter would not have been legitimate under international law.

The war in Vietnam was fought not only by the regular forces of North and South Vietnam, the United States, the Republic of Korea, and Australia; it also involved **guerrilla warfare**, supported by North Vietnam. This capitalized on North Vietnam's ties with the people in the countryside. By using antigovernment and ideological appeals, knowledge of the terrain, and the protective cover of the jungle canopy, these nonuniformed irregulars (or *guerrillas*) conducted a very successful campaign against the South Vietnamese government and its allies. This guerrilla warfare included terrorism, ambushes, rocket attacks, and sometimes even firefights with regular forces. These guerrillas were part of an insurgent movement or antigovernment **insurgency** that, coupled with the efforts of North Vietnamese regulars, eventually succeeded in winning the war and wresting control of the South Vietnamese government.

The former Yugoslavia provides another example of the important distinction between *civil* war and *interstate* war. Serbs opposed both the secession of "breakaway republics" and their recognition in the early 1990s by outside states as independent, sovereign states. From the Serbian perspective, the ensuing war among competing parties was really a civil war precluding any legal right to intervention by outside parties. Having been recognized as separate, independent, and sovereign states by UN members, however, Croatia, Slovenia, and Bosnia-Herzogovina were seen by other observers as engaging in a war among states against Serbia. As an interstate war, then, outside intervention by the UN, NATO, or other legitimate authorities acting in compliance with the UN Charter was presented as legitimate.

Humanitarian Intervention

In the absence of an invitation from the legitimate government of a state, even **humanitarian intervention**—using force to stop the fighting among competing groups, provide the necessary security to feed starving people, or halting ethnic cleansing—legally violates the principle of nonintervention in the domestic affairs of a state. The UN Charter does not give the Security Council authority to use force for humanitarian purposes *per se*. Armed intervention under UN auspices in the internal affairs of a state, however justifiable the humanitarian purpose might seem, is legitimate in this strict interpretation only if the problem cannot likely be contained, thus posing a threat to international peace and security.

The case of Kosovo in 1999 illustrates this point. No one denied that Kosovo was a province of Yugoslavia. The Serbs stated that whatever actions they took in the province were therefore an internal matter and outside intervention was a violation of Yugoslavian sovereignty. The Serbian policy of systematic ethnic cleansing, however, led to NATO military action on the grounds of humanitarian intervention and the claim that Serbian actions were a threat to regional peace and security. It is significant that NATO did not ask for the blessing of the United Nations for NATO's air campaign, given opposition within the UN Security Council on both political and legal grounds.

Humanitarian motives may genuinely accompany actions taken primarily for national-interest reasons. In other cases, however, humanitarian motives are presented as a pretext used by political leaders and diplomats in an effort to justify armed interventions done exclusively (or almost entirely) for national-interest reasons. Propagandists like to present humanitarian purposes for armed intervention to make the behavior seem less self-serving.

Because states usually intervene to serve their interests does not mean that they always do so for only self-serving purposes. They may wish to intervene

A P P L Y I N G   T H E O R Y

COMPETING CRITERIA FOR DECISIONS ON ARMED INTERVENTION

Events in 1989 brought an end to the cold war but not to armed intervention. Subsequent years have been marked by a continuation of armed intervention by outside states and multilateral coalitions of states as in responses to Iraq's armed intervention and takeover of Kuwait, civil strife in Somalia and Haiti, and genocide in the Balkan states and central Africa. Policy makers face decisions about whether or not to intervene with armed force to respond to aggression, prevent or stop genocide, restore order or maintain the peace.

Both economic and military capabilities as well as domestic political support (or opposition) typically are part of the decision-making calculus. We can also identify at least five additional and often competing criteria or factors typically weighed by policy makers considering armed intervention. Moreover political support for (or opposition to) armed intervention is often expressed in terms of one or more of these criteria:

SOVEREIGNTY

Under international law states are normally prohibited from intervention in the domestic affairs of other sovereign states unless requested by the legitimate government of the state subject to such intervention; however, use of force (including armed intervention) is allowed under the United Nations Charter:

- For collective security as when the Security Council authorizes using force in response to a contingency endangering international peace and security (Chapter VII, particularly Article 42) and
- For self defense or collective defense by alliances or coalitions of states as in responding to aggression against a sovereign state (Chapter VII, Article 51).

NATIONAL INTEREST

Armed intervention is an option often weighed against considerations of national interest and related national objectives. Some argue armed intervention should be pursued only if there is a vital national interest to be served. Even if one considers this criterion to be decisive, as many realists do,

there is no escaping the practical difficulty in trying to define precisely what the national interest (much less vital national interest) might be in a particular case. The national interest is subject to multiple interpretations, but even with this ambiguity it remains part of the decision making calculus.

HUMAN RIGHTS

A consensus has been forming mainly in the last half of the twentieth century that continues to the present and holds that human beings have rights that may supersede those claimed by sovereign states. This human rights consensus rests on increasing understanding and acceptance of respect for life, human dignity, and justice or fairness as universal ethical or moral principles that have global application to individuals, groups, and other categories or classes of human beings. Both unilateral and multilateral, voluntary assistance for relief in natural disasters is one manifestation of these principles in action. The enormous human and material cost suffered by the victims of mass destruction and atrocities throughout the twentieth century resulted in substantial growth in international law (codified by numerous treaties coming into force after World War II) which has come to (1) define certain civil or political, social, and economic rights and (2) prohibit certain acts defined as war crimes, genocide, and other crimes against peace and humanity. When such human rights violations are also understood to endanger international peace and security, there is clearer legal ground for humanitarian, armed intervention under UN Security Council auspices, following Chapter VII of the UN Charter.

EXPECTED NET EFFECT ON THE HUMAN CONDITION

Armed intervention has very real costs not just to people and property in states and societies subject to intervention, but also to the armed forces conducting such interventions. The extent of these costs usually cannot be known with certainty, but policy

(box continues)

APPLYING THEORY

makers nevertheless try to estimate what they are likely to be. It is extraordinarily difficult, if not impossible, to quantify with precision the net effect (benefits minus costs) on the human condition even after an armed intervention has occurred. Deaths and other casualties can be counted and property losses estimated but some human costs (for example, psychological damage) may not be known for many years, if then. The problem is compounded when one tries to estimate what these costs might be in advance of an armed intervention. Nevertheless this criterion typically plays on the minds of policy makers who contemplate whether armed intervention will better or worsen the human condition. At the very least expected net effect on the human condition can play on how an armed intervention is implemented. Using this criterion policy makers may select options expected to minimize or reduce adverse consequences to both armed forces and the peoples subject to their actions.

DEGREE OF MULTILATERALISM

As unilateral armed intervention, regardless of motivation or justification, has come increasingly into disfavor, policy makers have been more prone to look for multilateral support and cooperation in conducting armed interventions. UN Security Council mandates, for example, provide political and legal ground for proceeding. In the absence of such Security Council action, proceeding multilaterally under Article 51 as a collective-defense response is still viewed by most policy makers as politically preferable to unilateral action.

These criteria often compete with each other and choices concerning how much weight to give to one over the other have to be made sooner or later. That said, we are left with an analytical framework that specifies factors that typically are part of decisions to engage in armed intervention.

quite genuinely for humanitarian purposes or, consistent with their broad interests, to contribute to restoration of international peace and security. This seems to be the case of NATO intervention in Kosovo. Or they may wish to use military force in efforts against drug smugglers. In such cases states may weigh the costs and benefits of armed intervention or in terms of how well they serve the human condition.

In some cases the use of force for humanitarian purposes may cause even more bloodshed than if no intervention had taken place. In other cases the reverse is true: Armed intervention at relatively low cost may succeed in providing greater security and meeting human needs. The difficulty, of course, is that expected net costs or benefits to human beings are not always easy to estimate accurately.

LAW, FORCE, AND NATIONAL SECURITY

Quite apart from legal considerations, the question of *when* to use force in armed interventions is an important national security matter. Some argue that the sole criterion should be national interest, particularly if a vital interest is at stake. Domestic critics of post–cold war interventions by the United States in Somalia, Rwanda, and Haiti and the contribution of U.S. troops to the NATO peacekeeping operation in Bosnia and bombing campaigns in Kosovo and elsewhere in Serbia challenged U.S.

authorities, questioning whether sufficient U.S. interests were involved to bear the costs or risks involved, however worthy any of these ventures might have seemed to advocates justifying them on purely humanitarian grounds.

Legal restrictions are often overlooked when national interests or objectives are compelling. The French term **raison d'état** (or, in German **Staaträson**) refers to the rationale of justifying state policy only by the state's own interests or objectives. In 1914 Germany "justified" its invasion of Belgium on precisely these grounds. Germany had no particular quarrel with Belgium, which claimed a right to be neutral in the dispute between France and Germany. In a rare diplomatic admission in such circumstances, the German chancellor apologized for having to violate Belgian neutrality and thus its sovereignty but claimed that this was necessary in order to protect Germany from an attack by France across Belgium.[20]

The Belgian experience is reminiscent of the plight of the people on the Aegean island of Melos off the Greek coast when confronted by Athens. Melos had claimed a right to be neutral in the Peloponnesian War (431–404 B.C.) between Athens and Sparta. Recounting the events, Thucydides tells us how Athens tried to force Melos to join in an alliance against Sparta and its allies. When the Melians resisted, claiming the right to remain neutral, the Athenians responded that in the real world *might makes right:* "The strong do what they will and the weak do what they must."[21] Even though we may dispute the Athenian claim to any right based on its power position, they nevertheless had the capabilities to force the Melians into subjection, which they proceeded to do.

In a more recent example the leadership in Baghdad sought to justify the 1990 invasion of Kuwait, claiming that the territory of Kuwait really belonged to Iraq. The Iraqi leaders said that British colonialists, acting for their own purposes, had established Kuwait as a British "protectorate" (1897–1961) and had drawn the lines defining a border, thus artificially creating the oil-rich state of Kuwait. Provoked by a dispute over oil rights with Kuwait, Iraq was using its might in an effort to reestablish its "rights," annexing Kuwaiti territory as part of Iraq's historical patrimony or rightful inheritance.

Such an egregious act, however, stimulated an international collective response. Acting under UN auspices, an international coalition primarily under U.S. leadership (see Table 5.2) formed to counter Iraq's claims. Iraq was branded an aggressor and the coalition used force to expel Iraq's occupation forces from Kuwait. Granted, members of the coalition were motivated by their own oil interests in the region and concerned that Saudi Arabia or other Gulf states also might be invaded. But coalition members also denied Iraq's assertion of right through might. The coalition prevailed over Iraq in an armed intervention justified as a defensive measure to reestablish Kuwait and to restore international peace and security in the region. Although the United Nations is not a government with authority or power in itself to enforce the law against aggressors, it provided a convenient political and legal forum for coalition parties to take collective action on behalf of Kuwaiti rights, Saudi security, and their own interests.

---

[20]See Michael Walzer, *Just and Unjust Wars* (New York: Basic Books, 1977), p. 240; cf. Roderick Ogley, ed., *The Theory and Practice of Neutrality in the Twentieth Century* (New York: 1970), p. 74.

[21]See the Melian dialogue in Thucydides, *History of the Peloponnesian War*, Rex Warner, trans. (Harmondsworth, England: Penguin Books, 1954), pp. 400–408.

TABLE 5.2	MULTINATIONAL COALITION AGAINST IRAQ		
Argentina	Egypt	New Zealand	South Korea
Australia	France	Niger	Spain
Bahrain	Germany	Norway	Syria
Bangladesh	Greece	Oman	United Arab Emirates
Belgium	Hungary	Pakistan	United Kingdom
Canada	Italy	Poland	United States
China	Kuwait	Qatar	
Czechoslovakia	Morocco	Saudi Arabia	
Denmark	Netherlands	Senegal	

Note: Two other countries aided the coalition even though they did not directly participate in military action against Iraq: Japan, by sending medical teams to Saudi Arabia; and Turkey, by allowing coalition forces to use air bases in Turkey.

CONCLUSION

So many trees have been sacrificed to provide the paper for scholars and political leaders to pontificate on the causes of war and the use of force that many people do believe these are the defining issues in the study of international relations and world politics. Realists at least think so. So do peace researchers, many of whom view the world through pluralist lenses.

If it is any comfort, however, the world today is not the one described by Thucydides in the Melian dialogue. Over the centuries certain norms, laws, and rules of the game have been devised by clashing kings, prime ministers, chancellors, and presidents to influence, if not govern, their international contests. Using force is often seen by decision makers as a rational instrument of policy or means to attain their national objectives or serve their national interests. Accordingly political leaders do not bend to the logic and persuasiveness of just-war theory and international norms and law concerning armed intervention purely out of selflessness but rather due to enlightened self-interest. As the Athenians eventually learned, to their sorrow, ignoring even the most basic rules of international behavior—those regarding the conduct of war—ensures that one will be treated likewise once the tables are turned. In our world of such increasing dangers as nuclear proliferation and recurrent crises of authority that tempt external armed intervention, we can only hope that most states will see the logic behind the need in collectively abiding by a common set of rules to guide the conduct of their international relations.

Practicing World Politics

The Internet: Checking Out Some Web Sites on Security and the Use of Force

Supported by the Swiss government, the Zurich-based International Security Forum and the Center for Security Studies and Conflict Research have developed ISN, the International Relations and Security Network [www.isn.ethz.ch] as "a one-stop information service in the fields of international relations and security" that includes Internet links to a large number of international and nongovernmental organizations. Among these are the London-based IISS, the International Institute for Strategic Studies [www.isn.ethz.ch/iiss]; SIPRI, the Stockholm International Peace Research Institute [www.sipri.se]; and the Geneva-based UNIDIR, the United Nations Institute for Disarmament Research [www.unog.ch/UNIDIR]. The IISS is an "independent centre for research, information and debate on the problems of conflict" that publishes an annual *Military Balance* and *Strategic Survey* as well as *Adelphi Papers* and *Survival*, a journal on international security. SIPRI conducts research on arms transfers, arms production, military expenditure, military technology, chemical and biological weapons, European security, export controls, and other security topics and publishes an annual yearbook, research reports, and fact sheets. For a comprehensive set of Internet links to U.S. executive branch, Congressional, judicial, think-tank, media, defense industry, embassy, consulate, and international organization sites, visit the Center for Security Policy [www.security-policy.org].

The Washington-based American Committees on Foreign Relations [www.acfr.org], a grass-roots organization with committees in more than 30 U.S. cities, provides a list of American links to daily news sources, foreign affairs journals and magazines, think tanks, C-Span programs, Congressional links, columnists and opinion leaders. The government-funded U.S. Institute of Peace [www.usip.gov] sponsors academic research as do such nongovernmental organizations as the New York– and Washington-based Council on Foreign Relations [www.foreignrelations.org], which publishes the journal *Foreign Affairs* and various studies. The Chicago Council on Foreign Relations [www.ccfr.org] also provides a useful set of links to universities and institutes, international organizations, U.S. government and media links, and world affairs councils. For additional links see the New York–based Foreign Policy Association [www.fpa.org] and the Institute of International Education [www.iie.org].

KEY TERMS

force   *p. 142*
rational choice   *p. 143*

groupthink   *p. 147*

normative theory   *p. 156*

OTHER CONCEPTS

armed conflicts   *p. 142*
interstate war   *p. 142*
civil war   *p. 142*
armed intervention   *p. 142*
warfare   *p. 143*
decision   *p. 143*
suboptimal   *p. 144*

alliances   *p. 145*
strategy   *p. 149*
tactics   *p. 149*
military necessity   *p. 149*
deterrence   *p. 150*
principles of war   *p. 150*
mass   *p. 150*

surprise   *p. 150*
concentration of forces
   p. 150
economy of forces   *p. 150*
friction   *p. 152*
fog of war   *p. 154*
zero-sum   *p. 154*

ADDITIONAL READINGS

It is a daunting task to come up with a short list of books on war and force. A good beginning is Geoffrey Blainey's *The Causes of War* (New York: The Free Press, 1973). He examines theories of war using examples of actual conflicts dating back to 1700. A suggestion found on most lists is Kenneth N. Waltz's *Man, the State and War: A Theoretical Analysis* (New York: Columbia University Press, 1959). This work, which explicitly identifies different "images" or levels of analysis, has attained the status of a classic. The realist understandings of war and the use of force represented in this chapter owe much to the work of Kenneth Waltz.

Another classic study is Quincy Wright's *A Study of War* (Chicago: University of Chicago Press, 1942, 1964). An example of statistical analysis of causal variables and war is J. David Singer and Melvin Small, *The Wages of War, 1816–1965* (New York: John Wiley, 1972). Use of mathematical relations in developing an expected-utility theory is examined in Bruce Bueno de Mesquita, *The War Trap* (New Haven: Yale University Press, 1981).

A convenient summary of much of the war-causation literature is Greg Cashman, *What Causes War? An Introduction to Theories of International Conflict* (New York: Lexington Books, 1993). We would also recommend Richard Ned Lebow, *Between Peace and War: The Nature of International Crisis* (Baltimore: Johns Hopkins University Press, 1981) and the anthology edited by Robert J. Rotberg and Theodore K. Rabb, *The Origin and Prevention of Major Wars* (Cambridge: Cambridge University Press, 1989). An excellent overview of war and diplomacy is Gordon A. Craig and Alexander George, *Force and Statecraft* (Oxford, England: Oxford University Press, 1983). Also on the use of force as part of the diplomatic arsenal, see Alexander George, David Hall, and William Simons, *The Limits of Coercive Diplomacy* (Boston: Little, Brown, 1971). For a useful anthology of articles, see Kenneth N. Waltz (ed.), *The Use of Force: Military Power and International Politics*, 5th ed. (Lanham, Md.: Rowman & Littlefield, 1999).

INTERNATIONAL COOPERATION AND INTERNATIONAL SECURITY: INTERNATIONAL ORGANIZATIONS, ALLIANCES, AND COALITIONS

In order more effectively to achieve the objectives of this Treaty, the Parties, separately and jointly, by means of continuous and effective self-help and mutual aid, will maintain and develop individual and collective capacity to resist armed attack.

ARTICLE 3, THE NORTH ATLANTIC TREATY

Reacting in part to a territorial dispute over oil rights in Iraq's southern border area, Iraqi President Saddam Hussein surprised the world on August 2, 1990, when his military forces invaded oil-rich Kuwait. Seizing control, Iraq declared that Kuwait was really part of Iraq since British imperialists of an earlier period had created Kuwait artificially from land that was properly part of Iraqi *patrimony*. From the Kuwaiti perspective (and most outsiders shared their view), the invasion was clearly an act of aggression violating the sovereignty of a small state. Moreover the Iraqi move also posed a potential threat to Saudi Arabia and the delicate politics of oil. Policy makers in the United States and elsewhere saw Saudi Arabia as a country possessing the *world's* largest oil reserves, making it a key player in oil supply and pricing decisions within OPEC, the Organization of Petroleum Exporting Countries. Since viability of the global economy still depends on an adequate supply of oil, the idea that Iraq could gain control of a major source of the world's oil supply sent shivers up and down the spines of many national leaders.

What was to be done? Relying on diplomacy alone was difficult. Nevertheless both bilateral and multilateral efforts in the UN, Baghdad (the Iraqi capital), and elsewhere were made to seek peaceful resolution. Meanwhile to dissuade or deter further aggression, the United States led an effort under UN Security Council auspices to assemble a multinational coalition of military forces in Saudi Arabia and elsewhere in the Gulf region.[1] Since the Gulf is outside of the legally defined North Atlantic area, NATO was not in a position to respond. On the other hand European members of NATO coordinated their efforts in the Western European Union (WEU), an alliance not constrained geographically to Europe. The six-month military buildup in Saudi Arabia and the Gulf area, referred to as Operation Desert Shield, produced a formidable, multilateral array of ground, air, and naval forces.

The failure diplomatically and by show of force to persuade Iraq to withdraw from Kuwait finally led to launching hostilities against Iraqi forces on January 16, 1991. Operation Desert Shield had ended and Operation Desert Storm began. Sustaining relatively few casualties itself, the coalition imposed a crushing defeat on Iraq, forcing its occupation force from Kuwait and threatening Baghdad before hostilities ceased. Ten to twelve thousand Iraqi soldiers were killed in the air campaign and up to 10,000 more in the ground war. Devastation in the countryside was extensive due to aerial bombardment and actions on the ground. Although its human casualty losses were relatively light, the operation cost the coalition more than $100 billion.

---

[1]The name of the Gulf is itself in dispute between Arab states and Iran, the latter referred to historically as Persia. Not surprisingly Arab states prefer to use the term *Arab Gulf*. Non-Arab Iran refers to it as the *Persian Gulf*, the more commonly used term, due in large part to earlier nineteenth and twentieth century British usage when the United Kingdom considered the Gulf area to be in its sphere of influence. To avoid entanglement in this still-divisive issue, in this book we join the more recent convention of referring to this important area simply as *the Gulf*.

As in most wars human suffering in Iraq fell heavily on the common people whether they were Arabs, Persians, or Kurds. Kuwait was liberated, the oil fields secured (after wells were set aflame by retreating Iraqi forces), and Saudi Arabia avoided invasion. On the other hand Saddam Hussein was still in power and both Kurds in the north and Persians in the south remained in jeopardy at the hands of the Iraqi regime.

The Gulf War, nevertheless, is an example of international collaboration to respond to a change in the *status quo* initiated when Iraq invaded Kuwait. Members of different ***international organizations***—notably the Gulf Cooperation Council, the Western European Union, and Arab League—joined in coalition with still other countries. The coalition was not an established, standing alliance. Nevertheless it was assembled as a collective security response to what coalition members understood to be both a serious act of aggression against a small state and a threat to the world's oil supplics. Quite apart from the oil issue, small states elsewhere watched with great interest to see if the United States, other great and middle powers, and other small states would join forces to rescue a small state. After completing its tasks, the coalition disbanded.

ANARCHY, COOPERATION, HARMONY, AND DISCORD

As we have noted, international anarchy—the absence of central governance or world government in international relations—contributes to a sense of vulnerability on the part of all states and their peoples. One way to address security concerns under anarchy is for a state to rely on itself and increase its economic and military capabilities as discussed in Chapter Three. At a minimum the security goal is to deter aggression on the part of another state. This approach, however, assumes that the state has such capabilities at its disposal. An alternative approach is to collaborate with other states and pool resources toward the accomplishment of compatible goals. By such a process, the weak "I"—standing alone—becomes the stronger "we"—pulling together. In this chapter we begin to examine the logic, nature, and limitations of international cooperation. Although we do note the increasing importance of cooperative activities among such transnational, nongovernmental

international organizations (IOs) Coalitions that have a membership exclusively composed of states, which also leads some people to refer to them as ***intergovernmental organizations (IGOs)***; by contrast (and as the term implies), *nongovernmental organizations (NGOs)* are composed of private-sector individuals and groups.

ORGANIZATION OF PETROLEUM EXPORTING COUNTRIES (OPEC)

At a conference in Baghdad in 1960, five countries—Iran, Iraq, Kuwait, Saudi Arabia, and Venezuela—formed OPEC. With headquarters since 1965 in Vienna, Austria, OPEC now has eleven oil producing and exporting member countries—Algeria, Libya, Nigeria, Indonesia, Iran, Iraq, Kuwait, Qatar, Saudi Arabia, United Arab Emirates, and Venezuela. Previously active OPEC members included Ecuador (1973–92) and Gabon (1975–94). Acting as a cartel to serve member interests, OPEC ministers coordinate their oil production policies to help stabilize the oil market, while achieving for its members a satisfactory level of revenue from oil sales as well as an adequate return to those who have invested capital in the industry.

Semiannual ministerial meetings set agreed production targets. The most important OPEC objective thus is "to coordinate and unify petroleum policies among member countries." Rapid and dramatic increases in global oil prices in the 1970s were due to OPEC production decisions. Due in part to member-country needs for continuing revenue from oil sales, OPEC has taken a more moderate course since the 1970s in order to maintain adequate oil supplies to global markets. In practice oil production limits have been difficult to achieve and have not always been followed by member countries. Moreover new non-OPEC oil suppliers continue to add more oil to the global market.

Although there have been short-term increases in oil prices from time to time, the net effect since the 1970s, taking inflation into account, has been a real overall decline in the price of oil. Nevertheless OPEC has been more successful in cooperative activities than sugar, coffee, tin, and other commodity cartels. Cartel agreements are difficult to maintain since the parties are competing with each other for market share in regional and global markets at the same time.

organizations as Amnesty International or Doctors Without Borders, the focus here is primarily on cooperation among states and international organizations made up of states. This chapter will focus primarily on cooperation in terms of security; international cooperation in economic and social realms will be covered in Part IV.

We begin by clarifying what we mean by *international cooperation*. It is useful to frame the discussion in terms of *harmony* and *discord*, which can be understood as lying on opposite sides of a continuum. If generally harmonious relations exist over time between two or more states, then their policies typically aid the attainment of each other's goals; much bargaining usually is not required. Decisions in these relatively harmonious circumstances are made without negotiating most issues with the other states sharing these positive relations. Policy is influenced by a mutual understanding of each other's interests as well as points of difference. One example is relations since the nineteenth century between the United States and Canada, which share the longest demilitarized border in the world. Although Canadian and American interest and positions on issues are by no means

THE GULF WAR MULTILATERAL COALITION AND INTERNATIONAL ORGANIZATIONS

Truly a multilateral effort, a diverse array of close to fifty countries from around the world came together, contributing military, financial, or other resources totaling more than $100 billion. Although the United States assumed a leadership role both in the coalition and in the UN Security Council, Washington depended on global participation in the collective effort to liberate Kuwait and deter or dissuade any Iraqi moves against Saudi Arabia or other Gulf states. Some thirty-eight countries actually sent military forces.

International organizations also played an important role supporting the multinational coalition. Members of the Gulf Cooperation Council (GCC), an international organization of Arab oil producing states formed in 1981 with both U.S. encouragement and direct Saudi support, effectively pooled the combined security efforts of Saudi Arabia, Bahrain, Qatar, the United Arab Emirates (UAE), and Oman to liberate Kuwait, their fellow GCC member.

Deep divisions within the Arab world became apparent in a vote taken in the Cairo-based Arab League within a week of Iraq's August 2, 1990 invasion of Kuwait—discord that would be sustained throughout the effort. Egypt, Saudi Arabia, Kuwait, Morocco, and Qatar condemned the invasion, with Libya and Palestine joining Iraq in opposing any such condemnation. Yemen and Algeria abstained, with Jordan, Sudan, and Mauritania voicing their reservations. Tunisia absented itself from the proceedings.

Because the Gulf contingency was outside of NATO's geographically defined North Atlantic area, participating European members of the Western European Union (WEU) that sent military or other security forces to the region—notably the United Kingdom, France, Italy, Belgium, the Netherlands, Greece, and Spain—chose to use that organization as their principal forum for coordinating their combined efforts. Other national contributors of security forces included Canada, Denmark, and Norway (all NATO but not WEU members) as well as Argentina, Australia, and New Zealand. Financial contributions from Japan, Germany, and other countries were also an important part of this collaborative effort.

identical, a shared understanding of both overlapping and divergent perspectives facilitates maintenance of generally positive, cooperative relations.

At the other extreme, if substantial discord exists, then actors' policies hinder the attainment of other actors' goals and there is no incentive to change behavior. Cooperation, however, occupies a middle ground. It requires that the actions of separate individuals, organizations, or states be brought into conformity through a process of policy coordination that, if pursued successfully, can lead beyond mere coordination to extensive collaboration.[2] As such

---

[2]The following discussion draws from Charles A. Kupchan and Clifford A. Kupchan, "Concerts, Collective Security, and the Future of Europe," *International Security*, vol. 16, no. 1 (Summer 1991): 114–25.

INTERNATIONAL ORGANIZATIONS IN NORTH AMERICA

In addition to their combined efforts in NATO, Canada and the United States have collaborated militarily since the 1950s in what is now the North American Aerospace Command located in Colorado Springs, Colorado. An array of radars on land, at sea, and in airplanes as well as space-based detection devices provide early warning should bomber or missile attacks be directed against Canada or the United States. Cooperation in commercial matters among Canada, the United States, and Mexico occurs within NAFTA, the North American Free Trade Agreement. Since 1994 NAFTA secretariat sections in Ottawa, Washington, and Mexico City provide the administrative base for the NAFTA Commission and for implementing NAFTA provisions and managing or resolving trade disputes when they occur.

cooperation can itself be understood as a range of activities beyond merely consulting or coordinating at one end of the spectrum to full collaboration on the other end. Similarly discord includes a range of approaches: On the mild end of the spectrum, a party or parties may withdraw when possible from conflict situations or alternatively may decide to work at cross-purposes or even engage in obstructive activities or direct conflict. Along the spectrum between complete harmony and complete discord are eight categories we can identify that describe the degree of positive or negative interactions that characterize relations, whether in international or nongovernmental organization settings within or across state boundaries or among the governments of states themselves.

Complete Harmony	Zone of International Cooperation		Zone of International Conflict	Complete Discord		
← Increasingly Positive Activities			Middle Zone	Increasingly Negative Activities →		
Extensive collaboration	Working issues jointly	Coordinating	Consulting Notifying	Separating and withdrawing	Working at cross purposes	Obstructing actions Conflict

For cooperation to exist, each actor must change behavior *contingent* on changes in the behavior of others. Cooperation among states, therefore, does not necessarily spring from idealism or some altruistic belief in "the common good." Instead leaders believe that cooperation with other states maximizes benefits. In *game-theory* terms, this is a positive-sum orientation—one in which all parties stand to gain to one degree or another from cooperative or collaborative actions.

Cooperation or collaboration by states does not always serve benign, positive purposes toward others. Some states may join together in order to conquer other states just as the Germans and the Soviets did in 1939, when they invaded and divided Poland. Similarly some states may cooperate in order to exploit weaker states economically, a charge sometimes levied by developing countries against more advanced, industrial states.[3] The point to keep in mind, therefore, is that international cooperation is not necessarily benign, although many times it is. Not surprisingly cooperation among states relies heavily on diplomacy—a topic we explored in Chapter Four.

International cooperation may be a one-shot deal, such as an international relief effort to end a famine or the case of Poland mentioned above. Of interest to us, however, is cooperation that does not have such a short duration. In particular we are interested in international cooperation that has become *institutionalized.* By this we mean a *pattern of behavior that has become formally or informally organized and reflects certain rules and norms of behavior. Pattern* refers to behavior that occurs not once but repeatedly. *Formally organized* means that the rules and norms of behavior are reflected in the actions of a particular international organization, such as the United Nations or the North Atlantic Treaty Organization (NATO). These are goal-oriented, formal organizations with written charters, hierarchies, budgets, and letterheads. A number of international organizations have been formed to serve common regional interests. Most of these regional international organizations (see following box) have proven to be very durable, adapting to changes in circumstances over time.

Informally organized means that the rules and norms of behavior reflect and influence cooperation among states and transnational actors. It is not as if these rules and norms reside only within the bricks and mortar of formally constituted international organizations. The presence and effect of these values come to be understood and generally accepted by both states and nonstate actors in effect as part of an international culture—essentially as guidelines for the conduct of international relations. For example the concept of **multilateralism**—working issues jointly rather than *unilaterally* by a single state—has become the preferred way not only to cope with most issues on the global agenda but also the preferred means to construct collaborative mechanisms in international relations for attaining mutual gains.

Arrangements based on agreed norms are often grounded further in what are called *international regimes*. Examples include the set of agreed trade and commerce rules in the North American Free Trade Agreement, which progressively liberalize trade among Canada, the United States, and Mexico, opening and expanding trade by removing tariffs and other barriers; there is no single NAFTA headquarters located in one city, although secretariat sections are located in the capital cities of the three member countries. Another example is the agreement among states on generally accepted rules and norms of behavior concerning the treatment of diplomats; there is no International Organization of Diplomats to enforce such rules and norms. Whether formally or informally organized, however, institutions often *constrain activity* as well as *shape expectations*. Hence, as new issues arise, the way they are handled is influenced by existing international organizations and associated international regimes.

international regimes   Sets of rules agreed upon by states to govern their relations or conduct in specified issue areas such as trade and commerce, the exchange of money, environment, health, and so on. These international regimes are often associated with both international and nongovernmental organizations.

---

[3] *Ibid.*

REGIONAL INTERNATIONAL ORGANIZATIONS: A SAMPLER

Europe

Of all the world's regions, Europe has the most highly institutionalized set of international (intergovernmental) organizations, often with overlapping purposes and institutional jurisdictions (see Figure 6.A). Most extensive in the scope of its activities is the *European Union (EU)*. After a decision made in 1999, collective defense and other security functions of the *Western European Union (WEU)* are being absorbed by the EU as it develops its own common foreign and security policy alongside commitments to the *North Atlantic Treaty Organization (NATO)*. Security, trade and commerce, human rights, and preservation of diverse cultures are among the issues that concern the *Organization for Security and Cooperation in Europe (OSCE)*. For its part the *Council of Europe* promotes democracy and democratic values.

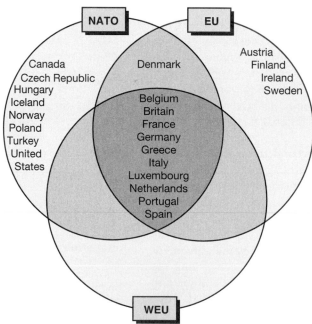

Figure 6-A   Overlapping memberships of international organizations

Source: "NATO Survey," *Economist,* April 24, 1999, p. 8.

The Americas

Canada, the United States, and Mexico are members of the *North American Free Trade Agreement (NAFTA)*. For their part Latin American states have also pursued economic integration goals among themselves, forming organizations such as the *Caribbean Community and Common Market (CARICOM)*, the *Andean Group* (a customs union composed of Bolivia, Colombia, Ecuador, Peru, and Venezuela), a Central American Common Market, and *Mercosur* in South America's "southern cone" composed of Argentina, Brazil, Chile, Uruguay, and Bolivia. Longest standing and most inclusive of regional international organizations in the Americas is the *Organization of American States (OAS)*. Indeed, multilateralism in the Western Hemisphere began with the Congress of Panama convened by Simón Bolívar in 1826, with delegates coming from Central and South America. Successor to both the International Union of American Republics (1890) and the Pan American Union (1910), the OAS was established in 1948 with its headquarters in Washington, D.C. Given these historical roots, the OAS qualifies as the oldest regional international organization in the world. Its objectives are to strengthen peace and security in the hemisphere; promote representative democracy; ensure the peaceful settlement of disputes among members; provide for common action in the event of aggression; seek solutions to political, juridical, and economic problems that may arise; curb hemispheric arms trafficking; combat corruption; fight narcotics and money-laundering; define fair telecommunications standards; and promote social, cultural, and sustainable economic development. An Inter-American Development Bank was set up in 1959 to provide capital for economic development. Principal OAS organs include a general assembly, meeting of consultation of foreign ministers, permanent council, the Inter-American Council for Integral Development, the Inter-American Juridical Committee, the Inter-American Commission on Human Rights, and a secretariat. Member states are Antigua and Barbuda, Argentina, the Bahamas, Barbados, Belize, Bolivia, Brazil, Canada, Chile, Colombia, Costa Rica, Cuba (excluded from participation since 1962), Dominica, the Dominican Republic, Ecuador, El Salvador, Grenada, Guatemala, Guyana, Haiti, Honduras, Jamaica, Mexico, Nicaragua, Panama, Paraguay, Peru, Saint Lucia, St. Kitts and Nevis, Saint Vincent and the Grenadines, Suriname, Trinidad and Tobago, the United States, Uruguay, and Venezuela. Not surprisingly, given its global and regional position, the United States has long played a major role in OAS deliberations and actions.

Middle East and Africa

Notwithstanding often major differences among its member countries, the Cairo-based *Arab League* formed in 1945 continues to promote pan-Arab goals. Members include Algeria, Bahrain, Comoros, Djibouti, Egypt, Iraq, Jordan, Kuwait, Lebanon, Libya, Mauritania, Morocco, Oman, Palestine, Qatar, Saudi Arabia, Somalia, Sudan, Syria, Tunisia, United Arab Emirates, and Yemen.

The best known and most inclusive of regional international organizations in Africa is the *Organization of African Unity (OAU)*. The OAU was established in 1963 at Addis Ababa, Ethiopia, its present headquarters and secretariat. Its objectives are to promote the unity and solidarity of African states; defend the sovereignty of member states; eradicate all forms of colonialism; promote international cooperation and human rights; and coordinate and harmonize economic, diplomatic, educational, health, welfare, scientific, and defense policies. The highest policy organ is an annual summit—the Assembly of Heads of State—with provision for extraordinary sessions when the need arises. An OAU council of ministers also holds two sessions a year. Given the diversity and often conflicting interests of many of its members, forging cooperation on many issues has been, to say the least, a very difficult and arduous process. OAU members are Algeria, Angola, Benin, Botswana, Burkino Faso, Burundi, Cameroon, Cape Verde, Central African Republic, Chad, Comoros, Côte d'Ivoire, Congo, Djibouti, Egypt, Equatorial Guinea, Eritrea, Ethiopia, Gabon, Gambia, Ghana, Guinea, Guinea-Bissau, Kenya, Lesotho, Liberia, Libya, Madagascar, Malawi, Mali, Mauritania, Mauritius, Mozambique, Namibia, Niger, Nigeria, Rwanda, Saharawi Arab Democratic Republic, Sao Tome and Principe, Seychelles, Senegal, Sierra Leone, Somalia, South Africa, Sudan, Swaziland, Tanzania, Togo, Tunisia, Uganda, Zambia, and Zimbabwe. Efforts to promote economic integration also have been made since 1975 by the sixteen members of the *Economic Community of West African States (ECOWAS)*: Benin, Burkina Faso, Cape Verde, Côte d'Ivoire, Gambia, Ghana, Guinea, Guinea-Bissau, Liberia, Mali, Mauritania, Niger, Senegal, Sierra Leone, and Togo.

East Asia and the Pacific

Regional international organizations are much less common in East Asia, a notable exception being the *Association of Southeast Asian Nations (ASEAN)*, which was formed in 1967 by Indonesia, Malaysia, the Philippines, Singapore, and Thailand to promote political and economic cooperation and regional stability. Other countries joining ASEAN include Brunei in 1984, Vietnam in 1995, Laos and Myanmar (Burma) in 1997, and Cambodia in 1999. In 1993, ASEAN members agreed to work to establish a free-trade area, eliminating most tariffs on manufactured goods. Following its annual ministerial meeting each July, ASEAN also consults with its ten "dialogue partners": Australia, Canada, China, the European Union, India, Japan, Republic of Korea, New Zealand, Russia, and the United States. In its early years ASEAN focused almost exclusively on economic matters and avoided security matters; however, in 1994 ASEAN helped form a twenty-two-member Asian Regional Forum (ARF) that meets annually at the ministerial level to promote regional stability and peace and to explore confidence- and security-building measures as well as the modalities of preventive diplomacy in the region.

The *Asia-Pacific Economic Cooperation (APEC)* is an association or process established in 1989 that promotes open trade and economic cooperation around the Pacific Rim. Participants in APEC include Australia, Brunei, Canada, Chile, the People's Republic of China (now including Hong Kong), Indonesia, Japan, Republic of Korea, Malaysia, Mexico, New Zealand, Papua New Guinea, Peru, the Philippines, Russia, Singapore, Taiwan, Thailand, the United States, and Vietnam. A multilateral forum in which heads of government and other government ministers meet and interact, APEC addresses economic and related issues of common concern in a continuing effort to promote economic growth. In addition to supporting national and international organizations managing financial crises, APEC seeks jointly to develop human capital, foster safe and efficient capital markets, strengthen economic infrastructure, harness future technologies, promote environmentally sustainable growth, and encourage the growth of small and medium-sized enterprises.

SOCIAL CONSTRUCTIVISM

Social constructivism is a theoretical perspective on international relations and world politics that understands such values or ideas as multilateralism as having been constituted or constructed over time so that they acquire legitimacy or acceptance as the way international relations and world politics are (or ought to be) conducted. Political leaders may choose to act unilaterally rather than multilaterally in concert with others, but when they do so they are acting contrary to the socially constructed norm that responses to problems, crises, or other issues properly are addressed by states collectively rather than individually by a particular state. In his book *Constructing the World Polity* (1998), John Ruggie discusses *multilateralism* as an example of an idea that, given its increasing and widespread acceptance, has become effectively institutionalized in day-to-day international relations and world politics.

Another example of a socially constructed norm in global society is **liberalism** in its economic application, the concept that open (if not entirely free) markets are preferable to erecting such market obsta-cles as tariffs or quotas, limiting imports or other barriers to trade and investment. Fundamental concepts such as the territoriality or sovereignty of states are also social constructions that over the centuries have acquired such standing that it is often assumed without any recognition that these concepts are in fact social constructions that evolved or developed over more than half a millennium!

These and other ideas about international relations and world politics do not exist somehow in nature. Instead they are of human origin or, in the language of social constructivists, these concepts are *constituted* or *socially constructed*. As social constructivist Alexander Wendt would have it, an anarchic world without central authority or world government allows for such social constructions, the world being what states (and others) choose to make of it. He expands on this idea in his book *Social Theory of International Politics* (1999).

Question: How would a Realist respond to this line of argument?

What options beyond unilateral efforts are there for states to help mitigate their sense of insecurity under conditions of international anarchy? Three broad options are world government and related world federalist designs, collective defense in alliances or less formal coalitions, and collective security as in collective enforcement of international law against aggressor states that violate the sovereignty of other states.[4] A fourth option is to build cooperative multilateral institutions not only for matters of defense and security but also to perform necessary functions in both regional and global contexts. We will discuss each in turn.

---

[4]For a classic treatment of world government, balance of power (collective defense), and collective security, see Inis L. Claude, Jr., *Power and International Relations* (New York: Random House, 1962).

World Government

Creating a **world government** involves the centralized management of international or world politics. In its most complete form, centralized law-making, judicial, and law-enforcement institutions would be established and states would agree to relinquish their control over foreign policy and national security, government finance, and other important matters to central authorities. Cooperation is institutionalized centrally, although substantial authority still may be exercised by local authorities.

As such world government has never occurred historically and is considered by many observers of international relations to be either an idealistic pipe dream or a recipe for a potentially domineering, authoritarian, global empire. By contrast advocates see it as a more effective means for managing conflicts regionally and globally, eliminating interstate war, and dealing with an increasingly complex agenda of global issues not easily addressed by the governments of sovereign states.

The idea of a world government to replace the anarchy inherent in international relations among sovereign states is not a new concept. The historical example that comes closest to world government is the Roman empire, but even that was geographically limited in scope and power. For his part, the philosopher Jean-Jacques Rousseau examined various eighteenth-century proposals for eliminating interstate war by reestablishing centralized government in Europe as had existed in the Roman empire. He concluded that however desirable such schemes might appear to be, there were just too many obstacles in the way of implementing them, making these ideas in his view decidedly impractical and unrealistic.

World federalists pursue a somewhat less ambitious approach to world governance. They look, in the short run at least, to establishing central institutions with practical roles to play. For example many world federalists advocate vesting an international court or tribunal with the necessary legal authority to hear and make judgments in international criminal cases. Relatively small, incremental steps like this are more practical in their view than larger constitutional schemes that would try to transform global politics overnight. Even if world government were eventually achieved by pursuing such a step-by-step approach, their vision is one in which substantial authority would still be retained by local government units. In world federalism, local government units would coexist alongside centralized global institutions with a federal division of powers or authority between central and state governments composing this world union.

Alliances, Coalitions, and International Organizations

A second option is to create a formal alliance or less-formal coalition with like-minded states. **Alliances** are coalitions of states, usually involving formal, long-term commitments; however, not all coalitions are alliances, at least not in the formal usage of the term. Thus NATO is an alliance that has been around for more than half a century. More than an alliance, NATO is also an international (or intergovernmental) organization with established institutions, bureaucratic processes and routines, and command structures that facilitate the performance of its activities. By contrast the coalition of states that formed in 1991 to counter Iraqi aggression against Kuwait (and to deter any such territorial moves by Iraq against Saudi Arabia) came into existence for these purposes only and subsequently disbanded. Even less-formal coalitions emerge from time to time as states pursue common security, economic, or other interests.

Alliances or coalitions can be offensive in character, as in World War II when Germany (then including Austria and other territories in central Europe) allied with Italy and Japan to form the Axis powers. Most alliances now, however, are defensive in orientation, pooling military forces and other resources for **collective defense**. Offensive alliances seek to upset the existing order or balance of power, whereas defensive alliances typically aim to maintain it, usually opting for the *status quo*—keeping things more or less the way they are.

This pooling of resources has the obvious advantage of spreading the burden of the costs of defense. According to realists, if states confront each other with relatively equal military capability, a balance of power exists and aggression is less likely to occur. A successful example of an alliance is the North Atlantic Treaty Organization (NATO), created in 1949 both to deter Soviet aggression during what had become a "cold" war and to incorporate the new Federal Republic of Germany into a security framework so that past aggressive behavior by Germany in two twentieth-century world wars would not be repeated. (The text of the North Atlantic Treaty is provided as an appendix to this chapter.)

Although allies and friendly states frequently have differences among themselves, the alliances and other coalitions they form do provide arenas or forums for both cooperative and collaborative activities. Even major disputes between allies as between Greece and Turkey, both members of NATO, are usually better managed within an alliance framework that allows other alliance members to participate in helping find mutually acceptable approaches to the problems at hand. Cooperation even in assisting allies to manage or settle conflicts, therefore, is to be found primarily within an alliance or other coalition. Allies or coalition partners work together to strengthen their individual and collective positions in competition with other states and opposing alliances or coalitions. In other words it is cooperation within an alliance and competition between an alliance or coalition and its adversaries that typically characterize these relations.

As noted earlier, less-formal coalitions may not have alliance status. The close relations that the United States has maintained with Israel, for example, include a formal agreement to cooperate on security matters that stops short of being a formal alliance. In large part it is the United States that has avoided formally allying with Israel, in fear that doing so would undercut the United States' ability to work with and influence Arab states. Although strains in U.S.-Israeli relations have shown themselves from time to time, Israeli need for U.S. support and American commitment to the survival of Israel have kept the bilateral coalition intact.

Other coalitions formed to exercise security functions under the UN Charter do not qualify as formal alliances. The multinational coalition formed in 1990 and 1991 to liberate Kuwait from occupation by Iraqi forces is an example. Although balance-of-power, collective defense considerations played a central role, the purpose was also to enforce a legal, collective security mandate under UN Security Council auspices. Once Kuwait was liberated, the coalition dissolved.

As noted, the North Atlantic Treaty Organization did not become directly involved in the Gulf War because its members saw the effort, however important, as falling outside the limits of NATO's geographic area of operations. Efforts by the coalition were supported, however, by another alliance not so geographically

◇ NATO—THE NORTH ATLANTIC TREATY ORGANIZATION ◇

NATO now has nineteen members, the most recent additions being the Czech Republic, Hungary, and Poland—countries previously within the Soviet sphere of influence and members during the cold war of the Soviet-led Warsaw Pact now seeking to define their security within the multilateral framework offered by NATO. This geographic expansion eastward by NATO remains controversial to the extent that such extensions are seen as threatening by the Russian Federation or other successor republics to the Soviet Union, which broke up at the end of 1991. The other sixteen members of NATO are the United States, the Federal Republic of Germany, the United Kingdom, France, Italy, Canada, Belgium, Netherlands, Luxembourg, Denmark, Norway, Iceland, Greece, Turkey, Portugal, and Spain.

As one British diplomat somewhat undiplomatically asserted at the time NATO was formed in 1949, the alliance was established with three purposes in mind: (1) to keep the Americans "in" (i.e., U.S. participation in assuring European security); (2) to keep the Russians "out" (i.e., containing the Soviet Union from further expansion of its sphere of influence into Western Europe), and (3) to keep the Germans "down" (i.e., from rising yet again as a threat to other countries in Europe). Undiplomatic as they sounded, these three phrases did capture three key security concerns among the charter members of NATO.

A regional international organization that performs collective defense functions consistent with Article 51 of the UN Charter, NATO's geographic scope is limited to the European and North Atlantic area. For its part the United States in 1949 did not want to be placed in the position of defending against attacks on British, French, Dutch, Portuguese, or Belgian colonies in Asia, Africa, or Latin America. As European empires were dismantled in the 1960s and subsequent decades, the United States tried to get NATO countries to support American efforts in such places as Vietnam or the Gulf; however, European countries (reluctant to engage in conflicts beyond the geographic scope authorized by the North Atlantic Treaty for NATO involvement) chose not to participate, identifying such contingencies as "out of area."

An attack against any NATO member is considered an attack against all. Although the North Atlantic Treaty provides for consultation by the allies if any member is threatened, in the event of such an attack there is no provision for an automatic use of force. Force may be used, but the alliance is pledged only to take "such action as it deems necessary . . . to restore and maintain the security of the North Atlantic area." Nevertheless the NATO alliance proved to be a substantial bulwark for maintaining peace in Europe during the cold war, routinizing collaboration among its members on security matters.

As a practical matter NATO's principal adversary during the cold war was the Soviet Union and the Soviet-led Warsaw Pact—an alliance formed in 1955 and composed of the Soviet Union, the German Democratic Republic (East Germany), Poland, Czechoslovakia, Hungary, Romania, and Bulgaria. The long cold war struggle over more than four decades was marked by crises and years of high tension interspersed with periods of *détente* or reduced tension. At the end of the cold war the Warsaw Pact was dismantled as the Soviet Union itself dissolved into the Russian Federation and other new states formed from its component republics, but NATO survived.

Questions were raised in the 1990s concerning NATO's post–cold war future, but the alliance proved useful as a means to secure continuing American commitment to European security. In the last half of the decade, NATO's well-developed organizational infrastructure facilitated carrying out military operations in the Balkans both in Bosnia-Herzegovina and in Kosovo. In the post–cold war era, NATO has also focused on its nonmilitary function in Article 2 to develop "peaceful and friendly relations by strengthening their free institutions" and promoting "economic collaboration."

NATO's headquarters is in Brussels, and its military arm is located near Mons in the French-speaking part of Belgium south of Brussels. The military arm is headed by an American Army or Air Force four-star general who holds the title of Supreme Allied Commander Europe (SACEUR) and also is the senior commander-in-chief of U.S. Forces in Europe (USCINCEUR). By contrast the position of Secretary General at NATO headquarters in Brussels is a civilian post held historically by European members of the alliance. In addition to serving as a *collective defense* alliance, NATO may also be called on under UN mandate to perform *collective security* and other security and peacekeeping tasks.

United Nations Security
Council in session.

constrained, the Western European Union (WEU), which was established in 1948, the year before NATO was formed. The WEU includes France, the United Kingdom, Germany, Italy, and other Western European powers, but by a 1999 agreement its functions are being absorbed by the European Union.

When they are successful, security is the **collective good** (or **public good** as it is sometimes called) produced by alliances. Canada and the United States formed a bilateral alliance in the 1950s known as the North American Air (now Aerospace) Defense Command (NORAD). For its part the United States maintains important bilateral alliances with a number of countries, including Japan and the Republic of Korea. Both Canada and the United States also belong to NATO with its nineteen formal members; some twenty-five other states in Central and Eastern Europe participate in NATO's Partnership for Peace program.

A key political question in alliances is who will pay—and how much—for the collective good. Because member countries of alliances differ in capabilities, their contributions cannot be equal. Quite apart from their greater economic capability to pay more, countries like the United States, which assume leading roles in alliances such as NATO, often pay proportionately more than countries playing less of a leading role. Some member countries pay a premium—more than their fair share—while others pay less, a reduced-fare price for the security provided by an alliance or other coalition. Politics within alliances such as NATO and other coalitions have often focused on burden sharing and the **free rider** problem, adjusting the distribution of costs among members in the interest of greater equity.

For some observers the very success of NATO spells its ultimate doom. The conditions that gave rise to NATO and sustained it for forty cold war years—the Soviet or communist threat—no longer exist. The Soviet Union collapsed in 1991 and its own military alliance involving Eastern European states, the Warsaw Pact, also dissolved. Cold war fears had encouraged cooperation in the West and prompted the European members of NATO to defer to broader U.S. foreign policy objectives. Furthermore it was under the umbrella of U.S. security guarantees that Western European economic recovery and development occurred. Without the Soviet threat, NATO was in search of a new

APPLYING THEORY

SECURITY AS A COLLECTIVE GOOD

The free-rider concept is an idea in public- or collective-goods theory—that "others" who make no payment or contributions themselves to providing the public or collective good are able to benefit from the contributions of one or a few who single-handedly or jointly provide the public good. As in the classic case of those who finance or build a lighthouse on a seacoast, the lighthouse provides a benefit to ships or ship companies that have not paid for the light they are using to guide themselves at night. Access to the light from a lighthouse cannot effectively be limited only to those who have paid for it; access is universal to any ship or boat passing by. So it is with providers of security who pay the costs for security that benefits others who pay nothing (free riders) or pay less than they otherwise would have to pay (referred to here as reduced-fare riders) for this public- or collective-goods benefit.

In practical terms this means that some countries pay far more than others (reduced-fare riders) for the security that an alliance like NATO provides. Nonmembers of NATO also benefit from the security it brings to the North Atlantic area even though they pay nothing for it. Another example is the North American Aerospace Defense (NORAD) alliance between Canada and the United States that provides early warning of attack on either or both countries. Canada has relatively less financial capability and thus spends far less than the United States does for the security both obtain from NORAD, much less than if Canada tried to provide for this security unilaterally—entirely on its own.

In the Gulf War, the United States assumed a leadership role in 1991 and assembled a multistate coalition in response to aggression by Iraq against Kuwait. All coalition partners participated in one way or another, but to different degrees. Some countries (notably Japan and Germany) did not send combat units but agreed to help finance the effort. Thus the costs of the effort were borne asymmetrically or unevenly, with some making greater contributions than others; some participated less—reduced-fare payers both financially or in terms of troop and other military force contributions. To the extent that nonparticipating states also benefited from the coalition's efforts to provide security in the Gulf region, they qualified as free riders. The amount and kind of contribution any one participant made depended upon individual state capabilities, the effectiveness of efforts by the United States and other coalition leaders to solicit these contributions, and the will of participating states to expend available resources for the venture.
Question: What incentives do great powers, such as the United States, need to provide security to other countries in the post–Cold War, twenty-first century?

role. Did NATO need a new threat or new set of risks to provide it a renewed sense of purpose and unity? It was initially thought that "political instability" might be an appropriate rallying cry. But for some observers NATO's inability to come to grips initially with the war in the former Yugoslavia was disappointing. Notwithstanding differences among the NATO allies, the organization eventually launched combined operations in the last half of the 1990s first in Bosnia-Herzegovina and then in Kosovo near the Albanian border. Others are wary about the future of democracy in Russia, believing NATO must continue in effect as an insurance policy against any significant change of regime or orientation in Russia that in the future might pose new threats to other states in Europe and the North Atlantic area.

Collective Security

A third approach involves the notion of **collective security**.[5] The essential idea of collective security is "all against one" as in a common law-enforcement or police action against an aggressor state. In a way the idea of collective security is like the posse of law-abiding citizens, popularized in the American West, who pooled their talents and other resources under command of state authorities to pursue law breakers. Unlike an alliance that is directed against an external threat, collective security is regionally or globally oriented. The purpose is to dissuade any state from breaking international law and committing aggression.

Under collective security arrangements, states retain ultimate control over their foreign policies but are pledged to confront any aggressor not with equal power, but rather with preponderant or overwhelming, collective use of force for international law-enforcement purposes. The threat of using such preponderant force as a means of law enforcement is viewed as a much more effective means to stop aggression and enforce international law than relying on a balance of power among competing states or alliances. Over time the success of collective security arrangements is aimed at mitigating the rivalry and hostility of an anarchic world composed of sovereign, independent, and often competitive states.

The emphasis in collective security, then, is on international law enforcement against aggressive or other illegal acts committed by states. As such it is understood as an alternative to alliance-against-alliance or balance-of-power mechanisms. Instead of one power coalition against another, collective security pools the capabilities of "law-abiding" states against aggressors and other international law breakers.

The actual scope of collective security cooperation varies along a continuum. At one end are arrangements involving all states and covering all regions of the globe—universal arrangements. Members agree to respond collectively to aggression wherever it occurs. At the other end of the continuum is a concert of the great powers of the day. Their interest in peace may be global in scope or limited to particular regions. Unlike many alliances, there is no binding, ironclad commitment to collective action. Decisions are often made through negotiations and the emergence of a consensus. Although a concert requires that its members share essentially compatible views on the desired nature of the international order, power politics and competition among member states still occur. Such competition, however, falls short of overt hostility. In order to make the distinctions between the universal and concert approaches to collective security clearer, we will discuss several historical examples.

Concert of Europe   The Concert of Europe, as we noted in earlier chapters, effectively lasted to a greater or lesser degree from the Congress of Vienna (1815), which was convened to put Europe back together after the defeat of Napoleon, until the Crimean War (1854). In 1815 the major players were the remaining great powers of the day: Great Britain, Russia, Austria, and Prussia (with territory in parts of present-

---

[5]The following discussion draws from Charles A. Kupchan and Clifford A. Kupchan, "Concerts, Collective Security, and the Future of Europe," *International Security*, vol. 16, no. 1 (Summer 1991): 114–25.

Practicing World Politics

Regional International Organizations and Alliances

It is worthwhile in any study of regional international organizations and alliances to check out their Internet sites. Following is an alphabetized list of addresses for a selected (but by no means complete) list of regional international organizations and alliances mentioned in this chapter:

- Andean Group [www.itcilo.it]
- Arab League [see http://haynese.winthrop.edu and www.ncusar.org for links]
- Asia-Pacific Economic Cooperation [www.apec.org]
- Association of Southeast Asian Nations [www.asean.org]
- Caribbean Community and Common Market [www.caricom.org]; Cent. America [www.sieca.org.gt]
- Council of Europe [www.coe.fr]
- Economic Community of West African States [www.cedeao.org]
- European Union [europa.eu.int and in the United States: www.eurunion.org]
- Mercosur (Common Market Southern Cone, South America) [www.mercosur.com]
- North American Aerospace Defense Command [www. spacecom.af.mil/norad]
- North American Free Trade Association [www.nafta-sec-alena.org]
- North Atlantic Treaty Organization [www.nato.int]
- Organization of African Unity [www.oau-oua.org]
- Organization of American States [www.oas.org]
- Organization for Cooperation and Security in Europe [www.osce.org]
- Organization of Petroleum Exporting Countries [www.opec.org]
- Western European Union [www.weu.int]

The UN also has regional economic commissions in Africa, Europe, and Latin America that maintain the following Web sites:

- Africa (Addis Ababa): [www.un.org/Depts/eca]
- Europe (Geneva): [www.unece.org]
- Latin America (Santiago): [www.ecla.org]

day Germany, Poland, and Russia). France was admitted in 1818. In keeping with the Concert approach, minor states were not members of this select circle, and the geographic interest of the members was limited to Europe. Disputes outside Europe stemmed from the often-competing colonial ambitions of the major powers.

The critical, underlying consensus was that all members would abide by the territorial settlement of 1815. The *status quo* was only to be changed by consensus. If collective action were to be taken, it would be done through informal diplomatic negotiations, not by some formal mechanism such as those stipulated by the League of Nations Covenant or UN Charter. Some observers believe this informality accounts for the nearly four decades of peace among the major European powers in the first half of the nineteenth century.

Collective management of relations, as under the European Concert system, could be accomplished, some thought, by invoking universally accepted legal principles and norms. As such, Concert diplomacy can be understood as an early expression of collective security. That there are law-breaking states that commit aggression or otherwise infringe on the sovereign prerogatives of other states was well understood. Law-abiding states, faced by aggression against any one of them, could band together to stop the violation. Any state could find security in the collective assurance that other states would come to its rescue. In sum the Concert of Europe is an example of an international regime—one with rules of organization and norms of behavior.

League of Nations   The idea of collective security was a cornerstone of the new League of Nations established in 1920 after World War I (1914–18). The League was an attempt to institutionalize multilateral efforts toward maintenance of peace and prevention of the awful carnage that had just been experienced. Great hopes were placed in the League. It was meant to include all countries and to resist aggression everywhere; it was meant to be *universal* in scope. Thirty-two states attended the initial meeting that established the League; by 1938, there were fifty-seven members. All states were represented in the General Assembly, but the League Council was an inner circle consisting of great-power permanent members and several smaller powers that served on a rotating basis.

According to Article 16 of the League Covenant, states that engage in an act of aggression shall "*ipso facto* be deemed to have committed an act of war against all other Members of the League." All states were required to impose collective economic and diplomatic sanctions against the aggressor. The use of military action, however, was to be decided upon by the Council, which would recommend what each member should contribute to the military force. As a practical matter, however, there were technical difficulties in defining aggression with sufficient legal precision or clarity to be a sufficient grounds for collective action in particular cases. Furthermore all Council recommendations had to be agreed on unanimously, so both temporary as well as permanent members in effect had veto power. States unwilling or unable for one reason or another to take collective action could (and did) hide behind these legal ambiguities. Genuine commitment by League members to collective security fell short. It was the League's inability to deal with the aggression of the Axis powers (Germany, Italy, and Japan) in the 1930s that led ultimately to the demise of the League of Nations and the outbreak of World War II in 1939.

The United States must also share a portion of the blame. The United States did not even join the League and was not a participant in the collective security system. President Woodrow Wilson had asserted extraordinary influence in the post–World War I settlements that led to enshrining collective security within the new League of Nations, but the U.S. Senate failed to ratify the League Covenant. As events would finally demonstrate, the League and its collective security system failed to keep the peace. World war began again in 1939 some twenty years after the first world war had ended.

United Nations   During World War II, diplomats charged with constructing a postwar international system drew lessons from earlier failures. The term "United Nations" was used by President Franklin D. Roosevelt in 1942 when

U.S. President Woodrow Wilson was a strong proponent of the League of Nations and its collective security mission. The League failed to keep the peace.

twenty-six states pledged their governments to continue fighting together against the Axis powers (Germany, Italy, and Japan). The UN Charter was drawn up by representatives of fifty countries at the United Nations Conference on International Organizations, which met in San Francisco in 1945. Delegates deliberated on the proposals worked out by representatives of China, the Soviet Union, the United Kingdom, and the United States at Dumbarton Oaks, Washington, D.C., from August to October in 1944. The charter was signed on June 26, 1945. The UN officially came into existence on October 24, 1945, when the charter had been ratified by the United States, China, France, the Soviet Union, the United Kingdom, and by a majority of other signatories.

As with the League, UN membership was to be universal in scope, all states participating in the General Assembly. Once again, however, the major powers at the time—the United States, United Kingdom, France, the Soviet Union, and China (the victors in World War II over Germany and Japan)—became permanent members of the Security Council. Article 42 of the UN Charter granted the Security Council the power to initiate collective military action. Veto power was also retained by the five permanent members. As a practical matter then, military force or other sanctions could never be directed under UN Security Council auspices against any of these five major powers because any resolution to that effect certainly would be vetoed by the major power affected.

While the UN did not abandon collective security as a concept, it was supplemented by both **preventive diplomacy** and collective defense. Preventive diplomacy seeks to prevent fighting from occurring in the first place. Accordingly the UN Security Council was granted legal and political authority to facilitate dialogue and negotiation between disputants.

As a form of international law enforcement, *collective security* seeks to dissuade states from committing aggression, which may entail taking offensive military operations against the designated aggressor; however, *collective defense*, supported by a legal framework allowed under Article 51 in the UN Charter, rests primarily on power and balance-of-power considerations. Alliances are formed to assure defense through mutual or collective efforts. If collective security and respect for international law fail to prevent aggression, states can still rely on their own power and that of their allies to provide defense. The central point is that the new United Nations retained the League's collective security or collective law-enforcement commitment but did not place exclusive reliance on it for assuring international security. States also would retain their sovereign rights to individual or collective defense in collaboration with other states in alliances or other power-based coalitions.

UN supporters contend that this significant modification of the League system has contributed substantially to the absence of world war since 1945. In times of high tension during the cold war the Security Council could not reach consensus on many issues. In these circumstances states could still rely on their respective collective defense alliances.

One major UN-sponsored military operation occurred during the Korean War (1950–53). This only came about because the Soviet delegation walked out of the meeting and was not present to veto a U.S.-sponsored resolution that committed troops to turning back the communist forces that had entered southern Korea in June 1950. Even in the most difficult cold war times, however, there was at least sufficient consensus in the Security Council to authorize a number of peacekeeping

THE OBJECTIVES AND STRUCTURE OF THE UNITED NATIONS

When states become members of the United Nations, they agree to accept the obligations of the UN Charter, an international treaty. According to the Charter, the United Nations has four basic principles: (1) to maintain international peace and security; (2) to develop friendly relations among nations; (3) to cooperate in solving international problems and in promoting human rights; and (4) to be a center for harmonizing the actions of nations. Some critics charge the United Nations has done a poor job in achieving these aims, whereas others charge the UN is doing too much and is a threat to the sovereign power of member states.

The UN has six main organs. The General Assembly, the Security Council, the Economic and Social Council, the Trusteeship Council, and the Secretariat are based at the UN headquarters in New York. The sixth organ, the International Court of Justice, is at The Hague, Netherlands.

The *General Assembly* consists of all member states. It meets as a deliberative body to consider pressing global problems. Each state has one vote. If the decision involves important matters involving peace and security, admitting new members, the UN budget, or the budget for peacekeeping, a two-thirds majority is required. Other issues require a simple majority. The Assembly cannot force any state to take an action, but the UN views Assembly recommendations as an indication of world opinion. The Assembly meets from September to December. When it is not meeting, its work is carried out by its six main committees and the UN Secretariat.

The *Security Council* is given the main responsibility for maintaining international peace and security and hence may meet at any time. There are fifteen Council members, with five—China, France, the Russian Federation, the United Kingdom, and the United States—permanent members. The other ten are elected by the General Assembly for two-year terms. In recent years there have been discussions about changing the composition of the Security Council. Decisions of the Council require nine yes votes. Each of the five permanent members, however, has veto power. When there is a threat to international peace, the Council generally first explores ways to settle the dispute peacefully, such as undertaking mediation efforts. If fighting has broken out, the Council may try to secure a cease-fire. If a truce or cessation of hostilities occurs, the Council may send in an international peacekeeping force to keep the opposing forces apart. The Council can also take measures to enforce its decisions, such as imposing economic sanctions or ordering an arms embargo.

As its title suggests, the *Economic and Social Council* coordinates the economic and social work of the UN. It is the central forum for discussing international economic and social issues and formulating policy recommendations. The Council receives input from numerous nongovernmental organizations that engage in lobbying and informational efforts. The Council has fifty-four members elected by the General Assembly for three-year terms. It meets one month each year, alternating between sessions in New York and Geneva, Switzerland. The year-round work, therefore, is carried out by subsidiary bodies and working groups. The Commission on Human Rights is one example, and other bodies focus on such issues as social development, the status of women, crime prevention, and environmental protection.

The *Trusteeship Council* was originally established to provide international supervision of eleven trust territories administered by seven member states. The Council's goal was to help these territories prepare for self-government or independence. By 1994 all of the trust territories had achieved this goal.

The *International Court of Justice* (also known as the World Court) is the main judicial organ of the UN. It consists of fifteen judges elected by the General Assembly and the Security Council. The Court decides disputes among member states, but participation in the proceedings is voluntary. If, however, a state agrees to participate, it is obligated to comply with the Court's decision.

The *Secretariat* carries out the substantive and administrative work of the UN as authorized or directed by the General Assembly, the Security Council, and other organs. The head official is the Secretary General. The UN staff totals some 8,700 persons drawn from 160 countries. Aside from the headquarters in New York, personnel are assigned to UN offices in Geneva, Vienna, and Nairobi.

It should also be noted that the United Nations Systems (see Figure 6.B) includes numerous functional units

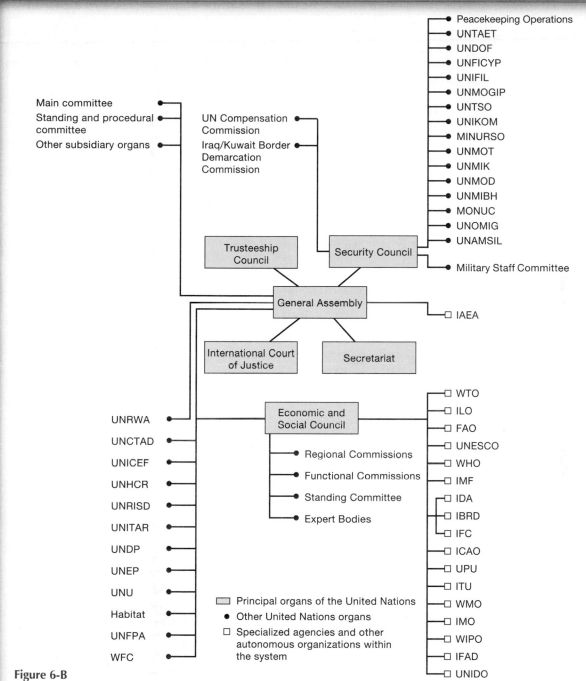

Figure 6-B

as well as the International Monetary Fund (IMF), the World Bank Group, World Trade Organization (WTO), and twelve other independent organizations known as "specialized agencies" linked to the UN through cooperative agreements. These other agencies include the World Health Organization (WHO), the International Civil Aviation Organization (ICAO), and the International Labor Organization (ILO). Capsule summaries of UN specialized agencies are provided later in this chapter.

Source: www.un.org/overview

missions to the Middle East, the Mediterranean (Cyprus), Africa, and Asia, where core interests of Security Council members were typically not at stake.

Nothing in the UN Charter forbids a state to help itself when Security Council measures fail to have the desired effect. Its inherent right as a sovereign state to defend itself either by its own means or in collaboration with others remains intact.

Multilateral Diplomacy   In a larger sense multilateral diplomacy in the United Nations as a whole (principal organs, their functional units, and specialized agencies) and in other international organizations has contributed to substantial progress in arms control, trade and commerce, health, human rights, environmental protection, and other socioeconomic issues. It was understood in 1945 that maintaining peace would involve much more than preventive diplomacy, collective security, and collective defense efforts. A lasting peace would have to rest on a much wider foundation of collaborative action, particularly on socioeconomic questions central to economics and identity. It was realized that progress in disarmament and arms control would also be crucial to advancing worldwide security. Much remains to be done as these issues continue to pose great challenges to diplomats.

Multilateral diplomacy also has been institutionalized in such regional organizations as the Association of Southeast Asian Nations (ASEAN), the Organization of American States (OAS), and the Organization of African Unity (OAU). Particularly noteworthy, however, is the degree of progress that has been achieved since 1945 in Europe—the creation of a Council of Europe to support democracy, a European Union of states committed to strengthening economic and political ties among its members, and periodic meetings within the Conference on Security and Cooperation in Europe (CSCE), now institutionalized as the Organization for Security and Cooperation in Europe (OSCE).

Since its formal establishment by negotiations culminating in the 1975 Act of Helsinki, the CSCE was understood until the end of the cold war more as a "process" than as yet another international institution. In the 1990s, however, members of the CSCE added a few institutions in Vienna, Prague, and Warsaw to support its work, renaming itself the *Organization* for Security and Cooperation in Europe. The core of the OSCE's work, however, remains a general commitment to dealing with security, socioeconomic, cultural, and human rights issues as part of a recurring multilateral agenda.

Multilateral diplomacy as an approach to managing both cooperative and conflictual relations has come a long way from the Concert system of the first half of the nineteenth century. Great experiments have been conducted, lessons have been drawn from these experiences, and modifications have been proposed and implemented. With the end of the cold war a number of observers predicted great things for the UN in terms of collective security and peacekeeping. The disintegration of Yugoslavia into warring national or ethnic factions, however, exposed weaknesses and problems within both NATO and the UN as well as in other international organizations such as the OSCE and European Union. In Yugoslavia and the Balkans, however, it was the greater institutionalization of NATO with its well established military command-and-control mechanisms as well as capabilities brought by U.S. participation that made NATO, along with the OSCE on civil functions, the alliance and international organizations of choice for these contingencies.

Limitations to Collective Security   Why has more not been accomplished by organizations concerned with collective security? Universal and concert approaches
to collective security suffer from at least six problems.[6] First is confusion about
what is cause and what is effect in the relation between collective security and
peace. Does collective security encourage peace, or does peace have to exist in
order for collective security arrangements to be instituted? In other words both
the League of Nations and the United Nations were created after exhausting,
devastating wars. These times of postwar positive expectations did not last very
long, and the usefulness of such organizations should be judged on how they perform in difficult (not just in good) times. When fascism reared its ugly head in the
1930s in Europe and Asia, the League ultimately failed. When the cold war began
in the late 1940s, many realists subsequently argued that the United Nations had
become more of an arena for Soviet-American competition than an ameliorating
factor in reducing East-West tensions.

Second is a gap between states' expressed commitments to collective security
and their actions. For a number of reasons states are sometimes reluctant to fulfill
their international commitments even when the act of aggression seems blatant.
Consider, for example, the international reaction to Iraq's invasion of neighboring
Kuwait in 1991. This would seem to have been an easy test for the efficacy of collective security—flagrant aggression by a dictatorial state against a country with
significant oil reserves. Yet there was a great deal of hand-wringing in capitals
around the world and it took U.S. leadership and some arm-twisting to put the
coalition together.

Third, timing is often a problem. Unlike an alliance, which traditionally has
an identified enemy, war plans, and joint training, collective security efforts do
not have these established elements. Consider again the Gulf War against Iraq,
which required six months of training and planning before Operation Desert
Storm was launched. The point is that putting together a coalition, deciding on
who contributes what, and devising a strategy take time, which may lead to a be-
lated military response.

Fourth, by relying on collective security's multilateralist response, there is always the possibility that the virtues of unilateralism (actions taken by one state)
will be overlooked. While a collective security effort offers the greatest amount of
pooled or collective power, it does so at the expense of flexibility. Numerous
states will doubtless want to influence policy decisions. A unilateral response—
such as on the part of the United States alone—provides less power but greater
flexibility. Perhaps the best combination was evident in the Gulf War, in which an
international coalition was formed under the leadership of the United States. The
United States got the coalition together and was decisive in planning the military
strategy for the campaign and actual deployment of coalition forces.

Fifth, as collective-security obligations typically call for some response, it is
possible that a minor war could escalate into a major war. For example a small war
between two states in Africa might not draw a great deal of international attention. On the other hand if there were an automatic collective security mechanism
in operation that demanded a response to any breach of the peace, the possibility
exists that with greater international involvement a small brushfire war might expand or escalate to become a larger regional or even global conflict.

---

[6]See Mark T. Clark, "The Trouble with Collective Security," *Orbis*, vol. 39, no. 2 (Spring 1995): 241
et passim.

Finally collective security can imply a commitment to the *status quo*. The Gulf War aside, concern for threats to the peace are paramount. Issues of justice tend to be secondary concerns. When questions of justice are ignored and blame is not assigned, there is a good chance that the collective security mechanism might break down due to disagreements among states on the legitimacy of the cause.

PEACEKEEPING: MANAGING AND CONTROLLING CONFLICTS

Peacekeeping can be understood as an extension of collective security thinking to cover conflicts that threaten international peace and security, particularly in the regions where these conflicts are being played out. Resolving conflicts involving states and nongovernmental parties are often decades-long projects at best, particularly when territorial issues are linked to competing national, ethnic, or tribal claims. Sometimes the most that can be achieved is to manage these conflicts—to contain and keep them from becoming violent as constructive steps are taken to address the difficult, divisive issues involved.

Since the end of World War II, even at the height of cold war tensions, important efforts have been undertaken to keep the peace by stationing multinational UN forces (so-called "blue helmets") or other national and multinational contingents on patrol in territorial border areas to provide a buffer or separation between conflicting parties and perform other functions necessary for the security and welfare of populations and the conflicting parties. At various times (and often for extended periods) one could find peacekeepers in such diverse places as the Mediterranean island of Cyprus, the Sinai desert, sub-Saharan Africa, the Balkan area of southeastern Europe, central Asia and Cambodia, or East Timor in Southeast Asia (see box on page 198).

UN **peacekeeping** forces have never been intended to fight wars. Accordingly they have usually been relatively small, lightly armed contingents, capable militarily only of modest defense of their own positions if they come under attack by any party. During the cold war peacekeepers were drawn from the national militaries of neutral or nonaligned states often with equal representation of NATO and Warsaw Pact members as well. Their purpose was to capitalize on the moral authority drawn from their position as peacekeepers accepted in principle by all contending parties. As such they were not to intervene in these conflicts, much less take sides. They were only to monitor the peace and to provide a necessary presence to dissuade the parties from resorting to force against each other.

Though never without problems, peacekeeping has worked best in these circumstances. A vexing problem, however, is what to do when a government collapses, civil war breaks out, no one is in charge, or widespread famine occurs. In such cases there are no parties to agree to a UN presence. This occurred in Somalia in 1993 when the regime collapsed and domestic disorder broke out. An international operation organized by the United States was initially dispatched to ensure the delivery of food supplies. Permission was not requested as Somalia was not a unified state but rather a collection of warring clans. What is known as *mission creep* subsequently occurred: the relief effort gave way to an attempt to enforce peace—a substantial expansion of the original humanitarian mission.

Two Irish UNIFIL peacekeepers confer beside a wall with portraits of Islamic leaders in a town of Lebanon.

UN mission in Bosnia-Hercegovina.

The UN Force in Cyprus has been deployed there since 1964.

Long-term civil unrest in East Timor came to a head in 1999 when residents of this former Portuguese colony taken by Indonesia in 1975 voted to become independent of Indonesia in a referendum watched by UN observers. Opposed to the outcome, elements of the Indonesian security forces cracked down on the East Timorese population, murdering residents and committing other human rights violations. With United Nations backing and concurrence of the Indonesian government in Jakarta, a multinational coalition led by Australia ultimately intervened to restore order.

The Somalia and East Timor cases typify the sorts of challenges the international community continues to face. Efforts have thus been undertaken to expand beyond the more limited peacekeeping or *peace-monitoring* roles to include *peace enforcement* and even *peacemaking*. "Blue helmets" lacked the military capability to perform these latter tasks, which are less peace oriented than they sound; they really amount to using force to "make the peace" or enforce it. Pressed by compelling circumstances, performance of these collective security tasks has evolved well beyond both the original, more limited understanding of peacekeeping and the forces detailed for that purpose.

FUNCTIONAL COLLABORATION IN SPECIALIZED AGENCIES, OTHER INTERNATIONAL ORGANIZATIONS, AND REGIMES

We have discussed three approaches to cooperation by which states and other actors have been urged by proponents to build security under conditions of international anarchy—eventually remove anarchy by pursuing world government and related world-federalist designs, organize collective defense in alliances or less formal coalitions, and provide collective security in its various dimensions including peacekeeping and observer missions.

A fourth approach is to build cooperative multilateral institutions not only for matters of defense and security but also to perform other important functions in both regional and global contexts. Aside from the United Nations organization with its six principal organs discussed earlier (the General Assembly,

❖ SELECTED PEACEKEEPING AND OBSERVER MISSIONS ❖

The United Nations and other peacekeeping missions or functional units summarized here and organized by region have detailed missions to perform that are specified typically in UN Security Council resolutions and the resolutions of such other international organizations in Europe as NATO and OSCE. The emergence of new contingencies and rapidly changing circumstances have made peacekeeping and observer missions highly fluid, with missions created seemingly overnight in diverse parts of the world—many to be disbanded (or merged with others) as soon as their immediate objectives have been completed. Others are left standing, sometimes for decades, depending on the purposes that remain to be served. For the latest information on peacekeeping and observer missions, check UN, NATO, and OSCE sources, including their respective Web sites. An excellent summary also can be found in the annual *Military Balance* published by the London-based International Institute for Strategic Studies and available in the reference sections of university and other libraries.

Current peacekeeping efforts include missions in almost every part of the world, presented by regions as follows:

Africa

UN Mission in the Democratic Republic of the Congo (MONUC)

- Established in December 1999
- Contributes to maintenance of civil order

UN Mission for the Referendum in Western Sahara (MINURSO)

- Established in April 1991 and headquartered in Laayoune, Morocco
- Designed to end dispute over future of Western Sahara between Morocco and separatist POLISARIO forces

UN Observer Mission in Sierra Leone (UNAMSIL)

- Established in 1999 and headquartered in Freetown, Sierra Leone
- Observes integration of former combatants into society and monitors civil order

Asia

UN Military Observer Group in India and Pakistan (UNMOGIP)

- Established in 1949 and headquartered in Rawalpindi, Pakistan, and Sringar, India
- Supervises India-Pakistan border in disputed Jammu-Kashmir area

UN Observer Mission in Georgia (UNOMIG)

- Established in 1993 and headquartered in Sukhumi, Georgia
- Monitors cease-fire in disputed Georgia-Abkhazia area

UN Mission of Observers in Tajikistan (UNMOT)

- Established in 1994 and headquartered in Dushanbe, Tajikistan
- Monitors Tajikistan-Afghanistan border area and Tajikistan interior

United Nations Transitional Administration (UNTAET)

- Established in 1999 and headquartered in East Timor
- Promotes peace, stability, and reconciliation and provides civil affairs and electoral units, as well as a civilian police component to recruit and train the new East Timorese police force, a military liaison component to undertake the necessary military liaison functions, and a public information component to provide information on progress made

Europe

UN Force in Cyprus (UNFICYP)

- Established in 1964 and headquartered in Nicosia, Cyprus
- Separates Greek and Turkish Cypriots and seeks to avoid recurrence of fighting since 1974 cease-fire

UN Mission of Observers in Prevlaka (UNMOP)

- Established in 1996 and headquartered in Dubrovnik, Croatia
- Monitors demilitarized Prevlaka peninsula in Croatia

UN Mission in Bosnia and Herzegovina (UNMBIH)

- Developed into its present form by UN actions taken since 1995; headquartered in Sarajevo, Bosnia-Herzegovina
- Monitors law enforcement, advises and trains law-enforcement personnel

NATO Stabilization Force (SFOR II)

- Established by NATO in 1998 to continue work of SFOR I; headquartered in Sarajevo, Bosnia-Herzegovina
- Separates combatant forces, controls air space, assists movement of refugees, and removes mines and other battlefield hazards

UN Interim Administration Mission in Kosovo (UNMIK)

- Established in 1999 and headquartered in Kosovo
- Tasks include administration of the province, promoting substantial autonomy and self-government in Kosovo, facilitating a political process to determine Kosovo's future status, supporting the reconstruction of key infrastructure and humanitarian and disaster relief, maintaining civil law and order, promoting human rights, and assuring the safe and unimpeded return of all refugees and displaced persons to their homes

NATO International Security Force for Kosovo (KFOR)

- Established in 1999 and headquartered in Kosovo
- Provides a secure environment to all ethnic groups, monitors the newly formed Kosovo Protection Corps, supports the UN mission in Kosovo (UNMIK) with its civil implementation tasks

NATO Albania Force (AFOR)

- Established in 1999 and headquartered in Plepa, Albania
- Mission to support UN High Commissioner for Refugees (UNHCR) and Albanian authorities to assist Kosovo refugees by constructing refugee camps, providing transportation and engineering support to repair transportation infrastructure, and assisting with electronic communications

OSCE Peace Missions

- Missions include Bosnia-Herzegovina, Croatia, Estonia, Georgia, Latvia, Moldova, Macedonia, Tajikistan, and Ukraine as well as efforts in Chechnya and Nagorno-Karabakh
- OSCE teams act as observers of conflict areas, mediators, and supervisors of elections

North Africa and the Middle East

UN Truce Supervision Organization (UNTSO)

- Established in 1948 and headquartered in Jerusalem
- Military observers have patrolled borders in such Arab-Israeli hot spots as Egypt, Syria (Golan Heights), the Lebanon, and Jordanian-Palestinian-Israeli areas

UN Disengagement Observer Force (UNDOF)

- Established in 1974 and headquartered in Damascus, Syria
- Supervises cease-fire lines between Israel and Syria since the 1973 war

UN Interim Force in Lebanon (UNIFIL)

- Established in 1978 and headquartered in Naqoura, Lebanon
- Separated Israeli and Lebanese forces, overseeing Israeli withdrawal from southern Lebanon in May 2000

(box continues)

UN Iraq-Kuwait Observer Force (UNIKOM)

- Established in 1991 and headquartered in Umm Qasr, Iraq
- Monitors demilitarized Iraq-Kuwait border since 1991 Gulf War ended

Other UN peacekeeping and observer efforts have included the following missions:

UN Observer Mission in Angola (UNOMA)

- Established in 1997 and headquartered in Luanda, Angola
- Continued work of earlier UN missions that began in 1991, mediating among conflicting Angolan groups and supporting development of government administration and public confidence

UN Assistance Mission for Rwanda (UNAMIR)

- Established in 1993 to monitor cease-fire agreement and to support and provide safe conditions for displaced persons

UN Mission in Haiti

- Established in 1993 to assist in implementing the agreement to transfer power back to a civilian government

UN Mission in Liberia (UNOMIL)

- Established in 1993 to assist in implementing a peace agreement

UN Operation in Somalia (UNOSOM II)

- Established 1992–95 to facilitate cessation of hostilities, maintain a cease-fire in order to facilitate a peace settlement, and provide humanitarian assistance

UN Protection Force (UNPROFOR)

- Established in 1992 to create conditions for peace and security required for the negotiation of an overall settlement of the Yugoslav crisis
- Turned mission over to NATO in December 1995

UN Transitional Authority in Cambodia (UNTAC)

- Established in 1992 to contribute to restoration and maintenance of peace and to support the holding of free elections
- Disbanded after UN-supervised elections in May 1993

UN Preventive Deployment Force (UNPREDEP)

- Established in 1995 and headquartered in Skopje, Macedonia
- Mission to monitor border areas in Macedonia

UN Civilian Police Support Group (UNPSG)

- Established in 1998 and headquartered in Vukovar and Zagreb, Croatia
- Mission to monitor police activities and return of refugees to their home areas

Security Council, Economic and Social Council, Trusteeship Council, International Court of Justice, and Secretariat), a large number of specialized agencies perform important tasks in a wide array of socioeconomic, human rights, and other human welfare tasks. Some of these are closely tied to UN organs while others are more loosely affiliated with the UN or tied to various regional international organizations.

What political analysts and other observers refer to as *international regimes* have typically grown up alongside these international organizations, providing generally understood or accepted norms or "rules of the road" to guide states, international organizations, and nonstate actors in dealing with even the most technical issues of common concern. The rules or norms that constitute these regimes typically have developed over time by customary practice or in some

A P P L Y I N G   T H E O R Y

 ## FUNCTIONALISM, NEOFUNCTIONALISM, AND EPISTEMIC COMMUNITIES

In his 1943 book *A Working Peace System*, David Mitrany identified certain functions that could not be performed by states single-handedly and thus were the basis for forming international organizations to perform them. The performance of such functions as mail delivery across borders, telecommunications, transportation, exchange of money, international trade and investment, and disease control require greater international institutionalization—the construction of functionally specific international organizations. The oldest of these are the International Telecommunication Union or ITU (as successor to the International Telegraphic Union that originated in 1865) and the Universal Postal Union or UPU established in 1874. Technological advances often have created new (or expanded old) functions. For example the airplane became the basis for a new civil aviation industry requiring transborder and transoceanic coordination among domestic civil aviation authorities and necessitating creation of an International Civil Aviation Organization (ICAO) to ensure security and air safety by both commercial and government passenger and cargo airplanes. Following this technology-driven logic, the ITU's agenda was not to remain static; its charter also grew as telecommunications technologies progressed beyond telephone and telegraph. Indeed, frequency use has become ever more complex as demand for assigned frequencies has increased with the advent of new modes of transmission—radio, television, and now satellites and the Internet. In short the ITU has had to expand its scope and the tasks it performs in managing the telecommunications function.

Building on Mitrany's **functionalism**—that functions give impetus to establishing the international organizations to perform these functions, Ernst Haas identified politics as the missing variable in Mitrany's for-

mulation. Haas and other **neofunctionalists** following his lead have put particular emphasis on the role played by politically connected, often technically specialized elites as carriers of integration and the construction and expansion of international organizations. In the examples used here, politically connected civil aviation or telecommunications experts are instrumental in the process of constructing, maintaining, and expanding their respective specialized agencies or international organizations—the ICAO and ITU—that regulate or facilitate operations in these sectors. Similarly economic and financial experts who both influence and respond to political authorities essential to bringing these international organizations online (and maintaining and expanding their tasks) have played central roles in developing such international organizations as the World Bank, International Monetary Fund, and World Trade Organization. For his part Peter Haas has focused research on the **epistemic communities** formed by specialists who communicate with each other across national borders, building professional relationships and associations in the often technical fields that define their common interests and concerns.

Question: Pluralists would argue that the increase in global interdependence should facilitate functionalist logic. How would a realist possibly respond?

epistemic communities Associations typically across national borders among knowledgeable persons or experts in particular (often technical) fields; these are networks of personal contacts established and maintained over time in various settings—international meetings and conferences, joint research projects, contacts in international and nongovernmental organizations, and direct communications facilitated now by the Internet.

cases have been specified more formally in multilateral agreements, treaties, or conventions.

Although nongovernmental organizations interact with security-related international organizations, they have proven to be particularly active participants in this human welfare domain of international organizational activity. NGOs influence the agendas of international organizations, many also monitoring closely their performance, holding them accountable for their actions in three principal ways: (1) directly by making their positions known to international organization officials; (2) indirectly influencing them through their links to the national governments of international organization member states; and (3) by publicizing their views via mass communications media—the press, radio, cinema, television, and most recently the Internet.

Even in the bleakest years of the cold war, functional collaboration within international organizations persisted, driven by the importance of the tasks on their agendas. Routinization of task performance also removed these issues from the international conflicts that otherwise divided countries and peoples. Cooperation thus survived even in periods of great international discord. Notwithstanding enormous frustrations at the time with conflicts in the Security Council that so constrained the United Nations as an effective multilateral actor in security matters, UN advocates at least found some compensation in the continuing work and contributions made by UN and other specialized agencies.

Finally we note the UN's role in holding a number of international conferences designed to build global consensus on important (though often controversial) socioeconomic and human rights issues. The approach is not new. Indeed, such efforts began in the 1960s in an effort to deal with trade and development priorities and cooperative strategies. The last decade of the twentieth century witnessed international conferences, for example, on education (1990), environment and development (1992), human rights (1993), population and development (1994), natural disaster reduction (1994), social development (1995), the advancement of women (1995), human settlements (1996), and food security (1996). Although not part of the formal deliberations, NGOs were also quite active, sometimes holding their own parallel conferences on the same topics in the same cities as the formal UN conferences.

CONCLUSION

In this chapter we have identified a spectrum between harmony and discord that characterizes the often insecure relations of states in an anarchic world. The emphasis, however, has been on the ways and means by which states cooperate in the regimes and international organizations they have constructed. Alliances and coalitions respectively are formal and less-formal types of international organization usually created with security purposes in mind. Other international organizations treat regional or functional issues relating not just to security but also to socioeconomic, human rights, and other human welfare issues affecting states and their peoples. Nongovernmental organizations are playing an increasing role in influencing and monitoring states and international organizations.

Four approaches to building security and cooperation include (1) building authoritative institutions to exercise a greater degree of world governance;

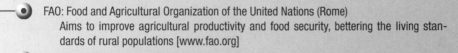

Practicing World Politics

Functional International Organizations as Specialized Agencies and Other United Nations Organs

We reduce here some of the confusion of the "alphabet soup" of international organizations that function as UN *specialized agencies* and other UN organs by presenting their abbreviations and also their full titles that indicate their functional focus. Even though the specialized agencies have independent standing, they are linked to the global purposes of the UN Economic and Social Council. In addition to library documents, books, articles, and other sources, their Web sites provide details concerning their missions, purposes, and activities.

Specialized Agencies

— ● **FAO: Food and Agricultural Organization of the United Nations (Rome)**
Aims to improve agricultural productivity and food security, bettering the living standards of rural populations [www.fao.org]

— ● **IAEA: International Atomic Energy Agency (Vienna)**
An autonomous intergovernmental organization under the aegis of the UN that works for the safe and peaceful uses of atomic energy [www.iaea.org]

— ● **ICAO: International Civil Aviation Organization (Montreal, Canada)**
Sets international standards necessary for the safety, security, and efficiency of air transport and serves as the coordinator for international cooperation in all areas of civil aviation [www.icao.int]

— ● **IFAD: International Fund for Agricultural Development (Rome)**
Mobilizes financial resources to raise food production and nutrition levels among the poor in developing countries [www.ifad.org]

— ● **ILO: International Labor Organization (Geneva)**
Formulates policies and programs to improve working conditions and employment opportunities and sets labor standards used by countries around the world [www.ilo.org]

— ● **IMF: International Monetary Fund (Washington, D.C.)**
Facilitates international monetary cooperation and financial stability (aims to maintain international liquidity) and provides a permanent forum for consultation, advice, and assistance on financial issues [www.imf.int]

— ● **IMO: International Maritime Organization (London)**
Works to improve international shipping procedures, raise standards in marine safety, and reduce marine pollution by ships [www.imo.org]

— ● **ITU: International Telecommunication Union (Geneva)**
Fosters international cooperation to improve telecommunications of all kinds, coordinates usage of radio and TV frequencies, promotes safety measures, and conducts research [www.itu.int]

— ● **UNESCO: UN Educational, Scientific, and Cultural Organization (Paris)**
Promotes education, cultural development, protection of the world's natural and cultural heritage, international cooperation in science, press freedom, and communication [www.unesco.org]

(box continues)

Practicing World Politics

UNIDO: UN Industrial Development Organization (Vienna)
Promotes the industrial advancement of developing countries through technical assistance, advisory services, and training [www.unido.org]

UPU: Universal Postal Union (Berne, Switzerland)
Establishes international regulations for postal services, provides technical assistance, and promotes cooperation in postal matters [www.upu.int]

WHO: World Health Organization (Geneva)
Coordinates programs aimed at solving health problems and the attainment by all people of the highest possible level of health, working in areas such as immunization, health education, and the provision of essential drugs [www.who.int]

WIPO: World Intellectual Property Organization (Geneva)
Promotes international protection of intellectual property and fosters cooperation on copyrights, trademarks, industrial designs, and patents [www.wipo.int]

WMO: World Meteorological Organization (Geneva)
Promotes scientific research on the Earth's atmosphere and on climate change and facilitates the global exchange of meteorological data [www.wmo.ch]

World Bank Group (Washington, D.C.)
Provides loans and technical assistance to developing countries to reduce poverty and advance sustainable economic growth [www.worldbank.int]
- IBRD: International Bank for Reconstruction and Development
- IDA: International Development Agency
- IFC: International Finance Corporation
- MIGA: Multilateral Investment Guarantee Agency

WTO: World Trade Organization (Geneva)
Administers WTO trade agreements, providing a forum for trade negotiations and handling trade disputes; monitors national trade policies; and offers technical assistance and training for developing countries [www.wto.org]

Other UN Organizations

Habitat: UN Center for Human Settlements (Nairobi)
Promotes housing for all, improving urban governance, reducing urban poverty, improving the living environment, and managing disaster mitigation and postconflict rehabilitation [www.unchs.org]

UNCTAD: UN Conference on Trade and Development (Geneva)
Main goals are to maximize the trade, investment, and development opportunities of developing countries, help them face challenges arising from globalization, and integrate them into the world economy on an equitable basis [www.unctad.org]

UNDCP: UN Drug Control Program (Vienna)
Provides leadership for all UN drug-control initiatives; works against illicit drug production, trafficking, and abuse; seeks service as a worldwide center of expertise and information in all fields of drug control; and provides technical assistance to help governments to establish adequate drug-control structures and strategies [www.undcp.org]

Practicing World Politics

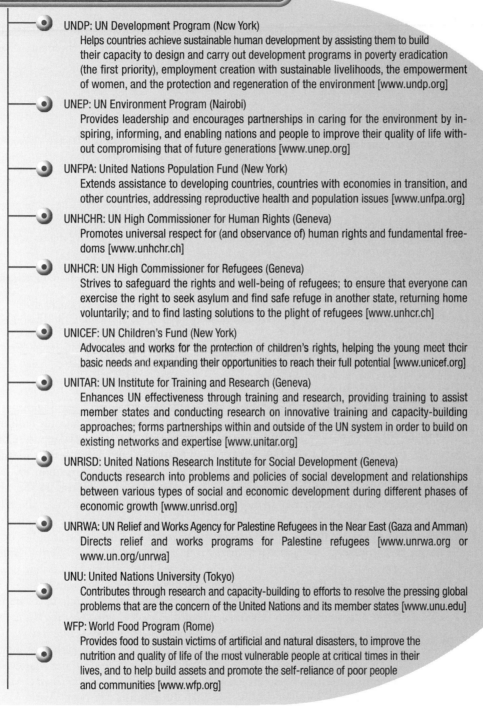

UNDP: UN Development Program (Ncw York)
Helps countries achieve sustainable human development by assisting them to build their capacity to design and carry out development programs in poverty eradication (the first priority), employment creation with sustainable livelihoods, the empowerment of women, and the protection and regeneration of the environment [www.undp.org]

UNEP: UN Environment Program (Nairobi)
Provides leadership and encourages partnerships in caring for the environment by inspiring, informing, and enabling nations and people to improve their quality of life without compromising that of future generations [www.unep.org]

UNFPA: United Nations Population Fund (New York)
Extends assistance to developing countries, countries with economies in transition, and other countries, addressing reproductive health and population issues [www.unfpa.org]

UNHCHR: UN High Commissioner for Human Rights (Geneva)
Promotes universal respect for (and observance of) human rights and fundamental freedoms [www.unhchr.ch]

UNHCR: UN High Commissioner for Refugees (Geneva)
Strives to safeguard the rights and well-being of refugees; to ensure that everyone can exercise the right to seek asylum and find safe refuge in another state, returning home voluntarily; and to find lasting solutions to the plight of refugees [www.unhcr.ch]

UNICEF: UN Children's Fund (New York)
Advocates and works for the protection of children's rights, helping the young meet their basic needs and expanding their opportunities to reach their full potential [www.unicef.org]

UNITAR: UN Institute for Training and Research (Geneva)
Enhances UN effectiveness through training and research, providing training to assist member states and conducting research on innovative training and capacity-building approaches; forms partnerships within and outside of the UN system in order to build on existing networks and expertise [www.unitar.org]

UNRISD: United Nations Research Institute for Social Development (Geneva)
Conducts research into problems and policies of social development and relationships between various types of social and economic development during different phases of economic growth [www.unrisd.org]

UNRWA: UN Relief and Works Agency for Palestine Refugees in the Near East (Gaza and Amman)
Directs relief and works programs for Palestine refugees [www.unrwa.org or www.un.org/unrwa]

UNU: United Nations University (Tokyo)
Contributes through research and capacity-building to efforts to resolve the pressing global problems that are the concern of the United Nations and its member states [www.unu.edu]

WFP: World Food Program (Rome)
Provides food to sustain victims of artificial and natural disasters, to improve the nutrition and quality of life of the most vulnerable people at critical times in their lives, and to help build assets and promote the self-reliance of poor people and communities [www.wfp.org]

(2) cooperating within alliances and coalitions to meet collective defense challenges; (3) participating in multilateral collective security and peacekeeping measures to advance the rule of law and international law enforcement in international relations; and (4) building consensus and expanding multilateral international organizations and regimes to deal functionally with the many diverse issues on the twenty-first century global agenda.

KEY TERMS

international organization (IO) *p. 175*	international regime *p. 179*	epistemic community *p. 201*

OTHER CONCEPTS

intergovernmental
    organization (IGO)
    p. 175
multilateralism   *p. 179*
social constructivism
    p. 182
liberalism   *p. 182*
world government   *p. 183*

world federalist   *p. 183*
alliance   *p. 183*
collective defense   *p. 184*
collective good   *p. 186*
public good   *p. 186*
free rider   *p. 186*
collective security   *p. 188*

preventive diplomacy
    p. 191
peacekeeping   *p. 196*
functionalism, functionalist
    p. 201
neofunctionalism,
    neofunctionalist   *p. 201*

ADDITIONAL READINGS

The literature on international organizations, alliances, coalitions, and regimes is extensive. We note the work of our friend, the late Werner Feld, and his colleague, Robert Jordan, *International Organizations: A Comparative Approach* (Westport, Conn.: Praeger, 1994) as well as the classic treatment of international organizations in Inis L. Claude, *Swords into Plowshares* (New York: McGraw-Hill). A companion to this is Claude's *Power and International Relations* (New York: Random House, 1962), which presents world government, balance of power, and collective security as alternative approaches to order in international relations. On integration related to both global and regional international organizations we have relied heavily on insights drawn from such works of Ernst B. Haas as his now-classic *Beyond the Nation State* (Stanford, Calif: Stanford University Press, 1964). On regimes, see Stephen D. Krasner, ed., *International Regimes* (Ithaca, N.Y.: Cornell University Press, 1983) and Volker Rittberger, ed., *Regime Theory and International Relations* (Oxford, England: Clarendon Press, 1993). On social constructivism, see John Ruggie's *Constructing the World Polity* (London: Routledge, 1998) and Alexander Wendt's *Social Theory of International Politics* (Cambridge, England: Cambridge University Press, 1999). An early presentation on epistemic communities is an article by Peter M. Haas, "Do Regimes Matter? Epistemic Communities and Mediterranean Pollution Control," *International Organization*, vol. 43, no. 3 (Summer 1989): 377–403. Finally, on the post–World War II history of UN peacekeeping, see William J. Durch, ed., *The Evolution of UN Peacekeeping* (New York: St. Martin's Press, 1993). On alliances, see Stephen M. Walt, *The Origins of Alliances* (Ithaca, N.Y.: Cornell University Press, 1987).

Appendix

The North Atlantic Treaty

*Washington D.C., 4 April 1949**

The Parties to this Treaty reaffirm their faith in the purposes and principles of the Charter of the United Nations and their desire to live in peace with all peoples and all Governments.

They are determined to safeguard the freedom, common heritage and civilization of their peoples, founded on the principles of democracy, individual liberty and the rule of law.

They seek to promote stability and well-being in the North Atlantic area.

They are resolved to unite their efforts for collective defense and for the preservation of peace and security.

They therefore agree to this North Atlantic Treaty:

Article 1

The Parties undertake, as set forth in the Charter of the United Nations, to settle any international dispute in which they may be involved by peaceful means in such a manner that international peace and security and justice are not endangered, and to refrain in their international relations from the threat or use of force in any manner inconsistent with the purposes of the United Nations.

Article 2

The Parties will contribute toward the further development of peaceful and friendly international relations by strengthening their free institutions, by bringing about a better understanding of the principles upon which these institutions are founded, and by promoting conditions of stability and well-being. They will seek to eliminate conflict in their international economic policies and will encourage economic collaboration between any or all of them.

---

*The Treaty came into force on 24 August, 1949, after the deposition of the ratifications of all signatory states.

Article 3

In order more effectively to achieve the objectives of this Treaty, the Parties, separately and jointly, by means of continuous and effective self-help and mutual aid, will maintain and develop their individual and collective capacity to resist armed attack.

Article 4

The Parties will consult together whenever, in the opinion of any of them, the territorial integrity, political independence or security of any of the Parties is threatened.

Article 5

The Parties agree that an armed attack against one or more of them in Europe or North America shall be considered an attack against them all, and consequently they agree that, if such an armed attack occurs, each of them, in exercise of the right of individual or collective self-defence recognized by Article 51 of the Charter of the United Nations, will assist the Party or Parties so attacked by taking forthwith, individually, and in concert with the other Parties, such action as it deems necessary, including the use of armed force, to restore and maintain the security of the North Atlantic area.

Any such armed attack and all measures taken as a result thereof shall immediately be reported to the Security Council. Such measures shall be terminated when the Security Council has taken the measures necessary to restore and maintain international peace and security.

Article 6*

For the purpose of Article 5, an armed attack on one or more of the Parties is deemed to include an armed attack

- on the territory of any of the Parties in Europe or North America, on the Algerian Departments of France[†], on the territory of Turkey or on the islands under the jurisdiction of any of the Parties in the North Atlantic area north of the Tropic of Cancer;

- on the forces, vessels, or aircraft of any of the Parties, when in or over these territories or any area in Europe in which occupation forces of any of the Parties were stationed on the date when the Treaty entered into force or the Mediterranean Sea or the North Atlantic area north of the Tropic of Cancer.

Article 7

This Treaty does not effect, and shall not be interpreted as affecting, in any way the rights and obligations under the Charter of the Parties which are members of the United Nations, or the primary responsibility of the Security Council for the maintenance of international peace and security.

Article 8

Each Party declares that none of the international engagements now in force between it and any other of the Parties or any third State is in conflict with the provisions of this Treaty, and undertakes not to enter into any international engagement in conflict with this Treaty.

---

[*]As amended by Article 2 of the Protocol to the North Atlantic Treaty on the accession of Greece and Turkey.

[†]On 16th January, 1963, the French Representative made a statement to the North Atlantic Council on the effects of the independence of Algeria on certain aspects of the North Atlantic Treaty. The council noted that insofar as the former Algerian Departments of France were concerned the relevant clauses of this Treaty had become inapplicable as from 3rd July, 1962.

Article 9

The Parties hereby establish a Council, on which each of them shall be represented to consider matters concerning the implementation of this Treaty. The Council shall be so organized as to be able to meet promptly at any time. The Council shall set up such subsidiary bodies as may be necessary; in particular it shall establish immediately a defense committee which shall recommend measures for the implementation of Articles 3 and 5.

Article 10

The Parties may, by unanimous agreement, invite any other European State in a position to further the principles of this Treaty and to contribute to the security of the North Atlantic area to accede to this Treaty. Any State so invited may become a party to the Treaty by depositing its instrument of accession with the Government of the United States of America. The Government of the United States of America will inform each of the Parties of the deposit of each such instrument of accession.

Article 11

This Treaty shall be ratified and its provisions carried out by the Parties in accordance with their respective constitutional processes. The instruments of ratification shall be deposited as soon as possible with the Government of the United States of America, which will notify all the other signatories of each deposit. The Treaty shall enter into force between the States which have ratified it as soon as the ratification of the majority of the signatories, including the ratifications of Belgium, Canada, France, Luxembourg, the Netherlands, the United Kingdom and the United States, have been deposited and shall come into effect with respect to other States on the date of the deposit of their ratifications.

Article 12

After the Treaty has been in force for ten years, or at any time thereafter, the Parties shall, if any of them so requests, consult together for the purpose of reviewing the Treaty, having regard for the factors then affecting peace and security in the North Atlantic area including the development of universal as well as regional arrangements under the Charter of the United Nations for the maintenance of international peace and security.

Article 13

After the Treaty has been in force for twenty years, any Party may cease to be a Party one year after its notice of denunciation has been given to the Government of the United States of America, which will inform the Governments of the other Parties of the deposit of each notice of denunciation.

Article 14

This Treaty, of which the English and French texts are equally authentic, shall be deposited in the archives of the Government of the United States of America. Duly certified copies will be transmitted by that Government to the Governments of the other signatories.

CONTROLLING GLOBAL ARMAMENTS

It is evident that when princes have given more thought to personal luxuries than arms, they have lost their state.

NICCOLÒ MACHIAVELLI, *THE PRINCE*, CHAPTER XIV

opular songs often reflect both the anxieties and aspirations or wishful thinking of their times. Fears of mass destruction were widespread during periods of high tension throughout more than four decades of the cold war that followed World War II. Focusing on national and ethnic strife, one song observed that "the whole world is festering with unhappy souls" and feared that "someone will set the spark off and we will all be blown away." Anxiety born of global insecurity also produced pockets of guarded optimism, reflected in the wishful thinking of another song:

> Last night I had the strangest dream I never dreamed before;
>
> I dreamed the world had all agreed to put an end to war.
>
> I dreamed I saw a mighty room and the room was filled with men,
>
> And the paper they were signing said they'd never fight again.

The people in the streets below were dancing round and round,

And guns and swords and uniforms were scattered on the ground.

Such sentiments also have ancient religious-cultural roots. In Judeo-Christian scripture, accepted as well by Muslims, is the optimistic expectation stated in song-like verse that nations one day

shall beat their swords into plowshares,

and their spears into pruning hooks;

nation shall not lift up sword against nation,

neither shall they learn war any more. (Isaiah 2:4)

Unfortunately much of recorded history is filled with accounts of war and its role in the rise and fall of empires, principalities, and states. As we noted in Chapter Five, there are various complementary and competing explanations for the causes of war. Whichever one we decide is most persuasive, it still seems that such conflict is here to stay. If, however, humanity is unable to eliminate the causes of war, perhaps something can be done to reduce the ability of states to wage war. Two suggested approaches have been disarmament and arms control.

DISARMAMENT AND ARMS CONTROL

Dealing with weapons in national arsenals is hardly a new problem confronting humanity in the twenty-first century. There have been efforts to promote general and complete *disarmament*—the dismantling and destruction of all forms of military weapons—or all weapons of a particular type (as in the elimination of nuclear, biological, or chemical weapons). How elusive has been the biblical challenge to turn all "swords into plowshares"—instruments of productivity rather than of human destruction! Nevertheless over the years people have joined together to protest the development and use of all types of weapons. It is assumed that the elimination of major weapons systems would, if not eliminate war, at least reduce its destructive capacity. This view is reflected in such populist movements as the Campaign for Nuclear Disarmament during the cold war.

disarmament Reducing to zero either all weaponry in national arsenals (as in general and complete disarmament) or all weapons of a particular type or kind (as in elimination of biological and chemical weapons).

Rarely is a state willing to disarm unilaterally (i.e., on its own initiative and being the only state to disarm). Although great schemes have been drawn up for general and complete disarmament—figuratively turning all swords into plowshares—this approach appears to have been too ambitious. As a practical matter diplomatic attempts to achieve disarmament have succeeded only (and even then not completely) when directed toward particular categories of weaponry such as agreed prohibitions against chemical and biological agents. Another example is the 1987 U.S.-Soviet Intermediate-Range Nuclear Forces (INF) treaty, which removed from Europe and destroyed an entire category of weaponry—all intermediate-range missiles capable of carrying nuclear weapons. After a fundamental change in government in the 1990s, South Africa decided to subscribe to the nonproliferation treaty and rid itself of the nuclear weapons secretly developed and procured by the previous regime.

Statecraft based on possessing weaponry and fielding armed forces, however, has been historically the more common norm. Far from viewing weapons as a cause of war, it is argued that they can serve a positive function in terms of not only protecting a state's national security, but actually maintaining the peace. *Si vis pacem, para bellum* (if you wish peace, then prepare for war) reflects the understanding that peace with neighboring and other states is best assured by a position or posture of military strength. If a state is relatively strong militarily, such strength in principle will deter or dissuade others who might be prone to attack. Hence weapons, it is argued, are actually necessary to maintain peace.

Both disarmament and arms control advocates are quick to point out, however, that such thinking, coupled with technological advances in weaponry, is in fact responsible for the carnage in two world wars that alone made the twentieth the bloodiest century in human history. Moreover advances in nuclear, chemical, and biological weaponry also threaten global destruction on a massive scale—a problem that remains on the twenty-first-century's global agenda. From this perspective military strength is hardly a reliable source of security. Arms races in which states compete to achieve security through acquisition of armaments and strengthened armed forces only worsen the global security problem. That more spending on security may actually worsen or undermine security is thus at the core of the security dilemma facing states and international and nongovernmental organizations concerned with such matters.

If complete global disarmament is viewed as an unrealistic goal, if not a fantasy, what about a more modest goal of placing restrictions on the number and types of weapons and curtailing their spread? Thus we enter the realm of *arms control*, viewed as a process designed to achieve such modest yet important measures as the following:

1. Reduce or put quantitative or qualitative limits on numbers, types, and locations of armed forces and their armaments or weaponry
2. Impose geographic or spatial limits on use or deployment of armed forces and weapons
3. Specify functional measures that facilitate communications and build confidence and security regionally or globally

Once instituted, these multilateral agreements constitute *international security regimes*. Somewhat more modest in scope than general and complete disarmament, these measures still offer rules and often a regional framework and thus

arms control   A negotiation process aimed at producing agreements on weapons and their use.

international security regimes   Sets of rules, many of which are legally binding, and associated institutions by which states regulate their conduct, such as arms control regimes.

some degree of structure to the development, acquisition, deployment, and use of armaments. Such agreements are typically aimed at one or more of the following:

- Curb arms race competition
- Achieve economic savings from reduced military expenditures
- Lessen the risk of war
- Reduce damage should war occur
- Enhance regional and global security

Once the almost exclusive preserve of states and their governments, arms control has become a central focus of nongovernmental organizations (NGOs) as well. Land mines placed during wars, for example, not only kill and wound soldiers, but also maim children and adult noncombatants who happen to stumble on these explosive devices long after wars have ended. Given this continuing danger, over a thousand local and international NGOs in more than seventy-five countries joined forces in the 1990s in an international campaign to ban land mines. British Princess Diana was among the many individual advocates of a treaty banning land mines. After much work by such public-spirited individuals and NGOs, 122 governments signed the Land-Mines Treaty in 1997. The treaty went into force in 1999; however, the United States and Russia, for the time being at least, are among the countries delaying signature of the accord because of their continuing reliance on these weapons. Indeed, if signed and ratified the treaty requires signatories to destroy all mines in national arsenals within four years, removing and destroying all of those already in the ground within ten years.

Critics note that states and coalitions of states may also see arms control as a way of gaining some strategic advantage over other states by getting them to agree to provisions that disadvantage them in arms race competition. Be that as it may, arms control regimes can also provide rules states agree to follow in their security relations with each other, lending some degree of order and providing greater security to an otherwise anarchical world lacking central authority or governance.

One example of an arms control regime, and a bold effort for its time, was defined in the Naval Limitation Treaty signed in Washington in 1922. This agreement bound the United Kingdom, France, Italy, Japan, and the United States to destroy some warships in their fleets and to accept strict numerical limits on the construction of new ones. Locations of allowable naval bases were specified, thus limiting expansion of overall capabilities to deploy and maintain fleets. In addition to these quantitative restrictions, qualitative limits also were imposed. Guns on smaller warships were limited in caliber to eight inches, thus restricting their destructive capabilities. Ships were also specified by type and allowable size. Total tonnage of aircraft carriers in any country's fleet was also subject to an overall limitation or cap. The naval-limitation regime established by this treaty failed in practice to prevent a naval arms race in the 1930s, spurred primarily by fascist regimes then in Germany and Japan. Nevertheless the treaty still stands as a model of how rules specifying both quantitative and qualitative limits can be incorporated in the construction of security regimes.

Given the large number of arms control agreements reached since the late 1950s, understanding the meaning and significance of what has been accomplished to date can be confusing. One way to cut through this thicket is to use the same three categories mentioned earlier to classify the provisions of arms control treaties and other agreements as those dealing with (1) quantitative and qualita-

Practicing World Politics

Disarmament and Arms Control

Disarmament and arms control have been on the United Nations agenda since its inception. In addition to the UN main Web page [www.un.org] including references to General Assembly Special Sessions on Disarmament (SSOD), check out the Geneva-based Conference on Disarmament (CD) through the UN Office at Geneva [www.unog.org] and the United Nations Institute for Disarmament Research also located in Geneva [www.unog.ch/UNIDIR]. Since the United States has been a key player in all but a few arms control efforts, see the U.S. State Department Web site and click on International Security and Arms Control [www.state.gov] for a compilation of treaties and other arms control agreements. See also the U.S. Institute of Peace [www.usip.org] for research and publications on arms control and other security matters.

The International Institute for Strategic Studies or IISS [www.iiss.org] is a nongovernmental organization located in London and composed of both members of governments and private citizens from around the world. Its annual publications, *Military Balance* and *Strategic Survey* (available for purchase through Oxford University Press or found in reference sections of many libraries for use by scholars, policy practitioners, students, and the general public), are valuable sources for research on arms control, disarmament, national military arsenals, and their uses. Other IISS publications include occasional monographs on particular international security topics known as *Adelphi Papers*, a professional journal containing scholarly articles on security called *Survival*, and single sheets focused on current security topics known as "Strategic Comments." For related information, see also another important nongovernmental organization, the Stockholm International Peace Research Institute [www.sipri.se] for its yearbook and other publications. With locations in Rome, London, Geneva, and at the American Academy of Arts and Sciences in Cambridge, Massachusetts, Pugwash Conferences [www.pugwash.org] bring together for discussions scientists and other "influential scholars and public figures concerned with reducing the danger of armed conflict and seeking cooperative solutions for global problems."

Other journals published by nongovernmental organizations that cover developments in arms control and disarmament include the Arms Control Association's *Arms Control Today* [www.armscontrol.org], the *Bulletin of the Atomic Scientists* [www.bullatomsci.org], and the *Arms Control Reporter* published by the Institute for Defense and Disarmament Studies [www.idds.org]. In addition to any online data provided, these sites also contain details on each organization's publications that can be found in libraries or by purchase or subscription.

tive limitations on armaments and armed forces and associated weaponry, including research, development, test and evaluation (RDT&E) of improved or new forms of weapons systems as well as other qualitative factors such as readiness, alert levels, or preparedness of military forces for combat; (2) geographic or spatial limitations on deployments or use of armed forces or particular weapons systems; and (3) functional mechanisms such as communications and other confidence- and security-building measures.

The largest number of agreements fall primarily into the first category of quantitative or qualitative restrictions on armed forces and armaments; however, a particular treaty or agreement may also have provisions that fall into one or both of the other two categories.

Rather than try to classify treaties or agreements in their entirety, our principal focus in Table 7.1 (p. 217), Table 7.2 (p. 220), and Table 7.3 (p. 221) is on how to classify and thus understand the most important provisions or terms of these arms control

◈ THE NOBEL PEACE PRIZE ◈

Swedish chemist Alfred Bernhard Nobel (1833–96) was a disarmament advocate who also invented dynamite, a nitroglycerine-based explosive. Nobel was concerned that explosive technologies usefully applied to building, mining, railroad, and other construction projects might have negative consequences in the development of ever more destructive weapons. The hope was that increasing destructiveness of weaponry would lead countries to avoid the use of force. Among other awards, his will established a grant "to the person who shall have done the most or the best work for fraternity between the nations, for the abolition or reduction of standing armies and for the holding and

promotion of peace congresses." The first of these annual Nobel Peace Prizes was awarded in 1901.

treaties and agreements. Table 7.1 contains a list of major arms control agreements, identifying in general terms the kinds of quantitative and qualitative restrictions they have imposed on national arsenals. Some arms control agreements are global in scope; others focus primarily on geographic regions such as Latin America or Europe, or particular places like Antarctica, the seabed, or outer space. These geographic or spatially oriented agreements are listed separately in Table 7.2. For a list of functional measures designed to enhance confidence and build security, see Table 7.3.

Functional Approaches to Conflict and Arms Control

Beyond quantitative, qualitative, and geographic restraints on armed forces and their armaments, another arms control mechanism is the construction of regimes that rely on functional approaches to controlling or managing conflicts. This includes establishing **confidence- and security-building measures (CSBMs)** that increase trust and reduce threat perceptions as well as maintaining effective communications even between adversaries in wartime. Multilateral peacekeeping missions under UN or other auspices may also contribute functionally as controls on the use of armed forces and armaments in conflict situations.

Communications as an arms control function has been a major focus of arms control efforts, particularly since the 1962 Cuban missile crisis that brought the United States and the Soviet Union to the brink of nuclear war. Clear, direct communications would have been helpful at such a dangerous time. Government leaders in Washington and Moscow had to rely instead on exchanging notes delivered by cable, with many hours lost in the process of transmission and translation. Even at that time telecommunications technology had more to offer than

TABLE 7.1	CONTROLLING ARMAMENTS: MAJOR ARMS CONTROL TREATIES AND AGREEMENTS

TREATY OR AGREEMENT	PRINCIPAL QUANTITATIVE AND QUALITATIVE RESTRICTIONS, LIMITATIONS, AND OTHER PROVISIONS: NUMBERS, TYPES, LOCATIONS, RESEARCH, DEVELOPMENT, TESTING, AND USE
Biological and Chemical Weaponry	
Chemical and Bacteriological Use (1925)	Prohibits *use* of asphyxiating, poisonous, or other chemical and bacteriological [biological] weapons
Production and Stockpiling	
Biological Weapons (1972)	Prohibits development, production, stockpiling, otherwise acquiring, or transfering biological weapons; requires destruction of existing stocks
Chemical Weapons (1993)	Prohibits development, production, stockpiling, transfer, acquisition, and use of chemical weapons; requires destruction of existing stocks; permits on-site inspections
Nuclear Weaponry: Testing and Transfer Restraints	
Test Bans	
Limited Test Ban (1963)	Prohibits nuclear weapons tests or other nuclear explosions in the atmosphere, outer space, or underwater [e.g., oceanic]
Threshold Test Ban (1974)	Prohibits underground nuclear weapons tests with yields greater than 150 kilotons; national, technical means of verification expanded by 1990 protocol to require advance notice and allow on-site inspections and measurement for tests greater than 35 kilotons
"Peaceful" Nuclear Explosions (1976)	Reaffirmed 150 kilotons limit on yield for nonweapons or "peaceful" nuclear explosions (PNE)
Comprehensive Test Ban (1996)	Proposes to eliminate *all* nuclear testing
Nuclear Nonproliferation (1968) and Safeguards	Nuclear weapons states agree not to transfer and nonnuclear weapons states agree not to receive nuclear weapons or weapons-related technologies; all parties agree to work toward nuclear disarmament
Protection of Nuclear Material (1980)	Holds states responsible for *secure* transit of nuclear materials used for peaceful purposes, providing standards and remedies

(continued)

TABLE 7.1 (CONTINUED)	

TREATY OR AGREEMENT	PRINCIPAL QUANTITATIVE AND QUALITATIVE RESTRICTIONS, LIMITATIONS, AND OTHER PROVISIONS: NUMBERS, TYPES, LOCATIONS, RESEARCH, DEVELOPMENT, TESTING, AND USE
Strategic Nuclear and Conventional Armaments	
SALT I (US-USSR Strategic Arms Limitation Talks: 1969–72)	
Defensive Forces	
• Anti-Ballistic Missiles (ABM) 1972 Treaty and 1974 Protocol	*Prohibits* deployment of ABM systems for territorial defense, allowing only limited ABM deployments for defense of a state's national capital or one ICBM-launcher complex; development, testing, or deployment of sea-based, air-based, space-based, or mobile land-based ABM systems; transfer of ABM systems or components to other states: *provides* for national technical means of verification while prohibiting concealment measures
Offensive Forces	
• Offensive Arms Limitations: Interim Agreement (1972)	*Prohibits* construction of additional fixed, land-based intercontinental ballistic missile (ICBM) and submarine-launched ballistic missile (SLBM) launchers or ballistic missile submarines; conversion of existing ICBM launchers from light to heavy types; *provides* for national technical means of verification (while prohibiting deliberate concealment measures) and relies on a Standing Consultative Commission to deal with compliance issues
SALT II (US-USSR Strategic Arms Limitation Talks: 1972–79)	Not ratified as a treaty, but treated as an executive agreement that put *quantitative* limits on ICBMs and SLBMs, heavy bombers, and air-to-surface and cruise missiles and *qualitative* restraints on modernization and conversion, testing and deployment of new systems (to include limits on numbers of reentry vehicles on ICBM and SLBM); advance notification of ICBM launches; allowing for national technical means of verification (while prohibiting deliberate concealment measures) and providing for the Standing Consultative Commission
Intermediate-Range Nuclear Forces (INF): US-USSR (1987)	Eliminates *all* intermediate-range (1,000–5,500 km) and shorter-range (500–1,000 km) ballistic and ground-launched cruise missiles and launchers

TABLE 7.1   (CONTINUED)

TREATY OR AGREEMENT	PRINCIPAL QUANTITATIVE AND QUALITATIVE RESTRICTIONS, LIMITATIONS, AND OTHER PROVISIONS: NUMBERS, TYPES, LOCATIONS, RESEARCH, DEVELOPMENT, TESTING, AND USE
Strategic Arms Reduction Talks (START): US-USSR, 1982–91	Reduces substantially strategic offensive armaments (ICBM, SLBM, and heavy bombers) to 1,600 each with associated warheads limited to 6,000 each [down from more than 12,000 nuclear warheads in U.S. and Soviet inventories]; warhead limits reduced subsequently to some 3,000; in 1992 Belarus, Kazakhstan, and Ukraine joined the Russian Federation and the United States in acceding to the treaty
Missile Technology Control Regime (MTCR) (1987 & 1993)	Establishes common export control policy and list of controlled items with intent to stop spread to other countries of ballistic and cruise missiles and technologies capable of delivering a 500-kilogram nuclear payload (1987) as well as chemical and biological weapons (1993) to a range of 300 kilometers or more (32 state participants)
Conventional Armed Forces in Europe (CFE) (1990)	Limits numbers, types, and locations in Europe of tanks, artillery pieces, armored combat vehicles, combat aircraft, and attack helicopters of all countries
UN Registry on Conventional Arms Exports (1991)	Compiles information provided by members on conventional arms transfers (exports and imports)
Wassenaar Arrangement (1996–97)	Requires arms exporting state participants to exchange information on arms sales and denials, working to minimize adverse impact on international and regional security and stability (33 state participants)
Land Mines (1997–98)	Requires signatories to destroy all mines in national arsenals within four years, removing and destroying all of those already in the ground within ten years

the systems governments were then using. The "hot-line" agreement reached in the following year established a direct communications link between the White House and the Kremlin, a system that would be expanded and modernized over the years as new telecommunications technologies became available.

Approaching arms and conflict control through communications and agreed procedures for managing crises to avoid their escalation to armed conflict have also been the inspiration for a set of nuclear accidents, incidents at sea, and prevention of nuclear war measures adopted in the early 1970s. The United States and the Soviet

TABLE 7.2	CONTROLLING ARMAMENTS AND CONFLICTS: LOCATIONAL OR GEOGRAPHIC LIMITATIONS AND RESTRICTIONS

TREATY OR AGREEMENT	GENERAL TERMS
Antarctica (1959)	*Allows* only peaceful, scientific, or other *nonmilitary* use of Antarctica; direct inspection by states of all facilities or aerial observation anywhere at any time; *provides* for open exchange of information from scientific investigation of Antarctica; *requires* advance notice to other parties of expeditions to and within Antarctica, stations in Antarctica occupied by its nationals, any military personnel or equipment intended to be sent (which are allowed only for scientific research or other peaceful purposes); *promotes* preservation and conservation of living resources; *prohibits* new territorial claims, nuclear explosions, or storage of radioactive waste materials
Outer Space (1967)	*Prohibits* orbiting nuclear or other weapons of mass destruction; military bases or maneuvers on (or national, sovereign appropriation of) celestial bodies; *provides* for damage claims and recovery of astronauts and objects launched into outer space
Latin America Nuclear Free Zone (1967)	Latin America defined as a nuclear weapons–free zone—prohibiting testing, use, manufacture, production, acquisition, or any other form of possession of nuclear weapons by Latin American states or anyone on their behalf
Seabed Arms Control (1971)	*Prohibits* nuclear or other weapons of mass destruction in the seabed or ocean floor and subsoil; *provides* for nondisruptive inspection of suspect facilities
Environmental Modification (1977)	*Prohibits* military or any other hostile use of environmental modification techniques having widespread, long-lasting, or severe effects as the means of destruction, damage, or injury to any other state
Conference on Security and Cooperation in Europe (1975 Helsinki Final Act); subsequent conference accords in Stockholm (1985) and Vienna (1991)	Specific to the Atlantic-to-Urals European area, conventional arms reductions (Table 7.1) are combined with a regime of confidence- and security-building measures

Union established risk reduction centers in 1987 in each other's capitals staffed by officials from both countries and agreed in 1988 on procedures for mutual notification of ballistic missile launches, both of which were efforts to strengthen communications mechanisms between the two principal nuclear powers.

Focusing on improved communications in crises as at other times also has been a model followed in efforts to establish security and cooperation in Europe. Growing out of periodic international conferences on security and cooperation in

TABLE 7.3	COMMUNICATIONS AND CONFIDENCE- AND SECURITY-BUILDING MEASURES: FUNCTIONAL APPROACHES TO CONTROLLING OR MANAGING CONFLICTS

TREATY OR AGREEMENT	GENERAL DESCRIPTION OF TERMS
U.S.-USSR "Hot Line" Agreement (1963); modernized (1971); expanded (1984)	Established in the wake of the 1962 Cuban missile crisis, the U.S. and USSR established and subsequently maintained and expanded direct communications links between Washington and Moscow
Nuclear Accidents: U.S.-USSR (1971)	Requires organizational and technical arrangements to reduce risk of accidental or unauthorized use of nuclear weapons; advance notice of missile launches extending beyond national territory; communications in the event of accidents
Incidents at Sea: U.S.-USSR (1972)	Provides cautionary measures to avoid collisions or other incidents at sea; prohibits simulated attacks on each other's ships; requires advance notification of actions on the high seas that are dangerous to navigation or to aircraft in flight
Prevention of Nuclear War: U.S.-USSR (1973)	Requires parties to refrain from the threat or use of force against each other or each other's allies that would endanger international peace and security, act to avoid military confrontations and the outbreak of nuclear war, and engage in urgent consultations if relations are in risk of nuclear conflict
Confidence- and Security-Building Measures (CSBMs): Atlantic-to-Urals European Area (1975, 1986, 1991)	Specific to the Atlantic-to-Urals European area, confidence- and security-building measures established in 1975 and 1986 were expanded substantially, requiring notifications of military exercises and allowing for observers; providing for exchange of information to include numbers, types, and locations of armaments, aerial reconnaissance, and announced and unannounced on-site inspections of military installations [measures when combined with limits on armaments (Table 7.1) effectively establish "transparency" or military openness, increased warning time should any party prepare to attack any other, and overall reduction in the risk of war]
Nuclear Risk Reduction Centers: U.S.-USSR (1987)	Establishes Nuclear Risk Reduction Centers in Washington and Moscow with communications links between the two and regular meetings between representatives of the centers at least once a year
Ballistic Missile Launch Notification: U.S.-USSR (1988)	Requires notification through the Nuclear Risk Reduction Centers at least twenty-four hours in advance of the planned date and launch and impact areas of any strategic ballistic missile launch; in the event of launch postponement, notice is good for four days

(continued)

TABLE 7.3	(CONTINUED)
TREATY OR AGREEMENT	**GENERAL DESCRIPTION OF TERMS**
Open Skies (1992)	Consistent with negotiated annual quotas, NATO and former Warsaw Pact countries agreed that in the European Atlantic-to-Urals area each had the right to conduct and the obligation to receive aerial reconnaissance flights by other parties

Europe (CSCE) that began in the early 1970s, a conflict-prevention center was one of the institutions created in the new Organization for Security and Cooperation in Europe (OSCE) established in the early 1990s. As with the CSCE, the OSCE includes the United States and Canada and virtually all European states, extending in geographic scope from the Atlantic to the Urals.

Efforts to improve communications also can be understood as one of a number of confidence- and security-building measures. The 1975 Helsinki agreement was the first major agreement of the CSCE process on security as well as on human rights and expanding cultural and commercial links across the barriers that then divided the European continent between East and West. The security "basket" of concern to us in this chapter contained a modest set of CSBMs calling for notification in advance of military exercises and provision for observation of these maneuvers. The idea behind adopting these measures and the construction of a CSBM regime was to avoid misunderstandings that could lead to war, lest military movements be misperceived as having immediate hostile intent when they were intended only as exercises for testing war plans or training military forces.

CSBM-regime expansion was the outcome of CSCE-wide meetings in Stockholm in the mid-1980s and Vienna in the early 1990s. One, which included only NATO and Warsaw Pact alliance members, was to negotiate CFE requirements concerning numbers, types, locations, and readiness or preparedness of military forces. The second included *all* CSCE participants and focused more specifically on expanding the CSBM regime. Agreements in Stockholm and Vienna expanded exercise-notification requirements, provided for increased rights by outside parties to observe military maneuvers, established rules for announced and unannounced inspections of military facilities to verify compliance or identify violations of CFE agreements, and, as mentioned earlier, formed a Conflict Prevention Center in Vienna to contribute to maintaining regional peace and security.

ARMS CONTROL, VERIFICATION, AND COMPLIANCE

Many of these arms control treaties and agreements address questions of **verification** and **compliance**. It's one thing to make agreements; it's another to live up to them. Verification of compliance with (or violation of) treaties or agreements is achieved in a number of ways, such as open admission of violations, on-site inspection by other parties, reports by reliable human-intelligence sources, or through **national technical means (NTM) of verification**. These means include advanced technical-intelligence capabilities on ground stations, aircraft, ships, and satellites or other space vehicles.

Alleged violations are presented in diplomatic exchanges in the expectation of bringing violators into compliance. As such verification (knowing what other countries are actually doing) can be understood as the first phase to be followed by what amounts to an enforcement phase in which compliance is sought if any of the parties is thought to be in violation of a treaty or agreement. For example the Standing Consultative Commission (SCC, a U.S.-Soviet bilateral forum located in Geneva) was created in the 1970s by the Strategic Arms Limitations Talks (SALT) to deal with compliance issues. Among the complaints the United States raised at the SCC was one dealing with strategic defenses. For years the United States complained publicly in this forum and elsewhere that a major radar station constructed at Krasnoyarsk in the former Soviet Union violated provisions of the Anti-Ballistic Missiles (ABM) Treaty. This issue was not resolved until the end of the cold war, when the Soviets finally conceded the point and dismantled the radar.

Another example of a dispute raised in the SCC was an exchange of allegations on obstruction of national technical means of verification used by each side to monitor the military activities of the other. By agreement in SALT, neither side was to obstruct these national technical means. The United States complained that the Soviets violated SALT accords by encrypting **telemetry** in missile tests—that is, putting into code the communications or signals sent by these missiles to ground stations monitoring their in-flight trajectories over the Soviet land mass. Although Soviet controllers could decode these signals, the practice obstructed American intelligence efforts to receive and interpret the same information.

Because analysis of intercepted telemetry was a national technical means used by both sides to assess missile characteristics or capabilities of the other, the

Radar and other aerospace data are monitored at the U.S.-Canada North American Aerospace Defense Command (NORAD) in Colorado.

United States contended that encrypting telemetry was a SALT violation. For their part the Soviets countered that the American practice of putting canvas or other protective tents or covers over missile silos violated the same provision. Even if the American claim—that these covers were for protection from rain or snow while performing repair or other maintenance functions—were true, the Soviets complained that covers of any kind or for whatever purpose obstructed their ability to photograph these missile launchers from satellites in space.

Eventually such issues were worked out or, if not resolved to the complete satisfaction of the parties, continued to be addressed. The important point here is that even during the height of the cold war, adversaries could meet formally to discuss and debate allegations of noncompliance. The SCC was an important mechanism for airing differences, if not always working them out very quickly. As such the SCC was a means for managing superpower disputes and maintaining the strategic-arms security regime.

Verification capabilities in post–cold war arms control regimes have been expanded substantially by providing for more open exchange of data on numbers, types, and locations of armaments—information that previously carried secret or even top-secret security classifications. States need not rely almost exclusively on national technical means of verification. Post–cold war arms control regimes typically allow direct observation by outside parties as a means of verifying, for example, the agreed destruction of tanks, missiles, or other weaponry. These regimes also usually provide for similar on-site inspections of military and other installations relevant to treaty or agreement provisions. In short there is greater **transparency** or openness in military matters in post–cold war regimes. Proponents see this greater transparency as a means of building trust or confidence even among adversaries.

ALTERNATIVE DETERRENCE DOCTRINES

Constructing or adhering to arms control regimes can be part of national strategies pursued by states that are designed to serve security and other interests and objectives. As suggested earlier, states may enter arms control negotiations for a number of strategic purposes, including curbing the arms race, achieving savings through trimming unnecessary defense expenditures, reducing the risk of war, reducing damage should war occur, or gaining some other advantage.

Our focus in this section is on nuclear armaments and the relation between arms control and *military (force-employment) doctrines* concerning **deterrence**, **defense**, and **warfighting**. Deterrence relations among the great powers that possess nuclear weapons seem relatively less important these days, nuclear deterrence questions receiving much less attention now than they did during the cold war. An improved climate of great-power relations and a wide array of strategic arms control achievements in the last half of the twentieth century have contributed substantially to international security and a reduced risk of general war in the twenty-first century.

At the same time, however, great-power strategic nuclear arsenals remain intact, even though the United States and the Russian Federation agreed to reduce strategic nuclear warheads by some 75 percent to about 3,000 each (from their cold war highs of more than 12,000 warheads apiece). Arms controllers still have a significant challenge to find ways to reduce nuclear arms below these still high levels without destabilizing deterrence relations and endangering international peace and security.

military (force-employment) doctrines   Doctrines that represent what military leaders and theorists understand to be the most effective ways and means of using force, whether to deter adversaries, to defend against them, or to engage them offensively and defensively in other combat operations that are part of warfighting.

We think it is useful to include here a review of how deterrence, defense, and warfighting theories or doctrines relate to existing nuclear weapons arsenals as well as the implications these doctrines have for construction, expansion, or maintenance of strategic arms control regimes. The continuing twenty-first-century importance of the topic is not only due to nuclear weapons remaining on the arms control agendas of the major powers possessing them, but also because India, Pakistan, and other countries have acquired (or may yet acquire) nuclear weapons capabilities, not to mention other chemical or biological weapons of mass destruction. Notwithstanding extensive, well intended efforts to avoid further spread of nuclear and other weapons of mass destruction, proliferation of such weapons and weapons-related technologies seems likely to continue.

Table 7.4 portrays alternative deterrence doctrines or forms of deterrence and relates these to different nuclear and other military-force requirements. *Finite or minimum deterrence* requires the smallest number of weapons. Possessing just a few weapons means, of course, that they are more vulnerable to being destroyed by an enemy than if a country has a larger number of such weapons in its arsenal, especially if these weapons are dispersed in different basing modes at different locations on land or at sea and thus are more difficult for an enemy to find and destroy.

By contrast to minimum deterrence, deterrence by *assured destruction* requires substantially more weapons, often in multiple-basing modes (for example in bombers and in land- or sea-based missiles) to assure that at least some weapons would survive a "first-strike" attack by an enemy and thus provide a capability for retaliating—a so-called second-strike capability.

Beyond assured destruction, even more weapons are required when one adds forces used for *defense to limit damage* in the event deterrence fails and war begins. Defense in this sense is actually a form of warfighting that calls for radars both for early warning of attack and to support combat operations using antiaircraft artillery, fighter interceptors with air-to-air missiles and other types of armament, and surface-to-air missiles against enemy bombers or fighter-bombers; land- or aerospace-based missiles or other projectiles directed against incoming missiles; offensive missiles or aircraft directed against enemy missile sites, launch-control centers or airfields to prevent them from launching missiles or aircraft sorties; and perhaps some civil-defense preparations as well.

The largest number of fully capable offensive and defensive forces, however, are called for in *deterrence by denial*—maintaining credible warfighting forces that would deny an adversary any reasonable expectation that it could attain its objectives by using force. Minimum deterrence and deterrence based on assured destruction rest on threats of punishment—that a would-be attacker will suffer retaliatory strikes. Although punishment to all sides is involved in any war, particularly a nuclear war, deterrence by denial is based on a different rational construction than deterrence based purely on threat of punishment.

Deterrence by denial means that going to war would not accomplish objectives sought and thus would make no sense to any enemy or other would-be adversary. To Clausewitz, as discussed in Chapter Five, war or other use of force by a state is a rational means to achieve particular political objectives. Consistent with the deterrence-by-denial doctrine, no useful purpose can be served by going to war with another country possessing credible warfighting forces and understood by its adversaries to have (and to be willing to use its) military capabilities at least to "prevail," if not win, any such contest. A capability to prevail or

finite or minimum deterrence A situation in which a country maintains a relatively small number of nuclear or other weapons of mass destruction for use in making deterrence threats.

TABLE 7.4	IMPLICATIONS FOR STRATEGIC ARMS CONTROL REGIMES OF ALTERNATIVE DETERRENCE OR DEFENSE DOCTRINES AND FORCE POSTURES

	STRATEGIC NUCLEAR DOCTRINES			
	MINIMUM OR FINITE DETERRENCE (NO REAL WARFIGHTING CAPABILITIES INTENDED; DETERRENCE ONLY THROUGH THREAT OF PUNISHMENT)	DETERRENCE BY ASSURED (OR MUTUALLY ASSURED) DESTRUCTION	DEFENSE BY DAMAGE LIMITATION (SOME WARFIGHTING CAPABILITIES)	DETERRENCE OR DEFENSE BY DENIAL (ROBUST WARFIGHTING CAPABILITIES)
Implications for Force Posture				
Offensive				
(bombers and other aircraft and missiles)	perhaps 100 or fewer nuclear weapons	large numbers of nuclear weapons	very large numbers of nuclear weapons	largest number and diversity of nuclear weapons
Defensive				
A. *Active* (artillery, fighter-interceptors, surface-to-air and antiballistic missiles, space-based systems, etc.)	none required	none required	some	robust, fully developed
B. *Passive* (radars, communications, civil defense, etc.)	minimal needs (for early warning)	minimal needs (for early warning)	substantial need (for civil defense and early warning)	robust, fully developed
Implications for Deterrence Stability	potentially unstable	usually considered the most stable	potentially unstable	usually considered the most unstable
Implications for Arms Control	most conducive to arms control limits or restrictions	caps possible on offenses; effort to block development of defenses	somewhat compatible with arms control efforts	least compatible with arms control limits

win effectively precludes an enemy any rational expectation of success. Denying adversaries virtually any possibility of goal attainment by using force is thus understood to deter war or other resort to use of force. We will now examine these concepts in greater detail.

Deterrence, Defense, and Warfighting

Military doctrine attempts to answer two key questions: (1) *What* military means shall be employed to protect a country? and (2) *How* shall they be employed? Doctrines concerning deterrence, defense, and warfighting involve either the threat or actual use of force. In deterrence the effort is merely to dissuade another state, through the threat of force, from doing something it has not yet undertaken; it is not actually required to change a course of action. This also may involve **extended deterrence** threats designed to protect allies. If deterrence fails, defense involves the use of military force to repel an attack. Warfighting is thus an *active* use of force for defense or to achieve other political-military goals.

The key point in this discussion related to arms control, however, is that the numbers and types of strategic nuclear and other weaponry a country has or may seek to possess is closely tied to the force-employment doctrines it adopts. The military forces (i.e., such **force posture** considerations as numbers, types, and locations of forces) required to deter, defend, or engage in warfighting depend heavily upon force-employment doctrines and related national security strategies. In the absence of change in doctrinal and strategic understandings and commitments, these national requirements effectively define the needs and limits of concessions that can realistically be made by negotiators in arms control talks.

By the 1990s, more than thirty years of talks had produced a regime or agreed set of rules on nuclear weapons test bans (that imposed at least a partial, qualitative restriction on nuclear weapons development), nonproliferation of nuclear weapons and weapons-related technologies, strategic arms limitation (SALT) and reductions (START), as well as elimination by the United States and the former Soviet Union of all intermediate-range missiles carrying nuclear weapons (INF). These agreements were not reached in a vacuum but were negotiated against force-posture requirements. In turn these requirements were tied to different conceptions of deterrence and defense or warfighting that had evolved over time.

Minimum or Finite Deterrence

As discussed earlier, the least-demanding alternative in terms of numbers of nuclear forces is minimum or finite deterrence, which requires only a relatively small number of nuclear weapons that can be used against an adversary. With only a few nuclear weapons (say one or more, but perhaps fewer than 100), a country cannot realistically choose to engage in actual warfighting, which requires a much larger arsenal with a full array of nuclear and nonnuclear offensive and defensive capabilities.

Understanding minimum or finite deterrence is particularly relevant in the present period of nuclear proliferation when a larger number of countries may acquire small nuclear arsenals. Because a minimum-deterrence country has only a relatively few nuclear weapons, its nuclear forces can be used effectively only to threaten attack against an adversary, typically against population centers or so-called **countervalue targets**. In a minimum-deterrence situation, there are not enough weapons to direct attacks at a large number of military or **counterforce targets** that would be struck if a country were trying to destroy or substantially weaken an enemy's warfighting capability. Hence minimum or finite deterrence can realistically be based only on a threat of punishment primarily to enemy populations should another country undertake aggression or other undesirable action as specified by the deterring state. Even if the genuine purpose is to deter war by such threats, aiming weaponry at population centers raises obvious moral questions.

A moral paradox is thus inherent in the sincere effort of arms control negotiators to reduce nuclear arsenals to minimum levels. A breakdown of deterrence in these circumstances could maximize the human cost of nuclear war. By contrast larger arsenals do allow for counterforce targeting as a way of reducing unnecessary death and destruction. The irony then is that fewer weapons, as in a minimum-deterrence posture, may be even more problematic morally than larger nuclear arsenals that can be directed more effectively against the larger number of military or counterforce targets, thus avoiding population centers whenever possible.

Critics are quick to point out, however, that such distinctions have little if any meaning when weapons of mass destruction are involved—that the distinction between civilian (countervalue) and military (counterforce) targets is difficult, if not impossible, to make when the destructiveness of such weapons can so easily spill over from military targets to adjacent or nearby cities, towns, or other settlements. Beyond direct losses of human life and property, severe damage to the environment including massive loss of animal and plant life are additional adverse consequences of using any weapons of mass destruction. The horrendous blast, radiation, and thermal or heat effects of nuclear weapons thus blur the distinction between counterforce and countervalue targets. Even if a state focuses on using nuclear weapons only against military or counterforce targets, massive **collateral damage (death and destruction)** to civil populations and property still cannot be avoided.

Minimum Deterrence as Strategic Doctrine for India, Pakistan, and Other New Nuclear Weapons States

Compared to the enormous size of U.S. and Soviet nuclear arsenals during the cold war (and the thousands of strategic nuclear weapons that still remain in their inventories), those belonging to the United Kingdom, France, and China then and now seem minimal indeed. Strategists have raised serious questions concerning the viability of such small national-deterrent capabilities and the stability of

Chakothi bazaar is seen deserted, twenty-eight miles north of Muzaffarabad, capital of Pakistan-held Kashmir, at the border of Pakistan and India. Most of the people left the border town because of shelling across the border.

deterrence relations based on them. These problems are compounded for India, Pakistan, or other countries newly acquiring nuclear weapons and related technologies because of the serious interstate conflicts in which they typically have been involved.

If nuclear weapons continue to proliferate in coming years, the countries acquiring them will likely have only relatively small arsenals to which minimum-deterrence concepts apply. In the experience of the original nuclear powers, minimum-deterrence doctrines establish a force posture with the fewest numbers of offensive forces. Because establishing an effective defense is both difficult and costly, new nuclear weapons states likely will come to rely primarily on the threat of retaliation as the basis of their deterrence with relatively few if any active defenses (fighter-interceptors, surface-to-air missiles, and antiaircraft artillery to shoot down enemy aircraft or missiles carrying these weapons). Nor is an effective antiballistic missile system (much less space-based or other strategic defenses) either attainable or affordable for most, if not all, of these countries in the absence of outside help by the United States or other technologically advanced, major military powers. Some passive defenses may be justified, such as radar (to give early warning of attack) or fallout shelters (to provide some civil defense), but the emphasis is on the offensive—maintaining, if possible, a credible retaliatory capability. Minimum deterrence also assumes a viable command-and-control mechanism that can make and implement nuclear weapons decisions in a timely manner.

Because minimum deterrence requires the smallest number of military forces of the several deterrence doctrines discussed in this section, it is the one most conducive to arms control limitations. If that is its principal advantage from an arms control perspective, critics of minimum deterrence emphasize that a smaller number of weapons also is more vulnerable to a comprehensive enemy attack aimed at destroying them before they can ever be used to retaliate. As mentioned previously, smaller numbers of weapons make strategic forces inherently more vulnerable to an effective enemy first strike, making minimum deterrence inherently less stable than an assured-destruction force posture. Its nuclear command-and-control authorities may not be up to the task of making and implementing reliable nuclear-employment decisions in a timely fashion. Moreover, decision makers under pressure in a country with just a few nuclear weapons, who believe their country is (or could be) under attack, might launch their few forces even before confirming that the attack was real. Fearing that virtually all of the country's retaliatory forces may be destroyed by an enemy before they can be launched in retaliation may lead a minimum-deterrence country to launch on warning of attack without having (or taking) the time to verify that an attack is actually underway—an extraordinarily dangerous position that can actually produce a war that otherwise would not have occurred! That is why many nuclear strategists consider minimum deterrence and tendencies for countries with these postures to launch on warning to be dangerous, unstable bases for deterrence relations.

To be effective, enough of the deterring country's offensive forces must be able to survive an enemy attack in order to launch a counteroffensive or retaliatory strike—a **second-strike capability**. The stability of deterrence relations is enhanced from this perspective by larger numbers of weapons in addition to other measures that enhance the survivability of nuclear retaliatory forces. When enough retaliatory forces are "survivable," national security decision makers need not act precipitously; they have time to weigh their options. Launch under attack (or even after attack) is possible for countries with survivable, second-strike capabilities.

Beyond numbers, additional measures to increase survivability include *hardening* (fortifying or shielding warheads or other components and placing missiles in reinforced-concrete underground silos), *mobility* (placing nuclear weapons on aircraft or in missiles on submarines), *dispersion* (spreading bomber bases and missile launchers over a wide geographic area), *diversification* (having a variety of nuclear delivery approaches, including aircraft, land-based missiles, submarine-launched missiles, or "standoff" missiles launched from an airplane or ship to targets perhaps hundreds or more miles away), and *strategic defense* (deploying antiaircraft and antimissile weapons systems designed to defend a country's retaliatory forces from attack).

These approaches involve technologies and expense well beyond the reach of most would-be nuclear powers in the first decades of the twenty-first century. As a result critics observe that the proliferation of small nuclear arsenals will result in inherently less stable, minimum-deterrence relations among medium-sized and small powers acquiring such weapons. This is another reason that arms control advocates feel so strongly about maintaining and expanding the nuclear nonproliferation security regime that forbids the transfer or acquisition of nuclear weapons and weapons technologies to nonnuclear countries, in exchange for a pledge by nuclear powers to work toward reducing their arsenals.

Stable deterrence depends on both capability and credibility. It is not enough to have a viable weapons capability as in a second-strike retaliatory, assured-destruction posture; if deterrence is to work, one's adversary must perceive a genuine will to use this capability—to retaliate if attacked. Some critics of minimum deterrence argue that smaller numbers not only undermine an adversary's perception that a deterring country could deliver a retaliatory strike but also raise questions as to a minimum-deterrent state's will ultimately to resort to nuclear strikes. Whether nuclear weapons have been used by an aggressor or not, why would such a minimum-deterrent state want to introduce them, when doing so would only invite retaliatory or further nuclear destruction?

In short critics worry about the stability of minimum deterrence when both capability and credibility can so easily be drawn into question. Defenders usually acknowledge these problems but argue that the horrendous consequences of using nuclear weapons and the uncertainty of calculations about such matters lead even the smallest nuclear weapons powers to be more cautious than critics contend.

Deterrence Through Assured (and Mutually Assured) Destruction and Defensive Efforts to Limit Damage

Assured (and mutually assured) destruction and defensive efforts to limit damage were dominant ways of thinking about deterrence between superpowers in the 1960s and 1970s during the cold war. For reasons presented in the previous two sections, many critics of minimum deterrence then and now have preferred a larger number of offensive nuclear-deterrence forces. Accompanied by hardening, mobility, dispersion, and diversification of these forces to enhance their survivability, the superpowers established and maintained a capability for second-strike assured destruction. In these circumstances neither side would be foolish enough to attack first. **Mutually assured destruction (MAD)** exists if both parties in a bilateral deterrence relation have a second-strike, assured-destruction capability against the other. If they do, the threat of punishment or destruction presumably is enough to deter both parties from launching (or even considering) a first strike.

Deterrence based strictly on assured destruction (or mutually assured destruction) requires a strong offense accompanied, as in minimum deterrence, by passive defenses for the earliest possible warning of attack and a viable command-and-control system able to make and implement nuclear-employment decisions in a timely fashion. A *stable* deterrence under these circumstances depends, paradoxically, on maintaining a condition of mutual vulnerability to a first strike, coupled with the assurance that comes from having sufficient survivable second-strike forces. The logic is that neither party would undertake a first strike against the other with the knowledge that doing so would invite unwanted retaliatory destruction.

The SALT accords in the 1970s between the United States and the Soviet Union were based, at least from the American point of view, on deterrence by this threat of mutually assured destruction. Caps were placed on strategic offense, specifying maximum numbers and types of missiles and bombers each side could have. At the same time severe restrictions were placed on strategic defenses, quantitatively limiting deployment of antiballistic missiles (ABMs) and qualitatively prohibiting space-based testing of strategic-defense components. Limitations on strategic defense were intended not only to curb the arms race but also to maintain the mutual vulnerability central to deterrence by mutually assured destruction.

Defense

The distinction between *deterrence* and *defense* became abundantly clear in the 1950s and 1960s. If deterrence broke down, what defenses would a society be able to muster? Hardened blast and fallout shelters could be part of a passive civil-defense plan. Active defenses that could destroy incoming bombers and missiles could be used to reduce or limit damage. Damage limitation could also be achieved by striking enemy missiles before they were launched (or by developing technologies to destroy them in the middle or terminal phases of their trajectories en route to targets). Of course the discussion of using active defenses or even offensive forces to limit damage made defense sound more and more like nuclear warfighting.

Children huddle below their desks in an American elementary school classroom during a "duck and cover" air raid drill in 1951.

In fact, damage limitation involved acquiring effective *area* and *point* defenses offered by antiballistic missile (ABM) systems or later by space-based systems as well as robust offensive systems with sufficient accuracy to take out enemy air bases and missile sites. There is a danger that one side may think its offensive and defensive "damage limitation" forces are strong enough to make a first strike against the other a feasible option. A credible **first-strike capability** includes not only a capacity to strike first but also an ability to nullify or reduce to "acceptable levels" the ability of an adversary to retaliate in kind.

Even if neither side in fact has such a credible first-strike capability, if either side perceived the other were on the verge of acquiring one, it might lead the disadvantaged party to act preemptively, starting a war before the other side achieved any strategic advantage. In short pursuing the development of damage-limitation forces is seen by many as potentially destabilizing. Even extensive civil-defense networks honestly designed to protect or defend populations in the event of war can be misinterpreted by an adversary as an indication of secret plans to develop a credible first-strike or warfighting capability. Thus developing or extending even passive defenses can be destabilizing, particularly when they are accompanied by existing active defenses and strong offensive capabilities.

In the SALT negotiations, arms control was used as one means of preventing the development of effective strategic defenses that, beyond their defensive value, also could be seen by an adversary as part of an effective warfighting arsenal. A good offense, after all, depends on having good defenses as well. Arms control agreements that limited nuclear warfighting capabilities were understood as contributing to the stability of deterrence relations.

Warfighting

In the late 1970s and 1980s talk turned more directly to developing nuclear warfighting forces that could win or at least "prevail" if deterrence broke down and nuclear war broke out. Credible nuclear warfighting capabilities were seen by some as another form of deterrence or, more generally, dissuasion. Although punishment would no doubt be involved, the primary focus would instead be on denial. From this perspective no would-be adversary would ever take on a country with nuclear superiority or at least an ability to fight and prevail in nuclear warfighting. Because adversaries would in effect be denied any rational purpose for engaging in nuclear war, they would be dissuaded from undertaking it in the first place. Hence another paradox of deterrence: The point of talking credibly about fighting and prevailing in a nuclear war is the belief that in so doing, that particular horrible possibility will never come about.

Force posture for effective nuclear warfighting capabilities is the least conducive to constructing arms control regimes. As in all warfighting, the aim of such a denial doctrine is to destroy or substantially weaken an enemy's war-making capability. Arms control restraints on numbers, types, and locations, as well as on research, development, test and evaluation (RDT&E) of weapons and weapons systems and other factors are an impediment to developing and deploying large numbers of offensive forces able to penetrate enemy territory and air space (as in employing "stealth" technologies that reduce or disguise the appearance on enemy radars of incoming aircraft and missiles) and destroy even the most hardened targets. This requires high accuracy in delivering bombs to target, using air bursts, ground bursts, and even earth-penetrating warheads, depending on the "hardness" and location of targets to be hit. Strategic offenses must also be accompanied by well developed and extensive active and passive defenses—objectives incompatible with most arms control agendas.

Moreover, research, development, test and evaluation as well as acquisition of substantial offensive and defensive nuclear warfighting capabilities were upsetting to the general population, which suffered understandably from cold war nuclear anxieties, made worse by saber rattling and other strong rhetoric between the United States and Soviet Union. Perhaps even more important were anxieties in the Soviet military high command that the United States was trying to achieve a credible first-strike capability and had the technological superiority to do so.

If this were so, Soviet second-strike forces were now potentially in jeopardy. Soviet command-and-control authorities considered shifting to a posture of launch on warning rather than waiting to confirm an attack until it was too late to retaliate. "Launch on warning" is, as discussed above, a highly unstable readiness posture compared to "launch after attack." The danger of false alarm (due to radar, computer, or other equipment malfunction), other accident, or miscalculation causing war to break out is less when time for command-and-control decisions is increased.

The End of the Cold War and Implications for Arms Control, Deterrence, Defense, and Warfighting Doctrines

The attitudes of Gorbachev and Yeltsin in the late 1980s and 1990s and the willingness of American leaders to trust them signaled a change for the better, making the international climate more conducive to arms control agreements of all kinds. Such agreements had implications for both defense and warfighting doctrines. Agreement under the Strategic Arms Reduction Talks (START) to reduce strategic nuclear weapons by about 75 percent as well as dramatically scaling back strategic defense plans also meant that both sides were, in effect, abandoning notions of deterrence or dissuasion by developing and maintaining robust nuclear warfighting capabilities. New arms control limitations and a U.S. decision to accept a strict interpretation of the ABM treaty that prohibits space-based testing of strategic defense components effectively put a lid on the nuclear arms race; however, proponents of deploying an effective national missile defense have called for renegotiating and amending the ABM treaty or, failing that, even abrogating it.

Nevertheless, the move away from planning to fight and prevail in nuclear warfare was a notable shift back to an earlier force posture compatible with mutually assured destruction deterrence doctrine. In a period of lower threat and risk of war, both the Russian Federation and United States agreed to put their strategic nuclear forces on less of a war footing, reducing alert and readiness levels to lower levels. Under heavy diplomatic pressures, the former Soviet republics have also agreed to disarm themselves of the nuclear weaponry they inherited after the formal breakup of the Soviet Union in 1992. With a strategic regime of quantitative and qualitative restrictions in place, deterrence relations among the major powers are more stable, the overall climate of post–cold war international relations is much improved, and the risk of general war among great powers has remained relatively low.

Deterrence Theory: Some Concerns

Reading military doctrinal statements can be a chilling experience for many people. Often written in a straightforward, technical manner, they are unsettling, particularly when they describe, often in matter-of-fact fashion, a possible nuclear exchange between states. Furthermore critiques of deterrence, defense, and warfighting theories or doctrines also make several other salient points.

First what is known as the *usability paradox* lies at the heart of U.S. nuclear weapons policy. Two key objectives of U.S. policy—to deter aggression against the United States and its allies and to prevent accidental war—require that U.S. nuclear forces be usable, but not *too* usable. In other words for deterrence to work, nuclear forces must be usable enough that an adversary is convinced that a U.S. nuclear response would be forthcoming if the United States or its vital interests were attacked. On the other hand, to prevent an accidental nuclear war, U.S. weapons must not be so usable that they could conceivably be launched by computer error or insane missile silo operators, or used in such a way that they provoke a fearful adversary to launch a preemptive attack. It is disturbing to note that a number of studies have suggested that the command-and-control systems of U.S. nuclear forces during the cold war were not without their problems.

Second, and perhaps even more disturbing, studies of the two most dangerous crises in the cold war—Cuba (1962) and the Middle East (1973)—suggest that leaders in both Moscow and Washington misperceived each other's motivations and intentions, making for much more dangerous situations than we had previously realized. Theories of deterrence, it is argued, may give leaders a false confidence that they can carefully calibrate their actions to those of an adversary, thus effectively communicating their intentions.

Finally there are major areas of concern involving nuclear weapons and the developing world. The key question is the extent to which the logic of deterrence as outlined here, essentially devised by American scholars and political leaders in relation to their cold war, then-Soviet counterparts, is equally applicable, for example, to Indian-Pakistani relations as to present-day U.S.-Russian relations. There is also concern over China's views on limited deterrence and the fact that Beijing is bent on expanding and modernizing its nuclear arsenal in the years ahead. Without China as a full player, both the nuclear nonproliferation and comprehensive test ban regimes are decidedly of less value. Notwithstanding presidential and executive branch assurances of the United States' continued compliance with these obligations, failure by the United States Senate to ratify the Comprehensive Test Ban Treaty does make it more difficult to keep these (and potentially other) parties in compliance with arms control regimes.

weapons proliferation
The spread of weapons and weapons systems to countries not previously possessing them (horizontal proliferation), or the accumulation of more and more weapons or weapons systems by particular countries (vertical proliferation).

WEAPONS PROLIFERATION

As suggested in references to India, Pakistan, and other countries newly acquiring weapons of mass destruction, the one topic that has dominated every international arms control agenda in the post–cold war era is the issue of *weapons proliferation*. There are five major areas of concern:

- Nuclear or radiological weapons
- Chemical weapons
- Biological weapons
- Ballistic missiles
- Advanced conventional weapons systems

Nuclear weapons and materiel, however, have dominated international debate and discussion.

Nuclear Weapons and Materiel

The cold war and the bipolar international system it created so completely dominated thinking about military security issues that the startling collapse in 1991 of the Soviet Union with its 33,000 nuclear warheads set governments, think tanks, and academe scrambling. During the cold war both superpowers entered into alliances and agreements with a number of states, providing security (as in extended deterrence provided to allies) in exchange for, among other things, the agreement not to pursue an independent nuclear weapons capability. But with the end of the cold war such security guarantees no longer seemed so secure as the former superpower rivals reassessed their foreign policies and domestic priorities. In Europe and the developing world, all states previously under the security umbrellas of either the United States or the Soviet Union began to reassess their positions. All expressed concern over the future of the nuclear arsenals and related technologies possessed by the Russian Federation and former Soviet republics.

Indeed, some 3,000 of these weapons were located in the former Soviet republics of the Ukraine, Kazakstan, and Belarus. Although Ukraine initially demonstrated some reluctance, all three finally did agree to relinquish control over nuclear warheads on their respective territories to Russia. This reluctance was partially due to a desire to extract Western aid concessions but stemmed primarily from Ukraine's concern over Russia's intentions, should Russia's relatively moderate leadership at the time under President Yeltsin be replaced in the future by a regime more threatening to Ukraine.

The physical security of the weapons in Russia and the former republics was also a problem, raising the specter of weapons being stolen and perhaps sold for private gain on the black market to states such as North Korea, Iran, or Iraq, which might be seeking to accelerate their own nuclear research and development efforts. There were (and continue to be) concerns about Russian and other nuclear weapons experts in the former Soviet republics who might transfer nuclear know-how to nonnuclear states. Many were left jobless by the demise of the Soviet regime and poor economic conditions in the post-Soviet period, and the fear is that some of these experts might be tempted to sell their expertise to foreign governments or terrorist organizations just to make ends meet, not to mention gaining great profit from such illegal ventures. Beyond legal prohibitions against nuclear technology transfers, finding proper employment and adequate compensation for these experts quickly became not just a Russian but also an international security concern.

The linchpin of the international non proliferation regime is the 1967 **Nuclear Non-Proliferation Treaty (NPT)**, in which the five declared nuclear powers at the time (the United States, the United Kingdom, the Soviet Union, France, and China) pledged not to export to nonnuclear states either nuclear weapons or nuclear weapons components or technologies. Other signatories agreed, as nonnuclear states, not to try to acquire a nuclear weapons capability in exchange for a commitment by the nuclear powers to negotiate in good faith on cessation of the nuclear arms race and the pursuit of nuclear disarmament. All parties that signed the treaty agreed to safeguards and inspections by the Vienna-based **International Atomic Energy Agency (IAEA)** of nuclear power plants and other nuclear facilities used for peaceful purposes. The purpose of these provisions, of course, was to reassure states that their neighbors were not secretly building nuclear weapons capabilities and thus persuading states to forgo pursuing weapons programs of their own.

Testing of nuclear weapons by India and Pakistan in 1998 added two more members to the nuclear club, although both are under enormous international pressure to hold back from deploying such weapons. It is assumed that Israel also has nuclear weapons capabilities. As noted earlier, South Africa developed these capabilities but chose to disarm itself of them after a significant change of regime. Likewise Brazil and Argentina appear to have moved away from developing nuclear weapons capabilities. Also mentioned earlier, after the breakup of the Soviet Union in 1992, three of the former Soviet republics (Belarus, Ukraine, and Kazakstan) relinquished nuclear weapons on their soil to the Russian Federation, which in turn were among those subject to destruction under the Russian-American START agreements.

Other states, unable to secure a weapons capability directly, still might be eager to augment their research and development programs with Russian or other foreign expertise. Nor is nuclear material secure. A state does not have to steal a weapon or purchase an actual nuclear weapon to become a worry to its neighbors. Arms reduction agreements between the United States and Russia under START require the dismantling of thousands of existing weapons. The two countries did decide to trim pre-1991 U.S.-Soviet strategic nuclear warhead totals by about 75 percent. This led, however, to the creation of a massive nuclear waste–disposal problem. It is estimated that by 2008 the Russians, who lack the processing facilities of the United States, will have had to dispose of some six tons of plutonium and thirty tons of enriched uranium.[1] Given its own interests also at stake, the United States has been willing to assist the Russian Federation in dealing with this issue.

Plutonium, an essential part of nuclear weapons, is not found in nature. It is a by-product of the same uranium that is used in a nuclear reactor. Plutonium, even if not weapons grade, could still be made into a low-yield "dirty bomb." Such a device could cause widespread devastation if detonated from the back of a truck. All sorts of such doomsday scenarios come easily to mind, with states as well as terrorist groups involved. But even the possibility of a black market in weapons and weapons-grade material is alarming. Nuclear smuggling of plutonium and other weapons-grade materials is pursued with relative ease when controls are lax, typically either to realize large financial gains by criminal elements, often linked to government or military officials with access to these ma-

---

[1]For ongoing coverage of this issue, go to www.iiss.org.

terials, or to supply terrorist groups or governments wanting to acquire or manufacture nuclear weapons with weapons-grade materials procured illegally in global black markets.[2]

How should a state respond to a credible terrorist nuclear threat? Refuse to negotiate and hope it is a bluff? Threaten to destroy the innocent people associated with the group's cause? If one country is unsure about what its neighboring rival has in its military arsenal, would it not have an incentive to acquire a nuclear weapons capability, perhaps in the name of deterrence?

As possession of nuclear weapons spreads, the possibility of inadvertent use increases, because new nuclear states are not likely to have as secure command and control over these weapons as did the major powers during the height of the cold war. In a crisis a state may be more likely to launch nuclear weapons against a neighbor, believing it must get in the first strike before its rival. This is known as a *preemptive strike*. Possible scenarios resulting from instabilities in such regions of the world as the Middle East or South Asia include the following:

- A regional war between two newly nuclear-armed states
- The rise of a regional nuclear-armed predator leading a major power (or major power–led alliance) to take action to thwart the predator's expansionist ambitions
- The loss of central government control over nuclear forces as a result of the political disintegration of the state, which could lead to a nuclear civil war or to a terrorist organization gaining control of one or more weapons

What can be done about the nuclear proliferation threat? One approach is on the *supply side*—prevention of the further spread of nuclear weapons or nuclear weapons technologies by prohibiting such exports by states already possessing these capabilities. On the *demand side* the aim is to improve regional security conditions so that states will be less likely to feel a need to acquire such weapons. Diplomatic efforts to persuade would-be nuclear powers from pursuing the acquisition of nuclear weapons or weapons technologies are demand-side measures. Thus in arms control usage the term *supply side* refers to countries already in possession of a particular weapon, weapons system, or related technology, whereas demand side refers to countries wishing to acquire any of these weapons, weapons systems, or technologies.

No doubt signaling their future intentions, India and Pakistan never signed the Nuclear Non-Proliferation Treaty, resulting in unilateral efforts by other states to deny certain technologies to these countries. Iraq, Iran, and Algeria have also been suspected of harboring nuclear ambitions, if not fully developed programs. At most the treaty to which neither was a party merely slowed India's and Pakistan's drive for nuclear weapons capability. On the other hand one reason Argentina and Brazil have renounced their desire to become nuclear powers may be

---

[2]Nuclear smuggling is not purely hypothetical. For example, in 1994 German police found six grams of plutonium-239 in a businessman's home and also found three men landing in Munich on a flight from Moscow carrying 363.4 grams of plutonium and 201 grams of lithium-6. In the same year, two former Soviet citizens and a Czech nuclear physicist were arrested in Prague and found to have three kilograms of highly enriched uranium-235. See Phil Williams and Paul N. Woessner, "Nuclear Material Trafficking: An Interim Assessment," *Transnational Organized Crime*, vol. 1, no. 2 (Summer 1995): 206–8.

due to the technological blockade on the part of supplier states. It should be noted that the NPT does not prohibit a state from conducting research and development of civilian nuclear-power programs. The obvious problem with this, however, is that such a program also can be used not only in developing expertise that can then be applied toward a weapons development program, but also in generating plutonium and other products that can be used in constructing nuclear weapons.

International faith in the power of the International Atomic Energy Agency (IAEA) to monitor suspected would-be nuclear powers was shaken in the early 1990s, when in the aftermath of the 1991 Gulf War the world learned the extent of Iraq's clandestine weapons program. Iraq had signed the NPT. This is one reason why Israel, an undeclared nuclear power, is still unwilling to sign the NPT. Efforts by North Korea to develop its own nuclear weapons became apparent when it announced in 1993 its intent to withdraw from the NPT regime in order to avoid an impending IAEA inspection of a suspect site. International pressure and subsequent negotiations kept North Korea formally within the NPT regime, although continued clandestine development of nuclear weapons by North Korea remains a major concern by other states.

Despite international efforts against proliferation, a few states have thus made some progress toward acquiring nuclear weapons. One danger, of course, is when a state feels threatened and engages in the preemptive destruction of another state's nuclear capabilities. This has happened twice—the Israeli attack on Iraq's reactor in 1981 and the U.S.-led coalition's attack on Iraq's nuclear facilities during the Gulf War in 1991. It is not certain how viable such an option would be in other cases. In 1981 a formal state of war existed between Israel and Iraq; however, in 1991 such attacks would have been unlikely, by contrast, had Iraq not just invaded neighboring Kuwait.

The demand side approach to nonproliferation involves *reducing motivations* to acquire nuclear weapons. The ideal solution is to eliminate the insecurity and fear among neighboring states. This has been the goal of the United States concerning the Arabs and Israelis. A complementary approach involves security guarantees. The United States, for example, has provided such a guarantee to South Korea as evidenced by the stationing of some 36,000 U.S. troops there. Likewise Japan has enjoyed a similar security guarantee from the United States as part of its extended deterrence security "umbrella" in east Asia. But that guarantee was made during the cold war as a measure to contain communism, and it is hard to believe that the United States or any other country would today make an equivalent guarantee to nonnuclear powers not already under the American security umbrella.

Chemical and Biological Weapons

Chemical weapons are much easier to produce than nuclear weapons, and they are found in the arsenals of most states. In January 1993, 130 countries signed the Chemical Weapons Convention (CWC), which revised and expanded the guidelines established by the 1925 Geneva Protocol. The tortuous negotiations began in 1968. Signers of the convention pledge not to develop, produce, acquire, stockpile, or transfer chemical weapons; not to use such weapons; and not to assist or encourage anyone to engage in such prohibited activity. States also pledge to destroy chemical weapons stocks and production facilities. Similar to the previously mentioned role performed by IAEA in the nuclear nonproliferation regime, one task for the new Organization for the Prohibition of Chemical Weapons (OPCW) is verification.

Despite the high lethality and effectiveness of biological weapons, they have not been used in modern warfare. As with chemical weapons, an international agreement also exists—the Biological and Toxin Weapons Convention (BWC), signed by some 150 states. The BWC forbids the production of biological warfare agents, but research is allowed for the purpose of producing vaccines and antidotes. Opportunities for cheating are plentiful. To date two states—Iraq and the former Soviet Union—designed programs to create biological weapons capabilities. The main drawback to the BWC is that it has no verification procedure, and hence efforts to control biological weapons lag far behind the international conventions that control nuclear and chemical weapons.

CASE & Point

BIOLOGICAL WEAPONS

The major international control mechanism for biological weapons is the Biological and Toxin Weapons Convention (BWC). The 1925 Geneva Protocol banned the use of "bacteriological methods of warfare," but it was not until 1969 that the United Kingdom offered a draft calling for the actual elimination of biological weapons. The United States supported the idea, and later that year U.S. President Nixon renounced the production and stockpiling of biological weapons. The United States and the Soviet Union agreed on a text banning the production of biological weapons, which was then submitted to the United Nations. In December 1971 the UN General Assembly approved a resolution supporting the convention. The key elements are

- No state shall develop, produce, stockpile, or acquire biological agents.
- Each state shall destroy existing stocks.
- No state shall transfer such agents.

The United States signed both the BWC and the Geneva Protocol in 1975. A 1986 Review Conference strengthened the procedures for consultation in case of concerns about compliance. Today some 150 states are signatories.

Point: The problem is lack of enforcement mechanisms, and it is estimated that ten to twenty-five countries now may possess or be seeking to develop biological weapons.

Since the Biological Weapons Convention was drafted in 1969, several things have changed. First the biotech revolution has made it possible for "designer" bugs to be crafted, raising the specter of a biological agent that could be impossible to combat, or one that could target a particular racial or ethnic group. Second the worldwide diffusion of technology makes the development of such agents possible for states that are unable to go the nuclear route but still feel vulnerable to attack by others.

Eliminating weapons of mass destruction, particularly chemical and biological weapons, remains a major arms control challenge. Progress has been made on regime construction through treaties and other agreements to outlaw the development, acquisition, and stockpiling of such weaponry. But implementation and enforcement is difficult, given the ease with which even nonspecialists can assemble such weaponry without detection. Governments wanting to produce and stockpile chemical and biological weapons may be identified through intelligence sources. By comparison, however, it is far easier to verify compliance or violations of nuclear nonproliferation regime rules than it is to identify chemical or biological weapons producers and stockpilers.

Ballistic Missiles

Global efforts have been undertaken to control the spread of nuclear, chemical, and biological weapons. The surest and fastest way to deliver such weapons is by **ballistic missiles**, and no similar global effort has been made to control the spread of these. Since their invention in the 1930s, guided ballistic missiles have been used in four wars: The Germans launched over 2,000 V-2 missiles in World War II; Iraq and Iran together launched over 1,000 in their 1980–88 war; the Kabul government used them against guerrillas during the Afghan civil war; and Iraq launched 80 modified Scud missiles against Israel and Saudi Arabia during the 1991 Gulf War. In all cases only conventional, high-explosive warheads were used, directed mainly against cities.

Beyond several hundred miles, however, ballistic missiles are a relatively inefficient means to deliver conventional munitions, hence the emphasis on nuclear warheads by the major nuclear powers during the cold war. For states without a nuclear capability, chemical weapons are easier to acquire or manufacture and more difficult to detect. While less deadly than nuclear weapons, they can still kill as many people as dozens of conventionally armed missiles. As the range of missiles increases, more and more countries are within an aggressor's target, a fact that feeds perceptions of international insecurity.

One attempt to deal with this development was the establishment in 1987 of the Missile Technology Control Regime (MTCR). The original seven members (the United States, Canada, France, Germany, Italy, Japan, and the United Kingdom) agreed to control the transfer of equipment and technology that could aid in the development of nuclear-capable missiles, defined as having payloads of at least 500 kilograms and a traveling distance of at least 300 kilometers. The regime has since expanded to thirty-two members, with Israel, China, and Russia committing themselves informally to follow the provisions without officially joining. Guidelines added in 1993 cover missiles capable of delivering chemical and biological weapons. Enforcement mechanisms, however, are lacking.

Conventional Weapons

The term *conventional weapons* suggests that these are of secondary concern compared to nuclear, chemical, and biological weapons. In fact conventional weapons have become ever more lethal, as was evident in the 1991 Gulf War and the bombing campaigns in Kosovo in 1999 and earlier in Bosnia and Hercegovina. Computer and guidance system advances have made it more likely that conventional warheads will be delivered with greater accuracy and thus have greater impact than in the past. It does not necessarily take professionally trained military personnel to operate some of these systems. Many surface-to-air missiles, for example, are portable, can be launched by an individual, and can bring down an airliner.

Much of the cold war was spent dealing with nuclear weapons questions that still remain on the arms control agenda. Conventional or nonnuclear armaments and military forces were also the subject of extensive negotiations during the cold war, particularly in Europe during the period of *détente* in the late 1960s and 1970s. With the end of the cold war, substantial progress has been made in regional security regime construction governing numbers, types, locations, and readiness of military forces in Europe.

Almost twenty years of mutual and balanced force reductions (MBFR) talks in Vienna between NATO and Warsaw Pact members produced very little in the way of results. By contrast, under the auspices of the Conference on Security and Cooperation in Europe (CSCE), the CSCE-wide Conference on Disarmament in Europe (CDE) in Stockholm during the mid-1980s and the Conference on Armed Forces in Europe (CFE) in Vienna during the late 1980s and early 1990s between members of the two alliances made major strides in arms control, particularly in relation to conventional forces. The CDE added to confidence- and security-building measures originally established in the 1975 Helsinki Final Act, which were enhanced still further in the early 1990s in CSCE-wide talks also in Vienna. For its part, members of the two alliances in the CFE produced an agreement specifying details of military force deployments, setting caps on numbers, types, and locations of armed forces and associated weaponry. As a result of these arms control agreements, European states were provided a militarily transparent or open environment affording increased warning time and thus reducing regional military threats substantially—an enhancement of international security through reducing the overall risk of war. Attention to armaments was coupled with political-military transparency involving the open exchange of information, on-site inspections, and other functional approaches to confidence- and security-building.

Although not yet attempted seriously outside of Europe, some arms control advocates see this European approach to regional security regime construction for conventional forces as having potential in such other troubled regions as the Middle East, the Gulf region, and both south and northeast Asia. Even though the conflicts that divide the parties cannot easily be resolved, the security of all can still be enhanced in the short run to the extent that adversary states in these regions can agree on a security regime to govern their military forces. As in Europe, such regimes could address numbers, types, locations, and readiness of forces, perhaps adding security- and confidence-building measures to the mix. Reducing the risk of war through these mechanisms—quite apart from efforts to increase trade and commerce or cultural and other exchanges—would improve the climate of relations, perhaps making conditions eventually more conducive to addressing underlying conflicts among states and societies or other actors or peoples in the region.

Arms transfers are another arms control–agenda item for the post–cold war period. Beyond immediate concerns about proliferation of nuclear weapons are concerns about

THE KALASHNIKOV AGE

*O*n Christmas Eve 1989, Charles Taylor marched into Liberia with a ragtag invasion force of some 150 amateur soldiers and set out to conquer the country. In the months that followed, Taylor seized control of the Liberian hinterland, exacting tribute from its inhabitants, recruiting additional soldiers, and killing all who stood in his way. As many as 200,000 people died in the cataclysm, and millions more were driven from their homes. Taylor had unleashed the most deadly combat system of the current epoch: the adolescent human male equipped with a Kalashnikov—an AK-47 assault rifle.

Since Taylor's invasion of Liberia, this deadly system has been employed with devastating effect in more than a dozen countries, producing a casualty rate normally associated with all-out war between modern, mechanized armies. In Algeria, Angola, Bosnia, Burundi, Cambodia, Chechnya, Colombia, Congo, Haiti, Kashmir, Mozambique, Rwanda, Sierra Leone, Somalia, Sri Lanka, Sudan, and Uganda, young men (and some women) equipped solely or primarily with AK-47s and other "light" weapons have produced tens of thousands—and sometimes hundreds of thousands—of fatalities.

Most of the casualties in these conflicts are non-combatants. Civilians constituted only five percent of the casualties in World War I, but they constitute about 90 percent of all those killed or wounded in more recent wars. Children have been particularly victimized by these conflicts: According to the UN Development Program, as many as two million children are believed to have been killed—and 4.5 million disabled—in armed conflict since 1987; another million have been orphaned, and some 12 million left homeless.

continued

IT'S BEEN SAID...

IT'S BEEN SAID...

Curbing the international production, stockpiling, and diffusion of small arms and light weapons must be a central feature of any strategy for preventing and controlling armed conflict. This does not mean cutting off the flow of arms altogether—established governments enjoy a right to self-protection under the UN Charter, and most will continue to produce or import some weapons for this purpose. But it should be possible to choke off the flow of black-market munitions to irregular forces and to restrict significantly the conditions under which governments can acquire arms through legal channels. Ultimately, it should be possible to block all but a small trickle of weapons to current and prospective belligerents in areas of persistent conflict.

Michael Klare, "The Kalashnikov Age,"
Bulletin of the Atomic Scientists
(January/February 1999), pp. 19–20.
Check out related articles at
www.bullatomsci.org.

the vast global armaments market. Both legal and illegal sales of armaments by and to states and nonstate actors continue on a truly massive scale. Critics observe that arms purchases deplete national resources that might otherwise be spent more productively on investment for economic development or other purposes. Moreover acquiring armaments beyond realistic defense needs fuels arms races that diminish (rather than enhance) the security of states and societies in a region.

Because the arms trade is a profitable business for many who engage in it, agreeing on rules to limit or constrain it has proven to be extremely difficult (see Table 7.5). Demand for weaponry continues to be very strong, and there is no shortage of suppliers willing and able to meet it. Moreover arms producing corporations and states can realize greater **economies of scale** when they have large export markets, which reduce the per-unit cost to producers of tanks, aircraft, or other expensive military hardware. In short the interests that favor a continuing and expanding global arms trade have proven far stronger politically than those arms controllers who seek construction of regimes to constrain or reduce the volume of trade and put limits on the kinds of arms that are traded globally and regionally. As indicated in Table 7.5 incentives to sell armaments are numerous; buyers are also motivated to import arms to strengthen their security, more cost effectively than if efforts were made to produce these weapons domestically.

The end of the cold war apparently has not affected the global arms market in conventional weapons. Over the last twenty years, a number of countries such as South Africa and Brazil have entered the global arms market as a way to earn revenue. As international competition has increased, there has been a remarkable globalization of the arms industry on the part of arms manufacturers. In the past arms industries were firms from different states competing against each other, often backed by their national governments. Firms would develop a complete weapons system and then attempt to sell it on the international market. This is no longer an accurate depiction of the arms market, given a series of transnational developments in recent years. Strategic alliances—loose agreements between firms to explore future collaboration or technology sharing—are one development. A number of major defense companies have taken the next step by establishing transnational joint venture companies in order to develop and build arms. Furthermore there have been a number of significant mergers and acquisitions in recent years, particularly among prime contractors in aerospace and other defense industries, resulting in greater concentration of capital in ever fewer multinational corporations.

The globalization of arms production has been encouraged by governments. In the aftermath of the cold war have come shrinking military budgets in most countries. Increased competition for sales in arms markets is responsible, at least in part, for downsizing and mergers. Many leaders believe that such transnational ties are necessary in defense-related industries to take advantage of technological

TABLE 7.5	THE POLITICAL ECONOMY OF THE GLOBAL ARMS TRADE				
	STATES AND ALLIANCES		**NONSTATE ACTORS**		
EXPECTED GAINS OR OBJECTIVES	SELLERS/ PRODUCERS	BUYERS	CORPORATIONS AND BANKS	RESEARCH GROUPS	TERRORIST REVOLUTIONARY GROUPS
Political					
Enhance security	X*	X			
Challenge governmental authority					X
Economic					
Increase revenue or profit from sales	X		X	X	
Assure return on capital (investments/ loans)	X		X		
Create jobs/reduce unemployment	X		X		
Generate new and spin-off technologies	X		X	X	
Achieve economies of large-scale production (lower unit costs of weaponry)	X	X	X		
Keep assembly lines open and running	X		X		
Secure market share	X		X		
Improve trade balance (export promotion)	X				

*The letter X denotes gains from arms trade that serve the interests of diverse actors.

developments around the world. These will help to maintain a cost-effective yet minimal research and development and production capacity to meet national defense needs. To remain insular and inward looking is to risk falling behind in important areas of research and development, yet another motivation for producing and selling arms.

MANAGING THE GLOBAL ARMS TRADE BY
CONSTRUCTING A CONVENTIONAL ARMS
CONTROL SECURITY REGIME:
THE WASSENAAR ARRANGEMENT

THE PROBLEM

Enormous amounts of money are involved in a global arms trade in which states and their respective corporations participate. The continuing demand for weapons as means to security creates substantial incentive for suppliers to the global arms market. Although export of armaments makes a contribution to defense needs of states not in a position to produce these weapons and weapons systems domestically, the magnitude of such arms transfers may have quite the opposite effect by fueling arms races, creating greater instability, and diverting national resources from investments in development or other positive purposes. We focus in this case only on trade in conventional arms—a term that includes all weapons except nuclear, biological, and chemical (NBC) arms.

THE GLOBAL ARMS MARKET: EXPORTERS AND IMPORTERS
The Supply Side

Data provided by the London-based International Institute for Strategic Studies (IISS) reveal the magnitude of the stake the world's largest arms producers and exporters have in the global arms trade market. On the supply side, just seven countries have 92 percent of global market share:

	Export Volume (US$ Billions)	Global Market Share
United States	26.514	48.6
France	9.804	17.6
United Kingdom	8.971	16.2
Russian Federation	2.854	5.1
Israel	1.252	2.2
Germany	0.834	1.5
China (PRC)	0.501	0.9

The Demand Side

Following is a summary by region indicating purchasers when known—where these armaments have been going:

	Import Volume (US$ Billions)	Global Market Share
Western Europe	18.340	32.9
Middle East & N. Africa	16.745	30.0
East Asia	13.236	23.7
Latin America	1.658	3.0
Sub-Saharan Africa	1.690	3.0
"Australasia"	1.554	2.8
South Asia	1.408	2.5
Central/Eastern Europe	0.782	1.4
Russia & Commonwealth of Independent States	0.391	0.7

Source: IISS, *Military Balance*, 1999–2000, pp. 280 and 283.

OBSTACLES TO AGREEMENTS ON REGULATING GLOBAL ARMS TRADE

As shown in Table 7.5, buyers and sellers, states and alliances, and nonstate actors all have major stakes in the global arms trade. Their expected gains and related objectives are both political and economic. Incentives to trade in arms far outnumber any disincentives.

TACKLING THE PROBLEM

Given global concerns about unregulated trade in arms and dual-use items (goods that have both military and nonmilitary applications), countries engaged in the arms production and export trade conducted negotiations beginning in 1994 in the town of Wassenaar in the Netherlands. Relatively modest in its demands, the outcome of these discussions in late 1995 and early 1996 nevertheless constituted a first step in a process—the so-called Wassenaar Arrangement, pledging thirty-three arms exporting countries to the following actions:

- Establish the Wassenaar Arrangement on Export Controls for Conventional Arms and Dual-Use Goods and Technologies
- Locate the headquarters and secretariat of the Wassenaar Arrangement in Vienna, Austria
- Meet on a regular basis in Vienna, the decisions being made by consensus
- Meet regularly to ensure responsible transfers of conventional arms and dual-use goods and technologies in furtherance of international and regional peace and security
- Promote "transparency" or openness with regular exchange of views and information on arms sales
- Achieve greater responsibility in transfers of conventional arms and dual-use goods and technologies, thus preventing destabilizing accumulations in national arsenals
- Enhance cooperation to prevent the acquisition of armaments and sensitive dual-use items for military end uses if the situation in a region or the behavior of a recipient state is or becomes a cause for serious concern
- Ensure that transfers of arms and dual-use goods and technologies do not contribute to the development or enhancement of military capabilities that undermine international and regional security and stability
- Maintain effective export controls for the items on agreed lists, which are reviewed periodically to take into account both technological developments and experience gained
- Exchange semiannual notifications of arms transfers, covering the same weapons categories used in the UN Register of Conventional Arms (battle tanks, armored combat vehicles, large caliber artillery systems, combat aircraft, attack helicopters, warships, and missiles or missile systems)
- Report arms transfers to other countries or denials of transfers to them of certain controlled dual-use items, preferably within thirty days (but no later than within sixty days) of the date of the denial
- Notify all participants, preferably within thirty days (but no later than within sixty days) of any approval by a participating state of any license to sell arms to a recipient state denied during the previous three years by another participating state

In addition to information exchange and compliance with notification obligations, parties to the Wassenaar Arrangement have been examining increased small arms trade often used in national and ethnic conflicts, illicit arms trafficking, and direct threats to commercial and other aircraft posed by the availability of man-portable air-defense systems (MANPADS), and the need for appropriate measures to prevent such weapons from falling into the wrong hands.

PARTICIPATION IN THE WASSENAAR ARRANGEMENT

The original thirty-three parties to the Wassenaar Arrangement agreed to welcome other participants, limiting Wassenaar club membership, however, to those producer-exporter states of arms or industrial equipment that (1) maintain nonproliferation policies, (2) adhere to relevant nonproliferation regimes and treaties, and (3) maintain effective export controls. The

continued

MANAGING THE GLOBAL ARMS TRADE BY CONSTRUCTING A CONVENTIONAL-ARMS CONTROL SECURITY REGIME: THE WASSENAAR ARRANGEMENT (CONTINUED)

lists of participants and nonparticipants that follow are categorized (using the same IISS data source) by annual volume of arms exports. The Wassenaar Arrangement and subsequent meetings are important first steps in tackling the conventional arms trade problem, but the Wassenaar Arrangement is limited not only by the modesty of its provisions but also by the fact that nine major or mid-level suppliers (especially China, Israel, Brazil, and North Korea) do not participate in the process at all.

Participant States in the Wassenaar Arrangement

Major Suppliers (annual arms exports US$1 billion or greater): France, Germany, Russia, United Kingdom, and United States

Mid-Level Suppliers (annual arms exports US$100 million–1 billion): Argentina, Austria, Belgium, Bulgaria, Canada, Czech Republic, Italy, Netherlands, Portugal, Spain, Sweden, Switzerland, Turkey, and Ukraine

Lower-Level Suppliers (annual arms exports under US$100 million): Australia, Denmark, Finland, Greece, Hungary, Ireland, Japan, Luxembourg, New Zealand, Norway, Poland, South Korea, Romania, Slovakia, and Turkey

Nonparticipants in the Wassenaar Arrangement

Major Suppliers (annual arms exports US$1 billion or greater): Israel and China

Mid-Level Suppliers (annual arms exports US$100 million–1 billion): Belarus, Brazil, Indonesia, North Korea, South Africa, and Yugoslavia

Lower-Level Suppliers (annual arms exports under US$100 million): Chile, Egypt, India, Iran, Jordan, Kazakstan, Kyrgyzstan, Malaysia, Mexico, Pakistan, Saudi Arabia, Singapore, Taiwan, Uzbekistan, and Zimbabwe

Point: High stakes in the global arms trade tend to make buyers and sellers reluctant to curb this market to any significant degree.

CONCLUSION

In this chapter we have examined a large number of disarmament and arms control efforts and agreements achieved during the last half of the twentieth century and continuing into the twenty-first century. The international security arms control regimes, established in the enlightened self-interest of states and supported by numerous nongovernmental organizations as well, give us institutions and rules concerning armed forces and armaments (many of which have the binding force of international law). Many arms control advocates see the task as having just begun, as they pursue a continuing, incremental effort to beat more swords into plowshares and in the process provide a greater degree of order to an otherwise anarchic world lacking central governance or authority.

KEY TERMS

disarmament   *p. 212*
arms control   *p. 213*
international security regimes   *p. 213*

military (force-employment) doctrines   *p. 224*
finite or minimum deterrence   *p. 225*

weapons proliferation   *p. 234*

OTHER CONCEPTS

confidence- and security-
   building measures
   (CSBMs)   *p. 216*
verification   *p. 222*
compliance   *p. 222*
national technical means
   (NTM) of verification
   p. 223
telemetry   *p. 223*
transparency   *p. 224*
deterrence   *p. 224*

defense   *p. 224*
warfighting   *p. 224*
extended deterrence
   p. 227
force posture   *p. 227*
countervalue targets   *p. 227*
counterforce targets   *p. 227*
collateral damage (death
   and destruction)   *p. 228*
second-strike capability
   p. 229

mutually assured destruction
   (MAD)   *p. 230*
first-strike capability   *p. 232*
Nuclear Non-Proliferation
   Treaty (NPT)   *p. 235*
International Atomic
   Energy Agency (IAEA)
   p. 236
ballistic missiles   *p. 240*
arms transfers   *p. 241*
economies of scale   *p. 242*

ADDITIONAL READINGS

A number of resources are available on the topics covered in this chapter. For annotated texts of arms control treaties and agreements, see Paul R. Viotti, *U.S. Foreign and National Security Policy* (Upper Saddle River, N.J.: Prentice-Hall, 2001, forthcoming); on other disarmament and arms control matters, see Stockholm International Peace Research Institute, *SIPRI Yearbook: World Armaments and Disarmament* (annual); U.S. Arms Control and Disarmament Agency, *World Military Expenditures and Arms Transfers* (annual); International Institute for Strategic Studies, *Military Balance* (annual); Arms Control Association, *Arms Control Today* (monthly journal); Institute for Defense and Disarmament Studies, *Arms Control Reporter*. This latter publication continually updates information on arms control negotiations, treaties, and regimes. See also Donald Kerr, *World Directory of Defense and Security* (Stockton Press); and Nicholas Rengger, ed., *Treaties and Alliances of the World*, latest ed. (Stockton Press). For reviews of arms control issues on the global agenda, see Jeffrey A. Larsen and Gregory J. Rattray (eds.), *Arms Control Toward the 21st Century* (Boulder, Colo.: Lynne Rienner Publishers, 1996); Barry Buzan and Eric Herring, *The Arms Dynamic in World Politics* (Boulder, Colo.: Lynne Rienner Publishers, 1998); and Andrew J. Pierre, ed., *Cascade of Arms: Managing Conventional Weapons Proliferation* (Washington, D.C.: Brookings Institution, 1998). We also recommend the monthly *Bulletin of the Atomic Scientists*.

   For a highly readable debate on nuclear proliferation, see Scott Sagan and Kenneth Waltz, *The Spread of Nuclear Weapons* (New York: W.W. Norton, 1995). Classics on the subject include Hedley Bull, *The Control of the Arms Race* (New York: Frederick A. Praeger, 1961, 1965); Thomas C. Schelling and Morton H. Halperin, *Strategy and Arms Control* (New York: The Twentieth Century Fund, 1961); as well as Schelling's *The Strategy of Conflict* (New York: Oxford University Press, 1963) and *Arms and Influence* (New Haven: Yale University Press, 1966); and Anatol Rapoport, *Strategy and Conscience* (New York: Schocken Books, 1964) and his later *The Origins of Violence* (New Brunswick, N.J.: Transaction Publishers, 1995).

INTERNATIONAL TERRORISM AND TRANSNATIONAL CRIME

*"We have gone around lost for a long time
but it will not be forever. . . .
The rich will come face to face with the poor
and between all the poor
we will bring you to bay
as if you were the thieving fox;
wait, just wait, you who starve my people to death.
I will kill you.[1]"*

**SONG POPULAR WITH THE REVOLUTIONARY SONS AND
DAUGHTERS OF PEASANTS IN PERU**

*"Today, American diplomats, law enforcement
officials, military personnel and others are called upon to
respond to assorted transnational threats that have
moved to center stage with the Cold War's end.
Combating these dangers—which range from terrorism,
international crime, and trafficking in drugs and illegal
arms, to environmental damage and intrusions in our
critical information infrastructures—requires
far–reaching cooperation."*

WHITE HOUSE COMMISSION (1997)

t the end of the path I noticed three young men engaged in what appeared to be idle conversation. I thought they were students waiting for the early morning classes to begin, and I greeted them cheerfully. Just as I was passing them, one of them called out my name.

"Mr. Cicippio!"

"I turned and they reached out for me. My heart hammering in my throat, I struggled to free myself. Then the butt of a pistol slammed into the back of my head, and the world came crashing in on me.

"I slumped forward onto my hands and knees, my vision a blur. I was able to make out my eyeglasses, lying smashed on the pavement and surrounded by drops of blood. When I reached out for them, one of the men kicked them away. A terrorist said, 'Don't raise your

[1]Simon Strong, *Shining Path: Terror and Revolution in Peru* (New York: Random House, 1992), p. 50.

head or I'll blow it off.' They picked me up and carried me, face down, into a university building and out the other side to an adjacent parking lot.

"They threw me into the rear of a small foreign automobile. A foot pressed down on my neck, pinning my head to the floor of the car. At that point, the events of my entire life passed before me.

"After a while we came to what appeared to be some sort of garage. It was damp and dark and smelled hellishly of car fumes. That place was where I would begin more than five years of cruel confinement, where the tortures of beating and hunger were secondary to those of loneliness, rage and bewilderment. Maddening boredom alternated with stark terror. I would be totally cut off from loved ones, never see the sun or stars, never read a newspaper or receive a letter."[2]

Joseph Cicippio, comptroller of the American University of Beirut,
taken hostage in Beirut, Lebanon April 12, 1986,
released December 2, 1991

Security matters are not just confined to states acting alone, in alliance with each other, or in adversarial relations with other states. Terrorism and crime are examples of security issues that cross national borders. In an increasingly globalized, interdependent world, states realize that such threats weaken their authority and also undermine the expansion of a global civil society. Hence such threats are best dealt with on a cooperative, multilateral basis. International conventions and organizations also have important roles to play in addressing these *international* security concerns.

TERRORISM

Throughout history ***terrorism*** has been one of the starkest expressions of rejection of authority. Terrorism, as politically motivated violence, aims at achieving a demoralizing effect on publics and governments. The very act of attacking innocents raises the shock value and sends a message that the government is unable to protect its own citizens. The concern is that over time terrorism eats away at the social-political fabric of many states, undermines democracy, provides a rationale for a government to delay democratic reforms, and can increase tension among

terrorism Politically motivated violence directed against noncombatants and designed to instill fear in a target audience.

[2]Joseph Cicippio and Richard W. Hope, *Chains to Roses* (Waco, Texas: WRS Publishing, 1993), pp. 8–9, 10.

states. The result is often the impression that the world is in a state of chaos and international order and authority are collapsing. It is understandable why terrorism is considered a major challenge to international security.

Terrorism is usually viewed as a weapon of the weak, so it is associated with such nonstate actors as clandestine terrorist groups and insurgencies. But our definition of terrorism is neutral and can be applied to any number of organizations. Terrorism has been used, for example, by drug traffickers in Colombia against government officials and has also been used by criminal organizations in Italy to intimidate judges. Furthermore terrorism can and has been a tool of statecraft. Indeed, down through the centuries, states have certainly terrorized many more people than have terrorist groups or insurgencies. In the 1970s and early 1980s, for example, a number of military regimes in Latin America utilized security forces to kidnap and murder systematically thousands of actual or suspected political dissidents in the name of "national security."

The focus in this chapter, however, is principally on nonstate actors who utilize violence to achieve political objectives; drug traffickers are discussed later in this chapter and the use of terrorism in the massive abuse of human rights on the part of state agents later in the book. In this chapter we also address state-sponsored terrorism that transcends state borders and is used against innocent foreign—as opposed to domestic—nationals.

Terrorism is certainly not new. In fact it is deeply embedded in history. The Zealots, for example, were a Jewish sect that appeared in A.D. 6 and assassinated local government officials in an attempt to ignite uprisings and drive the Romans out of Palestine. The effort failed and some 2,000 Zealots were crucified. Later turning to guerrilla warfare, they were finally crushed when their last mountain stronghold, Masada, was surrounded and 960 men, women, and children committed mass suicide. The Middle East also spawned the Assassins (A.D. 1090–1275), Muslims who killed the political rivals of the potentate for whom they worked. Historically the vast majority of terrorism in traditional societies was religiously inspired; indeed, terrorists often claimed they were carrying out the will of God. These historical examples are a good reminder that religiously inspired terrorism—a major contemporary concern—is certainly not new.

It was the French Revolution of 1789, however, that popularized the term *terrorism*. During this period terrorism was associated with the state. As dramatically depicted in Charles Dickens's *A Tale of Two Cities*, the guillotine was used to behead publicly those who were declared enemies of the state.

The nineteenth century witnessed the rise of secular (i.e., nonreligious) terrorism on the part of groups that were opposed to particular governments. During the 1800s, both the creative and destructive effects of the scientific and industrial revolutions became obvious in Europe and North America. Great wealth was created but also great poverty. The modern city was born; rural ways of life were changed forever. As humanity grew more confident in its ability to master nature, so too did it gain confidence in its ability to design and create the perfect society. For Karl Marx (1820–72) and other communists, such faith was evident in their vision of the ultimate victory of the downtrodden classes and the creation of a workers' paradise.

Other leftists, however, were impatient with the slow unfolding of history and wished to hasten the revolutionary process. Collectively known as *anarchists*, they pulled off a number of terrorist spectaculars. In the 1890s alone, victims included the presidents of France and Italy, the kings of Portugal and Italy, the prime minister of Spain, and the empress of Austria. Anarchists also attempted to assassinate

anarchists Individuals who advocate entirely voluntary human associations or communities, reject authority in general, and may or may not utilize violence against governments or their officials.

MIKHAIL BAKUNIN

Mikhail Bakunin was a nineteenth-century Russian anarchist. He is credited as the coauthor of the Revolutionary Catechism of 1869. Contemptuous of both Marxists and Liberals, he had great revolutionary hopes for members of the criminal groups, which he described in Robin Hoodish terms. For Bakunin a successful revolution required an alliance between the peasants and robbers. In his Principles of Revolution he wrote, "We recognize no other action save destruction though we admit that the forms in which such action will show itself will be exceedingly varied—poison, the knife, the rope, etc." Bakunin's coauthor of the Revolutionary Catechism was S.J. Nechaev. A former factory worker and student at St. Petersburg University, he wrote in the pamphlet's opening passage:

> The revolutionary is a lone man; he has no interests of his own, no cause of his own, no feelings, no habits, no belonging; he does not even have a name. Everything in him is absorbed by a single, exclusive interest, a single thought, a single passion—the revolution. . . . We are guided by hatred for all who are not the people. . . . We have an entirely negative plan, which no one can modify—utter destruction.

IT'S BEEN SAID...

the German kaiser and chancellor. What distinguished them from modern-day terrorists, however, is that their victims were almost always government officials, not innocent civilians. The Russian anarchist group known as the People's Will, for example, did not place bombs on railway platforms, kidnap schoolchildren, or shoot people in the knee to cripple them for life.

With the collapse of the major continental monarchies in Russia, Germany, and the Austro-Hungarian empire following World War I (1914–18), factional, ethnic violence and terrorism came to the fore. Under the banner of national self-determination, terrorist violence was particularly pronounced in Eastern and Central Europe. A somewhat similar process began to unfold in the so-called "developing world" during and especially after World War II. Having fought Nazi Germany, fascist Italy, and Japan in defense of freedom, Western leaders found it difficult to answer nationalist leaders in the colonial world who asked why their countries should not also be free from outside control. European reluctance to end colonial rule led nationalist movements, often with a terrorist wing, to fight British, French, and Portuguese domination. By the 1960s European colonial rule was effectively ended in most areas of the globe.

The cold war between the United States and the Soviet Union and their respective allies and supporters, however, lent an ideological cast to much of the terrorism from the late 1940s to late 1980s. Despite the fact that Karl Marx himself believed terrorism to be self-defeating, Marxist-Leninist teachings on revolution helped to inspire and justify revolutionary movements throughout the world and justify, to themselves at least, their use of terrorism. These movements included the Red Army Faction in Germany, Red Brigades in Italy, 17 November in Greece, Revolutionary Armed Forces of Colombia, Shining Path of Peru, Japanese Red Army, and New People's Army of the Philippines.

Particularly in Europe, terrorism became the basic *strategy* of the organization, meaning it was the defining signature of the group. In the Third World, however, terrorism was generally a *tactic* on the part of an insurgent organization, meaning it was simply one aspect of a larger revolutionary strategy that included paramilitary attacks on government forces, the liberation of territory, and the extensive use of propaganda.

Throughout the cold war insurgent organizations often combined Marxism-Leninism with old-fashioned nationalist appeals. Indeed, all successful revolutions, including Lenin's in Russia and Mao's in China, have relied extensively on such appeals. With the end of the cold war, however, most Russians acknowledged that their Marxist-Leninist vision for society was bankrupt. Furthermore, despite its socialist pronouncements, China experienced an economic boom as the state encouraged the development of a free market. These policies on the part of the two states most closely associated with Marxist-Leninist ideas on international revolution caused a predictable crisis of confidence for revolutionary movements around the world. Some simply condemned Russia and China for backsliding (Shining Path), while others experienced bitter internal divisions that weakened them (New People's Army). Now lacking a transnational ideological justification for their violent campaigns, other groups such as the Kurdistan Workers Party (PKK) shifted their emphasis away from Marxist ideology to more nationalist appeals.

Nationalism has always provided the dynamism of the various Palestinian organizations associated with terrorism. Despite couching their agenda in Islamic terms, organizations such as Hizballah (Party of God) in Lebanon, Hamas in the West Bank of Israel, and the Jihad group in Egypt are also fueled by nationalist sentiment. The expression of this sentiment is evident in their belief that other Western values have a corrupting influence on Islamic cultures, requiring an Islamic initiative or even revolution to rectify this situation. Indigenous political leaders in such countries as Egypt and Saudi Arabia are seen as having sold out to the West. Israel, despite its historical association with the region, is viewed as an outpost of Western interests and values. For some observers in the West, the ideological clash of democracy and communism during the cold war may be replaced by the clash of eastern and western civilizations.

Terrorism conducted within a particular state by and against the citizens of the same country can be termed *domestic terrorism*. Of greater interest to us, given our focus on world politics, is **international terrorism**. International terrorism is defined as terrorism involving the citizens or territory of more than one country. An example might help to clarify the difference. If the Jihad group (consisting of Egyptian citizens) bombs an Egyptian government building in Cairo, it is an act of domestic terrorism. If, however, the same group attacks foreign tourists visiting Egypt, it is an act of international terrorism. Similarly if the Jihad group went to Tunisia and killed an Egyptian diplomat, this would also be an act of international terrorism. Airline hijackings are perhaps the exemplar of international terrorism as the airplane invariably has passengers from a number of countries.

The United States became particularly concerned with international terrorism in the 1980s. As one of two superpowers with a military presence in many countries of the world and economic interests in virtually every country, it is not surprising that the United States has been blamed, rightly or wrongly, for all sorts of problems and has been viewed as an agent of military, economic, and cultural imperialism.

It has been in the Middle East that the United States has come face to face with international terrorism. Over the course of one year (1983) in Lebanon alone, 241 Marines were killed in the bombing of their barracks; the U.S. embassy was destroyed by a suicide truck bomb, costing seventeen lives; and U.S. citizens were repeatedly taken hostage by Hizballah. In 1985 there were several terrorist spectaculars, including the June hijacking of TWA flight 847 by Islamic extremists, which lasted seventeen days; the takeover of the *Achille Lauro* cruise ship by Palestinians in October, which resulted in the murder of a wheel chair-bound American tourist; and the December 27 attacks in the Rome and Vienna airports by the Abu Nidal Organization, which left eighteen dead and 114 wounded.

In December 1988 a bomb placed aboard Pan Am Flight 103 exploded over Lockerbie, Scotland, resulting in the death of 259 passengers and members of the crew. Conducted apparently by Libyan intelligence agents, this act of state-sponsored international terrorism, more than any other single terrorist incident, galvanized cooperation among Western governments. The bombing of the World Trade Center in New York City in February 1993, the nerve gas attack on Tokyo's subway in March 1995, and the bombings directed

international terrorism
Terrorist acts of violence that involve the citizens or territory of more than one country.

against the U.S. embassies in Kenya and Tanzania in August 1998 are more recent spectacular acts of international terrorism. In the remainder of this section we will examine the nature and extent of international terrorism and discuss the efforts of the United States and the international community to deal with it.

Causes of Terrorism

A great deal has been written on the causes of terrorism. But, as is often the case with human behavior, no single factor can be identified as the root cause. It is possible, however, to break down the major categories as follows:

Psychological Factors   Some analysts—not surprisingly they tend to be trained psychologists or psychiatrists—view some individuals who engage in terrorism as mentally disturbed. While the mental disorder perspective includes explanations rooted in such physiological factors as chemical imbalances in the brain, the main focus of attention is on the early childhood experiences of terrorists. Analysis of European terrorists points to such factors as abusive or unemotional parents, suggesting that terrorists are rebelling, perhaps, against parental authority figures as personified in their minds by the state.

While undoubtedly some terrorists exhibit pathological behavior, to dismiss all terrorists as mentally ill is simply wrong. In fact one thing most terrorists have in common is their normality. A young person with few life prospects may choose to join a terrorist organization for the expected thrill of life in the underground, or as a way to enhance his self-esteem by becoming a "defender of the community," or even simply as a way to earn money. Such prosaic possibilities have little to do with mental illness, and such psychological explanations often have the effect of downplaying terrorism's political component. As one former member of the Provisional Irish Republican Army stated, "The IRA gave these young men a sense of belonging, a status in their community, and a purpose, a cause to believe in and to fight and die for. These were young men without much hope of employment who had seen their communities devastated in sectarian attacks. Now that they were hitting back, their pride and dignity were restored."

Ideological Factors   Ideological explanations emphasize the power of ideas. Historically Marxism-Leninism has proven to be powerfully attractive to individuals who seek a framework that enables them to understand not only why injustices exist in a society but also how to end them. Terrorists, therefore, are "true believers," possessed by an idea that a better society can be created if only certain obstacles or threats can be eliminated. For Marxist-Leninists, this threat is the upper classes and bourgeoisie; for fascists it is often minority groups or foreign immigrants; for nationalists it is often colonialists; for religious extremists it is not simply foreigners but rather the values they represent that threaten the indigenous culture.

Environmental Factors   Explanations that examine *where* terrorism arises generally fall into one of two related categories: grievances and cultures of violence. Environmental grievances that affect a community can be social, political, or economic in nature. *Community* can be broadly defined, referring to either a particular economic class such as exploited peasants, or perhaps ethnic groups that have experienced political and economic discrimination over the years.

The Muslims of Lebanon, for example, particularly the Shia, have historically suffered from discrimination at the hands of the Christian Lebanese. Not only have the Shia been at the bottom of the economic ladder, but they have also been politically underrepresented in the government and parliament. Such grievances often fester for a long period of time and then erupt in bloody violence, as they did in Lebanon in 1976. In this particular case the Shia were energized by other factors such as the growing power of the Palestinians, particularly in southern Lebanon. Expelled from Jordan in 1970, many Palestinians fled to Lebanon, where they initially received a warm welcome. But as the Palestinians settled in, many Shia grew resentful when they also suffered from Israeli military reprisals directed against the Palestinians who were using southern Lebanon as a base of operations against Israel.

The second environmental source of terrorism can be termed **cultures of violence**. This does not refer to cultures that are somehow innately violent. Rather it refers to societies that have experienced high levels of communal violence over a number of years so that violence, not peace, becomes the norm. For young people growing up in Northern Ireland from the 1970s to the early 1990s, communal warfare and the presence of British troops and security forces on the streets were part of their everyday existence. Violence, not peace, was the *status quo*. Lebanon from the late 1970s through the 1980s represents a similar case. As communal violence continues, people may forget the original reason for conflict, and instead hatred becomes habitual and violence is a function of revenge.

The search for a single factor to explain terrorism is self-defeating. As with all human behavior, multiple factors come into play. To explain why any single individual turned to terrorism, one would have to consider the relative importance of psychological, ideological, and environmental factors. To assume that all terrorists are ideologically driven zealots is as much an over-generalization as it is to assume they are all mentally ill.

Furthermore, as time goes by, the continuation of a terrorist campaign has perhaps as much to do with maintaining the existence of the organization as it has to do with achieving the originally stated political objective. There is no reason to believe that terrorist organizations are any different from any other organization—the primary goal is organizational survival. For some individuals terrorism undoubtedly becomes a way of life. It is probable that the longer one is with the organization, the more important this factor becomes. Conversely it is likely that the most altruistic and ideologically driven members of the group are the newest recruits.

ASTRID PROLL

At age twenty-one Astrid Proll was one of the founders of the Red Army Faction in Germany in 1968. She protested against the Vietnam War, nuclear weapons, and the presence of U.S. troops in Germany and was an active participant in the Berlin subculture of the 1960s. She describes the founding of the RAF in the following manner:

It had a lot to do with the postwar conditions in Germany. We, the young generation, decided that we would never participate or keep quiet about something that was bad in society, as our parents had done. We hated our parents because they were former Nazis, who had never come clean about their past.

The Nazism had never been acknowledged; there had been no time to mourn. In the fifties there was the cold war; in the sixties, the cultural upheaval. We grew up with the American culture and their army sitting here, as the occupiers. It began with student protests. At the time we felt that the state was the oppressor, and that we had the right to use violence because we were the state's victims. But of course they managed to turn it around, so that we became the guilty ones and society the victims.

After the war, a lot of Nazis went straight into business again. They were everywhere—every second person was a Nazi, and they held powerful jobs in business and in the judiciary; the Nazis just continued their careers. At the height of the RAF, there were, I suppose, twenty or thirty activists, and there was a lot of sympathy for us because everyone knew someone who was either involved or supported people who did. It was something that everyone felt they had a responsibility to resolve.

Source: **Eileen MacDonald,** *Shoot the Women First* **(New York: Random House, 1991), pp. 209–10.**

IT'S BEEN SAID...

cultures of violence When violence becomes commonplace, it may acquire an acceptance or even legitimacy in a community or society.

Members of the Red Cross and Kenyan military remove a body from the collapsed building next to the U.S. embassy in Nairobi on August 11, 1998.

Extent of Terrorism

How much international terrorism has actually been conducted in the past two decades? How many persons have been injured? Should international terrorism be viewed as a threat to national and international security? How has terrorism changed over the years? We examine these questions by distinguishing between conventional terrorism and terrorism involving weapons of mass destruction.

Conventional Terrorism   We begin with conventional terrorism for the simple reason that except for the Aum Shinrikyo sarin gas attack in March 1995, all international terrorism in recent years has been of the conventional sort. What this means simply is that terrorists have essentially restricted their *modus operandi* to bombings, firebombings, arson, armed attacks, kidnappings, and vandalism. In fact the first three categories account for over 70 percent of all terrorist incidents from 1986 to 1998—bombings of various sorts are the preferred terrorist method of attack. The number of international incidents has fluctuated over time, but within a fairly narrow range (see Figure 8.1). Given the fact that these statistics cover the entire world, most people would probably be surprised at the low number. In fact the number of international incidents at the end of the 1990s was the lowest since 1971. So we seem to be faced with a paradox—just as the number of terrorist incidents drops to historical lows, terrorism has become a major international security concern.

Such statistics, however, obscure as much as they reveal. For example, the bombing of Pan Am Flight 103 in 1988, which killed 270 people, counts as a single incident, as does a Molotov cocktail tossed over the wall of the U.S. embassy in Bogota, Colombia, that same year. Similarly the 247 dead in the Nairobi bombing in August 1998 will statistically be treated the same as one of the periodic bombings of the Cano Limon-Covenas oil pipeline in Colombia in which no one is injured. In any given year, therefore, such statistics may underplay or overstate the political significance of a terrorist attack. It would perhaps be more

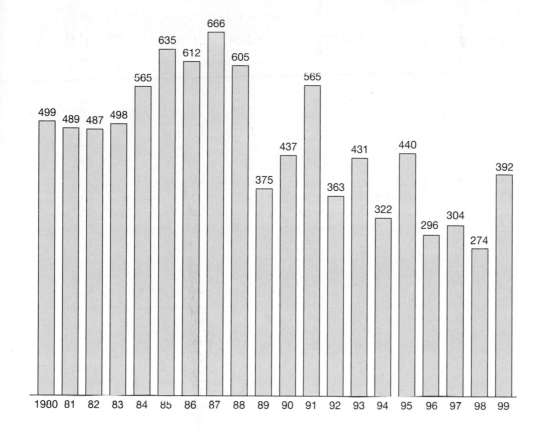

FIGURE 8.1   INTERNATIONAL* TERRORIST INCIDENTS
OVER TIME, 1980–99

*"International" refers to terrorism involving citizens or the territories of more than one country.
Source: U.S. Department of State, *Patterns of Global Terrorism 1999* (Washington, D.C., April 2000),
available at www.state.gov/www/global/terrorism/index

useful to examine the number of casualties resulting from acts of international terrorism over time (see Table 8.1). Again the numbers are hardly overwhelming.

What about terrorism conducted in the United States, domestic as well as international? With all the concerns over militias and millennialist cults, is this perhaps why terrorism has become such an important national security topic? Once again the figures are not particularly shocking. According to the FBI, total terrorist incidents per year from 1992 to 1998 totalled 3, 4, 0, 1, 3, 2, and 5.[3] There seems, therefore, to be a clear disjuncture between the actual amount of terrorism and the resultant government obsession with it.

To push the argument a bit further, what if two key incidents had not even occurred—Oklahoma City and Khobar Towers? There is no doubt that the bombing of the Alfred P. Murrah building in April of 1995 was the key catalyst for a dramatic intensification of U.S. government efforts to create and expand domestic programs to combat terrorism. The response involved more than an increase in the number of FBI analysts and agents devoted to counterterrorism. In Washington it was

---

[3]Federal Bureau of Investigation, *Terrorism in the United States 1998* (Washington, D.C., 1999).

TABLE 8.1	CASUALTIES CAUSED BY INTERNATIONAL INCIDENTS, BY REGION						

	NUMBER OF CASUALTIES						
REGION	1993	1994	1995	1996	1997	1998	1999
Africa	7	55	8	80	28	5,379	185
Asia	135	71	5,639	1,507	344	635	690
Eurasia	1	151	29	20	27	12	8
Europe	117	126	287	503	17	405	16
Latin America	66	329	48	18	11	195	9
Middle East	178	259	445	1,097	480	68	31
North America	1,006*	0	0	0	7	0	0

*High number is due to World Trade Center bombing.

Source: U.S. Department of State, *Patterns of Global Terrorism 1999* (Washington, D.C., April 2000), available at www.state.gov/www/global/terrorism/index.

recognized that "first responders" to a terrorist incident would not be federal or military forces, but rather local fire, police, and emergency medical personnel. Hence national security planning now involves local and state authorities to a degree never before experienced, a reality recognized in the Pentagon's Domestic Preparedness Program. U.S. counterterrorism policy, therefore, has had to move beyond deterrence, prevention, and punishment to include what is euphemistically termed *consequence management*. Similarly it is impossible to overestimate the impact on the U.S. federal government of the bombing of Khobar Towers in Saudi Arabia in June 1996. The Department of Defense in particular was moved to action by that incident. Since that time millions of dollars and countless hours have been devoted to improving *force protection*, a key Pentagon concept in its efforts to combat terrorism.

What, however, would U.S. national efforts look like today if a single individual, Timothy McVeigh, had decided not to strike out against the federal government a year after the bloody confrontation with the Branch Davidian religious cult in Waco, Texas? What if the shadowy Saudi Hizballah, suspected of conducting the Khobar Towers bombing, had failed in its mission? Would the United States be spending millions of dollars now and in the future to counter terrorism if these two incidents had not occurred? The political landscape could look very different.

Weapons of Mass Destruction Terrorism   One reason terrorism is proclaimed a top international security concern is that in recent years it has been coupled with another international security priority—the proliferation of weapons of mass destruction (WMD). Newspaper reports and Hollywood movies have highlighted the dangers posed by "nuclear leakage" from the former Soviet Union and fears as to where such material and scientific expertise may end up. It is bad enough if material falls into the hands of renegade states, but worse if terrorists get their hands on it. States have to fear retaliation should they employ such weapons. A small band of terrorists, however, might feel much more confident that they would be difficult to locate.

Raising the specter of terrorist use of nuclear weapons dates from the 1970s. Looking back, such studies are oddly reassuring. Utilizing the rational actor model associated with realist thinkers, it was assumed by analysts that terrorists recognized that the employment of such weapons was counterproductive in achieving political objectives and gaining public support for one's cause. As noted by Brian Jenkins, "terrorists want a lot of people watching, not a lot of people dead."[4] Such reasoning can be extended to the use of chemical and biological weapons.

Is this logic still applicable at the beginning of the millennium? Some commentators argue that self-sanctions against the use of weapons of mass destruction may have eroded over the years. It is necessary, however, to distinguish among different types of terrorist groups. With some degree of confidence, we can state it is unlikely such weapons will be utilized if we are talking about secular terrorist organizations with a political agenda that requires public support in order to succeed. Note the three critical adjectives—secular, political, and public. Nationalist-separatist movements, for example, often have political as well as clandestine terrorist wings. The terrorist wing may indeed be more likely to consider utilizing WMD for a number of reasons—violent-prone individuals are by definition drawn to operational cells; if cut off from broader society, internal dynamics tend to move a group toward extreme actions.[5]

The political wings of nationalist-separatist movements, however, also by definition have to take into account a number of factors. First there is the attitude of the core constituency they claim to represent. As horrible as the effects of bombings may be, crossing the nuclear, chemical, or biological threshold has emotional and psychological effects that go beyond the resultant physical devastation. Death by biological agents is simply viewed differently from death by conventional explosives. Second political leaders have to take into account the possibility of retribution against their own community. Third the employment of weapons of mass destruction would undoubtedly forsake any international sympathy and support for one's cause.

The limitations in such lines of argument stem from the fact that the universe of terrorist organizations has been restricted to *secular* groups with a *political* agenda requiring *public* support. What about religious groups? Islamic extremist organizations that engage in suicide bombings come to mind. It is often suggested that religious extremists differ from secular organizations in that the audience they are trying to impress is God, as opposed to a segment of the public. Hence religious convictions supposedly make it easier to engage in actions causing large numbers of deaths when the act is done in the name of God and supposedly with His blessing.

TERRORISM AS A THREAT

Some observers argue that international terrorism is overrated as a threat to national and international security. Others claim policy makers actually exacerbate the problem by giving it a high priority through public pronouncements, but then find that they are unable to fulfill their promises to prevent terrorist acts. As a result public anxiety increases and terrorists are further emboldened. When presidents and prime ministers appear on television to condemn terrorists' actions, they actually deliver what the terrorists want—publicity for their cause. Furthermore for an administration to become obsessed with hostages—as occurred from 1979–81 when Iran held U.S. diplomats—pushes into the background other national security concerns that are more deserving of policy-makers' attention. Terrorism, in other words, has to be placed in the larger context of national security.

As Jeffrey Simon has argued:

Terrorists have been quite successful in generating overreactions by U.S. presidents, the public, and the media during various terrorist attacks. The United States is today in a perpetual pre-crisis mode of thinking and acting about terrorism. The right incident—a hijacking, a major bombing, a hostage-barricade situation—at any time will touch off alarm bells throughout the country. The pattern has been repeated enough times in our recent past to be predictable.

Source: Jeffrey Simon, *The Terrorist Trap: America's Experience with Terrorism* (Bloomington: University of Indiana Press, 1994), p. 379.

IT'S BEEN SAID...

---

[4]Brian Jenkins, *The Potential for Nuclear Terrorism* (Santa Monica, Calif.: RAND, 1977), p. 8.
[5]See David C. Rapoport, ed., *Inside Terrorist Organizations* (New York: Columbia University Press, 1988); and Walter Reich, ed., *Origins of Terrorism* (New York: Cambridge University Press, 1990).

CHEMICAL AND BIOLOGICAL TERRORISM

The nerve-gas attack on the Tokyo subway by the Japanese Aum Shinrikyo cult in March 1995 led U.S. officials to overestimate the threat of mass-casualty attacks involving chemical or biological agents. In the United States, a mass-casualty attack with a chemical weapon has never occurred, and only one successful incident of biological terrorism has been reported. In 1984, members of the Oregon-based Rajneeshee cult deliberately contaminated restaurant salad bars in the town of The Dalles with salmonella bacteria, affecting 751 people temporarily with a diarrheal illness. Their objective was not to kill people but rather to sicken voters and keep them home so as to throw the outcome of a local election in the cult's favor.

U.S. policy makers and several outside analysts have predicted catastrophic consequences if a terrorist group or an individual—alone or with state sponsorship—ever mounts a major chemical or biological attack. These alarmist scenarios have been

IT'S BEEN SAID...

Such logic is not incorrect but simply incomplete. In fact religious groups have secular as well as sacred motivations. Hizballah, for example, is best known for its terrorist operations. Yet it also is represented in the Lebanese parliament and wants to be viewed as a legitimate political player. Such ambitions undoubtedly influence the group's approach to terrorism.

The religious groups most likely to utilize weapons of mass destruction, therefore, are probably not those associated with one of the world's great religions, but rather those that can be characterized as cults. In cults the focus of group loyalty and devotion is not so much to religious precepts as expounded by prophets who have long since departed this earth. Rather devotion is to a "living god" who issues edicts designed to enforce discipline and complete loyalty among followers. In other words the leader—not the message—is the focus of loyalty. When coupled with physical isolation and a view that outside society is corrupt and sinful, a cult can go one of two ways. Either it can withdraw into itself and avoid contact with the sinful outside world, or it can work to destroy and transform it. It is when a transformative agenda is coupled with the capability to produce weapons of mass destruction that a threat arises. Still the term *weapons of mass destruction* is more appropriately reserved for potential future events. Even including the Tokyo subway sarin gas attack, the record to date leads some analysts to speak more accurately of "weapons of mass disruption."

Perhaps the best argument for taking terrorism seriously as a threat to international security lies less in the historical record and more as a hedge against disturbing developing trends. We may well look back at the 1960s and 1970s with a certain degree of nostalgia. Groups that engaged in terrorism had stated political objectives that, however much one might disagree with them, were still fathomable. They developed a particular *modus operandi* and generally stayed with it. State sponsors were consistently the same nefarious lot. Analysts were perhaps no better than today in providing warning of impending terrorist acts, but at least there was a certain degree of confidence as to the limits to which groups would go to achieve their stated objectives.

Changing Nature of Terrorism

Today's terrorism is a multifaceted phenomenon consisting of a diverse array of actors, motivations, and tactics that evolves over time. Such a phenomenon requires equal ingenuity and flexibility on the part of those who study it or—as intelligence analysts, operators, and policy makers—deal directly with it. What is different today has been an evolution in the *who*, *why*, and *how* of terrorism. Each will be briefly discussed in turn.

Who Are Terrorists?   Examine any anthology on terrorism and you are bound to find discussion centered around the group as the unit of analysis. The subsequent classification scheme is invariably based on the group's essential goals or ideology—Marxist-Leninist, nationalist-separatist, fascist, religious. Typically terrorists utilize such nouns as "army," brigade," or "command" in the name of their organization in order to enhance the legitimacy of their cause by suggesting they view themselves as soldiers. Aside from anarchist organizations whose small numbers preclude a true division of labor, many larger terrorist groups indeed organize themselves along paramilitary lines and hence lend themselves to classic line-and-block organizational diagrams.

In the 1990s, however, a new category of analysis has been added. Referred to as *ad hoc* terrorists or "transient groupings," such entities consist of individuals who come together to plan and carry out a specific operation. The prime example involves Ramzi Yousef, mastermind of the 1993 World Trade Center bombing. Yousef entered the United States with a colleague and established contact with a diverse group of individuals. Prior to Yousef's arrival they could not be associated with a particular group. What they had in common was an association with a storefront mosque headed by Sheikh Abdel Rahman in Jersey City, New Jersey. Yousef acted as a catalyst, recruiting a sufficient number of individuals to carry out the World Trade Center bombing. He followed a similar *modus operandi* in the Philippines in late 1994, recruiting Islamic extremists for an ambitious plot to bomb a dozen aircraft and assassinate the pope on his visit to Manila. The point is that there was no "Ramzi Yousef Group" with a dedicated cadre of supporters, nor any official emblem, Web site, or published propaganda tracts.

A related phenomenon concerns what could be termed the *privatization* of terrorism. The exemplar is Usama bin Laden, much in the news following the bombings of the U.S. embassies in Africa. It is unclear if the bin Laden terrorist organization *per se* carries out all the terrorist activities attributed to the group. Bin Laden, the exiled son of a wealthy Saudi businessman, is also charged with helping to finance attacks against U.S. interests. In other words he facilitates, instigates, and inspires terrorist attacks. Perhaps the best way to think of him is as the private sector equivalent of a state sponsor of terrorism. Aside from published reports that Yousef stayed in one of bin Laden's safe houses, what the two have in common is both fought against the Soviets in Afghanistan and share a hatred of the United States.

It is unclear how many other Ramzi Yousefs are out and about plotting terrorist attacks. Perhaps he and bin Laden are anomalies as opposed to an emerging trend. What is apparent, however, is that it is becoming increasingly difficult to determine who is behind many terrorist attacks. If claims of responsibility are made, it is generally by a previously unknown group. It is possible that established groups carry out some of these attacks but are fearful of retaliation and hence prefer to remain silent. It is also possible, however, that we will witness more attacks by *ad hoc* groupings that have received encouragement if not financial and logistical support from individuals such as Usama bin Laden or states wishing to plead plausible deniability—not revealing their role in or knowledge of these activities.

Such a phenomenon obviously represents an extremely difficult intelligence target. It is one thing to collect against an established group organization—a group profile can be established and patterns of behavior or *modus operandi* can be

> based on the potential vulnerability of U.S. urban centers to chemical or biological attack and the growing availability of relevant technology and materials. But these scenarios have not drawn on a careful assessment of terrorist motivations and patterns of behavior. With more than a hundred terrorist organizations active in the world today, the challenge is to identify groups or individuals who are both motivated and capable of employing chemical or biological agents against civilians. Yet instead of examining historical cases in which terrorists sought to acquire and use such agents, the Clinton administration, as well as many outside analysts, developed threat assessments and response strategies in an empirical vacuum. Lacking solid data, they fell back on worst-case scenarios that may be remote from reality.
>
> *Source:* **Jonathan B. Tucker and Amy Sands, "An Unlikely Threat," *Bulletin of the Atomic Scientists*, v. 55, no. 4 (July–August 1999), www.bullatomsci.org/issues/1999/ja99**

IT'S BEEN SAID...

Saudi dissident Usama bin Laden.

A P P L Y I N G   T H E O R Y

❦ NETWAR ❧

When it comes to applying theory to terrorist groups, the most interesting work is done in the area of motivation and internal group dynamics, not the usual focus of international relations theorists. Realists tend to ignore terrorists, and pluralists simply list them as another transnational actor. The most interesting conceptual work on terrorist groups comes from national security theorists who see warfare in the future in terms of what is called **netwar**. Netwar "refers to conflicts in which the combatant is organized along networked lines or employs networks for operational control and other communications." The organizational form is not the classic hierarchical structure as reflected in line-and-block organizational charts. Rather netwar organizational forms may resemble "stars" that have some centralized elements, or "chains" that are linear, or most likely "all-channel" networks in which each principal node communicates and interacts with every other node (see Figure 8.A).

John Arquilla and David Ronfeldt argue, "Because of changes in the context of possible conflict, netwar will no doubt prove most attractive, for the near-term future, to nonstate actors. It is likely to become a policy tool of choice for ethnonationalists, terrorists, and transnational criminal and revolutionary organizations. Additionally, the rise of global civil society heralds the possibility that nongovernmental organizations associated with militant activism will become netwar combatants." Thanks to the worldwide information revolution, members of networks do not necessarily have to meet face to face. From the perspective of terrorists, security is therefore enhanced, and an organization could conceivably have support-

ers around the world. Netwar, therefore, denotes an emerging mode of conflict and crime at societal levels (within states and across borders) that involve measures short of war in which the actors use network forms of organizations, doctrine, strategy, and communication. These actors generally consist of dispersed groups who agree to communicate and act, perhaps without a central leadership or headquarters. It is suggested that hierarchical organizations such as states might be ill-equipped to deal with such organizational innovations.

To date, perhaps the best example involves the low-intensity conflict waged by the Zapatistas against the central Mexican government in the Yucatan. Netwar is evident in the decentralized collaboration among diverse Mexican and transnational (mostly U.S. and Canadian) activists who side with the Zapatista National Liberation Army (EZLN). The EZLN aims to affect government policy on human rights and other reform issues and have gained publicity for their goals with the aid of sympathetic nongovernmental activists. As Subcomandante Marcos has stated, the EZLN is not interested in taking over the state. Rather, "It is civil society that must transform Mexico—we are only a small part of that civil society, the armed part." Aided by the Internet, the EZLN and NGO activists have engaged in nonviolent action by utilizing the media to disseminate news, mobilize support, and coordinate actions [www.ezln.org].

Source: John Arquilla and David Ronfeldt, *The Advent of Netwar* (Santa Monica: RAND, 1996). See also Ronfeldt, Arquilla, Graham E. Fuller, and Melissa Fuller, *The Zapatista Social Netwar in Mexico* (Santa Monica, Calif.: RAND, 1998).

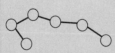

Chain
(Smugglers)

Star or Hub
(Drug cartel)

All-Channel
(Peace network)

FIGURE 8.A Basic Types and Levels of Networks
Source: John Arquilla and David Ronfeldt, *The Advent of Netwar*, MR-678-OSD (Santa Monica, Calif.: RAND, 1996), p. 49.

tracked and analyzed. *Ad hoc* groupings lack such signatures. How can a state collect information against a target if it doesn't even know the group exists? By definition an *ad hoc* grouping does not announce its presence.

Why Terrorism?   As noted, the possible motivations for individuals engaging in terrorism are diverse. They range from psychological and ideological to political, social, and economic grievances. As has been the case throughout recorded history, the mix and relative weight will vary depending on the individual and the group. Having said that, it appears that revenge was a prominent motivating factor in the 1990s. Whether directed against the U.S. government as a result of events in Waco or carried out by Islamic extremists who resent the pernicious influence of Western values on their societies, the potential for high casualties is always there. What is disturbing is that such attacks are not necessarily aimed at achieving a particular political agenda, but rather have the generalized goal of inflicting pain and suffering.

Religious motivation coupled with a desire for revenge is a particularly explosive combination—it makes it easier to justify in one's mind high numbers of casualties, whether they are military or civilian, government employees or tourists. In other words no one is an innocent, and no moral, ethical, or religious constraints apply. In fact religion often acts as a justification as opposed to a constraint on terrorist actions. Looking back over the past one hundred years, we have come a long way from nineteenth-century terrorist organizations such as the People's Will that targeted government officials and attempted to avoid killing innocent civilians. For many of today's terrorists, however, the death of innocents not only increases the shock value of the attack—an instrumental goal—but is an end in itself.

CASE & Point

THE JAPANESE SUBWAY ATTACK

In March 1995 morning commuters on several Tokyo subway lines were exposed to a poison gas attack that killed twelve people and injured hundreds more. The perpetrators were members of a Japanese religious cult, Aum Shinrikyo (Supreme Truth). Its charismatic half-blind leader, Asahara Shokou, had as a youth aspired to be Japan's prime minister but he failed to gain admittance to Japan's extremely competitive universities. In 1978 he opened a pharmacy and health food store, travelled through India and Nepal, and then returned to Tokyo and founded what became Aum Shinrikyo. By 1994 the cult claimed an estimated 10,000 members in Japan and 100,000 overseas. Its essential message was the corrupt nature of modern society and the need to destroy it.

Although more people have been killed by terrorist bombings in other incidents such as the Marine barracks in Beirut in 1983, the Tokyo gas attack was a watershed for several reasons. First it was the first large-scale terrorist use of chemical weapons against an urban target. As such it broke an operational and psychological barrier that terrorist groups had never crossed before. The fear is that the Aum Shinrikyo attack may encourage other groups to follow suit. Second Aum Shinrikyo is a religious organization, not a clandestine terrorist group seeking secular political objectives. The problem for governments is that such "millennialist" groups do not present political demands—their actions are carried out to bring about Armageddon, not to wring concessions from a government. Finally the group was amazingly well financed, had formed a number of front companies, and had built chemical factories employing highly trained scientists.

Point: Conventional images of the terrorist need to be modified.

How Terrorism Works   A great deal has been written in recent years on the potential terrorist use of weapons of mass destruction. This topic is part of a larger concern over the implications of our increasingly technologically reliant society. The subject can be discussed from the perspective of terrorist use of technology as well as from societies' reliance on it.

On the one hand technology certainly increases terrorist options. The media, for example, have always had a symbiotic relationship with terrorists—the latter provide the drama and the former the dissemination of the dramatic story to its readers and viewers. For some critics the electronic media in particular is to terrorism what oxygen is to a fire, almost deserving to be viewed as an unindicted co-conspirator. In recent years technological developments have provided terrorists with another communications option over which they have more control. The Internet hosts numerous Web sites for terrorist groups and their political fronts. Such sites are obviously a source of propaganda and a way to solicit financial contributions. They also hold the possibility of serving as a means of recruitment.

On the other hand the Internet also reflects the vulnerability of our technologically reliant society. In recent years there has been a steady drumbeat of journalistic and government reports analyzing the vulnerabilities of the air traffic and rail control systems, electrical power grids, government computer networks, and financial exchanges and banking records. Rather than having to be physically present at the chosen target, an adept hacker could be located on the other side of the world, using keystrokes to gain access to computer systems. While the alteration or wiping out of financial records may not have the visual impact or resultant fatalities of a car bomb, such computer hacking could obviously cause economic chaos. Dubbed **cyberterrorism**, hackers with such goals can use the Internet to access military, police, air traffic control, and other networks on which public safety depends.

To date such scenarios are mostly the province of novels and Hollywood thrillers. Yet such possibilities are being taken seriously by computer security experts and government investigative agencies. The dilemma is that in highlighting technological interdependencies and vulnerabilities, terrorists might be given ideas for new modes of disruption. But to ignore such possibilities reduces the incentives for the private sector and government to take preemptive action to reduce system vulnerabilities.

Practicing World Politics

The Internet: Checking Out Some Web Sites on Extremist Groups and Terrorism

Sympathizers of terrorist groups and radical organizations (and often the groups themselves) have created Web sites. The Colombian insurgency ELN, for example, is featured on a Web site at www.voces.org, and Peru's Shining Path is at www.blythe.org/peru-pcp. Hizballah, the Islamic extremist group based in Lebanon, can be found at www.moqawama.org. Sympathizers of Aum Shinryko present their views at www.aum-shinrikyo.com. As is often the case with the Web, sites tend to come and go with great frequency. For overviews of international terrorist groups, see the U.S. Department of State's site at www.state.gov/www/global/terrorism/index.html. Also check out the Web site www.terrorism.com that will hotlink you to other sites.

Final Observations   We conclude this discussion of the changing nature of international terrorism with two observations. The first is that one of the difficulties in discussing terrorism and international security is that a single event can immediately and dramatically shift perceptions of the relation between the two. Environmental degradation, progress toward global democratization, and even the spread of nuclear weapons allow one to identify and assess trends with some degree of confidence. In the case of terrorism, however, a devastating act by a single individual or small group can make current analyses irrelevant overnight. Perhaps more so than any other international security concern, relying on the historical record and simply projecting it into the future is problematical.

Second terrorist attacks may have an instrumental purpose such as driving the U.S. military out of Saudi Arabia, derailing the Israeli-Palestinian peace process, or intimidating a government into releasing jailed comrades. But such terrorist attacks often derive their real power from the psychological effects they produce on the public. While it is highly unlikely that any one individual might be a victim of a terrorist attack, events as far away as Nairobi or as near as Oklahoma City produce a feeling of vulnerability and uneasiness. Similarly government policies have the instrumental goal to deter, respond, and punish terrorists. We should not, however, underestimate the power of government policies to create a reassuring psychological effect among the public. National security is not simply an empirical fact, it is also a state of mind. It is therefore understandable why in recent years many governments have made what they view as prudent investments in efforts to respond to the evolving phenomenon of terrorism. Possible responses to international terrorism are worthy of further discussion.

Responses

Innumerable studies, articles, and reports have been produced over the years on the subject of how best to deal with the specter of international terrorism. Furthermore the issue makes the agenda of international governmental summits and United Nations resolutions, and it is a favorite topic of congressional hearings and vice-presidential task forces. Some of the most prominent suggestions include the following.

Eliminate Underlying Causes of Terrorism   This approach assumes that grievances lay at the heart of the problem. In a number of cases this seems possible. Spain, for example, devolved power to the Basque region, undercutting the appeal of the Basque separatist movement. The granting of limited political autonomy for the Palestinians in the West Bank and Gaza strip ended terrorism conducted by Yasir Arafat's branch of the Palestine Liberation Organization, although it fueled the fires of Islamic extremist organizations such as Hamas that oppose the peace process with Israel. Other organizations, however, such as Peru's Sendero Luminoso (Shining Path), may accept nothing less than total political and military victory, leaving little room to negotiate. The sheer amount of poverty and social ills found throughout the world always will provide a fertile ground for political discontent, which may be harnessed to terrorist violence. Nevertheless progress in accommodating the demands of some groups may reduce the likelihood that they will continue to resort to terrorist actions.

Counterattacks on Terrorism   This approach calls for military attacks on terrorist organizations and states that support them. Such an approach is appealing as it satisfies demands for punishment and justice and assumes the use of military force will act as a deterrent to further terrorist attacks. Complications with this approach, however, must be taken into account by policy makers. First of all excellent intelligence is required to locate members of terrorist groups that by definition are clandestine in nature. This is not easy to do. Placing an agent inside a terrorist group is no simple task—terrorists don't advertise for new members, and the vetting process is understandably quite rigorous. Satellite imagery might locate possible training sites in the countryside, but it is of limited utility in finding terrorists located in urban environments. Intercepting terrorist communications assumes one knows where to direct one's electronic gathering capabilities. When governments use technology only to locate and target terrorist groups, there is substantial risk of error with unintended, adverse consequences to nonterrorist groups.

Second, even if a government *can* locate terrorists, a military operation designed to eliminate them faces tactical and political challenges in its actual execution. For example, what if a group of terrorists is training at a site that is also used by the host government's paramilitary forces, a common occurrence? Is everyone targeted? If so, what of the political fallout regionally and internationally as photographs of "innocents" are provided to the world media? Would the government that launched the raid be willing to share the intelligence that presumably justifies the action with the public?

Finally military actions specifically directed against states supporting or engaging in international terrorism can result in retaliation and escalation. The best example of a military action against a state supporter of terrorism involved the U.S. bombing of Libyan facilities in April 1986. Designed to punish and deter Colonel Kaddaffi for the Libyan bombing of a West Berlin nightclub frequented by American military personnel, the Libyan government actually increased its support for terrorism; the agents it supported were implicated in the downing of Pan Am Flight 103 in 1988.

Impose Rule of Law   For many observers this is the critical pillar of any effective international antiterrorist policy. What is the purpose, they ask, in abandoning democratic principles and legal rights in the name of eliminating terrorism? Is the curbing of civil liberties worth it? History too often shows that in the name of combatting terrorism or subversion, temporary states of emergency evolve into dictatorial governments.

Governments can enforce the rule of law in two basic ways: through unilateral domestic efforts and through international cooperative efforts. The United States has used both approaches.

U.S. legislation designed to undercut terrorism also has implications for the U.S. government, U.S. citizens, corporations, and foreign governments and nationals. The Omnibus Diplomatic Security and Anti-Terrorism Act of 1986, for example, strengthens so-called *long arm statutes* that enable the Federal Bureau of Investigation (FBI) to arrest individuals overseas who are charged with committing a terrorist-related criminal act against U.S. citizens. Of particular importance is Section 6 (j) of the Export Administration Act that allows the Secretary of State to place a country on what has come to be known as the *Terrorism List*. If so designated, a whole host of sanctions are employed—no U.S. foreign assistance to the country, no export of weapons, and a negative U.S. vote that amounts to a veto in international economic institutions such as the World Bank or International Monetary Fund should they contemplate assistance to a country on the Terrorism List.

In terms of international legal efforts, states can pursue bilateral or multilateral approaches. An example of a bilateral agreement (between two countries) is the 1985 supplement to the U.S.–United Kingdom extradition treaty, which states that in certain crimes associated with terrorism (for example, skyjackings or the murder of diplomats) the defendant cannot claim he was engaged in a political act of conscience and hence not extraditable. For a government to accept this line of argument often led them to invoke the **political exception rule** that has traditionally been a source of tension among governments. This is in part because of different political agendas and foreign policy priorities but also because a number of European countries did not want to send a suspect to the United States where he or she might face the death penalty. But over the years this has become less of a problem, as the United States is quite willing to let a suspect be tried in a European court in lieu of extradition, and governments are less willing to accept the "political act of conscience" claims of terrorists.

An example of a multilateral or regional agreement is the 1977 European Convention on the Suppression of Terrorism, although it lacks an enforcement mechanism. Best known are various international agreements that states embody in domestic legislation (see following box). Examples include the Montreal Convention on the Marking of Plastic Explosives (1998) and a series of agreements dealing with skyjackings. The problem is that not all states sign such conventions, most obviously those that have been accused of supporting or conducting international terrorism, such as Iran, Libya, Syria, and Iraq. All states, however, can fall back on a particular international agreement—**Article 51** of the United Nations charter. This article states that "nothing in the present charter shall impair the inherent right of individual or collective self-defense if an armed attack occurs against a Member of the UN." Although this provision was originally intended as a legal basis for defense by sovereign states against aggression by other states, it can be broadly applied to defense against terrorist activity, whether or not it is state sponsored. All sovereign states thus reserve the right to engage in unilateral (or collective) military action against such threats.

International Cooperation   Perhaps even more important than formal legal agreements, however, are various efforts among states to improve international cooperation in the struggle against terrorism. Diplomatic progress, often painstaking and requiring enormous patience and persistence, can reduce the resorting to terrorism by most groups. This has occurred as an outcome of continuing negotiations concerning Northern Ireland and the Arab-Israeli peace process. An unintended, positive consequence of deliberations that resulted in the unification of Germany at the end of the cold war was the effective denial of sanctuary used by a number of terrorist groups operating from East Germany (the former German Democratic Republic).

◇ INTERNATIONAL AGREEMENTS ADDRESSING TERRORISM ◇

In addition to bilateral treaties and a number of United Nations Security Council and General Assembly resolutions, there are eleven major multilateral conventions related to states' responsibilities for combating terrorism. All require the prosecution or extradition of offenders.

Tokyo Convention (1963): Authorizes pilot to take measures if he or she believes a passenger is about to commit or has committed an action that threatens the security of the aircraft

Hague Convention (1970): Makes it an offense to threaten or seize an aircraft; requires states to punish perpetrators of hijackings

Montreal Convention (1971): Makes it an offense to perform an act of violence against a person or to place an explosive device on the aircraft

Convention of Crimes Against Internationally Protected Persons (1973): Defines such persons as diplomats, head of state, minister of foreign affairs, representative of an international organization

Convention on Physical Protection of Nuclear Material (1979): Criminalizes the possession, use, transfer, theft, or threatened use of nuclear material

Convention Against the Taking of Hostages (1979): Applies to cases in which hostages are used in an attempt to compel a state or international organization to take a particular act in order for the hostages to be released

Protocol for the Suppression of Unlawful Acts at Airports (1988): Extends provision of the Montreal Convention to airports

Protocol for the Suppression of Acts of Violence Against the Safety of Marine Ships (1988): Applies to terrorist activities on ships

Protocol for the Suppression of Unlawful Acts Against the Safety of Fixed Platforms Located on the Continental Shelf (1988): Established a legal regime applicable to fixed platforms (such as oil drilling platforms) that is similar to aviation regimes

Convention on the Marking of Plastic Explosives (1991): Provides for chemical marking to facilitate the detection of plastic explosives in order to combat aircraft sabotage

Convention on the Suppression of Terrorist Bombings (1997): Expands the legal framework for international cooperation in the investigation, prosecution, and extradition of persons who engage in terrorist bombings

Source: www.state.gov

Cooperation can take any number of forms—diplomatic support for another state's counterterrorist efforts, combined military operations, intelligence sharing, law enforcement cooperation, or security assistance and training. Such cooperation however, is not always easily achieved. A concern for international terrorism may be a common concern for most states, but its relative priority among foreign policy issues is not always the same. For example it was easy for Washington to call for stronger economic sanctions against Libya as the United States has few citizens living in that country and does not import Libyan oil. For the French and the Italians, however, this was not the case. Similarly Europeans often note that their geographical proximity to the Middle East means they are more likely than the United States to be the venue for terrorist actions on the part of Islamic extremists. Italy and France also play host to a large number of foreign nationals from this region.

In sum terrorism is a phenomenon that is here to stay—as history shows, terrorism doesn't end; rather it evolves. Often the instrument of groups or movements that perceive few, if any, other alternatives to serve their causes, terrorism for them becomes the purposeful or rational use of the irrational—bringing attention to their objectives through the intimidation and fear that terrorism evokes in target officials, populations, or institutions. A government simply cannot ignore terrorism even if it might wish to do so. With the advent of mass media and instantaneous communications—the so-called CNN effect—terrorist incidents in even remote parts of the globe are brought into our living rooms. It is inevitable that governments will have to address the clamor of questions raised by a press corps avidly covering all aspects of a newsworthy international terrorist incident.

To believe its underlying causes can be cured or its manifestations stamped out by military force is naive. Combatting international terrorism requires patience and the execution of a strategy combining a number of elements. In addition to gathering intelligence, using technologies of detection at airports and other locations, and employing law enforcement and military forces, such a strategy also has a place for diplomatic and conflict-resolution approaches that, if successful, reduce substantially the propensity of affected groups to resort to further terrorist activity. In an era of global interdependence when no state can be sure it will not fall victim to terrorist attacks, international cooperation is particularly important.

TRANSNATIONAL CRIME

Terrorist groups are not the only transnational threat to states. Organized crime, which traditionally has been viewed as a domestic problem for a few states, has become an increasing global concern. The threat is evident in a number of developments in the 1990s that have persisted into the new millennium:

- The Colombian drug cartels' assassination and bombing campaign designed to change their government's extradition policy (**Extradition** involves a government sending one of its citizens to another country for criminal prosecution.)
- Sicilian Mafia attacks on the Italian state and the murder of judges investigating organized crime
- The rise of criminal organizations in Russia and other areas of the former Soviet Union and Eastern Europe
- The dramatic expansion of international money laundering
- Reports of trafficking in nuclear materials in Europe
- The sale of pirated and counterfeit products, copyright, trademark, patent infringement and other forms of intellectual property violations

Transnational criminal organizations (TCOs) such as the Cali and Medellin drug cartels of Colombia and their bretheren in Mexico and elsewhere in the region that operate across state borders are both a cause and a consequence

Police officers escort Fabio Ochoa, a leader in the once-powerful Medellin drug cartel, down from a helicopter at the police airport in Bogota, Colombia, October 13, 1999.

of the development of the global market for illicit drugs, but other recent global developments have facilitated their spread:

- The end of the cold war broke down political and economic barriers between the East and West at the same time that attempts were being made to reform the criminal justice system throughout the former Soviet empire. Organized crime in Russia and each of the former satellites began to look beyond their respective borders for new markets and targets of opportunity.

- The development of free trade areas in North America and Western Europe (and movements to do so in Asia) occurred in tandem with the expansion of trade and transportation.

- The continual expansion of international telecommunications now allows for the easy electronic transfer of money.[6]

Underlying these trends is the fact that there is an insatiable demand for drugs. Estimates of the value of all global retail sales of illicit drugs ranges from $180 to more than $300 billion annually, making the drug trade one of the biggest commercial activities in the world.[7] In sum, one downside of the growth of global interdependence is the facilitation of the expansion of transnational crime in general and the drug trade in particular.

---

[6]Phil Williams, "Transnational Criminal Organizations: Strategic Alliances," *Washington Quarterly*, v. 18, no. 1 (1994): 57–72.

[7]See Paul Stares, *Global Habit: The Drug Problem in a Borderless World* (Washington, D.C.: Brookings Institution, 1996).

Terrorist groups and criminal organizations differ in one basic aspect: Terrorists tend to be more motivated by political objectives than criminals who pursue essentially economic goals. Terrorists very often wish to undermine a state, whereas criminals usually want to be left alone to pursue their criminal activities. Far from wanting to overthrow the capitalist system—the professed goal of many terrorists over the years—criminals embrace the market system and exploit it to their advantage. Instead of attacking governments and law enforcement agencies, they would prefer to corrupt and intimidate them.

There is reason to believe, however, that the traditional distinction between terrorists and criminals is eroding. Criminals at times resort to political violence to intimidate government officials, as seen in the assassination campaigns of the Medellin cartel and the Sicilian Mafia against judges in their respective countries. Conversely Shining Path in Peru has protected coca growers and shippers from government forces, reportedly receiving protection money from traffickers. Perhaps a better example is the Shan Army of Burma, which over the years has evolved from a revolutionary organization to little more than a cabal of drug traffickers.

This development is not unexpected. With the end of the cold war, Marxism-Leninism was discredited, and many revolutionary organizations underwent an identity crisis, losing their *raison d'être*. On a more practical level some terrorist organizations have lost state support and need to find an alternative source of income. It is not surprising that terrorist organizations, operating in such countries as Colombia, Peru, and Lebanon, which are the source of much of the world's illicit drugs, would become involved in the drug trade. On the other hand, as governments gear up to deal with the expanding transnational crime problem, it can be expected that criminals will resort more frequently to antigovernment violence as a means to intimidate and coerce policy changes.

If criminals essentially see themselves as businessmen, it is not surprising that they at times create strategic alliances that work to their mutual benefit. As with legitimate businessmen, the point is to reduce risk and improve profits. One example involves the relationship between the Colombian drug cartels and Mexican drug-trafficking families. Mexican criminal organizations have developed over the years an excellent smuggling infrastructure for transporting goods and people across the border into the United States. For the Colombians, employing the Mexican smuggling networks to get their cocaine into the United States lowers the risk of running afoul of U.S. drug interdiction efforts. For the Mexicans involved, the alliance allows them to share some of the profits of the cocaine industry, which has much higher profit margins than marijuana and other smuggled commodities.

A similar alliance has been developed between Mexican smugglers and Chinese criminal organizations that transport illegal immigrants seeking to enter the United States. The Colombians have also worked with Nigerian drug trafficking organizations, with the latter providing heroin to the Colombians in exchange for cocaine, which the Nigerians sell in Europe. Similarly the Sicilian Mafia and the

TRAFFICKING IN HUMAN BEINGS

Trafficking in human beings, especially women and children, across international borders for sexual exploitation and forced labor is an increasing crime problem as well as a grave violation of human rights. According to some estimates, each year between one and two million women and girls are trafficked around the world, with some 10,000 to 100,000 women trafficked East to West for sexual exploitation. The U.N. Commission on Crime Prevention and Criminal Justice has reported a dramatic increase in the abduction of children for commercial purposes by organized crime syndicates. Women and children caught in these trafficking rings are often forced to become prostitutes or domestic workers and are kept in illegal and unsafe working conditions. Some are held in virtual slavery, often punctuated by the threat or use of violence. This growing exploitation is not only an affront to human rights but also contributes to the transmission of HIV and other sexually transmitted diseases. Traffickers prey on women from developing countries as well as from states of the former Soviet Union and Eastern Europe who feel desperate because of economic conditions and the lack of economic alternatives.

Source: **White House Report,** *International Crime Control Strategy* **(May 1998), p. 22.**

IT'S BEEN SAID...

A DIFFERENT KIND OF INTERDEPENDENCE

The Republic of South Africa has unfortunately become an important hub for transnational criminal organizations engaged in narcotics trafficking due to the country's geographic location, porous borders, developed infrastructure, and overworked customs inspectors. Nigerian criminals play an important role by linking up with local South African gangs. Cartels in Colombia often receive semiprocessed cocaine from Bolivia and Peru and move it through Brazil. Nigerian drug mules then take the cocaine to Africa and into South Africa where contacts subsequently ship it to Europe. The Italian Mafia distributes the drugs in Western Europe while Russian gangs distribute the rest to Eastern Europe.

Hashish comes from Afghanistan and Pakistan through Kenya to Nigerian criminals in South Africa. LSD and ecstasy (XTC) comes to South Africa directly from the Netherlands and England respectively. In Southeast Asia Nigerian gangs, working with Chinese organized criminal elements known as Triads, move heroin from the "Golden Triangle" through South Africa and then into the West.

Source: U.S. Department of State, *Issues in Global Crime* (1998), pp. 17–18.

Point: Globalization is also reflected in the interdependence of transnational criminal organizations that operate in coalitions within and across the boundaries of countries throughout the world.

Colombians worked out an alliance in the late 1980s designed to aid Colombian entry into the European cocaine market. The Sicilians had a well established distribution system in Europe and knowledge of regional law enforcement capabilities; they were also making efforts to recapture a portion of the U.S. heroin market they had progressively lost to Asian suppliers.[8] Map 8.1 shows cocaine trafficking flows used by transnational criminal organizations.

How big a threat are such TCOs to national and international security? There is always the danger of threat inflation. Law enforcement and intelligence organizations, seeking to justify their mission and budget with the demise of the communist threat, may overstate the problem. To date it is apparent that such criminal alliances are alliances of convenience, with each organization asking "What's in it for us?" Such organizations are highly protective of their independence and markets, so there is no movement to create some sort of global criminal organization with central direction and enforcement mechanisms. In fact transnational criminal alliances have their strains and can fall apart just as legitimate international businesses have their disagreements.

But large-scale, organized criminal activity, though it is not designed to bring down a state and create a new political order, can have the pernicious and deadly effect of undermining the social fabric of a society and contributing to a host of financial and social ills and political crises of authority. This is particularly the case with narcotics trafficking and the attendant consequences of widespread drug abuse and the financial corruption of governments. Such dangers are particularly pronounced in countries struggling to escape from their authoritarian past but saddled with weak legal, financial, and democratic institutions.

How have governments responded? The nature of the response varies because different countries are faced with different degrees and types of threat. The

---

[8] *Ibid.*

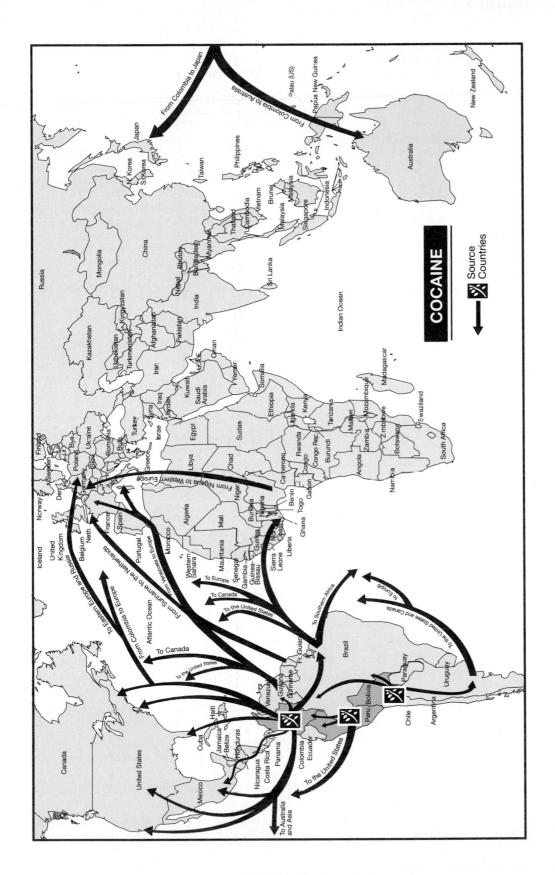

Map 8.1 INTERNATIONAL COCAINE TRAFFICKING FLOWS

Source: Office of National Drug Control Policy, *National Drug Control Strategy 1999* (Washington, D.C., 1999), p. 74.

273

INTERNATIONAL COOPERATION

On July 2, 1998, Hungarian mobster Tamas "Big Tom" Boros left his downtown office in Budapest just before noon. His cellular phone began to chirp and he stopped to answer it near a parked Fiat. At that moment eleven pounds of TNT packed in the car were detonated by remote control. Boros was obliterated, and his lawyer and two bystanders were killed. Twenty other people were injured.

Budapest, a Central European capital, has become the home to several dozen major Russian-speaking criminal gangs and also has become a key battleground in the struggle against transnational organized crime. Aside from arresting mobsters and passing a number of bills in parliament, Hungary has been cooperating with the U.S. Federal Bureau of Investigation (FBI). The FBI is training Hungarian and other Eastern European police in forensic and laboratory investigations. Since 1995 the United States has run the International Law Enforcement Academy in Budapest. Federal law enforcement officers train police officers from the former Soviet bloc, for example, on how to run undercover operations within the context of democratic institutions and the rule of law. Similar law enforcement academies are contemplated on other continents. Just as there has been a globalization of crime, there has been a globalization of law enforcement cooperation. Just as criminal organizations have become more interdependent, so too have law enforcement organizations at the working level.

A good example is Europol—the European Police Office—which aims at improving the effectiveness and cooperation of member states in preventing and combating terrorism, unlawful drug trafficking, and other serious forms of international organized crime. Authorized by the Masstricht Treaty on European Union (February 1992), limited cooperation began in January 1994 with the establishment of the Europol Drug Unit. Europol principally supports member states by facilitating the exchange of information through Europol liaison officers. To learn more visit the Europol website at www.europol.

Source: Peter Finn, "Gangs Find Budapest Appealing," *Washington Post*, December 21, 1998, p. A26.

Point: The end of the cold war has facilitated the rise of organized crime in Eastern Europe but there is also an increase in international police cooperation.

following case study illustrates the problems of international cooperation in the attempt to deal with transnational criminal behavior.

CASE STUDY: THE UNITED STATES, LATIN AMERICA, AND DRUGS

In the 1980s the U.S. government professed to follow a two-part strategy in its war on drugs, attacking the twin issues of supply and demand. The demand side dealt with such concerns as drug education, counseling, and rehabilitation. The supply side, on which we will focus, emphasized destroying crops at the source in Latin America, weaning peasants away from drug-related crops, and interdicting drugs before they could enter the United States. But the U.S. "drug war" ran afoul of competing national interests and faced a whole host of seemingly intractable problems.

The United States relies on the Peruvian, Bolivian, and Colombian militaries to carry out the fight against the drug traffickers, yet these militaries have repeatedly committed human rights abuses. Through military aid, the United States builds up the capabilities of institutions that in the past have undermined democracy through military *coup d'état*.

These same three countries suffer from dreadful economic problems. Bolivia, for example, experienced a decline in per capita income of 30 percent between 1980 and 1984, inflation at 24,000 percent in 1985, and the collapse of its major legal export, tin. By 1990, thanks to an economic stabilization program, inflation was brought down to 18 percent, the gross domestic product (GDP) grew 2.5 percent, and exports rose. Much of this relative success, however, depends on the coca trade, which accounts for as much foreign exchange as all other exports combined. Furthermore, although Bolivia's economic reforms eliminated some 45,000 state jobs in mining and public administration and factory layoffs totalled 35,000, the coca trade currently employs about 20 percent of the country's workforce, about 300,000 people.

Simply put, the U.S. war on drugs is also a war against a major segment of these Latin American economies. For a government to pursue such a policy risks public unrest, undermines authority, and threatens democracy. The top priority for Latin American political leaders is, understandably, economic and political stability, not what they see as the U.S. drug problem.

The situation is somewhat different in Colombia, where the Medellin cartel declared a "total war" on the state in 1989, leading to the death of over 400 police officers, 100 judges and assistants, and eleven journalists in a single year. The Colombian government draws a distinction between narcoterrorism and narcotics trafficking; they are certainly committed to reducing drug-related violence and responded vigorously to the attacks of the Medellin cartel.

Not only do states face competing national interests, but within such countries as Peru there are competing bureaucratic interests between the military and the police. In Peru, for example, bureaucratic competition is exacerbated by contradictory missions. The police, on the one hand, take the lead in counternarcotics efforts. Hence they seek to disrupt the cultivation and trafficking activities in the Upper Huallaga Valley in conjunction with the U.S. Drug Enforcement Administration. The military, however, is principally concerned with the Shining Path insurgency. As a result they hesitate to alienate peasant growers and so at times the military has thwarted counterdrug operations. A Peruvian general who was the former regional commander remarked: "There are 150,000 peasant coca-growers in the zone. Each one is a potential subversive. Eradicate his field and the next day he'll be one. . . . Most of my troops come from this area. In effect, the police were wiping out the livelihood of their families, while I was asking them to fight Shining Path, which was sworn to protect the growers. Shining Path looked like heroes."[9]

Even where U.S. in-country enforcement efforts have been somewhat successful, as in Peru and Bolivia, the result has been simply to spread coca production into other countries, such as Colombia, Brazil, Ecuador, Venezuela, and Argentina. And as U.S. interdiction efforts improved in the Caribbean and southern Florida, drug traffickers simply found alternative routes, such as coming through Mexico. Furthermore, by the late 1990s, a new generation of drug traffickers in Columbia became adept at using the Internet and other modern technology such as encryption, reversing the gains of earlier years that had crippled the older cartels. They also maintain a much lower profile, mix illicit and licit businesses, avoid engaging in terrorist attacks against the government, and operate in small autonomous cells. Rather than being hierarchically organized and integrated, Colombian traffickers contract out most of their jobs to specialists. It is estimated that there are now several hundred small cartels.[10]

Crop substitution has been proposed as a way to wean peasants away from coca growing, but the problem here is simply economics—coca often brings ten

[9]Kenneth E. Sharpe, "The Military, the Drug War and Democracy in Latin America: What Would Clausewitz Tell Us?" *Small Wars and Insurgencies*, vol. 4, no. 3 (Winter 1993): 72.

[10]Douglas Farah, "Drug Cartels Hold Tech Advantage," *Washington Post*, November 15, 1999, p. 1, 18.

COLOMBIA: CRISIS OF AUTHORITY

The year 2000 witnessed a virtual death watch for the government of Colombia. As the authority of the government began to wane, insurgents, drug traffickers, and vigilante groups grew more powerful. In November 1999 half the country's mayors threatened to resign because their districts had become ungovernable. Many residents of Bogota decided against leaving for the warmer climates of the country in December, fearful of running into insurgent groups or professional kidnappers. As one banker noted, "The security situation has gone from bad to worse. A few years ago when you heard about the war, you almost felt it was happening in a different country. You did not feel threatened. Now, though, everyone is on guard. You do not take the intercity highways, and you look twice before you leave your house." According to their own statistics, police fail to solve 95 percent of crimes, and most murders are not even investigated.

Two insurgent groups—the FARC (Revolutionary Armed Forces of Colombia) and the smaller ELN (National Liberation Army)—in the 1990s began moving into territory once under strong government control. The FARC has acted as a labor organizer in the coca fields, keeping the price of a bushel up while "taxing" the local farmers and providing a source of revenue for weapons and salaries. Believing the government is unable to protect them, rich farmers and businessmen created the Colombian United Self-Defense (AUC) unit, a rather bland name for what are in actuality death squads. These gangs of mercenaries and hit men terrify anyone who might have any sympathy for the rebels. The AUC constantly updates its "list," a roster of suspected collaborators who are taken to public places and executed. Having survived the violence associated with the Medellin cartel in the 1980s, Colombians hope they can once again right the ship of state and avoid falling further into political, social, and economic anarchy.

Source: Benjamin Ryder Howe, "Out of the Jungle," *The Atlantic Monthly*, May 2000, pp. 32–36. See also the superb and chilling three-part series on Colombia by Alma Guillermoprieto in *The New York Review of Books*, April 13, April 27, and May 11, 2000.

times the price of other crops. Coca is a hardy crop; one bush produces leaves four to six times a year for fifteen years. It is easy to harvest and process into paste, and drug traffickers make marketing easy for peasants by flying into remote airstrips and paying up front with U.S. dollars.[11]

How can governments combat transnational criminal organizations? As with all problems of world politics, there are no easy answers. One approach is to improve intelligence collection and analytical efforts, aiming at better understanding of TCOs, their networks, and means of doing business. This "mapping of the terrain" requires the sharing of information and intelligence among interested states. Interpol, a clearing house for police information based in Europe, is one example of such an enterprise. Another step is to develop joint programs and operations among those states that have the interest, will, and capability to make inroads in the power of TCOs.

Developing any strategy or policy requires taking into account the possible unexpected consequences of a particular line of attack to minimize the sorts of outcomes evident in counterdrug efforts in Latin America. One can also be critical of such rhetoric as "the war on drugs" or the "war on crime." Such military phrases imply that such problems can be solved once and for all—a naive hope—rather than reduced, a more reasonable goal. Finally, and perhaps most importantly, more progress can be made in curbing the *demand* for illicit drugs—the

---

[11]Sharpe, "The Military, the Drug War and Democracy in Latin America," p. 77.

market that gives incentives to criminal activity in the first place. It is not enough to wage war on the "supply side" without attending to the difficult social and other factors that lead people to buy and use drugs in the first place.

CONCLUSION

International terrorism has understandably received more headlines and news coverage than has transnational organized crime. A major terrorist incident, after all, is very dramatic. On the other hand it is unlikely we or anyone we know will ever fall victim to a terrorist attack. The impact of global crime, however, is much more pervasive. It is evident in the drug problems in our schools and society in general. Criminal activity has major financial consequences and, like terrorism, can threaten democratic institutions. This is particularly a concern in emerging democratic states.

Although one can debate the extent to which international terrorism and transnational organized crime are threats to international security, there is little doubt as to the key to a successful response. Unilateral actions by governments are the usual starting point. But multilateral and international efforts are indispensable in an age of increasing globalization and interdependence.

KEY TERMS

terrorism   *p. 250*   international terrorism   cultures of violence   *p. 255*
anarchists   *p. 251*   *p. 253*

OTHER CONCEPTS

netwar   *p. 262*   Article 51   *p. 267*   transnational criminal
cyberterrorism   *p. 264*   extradition   *p. 269*   organizations (TCOs)
political exception rule   *p. 269*
    p. 267

ADDITIONAL READINGS

The single best historical and conceptual overview of terrorism is Walter Lacqueur, *The Age of Terrorism* (Boston: Little, Brown, 1987). See also his more recent *The New Terrorism: Fanaticism and the Arms of Mass Destruction* (New York: Oxford University Press, 1999). We also recommend Bruce Hoffman, *Inside Terrorism* (New York: Columbia University Press, 1998); Walter Reich, ed., *Origins of Terrorism: Psychologies, Ideologies, Theologies, States of Mind* (Cambridge, England: Cambridge University Press, 1990). For a series of case studies of terrorist groups, see Martha Crenshaw, ed., *Terrorism in Context* (University Park, Penn.: Pennsylvania State University Press, 1995). On government responses, see Barry Rubin, ed., *The Politics of Counterterrorism: The Ordeal of Democratic States* (Washington, D.C.: Foreign Policy Institute, Johns Hopkins University, 1990). You might also wish to take a look at the journals *Terrorism and Political Violence* and *Conflict and Terrorism*. For academic articles on crime, see the journal *Transnational Organized Crime*. A recent anthology that takes an important regional focus is Tom Farer (ed.), *Transnational Crime in the Americas* (New York: Routledge, 1999).

AN EMERGING GLOBAL CIVIL SOCIETY: INTERNATIONAL LAW, INTERNATIONAL ORGANIZATION, AND GLOBALIZATION

> *Globalization involves the inexorable integration of markets, nation-states and technologies to a degree never witnessed before—in a way that is enabling individuals, corporations, and nation-states to reach around the world farther, faster, deeper and cheaper than ever before, and in a way that is also producing a powerful backlash from those brutalized or left behind by this new system.*
>
> **THOMAS L. FRIEDMAN, *NEW YORK TIMES* JOURNALIST AND AUTHOR OF *THE LEXUS AND THE OLIVE TREE***

> *The pursuit, attainment, and refinement of humane governance is the principal project of emergent global civil society, engaging both powers of reason and analysis, but also summoning the energies of imagination. . . . Humane governance can thus be achieved without world government . . . This is both the more likely and more desirable course of action.*
>
> **RICHARD FALK, CO-DIRECTOR, WORLD ORDER MODELS PROJECT**

CHAPTER 9

 n the summer of 1999, the Chinese government banned a vast, silent movement known as Falun Gong. Falun Gong is not a political organization designed to undercut governmental authority but rather an organization that synthesizes Buddhist, Taoist, and folk beliefs and whose distinguishing activity is collective deep-breathing exercises. Its tens of millions of followers include lower- and middle-class people plus communist party members who hope to achieve a healthier and happier life. The Chinese government was unable to arrest the leader of Falun Gong for a simple reason—he lives in New York City. But with the Internet's e-mail capability, this geographic separation from his followers did not pose a significant obstacle to communication.

Similarly when various nongovernmental organizations decided to protest against the World Trade Organization in Seattle, Washington, in November 1999, and against the World Bank and International Monetary Fund, Washington, D.C., in April 2000, the Internet

Study in contrast: Athletic official in traditional dress using cell phone in Ulan Bator, Mongolia.

provided a means to coordinate strategy well before these organizations arrived. No matter the culture or nationality, persons with a common interest, faith, or agenda are able to share ideas and concerns without ever having to meet face to face. A sense of community, therefore, does not necessarily have to arise from the close proximity of individual members—virtual communities can arise from online connections.

Ours is a complex, multicultural world, divided into separate states with people constituting different societies around the globe. Societies in some states have distinct cultures and national identities. Others are decidedly multicultural, sometimes with multiethnic or multinational identities. Moreover cultures and identities are not always confined by state boundaries but frequently overlap these artificial state lines that otherwise separate or divide peoples.

Culture, particularly the general values we have in common and the associated identities we hold, is an attribute we can identify both within and across societies. In this chapter, however, we focus on the emergence in the last 500 years or so of an increasingly global society. Themes will be introduced that we discuss at greater length in subsequent chapters. An emerging global culture, coexistent with cultures within and across states and their societies, has also been a foundation for forming consensus or agreement on the formulation of international law to guide, direct, or govern the behavior of states, international and nongovernmental organizations, and other actors.

Global society becomes civil society to the extent that values or norms gain legitimacy and become widely accepted, some even acquiring the force of law. Use of the term *civil society* in "domestic" societies within states implies that behavior of people within these societies is subject to the rule of law. So it is with a still-emergent global civil society.

THE GLOBALIZATION OF INTERNATIONAL RELATIONS AND WORLD POLITICS

globalization The continual increase in transnational and worldwide economic, social, and cultural interactions aided by advances in technology.

Globalization refers to enormously increased transnational and worldwide interactions in virtually every human pursuit. This globalization owes much to great advances in technology or know-how, especially in transportation, communications, and related technologies. Widespread application of these technologies has already transformed the ways in which we do business and interact with each other. In trade we now engage in global marketing, sales, and delivery of goods and services; in finance we transfer large amounts of money instantaneously across the globe. In science we use computers (and supercomputers) in analysis of data and exchange information globally through the Internet and other media on findings in such diverse fields of inquiry as astrophysics and the exploration of space, quantum mechanics and the behavior of subatomic particles, and chemistry, biology, and medicine as we pursue genetic research and look for anti-cancer and other disease remedies.

Indeed, advances in technology, particularly during the last 500 years, have shrunk the globe dramatically and likely will continue to do so throughout the twenty-first century. Let's take a quick look back and see where we've come from. Larger sailing ships and improved celestial navigation in the late fifteenth century facilitated global transportation for exploration, trade, and commerce (and warfare). The invention of the sextant in 1731 made it possible to locate geographical position by measuring the degrees of elevation of the sun or stars above the horizon, further expanding exploration, trade, and cultural exchange.

Technologies further enhancing this mobility were products of the nineteenth-century industrial revolution that brought the wood- and coal-fueled steam engine for use in steel-clad ships engaged in global seaborne transit, augmented by railroads that quickly came to link and crisscross continental land areas. The late nineteenth and early twentieth centuries witnessed the harnessing of electricity, and the development of the internal combustion engine that substantially replaced horses, horse-drawn wagons and carriages, and bicycles with automobiles, trucks, and buses as the principal means of overland road and highway transportation.

Coal was augmented by the development of petroleum-based gasoline or diesel fuels that then became the principal energy sources not only for the road and highway transportation mode but also for railroads, ships at sea, and aviation. After World War II nuclear energy found limited use in submarines and some surface warships, extending significantly their operational range. Development of the jet engine in the 1940s replaced most propeller-driven engines in both military and civil aviation.

Electricity also brought the development of light bulbs, the vacuum tube, and the ability to send electronic signals, innovations that matched advances in transportation. The gradual development of new communications technologies began in the mid-nineteenth and early twentieth centuries with the development of the telegraph and then the telephone (carried by above- and below-surface wires and even undersea cable linking continents), radio and radar, and by the late 1930s and 1940s, the development and marketing of black-and-white television. Color television and vacuum-tube, mainframe computers emerged in the 1950s and 1960s, enhanced by the development in the 1960s and 1970s of transistors and solid-state technologies that largely replaced reliance on vacuum tubes in computer and most communications applications. Use of Earth satellites developed since the late 1950s for military and commercial purposes were enhanced by new semiconductor, microchip, and related microelectronic technologies in the 1980s and 1990s, pushing computers and telecommunications to ever-higher levels.

The Internet

Information age gurus argue that the Internet epitomizes the globalization process. One analyst who cautions against making sweeping assumptions about the impact of the Internet on politics and global society is Andrew Shapiro, director of the Aspen Institute Internet Policy Project [ashapiro@interport.net]. Following are a few of his observations:

"The Internet Is Inherently Democratizing": Wrong. Pundits and politicians alike are fond of making this claim, but it is an empty truism and a dangerous one at that. The Internet does have strong democratic proclivities. As a vast forum that encourages "many-to-many" interaction, the Net makes it possible for citizens around the world to participate in public dialogue. Its decentralized structure helps individuals bypass gatekeepers and control the flow of information and goods. . . . Yet these features are shaped by malleable computer code and subject to alteration, often in ways that may not be obvious to nontechies. Saudi Arabia, for example, did not give its citizens online access until it had effectively tinkered with the code of the Net to filter out all "objectionable" material. And Iran programmed the chat rooms of its closed online network so that only two people could speak to one another at a time.

"Governments Cannot Effectively Regulate Cyberspace": Think again. For years, creative cyber-rights advocates have tried to elude draconian regulation of the Internet by pushing the idea that online interactions occur on some distant frontier beyond the reach of "meatspace" governments. Not only is state regulation of cyberspace illegitimate, it simply cannot be done. As a defense against censorship, it is a clever argument. But for the most part, it is just not true. In addition to wielding an iron hand, authoritarian nations are increasingly adopting a more

IT'S BEEN SAID...

sly silicon touch in order to control what their citizens can read and hear online. Filtering software and protocols may make censorship easier than in the predigital era. Instead of confiscating underground books or pamphlets, governments can simply route all Internet communication through electronic gateways known as proxy servers. These powerful computers act as high-tech sieves, sifting out whatever is deemed subversive or offensive. China uses proxy servers to exclude a good deal of foreign content—from dissident sites to, on occasion, the New York Times *and CNN.*

"The Internet Will Enhance Cross-Cultural Understanding and Empathy": Not necessarily. If we were to use the Net to open ourselves up to new social and cultural experiences, we could do wonders for cooperation and mutual understanding at the local, national, and international levels. But the ability the Net gives us to endlessly filter and personalize information means that, more than ever before, we can also build virtual gated communities where we never have to interact with people who are different from ourselves. . . . If this happens, communal conversations could be cut up into an endless number of isolated exchanges. Local activists would have difficulty competing with virtual communities for the attention of their neighbors. Even as the global nature of the Net promises to let us shrink the world, compromise between different nations and peoples may be more difficult if we replace fading national borders with new ones based on prejudice and self-indulgent preference."

IT'S BEEN SAID...

Advances in wireless technology went well beyond earlier "walkie-talkies" and limited-range field telephones to mass marketing in the 1990s of portable, handheld cellular telephones for routine domestic and limited transnational use—satellites even allowing for global communications for those able to afford this extended, worldwide coverage. These new technologies, of course, have also found their way into vehicles of every sort as well as the navigation and communications machinery of transportation systems on land, at sea, and in the air. A far cry from using sextants and other mechanical, radio, radar, or electronic-based devices for measuring location of a ship or airplane, Earth satellites can now be used with extraordinary accuracy in determining precise geographic position at any point in time.

Transmission via satellite of telephone, radio, television, and other electronic signals has literally made routine a diverse variety of worldwide links of human beings that outside of science fiction were inconceivable to most people just two or three decades ago. Sometimes portrayed as an "information superhighway," the Internet or World Wide Web that emerged for widespread use in the 1980s and 1990s is really still in its infancy. We can expect that most of the limitations of bandwidth, speed, and other technicalities will be overcome in the next five to ten years, substantially enhancing information transit in all modes including television, but also facilitating widespread use globally of these new applied technologies.

Already the impact of transportation and telecommunications advances on movement of peoples, the flows of their economic resources, and transmission of their ideas has been enormous. The outlines of a more cosmopolitan worldview are apparent to many observers (a number would characterize themselves as *pluralists*) who see the world as having been fundamentally changed, not just in the last 500 years, but especially in the last half century. States are still around and remain important, if not always the most important actors. We see states interacting in interdependent, often interconnected relations with each other and with an increasing number of international and nongovernmental organizations (including multinational corporations and financial institutions). All of these rely on global transportation and telecommunications networks to do their work and now have greatly expanded capabilities to facilitate their diverse efforts. Even individuals and small groups can utilize these technologies to expand their impact.

THE EMERGENCE OF A STATE-CENTRIC GLOBAL SOCIETY

Taking the longer view, advances in transportation, communications, and other technologies over the last 500 years also witnessed the rise of states as the major actors in international relations. Certainly these technologies, coupled with similar developments in armaments of all kinds (including increasing mobility of armed forces on land or at sea), put governments in a better position to expand their effective authority within the territorial boundaries of their respective societies, also expanding their links and interactions with other states and societies in both peacetime and warfare. The emergence of nationalism in eighteenth- and nineteenth-century Europe and in the Western Hemisphere contributed to greater differentiation among societies with diverse cultures and identities as increased movement and communications of peoples and their governments occurred within the territorial borders of states. Extension of this mobility beyond the borders of states also called for some agreement on rules to govern commercial activity and matters relating to war and peace.

A cosmopolitan view of society was certainly present in Europe during the Middle Ages even though, as a practical matter, most people spent their lives in the local areas related to their position in feudal society. Nevertheless travel by lords and knights was not uncommon (some even engaged in the Crusades against Muslims occupying much of the Holy Land in what we now call the Middle East). The idea of a Christendom as an all-encompassing European society was common to the medieval mindset even as daily life often witnessed strife among different feudal communities.

Although difficult given the technologies of the day, travel was not restricted to the upper stratum. Even peasants were known to travel in large numbers, if only once in a lifetime, on pilgrimages to holy sites. Of course soldiers and sailors also crossed the English Channel for campaigns in England or France or descended from northern Europe in forays to the south. Indeed, Scandinavian Norsemen or Vikings made their presence felt in Britain and Ireland as well as on the European continent, particularly in coastal areas.

Increased commerce associated with advancing transportation technologies at sea raised questions concerning rights of navigation through the coastal waters of different states as well as the modalities by which goods would be bought and sold—imported and exported across territorial boundaries. Although territorially a rather small state, Holland had already emerged as a major sea-based commercial center by the sixteenth and seventeenth centuries. With its "head" turned toward the sea and its "back" turned toward the rest of Europe, it is not surprising that the idea of **international law** or law among nations would gain prominence in Holland.

Hugo Grotius (1583–1645), both a scholar and very practical man living in the Dutch commercial town of Delft, turned his attention to these concerns of governments, trading companies, and businesses of newly formed states in his day—commercial issues and matters of war and peace. Writing in the wake of the horrors of the Thirty Years' War, Grotius offered formulations of law drawn from several sources. One can see the influence on Grotius of the philosophical and historical legacy of a Roman imperial **jus gentium** (a law to govern relations among

> *Another concern stemming, at least in part, from globalization is the rapid disappearance of languages. There are about 6,700 languages worldwide, and many linguists claim that at least one disappears every two weeks. "The only ones that are safe have some kind of power or state support, or have sheer numbers on their side," said linguist Michael Krauss, director of the Alaska Native Language Center in Fairbanks. "That's less than 200 languages." Many linguists believe half of the rest will be gone in 100 years.*
>
> *In Australia, 90 percent of what used to be 250 languages are moribund, and in the Amazon jungle, 82 of the 100 to 150 languages used there appear doomed. The reasons? Cultures that had been isolated now have access to the Internet, but only in a foreign language. Economic factors may draw people to a more powerful neighbor, but such opportunities can only be seized if one knows a different language. Furthermore, modern mobility has encouraged intermarriage and often young people see no need to study the esoteric language of one of their parents. Finally, English has become the global language of commerce and the purveyor of popular culture.*
>
> Question: *How do you assess the pros and cons of increasing globalization?*
>
> *Source:* **Andrew L. Shapiro, "The Internet,"** *Foreign Policy,* **(Summer 1999): 14–27;** **"Saying the Words That Save a Culture,"** *Washington Post,* **August 9, 1999, p. 1.**

IT'S BEEN SAID...

A P P L Y I N G   T H E O R Y

ASSESSING THE ROLES OF STATES AND NONSTATE ACTORS

Theorists, pluralists as well as realists, cannot ignore states and their interactions even as we expand our focus to include nonstate actors with channels of inter-action that both crisscross and surround *international* or, more precisely, *interstate* relations. Our vision of the world need not be either-or. States (and interstate rela-tions) coexist and interact with other units in diverse and complex patterns of interactions. To say the least states have not yet withered away, however desirable they may or may not be. Most observers thus concede that states remain central players along with interna-tional and nongovernmental organizations in the world politics of global society, whatever may be true at present or in the future concerning any transformative role played by nonstate actors.

An important early work (1971) making the case for taking nonstate actors seriously was by Robert O. Keohane and Joseph S. Nye Jr. Both authors have contin-ued over the years to investigate the complexity of world politics, recognizing the centrality of the state yet sensi-tive to the impact of transnational interdependence and nonstate actors on world politics. About 5,000 inter-national NGOs lobby states and international organiza-tions, some to promote international cooperation, others to keep states from interfering with the activities of pri-vate citizens. There are also some 7,000 multinational corporations (MNCs) with subsidiaries that have gross sales larger than the gross domestic product (GDP) of even some major countries. Finally, loosely organized transnational alliances involving dissident movements played important roles in toppling communist regimes in Eastern Europe in 1989.

The biggest problem with most works on transna-tional actors is that they tend to be highly descriptive but with low theoretical content. The key question to ask about transnational actors is *How and when can trans-national actors change policy?* A number of scholars in recent years have attempted to answer this question. A major focus of theoretical and empirical work is on how domestic structures—the political institutions of the state, societal structures, and policy networks that link the two—affect the policy impact of transnational actors. The basic argument is that under similar international conditions, differences in domestic structures determine the variation in the policy impact of transnational actors. The extent to which transnational actors gain access to political systems seems to be primarily a function of the state structure. The hypothesis is that the more central-ized the state structure, the less access points trans-national actors have to penetrate and influence the institutions of the state. Conversely states with "weak" political institutions should be easier to influence. Hence we would expect human rights organizations to have the most difficulty in establishing contact with dis-sident movements in countries with authoritarian sys-tems, such as Eastern Europe while under communist rule from the late 1940s to 1990. The more fragmented the state structure, the less a state is able to resist or con-trol the influence of foreign transnational organizations. This is the case with many Third World countries.

Question: Given the federal structure of the United States and its separation of powers, do you think the United States qualifies as a "weak" state? If so, accord-ing to the domestic structure theory, transnational ac-tors should have an impact on policy.

These points are raised and more fully discussed in Thomas Risse-Kappen, ed., *Bringing Transnational Relations Back In: Non-State Actors, Domestic Struc-tures and International Institutions* (Cambridge, England: Cambridge University Press, 1995). See also the seminal work by Robert O. Keohane and Joseph S. Nye Jr., eds., *Transnational Relations and World Politics* (Cambridge, Mass.: Harvard University Press, 1971).

diverse peoples in the ancient Roman empire) as well as **natural law** thinking. Natural law is a philosophical view that claims there are laws inherent in nature that transcend any laws made by mere mortals. Such thinking is closely tied to the writings of Augustine, Aquinas, and other Christian writers of the late Roman empire and Middle Ages. Grotius also knew how to make general principles and

APPLYING THEORY

INTERNATIONAL RELATIONS AND THE ENGLISH SCHOOL

A number of scholars often identified as the "English School" draw from a rich intellectual tradition marked by such twentieth-century English luminaries as E. H. Carr, who wrote in the 1930s and 1940s (his best-known book is *The Twenty Years' Crisis* on international politics in the period between World Wars I and II), and Martin Wight, whose writings and lectures in the 1950s inspired another generation of scholars. These included the late Hedley Bull, Adam Watson, and Adam Roberts. Rather than studying an international *system* as many Americans do, scholars in the English school prefer to view international relations and world politics as taking place within a global *society*. Such present-day English School writers as Adam Roberts and Geoffrey Best, for example, have addressed human rights, interstate warfare, and national and ethnic strife as among the central issues facing states in a worldwide or global-society context.

The English School relies on traditional insights drawn from history, philosophy, and law. Order in this worldwide anarchical society doesn't just occur on its own. Political leaders create balances of power, establish rules of customary behavior out of enlightened self-interest, or subscribe to universal norms based on common moral understandings. Concerning power and balance of power, look to Machiavelli or Hobbes; for the regulation offered by international law or other rules as in international regimes, the influence of Grotius or Grotian thought is evident (Grotius's writings earned him the customary title "father of international law"); and the quest for universals as normative bases of state behavior in global society invokes the *idealist* aspirations of Kant and other moral philosophers.

That ideas and values or norms play a part in international relations alongside interest and power considerations constitutes a blend, but also a tension between realist and ***idealist*** understandings. To Carr, policy in the real world is made subject to (and as the outcome of) such tensions—an insight core to understanding international politics. The realist who puts exclusive focus on power and interest considerations was as unrealistic to Carr as the utopian who puts total reliance on moral norms.

Based on his interpretation of work by the English writer Thomas Hobbes (1588–1679) and his Dutch contemporary Hugo Grotius (1583–1645), Hedley

Bull's own work blends both Hobbesian and Grotian traditions. Consistent with his mentor Martin Wight's earlier contributions, Hedley Bull identified three traditions of thought in his now classic 1977 book *The Anarchical Society*:

1. "Hobbesian" or realist—referred to earlier by Wight as "Machiavellian" (a reference to the realist writings of the Italian writer Machiavelli, 1469–1527)
2. "Grotian" or internationalist
3. "Kantian" (or universalist)

Indeed, Bull argued that order in an *anarchical* global society (one without world government or other central authority) rests on both the balance of power and agreed international rules or norms (some of which have the standing of law among sovereign states). Consistent with Carr's view, Bull seemed decidedly less optimistic about prospects for achieving the vision offered by the renowned East Prussian scholar Immanuel Kant (1724–1804), who anticipated an international order based on universally accepted moral norms.

In the global society that emerged after several centuries of development, sovereign states emerged historically as the principal actors. In his book simply titled *Sovereignty*, F.H. Hinsley explores the historical and philosophical development of this key attribute of states as they interact in what Bull portrayed as an international, anarchical society. For his part Adam Watson has observed how these European understandings of the sovereign state as core to politics spread throughout the world during the colonial and imperial periods to become the global understandings that underlie present-day world politics.

Questions: Do you think writers in the English School are more appropriately associated with the realist or pluralist images of international relations and world politics? Could you make the case that they straddle these two images?

idealist   One who sees values or human preferences such as justice or a desire for world peace as potentially decisive and capable in themselves of overcoming obstacles to their realization; referred to by critics as "utopians."

customary practice central to his constructions of legal rules of the road for states in a newly emerging, state-based European society. Thanks to the colonial and imperial extension of European states in the eighteenth, nineteenth, and twentieth centuries, this would eventually move closer toward a global society of peoples within states.

Aided by new transportation and communications technologies, territorial states became the principal actors in this new international societal order. Following Grotius and other writers, international law developed rapidly in two principal areas—economic (mainly trade and commerce) and security matters of war and peace (including diplomacy). For example, following Grotius, the territorial sea came to be defined by a three-mile limit extending from the shoreline of the coastal state. The reason three miles was chosen was that artillery technology of the time limited the range of a cannon ball to about three miles, the practical distance then that any country could expect to defend from the shore without actually going to sea. Principles of just war (limits on conduct *of* and *in* warfare developed by Cicero, Augustine, Aquinas, Gentili, Suarez, and other philosophers over more than 1,500 years of western civilization) now became matters of international law, not just moral preachings. Ideas concerning mutual respect for the welfare of foreign diplomats and their embassies and consulates now became legal obligations based on the customary practice of states.

INTERNATIONAL LAW AND MULTILATERAL INSTITUTIONS

As certain values and norms have gained legitimacy and acceptance on a global scale, many of these have also acquired legal status. For example, understanding, acceptance, and growing commitment since World War II to such ethical principles as respect for life, human dignity, and justice or fairness as global norms have motivated efforts to construct and expand international law on human rights.

Treaties or *conventions* are the most concrete forms of international law. Governments, as agents of the sovereign states they represent, contract when they sign and ratify treaties or international conventions to be bound by mutual agreement to the terms of these documents. The ancient idea from Roman times that treaties are binding (in Latin, *pacta sunt servanda*) finds practical application in global civil society in the construction of international law on human rights, defining civil and criminal jurisdictions of legal accountability, managing the global environment, and reducing environmental degradation. At the same time the more traditional domains of international law on matters of security in war and peace as well as commerce are expanding in an increasingly global economy.

Another important source of international law is *customary practice* over time (such customary international law often becoming codified later in treaties or conventions). *General principles* inform our understandings of international law, particularly for those who turn to a natural law tradition that sees universal principles of law as discoverable by applying human reason. Finally we rely on the *writings of jurists*—justices and judges—whose legal opinions in cases before international as well as domestic courts bring all of these sources into sharper focus. Legal precedents are important in establishing wider legitimacy

South Korean President Kim Dae-jung makes a keynote speech at the beginning of the 1999 Seoul International Conference of Non-Governmental Organizations (NGO) at the Olympic Stadium in Seoul, Monday, October 11, 1999. Activists from more than 100 nations gathered to discuss human rights, land mines, hunger, and refugees at the conference.

and acceptance of the rule of law on an ever-increasing number and diversity of issues in international relations and world politics.

Some ideas or norms in global civil society over time may become institutionalized as the legitimate and accepted ways and means of conduct in international relations and world politics. For example John Ruggie has observed how *multilateralism* has become the preferred way of dealing with issues on the global agenda. Rather than resorting to unilateral actions by individual states, these issues are thought to be addressed more properly (and functionally more effectively) in the international organizations to which states belong and in other multilateral settings. These settings are increasingly open not only to states, but also to nongovernmental organizations, groups, and even individuals. The idea of global civil society is thus an ever more cosmopolitan or pluralist vision of the ways and means of conducting international relations and world politics.

Not only do ideas become *institutionalized*—accepted as the appropriate or legitimate ways in which states and nonstate actors expect (or are expected to) behave, but these ideas often become *embedded* in (meaning an integral part of) both international and nongovernmental organizations in which states or their citizens participate and interact with one another. For example the United Nations organization or any of its specialized agencies provide a multilateral forum, procedures, and processes for dealing with the wide range of issues in which states and nonstate actors engage.

CONSTRUCTING GLOBAL CIVIL SOCIETY: A MULTICENTURY PROJECT

The two oldest fields in the construction of the rule of law in global civil society are security or war and peace issues and economic or commercial matters. The newest (and much less developed) fields are human rights, the environment, and holding individuals accountable and offering them standing in both civil and criminal cases before global and regional courts. As regional and global cultures emerge that specify values and realize consensus on such matters, this consensus provides a more solid ground or foundation for formulating international law.

multilateralism An institutional form that coordinates relations among three or more states (and other actors involved in the process) on the basis of generalized principles of conduct. Example: In trade, the most-favored nation (MFN) principle forbids discrimination among countries producing the same product for export.

INSTITUTIONALIZED IDEAS AND THE SOCIAL CONSTRUCTION OF GLOBAL CIVIL SOCIETY

Norms that become established in the form of either tacitly accepted understandings or explicitly agreed upon rules (some of which have the binding quality of international law) lie at the foundation of **international regimes** (voluntarily agreed sets of principles, norms, rules, and procedures concerning diverse issues—human rights, war and peace, commercial transactions, etc.) and their servicing institutions. These regimes and institutions are the outcome of human design efforts intended to provide an authoritative basis for regulating or at least influencing the behavior of both state and nonstate actors. So understood, the development of global society is a **constructivist** enterprise.

Alexander Wendt and other social constructivists portray self-help, power politics, and similar concepts as having been socially constructed under the anarchy of international relations and world politics and as such not necessary or essential attributes of international politics. For example the realist view that states are on their own as sovereign entities relying on "self-help" to achieve their objectives is an institutionalized idea—one of various structures of identity and interest that may exist under anarchy. Indeed, Wendt sees such collective meanings (or institutionalized ideas) as constituting the structures that organize our actions. The key point is that systems do not have an independent existence; they are what people make (or have made) of them.

To John Ruggie, another social constructivist, multilateralism is another example of an institutional form and as such a social construction often embedded in international organizations constituted around this value. To the extent that multilateralism becomes an established way of conducting international affairs, this institutional form effectively influences or channels the course of subsequent actions taken by states. Ideas matter and thus constructivists see the building blocks of the international reality we construct as not just a function of bricks and mortar, financial, and other tangible or *material* considerations, but also (and perhaps more importantly) they are a function of *ideational* factors. Such ideational factors include culture, norms, and ideas as well as the reflective acts of social creation that we put in more concrete form in the global institutions we construct.

Question: How do you think realists would respond to this perspective?

For extensive presentations of their social-constructive perspectives, see Alexander Wendt, *Social Theory of International Politics* (Cambridge, UK: Cambridge University Press, 1999) and John Gerard Ruggie, *Constructing the World Polity: Essays on International Institutionalization* (London: Routledge, 1998).

Diplomacy and Security: Matters of War and Peace

The emergence of sovereign states in fifteenth-, sixteenth- and seventeenth-century Europe focused attention on the ways and means of diplomacy or communications among states, their security concerns, and the conduct of relations among them in both war and peace. Consistent with the writings of Jean Bodin (1530–96), Hugo Grotius (1583–1645), and other legal scholars, international law came to define the **sovereignty** of a state as conveying a right to exercise complete jurisdiction on its own territory as well as a right to be independent or autonomous in conducting foreign policy or international relations. Although they may be unequal in power and position in international relations, sovereign states enjoy legal equality as members of the United Nations and other international organizations. Indeed, Article 2, Section 1 of the UN Charter states clearly and unequivocally that the "Organization is based on the principle of the sovereign equality of all its Members." As we already discussed in Chapter Four, routines and procedures for diplomatic representation became established practice over time and thus served as a customary basis for international law. States came to accept as a matter of international law the immunity from arrest or prosecution of foreign diplomats and the extraterritorial idea or legal fiction that the small parcel of land on which an embassy, consulate, or other diplomatic mission was located was to be secured and respected as subject to the sovereign prerogatives of the foreign country as if it were its own territory. Although long established as customary international law, these and other rules governing diplomacy finally were specified formally as treaty obligations in the Vienna Conventions on Diplomatic and Consular Relations in 1961 and 1963 respectively.

Nongovernmental organizations, other groups, and individuals in their private capacities can influence decision making and implementation of foreign and national security policies, but diplomacy and war and peace matters are primarily the domain of states and international organizations made up of states. Grotius wrote about war and peace, drawing from the moral tradition in western thought we have already discussed in Chapter 5. That use of force in war must be justified (*jus ad bellum*) and that states engaged in warfare are obligated to observe limits and practice right conduct (*jus in bello*) thus acquired legal (in addition to moral) standing through the work of Grotius and other writers.

Efforts began in the late nineteenth century to codify and expand upon these principles, which resulted initially in the Hague Conventions of 1899 and 1907 that specified certain legal obligations as well as illegal conduct in warfare. Reacting to the enormous carnage of World War I that had devastated Europe between 1914 and 1918, signatories of the Covenant of the League of Nations tried to find in the concept of collective security an alternative to war and the use of force in international relations. As already discussed in earlier chapters, collective security was understood as amounting to collective law enforcement. Since aggression against a sovereign state was illegal, law-abiding states would come together, pooling their resources to take appropriate action against any law-breaking aggressor state. The Pact of Paris or General Treaty for the Renunciation of War (more commonly referred to as the Kellogg-Briand Pact) took matters a substantial step further in 1928 by declaring resort to war as an illegal activity.

Practicing World Politics

The Internet: Checking Out Some Web Sites on World Federalism

Formed more than half a century ago, the World Federalist Association or WFA [www.wfa.org] is a nongovernmental organization in the United States that seeks to abolish war, preserve a sustainable global environment, and provide a just world community through the development of enforceable world law. Its agenda also includes working toward an effective democratically elected federal system of global governance and moving to a system of world law that applies to individuals as well as nation-states. The WFA works with counterpart organizations in other countries that are part of the World Federalist Movement. Links to such national sites in Canada, Sweden, Japan, Germany, and the Netherlands as well as to Young European Federalists and other NGOs can be found on the WFA site.

However well intended, this legal approach to security and matters of war and peace failed to prevent acts of aggression in the 1920s and 1930s, as well as the onset of a second world war in 1939. After World War II, the United Nations Charter retained collective security as collective law enforcement but supplemented it by recognizing the inherent right of sovereign states to use force to provide for their individual or (joining with other states in alliances or coalitions) their collective self-defense. On the conduct of warfare itself, the tradition of the Hague Conventions was revived in the formulation by treaty of obligations and limits in the Geneva Conventions on the Laws of War of 1949. These laws of war were formulated with interstate wars in mind but fell short in addressing civil wars and other armed conflicts that may occur within or across boundaries of states. Accordingly two protocols to these conventions signed in 1977 extended coverage of laws of warfare to cases of "armed conflict not of an international [i.e., interstate] character."

Security issues have also been a major growth area in global civil society since World War II as indicated by the extraordinary proliferation of arms control agreements and treaties emerging from exhaustive diplomatic efforts over the last half of the twentieth century and continuing to the present day. These have already been treated at length in Chapter Seven, detailing rules that can be categorized as (1) qualitative and quantitative restraints or armaments; (2) geographic (or spatial) limitations on deployment and use of weaponry; and (3) such functional approaches as maintaining reliable telecommunications links and adopting such confidence- and security-building measures (CSBMs) as the direct exchange of military information, conduct of aerial reconnaissance and on-site inspections, notification of military exercises with foreign observers at these maneuvers, and staffing of conflict prevention centers intended to reduce the likelihood of misperceptions and miscalculations that could lead to war.

Economic and Commercial Matters

A culture in global society dealing with economic or commercial matters also has deep roots. Certainly Grotius and other contributors made commerce a core focus in developing rules to govern trade. Early rules that acquired legal standing under international law were that ships carrying cargoes were free to transit the high seas without interference. Moreover piracy threatening international commerce was understood as a crime against the law of nations punishable by any state. Rules that emerged in customary practice governing the responsibilities of exporters to deliver and importers to pay for the goods they buy reduced to a routine how commercial traders conduct their business. Also contributing to the expansion of trade was developing most-favored nation (MFN) status as a diplomatic measure, granting other countries (and their firms) a right to sell their products at the same low level of tariff or tax as was imposed on imports from their "most-favored" trading partners.

Similarly international law came to require nondiscriminatory treatment of foreign investments. Such properties may be expropriated or taken by a host country's government for some legitimate public purpose (such as putting in a highway across privately owned properties). Let's say, for example, that as part of its economic development plan the Ecuadoran government has decided to put in a new highway directly across Guayaquil, one of the country's coastal cities. This will require the government to nationalize or take for public use all private properties in the path of the proposed highway, giving the owners monetary compensation for their losses, typically the market values of properties seized. It is not enough just to compensate domestic property owners: international law also requires the government to give fair or just compensation to foreign property owners as well.

Practicing World Politics

The Internet: Checking Out Some Web Sites on Economically Oriented International Organizations

Such international organizations as those referred to in the text perform substantial economic or commercial roles in global civil society. Most of these and other specialized United Nations agencies can be found on the World Wide Web by their abbreviated organizational names followed by .org or in some cases .int [www.icao.org], [www.imo.org], [www.itu.org], [www.wto.org], [www.imf.org], and [www.worldbank.org]—the last of these the more commonly used nickname substituted for its more formal designation as the International Bank for Reconstruction and Development.

Since the end of World War II international law on economic and commercial issues has continued to grow. The General Agreement on Tariffs and Trade (GATT)—now the World Trade Organization (WTO)—located in Geneva has reduced taxes and quotas or limitations on imports as well as other barriers to trade in treaties or other agreements that effectively have the force of international law. Other international organizations and UN specialized agencies like the World Bank and International Monetary Fund, both located in Washington, D.C., follow legal procedures and processes in lending capital respectively for economic development or for maintenance of international **liquidity**—cash needed from time to time by national treasuries and their central banks to settle financial obligations due to the national treasuries of other countries, thus maintaining the viability and facilitating the exchange of national currencies used in international commerce.

International transportation is subject to rules with the effect of law made by member states and staffs in UN specialized agencies—the International Civil Aviation Organization (ICAO) in Montreal and the International Maritime Organization (IMO) in London. Similarly another UN specialized agency, the International Telecommunication Union (ITU) in Geneva, has regulatory authority on international use of telecommunications frequencies. A more recent example of continued growth in international law concerning economic or commercial matters is the Anti-Bribery Treaty negotiated within the Organization for Economic Cooperation and Development (OECD)—an international organization composed of First World, "rich," advanced industrial countries. The treaty obligates its signatories to pass laws prohibiting corporations seeking contracts from paying bribes to government officials.

"Growth Areas" in International Law: Human Rights and the Environment

Prior to World War II international law dealt primarily with security, diplomatic, and economic or commercial matters. As indicated in the previous two sections, these domains have continued to expand substantially since 1945. Human rights and the environment, however, are the new "growth" areas for extending international law within global civil society. These topics will be discussed in greater detail in Chapters Twelve and Fourteen, but some basic background is appropriate at this point.

Human Rights   The Holocaust in Germany and other areas in Europe under the National Socialist (Nazi) regime's influence or control in the 1930s and 1940s cost some six million Jews their lives and forced millions more to flee their homes, leave their property behind, suffer extreme trauma, and sustain enormous psychological damage. Additional millions of Slavs, Gypsies, homosexuals, regime opponents, and others deemed undesirable by the regime were also sent to labor or concentration camps. Also stirring the human conscience were reports of atrocities in Asia and the Pacific, particularly those conducted by the Japanese military against Chinese and other Asian peoples. Moreover all of these losses were in addition to the tens of millions killed in the war itself. Reflection on these horrific human losses led to calls for action to preclude any such occurrence from ever happening again.

One immediate response was to hold perpetrators accountable in the Nuremberg and Tokyo war crimes trials held in 1945 and 1946. In addition to crimes against the laws of war, two other categories were delineated in 1945 by the United States, the United Kingdom, France, and the Soviet Union: crimes against the peace (as in planning and waging a war of aggression) and crimes against humanity (such inhumane acts against civilian populations as murder, extermination, enslavement, and deportation). Though criticized by some as merely a case of the victorious holding the vanquished accountable, the trials did set an important precedent by holding individuals *internationally* accountable for criminal acts.

The trials were followed in 1948 by two important agreements: (1) a United Nations Genocide Convention that defined this crime against the law of nations as being one committed "with intent to destroy in whole or in part, a national, ethnic, racial or religious group, as such" and (2) a UN General Assembly Universal Declaration of Human Rights discussed in greater detail in Chapter Fourteen. These initiatives in effect set a human rights train in motion leading over several decades to international agreement in the UN General Assembly on a number of important treaties: an International Convention on the Elimination of All Forms of Racial Discrimination (1965), a Covenant on Civil and Political Rights (1966), a Covenant on Economic, Social, and Cultural Rights (1966), an International Convention on the Suppression and the Punishment of the Crime of Apartheid (1973), a Convention on the Elimination of All Forms of Discrimination Against Women (1979), a Convention Against Torture and Other Cruel, Inhuman, or Degrading Treatment (1984), and a Convention on the Rights of the Child (1989). Regional human rights efforts were also central in the Act of Helsinki (1975) within what is now the Organization for Security and Cooperation in Europe.

Universal acceptance of these sweeping provisions as international law, of course, is a decades-long process requiring both signature and ratification of these treaties. What they do represent, however, is a growing consensus in global civil society on the universal norms that should guide human conduct and protect human rights no matter where one resides or travels.

Environment   A growth area in the construction of international law for global civil society is the physical environment within which human beings, plants, and animals live. Pollution and other forms of environmental degradation as well as

A P P L Y I N G   T H E O R Y

HUMANE GOVERNANCE AND THE WORLD ORDER MODELS PROJECT (WOMP)

Princeton Professor Richard Falk and Saul Mendlovitz codirect the World Order Models Project (WOMP), which seeks a world characterized by "humane governance." Quite apart from whether or not the twenty-first century witnesses establishment of world government or other forms of international organization, the multinational participants in WOMP identify ten tasks that define its humane governance vision: (1) "taming" war as a first step, (2) eventually abolishing war, (3) making individuals in authority accountable internationally for war and human rights violations, (4) constructing an effective collective security system, (5) establishing globally the rule of law, (6) effecting revolutionary or other social change through nonviolence, (7) protecting human rights, (8) managing the global environment, (9) promoting a fully participative "positive citizenship" concept that combines global identity and commitment to both nonviolence and human rights, and (10) realizing in practice cosmopolitan democracy as the essential basis of global civil society. For further information, see www.princeton.edu and go to the Center for International Studies, World Order Studies Program.

depletion of nonrenewable resources are global concerns on a planet of some six billion people, many of whom suffer from poverty, malnutrition, and little or no access to adequate health care. At the same time populations continue to grow and demands for better levels of living continue to rise. Pressures on the environment are enormous as we try to sustain the economic development that is so necessary for improving the welfare of human beings and other forms of life on Earth.

Notwithstanding the high aspirations of environmental advocates, efforts to construct international law on such matters have been extremely difficult. For one thing asymmetric or uneven development and distribution of wealth and income around the world create diverse interests and purposes. Poorer countries understandably want to be able to pursue their economic development plans with as few environmental obstacles as possible. For their part richer countries already consume a disproportionate share of resources, the high levels of production they sustain contributing substantially to resource depletion and environmental degradation.

Not only are interests divergent, but scientific efforts to find remedies or viable approaches to reducing environmental degradation have been clouded by uncertainties as to both cause and effect. Nevertheless relatively modest agreements have been reached on such matters as ozone-layer depletion and global warming or climate change. For example, understanding that such chlorofluorocarbon (CFC) uses as freon in refrigerators and aerosol propellants in spray cans are causes of ozone-layer depletion, negotiators finally reached an initial agreement in 1987 in the Montreal Protocol to put limits on (in an effort to phase out) CFC emissions. The parties have continued to address the matter, amending the protocol in 1990, 1992, 1995, and 1997.

Although the science behind climatic change is not as clear, a growing scientific consensus holds that a principal cause of global warming is continued emissions of carbon dioxide and other greenhouse gases produced in particular by industrial and other burning of fossil fuels (coal, petroleum products, and natural gas). These greenhouse gases work in effect as an atmospheric blanket that retains heat from the sun's rays. Signatories of the Kyoto Protocol (1997) pledged to reduce their production of such gases by the year 2012 by 5.2 percent compared to 1990 emissions levels. The Kyoto Protocol is the product of a continuing process of negotiations within the UN Framework Convention on Climate Change (1992).

CONCLUSION

In this chapter we have taken a broad view over more than half a millennium at the emergence and development of global civil society. Technological advances have facilitated bringing diverse peoples around the globe into ever greater and more frequent contact in economic or commercial, cultural, and social matters. As these peoples increasingly interact with each other on diverse issues, we can identify the gradual development over time of some common norms or understandings. Notwithstanding diverse cultural understandings and views as we compare and contrast different societies and identities within and across state boundaries throughout the world, consensus on at least some common values or preferences has emerged over time. This constitutes a culture within a global civil society that serves as a basis for constructing and maintaining international law and international organizations. The rule of law in a global civil society focuses not just on the more traditional, state-centric sectors—security, diplomacy, war and peace, and economic or commercial matters—but also on newer "growth areas" such as human rights, the environment, and individual standing and accountability before international courts. The idea of global civil society has a long way to go before matching what has been achieved within the domestic civil societies of most states, but it is worth taking stock of what has been done since World War II as work on this project continues well into the twenty-first century.

KEY TERMS

globalization   *p. 280*   idealist   *p. 285*   multilateralism   *p. 287*

OTHER CONCEPTS

international law   *p. 283*   international regime   sovereignty   *p. 288*
jus gentium   *p. 283*   *p. 288*   liquidity   *p. 291*
natural law   *p. 284*   constructivist   *p. 288*

ADDITIONAL READINGS ～

Thomas L. Friedman portrays globalization as "the integration of capital, technology, and information across national borders in a way that is creating a single global market and, to some degree, a global village." Central to his thesis is the dynamic "tension between the globalization system"—represented metaphorically by the Lexus (high-technology, capital-intensive manufacture of quality automobiles)—and "ancient forces of culture, geography, tradition, and community" symbolized by his reference to the olive tree. See Friedman's *The Lexus and the Olive Tree* (New York: Farrar, Strauss, Giroux, 1999). On development in an emergent global civil society of global norms, rules, and international law that it is hoped will constitute *humane governance*, see Richard Falk, *On Humane Governance: Toward a New Global Politics* (University Park: University of Pennsylvania Press, 1995). On rules that constitute regimes in global civil society, see Robert J. Beck, Anthony Clark Arend, and Robert D. Vanderlugt (eds.), *International Rules: Approaches from International Law and International Relations* (New York: Oxford University Press, 1996). On developments in international law covering war and peace, the global economy, human rights, the environment, and individual criminal or civil accountability before international tribunals, see the latest edition of D. J. Harris, *Cases and Materials on International Law* (London: Sweet and Maxwell, 1973, 1991).

GLOBAL ECONOMY: POLITICS AND CAPITALISM

"A world-economy, capitalist in form, has been in existence in at least part of the globe since the sixteenth century. Today, the entire globe is operating within the framework of this singular social division of labor we are calling the capitalist world-economy."

PROFESSOR IMMANUEL WALLERSTEIN

CHAPTER

10

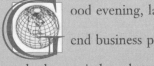ood evening, ladies and gentlemen. Welcome to "Capital Recap"—your week-end business program on global commerce. Here's the latest from Wall Street and other capital markets. . . .

After an eighteen-month decline, the *bears* are in retreat as the *bulls* are finally taking center stage. Both the Dow and NASDAQ are up about 15 percent over the past two weeks, 10 percent this past week alone! The Fed's decision last week to cut the discount rate by another quarter of a point, coupled with this week's news of increased earnings last quarter in blue-chip and technology stocks, boosted the rally already under way.

Even small-capitalization stocks are up, seen by many as good buys, given their reports of increased sales figures but still low price-earning ratios. Bonds are steady as mutual funds and other large institutional buyers so far have held them while moving their large cash reserves into equities.

It may still be too early to tell, but White House officials are saying the recession is over!

In any event the dollar is up against the Euro, yen, and other major currencies on news that although the American economy is rebounding, the U.S. trade deficit has narrowed—exports gaining slightly with imports so far remaining down.

Checking with overseas capital markets, Hong Kong's Hang-Seng and, not to be outdone, both the German Dax and English FTSE indexes are also up, responding to strong macroeconomic indicators in East Asia and Europe and following the trend being set on Wall Street.

Now let's turn to our guests for their comments on these late-breaking developments. . . .

Once the domain of a few experts, the workings of the global, capitalist economy are now of interest to many who tune in to television and radio reports, read the financial press, and consult the Internet. We have witnessed in recent years an enormous expansion in number and diversity of stakeholders in capital markets who consult brokers or engage in online trading of stocks and bonds, channel resources into mutual funds, and trade on commodity and currency markets as well. Not restricted to domestic firms, the capital they control travels the globe at lightning speed as they seek investment opportunities or recoil when they think their capital is in jeopardy.

GLOBAL POLITICAL ECONOMY

If war is too important to be left to the generals—as government leaders, diplomats, and many political scientists have believed—then economics may be too important to be left only to businesspersons or economists. Economic questions tend to become politicized rather quickly because the stakes are high, some questions seem to require some authoritative or governmental response, and competing parties do not see these issues the same way.

In a deeper sense the economy cannot really be separated from politics. Even the *laissez-faire* (or *laisser faire*, in French meaning "to leave alone") stance, believing that governments should not intervene in the marketplace, leaving such affairs to private interests, is a political decision. The degree to which a more intrusive role for government is allowed or preferred—buying and selling in currency and other markets to affect exchange and interest rates or other prices, letting contracts to private-sector suppliers of goods and services, regulating commercial transactions, or in the extreme, actually directing output levels or production quotas and prices—is also subject to authoritative or political choice.

Many of those who have favored economic *laissez-faire* policies have presented economics as if it were entirely separate from politics. Although we place high value on economic theories that have contributed to explaining and predicting how markets, national economies, and global commerce function, we think a more accurate and comprehensive understanding is served by incorporating political variables into these presentations. We prefer the term ***political economy***, which captures the very essence of what is at stake either domestically or globally—the intersection of politics (or authoritative choice) with economics, which is concerned with seemingly unlimited wants in a world marked by a relative scarcity of resources.

Political economists, then, begin either as *economists*, who understand the political nature and implications of economic issues for politics, or as *political scientists*, who understand the importance of economics in political questions and reject the notion that economic issues are in any way unimportant or inconsequential and thus "low" politics. Because of their salience, economic issues can occupy extremely high places in national and global policy or on political agendas. As global economic interdependence grows and globalization trends persist, this will continue to be the case.

political economy   The intersection of politics (or authoritative choice) with economics, which is concerned with seemingly unlimited wants in a world of relative scarcity of resources.

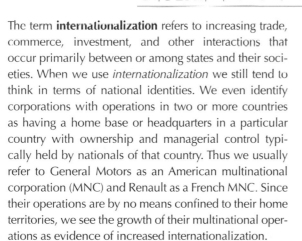

ARE INTERNATIONALIZATION AND GLOBALIZATION THE SAME THING?

The term **internationalization** refers to increasing trade, commerce, investment, and other interactions that occur primarily between or among states and their societies. When we use *internationalization* we still tend to think in terms of national identities. We even identify corporations with operations in two or more countries as having a home base or headquarters in a particular country with ownership and managerial control typically held by nationals of that country. Thus we usually refer to General Motors as an American multinational corporation (MNC) and Renault as a French MNC. Since their operations are by no means confined to their home territories, we see the growth of their multinational operations as evidence of increased internationalization.

By contrast **globalization** transcends or goes beyond states and their respective corporations, taking a broad or global view of such matters. As firms begin to lose exclusive national identity, they perform as actors on a world or global stage. Indicative of increasing globalization are mergers of MNCs in one country with MNCs in another country as well as increasing diversity in ownership with shares of stock in a particular country owned by nationals from different countries. Aided by advances in telecommunications and transportation technologies, exchange and transfer of information anywhere in the world are instantaneous and human beings are able to close geographic gaps that historically have divided and kept them apart. For example, as globalization increases, measurements of economic or commercial activities purely on a state-by-state basis begin to lose their significance as we come to think in world (or at least regional) terms. Thus we become more interested in trade and other forms of commerce within and between North America, the European Economic Area, or East Asia and the Pacific than we do about purely national economic data. Of course, as discussed in Chapter Nine, globalization is not just a matter of economics, but also deals with international security, human rights, the environment, and many other pressing topics on the global agenda.

THE EMERGENCE AND DEVELOPMENT OF CAPITALISM AS A WORLDWIDE FORM OF POLITICAL ECONOMY

As noted in Chapter Two, *capitalism* as a **mode of production** or form of political economy gradually emerged in Europe during the late Middle Ages into the Renaissance, eventually displacing **feudalism**. Feudal political economy concentrated agricultural and other production in small communities, carried out by peasants under the protection of lords or aristocratic landholders on whose estates they worked. These communities were largely self-sufficient economically. Some provided the protection of castle walls against marauding bands or other intruders. Relatively little need for trade existed in a feudal society, other than for a few spices, silks, or other commodities not produced locally. Feudal markets for exchange of goods and services therefore were marginal or relatively unimportant compared to those that arose under capitalism.

The focus of daily life under feudalism was on the local community as headed by local barons, dukes, and kings. Standing as exceptions to this inward focus were once-in-a-lifetime pilgrimages to holy shrines or intermittent participation in the Crusades. The Crusades to the Middle East during the late Middle Ages were Christian Europe's quest to wrest control of the Holy Land from Islam. No doubt these experiences fostered some continuing interest in commerce with the outside world, but even more significant was the change in social structure and economic activity marked by the emergence of towns.

Markets emerged as these towns sprang up near the castles or estates that had been the centers of feudal life. Townsmen (or *burghers*, as they were called in the German-speaking states) traded the goods and services that they and others produced. They would become the core of a new middle class between the landowning aristocracy and the peasantry or farm people tied to landed estates in the countryside. This new middle class of townsmen or burghers was labeled in French the *bourgeoisie* or more commonly in English the "capitalist class."

Trade among towns and cities increased substantially as markets became more important throughout Europe. Examples of early urban centers of market activity, including banking, are such fourteenth- and fifteenth-century trading cities as Venice and Bruges, in modern-day Italy and Belgium respectively. Printing presses and other tools and hand-operated machines were the new technologies that contributed to production in towns and urban settings, even as agricultural production remained centered in the great landed estates of the passing feudal era. We can see evidence of these feudal and early capitalist political economies in the castles and usually well-preserved or restored old centers of late medieval and Renaissance towns and cities throughout modern-day Europe.

capitalism An economic system, form of political economy, or mode of production that emphasizes money, market-oriented trade, capital investment for further production, and a set of values or culture legitimating investment and market-oriented behaviors.

Identifying the Attributes of Capitalist Political Economy

Attributes of emerging capitalism included **markets** and **money**, but these were not new. Although less important in feudalism, markets and money were the bedrock of ancient forms of political economy to be found, for example, among Phoenicians, Egyptians, Greeks, Persians, and Romans. Money provided a *standard of value* for buying and selling in markets and a *store of value* that could be held until needed for spending at a later time. These functions were essential to commerce in ancient market economies that relied so heavily for production on human (including slave) labor. Even the technologies for harnessing animal labor, especially for agricultural production, were late in coming and would not be fully developed until the feudal period of the Middle Ages.

Investment as an Attribute of Capitalism   What distinguishes capitalism from feudal and ancient political economies is its greater need for **investment**. Advancing technologies that produced the machinery and tools of early preindustrial capitalism would be followed by a late eighteenth- and nineteenth-century industrial revolution that began in the United Kingdom. This soon spread to France, the German states, and elsewhere on the European continent and the Americas, particularly the United States. The tools and hand-operated machines of early capitalism, the heavy machinery of industrial capitalism, and the high-technology machinery and computers or artificial intelligence of advanced or postindustrial capitalism all require that substantial amounts of savings be put aside for investment in these tools and machinery that are essential to production.

If we consume all that we were capable of producing, there would be nothing left for investment or for the purchase of new plants and machinery. An airline that as a service industry provides transportation of passengers or cargo needs to invest in new airplanes and airport facilities not only to expand its present business but also to maintain and eventually replace aging equipment or facilities. An industry producing goods (for example, automobiles, personal computers, and other manufactured and agricultural products) faces the same need to invest in new factories or plants and machinery. So it was in preindustrial capitalism when some time, effort, and resources or savings had to be put into crafting, purchasing, and maintaining the tools and hand-operated machines used in the production of goods and services.

The plants, tools, and machinery that are essential to the production of other goods and services are referred to by economists as **capital goods**. Capital goods have no value to us in themselves other than their contribution to the production of other goods or services we do value or want to produce for consumption. A lathe used in cutting or shaping metal or wood in manufacturing, an airplane used to carry passengers or move cargo, a printing press used by a publisher of books or newspapers, and a computer and software used by a writer for word processing are examples of capital goods. We do not consume everything we produce, but put our profits from sales, salary, or other income from earlier production into new investments in capital goods for further or future production.

Two important components of **gross national product (GNP)**—a measure of the aggregate size of a national economy—are annual *consumption* and *investment*. Measured in dollars or other currency, how much has been spent on goods and services and how much has been saved or set aside for capital investment—the purchase or acquisition of capital goods for future production? Capitalist economies that do not invest sufficiently tend to decline or experience a drop in production, consumption, and standard or level of living. To maintain or expand present levels of production, consumption, and living standards, capitalist economies require sufficient **capital formation**—new and continuing investment in capital goods for production and consumption. The box on page 302 examines gross national product (GNP) and **gross domestic product (GDP)** in greater detail.

A Commercial Culture as Attribute of Capitalism   The late nineteenth- and early twentieth-century German political sociologist Max Weber observed how the emergence of capitalism was also accompanied by a new set of social values

THE WEALTH OF A NATION AND ITS
 PRODUCTIVE CAPACITY: GROSS NATIONAL
PRODUCT AND GROSS DOMESTIC PRODUCT

Adam Smith observed that the wealth of a nation was not to be found in its stock of gold and other treasure; it was to be found instead in the productive capacity of its economy—that is, the total of goods and services that could be produced. Gross national product (GNP) is now a commonly used annual measure that captures the essence of Smith's idea.

GNP is the total or aggregate of goods and services produced in a state in a given year. We can compute it by summing the dollar amounts of the following:

1. Domestic consumption of goods and services (C)
2. Investment (I) of surplus or savings—additions to the capital stock used for future production
3. Government spending to purchase goods and services (G)
4. Exports of domestic production (X) minus imports of foreign production (M)—a subtraction that also takes account of the contribution of foreign-produced goods and services to domestic production and consumption levels

Demonstrated national productive capacity		Consumption		Investment		Government Spending		Trade Balance
GNP	=	C	+	I	+	G	+	(X − M)

Gross domestic product (GDP) is a more refined measure that subtracts national earnings from foreign investments in other countries. After all, domestically owned capital invested abroad contributes to *foreign*, not *domestic* production. GNP counts returns from such investments; GDP does not.

GDP = GNP − returns on foreign investments

In addition to statistical problems in counting accurately the sum of commercial transactions, neither GNP nor GDP accurately captures production of goods and services not traded in the marketplace. Because goods and services produced and consumed in a household cannot be measured directly, GNP and GDP are criticized for understating aggregate or total domestic production. This is particularly acute in Third World economies that typically have a higher proportion of household production and consumption.

Consistent with Smith's focus on the wealth of *nations*, GNP and GDP are aggregate measures at the state and society level. In an interdependent and interconnected global economy, some critics claim that measures of demonstrated productive capacity at regional, global, or other levels of aggregation may well be more appropriate, particularly since globalization trends that accelerated in the twentieth century have continued into the twenty-first century.

supportive not only of market-oriented trade and monetary activities, but also of the savings and investment function so essential to capitalism. Church teachings in the Middle Ages had held that the righteous did not commit the sin of usury, which was defined as earning interest from loans, or by making profit on sales.

Religion is so deeply embedded in a society's culture or set of values that it is often difficult to distinguish between values that have a religious grounding and those that do not. The antimarket religious orientation of Church authorities was perfectly consistent with the feudal political economy, which did not rely heavily on markets anyway. Weber observed how the rise of capitalism was encouraged by a revolution in religious thought on economic matters. This was a product of the Reformation that he referred to as a "Protestant ethic" or "spirit of capitalism."[1]

The importance of the individual in Lutheran thought, for example, was a liberal idea consistent with the new capitalist political economy that would come to rely so heavily on individual initiative in the marketplace. Calvinist or puritanical ideas held that hard work was good and that one ought to lead a productive but prudent life. Further it was held that one ought not to consume all that one produced but should invest the savings of money originally earned from hard work (thus putting one's money to work as well). Earning a fair profit or a fair return on loans and investments were now legitimate in the new religious teachings.

Weber observed that eventually the religious underpinnings of these new market-oriented values in an emerging capitalist culture would be forgotten. The important point for us, however, is to recognize that as a form of political economy, capitalism has its own "culture" or set of supporting values, just as European feudalism had. Capitalism legitimizes profit-making enterprises and allows for interest on loans and returns on investment that are essential to its functioning. Indeed, worldly success was believed by some Protestant sects to be a mark of one's membership in the "elect," who were predestined to enjoy eternity in heaven. Poverty was not seen as a sign of God's favor.

Setting religious underpinnings aside, the new commercial ethic oriented members of society in a deeper sense *to produce above consumption needs* and *to accumulate savings, thus increasing wealth available for investment*. In the secular European and American commercial cultures, the religious sources of these ideas may have been forgotten, but the ideas spawned by these religious understandings decidedly were not lost. Indeed, these ideas related to work, savings, and investment were retained in a commercial culture accepted by people of diverse religious identity as well as by those claiming no religious preference.

After all, investment is the "fuel" that drives the capitalist "engine." If capitalist economies are to be maintained and grow, there is a continuing and seemingly never-ending need for more investment in capital goods. Indeed, one of Weber's principal insights was to identify capitalism's dependency on a commercial culture that treats market-oriented activities as legitimate, encourages hard work, and promotes a propensity to save and invest. This was as true in preindustrial capitalism as it is in the more advanced forms of industrial and postindustrial capitalism that continue to require enormous amounts of investment in capital goods.

The Passing of Feudalism and the New Politics of Capitalism, Mercantilism, and Liberalism

As capitalism gradually displaced feudalism, states were also emerging as a new political unit. Notwithstanding a serious fifth-century schism in the waning days of the Roman empire between the Christian Church in the West at Rome and what became the Orthodox Christian Church in the East at Constantinople (Istanbul in present-day Turkey), the Western European feudal idea of unity in Christendom survived throughout the Middle Ages. The fifteenth- and sixteenth-century Protestant Reformation, however, split Christendom in Western Europe

---

[1]For a readily available edition in English, see Max Weber, *The Protestant Ethic and the Spirit of Capitalism* (New York: Charles Scribner's Sons, 1958, 1976).

along the new state lines as warring princes chose either Protestant or Catholic professions of faith.

Notions of feudal unity in Christendom gave way eventually to a more fragmented order of sovereign states that declared themselves independent of any claims to superiority by either religious or temporal authorities, pope or emperor. The old idea that emperor and pope stood at the top of an earthly hierarchy composed of many small feudal communities, dukedoms, kingdoms, and other principalities no longer conformed to the new reality. The 1648 Peace of Westphalia that ended the Thirty Years' War concluded that the religion of the inhabitants would be determined by the prince or temporal authority in any given realm—in Latin, *cujus regio ejus religio* (the religion of the inhabitants of the realm as being determined by the ruler) captured this new idea. The authority of princes in these new political units called states was indeed supreme if even religious matters could be determined by them.

States thus displaced the landed estate or feudal community in the new European political and economic order that emerged. The monarchs in these new states gradually accumulated more and more central authority within their realms. As a matter of state policy, kings and queens favored international trade that enriched them and their governments. If one visits the churches and other well preserved buildings in Toledo, the imperial capital of Spain, one can see in the altars and other artworks vast amounts of gold, precious gems, and other treasure acquired primarily by sixteenth-, seventeenth-, and eighteenth-century Spanish monarchs as they pursued the mercantile policies of early capitalism.

In addition to acquiring new gold from mines in New World colonies, mercantilists acquired gold from running a favorable balance of trade and stored it in national treasuries. Hoards of gold, silver, and other precious metals accrued in national treasuries from the profits or royalties from commercial transactions conducted by state-chartered corporations and other traders. Sometimes such treasures were retained by these national firms as a store of value to finance future purchases required in their business ventures. The ideal in **mercantilism** was for traders to sell more than they bought, requiring others to pay for their purchases with gold or silver, which then could be added to the national treasure.

The Scottish political economist Adam Smith took issue with the mercantilist view in *The Wealth of Nations*, which he published in 1776. Smith argued that national wealth in capitalism was not to be found in the treasure that accrued in treasury vaults. Rather wealth was to be found in the *productive capacity of economies*, which was increasingly to be found in their capital stock along with labor and other resources that are the **factors of production**. His was a **liberal** view of capitalist political economy, emphasizing **free markets** in which governments took a hands-off or *laissez-faire* approach, allowing nongovernmental, private firms and individuals to buy and sell in the marketplace without interference by state authorities.

After all, state authority or government in European feudalism had been in the hands of land-owning aristocrats. In many instances state authority had been used against the bourgeois or commercial interests of the new middle class. Consistent with the political liberalism of John Locke and other writers discussed in Chapter Fourteen on human rights, Smith's economic liberalism supported the interests of the new middle class by holding that free-market enterprises were far more likely to increase national wealth.

Adam Smith, author of *The Wealth of Nations* (1776).

CLASSICAL POLITICAL ECONOMY

Of the classical economists, two of the best known are Adam Smith (1723–90) and David Ricardo (1772–1823). In his monumental work *An Inquiry into the Nature and Causes of the Wealth of Nations* (1776), Smith rejected mercantilism in favor of productive capacity as the proper measure of a nation's wealth. Smith understood the importance of producing tools, machinery, or other *capital goods*, but still relied on a labor theory of value—that is, the value of what is produced is the result of labor put into the production process. Indeed, Smith argued that efficiency can be enhanced significantly with specialization and a **division of labor**.

Ricardo extended Smith's analysis, criticizing aristocratic or other landholding interests for putting an unwarranted cost on production and for restraining international trade through tariffs and other protectionist measures that favored their agricultural interests. Arguing that free trade allowed for national specialization in accordance with **comparative advantage**, Ricardo saw that great gains in overall or aggregate production would come from allowing international markets to operate

without government interference favoring particular class interests. Of course, Ricardo's free-trade prescription favored the newly emergent capital-owning class, which put its capital to work in manufacturing and would benefit from free markets in which to sell its products. Ricardo's major work was *Principles of Political Economy and Taxation* (1817). A free-trade advocate, Ricardo also advanced his cause as a member of the British parliament.

Consistent with both Smith's and Ricardo's analyses, Karl Marx (1818–83) accepted the same labor theory of value but focused on what he understood to be the exploitative character of class relations. Smith had referred to classes as various "orders" in society, understanding as did Marx later that classes had played an historic role in the political economy. Marx expanded Ricardo's criticisms of the aristocracy to include capitalist and other classes that have been dominant over the course of human history. Marx also understood capitalism as a worldwide form of economy with commercial implications on a global scale.

In serving their own interests, capitalists would have to compete with other self-oriented buyers and sellers in the market place. Competition among free traders would force firms and individuals wanting to stay in business to be more efficient without government interference, thus supplying the market with quality goods and services at lower, more competitive prices. Instead of government direction, an invisible hand of market competition would force these efficiencies, resulting in greater productivity and thus wealth for the nation as a whole than could be acquired under mercantilism.

Following Smith's lead as a classical political economist in the economic liberal tradition, the early nineteenth-century English writer David Ricardo even more explicitly favored the new commercial middle-class or bourgeois interests against those of the aristocracy. He complained that land-owning aristocrats contributed virtually nothing to capitalist production in exchange for the rents they collected as mere owners of land used by others for productive enterprise. As such, aristocrats were a drag on capitalist economies.

Moreover **protectionism** (typically in the form of tariffs or taxes on imports) favored these agricultural interests and denied firms and individuals the freedom to buy and sell at market prices without restriction across national frontiers. Tariffs and other barriers to **free trade** both protected and encouraged inefficient producers. Pushing Adam Smith's economic liberalism beyond the borders of the

WHAT IS CAPITAL AND HOW IS IT FORMED?

The term *capital* refers to one of three *factors of production*, the other two being labor and land (or natural resources). Production of any good or service involves combining various amounts of these three factors. Some products are referred to, for example, as labor-intensive or capital-intensive depending on the relative proportion of labor or capital used in production of a particular good or service. Thus making handwoven carpets from yarns (from the "land" as in wool, cotton, or other resources drawn in turn from agricultural production) is highly labor-intensive, using relatively little capital. By contrast, because manufacturing carpets in factories requires purchasing and putting specialized machinery to work using the same yarns, we say it is far more capital-intensive than making handwoven carpets.

Capital is often in the form of equipment or *capital goods* essential to the production of other goods and services. We also refer to *finance capital* that can be used for investments in factories, machinery and other production equipment, computers, research and development of products, and delivery systems—roads and trucks, railroads and trains, airports and airplanes, seaports and ships, all of which require large capital expenditures. Industrial and advanced-technology economies that depend on so much machinery and other production equipment and delivery systems require vast amounts of capital to sustain production and foster economic growth.

If we spend or consume everything (or even more than) we produce, there will be nothing left over for capital investment. *Savings* are generated when we consume less than we produce. For example if you earn a wage or receive profits from a business and spend it all not just on the essentials (food, clothing, and shelter), but also on luxury or nonessential goods and services, then nothing will be left for savings and investment. If you don't spend everything you earn and set aside some of these earnings for savings, then these savings are available as finance capital for investment in capital goods necessary for future production.

Similarly we save (set aside for future use) some machines or equipment used as capital goods, which normally serve no other purpose or practical value than to produce other goods or services. A *lathe* is an example of a capital good; it is a machine used in manufacturing other products—cutting or shaping materials such as wood, metal, or plastic by holding and turning or rotating them against a cutting tool. In addition to shaping, lathes can be used to make threads, drill holes, and grind or polish materials.

On the other hand, other types of equipment or machinery may have purposes other than just contributing to further production of goods or services. An automobile used for pleasure, for example, is not a capital good as pleasure driving is a consumption, not an investment activity. Miles driven for sightseeing depreciate the car's value through use (it wears out over time) without any contribution to producing other goods or services; however, the same car put to use for production of services—let's say by converting it into a revenue-earning taxi for transporting passengers—is now a capital good because its use is no longer for pleasure or consumption; it is now an essential part of a business that provides taxi services. The taxi used to transport passengers will need capital expenditures for maintenance and repair, but a portion of the revenues its use brings in can be allocated to pay these costs as well as fund purchase of a replacement taxi when it wears out or no longer can be of service for business use.

In short both capital goods and finance capital are necessary not only for manufacturing various products, but also for providing services as in taxi, car-rental, airline, banking, telecommunications, or other service industries. Capital is "formed" typically from business or private earnings set aside as savings. Capital formation becomes a problem when national savings rates are too low (typically when consumption is very high). In such circumstances, attracting the savings of people and firms in other countries in the form of investment or loans may be necessary if current production levels are to be sustained, not to mention fostering economic growth in production capacity.

Direct investment occurs when, for example, capital is used to purchase or pay for factories, equipment, or other capital goods essential for production. Portfolio investment is when capital takes the form of investment in such securities as stocks, bonds, or bank assets, which can then be used by corporations to fund their capital expenditures in existing or new plant and machinery. Governments, of course, also raise capital by taxing earnings or sales or borrowing (as in getting loans from banks or issuing bonds in capital markets). This capital may be subsequently allocated for investment expenditures on such projects as research and development of new production-related technologies in manufacturing, agriculture, health care, or other sectors, and on construction of roads and bridges, schools, hospitals, and the like.

state, Ricardo argued that international trade free of such government interference would have the same positive effect on productivity as free trade in domestic political economies.

Aggregate productivity would increase, Ricardo maintained, as more efficient producers specialized in producing those goods and services in which they had a comparative advantage. Ricardian theory held that free trade would favor the most efficient producers, regardless of their country of origin, who in competitive markets were in a position to offer the lowest prices for any given good or service. The resulting specialization by this market-driven efficiency criterion would amount to an international division of labor in the overall production of goods and services for the market.

In a classic example used by Ricardo, producers in England enjoyed a comparative advantage (or were more efficient) in cloth production and thus should specialize in it. Producers in Portugal, however, retained a comparative advantage in the production of wine and thus should specialize in that. More cloth and wine could be produced through such specialization and division of labor than if both were produced in each country.

Comparative advantage was an idea that also served the interests of the commercial middle class in the United Kingdom which, as the first country to undergo an industrial revolution, had already acquired a comparative advantage in textiles and other manufactures. Free-trade theory also undermined the interests of British aristocrats who, with the repeal of the Corn Laws in 1846, no longer could rely on the protection of their less-efficient agricultural sector. Over time peasants left the countryside for urban employment in factories owned by the new capitalists.

The Progressive Globalization of Capitalism

The seventeenth and eighteenth centuries marked the first wave of imperial expansion from Europe that focused on acquiring colonies in the New World of the Americas. The British, French, Dutch, Spanish, and Portuguese were the key players. Mercantilist policies dominated in this early stage of capitalism as colonial powers sought trade and commercial advantages over each other.

In the process of acquiring and maintaining these colonies, settlers and successive generations brought with them European political and economic ideas that took root in the new world. As colonies gained their independence in the late eighteenth and early nineteenth centuries, new states formed with claims to sovereignty following the European or "Westphalia" model. Along with the state, the elements of market capitalism were also transferred. The political economy of states and societies in the Western Hemisphere resembled those of the European countries that had organized and cultivated them.

The second wave of nineteenth- and twentieth-century **imperialism** effectively spread capitalist political economy throughout the globe to distant parts of Africa, Asia, and the Pacific. The same European powers along with Germany, Belgium, and the United States were the players in the second wave of imperial expansion that established new colonies or other territorial holdings. Corporations and banks from imperial countries were transnational actors, which operated globally just as state-chartered firms had done in the first wave of imperial expansion.

Motivated primarily by mercantilist policies, colonial empires were constructed to serve the commercial advantage of the colonial power. At the same time, European and American administrations and firms transferred their ideas about capitalist political economy throughout the world. As colonies in Africa, Asia, and the Pacific became independent, particularly in the first quarter-century after World War II, their capitalist political economies were often linked by **neo-colonial** ties with the former colonial power.

Nevertheless the effect of the second wave of imperialism and the decolonization that followed was to complete the *globalization of capitalism* and capitalist political economy. **Multinational corporations** or **MNCs** (firms that own and manage economic units in two or more countries) and multinational banks headquartered in the world's largest economies operated alongside firms in the markets of these new states.

Even communist or socialist states in Central and Eastern Europe, China, Cuba, and elsewhere that experienced revolutions led by those seeking to overthrow capitalism were forced to adopt what some political economists refer to as a particular (sometimes brutal) form of state capitalism.[2] Instead of privately owned capital being at the core of the domestic political economies of these countries, capital was expropriated in the name of the "people" from private owners. It was concentrated in the hands of state authorities in centrally planned or controlled economies following a Leninist political design of "democratic centralism" within a ruling-party apparatus.

Most people accepted the claims by these regimes that they had rejected capitalism. Socialist regimes established in these countries led to their categorization as a Second World apart from advanced capitalist, industrial and postindustrial political economies in the First World and those of less-developed, predominantly capitalist countries in the Third World. The separate categorization of Marxist-Leninist or socialist regimes as noncapitalist or anticapitalist, authoritarian or command economies is still the consensus view.

By contrast some political economists have disagreed, noting that in fact these Leninist regimes had succeeded only in overthrowing *free-market* capitalism in which capital was privately owned, the most common form of capitalism. Political economists who adopt this view note that the centrally planned and directed political economies of these Leninist regimes still remained part of a worldwide capitalist political economy and retained in their domestic political economies a capitalist reliance on markets, money, and investment subject to state direction or control with a supporting commercial culture expressed in a Marxist-Leninist, materialist ideology.

Since the Bolshevik Revolution in Russia in 1917 and throughout the cold war, political regimes in these countries claimed to have established socialism and to be on the way toward achieving the goals of communism—production from each member of society according to his or her ability and distribution to each according to need. As a practical matter, however, these Leninist political economies still depended on markets, money, and capital investment—all of which were tightly controlled by regime authorities who set production goals

---

[2]For an early representation of this idea, written in a different context or time frame of the 1930s and early 1940s, see Frederick Pollock, "State Capitalism: Its Possibilities and Limitations" in Stephen Eric Bronner and Douglas MacKay Kellner, eds., *Critical Theory and Society* (New York: Routledge, 1989), pp. 7–8 and 95–118. In *state capitalism* Pollock sees the essential elements of capitalist investment and production in place even as state or party authorities constituting a new class of central planners take over capital investment, pricing, and distribution functions previously left to markets in what he calls *private capitalism*. Pollock does not claim credit for the idea but does provide a useful synthesis or model in which he specifies, following Max Weber, the ideal typical attributes of state capitalism.

and prices. State capitalism is not *free-market* capitalism, but it bears the marks of capitalism all the same.

As with free-market capitalism, investment in capital goods is also a central function in state-capitalist economies. Unlike free-market political economies, however, state-capitalist economies reserve to central authorities key decisions on investment (as on most other matters of importance). For example collectivization of agriculture in the Soviet Union in the 1930s during the Stalinist period—expropriating land and putting peasants on collective farms—was the model followed in Eastern Europe, China, and Cuba. Some political economists see this agricultural collectivization not just as a means of enhancing agricultural productivity, but also as a way for state authorities to extract or collect the "surplus value" or profit produced by these peasants, reallocating much of it to investment in heavy industry, the military, or other economic sectors favored by regime authorities.

The end of the cold war resulted in the abandonment of Leninist and state-capitalist forms of political economy by most of these states and societies. Experiments, some not always very successful, were undertaken with different forms of free-market capitalism. Some of these included a strong social-democratic component with some state ownership of industries, utilities, or other means of production. Others have had little or no government ownership and a much less generous provision for the kind of social security taken for granted in the more advanced Western welfare states. The underlying cultures in these different societies are decisive in determining the degree to which regimes in these states will privatize their economies and the emphasis they will place on achieving social-democratic or welfare-state goals.

The globalization of capitalism in the present-day world is one in which money, markets, and investment are central attributes. As Weber understood, an orientation to work, productivity, and a propensity to save and invest remain key cultural values essential to the effective functioning of capitalist political economies anywhere. At the same time, beneath the surface of global capitalism is a world of great diversity. Capitalist political economies do differ substantially from country to country. There are differences in commercial and political values that affect the way business is conducted and the political, social, and economic choices that are made.

For example the United States probably has (by choice) the least generous and Switzerland and Sweden, also by choice, have among the most generous welfare states of any of the advanced capitalist political economies. On the issue of privatization versus socialization (or public ownership of the means of production), Switzerland is much closer to the United States, with most production capital in private hands. Sweden has widespread private ownership of both small and well-known, large firms such as Saab and Volvo, the latter now internationalized given its passenger-car merger with Ford. On the other hand state subsidies of private industries and outright public ownership of other firms is much more prevalent in Sweden, as it is in other northern European countries with strong social-democratic expectations.

To illustrate how commercial culture and the structure of government-private sector relations can vary, we can compare the United States with Japan. As in the United States, most of the Japanese economy is in private hands, but the relation between Japanese firms and their government is close-knit, with direct coordination and state subsidies widely accepted as perfectly legitimate within the Japanese commercial culture. The Ministry of International Trade and Industry (MITI) has

Pedestrians stroll in front of a large Wal-Mart store in Shenzhen, China.

been widely studied for the role it has played in advancing the global competitiveness of Japanese industry.

Although there are U.S. government subsidies and government-industry partnerships for research and development as well as other contracts with private-sector firms, the underlying American commercial culture generally views government intervention in the market with skepticism. As a result no U.S. equivalent institution to MITI for coordinating government-industry relations exists. Suggestions that the United States emulate or copy the Japanese (or, for that matter, French) government-industry, joint-planning approach to market competitiveness are strongly resisted by many in the United States. By contrast almost all other advanced industrial countries have ministries or agencies concerned with advancing the global competitiveness of their national industries. Quite apart from balance-of-payments considerations, government involvement in these countries typically tries to optimize employment of the national labor force as well as assure sufficient returns to domestic owners of capital invested in these enterprises.

Although there are similarities, the ways in which multinational corporations and banks operate and interact on a global basis also reflect the diversity of the underlying commercial cultures they represent. Some will be more likely to form alliances or even **cartels** with other firms much as they are accustomed to doing in their domestic markets. Other firms, reflecting fiercely competitive and free-market-oriented values in their domestic commercial cultures, are likely to act in the same way abroad.

On the other hand there can also be convergence of multinational corporate orientations across cultures on such issues over time. Globalization has also meant an increasing concentration of capital as competition for market share has driven some firms to seek strategic alliances or mergers and acquisitions. For example, in reaching out to global markets, American multinationals like United Airlines have organized strategic alliances with other non-U.S. airlines—Air Canada, Air New Zealand, All Nippon Airways, Ansett Australia, Lufthansa, SAS, Thai International, and Varig, as well as regional alliances with still other carriers. Other major carriers have done much the same thing. In the automotive industry U.S. multinational Chrysler has merged with German Daimler Benz to form "Daimler Chrysler" and U.S. multinational automaker Ford has acquired Swedish Volvo cars. Although adaptation can be difficult, these alliances and mergers have forced often very diverse corporate cultures to grapple with the challenges of building fully collaborative alliances and organizations compatible with their diversity in national and corporate perspectives.

THE TWENTIETH-CENTURY DEBATE ON GLOBAL COMMERCE

A knowledge of historical background of the emergence and globalization of capitalism is essential to understanding twentieth-century arguments among economic liberals, mercantilists, post–World War II neomercantilists, and world-system theorists. After the heyday of economic liberalism in the late nineteenth and early twentieth centuries, the period between the two world wars was marked by a revival of mercantilist ideas. Countries erected high tariffs and other barriers to trade to protect domestic industries and agricultural sectors from foreign competition. They also **devalued** their currencies in an effort to secure a price advantage for domestic industries, making exports cheaper to foreign buyers while making imports more expensive to domestic buyers. It was a game all countries could play, and most did as they engaged in successive rounds of competitive devaluations.

The aim was to run a favorable balance of trade—exporting or selling more than was imported or bought from abroad, regardless of the effects of such policies on foreign producers. As in the mercantilist period, relatively more successful players could be identified by the amount of gold or other monetary assets they accrued from positive trade balances. Referred to by economic liberals as "beggar-thy-neighbor" policies, protectionism and competitive-devaluation policies resulted in an enormous reduction in the volume of trade during the 1930s as each country strove to avoid purchasing other countries' exports. No country really won in this game; all experienced economic depression and the loss of productivity. Indeed, as Adam Smith had observed a century and a half before, the wealth of nations was not to be found in their gold stocks.

Any trade that did go on tended to occur in mutually exclusive trade blocks—for example, Germany at the core of Central European trade, Britain within its empire and commonwealth, the United States in North America and the Caribbean, and Japan in its East Asian "coprosperity" sphere. Many historians have identified the breakdown of economic liberalism and the formation of political-economic blocks in the 1930s as contributory causes of World War II. In any case this was widely believed, particularly among British and American policy makers who were charged with constructing a postwar global economy based on liberal principles.

Their objective was to establish an open trading and commercial environment on a global basis, rather than to repeat the experience of the interwar period. *International economic regimes* or sets of rules governing commerce were established, as were international organizations charged with implementing

THE INFORMATION REVOLUTION

The Information Revolution is now at the point which the Industrial Revolution was in the early 1820s, about forty years after James Watt's improved steam engine (first installed in 1776) was first applied, in 1785, to an industrial operation—the spinning of cotton. And the steam engine was to the first Industrial Revolution what the computer has been to the Information Revolution—its trigger, but above all its symbol. Almost everybody today believes that nothing in economic history has ever moved as fast, or had a greater impact than, the Information Revolution. But the Industrial Revolution moved at least as fast in the same time span, and had probably an equal impact if not a greater one.

Source: Peter Drucker, "Beyond the Information Revolution," *Atlantic Monthly*, October 1999, pp. 47–48.

IT'S BEEN SAID...

the three-part grand design, which included free or open *trade*, *monetary* means for maintaining the currency exchange essential to commerce, and capital *investment* for economic development.

Attempts to establish an International Trade Organization (ITO) as a key institution for a free- or open-trade regime failed when opposition at the time, particularly in the United States, described such a plan as too socialistic. There was the possibility that an ITO would become too strong and intervene against corporate or national interests. Although the ITO idea failed, a General Agreement on Tariffs and Trade (GATT) was established.

In succeeding decades, GATT negotiation rounds worked painstakingly to reduce tariffs and other barriers to trade. In turn the GATT has been succeeded since the 1990s by the World Trade Organization (WTO), an institution given the task of continuing the work of reducing barriers to trade and fostering as open a trading environment on a global basis as possible. Trade liberalization will not be an easy task, as some political economists see growing tendencies to form competing European, American, and Japan-East Asian trade areas. Trade areas are not inherently bad for simple geographic reasons; internal trade within North America, within Europe, and within Asia usually tends to be greater than their external trade with other areas. Enhancing such trade within regional areas can be beneficial, but free-trade advocates worry lest these trade areas become mutually exclusive trade blocks as they were in the 1930s. The challenge for the WTO and other organizations will be to maintain global trade across regions on as open a basis as possible even as efforts are made at the same time to enhance intra-regional trade. At the same time (and responding to public pressures), the WTO and other international organizations concerned with global commerce will be called on to accommodate to a greater degree than in the past to demands from both labor and environmental interests adversely affected by the increasing globalization of capital and commercial transactions.

Creating an international monetary regime and an International Monetary Fund (IMF) was much easier than constructing a trade regime. Competitive devaluations, such as those that had occurred during the interwar period, were forbidden and exchange rates of one currency for another were to be stable. This was set forth by the Bretton Woods regime, named for the New Hampshire location where the international agreement was reached in 1944. The IMF was to maintain international **liquidity**, helping states with insufficient foreign cash reserves by making short-term loans, enabling them to balance their books in the event of a shortfall in foreign currency reserves or other monetary assets. For example if a country had a negative trade balance and insufficient funds to cover the cost of imports in excess of export earnings, it could borrow from the IMF. In the absence of IMF lending, it might have been forced to put up trade barriers against further imports, thus cutting off trade, to the disadvantage of other countries.

The international monetary regime changed in the 1970s from relatively fixed exchange rates under Bretton Woods to a regime of "managed flexibility" or floating exchange rates subject to currency-market interventions by central banks. The IMF, however, remained in place as a monetary lending agency with purpose and capacity to maintain international liquidity. In a regime in which exchange rates are set in currency markets, central banks and national treasuries may choose to intervene in these markets unilaterally or, more likely, in concerted, multilateral actions. They intervene in order to buy and sell national currencies so as to affect their price or exchange rate, in turn affecting prices of goods and services. To do so effectively may require borrowing foreign currencies from other countries or from the IMF. For example Mexican efforts in the 1990s to defend the peso's value required borrowing dollars or other **hard currencies** from the IMF, the United States, or other countries.

Finally a multilateral capital-investment regime was established after World War II with the World Bank as its principal agency. The formal and original title of the World Bank—International Bank for Reconstruction and Development (IBRD)—reflects its original purpose, which was to rebuild war-torn economies in Europe and Asia. Its task in more recent decades, however, has been to lend capital for development purposes to capital-poor, Third World countries with an eye to integrating them more effectively in an open and global political economy. Efforts by the World Bank are supplemented by regional development lending banks, such as the Inter-American Development Bank (IADB) and Asian Development bank (ADB) as well as bilateral loans from capital-rich to capital-poor countries.

 ## THE OEEC BECOMES THE OECD

The Organization for European Economic Cooperation (OEEC) was formed in 1948 in Paris in the aftermath of World War II to facilitate capital-investment flows (U.S. assistance under the Marshall Plan as well as Canadian aid) to rebuild European economies. Aims at the time were to promote trade and monetary cooperation among member countries, fostering production and the economic reconstruction of Europe, promoting trade by reducing tariffs and other barriers, considering formation of a customs union or free-trade area, and exploring arrangements for regional monetary payments on a multilateral basis.

Immediate postwar economic reconstruction in Europe largely completed, an expansion of scope took place 1961 with the formation of the Organization for Economic Cooperation and Development (OECD) to replace the OEEC, but still with Paris-based headquarters. Along with OEEC members, the United States and Canada became members in their own right. Admissions are no longer confined to Europe, and there are now twenty-nine member states from around the world committed to market economy, pluralist

democracy, and respect for human rights. The original or charter OECD members from 1961 are Austria, Belgium, Canada, Denmark, France, Germany, Greece, Iceland, Ireland, Italy, Luxemburg, the Netherlands, Norway, Portugal, Spain, Sweden, Switzerland, Turkey, the United Kingdom, and the United States. Of this group, only Austria, Canada, and the United States were not members of the earlier OEEC. Members joining the OECD later are Japan (1964), Finland (1969), Australia (1971), New Zealand (1973), Mexico (1994), Czech Republic (1995), Poland (1996), Hungary (1996), and the Republic of Korea (1996).

Often referred to now as the rich countries' club, the OECD fosters strong economies in its member countries and works to expand free or open trade and contribute to economic development not only in advanced-industrial and postindustrial, but also in developing countries. With a truly global view, the OECD now focuses its efforts on the increasingly global economy. For further and up-to-date information, check out the OECD's official Web site [www.OECD.org].

Practicing World Politics

International Organizations and the Global Economy

For a preview of international institutions covered in greater detail in Chapters Eleven and Twelve, check out Web sites for the World Bank group in Washington, D.C. [www.worldbank.org], the International Monetary Fund also in Washington [www.imf.org], and the World Trade Organization in Geneva [www.wto.org]—all specialized agencies in the United Nations system. The principal UN organ responsible for global economic matters is the UN Economic and Social Council [www.un.org]. Other UN organs and specialized agencies dealing with economic or commercial matters on a global basis include those specializing on the following:

- *Different aspects of economic and commercial development and production, energy, copyrights, and patents*—UN Development Program in New York [www.undp.org]; UN Environment Program in Nairobi [www.unep.org]; the Food and Agricultural Organization of the UN in Rome [www.fao.org]; the International Fund for Agricultural Development also in Rome [www.ifad.org]; the UN Industrial Development Organization in Vienna [www.unido.org]; the UN Conference on Trade and Development in Geneva [www.unctad.org]; the International Atomic Energy Agency in Vienna [www.iaea.org]; and the World Intellectual Property Organization in Geneva [www.wipo.int]

- *Labor and related human issues*—the International Labor Organization in Geneva [www.ilo.org]; the UN Institute for Training and Research [www.unitar.org]; and the UN Research Institute for Social Development [www.unrisd.org] both in Geneva; the World Health Organization in Geneva [www.who.int]; Habitat, the UN Center for Human Settlements in Nairobi [www.unchs.org]; World Food Program in Rome [www.wfp.org]; the UN Population Fund in New York [www.UNFPA.org]; the UN Drug Control Program in Vienna [www.undcp.org]; and the UN Children's Fund in New York [www.unicef.org]

- *Transportation*—the International Maritime Organization in London [www.imo.org] and the International Civil Aviation Organization in Montreal [www.icao.int]

- *Communications*—the Universal Postal Union in Berne [www.upu.int] and the International Telecommunication Union in Geneva [www.itu.int]

Details on UN organ and specialized agency roles and missions found at these Web sites are also summarized in Chapter Six. The UN also has regional economic commissions in Africa (Addis Ababa) [www.un.org/Depts/eca], Europe (Geneva) [www.unece.org], Latin America (Santiago) [www.ecla.org], and Asia and the Pacific (Bangkok) [www.unescap.org].

Regional international organizations dealing primarily with economic or commercial matters include in the Americas, the Andean Group [www.itcilo.it], Caribbean Community and Common Market [www.caricom.org], Mercosur (Common Market Southern Cone, South America) [www.mercosur.com], and the North American Free Trade Association [www.nafta-sec-alena.org]; in Asia and the Pacific, the Asia-Pacific Economic Cooperation [www.apec.org] and the Association of Southeast Asian Nations [www.asean.org]; in Africa, the Economic Community of West African States [www.cedeao.org]; and in Europe, the European Union [europa.eu.int; U.S. Web address is www.eurunion.org]. Other international regional organizations for which economics is one among a wide range of agenda items include the Organization of African Unity [www.oau-oua.org], the Organization of American States [www.oas.org], and the Organization for Security and Cooperation in Europe [www.osce.org]. Regional lending institutions include the Asian Development Bank [www.adb.org], African Development Bank [www.afdb.org], Inter-American Development bank [www.IADB.org], and the North American Development Bank [www.nadb.org].

The best way for capital-poor countries to borrow for investment purposes is at concessionary rates of interest, that is, below market rates from long-term lenders such as the World Bank, other international lending institutions, or foreign governments. Loans at concessionary rates for development purposes are really a form of grant or foreign aid. If they are prudent, borrowing countries will set aside a portion of the concessionary loan, investing it at higher market rates and allowing compound interest over time to produce the funds needed to pay off the loan when due.

Unfortunately, heavy borrowing in the 1970s and 1980s by Third World countries—often at market interest rates from privately owned multinational banks and foreign governments—left many Third World countries deeply in debt. The heavy interest payments were burdens on their domestic political economies. Moreover much of the money borrowed was not spent for development, or when it was, was not always allocated to sound projects. As a result many of the expected economic gains for which the loans were originally requested were not realized either. Although many lenders offered refinancing and debt relief to borrowers so they could avoid default, the burden was reduced and crisis avoided primarily by the gradual reduction in global interest rates in the 1980s and 1990s.

THE NORTH-SOUTH DIVIDE

The extraordinarily large gap in technology, capital, and levels of living between advanced industrial and postindustrial countries of the "North" and those in the "South" where most people live is a striking characteristic of the present-day global political economy. French socialists first started using the expression *Third World* in the 1960s to denote the most populous category of the world's peoples, in much the same way as the term *third estate* in French history and culture refers to the masses of people who at the time of the French Revolution in 1789 were decidedly less well off than those in the upper classes. This original usage of Third World thus had a positive connotation because it carried the implication that improvement in life conditions for the world's masses was still possible, whether by revolution or other means. In more recent years, however, the term has fallen into disfavor among those who feel the term devalues or puts lower-income countries in a third-rate position.

In any event in this chapter and throughout this volume we use these terms descriptively without any intended connotation. *First World* and *North* are used interchangeably to refer to high-income countries that with a few exceptions lie in the Northern Hemisphere. *Third World* or *South* are also interchangeable terms that reflect that most middle- and low-income countries are in the Southern Hemisphere. As a practical matter the term *Second World* that during the cold war referred to the Soviet Union and other centrally planned, Marxist-Leninist political economies has much less usage today.

A world profile using United Nations and World Bank data (see Table 10.1) divides countries by level of economic development into high-, middle-, and low-income categories. As is immediately apparent from a review of the data, the disparities are enormous. Take a look at Table 10.1, which shows dramatically how human conditions vary. Adjusted for inflation and to reflect purchasing power parity, real per capita income in 45 high-development, high-income countries, for example, is still seven times the average in 94 middle-income countries, and more than 20 times the average in 35 low-income countries (32 of which are in Africa). Other indicators of level of living show literacy at close to 100 percent in high-income countries, but only half that in low-income countries, the middle-income countries splitting the difference. Food calories in the

A P P L Y I N G   T H E O R Y

⪧ A RADICAL CRITIQUE ⪦

The theory of the dual economy (dualism) asserts that every economy, domestic and international, must be analyzed in terms of two relatively independent sectors: a modern, progressive sector characterized by a high level of productive efficiency and economic integration, and a traditional sector characterized by a backward mode of production and local self-sufficiency. The theory argues that the process of economic development involves the incorporation and transformation of the traditional sector into a modern sector through the modernization of economic, social, and political structures. Global integration of markets and institutions is the consequence of an inexorable movement of economic forces toward higher levels of economic efficiency and global interdependence. Individualism, economic rationality, and maximizing behavior drive out age-old values and social mores. [Robert Gilpin, summarizing the liberal perspective on modernization and development, in *The Political Economy of International Relations* (Princeton NJ: Princeton University Press, 1987), p. 66.]

World-system theorists were interested in the nature and effects of globalization long before the end of the cold war and the subsequent popularization of the term. These theorists attempt to explain the economic, political, and social development of regions throughout the *entire* world. Developed and underdeveloped states, winners and losers, are all examined. World-system theorists point to the persistence of **uneven development** and the fact that some areas of the globe

(particularly in the euphemistically termed *developing world*) are not part of the previously mentioned "inexorable movement of economic forces toward higher levels of economic efficiency." Africa, for example, is not unique, its fate somehow detached from the operation of the global economy. To the contrary, they argue that its experience is an integral part of the capitalist world-system. Third World underdevelopment and exploitation are actually *central* to maintaining the present structure of dominance in the capitalist world-system. The first priority, therefore, is to understand this global system from a historical perspective. Only then can the fates of particular societies or regions of the globe be understood.

Advocates of this view are not necessarily Marxists, and in fact some adherents differ from classical Marxism in key respects. But world-system theory is essentially grounded in the Marxist conception of social reality because of its emphasis on the primacy of the economic sphere and the role of class struggle. Rather than focusing on domestic class structure, however, the emphasis is on an international hierarchy and the struggle among states and transnational classes.

The writings of Immanuel Wallerstein represent the most ambitious world-system work and have been the catalyst for an extensive amount of subsequent research. In attempting to understand the origins and dynamics of the modern world economy and the existence of worldwide uneven development, he aspires to no less than a

poorest countries are two-thirds of those supplied to the richest countries, grams of protein only about half. Diseases such as tuberculosis are still major afflictions in poor countries and the supply of medical providers—physicians and nurses—is a fraction of those available in high-income countries. Given these conditions as well as high infant mortality, it is hardly surprising that life expectancy declines from 77 years in high-income countries to 66 and and just over 50 years respectively in middle- and low- income countries.

That the few consume the most is apparent when we examine per capita energy-consumption levels. Industries, other businesses, and individuals in the less-populated North consume more than five times as much energy (measured in kilograms of oil or equivalent) per person as those in middle-income countries and more than twelve times as much as those in low-income countries in the South. The same disparities in consumption between North and South apply for other

A P P L Y I N G   T H E O R Y

historically based theory of global development, which he terms **world-system theory**.

Wallerstein begins by analyzing the emergence of capitalism in Europe, tracing its development into a capitalist world-system that contains a *core*, a *periphery*, and a *semiperiphery*. The core areas historically have engaged in the most advanced economic activities, such as banking, manufacturing, technologically advanced agriculture, and ship building. The periphery has provided raw materials—minerals, timber and the like—to fuel the core's economic expansion. Unskilled labor is repressed, and the peripheral countries are denied advanced technology in those areas that might make them more competitive with core states. The semiperiphery (somewhere in between the core and periphery) is involved in a mix of production activities, some associated with core areas and others with peripheral areas. The semiperiphery also serves a number of other functions, such as being an outlet for investment when wages in core economies become too high. Over time particular countries or regions of the world may gravitate between core, peripheral, and semiperipheral status.

Class structure varies in each zone depending on how the dominant class relates to the world economy. Contrary to the liberal economic notion of specialization based on comparative advantage, this division of labor *requires* as well as *increases* inequality between regions. States in the periphery are weak, in that they are unable to control their fates, whereas states in the core are economically, politically, and militarily dominant. The basic function of

the state is to ensure the continuation of the capitalist mode of production.

Given the inexorable nature of capitalism, Wallerstein and his followers were probably less surprised than most theoreticians at the virtual collapse of most of the communist Second World. In a post–cold war volume, Wallerstein attempts to place the events of 1989 in historical perspective. Liberalism—an ideology he identifies as associated with the capitalist world-system—has served as a "legitimating geoculture." On North-South relations, he depicts the North's wealth as largely "the result of a transfer of surplus value from the South." Vulnerability in a capitalist world economy comes from "a ceaseless accumulation of capital" that approaches its limit "to the point where none of the mechanisms for restoring the normal functioning of the system can work effectively any longer." Grossly unequal distribution of material gains contributes to multiple strains in the world-system and undermines state structures, notably "their ability to maintain order in a world of widespread civil warfare, both global and state level." Hence Wallerstein sees a direct connection between the continual deepening of global capitalism, crises of political authority, and increased conflict.

Question: Is this radical critique persuasive in undermining the more optimistic liberal view that modernization and development processes are improving the human condition?

Source: Immanuel Wallerstein, *The Capitalist World-Economy* (Cambridge, Eng.: Cambridge University Press, 1979), and *After Liberalism* (New York: New Press, 1995).

nonrenewable resources. Measured per capita the North is also the heaviest-polluting group. The higher levels of living enjoyed by people in the North come at a very high price indeed.

High-income countries have remained highly urbanized even as high-technology, capital-intensive, information-based services have displaced many labor-intensive industries. Low- and middle-income countries have also experienced a substantial shift in recent decades from agriculture to urban-centered industry and services. In pursuit of a better life and responding to the labor demands of new industries, people in low- and middle-income countries have become more urbanized, many leaving the countryside and their rural way of life behind. But many (if not most) have not found a better life in the cities as the rapid urban in-migration has overloaded the capacity of many governments to provide even such essential services as clean water and sanitation.

| TABLE 10.1 | GLOBAL POLITICAL-ECONOMIC AND SOCIAL INDICATORS: A WORLD PROFILE |

	Level of Development:		
	LOW INCOME	MIDDLE INCOME	HIGH INCOME
Number of Countries in Sample	35	94	45
Aggregate Economic Performance			
Gross National Product (GNP in billions of US$)	$177.8	$ 5,037.7	$24,193.6
Annual Real Economic Growth Average annual percent increase in real GNP (1975–95)	2.3	3.6	2.7
External Debt (as percent of GNP)	93.4%	32.9%	36.0%
Net Official Development Assistance Received (ODA as percent of GNP)	10.5%	0.6%	0.1%
People, Income, and Opportunities			
Population (millions)	636	4,089	1,018
Real GDP per Capita (1997) Annual Income per Person (US$)	$982	$3,327	$21,647
Gender Opportunities/Empowerment Real Per Capita Annual Income (US$) for Women	$691	$2,220	$15,827
Percent of Seats in Legislature by Women	8.9%	10.0%	17.3%
The Human Condition			
Nutrition (per capita daily supply) Total Food Calories per person Total Protein in grams per person	2,145 51.0	2,695 69.6	3,347 102.7
Health Tuberculosis Cases per 100,000 people Doctors per 100,000 people Nurses per 100,000 people	100.7 13 45	75.2 108 175	19.6 244 662
Life Expectancy (age in years)	50.6	66.6	77.0
Literacy (adult)	48.5%	75.9%	98.3%
Education: Enrollments as percent of Relevant Age Groups Primary Schools Secondary Schools	56.6% 28.4%	90.7% 65.1%	99.3% —

TABLE 10.1   (CONTINUED)

	Level of Development:		
	LOW INCOME	MIDDLE INCOME	HIGH INCOME
Population, Economic Development, and Environment			
Population Growth Rate			
1975–97	2.7%	1.8%	0.7%
Expected/Projected to 2015	2.3%	1.1%	0.4%
Level of Technological Development			
Scientists/Technicians per 1000 people	—	0.7	3.8
Per Capita Annual Energy Consumption			
Kilowatt hours per person	91	1,147	8,550
Kg oil or equivalent per person	400	902	4,977
Pollution (carbon dioxide emissions)			
Metric tons per person	0.3	2.8	11.7
Economy and Society			
Percent of Output (GDP) by Economic Sector			
Agriculture	32%	13%	2%
Industry	30%	37%	34%
Services	38%	50%	64%
Urbanization (percent of population in cities)	1975 1997 15.6% 27.5%	1975 1997 29.7% 41.2%	1975 1997 72.9% 77.9%

Source: United Nations Development Programme (UNDP). Data are taken from numerous tables in the UNDP's annual *Human Development Report, 1999* (New York: Oxford University Press, 1999); cf. the World Bank's annual *World Development Report*, also published by Oxford University Press.

A Look Ahead

A few further comments are in order concerning the future of international cooperation in the economic realm. Historically when we think of international cooperation, we think of cooperation among states: Consider the post–World War II creation of the IMF, the World Bank, and the construction of international regimes. The dominant paradigm or image among political leaders traditionally has been one of national economies facing the outside world, paralleling the realist perspective of states as the key unit of international relations.

It can be argued, however, that this distinction between national and international economies is outdated. As noted here and in Chapter One and Chapter Nine, a remarkable globalization of financial markets has occurred, eroding the

A P P L Y I N G   T H E O R Y

TECHNOLOGY, COMPETITIVENESS, AND GLOBAL POLITICAL ECONOMY

Economic growth in late twentieth-century economies is profoundly influenced by innovations and upward shifts in technology. A number of economists have been re-examining conventional (or neoclassical) thinking that focuses primarily on investment capital and labor inputs to production processes, giving relatively less attention to technology or knowledge-based inputs.

The conventional view that at a certain point each new input of capital or labor results in successively smaller gains in production—so-called "diminishing results"—is challenged by economists who see investment in technology or knowledge capital as actually producing "increasing returns." The new thinking extends views developed in the 1930s and 1940s by economist Joseph Schumpeter, a contemporary of John Maynard Keynes, who addressed the impact of technological innovation on business cycles.

Investments in technology are very costly; however, they are seen as crucial determinants of economic growth and future competitiveness in the global economy. Governments have been active players along with business enterprises in pursuing technological development, particularly high technologies with application in such knowledge-intensive industries as electronics, computers, and telecommunications.

Know-how in advanced materials, superconductors, semiconductors, computers, and lasers has very real market applicability. Payoffs in these sectors are potentially not only greater but also increasing compared with similar investments in machines for lower-technology manufacturing enterprises. The implication is that countries and firms able to work in this high-technology sector will reap the greater rewards of knowledge-intensive production.

Question: Is it inevitable that such a trend will increase the development gap between the First and Third Worlds?

ability of states to control their "national economies."[3] Similarly in terms of production, it becomes difficult to determine exactly what is an "American" product. For example in the 1990s an American consumer paying $20,000 for a Pontiac Le Mans would have seen $6,000 of that sum going to South Korea for parts and operations, $3,500 to Japan, $1,500 to Germany, and an additional $1,400 to other suppliers of products and services in these countries. Less than $8,000 went to pay for goods and services in the United States.[4]

It is possible that we may soon witness further political fallout from the increase in global economic interdependence. First, now that economic barriers among the advanced capitalist states have been reduced significantly, differences in domestic economic structures—government policies and patterns of private sector industrial organization—may become more important. The best example involves U.S. criticism of Japan's domestic economic structure and policies that aggressively push Japanese exports and make it difficult to import foreign goods and services. A key aspect of support for the postwar international economic order has been a domestic social compact between state and society in many countries in which support for an open-international market is balanced by domestic programs

[3]See Benjamin J. Cohen, "Phoenix Risen: The Resurrection of Global Finance," *World Politics*, vol. 48, no. 2 (January 1996): 268–96.

[4]Robert Reich, *The Work of Nations* (New York: Knopf, 1991), note 44, p. 113.

designed to support workers with unemployment compensation, retraining, and other benefits as part of a social "safety net." High and increasing costs have made it increasingly difficult for governments to live up to their end of the domestic bargain.[5] As a result political criticism of free trade has increased.

Second, even if unilateral protectionism does not come about, regional trade and other economic arrangements run the risk of becoming mutually exclusive camps if members turn inward and away from interdependent relations within broader global markets. Such blocks could evolve in North America, Europe, and the Far East.

Third, the growing North-South economic divide is a challenge not only to a truly global economy, but also a threat to an emerging global civil society. Economic and social inequality continues to be an important feature of world politics. If populations continue to grow so rapidly, capitalist political economy will be put to the test as resource and environmental constraints make sustainable development extraordinarily difficult in many areas of the Third World.[6] The domestic, regional, and international political repercussions could be significant.

In sum maintaining an open global financial and trading environment consistent with liberal or openness principles is a substantial challenge in coming decades in a world that could just as easily move in the opposite direction.

CONCLUSION

In this chapter we have examined some of the key concepts and issues associated with the global political economy. As we noted in Chapter One, when people speak of the expansion of global interdependence, very often they are referring to economic interdependence. Particularly since the end of World War II, the world has been increasingly caught up in a web of economic relations, the extent and density of which were heretofore unknown. Furthermore economic interdependence has progressively worked to undermine the claims of governments that they have the ability to protect national economies from the effects of the larger, global political economy. The notion of economic independence is rapidly fading as international economic issues become domestic political issues and vice versa. Globalization is having an enormous impact.

As we have noted, however, the benefits of global economic interdependence and interconnectedness are uneven. Some states prosper more than others. As in earlier years the Third World or the South continues to be trapped in poverty. Already beset by problems of political legitimacy, many such regimes see their authority further eroded by an unforgiving global economy that rewards those with highly trained and adaptable work forces with access to the most modern technology. For every Singapore or Malaysia, there are five Sierra Leones or Sudans. So despite growing global economic interdependence, this does not mean a global economic leveling is occurring. The gap between North and South

---

[5]John Gerard Ruggie, "At Home Abroad, Abroad at Home: International Liberalisation and Domestic Stability in the New World Economy," *Millennium: Journal of International Studies*, vol. 24, no. 3 (Winter 1995): 507–26.

[6]See Andrew Hurrell and Ngaire Woods, "Globalisation and Inequality," *Millennium: Journal of International Studies*, vol. 24, no. 3 (Winter 1995): 447–70.

continues to widen and there remains the danger of mutually exclusive, regional economic trading blocks forming in the more advanced areas of the world that compete with one another.

KEY TERMS

political economy *p. 299*   capitalism *p. 300*

OTHER CONCEPTS

internationalization *p. 299*
globalization *p. 299*
mode of production
    p. 300
feudalism *p. 300*
markets *p. 300*
money *p. 300*
investment *p. 301*
capital goods *p. 301*
gross national product
    (GNP) *p. 301*
capital formation *p. 301*

gross domestic product
    (GDP) *p. 301*
mercantilism *p. 304*
factors of production
    p. 304
liberal *p. 304*
free market *p. 304*
division of labor *p. 305*
comparative advantage
    p. 305
protectionism *p. 305*
free trade *p. 305*

imperialism *p. 307*
neocolonial *p. 308*
multinational corporation
    (MNC) *p. 308*
cartel *p. 310*
devalue *p. 311*
liquidity *p. 312*
hard currency *p. 313*
uneven development
    p. 316
world-system theory
    p. 317

ADDITIONAL READINGS

A classic reading, worth pursuing in serious study, is Adam Smith, *The Wealth of Nations* (1776). Among the available editions are those from Oxford University Press and University of Chicago Press, both 1976. Many cite Smith, but few have actually read him and understand the context and meaning of this work. The first three of the five "books" or parts are the most important; however, his classic reference to invisible hand is to be found in the fourth book. Smith's earlier (1759 and 1761) *Theory of Moral Sentiments* (Indianapolis, IN: Oxford University Press, 1976) presents his understandings about how moral values relate to political economy in society. Smith's works have also been reprinted by Liberty Fund, Inc. (Indianapolis, IN). Max Weber's *Protestant Ethic and the Spirit of Capitalism* (NY: Charles Scribner's Sons, 1958, 1976), written as a challenge to Marx's more material explanation for the emergence of capitalism, formulates the hypothesis that religious ideas that eventually became secularized in modern commercial culture were at least as important as material factors, if not more so. See also Weber's classic *Economy and Society* (Berkeley: University of California Press, 1968, 1978). Two books on the development of different forms of capitalist political economy including ideas and practical realities in relation to public versus private ownership of the means of production are Karl Polanyi's *The Great Transformation* (Boston: Beacon Press, 1944, 1957) and Joseph A. Schumpeter's *Capitalism, Socialism, and Democracy* (New York: Harper and Row, 1942, 1976). Another good read in this genre is Albert O. Hirschman's *The Passions and the Interests: Political Arguments for Capitalism Before Its Triumph* (Princeton, N.J.: Princeton University Press, 1977, 1997).

For an overview of international political economy, see Robert Gilpin, *The Political Economy of International Relations* (Princeton, N.J.: Princeton University Press, 1987), Robert O. Keohane and Joseph Nye, *Power and Interdependence* (Boston: Little Brown, 1977), and James A. Caporaso and David P. Levine, *Theories of Political Economy* (New York: Cambridge University Press, 1992). Among his many valuable works, but particularly relevant to the historical twentieth-century discussion in this chapter, is Charles Kindleberger's *The World in Depression, 1929–1939* (Berkeley, Calif.: University of California Press, 1973).

A useful textbook, published in several editions by Prentice-Hall and particularly strong in international political economy, is *Continuity and Change in World Politics* by our University of Denver colleague, Barry Hughes. A comprehensive treatment of international political economy focusing on concepts and theories, global trade and montary systems, multinational corporations and North-South relations, technology and domestic sources of national economic behavior, and business cycles and globalization is Robert A. Isaak, *Managing World Economic Change: International Political Economy*, 3rd ed. (Upper Saddle River, N.J.: Prentice Hall, 1991, 2000). Other textbooks in various editions are Susan Strange, *States and Markets* and Joan Spero, *The Politics of International Economic Relations* (both New York: St. Martin's). For a useful anthology of selected readings on various topics in international political economy, see David N. Balaam and Michael Veseth, *Readings in International Political Economy* (Upper Saddle River, N.J.: Prentice-Hall, 1996).

On equity and social justice in global political economy, see George Demartino, *Global Economy, Global Justice: Theoretical and Policy Alternatives to Neolib eralism* (London: Routledge, 2000). Cf. David P. Levine, *Wealth and Freedom: An Introduction to Political Economy* (N.Y.: Cambridge University Press, 1995).

THE POLITICAL ECONOMY OF INTERNATIONAL TRADE, MONEY, AND REGIONAL INTEGRATION

"Economic interdependence among nations places a premium on frameworks and institutions. I am sure we would all prefer the rule of law over the law of the jungle. I am confident we would choose sustainable gains, within a stable and predictable system, over an unstructured and unregulated global environment. We need rules of the road and norms to guide relations between individuals and communities. This is as true of the global village as it is of the village each of us may have come from."

KOFI ANNAN, UN GENERAL SECRETARY

he following report appeared in the "Weekly Piracy Report, 5/16/00" of the ICC Commercial Crime Services (www.iccwbo.org):

- Ships calling at the Indonesian ports of Belawan, Jakarta, Merak, Samarinda, and Tanjong Priok have reported numerous pirate attacks while at anchor and at berth. Attacks have also been reported at Chittagong, Mongla, and Chennai.

- "MT Global Mars" departed Port Kelang in Malaysia on 22.02.2000 for Haldia, India with 6,000 metric tons of palm oil products. Her last reported position was 07 32N-97 24E at 1400 on 23.02.2000. Since then there has been no contact with the vessel. The vessel was hijacked by pirates on 23.02.2000. The eighteen crew (eight from South Korea and ten from Myanmar) were set adrift in a small boat.

- All vessels are advised to maintain antipiracy watches and report all suspicious movements of craft. Piratical attacks should be immediately reported to the Piracy Reporting Centre, Kuala Lumpur, Malaysia.

International **trade**—**exporting** and **importing**—can indeed be dangerous business. Carrying valuable cargoes across troubled waters and up and down rivers was a centuries-long struggle between trading companies and their ships' captains and crews and bands of pirates making robbery their central occupation. Tales heard ashore from the safety and comfort of firesides at home (and far from the reality of fighting, life and death, and material gain and loss) were engaging and the colorful characters daring.

Among the pirates, Jean Laffite and Blackbeard (Edward Teach) became legendary and Robert Louis Stevenson immortalized Long John Silver in his fictional *Treasure Island*. Sir Walter Scott and James Fenimore Cooper also entertained their readers with novels about piracy on the high seas complete with sword fights among swashbuckling sailors, skull-and-crossbones pirate flags, and ominous, suspense-filled narratives. "Hang 'em from the yardarms at first light!" became a classic refrain in novels (and later in cinema) when it came to giving pirates their just due.

Piracy at sea is anything but new. The political leadership in ancient Rome, for example, sent ships to stop the piracy that had long plagued Mediterranean commerce since the first century B.C. Decline of the Roman empire several centuries later removed a major obstacle to pirates and piracy, which returned with a vengeance to challenge commerce in succeeding centuries.

Responding to growth in the volume and importance of trade in modern times, national navies were mobilized to protect **international commerce**. Portrayed as a threat to humankind, piracy was seen under customary international law as a crime against all nations, a capital offense, enforceable by any of them. In a quest against pirates governments sent out their newly formed deep-water navies, capable of combat operations on the high seas far away from national shore lines.

The record of international law enforcement, however, was mixed. Sometimes states encouraged attacks on commercial ships of their enemies—referred to technically as **privateering** rather than *piracy*, but potentially just as devastating to international commerce. Pirates of the Caribbean were joined by prominent sixteenth-century English buccaneers such as Sir Francis Drake (c. 1540–96) and Sir John Hawkins (1532–95). They directed much of their energies toward disrupting Spanish commerce but also participated in the terrible slave trade then rampant. Privateering played a role in the late sixteenth-century English-Spanish struggle that culminated decisively in 1588 with the sinking of the Spanish *armada* of national warships by England. This loss of naval power spelled the beginning of the displacement of Spain as a power in the New World, a retreat that ultimately was not completed until the 1820s in the period of national independence movements in Latin America.

In the 1600s and 1700s, countries such as England engaged only in selective law enforcement against pirates, in effect tacitly encouraging pirates to direct their efforts against the commerce of enemy states such as Spain. By contrast a stronger law-enforcement consensus emerged in the nineteenth century. Beginning in 1803, marines aboard U.S. Navy ships took action against pirates operating from North African ports—an action commemorated in a famous refrain in the U.S. Marine Corps hymn—"to the shores of Tripoli."

After the Anglo-American War of 1812 and the subsequent defeat in Europe of Napoleon's armies, the U.S., British, and Dutch navies, and later the French fleet, coalesced to fight and win the war against piracy in the Mediterranean waged from North African locations. Two other major concentrations of pirates in the nineteenth century were the Persian (or Arab) Gulf, where pirates had found refuge in settlements referred to collectively as the Pirate Coast, and the strategic Straits of Malacca through which most European shipping passed to and from the Far East. In the 1820s London dispatched the Royal Navy to the Gulf to stop pirates from preying on British and other shipping en route to (or coming from) India, China, and elsewhere in Asia and the Pacific.

Diplomacy combined with the force of the Royal Navy resulted in truces signed with local Arab rulers (or sheikhs), assuring British protection of Arab "city states" (and formally renaming the area the "Trucial" Coast) in exchange for agreement by the local sheikhs to deny refuge to pirates. More difficult was curbing piracy in the Far East in the Straits of Malacca, a narrow corridor between present-day Singapore and Malaysia on the north side and Indonesia on the south through which most British, French, Dutch, and Portuguese commerce passed. The Malacca coast on the Asian mainland and seemingly countless islands in the Indonesian archipelago provided ample harbor to pirates. Only when greater naval presence in the region was established were pirates kept at bay.

Though decidedly less common today than in earlier times, piracy continues to be a threat to trade even in the twenty-first century with occasional incidents reported at sea. Brigandage or robbery of overland shipments as well as hijackers commandeering aircraft also continue to pose present-day challenges to public and private interests as well as to national law-enforcement authorities concerned with international commerce and threats to civil aviation.

The point we want to make is that trade has always been linked with world politics. In this chapter we will deal with trade, money, and regional integration projects designed to enhance international commerce. For those new to the subject, the large number of concepts introduced here may be a particularly challenging introduction to a complex, technical subject. Because the authors view economics as much too important to be left just to economists, we think the subject deserves greater attention than even the scope of this volume allows. Indeed, the study of international relations and world politics cannot be complete in our view without greater understanding of political economy in an increasingly globalized world. We start out by providing the conceptual basics in terms of international trade.

CLASSICAL TRADE THEORY AND COMPARATIVE ADVANTAGE

Piracy and other illicit activities emerged early as threats to international commerce. But why do countries trade in the first place? One answer is provided by classical trade theory drawn from the writings of David Ricardo (1772–1823) and others. Classical trade theory predicts that countries (their corporations and their other firms) will tend *ceteris paribus* (i.e., other things "equal" or held constant[1]) to produce and export those products in which they have a ***comparative advantage*** and at levels determined by both their productive capacities and

comparative advantage In classic trade theory, the concept that countries will produce and export to other countries those products that they can produce relatively more efficiently than can their trading partners.

---

[1]Economists often use the term "other things equal," or in Latin *ceteris paribus*, as a caveat or warning that the model they are describing or the argument they are making contains simplifying assumptions—for example, that factors held as constants in a model or argument are variables in the real world that could otherwise affect the predicted outcomes.

the demand for these products in domestic and external (regional and global) markets. If there were no differences in efficiency of production and domestic production capacity were sufficient to meet demand, in theory there would be no trade at all.

For countries or their business firms to engage in international trade requires some reason or rationale for doing so. Thus trade depends upon *differences*, not sameness in relative efficiency and capacity of production among two or more countries and their businesses actively engaging in the buying and selling of diverse goods and services—the products they trade regionally or globally.

The reason we give so much attention in this chapter to understanding the economics of trade is that it is so important to countries worldwide. The importance of trade in national economies is apparent in Table 11.1, which depicts exports and imports as a percentage of total domestic economic production as measured by GDP. As noted in Chapter Ten, it should not surprise us that anything so important as economics is also highly *political*. Politics is core to economics as peoples, their governments (and the international and nongovernmental organizations they form) inevitably become involved to a greater or lesser degree in the decisions they make about budgets, money, trade, investment, and other commercial matters. Particularly for states, as we noted in Chapter Three, economic capabilities are one indicator of overall state power, and hence of interest to realists and pluralists alike.

Some people think governments have a constructive role to play in managing their economies and working with other governments to manage regional and global commerce. Others prefer a *laissez-faire* approach, minimizing government participation or interference in the marketplace, whether domestically or globally. Having said that, most *laissez-faire* advocates concede that government treasuries and their central banks wind up playing an instrumental role in global commerce by managing the national supply of money and assuming obligations to make payments to other countries that come from international trade, investment, and other commercial or financial transactions. These transactions are summarized in the box on page 332. Governments, their courts, and their law-enforcement authorities also play a pivotal role in defining, enforcing, and adjudicating disputes concerning property rights. However we look at it, it is difficult to talk about trade and commerce without talking about politics and the roles played by governments and international organizations.

A Rolls Royce dealership in Moscow.

TABLE 11.1   INTERNATIONAL TRADE

Exports and imports are an important part of national economies, although some countries are relatively more dependent on their trade sectors than others. For example Germany's exports are 24 percent of its GDP. By contrast, although the United States is the world's largest exporter, exports amount to only 12 percent of its GDP. As discussed in Chapter Ten, when exports are greater than imports, the dollar difference adds to GDP. Conversely if imports exceed exports, GDP is reduced by that dollar difference. The following table depicts the relative importance of trade in a representative sample of countries organized by level of development or size of economy and by region.

COUNTRIES	EXPORTS (US$ MILLIONS)	EXPORTS AS PERCENTAGE OF GDP	IMPORTS (US$ MILLIONS)	IMPORTS AS PERCENTAGE OF GDP
HIGH INCOME/ DEVELOPMENT				
Group of Seven				
United States	856,000	12	965,700	13
Japan	456,889	10	432,269	9
Germany	569,614	24	541,018	23
France	368,605	24	328,652	21
Italy	324,046	27	260,606	21
United Kingdom	340,685	30	349,600	30
Canada	234,297	40	211,487	36
Other European				
Austria	93,400	41	94,628	41
Belgium	183,718	68	171,012	64
Czech Republic	29,950	58	32,208	63
Denmark	64,916	35	56,229	31
Finland	47,347	38	37,251	30
Greece	18,841	15	29,295	24
Ireland	53,981	76	43,237	61
Luxemburg	15,467	91	13,729	81
Netherlands	212,504	54	187,182	47
Norway	64,230	41	50,620	32
Poland	35,616	26	41,170	30
Portugal	33,658	31	41,672	38
Slovakia	10,976	56	12,366	64
Spain	148,125	26	143,065	25
Sweden	100,672	40	83,713	33
Switzerland	106,413	36	94,088	32
Other Regions				
Argentina	29,318	9	34,899	11
Chile	20,716	27	22,540	29
Costa Rica	4,360	46	4,529	48
Israel	31,065	32	43,873	45
Republic of Korea	168,683	38	171,085	39

(table continues)

TABLE 11.1   (CONTINUED)

COUNTRIES	EXPORTS (US$ MILLIONS)	EXPORTS AS PERCENTAGE OF GDP	IMPORTS (US$ MILLIONS)	IMPORTS AS PERCENTAGE OF GDP
Other Regions (cont'd)				
Kuwait	15,974	53	12,407	41
New Zealand	18,921	29	18,337	28
Uruguay	4,511	23	4,563	23
MEDIUM INCOME/ DEVELOPMENT				
Latin America				
Brazil	61,982	8	83,556	10
Colombia	14,553	15	17,422	18
Mexico	121,772	30	121,896	30
Nicaragua	803	41	1,294	66
Panama	7,759	94	7,520	91
Peru	8,182	13	10,617	17
Venezuela	25,735	29	17,692	20
Asia				
Cambodia	920	30	1,281	42
China	207,303	23	166,759	18
India	44,107	12	59,230	16
Indonesia	60,106	28	60,700	28
Malaysia	92,877	94	91,360	93
Thailand	72,382	47	71,340	46
Kazakhstan	7,810	35	8,280	37
Pakistan	10,009	16	12,955	21
Philippines	40,284	49	48,777	59
Vietnam	11,480	46	13,443	54
Other Regions				
Egypt	15,251	20	18,820	25
Hungary	20,801	45	21,013	46
Romania	10,359	30	12,802	37
Russian Federation	102,196	23	90,065	20
Saudi Arabia	62,991	45	43,017	31
South Africa	35,848	28	34,365	27
Turkey	46,675	25	57,698	30
LOW INCOME/ DEVELOPMENT				
Africa				
Angola	5,196	68	5,003	65
Côte d'Ivoire	4,777	47	4,055	40
Congo (Dem. Rep. of)	1,463	24	1,350	22

TABLE 11.1 (CONTINUED)				
COUNTRIES	EXPORTS (US$ MILLIONS)	EXPORTS AS PERCENTAGE OF GDP	IMPORTS (US$ MILLIONS)	IMPORTS AS PERCENTAGE OF GDP
Africa (cont'd)				
Ethiopia	1,017	16	1,682	26
Mali	644	25	889	35
Mozambique	500	18	937	34
Nigeria	16,286	41	13,677	34
Senegal	1,481	33	1,730	38
Tanzania	1,259	22	2,118	36
Uganda	826	13	1,335	20
Zambia	1,276	33	1,474	38
Other Regions				
Bangladesh	5,075	12	7,656	18
Laos	418	24	721	41
Yemen	2,489	44	2,966	52

Source: United Nations Development Programme (UNDP) as published in *Human Development Report, 1999* (New York: Oxford University Press, 1999), pp. 45–48.

Consistent with Ricardian thinking (see page 334), the **Heckscher-Ohlin theorem** developed early in the twentieth century holds that because different countries have diverse factor endowments—different amounts and quality of *land, labor,* and *capital,* they likely will export those goods or services in which their combination of these production factors gives them a comparative advantage. For example producers in some countries having sufficient labor and a favorable climate might specialize in agricultural production, whereas producers in other countries with larger capital endowments might specialize in manufactured goods and services such as banking.

Capital-rich countries may or may not be rich in land or other natural resources, but their capital may still give them decided advantages over other countries that are natural resource-rich countries. For example oil production, refineries, and transport by ships at sea and pipelines across land areas (as with mining and marketing of other mineral commodities) require large amounts of capital. The same is true of agriculture.

We still often think of agriculture—raising animals and the growing and harvesting of plants for food and other purposes—as a labor-intensive enterprise favoring countries with good soil, favorable growing climate, and abundant populations willing to work on their own land or on larger farms and ranches owned by agribusiness interests. Historically this has been the case. Even today the composition (proportion of GDP) of many Third World economies remains 30 percent or more agricultural compared to advanced-industrial or postindustrial, First World economies that are perhaps just 1 to 3 percent agricultural.

On the other hand, the capital-rich United States and other First World economies tend to be relatively more efficient in agricultural production because

TRADE AND PAYMENTS BALANCES: AN OVERVIEW OF INTERNATIONAL COMMERCIAL ACCOUNTING

The *balance of trade* or *current account* (b) refers to exports (X) minus imports (M) of goods (merchandise trade) and services across national borders during a specified period of time (typically a month, quarter [three months], or year). Thus if Japan has exported more than it has imported in a given year, it is said to have run a **surplus** or positive balance of trade. By contrast if the United States imports more than it exports over the same period of time, it is said to have a **deficit** or negative trade balance.

$$\begin{array}{ccccc} \text{Balance of Trade} & & \text{Exports} & & \text{Imports} \\ b & = & X & - & M \end{array}$$

The trade balance or current account is only one of several accounts in a country's overall **balance of payments**. Net investment, the *capital account*, is another. This is the difference between capital investment by domestic investors in foreign countries and capital investment by foreign investors in the country's domestic economy.

Unilateral transfers is a third account. This refers to grants or other transfers received by a country's government (e.g., foreign aid) or residents (e.g., social security or other pensions received) from foreign governments minus grants or other transfers sent by the country's government to other governments or to residents living in other countries.

Finally there is the *official reserves* account (referred to historically as the gold account) composed of assets used to balance payments with other countries; these are generally gold, foreign currencies, and special drawing rights (SDRs) from the International Monetary Fund (IMF) that can be counted as official reserves. If after adding up the balances in the other accounts there is a net deficit, the balance can be made up by sending official reserves to other countries. On the other hand if the sum of a country's other accounts shows a surplus, other countries may be called upon to transfer a portion of their reserves to add to the official reserves of the surplus country.

$$\begin{array}{cccccccccccc} \text{Balance} & & & \text{I} & & \text{II} & & \text{III} & & \text{IV} & & \\ \text{of} & (B) & = & \text{Current} & + & \text{Capital} & + & \text{Unilateral} & + & \text{Official} & = & 0^* \\ \text{Payments} & & & \text{Account} & & \text{Account} & & \text{Transfers} & & \text{Reserves} & & \end{array}$$

BALANCE OF PAYMENTS IN OUTLINE FORM

I. *Current Account* (Goods and Services)
   A. Examples of Credits/Positive Entries (+):
      1. Merchandise exports (goods)
      2. Transportation abroad provided by domestic carriers (airplanes, ships, etc.) and paid for by foreigners
      3. Expenditures by tourists from foreign countries
      4. Financial services and insurance provided by domestic banks and other firms to (and paid for by) foreigners
      5. Interest, dividends, and other financial payments received by domestic residents from abroad
      6. Spending by foreign governments (e.g., the costs of running their embassies and other missions, making official visits, stationing troops if any, and various other activities)
   B. Examples of Debits/Negative Entries (–):
      1. Merchandise imports (goods)
      2. Transportation abroad provided by foreign carriers and paid for by residents
      3. Expenditures by residents as tourists in other countries
      4. Financial services and insurance provided by foreign banks and other firms to (and paid for by) domestic residents
      5. Interest, dividends, and other financial payments made to foreigners
      6. Spending by the government in foreign countries (e.g., the costs of running their embassies and other missions, making official visits, stationing troops if any, and various other activities)

II. *Capital Account*
  A. Examples of Credits/Positive Entries (+):
    1. Increase in foreign-owned deposits or accounts in domestic banks, brokerage firms, or other financial institutions
    2. Decrease in domestically owned deposits or accounts in foreign banks, brokerage firms, or other financial institutions
    3. Purchase of domestic stocks, bonds, or other securities by foreigners
  B. Examples of Debits/Negative Entries (−):
    1. Decrease in foreign-owned deposits or accounts in domestic banks, brokerage firms, or other financial institutions
    2. Increase in domestically owned deposits or accounts in foreign banks, brokerage firms or other financial institutions
    3. Purchase of foreign stocks, bonds, or other securities by domestic residents
III. *Unilateral Transfers* (Gifts or Grants)
  A. Examples of Credits/Positive Entries (+):
    1. Grants, contributions, or pensions received from nongovernmental foreign sources

    2. Grants or other payments (including pensions) received from foreign governments
  B. Examples of Debits/Negative Entries (−):
    1. Grants or contributions made to foreigners or residents in foreign countries (e.g., pensions)
    2. Grants or other payments made to foreign governments
IV. *Official Reserves* (gold, foreign currencies, SDRs)
  A. Credits/Positive Entries (+):
    1. Export of reserves, thus reducing payment amounts due to foreign countries as a result of net deficits in the other three accounts (current account, capital account, and unilateral transfers)
  B. Debits/Negative Entries (−):
    1. Import of reserves, thus reducing payment amounts due by foreign countries as a result of net deficits in the other three accounts

*Balance of payments equals zero with overall surpluses or deficits in the first three accounts compensated by transfers (gains or losses) of official reserves in the fourth account.

capital has been effectively substituted for higher-cost labor in these countries. Indeed, mechanization of agriculture, coupled with agricultural research and development of growing-and producing technologies require vast amounts of capital, which they have in relatively more abundant supply than Third World countries do. Such technologies include using chemicals as fertilizer and for insect or pest control, developing plant hybrids with greater or more diverse crop yields, and the more controversial area of genetically engineering new plant and animal forms by altering DNA or cell content.

Thus capital-intensive agriculture becomes a comparative cost advantage for many capital-rich countries. Moreover governments in these countries, enjoying ample access to capital through taxation or borrowing, have also subsidized the politically influential agricultural sectors in their countries. Not surprisingly, in the absence of tariffs, quotas, or other barriers, these capital-rich countries are prone to export agricultural produce to each other and even to Third World countries! In a capitalist world economy, we should not be surprised that decisive advantages even in agriculture often go to capital-rich countries.

Another related objection to classical trade theory is that it ignores unequal **terms of trade**. Beginning in the 1960s, Latin American and other economists complained that Third World, less-developed countries of the South were in a decidedly disadvantageous position compared to more advanced, industrial countries of

terms of trade   Ratio of export prices of one country to those of another, which tells us in effect the amount of revenue from a country's export sales *to* the other that can be used to pay for imports *from* the other.

APPLYING   THEORY

CLASSICAL RICARDIAN THINKING ON PRODUCTION, COMPARATIVE ADVANTAGE, AND TRADE

To understand classical trade theory and the concept of comparative advantage, it helps to simplify things a bit. So let's pretend there are only two countries in the world (*Insula* and *Terra*), each capable of producing the same two products. Many texts illustrate the concept of comparative advantage as affecting the trade of cloth versus wheat or wine versus textiles, but we will modernize the example by referring to the trade of semiconductors versus lumber. (Semiconductors used in computers and other high-technology applications conduct electricity better than insulators, but not as well as good conductors do.)

Insula is an island country with small, well-tended forests and other natural resources. Terra, a continental country, also has natural resources and vast forest lands. Let's assume each country uses the factors of production (land, labor, and capital) it has to produce just two products—semiconductors and lumber. It takes land (or natural resources) to produce them: Silicon or other crystalline substances are used to manufacture semiconductors (used in computers and other advanced technologies) and forests with trees of one kind or another are necessary to produce lumber (used in construction, manufacture of paper, and for many other applications).

In the real world, of course, even the smallest national economies produce more than just two products and many national economies are able to produce and compete in the sale in regional and global markets of a large number of products. They use money to buy and sell, import and export. To keep things simple, however, let's assume that these countries **barter** or exchange one product for another without using money. We omit in this discussion the effects of such variables as different levels of domestic demand, different size economies and scale of production, changes in exchange rate that affect prices (a topic discussed later in this chapter), and government intervention (as in subsidizing production or imposing tariffs or quotas to protect and encourage domestic production of a particular product). Rather, in order to understand classical free-trade theory and its predictions, it is helpful to reduce the trade puzzle to its

basic essentials—production tradeoffs of just two products produced and traded between just two countries *ceteris paribus* (i.e., holding all other factors constant or "equal").

Production Possibilities

In addition to land and other natural resources, both semiconductor and lumber production rely heavily on labor (or human resources, especially *skilled* labor) and capital in the forms of machinery, work space, and finance for these enterprises. Take a look at the graphic presentation of production possibilities for the two countries in Figure 11.A. The diagonal lines on both graphs represent the maximum possible combinations of semiconductors and lumber that can be produced separately by Insula and Terra.

If Insula produces only semiconductors (putting *all* of its available land, labor, and capital to that purpose), the most it can produce is 100,000 units, but no lumber at all is produced at that level of semiconductor production. If Insula wants to produce at least some lumber, it will have to reduce semiconductor production a bit to free up some land, labor, and capital, reallocating these to lumber production. On the other hand if Insula forgoes semiconductor production entirely and produces only lumber, the most lumber it can produce is 50,000 units.

As a practical matter, however, firms in Insula actually produce *both* lumber and semiconductors, as depicted on the graph by point I: 25,000 units of lumber and 50,000 semiconductors. A similar analysis for Terra reveals a maximum production possibility of *either* 100,000 units of lumber *or* 50,000 semiconductors with *actual* production, point T, being a combination of 50,000 units of lumber and 25,000 semiconductors.

The *marginal* tradeoff between producing semiconductors and lumber for Insula is 2:1—for every two units of reduced semiconductor production, Insula can free up enough land, labor, and capital to produce one more unit of lumber instead. The reverse is also true: For every unit of reduced lumber production, Insula can allocate enough land, labor, and capital to produce two more

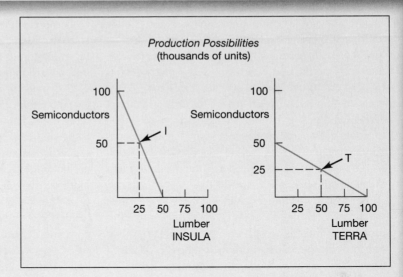

FIGURE 11.A

semiconductors instead. (We can also see this by look-ing at the downward or negative slope of the diagonal line, which is 2.0.)

By contrast Terra's *marginal* tradeoff between pro-ducing semiconductors and lumber is 1:2—for every unit of reduced semiconductor production, Terra can free up enough land, labor, and capital to produce two more units of lumber instead. Alternatively if Terra for-goes two units of lumber production, it will have enough land, labor, and capital to produce one more semiconductor instead. (Again we can also see this by looking at the downward or negative slope of the diag-onal line, which is 1/2 or 0.5.)

Comparative Advantage and Specialization

These tradeoffs show us how Insula, compared to Terra, is relatively more efficient in producing semiconduc-tors than lumber (it can produce two more semicon-ductors for every unit of lumber production it forgoes) and Terra is relatively more efficient in producing lum-ber than semiconductors (for every unit of semicon-ductor production it forgoes, it can produce two more units of lumber). Put another way efficiency in produc-ing semiconductors allows Insula to produce them less expensively than Terra can. Terra's comparative advan-tage in lumber allows it to produce lumber less expen-sively than Insula can.

The idea of *tradeoffs* is captured by the term **oppor-tunity costs**. If a country (or more specifically, its cor-porations or other firms) choose to invest their capital and allocate labor and other resources to production of some quantity of semiconductors, the same capital and labor will not be available for production of some quantity of lumber (or other products). If Insula allo-cates *all* of its production to semiconductors, it will not have any labor or capital left to cut trees, process, and deliver lumber to market. Inability to produce *any* lum-ber because production factors have been allocated to producing only semiconductors is referred to as an op-portunity cost. As a practical matter, of course, produc-tion decisions in the real world are usually not all-or-nothing decisions. Instead a country may allo-cate its capital, labor, and natural resources to produc-tion of different amounts of semiconductors, lumber, or other products. Still, as the model depicts, Insula's de-cision this year to produce 50,000 semiconductors and 25,000 units of lumber (point I) also means it is forgo-ing (as "opportunity costs") the production of up to an additional 50,000 semiconductors *or* up to an addi-tional 25,000 units of lumber it could produce if a de-cision were made respectively either to produce more semiconductors (and less lumber) *or* more lumber (and fewer semiconductors).

(box continues)

A P P L Y I N G   T H E O R Y

In any event if both countries choose not to trade with each other and sustain their current production levels of both products (points I and T respectively), their total production will be 75,000 semiconductors (50,000 for Insula and 25,000 for Terra) and 75,000 units of lumber (25,000 for Insula and 50,000 for Terra). On the other hand if each specializes according to comparative advantage, total production of semiconductors and lumber can be increased from 75,000 to 100,000 units of each product—the maximum production possibility (see Figure 11.B).

Because of this difference in efficiency in the use of the three factors of production and consequent cost of production, there is an opportunity for trade. If the two countries do specialize in producing those products in which they enjoy a *comparative advantage*—those in which they are relatively more efficient as producers—aggregate or total production of both products can expand substantially. Assuming Insula needs the 50,000 semiconductors it now produces for domestic use, if production of semiconductors is increased to 100,000 (its maximum production possibility), it can increase its consumption or use of semiconductors somewhat but still have enough left over for export to Terra. Similarly, by specializing in lumber production, Terra can also increase its consumption of lumber somewhat but still have enough left over for export to Insula.

Based on prespecialization production levels, Insula can expect an export market or demand in Terra for at least 25,000 semiconductors and Terra can expect an export market or demand in Insula for at least 25,000 units of lumber. In fact Terra may wish to import more than 25,000 semiconductors and Insula may wish to import more than 25,000 units of lumber. Insula and Terra are able to exchange (or barter) these two products at a "price" or trade ratio advantageous to the parties. Again both countries can consume more domestically and still have enough left over for export to the other. Because more is produced less expensively through specialization, both countries engaging in trade can benefit mutually from this increase in production—an ability to consume more of both products than was possible before specialization of production. In this example the welfare of both countries is better off *after specializing* in production and export of semiconductors and lumber than it was before they did so. *The Bottom Line: Classical trade theory tells us* ceteris paribus *that countries tend to produce for export those products they produce most efficiently—those in which they enjoy a comparative advantage.*

In principle, in a free-trade environment both countries allow buying and selling and importing and exporting to proceed without any politically imposed

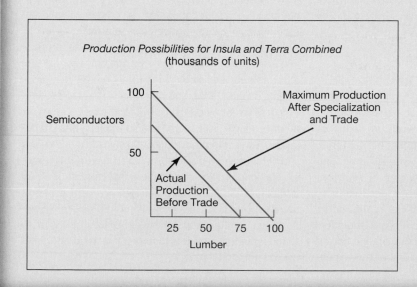

Production Possibilities for Insula and Terra Combined
(thousands of units)

FIGURE 11.B

restrictions or other obstacles—no tariffs, quotas, government subsidies to domestic producers, or any other barriers to trade. Whether applied on a regional or global basis, *the claim of classical trade theory is that if we allow free, unencumbered trade, countries will tend to specialize in production of those products (goods and services) in which they have a comparative advantage*. A world in which the most efficient producers of particular products tend to specialize in production of them results in maximizing or optimizing aggregate, worldwide production, thus enhancing global welfare. As critics are quick to point out, however, enhancing aggregate production through specialization and free trade does not mean an equal or even equitable distribution of these gains. Some countries and their businesses clearly benefit more than others.

Work by Eli Heckscher in 1919 and Bertil Ohlin in 1933 noted that trade occurs due to different concentrations or intensities of factors of production among countries—so-called *factor endowments*. A given country tends to export those products that are "intensive" in the factor it has in relative abundance compared to other countries. Thus the Heckscher-Ohlin theorem predicts that capital-rich countries tend to export such capital-intensive products as manufactured goods, whereas land or natural resource-rich countries tend to export **commodities**—minerals or agricultural products. The abundance of oil in Saudi Arabia and other oil-rich countries, for example, accounts for them being the world's largest oil exporters.

A challenge to the Heckscher-Ohlin theorem was raised in 1953 by Wassily Leontief in an empirical or factual study of trading relations, suggesting that other variables not accounted by Heckscher and Ohlin also affect trading outcomes. Subsequent studies lead many to conclude that the Heckscher-Ohlin theorem seems to capture an important part of the explanation of why and what states trade, but only a part. Other factors also need to be taken into account.

commodity Broadly, any article that is bought or sold; agricultural products, metals, and other minerals are often referred to as commodities and are traded in bulk on commodities exchanges.

the North. Economists like Argentine Raúl Prebisch observed that countries in the South export raw materials and agricultural commodities that tend not to increase (or even tend to decline) in price, whereas countries in the North gain an advantage from production and export of manufactured goods that tend to increase in price.

To address this and other trade problems, Third World countries have sought trade preferences from rich countries. Trade preferences can take the form of assurances by First World countries that they or their businesses will buy at least a certain minimum quantity of Third World products. Alternatively they may agree to give trade preferences—not to impose tariffs, quotas, or other barriers against Third World exports even as these countries retain such barriers against imports from the First World.

For their part the European Union (EU) countries have developed by political agreement the most extensive set of trade preferences in Africa, the Caribbean, and the Pacific (the so-called "ACP" countries), many of which were former colonies of EU members. In addition to benefits derived by Third World countries from these measures, trade preferences and cooperative monetary measures also tie them economically to the countries granting these favors. Critics thus see extensive trade preferences as a means of maintaining neocolonial, political-economic relations that also convey substantial advantages to First World countries. Defenders see little or nothing wrong with trade preferences or arrangements that benefit both sides, however unequally.

NEOCLASSICAL AND SUBSEQUENT ECONOMIC THOUGHT ON HOW THE GLOBAL POLITICAL ECONOMY WORKS ⁓

What we now call **neoclassical** economic theory refers to late nineteenth- and early twentieth-century developments in economic thought that departed from the labor theory of value and other approaches advanced by Adam Smith, David Ricardo, and other classical economists (see Chapter Ten). English economist Alfred Marshall (1842–1924) and French economist Leon Walras (1834–1910), although often at odds with each other, were particularly prominent early neoclassical contributors.

Instead of seeing the value of a good or service as determined primarily by the human labor put into its production, neoclassical economists see *value* in a market context—price as the outcome of **demand** for and **supply** of particular products. As such value is to be found in relative abundance or scarcity and in the utility buyers and sellers place on the goods or services they seek (demand) or provide (supply) to markets. Utility and marginal utility (the value to be found in each additional unit of a good or service) thus became key concepts in market analysis, with the equilibrium price dependent on the intersection of demand and supply curves representing quantities sought or provided at alternative prices in different types of markets (e.g., models of "perfect" or "pure" competition among many sellers, oligopoly among a few sellers, and monopoly dominated by one seller).

Bringing the ideas of earlier economists together, Marshall and Walras dealt with different aspects of market equilibrium as a conceptual device for understanding market forces. Although Smith, Ricardo, and other classical writers certainly dealt with individuals and firms as units in the marketplace, they also placed relatively more emphasis in their work on understanding the functioning of the economy as a whole (the subject of *macroeconomics*) whereas neoclassical economists focus relatively more on how purchasers (consumers or buyers) and suppliers (firms or sellers) interact in the marketplace (the subject of *microeconomics*).

Neoclassical economic theorists have developed and explored the applicability of such *microeconomic* concepts as *elasticity* of demand and supply—the expected response to changes in price (or income) with respect to quantities of a product buyers want to purchase or suppliers want to sell; *externalities*—the positive or negative impacts (benefits or costs) of market behaviors on others; *efficiency* and optimization of utility, production, allocation of resources, and performance of other market activities; and *rational expectation*, *public choice*, and *collective goods theories* that provide a basis for explaining or predicting market behaviors. Other important analytical concepts introduced by neoclassical economists to provide understanding of market processes include *marginal cost* (the cost of producing and supplying an additional unit), *marginal revenue* (the amount earned from sale of an additional unit), and *diminishing marginal returns*, or more simply, *diminishing returns* (that each additional unit of land, labor, or capital put into production—holding all other factors constant—will produce proportionately somewhat less of a product than the previous unit of land, labor, or capital). In all of this work, most neoclassical theorists have made heavy use of both mathematics (stating economic ideas symbolically in algebraic equations) and statistics, in what is usually referred to as *econometrics*.

At the same time other economists have also made substantial contributions to *macroeconomic* theory. Directly influenced by Marshall's earlier work, John

macroeconomics The branch of economic theory that deals with attempting to understand and explain the functioning of the economy as a whole, typically involving such aggregates as money supply and GNP or GDP.

microeconomics The branch of economic theory that deals with how purchasers and suppliers interact in the marketplace, which is sometimes referred to simply as price theory.

Maynard Keynes (1883–1946) and his followers have taken a macroeconomic view, dealing with *aggregate* demand and supply for an entire economy taken as a whole and exploring, for example, how demand is stimulated or dampened when government spends and taxes (**fiscal policy**) and influences the money supply and interest rates (**monetary policy**). Keynes also participated in laying political plans in 1944 for global actions through an International Monetary Fund (IMF) to assure international monetary flows and facilitate currency exchange so essential to international commerce (discussed more completely later in this chapter). Often at odds with Keynesian economists, the work of Milton Friedman and other **monetarists** has focused on how the supply and velocity or flow of money in an entire economy affect production and supply as well as demand for what is produced. For his part Joseph Schumpeter (1883–1950), a contemporary of Keynes, also took a macroeconomic perspective, particularly in his exploration of how changes in technology, innovation and other factors influence business cycles as well as the political-economic view in his work on how capitalism and socialism relate to democracy and democratic ideas.

These and other economists have made very important contributions to macroeconomic theories and concepts, but in our view have had an even greater impact on microeconomic theorizing. Originally formulated more with local or domestic markets in mind, microeconomic theories and concepts developed by neoclassical economists have increasing applicability to the global political economy. Markets for many goods and services now have truly worldwide scope. Microeconomic theory offers explanation of the exchange value (or price) of currencies in relation to each other as well as an account of the expected effects of governmental subsidies, regional integration, tariffs, quotas, or other barriers to trade—issues of enormous political importance, given the high economic stakes states, firms, consuming publics, and others have in such matters. In short neoclassical and other theorists have continued to expand our understanding of the global political economy beyond the foundational insights offered by classical writers.

Trade and "Increasing Returns" from Specialized, Large-Scale Production

Classical Ricardian free-trade theory (amplified by the already discussed Heckscher-Ohlin theorem concerning relative factor endowments) focuses primarily on cost differences among producers. If a country is relatively more cost-efficient at producing a particular good or service, it will tend to specialize in producing and exporting what is not consumed or used domestically. Or so says classical theory. It is the *differences* among countries that explain trade. In the absence of government intervention to put tariffs, quotas, or any other obstacles in the way of trade, countries will tend to specialize in producing those products in which they enjoy a comparative cost advantage relative to other producers. The result, then, of relegating production to the most efficient producers is, in principle, to maximize total productive capacity or aggregate output of goods and services, enhancing global welfare, however uneven the distribution of these gains from specialization and trade may be.

Not so fast, say some economists. Ricardian theory goes part way, but does not really provide a complete answer to why countries trade. Instead of focusing just on differences in production cost efficiencies, we also need to understand how **economies of scale** influence marketing and production for export trade. That the average cost per unit of producing a million semiconductors typically is less than when a production line is set up to produce only a thousand is an example of an economy or unit-cost reduction based on large-scale production. Existing producers, large or small, of particular goods and services thus may look globally to expand their markets and enjoy increasing gains from export trade, dramatically increasing sales by finding many more customers that can be served efficiently by increasing substantially the overall level or scale of domestic production.

In the 1930s and 1940s economist Joseph Schumpeter, a contemporary of John Maynard Keynes, addressed the impact of technological innovation on business cycles. Clusters of new technologies displace older technologies in a process of "creative destruction." Economic growth, particularly in early twenty-first-century advanced-industrial and postindustrial, information- or knowledge-based economies, is profoundly influenced by such innovations and upward shifts in technology. Likewise a number of economists have been reexamining conventional (both classical and neoclassical) thinking that focuses primarily on investment capital, labor, and natural resource inputs to production processes, giving relatively less attention to technology or knowledge-based inputs that, in fact, are increasingly important.

Investments in technology usually are very costly; however, they are seen as crucial determinants of economic growth and future competitiveness in the global economy. Governments have been active players along with business enterprises in pursuing technological development, particularly "high technologies" with application in such knowledge-intensive industries as electronics, computers, and telecommunications. Know-how in advanced materials, superconductors, semiconductors, computers, and lasers has very real market applicability. Payoffs in these sectors are potentially not only greater, but also increasing compared with similar investments in machines for lower-technology manufacturing enterprises. The implication is that countries and firms able to work in this high-technology sector will reap the greater rewards of knowledge-intensive production.

MIT economist Paul Krugman is prominent among those who have raised theoretical challenges to classical Ricardian trade theory. Krugman is careful to note, however, that focusing on increasing gains as motivation for export trade is a supplement to (not a replacement for) comparative-cost considerations that have dominated our explanation or understanding of why trade occurs.[2] Engaging in trade for increasing gains is not a new idea, but as Krugman suggests, we may not have given it sufficient consideration.

The increasing-gains argument, however, may actually matter more than merely enjoying a comparative-cost advantage, particularly for high-technology products in some markets in which certain firms have already well established themselves. It is difficult, although not impossible of course, to start up a new firm and achieve a strong market position when one or a few large firms with ready access to capital already dominate a particular market. It is even harder to compete when new, fast-changing high technologies are difficult to acquire and develop into marketable products that can be produced at sufficient scale to be cost (and price) competitive.

By contrast, because of their ready access to capital, large, established firms in industries with increasing returns to scale are usually quite able not only to beat start-up competition, but also to grow even larger and realize ever-increasing gains from expanding their export-market positions.

---

[2]For example see Paul R. Krugman, *Rethinking International Trade*, (Cambridge, Mass.: MIT Press, 1990, 1994).

Some telecommunications and other information-technology enterprises may be different. In this regard it is a world market still open to technological innovations advanced by individual entrepreneurs. Indeed, some start-up firms with high-technology applications have been successful challengers to established, large-scale firms, but even these players have had to secure substantial access to capital to finance and expand their efforts by selling stocks and issuing bonds in financial markets. Table 11.2 contains a list of some of the world's most prominent multinational corporations, each of which typically has a main headquarters in one country but is deeply involved in trade as well as manufacturing and other operations in a number of countries.

Aviation is a good example of a market in which only a few firms dominate globally. In fact, mergers and acquisitions of existing firms have continued to reduce the numbers of these large firms to just a few. Capital for production of aircraft and related high-technology products is thus increasingly concentrated in fewer corporations. Thousands of smaller firms offering specialized products are therefore increasingly dependent for contracts on a declining number of major producers. In order to compete on a scale with such U.S. giants as, for example,

Muslim women at a fast-food restaurant in Kota Bharu, Malaysia.

TABLE 11.2   MULTINATIONAL CORPORATIONS

Some of the most prominent firms in the global economy at the beginning of the first decade of the twenty-first century, organized alphabetically by sector or type of business, are listed here. **Multinational corporations** or **MNCs** are firms typically with main headquarters in one country but production or other operations in two or more countries; they play an increasingly important role in all aspects of the global economy. Ownership of these MNCs by nationals of different countries holding shares of stock or other stakes has also increased as the world economy has become more globalized. MNCs cover the globe in search of natural and human resources and markets, their operations bridging borders and often bypassing government regulation. They are also important carriers of technology and technological innovation. The following list is a representative sample, by no means a complete listing.

Information Technology

America Online (US)
Cisco Systems (US)
Dell (US)
EDS (US)
Hewlitt-Packard (US)
IBM (US)
Intel (US)
Microsoft (US)
SAP (Germany)

Electrical/Electronic

General Electric (US)
Matsushita (Japan)
Nokia (Finland)
Philips (Netherlands)
Siemens (Germany)

Telecommunications

AT&T (US)
BT (UK)
Lucent Technologies (US)
SBC Communications (US)
Vodafone (UK)

**Engineering/Aerospace/
   Automotive**

ABB (Switzerland/Sweden)
BMW (Germany)
Boeing (US)
Bosch (Germany)
Bridgestone (Japan)
Cooper Tire & Rubber (US)
Daimler Chrysler (Germany)
Ford (US)

General Motors (US)
Honda (Japan)
Mannesmann (Germany)
Mitsubishi (Japan)
Toyota (Japan)
Volkswagen (Germany)

Financial

AIG (US)
Axa (France)
Berkshire Hathaway (US)
Chase Manhattan (US)
Cigna (US)
Citigroup (US)
Credit Suisse (Switzerland)
Deutsche Bank (Germany)

(table continues)

TABLE 11.2	MULTINATIONAL CORPORATIONS (CONTINUED)

Financial (continued)
GE Capital (US)
Goldman Sachs (US)
HSBC (UK/Hong Kong)
JP Morgan (US)
Lloyds TSB (UK)
Merrill Lynch (US)
Morgan Stanley Dean Witter
   (US)

Pharmaceuticals/Health Care

Glaxo Wellcome (UK)
Johnson & Johnson (US)
Merck (US)
Novartis (Switzerland)
L'Oréal (France)
Pfizer (US)
Roche (Switzerland)

Retail

Amazon (US)
Carrefour (France)
Gap (US)
Home Depot (US)
Nike (US)
Seven-Eleven (US)

Sony (Japan)
3M (US)
Whirlpool (US)
WalMart (US)

Energy/Chemical

Akzo Nobel (Netherlands)
BASF (Germany)
Bayer (Germany)
BP Amoco (UK)
Dow Chemical (US)
DuPont (US)
Enron (US)
Exxon-Mobil (US)
Royal Dutch Shell
   (Netherlands/UK)
Schlumberger (US)

Natural Resources

Alcoa (US)
Bemis (US)
International Paper (US)
Nucor (US)
Pechiney (France)
Rio Tinto (UK/Australia)

Transport

Air France (France)
American (US)
British Airways (UK)
Delta (US)
Lufthansa (Germany)
TNT Post Groep (Netherlands)
United Airlines (US)
UPS (US)

Food/Beverages/Leisure

British American Tobacco (UK)
Cargill (US)
Coca Cola (US)
Danon (France)
Disney (US)
Fuji (Japan)
Heineken (Netherlands)
Kodak (US)
McDonald's (US)
Nestlé (Switzerland)
Pepsico (US)
Philip Morris (US)
Procter & Gamble (US)
Unilever (Netherlands/UK)

Source: Based on a survey of business leaders, the *Financial Times* publishes an annual list of the "world's most respected companies." See the December 7, 1999, issue as well as www.ft.com/ftsurveys. Some business categories have been combined or deleted and a few firms have been added to the *Financial Times* list.

Lockheed-Martin and Boeing-McDonnell Douglas, European producers have pooled their efforts in joint development and production agreements for both civil and military aircraft, thus effectively reducing even further the total number of competitors in global markets.

The automobile market is another example. Transnational mergers between Chrysler (a U.S.-based multinational corporation) and Daimler-Benz (the German automobile producer) along with a similar agreement between Ford (another U.S.-based multinational) and Volvo (a Swedish firm) underscore market incentives to remain competitive and realize increasing gains by pooling technologies and other forms of capital.

Existing large-scale producers motivated by the prospects of increasing gains have a decided trade advantage, quite apart from any comparative-cost considerations suggested by classical theory. Following the same logic, of course, even smaller firms marketing specialized products seek to increase both their domestic- and export-market shares to achieve increasing gains. Although not yet fully developed, new thinking on trade and other aspects of the global economy thus challenges old theoretical assumptions and predictions, provides new explanations, and aims to expand our understanding of how international and global trade actually works.

Impacts on Trade of the Volatility of Money

Classical free-trade theory also assumes the neutrality of money, which hardly seems to be the case in the real world. By "neutralizing" money, in classical trade theory the exchange of goods and services is influenced only by production cost and related considerations, not fluctuations in the value or exchange rates of currencies. In the earlier example in which the fictional countries Insula and Terra bartered semiconductors and lumber (see box on page 334), no consideration was given to the value of currencies. Again, following classical theory, it is comparative production costs, not changes in the value of money, that are supposed to drive consequent changes in the direction, volume, and types of products traded.

But in the real world the value of money *does* fluctuate with consequent effects on prices. One country's currency may be worth *more* than another country's currency today than yesterday, but it may be worth *less* tomorrow. Unfortunately the prices at which goods and services are traded also change when ***exchange rates*** between currencies also change. Let's look at an example. If one U.S. dollar could purchase 120 Japanese yen last week but today can only purchase 110 yen, we say the dollar has **depreciated** in relation to the yen. Put another way the yen has **appreciated** in relation to the dollar over the same period. A week ago 120 yen could buy one U.S. dollar, but now the same 120 yen can buy about $1.09.

Let's see how a change in exchange rates affects prices. A Japanese importer wanting to buy a Ford automobile costing $25,000 last week at an exchange rate of 120 yen to the dollar had to come up with 3 million yen. This week the same $25,000 Ford can be bought at 110 yen to the dollar for 2,750,000 yen—a saving to the Japanese importer of 250,000 yen (about $2272.72 at this week's exchange rate). Savings on the car are to the benefit of the Japanese importer; however, the American exporter is paid the same amount ($25,000) this week as last week. The real gain to the American exporter, of course, is the degree to which Japanese importers are willing to buy more Fords at 2,750,000 yen than they would at 3 million yen. Other things equal, more sales at the same dollar price mean more revenue and profits to Ford and Ford retailers.

Economists describe the impact on markets (and export-import positions) of exchange-rate changes by referring, as in the Ford case discussed earlier, to the **price elasticity of demand** in the Japanese market for Fords. For example if demand for Fords increases substantially with a small decline in yen price, and as a result many more are purchased, elasticity is said to be high. The American exporter realizes great gains from increased sales due to a reduced price in yen to Japanese. The American exporter's gain is not caused by increased efficiencies or reduced production costs on the American side. The gain in sales is purely due to a change (a decline) in the dollar-yen exchange rate. This effect is less if Japanese demand for Fords is not very elastic in relation to price, or worse from the American perspective, is perfectly inelastic—demand stays the same (does not change at all in relation to price).

A change in exchange rates can be looked at two ways—two sides of the same coin, if you will. On one side we see the dollar depreciating in value from 120 to 110 yen. On the other side we see the yen appreciating in value from last week's

exchange rate   The price of one currency in terms of another; for example, it may take $1.60 (U.S.) to purchase a British pound, or put another way one U.S. dollar at this exchange rate will buy 0.625 of a pound.

◇ EXCHANGE RATES ◇

An *exchange rate* is merely the price a currency can be bought at (or sold for) using another currency. Although exchange-rate arithmetic may seem confusing at first, it's really not so difficult to figure out if we treat a currency just like any product traded in markets and we take a few moments to sort out how it is priced. Tourists are forced to do this when they travel abroad.

If the British pound (often referred to in currency markets simply as *sterling* and abbreviated as £) can be traded for $1.60, we refer to this as the sterling-dollar exchange rate (£ 1.0 = US$1.60). Put the other way one U.S. dollar can buy 0.625 of a pound—an exchange rate of US$1.00 = £ 0.625. This is how to switch from one exchange rate to the reverse:

$$£\,1.00 = US\$1.60$$

thus, reversing what is on either side of the = sign

$$US\$1.60 = £\,1.0$$

and

$$US\$1.00 = \frac{£\,1.0}{1.60} = £\,0.625$$

In the example used in the text, the dollar-yen exchange rates are US$1.00 = 120 yen (for last week) and US$1.00 = 110 yen (today)—a *depreciation* in the value of the dollar in that the same dollar buys fewer yen today than it could a week ago. Put the other way last week's yen-dollar exchange rate can be expressed as 100 yen equaling about $0.83 last week, but increasing to about $0.91 today—an *appreciation* in the value of the yen.

The exchange rate of a currency (its price in relation to other currencies) fluctuates in financial markets in response to shifts in demand for (and supply of) them in much the same way as commodities do. Currencies in demand *ceteris paribus* tend to rise in price; a drop in demand means its exchange rate in relation to other currencies falls. When governments or their central banks make the authoritative or political choice to increase or decrease the supply of their currencies by selling or buying them in open-market operations, they also can impact exchange rates for these currencies. These effects are summarized in Figure 11.C.

The intersection of the demand and supply curves is the equilibrium exchange rate in a particular financial market. The dashed lines represent alternative demand and supply curves. Look at what happens to exchange rates when the levels of demand and supply go up (increase) or go down (decrease).

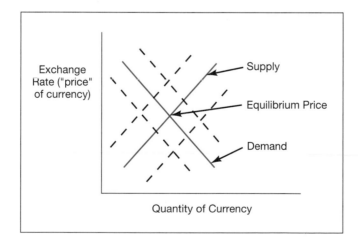

FIGURE 11.C EFFECTS OF SUPPLY AND DEMAND ON CURRENCY EXCHANGE RATE

yen-dollar exchange rate when it took 120 yen to buy a dollar; today it takes only 110 of a "stronger" yen to buy a dollar. To put it another way last week 100 yen were worth about $0.83 (since it took 120 yen to buy a dollar, 100 yen bought only a fraction of a dollar: 100/120 = 0.833). By contrast today the same 100 yen are worth about $0.91—an increase in value of about $0.08 (since it now takes just 110 yen to buy a dollar, 100 yen now buys a larger fraction of a dollar: 100/110 = 0.909).

Now let's turn the tables and look at the position of a Japanese exporter (and its U.S. retailer or dealer) of Honda automobiles. At 120 yen to the dollar, a Honda with a 3 million yen retail price that arrived by ship in Los Angeles last week can be sold for $25,000, competing directly with a $25,000 Ford. On the other hand, at an exchange rate of just 110 yen to the dollar, if the export manufacturer of the same type Honda arriving in Los Angeles today is to receive the same profit margin in yen, it will have to raise the retail price in the U.S. market by more than $2,200. The Honda will be less competitive in this circumstance not due to any change in quality or cost of production but solely because a change in exchange rate has had an adverse impact on its price. In an elastic market in which U.S. consumers are willing to substitute Fords for Hondas, a price rise can adversely affect Honda's market position, undercutting its sales and revenues.

Given the dollar's decline in value (it now buys only 110 yen compared to 120 yen last week), if the Japanese exporter and its U.S.-based retail dealer judge the American market to be inelastic, the price increase due to the exchange-rate change can be passed directly onto the consumers. On the other hand if the U.S. market for Hondas is elastic, the exporter and retailer may choose for the time being to hold the American price at $25,000 and absorb more than $2,200 in lost revenue between them on the sale of each vehicle. (Of course, how the loss is distributed is subject to contract or negotiation between the export manufacturer and the importing dealer. Thus Honda can reduce the price in yen the dealer is charged or the dealer will have to reduce its dollar profit margin on each Honda it sells.)

Why Should We Care?

To sum up, *exchange rates are important to know about precisely because changes in them directly affect prices and thus the revenues earned from international trade.* Political decisions or actions taken by governments and their central banks either unilaterally or coordinated multilaterally with their counterparts in other countries thus can affect exchange rates, export-import prices, and the terms of trade. If a country's currency *depreciates* or falls in relation to other world currencies, the prices of the products its firms export become cheaper (and thus more competitive) in foreign markets. At the same time foreign goods its firms and individuals import become more expensive in domestic markets. On the other hand if a country's currency *appreciates* (or becomes more valuable in relation to other currencies), its firms and people may buy and import more from abroad at lesser prices, but the prices of its exports rise and thus become less competitive in foreign markets. Because government and central bank actions can have such effects on the livelihoods or welfare of exporters, importers, and those who produce or own the goods and services traded, changes in prices or currency values are not just economic, but also highly political decisions.

Indeed all of this becomes very political when governments (or their central banks) choose to intervene in global currency markets to maintain, increase, or

EXPORT TRADE, FLUCTUATING PRICES, AND THE ELASTICITY OF DEMAND

Price elasticity of demand is a concept used by economists to measure how changes in price affect the demand for a product in particular markets for that product. For example if the price of coffee goes too high, will many coffee drinkers reduce their purchases of coffee, perhaps substituting tea? If so we might describe the demand for coffee as being very elastic with respect to price. Alternatively, are coffee drinkers so committed that they may grumble about a price rise but still continue to buy in comparable numbers? If so we say coffee demand seems to be relatively inelastic with respect to price.

The demand for a particular product like coffee may be elastic in some markets but inelastic in others. This is an important distinction for export trade just as it is for sales in domestic markets. Setting aside other factors that influence sales in domestic and export markets, revenue earned from sales depends upon price and elasticity of demand. An inelastic market for coffee may tolerate an increase in prices, but raising prices in an elastic market likely will produce substantial reduction in sales. Conversely a decline in price in elastic markets likely will result in increased sales.

Price elasticity of demand (E) may be expressed simply as a function of changes in price (P) and quantity of demand (Q) for a particular product:

$$E = \frac{\text{Percentage change in Q}}{\text{Percentage change in P}}$$

Thus if an increase in the export price of coffee from $5 to $6 a pound (a 20 percent increase) produces (or is expected to produce) a 30 percent reduction in the volume of monthly export sales (say from 100,000 to 70,000 pounds), the price elasticity is

$$E = \frac{(100,000 - 70,000)/100,000}{(\$6 - \$5)/\$5} = \frac{0.3}{0.2} = 1.5$$

Revenue from export sales of coffee in this market declines from $500,000 (100,000 pounds exported at $5 a pound) to $420,000 (70,000 pounds exported at $6 a pound), an $80,000 *loss* in sales revenue by the exporter. By contrast if the export market for coffee were completely *inelastic*, a decline in price would have no impact on sales and elasticity would be zero:

$$E = \frac{(100,000 - 100,000)/100,000}{(\$6 - \$5)/\$5} = \frac{0.0}{0.2} = 0.0$$

In this case an increase in export price increases revenue from $500,000 to $600,000—a *gain* for the exporter of $100,000.

Quite apart from price, elasticity can also be calculated for changes in income levels in particular markets, that is, an income *elasticity of demand*. An increase (or decrease) in incomes may affect demand for some products, but less so for others. For example, demand for goods and services considered to be luxury items tends to be relatively more sensitive to changes in income levels than is demand for the necessities of daily life. The concept of market elasticity is not just limited to demand but also can be calculated for the supply side. Thus *price elasticity of supply* refers to whether and by how much an increase (or decrease) in market price for a particular product provides incentive for increased (or decreased) production and supply of a product such as oil to domestic or export markets.

decrease a currency's exchange value. For example in the mid-1980s U.S. monetary authorities (in the U.S. Treasury and Federal Reserve Board, the central banking authority that oversees the U.S. banking system) perceived that just as in the 1960s and early 1970s, the dollar had become too **overvalued** in relation to other major currencies. Put simply an overvalued dollar meant that U.S. firms and individuals could import foreign products too cheaply while U.S. exports were too "pricey" or expensive to foreigners. The decision to depreciate and thus reduce the foreign buying power of the dollar (making foreign goods pricier to Americans) also made U.S. products cheaper to foreigners. This sounds at first like a charitable gesture or good deal to foreigners by U.S. monetary authorities. On closer examination, however, it was a case of "charity begins at home."

Jobs were at stake. An overvalued dollar meant U.S. consumers would tend to pass up buying U.S.-made products in favor of foreign-made goods of comparable quality but priced at a discount only because of an overvaluation in dollar-foreign currency exchange rates. As a result overall U.S. purchases from other countries were far greater than American sales abroad—a national trade imbalance deeply in red ink. Even more important from a domestic political perspective, however, imports of foreign products stimulate production (and employment) in other countries but tend to dampen or reduce domestic production with consequent losses of jobs. Labor unions argued that jobs were being lost to producers in other countries. Some put it this way: Overvaluation of the dollar tends to shift production to other countries with job creation abroad to replace jobs cut at home, in effect exporting jobs.

U.S. monetary authorities might have tried to depreciate the dollar unilaterally—by themselves—but instead worked the issue multilaterally, negotiating

PURCHASING-POWER PARITY AND PRICING HAMBURGERS, FRIES, AND COLA

Classical trade theory assumes the neutrality of money. As demonstrated in the text, however, exchange rates can get out of whack and adversely affect trade that otherwise would be based on comparative advantage with lower-cost, more efficient producers specializing in production of certain products. In the real world some currencies are overvalued (overpriced in terms of their exchange rates with other currencies), and others are undervalued (underpriced in terms of their exchange rates with other currencies).

To be neutral money should be in *parity* or roughly the same in purchasing power to buy goods and services in one country as in another. A practical but amusing way to measure purchasing-power parity is to compare how much it costs to buy the same hamburger, fries, and cola in one country as in another. If money is really neutral and production and marketing costs are roughly the same, the hamburger, fries, and cola should cost or be priced about the same regardless of which currency one uses. This is what is meant by purchasing-power parity—the equivalent values of all currencies should in principle buy about the same number or amount of the same goods or services.

In 1983 the *Economist*, a weekly news magazine, developed its "Big Mac" index—a play on one of the

McDonald's hamburger offerings—as an indicator of what exchange rates should be (and might well become). The index is calculated and published in the magazine from time to time. In principle the price of the Big Mac *ceteris paribus* should cost about the same everywhere, but that is usually not the case. In some countries it is decidedly higher or lower than others. If the local currency is overvalued in relation to the dollar, the Big Mac tends to be cheaper (i.e., an overvalued currency goes further; it can purchase a Big Mac less expensively) than in another country with an undervalued currency (more of which is needed to purchase the same Big Mac).

For example one publication of the index suggested that many European currencies, in particular the Euro, were overvalued in relation to the dollar—that Big Macs were much cheaper in these countries than in the United States. Subsequently the exchange value of the European currencies dropped, bringing them much closer to purchasing-power parity with the dollar. "See, we told you so," said writers for the *Economist*. Critics have advocated the *Economist* move away from its Big Mac index to a more diverse, market-basket calculation using a number of products.

with their treasury and central bank monetary-authority counterparts in other countries to collaborate in depreciating the dollar. This meant refusing to defend the existing exchange rates between the dollar and other countries, instead letting the dollar slide or helping it down the depreciation road to a new, lower level at which valuation or purchasing power of the dollar and other countries would at least be closer or somewhat more comparable. *The Bottom Line: Consistent with classical trade theory, the effort to adjust exchange rates in this way is designed to achieve greater purchasing-power parity* (see box on p. 347) between the dollar and other currencies because this shifts competition from artificial, exchange-rate considerations to such factors as efficiency, cost of production, and quality.

An International Monetary Regime for Financing International Commerce

In day-to-day international commerce, government agencies, business firms, other groups, and individuals use domestic currency to buy foreign currencies to finance the purchase of goods and services imported from abroad, to loan or invest money in foreign countries, or to have money to spend there. Similarly foreign government agencies, foreign business firms, other groups, and individuals living abroad use their currencies to buy currencies in other countries needed to conduct the same kinds of transactions. Currencies, usually in the form of deposits in banks and other financial institutions, thus readily move back and forth across national boundaries.

Rules governing the exchange of currencies and conditions for loans have evolved over time, as have the international organizations tasked by member countries with implementing or enforcing them. The sets of rules and institutions associated with them constitute what we can refer to as an ***international monetary regime***, which has as its purpose providing financial arrangements so essential to maintaining and expanding trade and other forms of international commerce.

In earlier centuries currencies were often defined as being equivalent in value to a fixed weight of some precious metal like silver or gold. In the late nineteenth and early twentieth centuries, for example, a U.S. dollar could be exchanged for 1/20th of an ounce of gold. Put another way it took $20 to buy an ounce of gold from the U.S. Treasury. Stated formally the dollar's gold parity (a technical term) was $20 an ounce. At the same time the value of the British currency (the pound sterling) was also defined as a fixed weight of gold. Countries willing to exchange their currencies for gold on demand were said to be on a gold standard.

In fact relatively little gold was actually exchanged, since countries found it more convenient instead to exchange each other's currencies as needed to finance trade and other forms of international commerce. Knowing what the exchange rate was between the U.S. dollar and British pound was easy to calculate, since both were defined in terms of specified weights of gold. Thus at the time it took about $4.87 (more precisely $4.867) to buy one British pound note. At the core of the international monetary regime at the time was what amounted to a gold-exchange standard.

In the late 1800s and early 1900s the United Kingdom enjoyed financial prominence in Europe and throughout the world. Given its standing and its access to capital throughout the world, the Bank of England as a central bank not only

international monetary regime Financial rules, regulations, and institutions agreed on by states to facilitate international trade and commerce.

managed the British currency—the pound sterling, which was readily convertible into a fixed quantity of gold—but also effectively the worldwide international monetary regime. Other countries often held deposits of the pound sterling as **reserves**, which could be used to finance their trade and other purchases abroad. Holding sterling deposits as reserves was actually preferable to holding gold since these sterling deposits could even earn interest. Because of its pivotal role in the international monetary regime of the time, sterling came to be regarded in effect as a key currency.

This is how the Bank of England managed the international monetary regime at the time. Because foreigners understood and respected the financial soundness of the Bank of England and the economy it represented, whenever the Bank of England wanted to attract foreign currencies to enhance its own reserves in order to make payments to other countries, it could do so simply by raising its interest rate—referred to technically as its *discount rate*.

As a central bank, changes in the rate it charged to other British banks would impact their own interest rates as well. By raising its discount rate, the Bank of England in effect encouraged the sale of sterling to holders of foreign currencies seeking greater earnings due to higher interest rates to be found in British financial markets. Put another way holders of foreign currencies would readily use these holdings to buy sterling for deposit in British banks, thus taking advantage of higher British interest rates. In turn many of these foreign currencies would wind up in the Bank of England's reserves as British banks exchanged them there for sterling.

During World War I (1914–18) budgetary requirements to finance the war effort forced Britain (and other countries) to abandon the gold-exchangeability of their currencies. Wartime controls on currency expenditures were eventually removed when the war ended as the United Kingdom tried to reassume its prewar role as manager of a restored international monetary regime. Although the United Kingdom still retained its worldwide empire, Britain's capital base had been significantly eroded by heavy borrowing necessitated by massive wartime expenditures. The United States, although it possessed the capital base to assume the international-monetary management role, was unwilling to do so. Given its financially weakened position, Britain had great difficulty performing the monetary-management role in the 1920s and finally was forced to abandon the effort in 1931 with the onset of a worldwide economic depression.[3]

During the 1930s, countries often resorted to currency **exchange controls** to limit the amount of money spent abroad, thus avoiding payments obligations. At the same time imports were restrained by high tariffs, quotas, and other barriers to trade. It was a period described as "beggar thy neighbor" as countries turned inward to protect themselves no matter what the expense might be to other countries. Countries also devalued their currencies in an effort to make imports more expensive to firms and individuals at home while at the same time promoting their exports by making them cheaper to foreigners.

The United States did this by raising the price of gold from $20 to $35 an ounce. Raising the official price of gold amounted to a devaluation of the dollar. The process was a bit complicated, but here is how it worked. The exchange value of the dollar depended upon its gold value. Following the increase in gold price,

---

[3]For an excellent discussion of this period, see Charles P. Kindleberger, *The World in Depression, 1929–1939* (Berkeley, Calif.: University of California Press, 1973).

Americans now had to pay $35 for the same amount of foreign goods and services that they previously bought with an ounce of gold when it was priced at $20—in effect a 75 percent increase in the price of imports. At the same time foreign purchasers got a good deal designed to promote exports, since the foreign currency equivalent to an ounce of gold now bought $35 worth of American goods and services instead of just $20 worth. Of course more than one country could play this game, and many did. As a result round after round of **competitive devaluations** characterized the 1930s as each country tried to establish a trade advantage over others—maximizing exports and minimizing imports. It was a zero-sum political game that countries played, seeking gains at the expense of others.

The net effect of such policies was a drastic reduction in international trade and foreign investment as the worldwide economy continued to stagnate. These economic events were followed in a few years by the onset of another world war in 1939, which many observers at the time and since have understood at least partly as a consequence of the self-serving, nationalistic or neomercantilist political-economic policies pursued throughout the 1930s.

Lessons drawn from this experience led during World War II to political plans for establishing a new international monetary regime that would make possible a re-opening of international trade and investment across national borders. Instead of *zero-sum* thinking, achieving positive gains through expanded trade and commerce took center stage. In game-theoretic terms, there was a visible shift from the zero-sum political game of the Depression years to a positive-sum political game to guide country players in the postwar period. All could gain in principle from international monetary collaboration.

One outcome of this thinking was establishment of an International Monetary Fund (IMF) by international agreement at a conference held in 1944 at Bretton Woods, New Hampshire. British economist John Maynard Keynes and his American counterpart, Harry Dexter White, were the key proponents of alternative plans. In proposing to allow the new IMF political authority to create reserves (to which Keynes and his followers gave the nickname *bancor*), the Keynes plan was far more liberal than the White plan, which preferred to rely on gold and key currencies for reserves and opposed conferring any such reserve-creation authority on the new IMF. Given the political-economic prominence of the United States in these negotiations, the American view was more influential in determining the final outcome. Nevertheless a version of Keynesian thinking was evident in the 1960s when member countries authorized the IMF to create SDRs or Special Drawing Rights (see the discussion of SDRs later in this chapter).

The task the IMF was given at Bretton Woods, which prevailed during the institution's first quarter-century, was to oversee and manage an international monetary regime of relatively fixed exchange rates. It did this by relying on key currencies like the U.S. dollar, which were readily exchangeable into gold or other currencies. As such a new gold-exchange standard came into existence with the U.S. dollar at its center—in effect a dollar-gold-exchange standard with the dollar still priced at its 1934 level of $35 an ounce. As in the sterling-gold-exchange standard of the late nineteenth and early twentieth centuries, relatively few actual gold exchanges occurred among national monetary authorities. Most countries held their reserves in the form of U.S. dollar deposits, understood to be at least as good as gold, or even better since these deposits also earned interest.

This would last until 1971 when the United States, confronted by long-standing balance-of-payments deficits and now a substantial deficit in its trade balance as well, decided to go off the gold-exchange standard and made the uni-lateral political choice to abandon fixed exchange rates. It allowed the value of its currency to **float** or be set based on market supply and demand. American offi-cials complained that over the years the dollar had become overvalued, which as a practical matter meant that U.S. exports were too expensive to foreigners and im-ports too cheap to Americans. As a result the volume of U.S. exports could not keep up with the ever-increasing volume of American imports. By contrast many other countries were seen as having undervalued currencies, giving them a deci-sive trade advantage—promoting their exports to (while discouraging imports from) the United States.

With its trade balance slipping into deficit, American officials chose to devalue the dollar by letting its value float, depreciating it in currency markets. Since the exchange value of many other currencies were tied to what had become a floating dollar, their values also fluctuated. A new international monetary regime of flexible exchange rates had come into existence. Fierce debates, however, occurred among monetary authorities as to just how flexible these rates should be.

Fixed exchange rates were credited with having contributed to the enormous growth in international commerce since the end of World War II. On the other hand they were also blamed for leading to financial crises when currencies were viewed in currency markets as either overvalued or undervalued in relation to other currencies. A compromise position, managed flexibility, allows for some in-tervention in currency markets by monetary authorities to stabilize or otherwise influence exchange rates.

Faced with what they understood as destabilizing fluctuations in exchange rates, in the 1970s and 1980s members of the European Communities (EC) de-veloped a monetary arrangement to stabilize rates among themselves even as their currencies floated collectively in relation to the dollar. As the EC became incor-porated in the 1990s in a new European Union (EU), an outgrowth of earlier monetary collaboration was the establishment of an economic and monetary union. This included a common central bank located in Frankfurt managing a new currency, the *Euro*, viewed as the leading competitor or potential competitor to the dollar as a global key currency.

International Organizations and International Monetary Regime Maintenance

The IMF has its headquarters in Washington, D.C.—separate from but physi-cally next to the World Bank, which also has its headquarters in Washington. Although the World Bank specializes in making loans for investment in economic reconstruction and development (see Chapter Twelve), the focus of the IMF is on the finance of trade—assisting member countries to manage their payments obligations to each other. Another institution, the Bank for International Settle-ments (BIS) in Basel, Switzerland, is a bank for central bankers who engage in buying, selling, lending, and borrowing each other's currencies as needed to sus-tain international commerce.

Established in 1930, BIS members include many of the same countries that belong to the IMF. Governments and their treasury officials are typically the principals in the IMF, whereas central bankers are the main players in the BIS. Over the years central bankers participating in the BIS have played an active, often pivotal role in actually making some of the financial arrangements agreed to by treasury and other government officials of IMF member countries.

The International Monetary Fund building in Washington, D.C.

If there is a shortfall in the supply of foreign currencies available, banks (and governments) can turn to their central banks—national institutions that service the banking needs of both member banks and government treasuries. Countries normally keep reserves of foreign currencies (and gold that can be used to buy these currencies), but sometimes these reserves become depleted, as when charges for imported goods and services and other payments far exceed earnings from exports and other sources. When that happens member countries can draw on their accounts or borrow from the International Monetary Fund (IMF), which is in a position to keep its members in cash (i.e., maintain international liquidity).

The IMF makes advances of hard currencies that can readily be exchanged for whatever currency may be needed to finance transactions. As the IMF itself likes to say, it operates in much the same way as a credit union by offering its member countries a variety of different kinds of loans and other mechanisms to meet their financial needs. If countries did not have such a source of short-term finance for balancing their payments, they likely would be forced to impose exchange controls, severely limiting the amount of domestic currency used to acquire foreign currencies, thus restricting purchases from abroad and disrupting international commerce.

Advances by the IMF are just that—advances that must be repaid, usually with interest. The IMF has about $300 billion in deposits by its members, which it can use to provide hard currencies to members in need. The amount of each country's required deposit or "quota" is different depending on the size of its economy and trade requirements. The quota size also determines the voting power a member has on the board of governors that provides policy guidance and direction to the executive board, the IMF managing director, and the IMF staff. In effect this gives political primacy in the IMF to countries with the largest economies, notably the United States and other Group of Seven members. With

---

INTERNATIONAL LIQUIDITY AND CURRENCIES

Liquidity is a financial term referring to having cash available or an ability to raise such funds readily by selling assets. Maintaining international liquidity, a central IMF task, means providing member countries in need with access to financial assets that can be exchanged for currencies necessary to meet their payments obligations. Financial assets held as reserves by national monetary authorities include gold, SDRs (see box on p. 353), and **hard currencies**.

Hard currencies are those major currencies (i.e., the U.S. dollar, British sterling or pound, Japanese yen, German mark, French franc, and now the European Union's Euro) readily accepted and used by countries for making their payments transactions. What made them *hard* in earlier times was their convertibility to gold (or dollars that in turn were readily convertible to gold) by national treasuries or at their central banks. By contrast **soft currencies** lacked this convertibility and thus were less accepted.

Now we refer to hard currencies simply as those readily accepted and exchangeable for one another and thus easily used to buy any country's currency whenever needed. In an effort to improve their acceptability, monetary authorities of countries with soft currencies sometimes peg or link these currencies to the dollar or one or another of the hard currencies, allowing their soft currencies to rise and fall in value in the same way as the leading hard currencies do. As a result their otherwise soft currencies are more readily accepted in commercial transactions.

◈ ⬧ SPECIAL DRAWING RIGHTS (SDRs) ⬧ ◈

Policy makers in the 1960s and 1970s addressed the availability of reserves to finance payments in international trade, concluding that reliance on growth in gold, dollars, and other hard currencies was not sufficient. Building on ideas set forth earlier by John Maynard Keynes and other economists, the IMF was authorized by its member countries to create **Special Drawing Rights (or SDRs)**, dubbed by journalists at the time as "paper gold." In fact SDR allocations to each IMF member country amounted to a new line of credit that could be drawn on without challenge in a time of need. Because countries having SDRs in their IMF accounts can readily exchange them at any time for *hard currencies* like the U.S. dollar, Japanese yen, and other **convertible currencies**, they are "as good as gold" and thus also can be included as part of a country's official reserves in the same way that gold and hard currencies are counted. So far the IMF has been authorized to create and allocate SDRs worth a total of about $30 billion.

18 percent of the vote, the United States has the largest number of votes. Given the requirement for an 85 percent voting majority on important matters, the European Union members voting as a block and the United States voting alone all enjoy the political advantage of an effective veto on major policy questions and other organizational decisions.

Each member of the IMF meets its contribution quota by putting on deposit 25 percent of the amount in convertible currencies, gold, or SDRs—Special Drawing Rights (see box on this page), and the remaining 75 percent of the quota by deposit of the country's own currency. When in need the first 25 percent can be drawn without question (which amounts to a line of credit), but drawings beyond that amount are usually subject to certain conditions.

These conditions are the politically difficult part. In time these IMF-prescribed remedies are expected to lay a firm basis for producing a viable economy able to sustain growth and finance trade. In the short run, however, these measures often call for substantial government belt tightening—tighter fiscal policies (e.g., cutting expenditures and increasing taxes) and tighter monetary policies (e.g., raising interest rates and constraining growth in the domestic money supply). Unfortunately such policies designed to dampen economies, cut inflation, curb imports, and foster greater efficiency in use of factors of production—so-called **structural adjustments** in the fundamental elements of an economy—also impose enormous costs. Businesses, for example, may not readily find capital to finance plans for expansion or may even close, and workers may lose jobs and have difficulty finding new employment. These economically difficult times brought on by such IMF-prescribed austerity measures may well have politically explosive consequences for governments complying with IMF loan conditions. The IMF has also been the target of much criticism for insisting on these stringent requirements as conditions for advances to borrowing countries. Critics see these structural adjustment measures as retarding economic growth and development in Third World countries with unfair, often dire consequences to the peoples affected by these policies.

From the IMF perspective, exchange controls (see box on p. 354) come at a great cost. If countries in economic difficulties impose exchange controls (as many did before the IMF became effective as a lending agency), the net effect will be reduction in

THE EFFECTS OF NATIONAL MACROECONOMIC POLICIES

Fiscal policies deal with government budgetary matters (how much and how to tax and spend), whereas *monetary policies* address government measures that affect size and growth of the money supply and level of interest rates. Together fiscal and monetary policies are sometimes referred to as *macroeconomic policies* because they affect the national economy taken as a whole.

No matter how necessary imposing fiscal and monetary restraints may seem to finance experts, compliance with loan conditions can be extraordinarily difficult. Certainly this was the case for Indonesia, Thailand, South Korea, and other countries caught in the Asian financial crisis during the late 1990s. For its part, however, Malaysia found its own way out of IMF-imposed austerity by breaking IMF rules and imposing *exchange controls*—limiting the amount of *ringit*, the Malaysian currency, that could leave the country and be spent abroad. By adopting this monetary policy, Malaysia managed its payment obligations through government actions to limit the amount that could be spent abroad for imports or other purposes.

Imposing exchange controls is a monetary policy for managing a country's payments obligations to other countries. These controls usually take the form of domestic banking regulations in Country X that limit purchase of foreign currencies that can be used to finance imports, other purchases, or investments abroad. People leaving a country also are limited in the amounts of the country's currency they physically can take with them lest these funds be spent abroad. With less money spent abroad, there are fewer payment obligations to meet when the central banks or treasuries of other countries seek hard currencies or other reserves in exchange for amounts of currency from Country X they have acquired.

As discussed earlier, trade of goods and services in classical theory is based on differences in cost of production and market value of products themselves, not on the value of money used to purchase them. Thus it was convenient for classical economic theorists to assume the neutrality of money—that money has no independent impact on the costs of production or market value of goods and services. In fact money is anything but neutral in the real world. Changes in exchange value, for example, have a direct influence on the prices of exports and imports and thus on the demand for and supply of them. Accordingly governments and their national monetary policies do influence both domestic and international trade (see box on the next page).

externalities Positive or negative effect on others of decisions made or actions taken, as when a state makes a monetary or trade decision which, however much it may benefit the state and its economy, has a negative effect on the economy of other states.

imports and thus on the global volume of trade, adversely affecting economic growth as well. Moreover other countries can no longer sell their products freely to countries limiting imports through exchange controls. When export sales go down, profits and jobs are lost. These are real costs borne by other countries, which economists refer to as negative ***externalities***.

Resorting to exchange controls thus runs the political and economic risk that countries adversely affected by this policy may choose to retaliate economically by discriminating against the exports of countries adopting such measures. In short, those opposing resort to exchange controls as a way of managing a country's payments not only see such a policy as reducing the volume of trade, but also argue that it is an unfair way of shifting some of the costs of structural adjustments in one's own economy to the shoulders of others. Be that as it may, defenders of managing a country's payments through exchange controls see it as a more desirable, somewhat less intrusive remedy than either bearing the social and political consequences of fiscal and monetary austerity, or worse yet, directly blocking trade by imposing high tariffs or quotas against imports from other countries—an approach sure to invite retaliation in kind.

DOMESTIC EFFECTS AND EXTERNALITIES OF NATIONAL MONETARY POLICY

Following is a list of domestic and external effects of political choices to change a country's monetary policy—specified here in terms of both interest rates (the cost of borrowing money) and the money supply (the amount of money in circulation).

INTEREST RATES UP
(tightening monetary policy;
growth in money supply decreased)

INTEREST RATES DOWN
(loosening monetary policy;
growth in money supply increased)

Domestic Effects (ceteris paribus)

- *Dampens domestic economy*; slows growth by raising the cost of capital (e.g., borrowing capital for investment in productive enterprises is more expensive at higher interest rates)
- *A curb on inflation* (slower growth/less demand tends to keep prices stable or at least slow price increases; less money in circulation means there is less to spend)
- *Increases fiscal cost of servicing national debt* (government pays more interest given higher rates)
- *Encourages short term net capital inflow* (as when capital flows in to take advantage of relatively higher interest rates domestically)
- *Tends to increase exchange value of domestic currency* (increasing capital inflows to take advantage of relatively higher interest rates tends to increase demand for country's currency)
- *Stimulates imports; discourages exports* (i.e., higher exchange value means imports tend to be cheaper domestically, exports more expensive to foreigners)
- *Discourages long-term investment in domestic economy by foreigners* (i.e., cost of domestic assets more expensive when purchased with foreign currencies)

- *Stimulates domestic economy*; encourages growth by lowering the cost of capital (e.g., borrowing capital for investment in productive enterprises is cheaper at lower interest rates)
- *Could spur inflation* (faster growth/greater demand tends to put upward pressure on prices; more money in circulation means there is more to spend)
- *Decreases fiscal cost of servicing national debt* (government pays less interest given lower rates)
- *Encourages short-term net capital outflow* (as when capital flows out to take advantage of relatively higher interest rates abroad)
- *Tends to decrease exchange value of domestic currency* (increasing capital outflows to take advantage of relatively higher interest rates abroad tends to decrease demand for country's currency)
- *Stimulates exports; discourages imports* (i.e., lower exchange value means exports tend to be cheaper to foreigners, imports more expensive domestically)
- *Encourages long-term investment in domestic economy by foreigners* (i.e., cost of domestic assets cheaper when purchased with foreign currencies)

External Effects (ceteris paribus)

- *Stimulates foreign production* by promoting imports (see previous examples)
- *May "export" inflation* by dampening domestic economy while stimulating foreign production for export
- *More difficult for Third World and other debtors to pay their obligations*

- *Dampens foreign production* by promoting exports (see previous examples)
- *Tends to dampen inflation pressures abroad* by stimulating domestic production and curbing imports
- *Easier for Third World and other debtors to pay their obligations*

Political Choices: How Much Capital Should the IMF Have and for What Purposes?

Decisions on how much capital the IMF should have and for what purposes are essentially political choices made by member countries represented in the IMF's board of governors and its executive board. Indeed, the IMF's central function is to have the necessary funds available to lend to countries in balance-of-payments difficulties, thus precluding their resort either to erecting tariffs, quotas, and other barriers to trade or to imposing exchange controls. The IMF also facilitates dismantling exchange controls already in existence when countries are making the adjustments necessary to open their domestic economies and participate more fully in global trade and other forms of commerce.

To do all this—as a practical matter to be able to perform its core task of maintaining international liquidity as well as make funds available for other purposes specified by international agreement of its member countries—the IMF requires enormous capital resources. Because 75 percent of the quota contributions made by member countries is in their own currencies, the amount of "hard currency" available for lending is considerably less than half of some $300 billion the IMF has on deposit from quota subscriptions.

IMF lending resources were initially expanded in the 1960s when a new mechanism, the General Arrangements to Borrow (GAB), was constructed to supplement drawings on quotas. Eleven capital-rich countries originally put up GAB funds, which now total about $23 billion that can be lent to IMF members needing balance-of-payments assistance. Following the same model, twenty-five member countries decided to contribute hard currencies to another facility, the New Arrangements to Borrow (NAB), which was established in 1997, doubling total resources available under these arrangements to a combined total of some $46 billion.

The IMF also has a gold stock of more than 100 million fine ounces (its market value fluctuates from day to day, but at say, $300 an ounce, this is worth more than $30 billion), which the IMF board of governors can authorize be sold to acquire hard currencies. The political decision to create Special Drawing Rights or SDRs—so-called "paper gold"—and allocate them to member countries (see box on SDRs earlier in the chapter) also expanded capital resources that now amount to close to an additional $30 billion.

As a lending institution, the IMF charges interest on drawings or borrowing of its funds. Member countries actually earn interest on their quota contributions when their currencies are borrowed by other countries. The interest rates charged to borrowing countries, however, are truly **concessionary**—well below rates countries would be charged if they borrowed in financial markets. Over the years the specific purposes for which the IMF may lend funds have expanded substantially, particularly for low-income, less-developed countries.

For example since the 1980s some eighty low-income, less-developed countries have been eligible to receive special treatment by borrowing funds for ten-year terms from the IMF's Enhanced Structural Adjustment Facility at below-market or concessionary interest rates (just one-half of one percent). The condition for such loans is that borrowing countries use the money for structural adjustment tasks—implementing a three-year program designed to provide a foundation for sustained economic growth, thus enabling them to meet their payments obligations. A total of close to $10 billion in loans has been disbursed to more than fifty needy countries by this facility with new lending projected at more than a billion dollars a year. The source of these funds is from capital-rich and other more economically developed countries willing to contribute.

The IMF may extend contingency lines of credit to countries not presently in balance-of-payments difficulties, but that are concerned that the effects of financial turmoil in other countries might spread to them. The IMF also has special lending authority for countries recovering from war and other civil conflicts as well as emergency assistance or compensatory financing when earthquakes, hurricanes, floods, droughts, frosts, insect and other pest infestations, or other natural disasters adversely affect exports or disrupt normal trade and payments transactions. The IMF not only lends money in such circumstances but also renders technical assistance toward establishing or reestablishing the financial infrastructure that may have been destroyed or weakened by political or economic turmoil brought on by natural disasters or armed conflict.

Understanding itself as an agent for global trade and commerce, the IMF sees this role as encompassing technical tasks as well as fostering market-oriented values in member or would-be member countries willing to avail themselves of such assistance. Accordingly the IMF contributes to developing effective central banking and treasury institutions, collecting and refining statistical data on economic activities, and training officials who can perform technical monetary tasks. Perhaps even more significantly, as an agent of socialization the IMF joins other international organizations and governments in efforts to integrate these officials within an expanding, worldwide culture of values shared by professionals or technical experts dealing with monetary matters so essential to sustaining and increasing global trade and other forms of commerce. These technical experts can be understood as constituting an **epistemic community** conversant with each other across state boundaries whether in direct meetings or by telecommunications.

An International and Global Trade Regime

Just as an international monetary regime sets forth rules for the exchange of currencies and the finance of international commerce, an international trade regime also has rules relating to how exports and imports are bought and sold, transported, paid for, and delivered. Many of these rules have standing as customary international law and are enforceable in suits brought in national courts.

As discussed in Chapter Nine, the topic of rules for international commerce is not a new one. Grotius (1583–1645) addressed the topic and both customary international law and the Law of the Sea Treaty identify territorial waters, define rights of passage for commercial vessels, and underscore the primacy of freedom of navigation on the high seas. Similar rules with the force of international law apply to trade across land and by air.

As discussed in Chapter Ten, political opposition, particularly in the United States, blocked efforts after World War II to establish an International Trade Organization (ITO) as a companion institution to the International Monetary Fund and World Bank. Instead negotiating arrangements known as the General Agreement on Tariffs and Trade (GATT) produced periodic international conferences (or *rounds* as they were called) that worked toward reduction of tariffs, quotas, and other barriers to trade, especially those erected in the 1930s when protectionist sentiments had reigned supreme.

Even in the absence of an international organization or specialized agency for trade, participating countries (including the United States) made great progress in liberalizing global trade—opening markets between and across national borders. Nevertheless, open-trade (if not entirely free-trade) advocates still saw much work to be done. In addition to further reductions in trade barriers, curbing bribery or other illicit practices and assuring global respect for intellectual property rights (patents and copyrights) are issues high on the agenda of both private interests and those wishing to promote growth in international commerce. Moreover advocates want to head off fears of trade wars or any thought of return to the mutually exclusive, regional trading blocs that had prevailed in the 1930s. Bringing many newly market-oriented countries into the global trading regime was another important motivation in the 1990s for moving beyond GATT to forming a new World Trade Organization (WTO).

With more than 130 member countries (and others waiting to join), the main function of the WTO, headquartered in Geneva, is "to ensure that trade flows as smoothly, predictably and freely as possible." In addition to agreements reached on trading rules, member countries may bring complaints against other members to the WTO's dispute-settlement process. WTO official tasks include "administering trade agreements, acting as a forum for trade negotiations, settling trade disputes, reviewing national trade policies, assisting developing countries in trade policy issues through technical assistance and training programs, and cooperating with other international organizations."

Major disputes do surround the WTO, as evidenced by demonstrators at a WTO ministerial meeting held in Seattle in 1999. WTO opponents were highly critical of trading policies that in their view do not afford sufficient weight to protecting the environment. Labor interests challenged WTO policies that open trade at the expense of workers who lose their jobs in what they argue is unfair global competition brought on by corporate exploitation of foreign workers who are paid very low wages and often suffer poor working conditions in labor-intensive industries abroad. Environmental activists and labor rights advocates thus found common cause in these anti-WTO demonstrations.

These challenges from outside the WTO are matched by conflicts within. Not only are unfair trade practice complaints frequently made by member countries against each other, but members also differ philosophically on practical goals. Some members like the United States argue for open markets as free as possible of government intervention or protectionism. Other members argue not so much for free trade but rather for managed trade that avoids some of the environmental, labor, and other pitfalls encountered in a free-trade environment. From this perspective the WTO can serve as a forum for discussing and negotiating managed-trade arrangements in which governments intervene in markets to reduce costs to interested parties.

REGIONAL ECONOMIC INTEGRATION
AND GLOBAL COMMERCE

A positive view of the global political economy sees some hope in both worldwide and regional economic integration efforts. As discussed in Chapter Six, **functionalists** note that international organizations are formed from the recognition that

CASE & Point   CHINA

If there is one country that figures prominently in the speculation of what international relations and world politics will look like in the next few years, it is China. Despite unprecedented access to China in the past twenty years by scholars, businesspeople, journalists, diplomats, and tourists, the country conjures up many different and conflicting images. For some China is epitomized by its economic miracle and the skyscrapers of Shanghai, the spread of cell phones, and dusty construction sites. Much has changed under the communist rulers. Others point to the repression of pro-democracy demonstrators in Tianamen Square in 1989 and the continual repression of dissidents as evidence of the "real China." From their perspective little has changed under the communist rulers. The diversity and complexity of this giant country provide evidence to support almost any point of view.

What most observers would probably agree on, however, is that the single biggest challenge for the current Chinese leadership is the need to deliver continual economic growth or risk political turmoil. The economic reforms that began in the late 1970s generated catch-up growth—gains from disbanding agricultural communes and the resultant influx of cheap labor to low-end manufacturing firms made for double-digit economic growth. Those days are gone as growth rates in the manufacturing sector have slowed and agricultural productivity has reached its limits due to a severe shortage of water. The gap in the standard of living between the city and the countryside is a serious problem as is the growth in corruption and widespread environmental degradation.

Just as observers have disagreed on China's recent past, they have presented sharply different perspectives on China's future military, political, and economic developments and their implications for international affairs. Some see China as not only a threat to regional peace and stability in Asia, but also as a potential global hegemonic power in the decades ahead. Using the term of the realist scholar Arnold Wolfers, China is seen by some as a "non-status quo power" that threatens to upset the political-military balance in Asia. Both South Korea and Japan look nervously to the West, continuing to rely on U.S. security guarantees. Chinese saber-rattling directed against Taiwan and threats of coercive reunification, the modernization of its strategic-weapons program, and the export of military technology to so-called "rogue states" have been cause for disquiet if not alarm on the part of some self-professed realists.

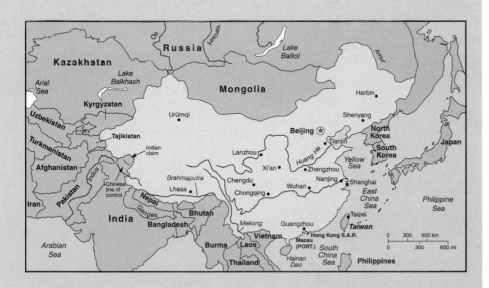

FIGURE 11.D

(box continues)

Why offer China, it is asked, the benefits of international trade if such action shores up its economy and will make China a more formidable foe in the future?

Others argue that China as a military threat is overdrawn, and that if it should ever become a truly global threat, it would not happen for many years to come. In fact instead of worrying about China as a powerful actor on the international stage, some claim we should worry about a very different sort of problem—the possibility of China being too weak. A weak China would also pose significant security concerns. From a Chinese perspective a strong state and a unified society are as much an imperative today as they were for Machiavelli's contemporaries in fifteenth- and sixteenth-century Italy. History demonstrates that a weak state and a divided nation invite foreign aggression. To prevent civil strife from erupting and the country from fragmenting into warring fiefdoms, a strong state is required. From the Chinese point of view there is a link between internal and external security and hence a concern over the territorial disintegration of China brought about by economic, social, and political pressures. What the Chinese leadership is counting on, therefore, is that the forces of economic decentralization will not lead to demands for political decentralization.

In recent years foreign scholars have begun to analyze possible centrifugal forces in China, realizing that the dissolution of China would have repercussions within as well as beyond its borders—damage the prosperity of one-fifth of humanity, lead to massive migration, and destroy East Asian stability. The possibility may seem far-fetched to some, but so did the possibility of the disintegration of the Soviet Union.

Economically some see China simply as a vast market, its 1.3 billion citizens potential customers for a wide variety of consumer goods. International businesses, the United States, the European Union, and other advanced industrial countries lobbied for China's admittance to the World Trade Organization (WTO). Bipartisan U.S. political support resulted in Congress granting permanent normal trading relations (PNTR) status to China in May 2000. Both China and its trading partners, it was claimed, would benefit in economic terms from the tariff-reduction and market-widening proposals. But there was a political argument as well—by bringing China into the global trading system it will no longer be the self-isolated Middle Kingdom but rather a vested partner in a stable global economic system. This follows the logic of economic liberalism and arguments for the pacifying effects of global interdependence. Furthermore, although not usually voiced, is the view that economic development will help to undermine the authoritarian regime in Beijing. Trade with foreigners will supposedly add pressure to the further development of the rule of law. Hence supporters of PNTR status for China managed to combine economic self-interest with claims of being supportive of human and political rights in China.

Some realist critics dismiss the economic liberalism argument as historically unfounded and empirically incorrect. The simple proposition that the benefits of economic exchange make war too costly to pursue seems intuitively plausible, yet in an anarchic world fear will be ever-present and hence so will be the possibility of war.

Other critics, however, take a different tact, arguing that in the pursuit of trade benefits the world is too willing to overlook China's human rights abuses. By granting PNTR and admitting China to the World Trade Organization, advanced industrial states were in effect placing their seal of approval on the regime. Why, it was asked, should the advanced industrial democracies give up a carrot (admittance to the WTO and PNTR) that could be used to improve human rights in China?

Point: Too often we read interpretations of China only from outsiders. For Chinese perspectives that deal with the topics mentioned here, see Yong Deng and Fei-Ling Wand, *In the Eyes of the Dragon: China Views the World* (Savage, MD: Rowman and Littlefield, 2000).

certain tasks need to be performed, such as monetary exchange, trade, multilateral investment, mail service, or parceling out telecommunications frequencies. **Neofunctionalists** focus on the *political* processes orchestrated by politically connected specialists or elites. To the neofunctionalist, integration doesn't just happen, it arises by design.

An internal logic to the economic integration process identified by neofunction-alists is apparent in the European integration experience. For example, free trade and commerce in the 1950s expanded in one economic sector (a customs union known as the European Coal and Steel Community or ECSC), but commercial transactions and ties also spilled over into other economic sectors that in turn were used by commercial and politically connected elites in 1958 to create an enlarged European Economic Community (EEC) as well as a European Atomic Energy Community (EURATOM) to advance peaceful, economic uses of nuclear energy. The ECSC, EEC, and EURATOM—referred to collectively as the European Communities (EC)—carried out their integration tasks for more than thirty years before being incorporated into what is now referred to as the European Union (EU).

These elites had made no secret of their objectives and plans for constructing a new Europe. In the first decade or so after World War II Jean Monnet and

Practicing World Politics

Checking Out Web Sites on International Organizations

International organizations play important roles in trade and monetary aspects of global and regional economies. Visit some of their Web sites:

Global

- World Trade Organization [www.wto.org]
- International Monetary Fund [www.imf.org]
- Bank for International Settlements [www.bis.org]
- World Bank [www.worldbank.org]
- UN Conference on Trade and Development [www.unctad.org]
- World Intellectual Property Organization [www.wipo.int]
- Organization of Petroleum Exporting Countries [www.opec.org]

Regional

- Andean Group [www.itcilo.it]
- Asia-Pacific Economic Cooperation [www.apec.org]
- Association of Southeast Asian Nations [www.asean.org]
- Caribbean Community and Common Market [www.caricom.org]
- Economic Community of West African States [www.cedeao.org]
- European Union [europa.eu.int and in USA www.eurunion.org]
- Mercosur (Common Market Southern Cone, South America) [www.mercosur.com]
- North American Free Trade Association [www.nafta-sec-alena.org]

UN Regional Economic Commissions

- Africa (Addis Ababa): [www.un.org/Depts/eca]
- Europe (Geneva): [www.unece.org]
- Latin America (Santiago): [www.ecla.org]

Robert Schuman from France and German Chancellor Konrad Adenauer were among the important advocates of a new Europe. Reacting to the devastation wrought by two world wars, they were trying to put in place an alternative set of positive, constructive relations among former enemies. By fostering economic integration efforts they were trying at a very practical level to establish new, cooperative links between France and the Federal Republic of Germany, core players in the continental European economy. Theirs was an incremental, step-by-step strategy for attaining economic integration goals over time. A principal motivation was their expectation of a positive impact on *political* relations among European states to be drawn from progress toward greater economic integration.

Another example of spillover occurred when a common agricultural policy (CAP)—painstakingly developed in the late 1960s and early 1970s to set farm

---

TABLE 11.3   A REGIONAL INTEGRATION LADDER

Descent on the ladder denotes movement from relatively shallow to ever-deeper levels of integration. Participants may choose to minimize the degree of integration, staying on upper rungs, or they may decide to deepen the level of integration by moving to lower rungs.

		CHARACTERISTICS (CHARACTERISTICS ARE CUMULATIVE AS RUNGS DESCEND)
First Rung	*Free-Trade Area*	*Goal:* no tariffs or other trade barriers (e.g., North American and European Free Trade Areas [NAFTA and EFTA])
		+
Second Rung	*Customs Union*	*Goal:* common external tariff against imports (e.g., European Economic Community, EEC, established in 1958)
		+
Third Rung	*Common Market*	*Goal:* free movement of factors of production (land, labor, and capital) within integration area (e.g., Europe 1992, Single European Act)
		+
Fourth Rung	*Economic and Monetary Union*	*Goal:* common currency and integrated economic policies (e.g., European Union Treaty agreed to at Maastricht in 1991, also calling for common foreign and security policy; implemented by Amsterdam Treaty signed in 1997 and effective in 1999)
		+
Fifth Rung	*Full Political Union*	*Goal:* complete economic and political integration (e.g., federations like the United States, a model for some advocates of European integration, but others oppose stepping into this deepest form of integration)

prices and price supports within the EEC—came apart. The key precipitating event was when the dollar, to which European currencies were then tied, was allowed to fluctuate in value. To reconstruct a new CAP, integration spilled over into the monetary sector with the creation of a European Monetary System to stabilize currency exchange rates, a necessary step to stabilize prices for agricultural commodities traded within the EEC (see Table 11.3).

Integration also can occur in response to external challenges. Movement from a Customs Union to a Common Market in 1992 and achievement of a European Economic and Monetary Union are not driven by the internal logic indicated by neofunctionalist theory. It is more a calculation by politically relevant elites that Europe will have to deepen the level of economic integration in order to remain competitive with the United States, Japan, and other countries in twenty-first-century high-technology and other global markets.

Deepening the level of integration competes with *widening* membership in the European Union (see Table 11.4). As more members are added to the European Union, economic disparities increase, making it difficult to achieve greater integration. This is particularly true if new members at lower levels of economic development from eastern and southern Europe are added. Advocates of deepening integration argue against full membership for less-developed European countries, proposing associate membership arrangements instead.

Our focus in this section has been on European economic integration because it is the region that has made the most progress toward these goals. By contrast the North American Free Trade Agreement (NAFTA), the West African Economic Community (ECOWAS), the Common Market in the Southern Cone of South America (MERCOSUR), the Andean Group, the Central American Common Market (CACM), the Association of Southeast Asian Nations (ASEAN), and other regional integration organizations are much more modest efforts that do not even have as an objective the levels that already have been achieved in Europe, much less those that are anticipated by European integration advocates.

For example the much-celebrated Canada-Mexico-United States NAFTA accord has only the relatively modest ambition of gradually establishing a regional free-trade area. In this context it does also provide for greater mobility of capital and some harmonization of business practices and standards. As yet there has been no serious discussion, however, of moving to a customs union with a common

---

TABLE 11.4   AN EVER-WIDER EUROPEAN UNION

Will *widening* membership in the EU make *deeper* integration more difficult?

Charter Members	Joined in 1973	Joined in 1986
Belgium	Denmark	Portugal
France	Ireland	Spain
Germany	United Kingdom	
Italy		Joined in 1995
Luxemburg	Joined in 1981	
Netherlands		Austria
	Greece	Finland
		Sweden

A P P L Y I N G   T H E O R Y

INTERDEPENDENCE, INTEGRATION, AND GLOBALIZATION

As noted earlier in the book, the term **interdependence** means different things to different people. It is not always considered desirable. Some realists, for example, see interdependence as the *vulnerability* of one state to another—something to be avoided, reduced, or at least minimized. By contrast a common view among theorists we label pluralists is that interdependence merely reflects the *sensitivity* of one state (or actors within that state) to actions taken by other states (or actors within those states). Raising interest rates in one state, for example, may affect the financial markets in other states. Although there are costs associated with interdependence, benefits to either or both parties may outweigh these costs. Thus interdependence is not necessarily only a matter of one country's vulnerability to another.

On balance pluralists tend to emphasize the benign or positive implications of interdependence. They also focus on the multiple channels that connect societies, including interstate, transgovernmental, and transnational relations. Interdependence in this sense underscores the *interconnectedness* of states and other actors. As such **integration** can be understood as a process resulting in greater interconnectedness or interdependence of both state and nonstate actors. Pluralists see increased interdependence in European and other regional integration projects as well as in the construction of international trade and monetary regimes on a global basis. Interdependence is also central to our understanding of the progressive globalization of the world political economy discussed in this chapter as well as in Chapters Nine, Ten, and Twelve.

external tariff, much less a common market that would allow for the free flow of labor across borders. We should not be surprised when European Union members experience difficulties agreeing to establish and sustain an economic and monetary union with a common currency—a much deeper level of integration than ever attempted in other regional integration projects.

Developing and maintaining trade within a region can (but need not) divert trade or displace other commercial relations outside of the regional context. To the extent that they create trade and promote economic development, regional efforts—however ambitious or however modest—do contribute to the continued functioning of capitalist political economy on a global scale.

CONCLUSION

Economics has been called the dismal science not just because of an inherent pessimism accompanying many economic theories or theorists but also because of a certain opaqueness of presentation seemingly impervious to penetration by general readers. To many people economics may well be a dismal science, but it is nonetheless an enormously important undertaking if we are to understand what is taking place in an increasingly globalized world. The importance of economics underscores its link to politics—in particular the processes leading to authoritative decisions and implementation of economic policies by governments and international organizations. That is why the focus in the chapters in Part IV is on *political economy*, a term that explicitly recognizes the political dimension of economic matters in domestic as well as international and global contexts.

KEY TERMS

comparative advantage
  p. 327
terms of trade   p. 333
commodity   p. 337

macro- and microeconomics
  p. 338
exchange rate   p. 343

international monetary
  regime   p. 318
externalities   p. 354

OTHER CONCEPTS

trade, exports, imports
  p. 326
international commerce
  p. 326
privateering   p. 326
Heckscher-Ohlin theorem
  p. 331
surplus, deficit   p. 332
balance of payments
  p. 332
barter   p. 334
opportunity cost   p. 335
neoclassical economics
  p. 338
demand, supply   p. 338
fiscal policy, monetary
  policy   p. 339

monetarists   p. 339
economies of scale   p. 339
multinational corporation
  (MNC)   p. 341
depreciate, depreciation
  p. 343
appreciate, appreciation
  p. 343
price elasticity of demand
  p. 343
overvalued, undervalued
  currency   p. 346
reserves   p. 349
exchange controls   p. 349
competitive devaluations
  p. 350
float   p. 351

liquidity   p. 352
hard, soft currencies
  p. 352
Special Drawing Rights
  (SDRs)   p. 353
convertible currencies
  p. 353
structural adjustment
  p. 353
concessionary   p. 356
epistemic community
  p. 357
functionalism   p. 358
neofunctionalism   p. 360
interdependence   p. 364
integration   p. 364

ADDITIONAL READINGS

For further background reading, see Robert Gilpin's chapters on international political economy, money and international finance, trade, and multinational corporations in *The Political Economy of International Relations* (Princeton, N.J.: Princeton University Press, 1987). Robert O. Keohane and Joseph S. Nye deal with trade, money, and the oceans in *Power and Interdependence* (Boston: Little Brown, 1977), and Keohane focuses on institutions and theories of cooperation in the world political economy in his *After Hegemony* (Princeton, N.J.: Princeton University Press, 1984).

A widely used text presenting even the most difficult and complex international or global economic ideas in plain English is Paul R. Krugman and Maurice Obstfeld, *International Economics: Theory and Policy* (Reading, Mass.: Addison-Wesley, 1997). Also easily read are H. Robert Heller's relatively short *International Trade: Theory and Empirical Evidence* (Englewood Cliffs, N.J.: Prentice-Hall, 1968) and Charles P. Kindleberger's now classic, nonmathematical presentations on international political economy that include *Foreign Trade and the National Economy* (New Haven, Conn.: Yale University Press, 1962), *Power and Money* (New York: Basic Books, 1970), *The World in Depression, 1929–1939* (Berkeley, Calif.: University of California Press, 1973), and *A Financial History of Western Europe* (London: Allen & Unwin, 1984). For a highly readable account of the development of both classical and neoclassical thought in economics, read the latest edition of Robert B. Ekelund Jr. and Robert F. Hebert, *A History of Economic Theory and Method* (New York: McGraw-Hill, 1975, 1997). See also the chapters on trade and finance in David N. Balaam and Michael Veseth, *Introduction to International Political Economy*, 2nd ed. (Upper Saddle River, N.J.: Prentice Hall, 2001).

THE POLITICAL ECONOMY OF INVESTMENT AND SUSTAINABLE DEVELOPMENT

"If the earth does grow inhospitable toward human presence, it is primarily because we have lost our sense of courtesy toward the earth and its inhabitants, our sense of gratitude, our unwillingness to recognize the sacred character of habitat, our capacity for the awesome, for the numinous quality of every earthly reality."

THOMAS BERRY, *THE DREAM OF EARTH* (1988)

Technology in the form of computers and information drives growth in advanced-industrial and postindustrial service economies in increasingly globalized markets. Given these circumstances, the gap between capital-poor and capital-rich countries grows wider and wider. Prospects of narrowing much less closing the gap seem dimmer and dimmer. "The rich get richer and the poor stay poor (or worse, get poorer)." Or so says the conventional wisdom.

But according to some optimists, these are different times. They see harnessing information technology for productive purposes as by no means the exclusive preserve of capital-rich countries. They see possibilities in at least some less-developed, lower-income economies that acquire the know-how in advanced-production processes that capitalize on information technologies—putting labor and natural resources to work and leapfrogging to ever-higher levels of production and productivity. In Panama, for example, women weave intricate animal or geometric designs on shirts and dresses. "Weaving *molas* is an important part of my life," one young Panamanian notes, "This is more than just a *mola*. It is part of women's development, of our economic well-being, and most important of Panamanian culture." She and her colleagues were speaking at a UN-sponsored program designed to teach computer technology in order to sell their products on the Internet. In doing so they bypass the retailers and retain 60 to 70 percent of their profit as opposed to the 10 percent they would get through retailers.[1]

Naysayers are quick to point out that any such gains, if achieved at all, will no doubt be reserved for only a small segment of populations in the Third World economies of the South. Advanced information-based technologies are labor saving, but labor is precisely what Third World countries have in abundance. These pessimists (or are they only being realistic?) see dual economies as the best that can reasonably be achieved—a minority of 30 percent or more relatively well off, with the majority of the population still suffering from varying degrees of poverty. Vast numbers of people measured in billions or hundreds of millions (as in China and India) with high population growth rates pose formidable challenges not so easily met. Notwithstanding substantial gains, some 80 percent of China is still a peasant society. According to the pessimists the advantages still go to the already capital-rich countries of the North with their smaller, relatively well-educated and trained labor forces.

Social justice demands better levels of living than most of the world's more than six billion people now enjoy. Human rights to a full life and socioeconomic well-being require not only ***sustainable economic development*** and growth on a truly global scale but also a more equitable distribution of wealth—lofty objectives sought by economic development advocates. To the contrary, wishful think-

sustainable development
Economic growth that continues over time and also improves social conditions but does not deplete natural resources or cause environmental damage that undermines or precludes continuing economic growth.

---

[1]World Bank, available at www.un.org/Pubs/ourlives/bank.htm

ing aside, pessimists see economic growth as both consuming resources that cannot be replaced and polluting the environment, making it extraordinarily difficult (if not impossible) to sustain growth much less extend economic development to all the world's peoples.

Beyond assuring some basic, minimum level of living, is the world (or at least large parts of it) to abandon the effort, get off the ever-increasing growth-and-development train, and seek some new way of defining the quality of life? It is an interesting thought, taken more seriously by those who see the exhausting pace prescribed by market capitalism as having eroded core values and the overall quality of life. For understandable reasons more low-income countries still seem eager to get better seats on—not get off—the growth-and-development train. Progression from local to express and then to "bullet-train" class seems to be the more common worldwide aspiration. But how realistic is this goal?

THIRD WORLD POVERTY AND CAPITAL FORMATION

Most of the Third World is, quite frankly, invisible to the West. When it makes the news it is invariably bad news—poverty, wars, famines, AIDS. The facts are stark and difficult to comprehend. Approximately 1.2 billion people—a fifth of humanity—subsist on less than one dollar a day. Women and children account for the majority. Seven hundred million people live in the forty-two most indebted, poverty-stricken countries. Even though barter exchanges of one agricultural good for another is the common way of subsistence as opposed to the use of currency, living standards are appallingly low compared to that of the industrialized North. Malnutrition accounts for the fact that 30 percent or more of children under five years old suffer from severe or moderate stunting and contributes to more than half of the deaths of children under five years old in developing countries.[2] Examples of extreme poverty are found throughout the Third World, but particularly in more than thirty African countries identified in data collected by the UN Development Programs (see Table10.1 on p. 318).

As mentioned in Chapter Ten, Adam Smith (1723–90) saw the wealth of nations lying not in their stock of gold or other treasure, but rather in their

[2]UNICEF, *The State of the World's Children 2000* (1999), available at www.unicef.org/sowc.

> If it were true that the poor were just like the rich but with less money, the global situation would be vastly easier than it is. As it happens, the poor live in different health conditions and must overcome agronomic limitations that are very different from those of rich countries. Those differences, indeed, are often a fundamental cause of persisting poverty.
>
> **Jeffery Sachs, Harvard University economist, as cited in "Helping the World's Poorest," *Economist*, August 14, 1999, p. 17.**

IT'S BEEN SAID...

productive capacity—effectively combining *capital* with *land* (natural resources) and *labor* (human resources) for production of goods and services. Figure 12.1 shows the distribution of GNP (gross national product per capita) in the world. All countries have labor, yet in many countries of the Third World it is uneducated and poorly trained. Land may be essentially deserts, mountains, and jungles, with natural resources few and far between. Capital formation on a national basis depends heavily on domestic savings, but millions of people are more worried about their next meal than saving for the future. Of these three *factors of production*, it is the stock of capital that not surprisingly figures most prominently in capitalism and in discussions of how to jump-start Third World economic development.

For years states and international organizations have provided a total of approximately $1 trillion in aid to the Third World. The logic was straightforward. It was assumed that such aid would boost recipient countries' growth rates and hence help millions escape poverty. Unfortunately many studies have failed to find a strong link between the amount of aid and faster economic growth. Why not? First a good deal of the aid was not really concerned with stimulating economic growth. During the cold war the Soviet Union, United States, and its allies were primarily concerned with propping up friendly governments. To this day Israel and Egypt are the two major recipients of U.S. foreign aid. Nor were the economic and financial competencies of governments a primary consideration. Second, donors often send inappropriate types of aid. Some, for example, prefer to direct aid to conspicuous prestige projects such as dams. Even small donations are regularly ill-advised—Somalis have received heartburn pills and Mozambican peasants high-heeled shoes. Nomads of northwestern Kenya, long pestered by poorly planned charitable projects, refer to their own government as well as foreign aid workers as *ngimoi*: "the enemy." Third, wars in the Third World often destroy the best-laid development plans. Finally there is no doubt that corruption, incompetence, and poor economic policies have squandered large amounts of donor cash.[3]

Yet all is not hopeless. Botswana, for example, gained independence in 1966. At the time one British official rather undiplomatically termed it "a useless piece of territory." Foreign aid initially kept the new government going. Then diamonds were found in the desert, but the government did not squander its newfound wealth. Profits were ploughed into infrastructure, education, and health care. Foreign investment was welcomed and private business allowed to flourish. Aid projects proceeded only if it were likely they would provide sustainable development. From 1966 to 1991, Botswana's economy grew at one of the fastest rates in the world. A key reason was the fact that government ministers were for the most part honest and competent. As the economy slowly diversified, aid donors began to look for other, needier recipients.[4]

factors of production
Land, labor, and capital are essential elements that are combined to produce the goods and services that constitute economic output.

---

[3]"Helping the Third World," *Economist*, June 26, 1999, p. 24.
[4]Ibid.

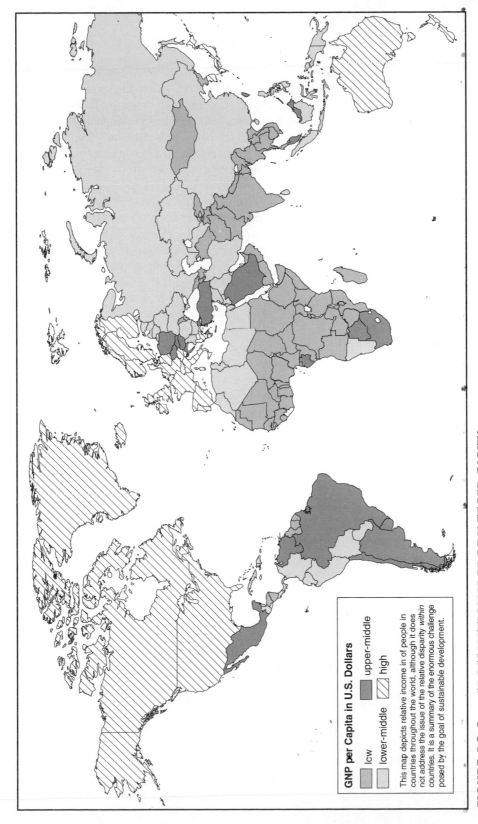

FIGURE 12.1   GROSS NATIONAL PRODUCT PER CAPITA

GNP per Capita in U.S. Dollars

low
upper-middle
lower-middle
high

This map depicts relative income in of people in countries throughout the world, although it does not address the issue of the relative disparity *within* countries. It is a summary of the enormous challenge posed by the goal of sustainable development.

Sources of Capital

In addition to grants and loans by governments and nongovernmental organizations, a conventional source of multilateral aid has been the World Bank. Formally the International Bank for Reconstruction and Development (IBRD), the institution was established along with the International Monetary Fund (IMF) at an international conference at Bretton Woods, New Hampshire, in 1944. The World Bank's immediate post–World War II goal was economic recovery and reconstruction of major European and Asian economies devastated by the war. Located in Washington, D.C., next to the IMF, the World Bank's focus since the 1950s and 1960s has been on loans for economic development to capital-poor countries. The World Bank's capital comes from contributions—a multilateral form of foreign assistance by capital-rich member countries that want to use this institution as a vehicle for lending to less-developed countries. Since it began operations after World War II, the World Bank has loaned more than $400 billion. In addition to loans at near-market rates, the World Bank engages in extensive lending at **concessionary**, below-market rates to capital-poor countries through its affiliate, the International Development Association (IDA). World Bank loans for private-sector projects in developing countries are made through its International Finance Corporation (IFC) affiliate.

To facilitate lending and direct investment to countries where investors fear takeover of their assets by **nationalization** or **expropriation** or face political instability or other political risks, the Multilateral Investment Guarantee Agency (MIGA) is an investment-insurance affiliate that provides political-risk insurance programs. Disputes between governments and private investors can also be submitted for mediation or conciliation to the World Bank's International Center for Settlement of Investment Disputes (ICSID).

Regional lending for development also occurs through such separate international organizations as the Inter-American Development Bank (IADB), Asian Development Bank, African Development Bank, and now the North American Development Bank. Privately held investment banks are also participants, often benefiting from research on investment projects undertaken by multilateral institutions. Table 12.1 charts investment capital for development in selected countries.

Multinational corporations (MNCs), investment firms, and international banks seeking profits or returns on investment are an additional source of capital. Annual revenues of many MNCs are larger than the GDPs of many states. MNCs are also a potential source for the transfer of technologies they use in their production processes if carried out in Third World countries. Of course proprietary interests of the MNCs often lead them to maximize their profits while minimizing technology transfers. Nevertheless they are an important source of capital as well as training for domestic labor forces. Of course, continuing and seemingly endless debate goes on between MNC advocates, who see these corporations as well as domestic firms providing jobs and contributing substantially to development, and those who contest this view, seeing MNCs as essentially predatory, engaging in whatever levels of exploitation governments and local elites will tolerate. Critics claim that one reason MNCs organize their operations multinationally is to avoid or circumvent obstacles or barriers imposed by particular states (see the box on p. 375 on transfer pricing). Nevertheless private direct

TABLE 12.1	INVESTMENT CAPITAL FOR DEVELOPMENT IN SELECTED COUNTRIES

Development depends on the investment of capital, whether this capital is created domestically or comes from other countries. In this table "net" flows refer to inflows of investment capital from abroad minus outflows of capital to other countries. As the term implies, *direct investments* refer to funds put directly into businesses or other enterprises by investors. By contrast *portfolio investments* refer to investors purchasing stocks or bonds. The funds raised by such sales are available for investment by firms issuing these stocks or bonds. A measure of the relative size of total net investment flows going into a particular country's economy is to calculate them as a percentage of gross national product (GNP) in a given year. The list in the table is a sample of countries selected based on availability of data and as representative of net investment flows into national economies of varying size and level of development in different regions.

COUNTRIES	GNP (US$ BILLIONS)	NET FOREIGN DIRECT INVESTMENT FLOWS (US$ MILLIONS)	NET PORTFOLIO INVESTMENT FLOWS (US$ MILLIONS)	TOTAL OF NET INVESTMENT FLOWS AS PERCENTAGE OF GNP
HIGH INCOME/ DEVELOPMENT				
Republic of Korea	485.2	2,341	2,704	1
Chile	70.5	5,417	1,525	10
Czech Republic	54.0	1,301	221	3
Argentina	319.3	6,327	11,250	6
Uruguay	20.0	200	451	3
Costa Rica	9.3	500	41	6
MIDDLE AND LOW INCOME/ DEVELOPMENT				
Latin America				
Brazil	784.0	16,330	5,056	3
Mexico	348.6	12,101	2,526	4
Panama	8.4	340	461	10
Peru	63.7	2,000	−110	3
Asia				
Bangladesh	44.1	145	11	<1
China	1,055.4	45,300	11,787	5
India	357.4	3,264	4,035	2
Indonesia	221.5	5,350	3,417	4
Malaysia	98.2	3,754	2,014	6
Thailand	165.8	3,600	1,418	3
Kazakhstan	21.3	1,320	400	8
Pakistan	64.6	800	627	2
Vietnam	24.0	1,200	−94	5

(table continues)

TABLE 12.1   (CONTINUED)

COUNTRIES	GNP (US$ BILLIONS)	NET FOREIGN DIRECT INVESTMENT FLOWS (US$ MILLIONS)	NET PORTFOLIO INVESTMENT FLOWS (US$ MILLIONS)	TOTAL OF NET INVESTMENT FLOWS AS PERCENTAGE OF GNP
Other Regions				
Côte d'Ivoire	10.2	50	18	1
Egypt	72.2	834	1,813	3
Hungary	45.8	2,085	598	6
Romania	31.8	1,224	422	5
South Africa	130.2	1,705	2,016	3
Turkey	199.3	606	2,552	2

Source: Adapted from United Nations Development Programme (UNDP) data for 1997, in *Human Development Report, 1999* (New York: Oxford University Press, 1999), pp. 49–52 and 180–83.

investment, portfolio investment, and bank lending accounted for approximately $145 billion dollars in capital investment in Third World countries during 2000. Net private capital flows to emerging economies from 1995 to 2000 are illustrated graphically in Figure 12.2.

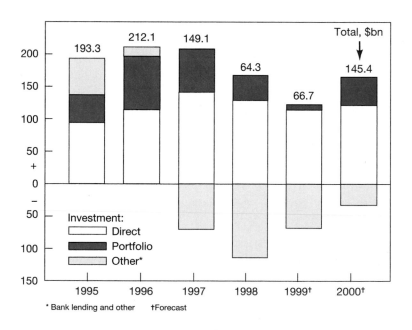

FIGURE 12.2   PRIVATE CAPITAL FLOWS TO AND FROM EMERGING ECONOMIES, $BN
Source: "Uncertain Prospects," *Economist,* April 24, 1999, p. 23.

MNCS, POLITICS, AND THE STATE: THE COMPLEX CASE OF TRANSFER PRICING

It is fair to say that since the end of World War II, the most controversial aspect of international political economy has been the rise of the multinational corporation (MNC). Some see MNCs as eventually superseding the nation-state, muting nationalism by providing economic benefits to all. Others view MNCs as rapacious imperialists, exploiting the weak and poor in their quest for greater profits. The truth is somewhere in between these two views. In direct, open conflict between MNCs and the state, the state will in principle generally prevail, as it always has the option of closing down the corporation's operations. MNCs realize this and prefer to avoid such confrontations. Conflict between states and MNCs therefore tends to be more subtle and is usually reported on the business page, not the front page, of daily newspapers.

To illustrate potential conflict between a state and a multinational corporation, consider the following scenario. XYZ Corporation's automobile assembly plant **subsidiary** in the country of Ruralia needs to import engines, computer parts, and other higher-technology components manufactured in XYZ subsidiaries located in more industrially developed countries.

As it turns out there is a difference in tax rates on profits in these countries. Because XYZ Corporation is a rational actor that tries to maximize its gains (or minimize its losses), the corporation can be expected to reduce its tax exposure—maximizing legally the amount of profit it makes in countries with lower tax rates. It may choose to do this through **transfer pricing**—increasing or decreasing the prices its subsidiaries charge each other for components.

Its assembly plant is in low-tax, less-developed Ruralia, a country chosen both because of its relatively low taxes and an abundant supply of relatively unskilled, lower-cost labor. The local government has intentionally set the tax rate low to attract investment by multinational corporations as part of its own economic development plan.

Although the Ruralian government would like XYZ Corporation to put in more than just an assembly plant, it recognizes that at least the assembly plant will employ a substantial number of Ruralians who would not otherwise have these jobs. Opponents who see XYZ and other MNCs as exploiting local labor, damaging the environment, or imposing foreign cultural preferences on Ruralians are not as strong politically as local investors and businesses that favor the plant. Some of these interests will participate in the venture directly, whereas others expect to gain indirectly due to the plant's positive contribution to local economic growth. The argument in favor of XYZ is that foreign investment contributes to a rising tide that raises all ships.

Thus, notwithstanding some domestic opposition, XYZ's investment in an assembly plant is compatible with both corporate and state objectives. In short, XYZ Corporation and the Ruralia government are rational (or purposive) actors seeking to make a good business deal. One side may get the better deal, but both see the investment as a potential or expected gain.

Manufacturing computers, carburetors, or other engine components that involve higher technologies, by contrast, requires greater capital investment in machinery, employing relatively fewer but higher-skilled and higher-paid workers than those needed for assembly plants. Countries like Industritania with higher-skilled and higher-paid labor forces are often higher-tax countries as well.

In this circumstance the corporation's internal sales prices of computers, carburetors, or other engine components needed by the assembly plant subsidiary in Ruralia are set legally at or near cost, thus minimizing profit from producing these components in the high-tax country. Setting lower prices also reduces the tariff or tax that must be paid on the value of components imported by the assembly plant subsidiary in Ruralia, which has relatively high tariffs to protect its new, emergent industries as they compete in global markets.

When the automobiles have been assembled in Ruralia, they are sold or exported at market prices. Because components were imported so cheaply and labor and other production costs were also held

(box continues)

down, profit as the difference between revenue from sales and the overall costs of production is maximized in Ruralia and minimized in Industritania. Because of liberal capital outflow rules, XYZ Corporation spends some of its gain on new investment in Ruralia but moves most of it out of the country, using some to finance investments in other subsidiaries and **repatriating** the rest to its corporate headquarters to pay corporate shareholders and other stakeholders.

In this example Industritania lost tax revenue on profits: Had components manufactured there been exported at market prices well above cost, revenues would have been higher. XYZ Corporation can expect the Industritanian government to object, particularly if XYZ exports components to its Ruralia subsidiary *below* production cost, thus avoiding payment of any tax at all to Industritania. On the other hand Ruralia gains by having more profits to tax, even though its tax rate remains low.

When their interests diverge, governments may try through policy, law, and regulation to control multinational corporate operations. The complexity of financial transactions such as transfer pricing among subsidiaries of the same corporation in several countries makes regulation extraordinarily difficult. Moreover, if the corporation finds local government too hostile, it may choose to close its plants and take operations elsewhere.

Another important source of capital for developing countries is from export trade—a positive trade balance that occurs when the revenue from exports exceeds outlays for imports. Capital earned from trade is thus available for investment or other purposes. On the other hand if outlays for imports exceed revenues from exports—a negative trade balance—this is a net drain on capital, making less capital available for domestic investment or other purposes. Excessive military expenditures on imported armaments or other unnecessary purchases of luxury goods from abroad also divert capital from investment. Not all imports, however, come at the expense of development. Imports of capital goods used in domestic production of goods and services may be essential to advancing economic growth. Because trade is so important to development, it is not surprising that many Third World countries in the South seek **trade preferences** from advanced industrial countries in the North. (See the more detailed discussion of trade preferences later in this chapter.) They also see capital gains to be had from pro-growth policies in First World countries—prosperity in the North that makes firms and individuals in First World countries more likely to import from Third World countries, invest in them, and even spend leisure time and money there as tourists.

Payments of interest and principal on loans to foreign governments or banks also constitute a substantial drain on capital, particularly if developing countries have borrowed too heavily. When global interest rates take a significant turn upward, additional strain is placed on Third World countries trying to service (make payments on) existing debt or refinancing and securing new loans. Countries facing financial difficulties, perhaps in danger of being forced to default on their loan payments, often seek debt forgiveness (see Table 12.2 and Figure 12.3, p. 379).

Failing that they ask for cooperation from governments or international or private lending institutions as they try to reschedule or refinance these obligations with new long-term loans at concessionary, below-market interest rates. As noted in Chapter Eleven, such concessionary loans are really a form of grant aid

TABLE 12.2	FOREIGN AID, DEBT, AND ECONOMIC DEVELOPMENT

Net official development assistance (ODA) or aid from governments and international organizations is an important source of investment capital for many developing countries. Borrowed funds are also an important source of capital for investment. Properly invested, such funds can contribute to economic development. Whether invested wisely or not, *servicing* debt (making payments of interest and principal on time) can be a heavy burden, particularly for countries that find themselves overextended. One indicator of debt burden is to calculate total debt as a percentage of gross national product (GNP) for a country's economy as a whole. Another indicator is the *debt service ratio*, the percentage of export earnings in a given year used to make payments of interest and principal on all external borrowings. All such debt payments, of course, constitute a drain on capital that otherwise would be available for further domestic investment. This table gives a sample of countries selected based on availability of data and as representative of debt burdens in national economies of varying size and level of development in different regions.

COUNTRIES	TOTAL AID RECEIVED (NET ODA) (US$ MILLIONS)	TOTAL AID RECEIVED AS PERCENTAGE OF GNP	TOTAL EXTERNAL DEBT (US$ MILLIONS)	EXTERNAL DEBT AS PERCENTAGE OF GNP (US$ MILLIONS)	DEBT PAYMENTS AS PERCENTAGE OF EXPORTS (DEBT SERVICE RATIO)
HIGH INCOME/ DEVELOPMENT					
Chile	136	0.2	20,384	42.4	20.4
Czech Republic	107	0.2	21,456	41.8	14.1
Argentina	222	0.1	50,946	38.7	58.7
Uruguay	57	0.3	6,652	33.6	15.4
Slovakia	67	0.3	9,989	51.7	12.2
Poland	641	0.5	33,307	29.5	6.1
MIDDLE AND LOW INCOME/ DEVELOPMENT					
Latin America					
Brazil	487	0.1	193,663	24.1	57.4
Colombia	274	0.3	31,777	34.4	26.6
Mexico	108	<0.1	149,690	38.4	32.4
Panama	124	1.5	6,338	75.4	16.4
Peru	488	0.8	30,496	48.8	30.9
Venezuela	28	<0.1	35,542	41.6	31.3
Asia					
Bangladesh	1,009	2.3	15,125	35.1	10.6
China	2,040	0.2	146,697	16.6	8.6
India	1,678	0.4	94,404	24.9	19.6
Indonesia	832	0.4	136,174	65.3	30.0

(table continues)

TABLE 12.2   (CONTINUED)

COUNTRIES	TOTAL AID RECEIVED (NET ODA) (US$ MILLIONS)	TOTAL AID RECEIVED AS PERCENTAGE OF GNP	TOTAL EXTERNAL DEBT (US$ MILLIONS)	EXTERNAL DEBT AS PERCENTAGE OF GNP (US$ MILLIONS)	DEBT PAYMENTS AS PERCENTAGE OF EXPORTS (DEBT SERVICE RATIO)
Malaysia	—	—	47,228	50.5	7.5
Thailand	626	0.4	93,416	62.6	15.4
Kazakhstan	131	0.6	4,278	19.5	6.5
Pakistan	597	1.0	29,665	47.5	35.2
Philippines	689	0.8	45,433	53.0	9.2
Vietnam	997	4.1	21,629	89.4	7.8
Other Regions					
Côte d'Ivoire	444	4.7	15,609	165.3	27.4
Egypt	1,947	2.5	29,849	39.0	9.0
Hungary	152	0.3	24,373	55.0	29.7
Nigeria	202	11.0	28,455	75.6	7.8
Romania	197	0.6	10,442	30.2	15.7
Russian Federation	718	0.2	125,645	28.7	6.5
South Africa	497	0.4	25,222	20.0	12.8
Turkey	—	—	91,205	47.1	18.4

Source: Adapted from United Nations Development Programme (UNDP) data for 1997, in *Human Development Report, 1999* (New York: Oxford University Press, 1999), pp. 193–96.

since interest earned from a proportion of the loan invested at higher market rates can actually be used to service the loan. Debtor countries do have some leverage over their lenders, however. Because lenders stand to lose all if borrowers default, the former are usually willing to accommodate reasonable requests from the latter, particularly if these concessions give some assurance that the loan eventually will be repaid. Figure 12.4 and Table 12.3 (p. 380) show foreign sources of capital and foreign aid donors to developing countries.

TRADE AND DEVELOPMENT

NIEO A policy resolution of developing countries calling for a new international economic order—an international economic system more favorable to their interests.

Aside from aid, loans, investment, and debt forgiveness, trade preferences have been a key element of the agenda for a *New International Economic Order (NIEO)* advanced by Third World countries in the South and articulated over several decades in the UN Conferences on Trade and Development (UNCTAD) and in other forums. Efforts that began in the 1960s and 1970s to build an NIEO looked for ways to bridge the great North-South divide. It is not surprising that

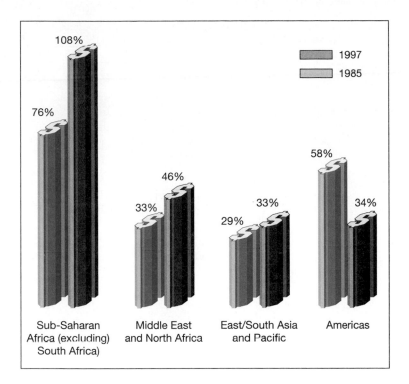

FIGURE 12.3 DEBT INCREASES AND DECREASES (EXTERNAL DEBT OF DEVELOPING COUNTRIES AS A PERCENTAGE OF GNP BY REGION)
Source: UNICEF, *The Progress of Nations 1999.* www.unicef.org/pon99

A New International Economic Order (NIEO)?

The arrows in this figure depict the direction of net capital flows less-developed countries in the South prefer. Critics note that net capital flows in fact often move in the opposite direction when MNCs send their profits or returns on investments back to the North, and when countries in the South run negative trade balances and must repay their loans (often at market rates), and owners of capital in the South choose to invest in the North where they expect to realize greater returns.

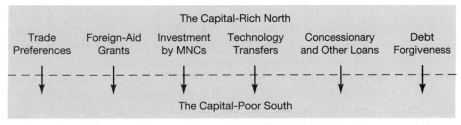

FIGURE 12.4 FOREIGN SOURCES OF CAPITAL

TABLE 12.3	PRINCIPAL FOREIGN AID DONOR COUNTRIES: OFFICIAL DEVELOPMENT ASSISTANCE (ODA)

Official Development Assistance (ODA) from the North is an important source of capital for investment in the South and in other countries receiving such aid. In addition to examining the total or aggregate amount of foreign aid disbursed for development purposes, two other indicators of the degree of commitment of capital-rich countries to development assistance are ODA as a percentage of total economic capability or gross national product (GNP) and also as measured on a per person (or *per capita*) basis, dividing total ODA from each country by its population.

COUNTRIES	TOTAL ODA (US$ MILLIONS)	ODA AS PERCENTAGE OF GDP	ODA (US$ PER PERSON IN DONOR COUNTRY
Group of Seven			
United States	6,878	0.09	30
Japan	9,358	0.22	79
Germany	5,857	0.28	87
France	6,307	0.45	125
Italy	1,266	0.11	33
United Kingdom	3,433	0.26	55
Canada	2,045	0.34	64
Other Donor Countries			
Australia	1,061	0.28	59
Austria	527	0.26	72
Belgium	764	0.31	88
Denmark	1,637	0.97	342
Finland	379	0.33	81
Ireland	187	0.31	51
Luxemburg	95	0.55	226
Netherlands	2,947	0.81	212
New Zealand	154	0.26	38
Norway	1,306	0.86	308
Portugal	250	0.25	25
Spain	1,234	0.23	34
Sweden	1,731	0.79	222
Switzerland	911	0.34	148

Source: Adapted from United Nations Development Programme (UNDP) data for 1997, in *Human Development Report, 1999* (New York: Oxford University Press, 1999), p. 192.

the General Assembly was at the core of NIEO efforts, since Third World countries have had a controlling majority there after decolonization and the creation of new states in Africa and Asia in the 1960s tipped the balance of votes in that chamber toward the South.

One of the things most Third World countries wanted from the North was generous trade preferences. In a challenge to Ricardian free-trade theory as a basis for policy, discontent was expressed concerning the uneven or asymmetric distribution of wealth created through free trade—an arrangement that clearly favored the North. For one thing, as discussed in Chapter Eleven, the terms of trade between exporters favor the North's manufactured and higher-technology goods and services over the single-commodity agricultural or mineral exports or relatively low-technology manufactures offered by most Third World countries. Prices for these Third World exports barely hold their own or tend to decline over time. By contrast First World manufactures and higher-technology goods and services tend to hold their own or increase in price over time.

One approach to securing more favorable terms of trade is to form a **cartel** or joint arrangement that allows member states to influence the price of a commodity by regulating its supply to the world market. Efforts to form cartels among coffee producers and tin or other agricultural and mineral exporters have been relatively unsuccessful due to difficulty in enforcing compliance with cartel production targets and quotas. The ready availability of substitute suppliers outside of cartel arrangements has compounded these difficulties. Moreover a rising price for one mineral or agricultural product may lead consumers to substitute and import another less-expensive product. If coffee becomes too high in price, for example, some consumers may switch to tea.

One exception to this generally negative record for cartels, at least for a few years, was the Organization of Petroleum Exporting Countries (OPEC), a cartel that was successful in substantially raising the world price of oil in the 1970s. These "oil shocks," as they were called, immediately and dramatically improved the terms of trade of cartel members; however, the industrial world's heavy dependence on imported oil at ever-higher prices significantly raised overall costs of production in oil buying countries and thus contributed to fueling inflation on a global scale. Efforts were undertaken to find new oil supplies and to develop alternative energy sources. Powerful First World countries also brought great pressures to bear on those OPEC members they could influence.

The dollar price of oil was relatively static in the 1980s and 1990s, actually declining in real terms when we take inflation into account. The OPEC cartel thus has not been as successful as in its early years due to a number of factors. First rivalry among OPEC members and a desire to produce more oil for export than allowed by cartel agreements kept OPEC production targets higher than they might have been and effectively added enough oil to world supplies to keep prices from rising. Due in part to its security and economic relations with the United States and other Western countries, Saudi Arabia (which has the world's largest oil reserves) has remained committed to maintaining an ample supply to world markets. Second development of oil fields under the North Sea between Britain and Norway, at Prudhoe Bay in northern Alaska, and more recently in the central Asia-Caspian Sea area have added to world oil supplies. Finally, although aggregate demand for oil has continued to increase over the decades, it is less than what it would have been thanks to some development of alternative energy sources and energy-efficiency measures.

Because of largely unsuccessful efforts to affect world prices through cartel formation and continuance of adverse *terms of trade* for much of what it produces for export, the South has sought trade preferences from the North as part of the NIEO. The argument is that beginning or infant industries in the South may need the protection of tariffs or other barriers to trade until they have grown sufficiently to be competitive in global markets. At the same time these countries want advanced industrial or postindustrial societies not to discriminate against Third World exports by imposing trade barriers against them. Third World

terms of trade The ratio of export prices from one country to those of another. Developing countries claim that over time, the prices of their commodities and other exports tend to fall while the price of manufactured goods exported to them by advanced industrial countries tends to rise.

countries in effect have argued for unfettered access to First World markets for their exports, without fear of reprisal if in the early stages of industrialization they are allowed to discriminate against First World exports.

Foreign-exchange earnings that come from exports can be used to purchase capital goods from the advanced industrial and postindustrial economies that produce them. Indeed, trade balances favorable to a Third World country are an important source of capital that can be invested for economic development purposes. By contrast, when Third World countries continue to run negative trade balances, capital that could have been invested in their domestic economies is drained off. That is why favorable terms of trade are so important, particularly to Third World countries trying to acquire capital for industrial or other economic development.

Special trade arrangements have in fact been made and preferences granted, most notably under agreements known as the Lomé Conventions (named for negotiations conducted in the African country of Togo) by European Union members with Third World "ACP" countries in Africa, the Caribbean, and the Pacific, many of which are former colonies of European powers. As mentioned in Chapter Eleven, critics have been quick to claim that these trade concessions, although of some benefit to the South, also effectively tie these states to the former colonial powers in what amount to **neocolonial** relations that work to the net advantage of Europe.

A great frustration to many in Third World countries, therefore, is the degree to which they are caught in a seemingly inescapable structure of **dependency** on capital-rich First World countries. There seems to be no escape. Adverse terms of trade are difficult to reverse and producing qualitative manufactures that will compete favorably with those produced by firms in technology-endowed and capital-rich countries is a formidable task. Some **newly industrializing countries (NICs)**—for example South Korea, Taiwan, Singapore, Hong Kong (now part of China), and Brazil—have been able to break into world markets for manufactures or such technology-intensive services as banking and insurance by combining substantial domestic capital formation, imported technologies, and access to a lower-wage but skilled and conscientious labor force.

Most Third World countries have not been so successful, as their domestic firms find it difficult to compete in global trading markets. Some have formed regional free-trading areas such as the Economic Community of West African States (ECOWAS) among lower-income countries in West Africa, the Southern Cone Common Market (MERCOSUR) in South America, the Andean Group, the Caribbean Community and Common Market (CARICOM), the Central American Common Market (CACM), and the Association of Southeast Asian Nations (ASEAN). For its part Mexico has joined the United States and Canada, two First World countries with about ten times its per capita income, in a North American Free Trade Agreement (NAFTA). Given these economic asymmetries in levels of development, Mexico has faced substantial difficulties, as reflected in its having to defend the peso, its currency, with heavy foreign borrowings from time to time. Mexico's hope, of course, is that NAFTA will be a means of access to capital and to the huge, relatively wealthy Canadian and American markets for selling its goods and services over the long term.

Critics contend, however, that by joining NAFTA Mexico is locking itself further into a structure of dependency. From this perspective unfavorable terms

CASE

THE INTERNET AND THE THIRD WORLD

An important reflection of globalization is the spread of global communication. The Internet epitomizes this global connectivity. But what about the Third World? Developing countries lack easy access to computers, infrastructure to support their use, and skilled users. Does the Internet therefore represent yet again a technological advancement that leaves the poorest of the world even further behind? As a result of the Rio Conference in 1992, the UN Development Programme (UNDP) launched the Sustainable Development Networking Programme (SDNP) designed to help bridge the information gap between the haves and have-nots. The program was met with much initial skepticism both within and outside the United Nations. How, it was asked, does information technology aid sustainable development? How does one get an illiterate farmer from his field to a computer? The answer is, "You don't."

The key intermediaries are NGOs that pass on useful information to the farmer. In Mexico, for example, the SDNP has established an information center for corn producers where farmers can learn online what the market price of corn is in the capital. The goal is to help them avoid underselling their crops. Similar information centers have been established in Jamaica, Guatemala, Honduras, and Costa Rica. The long-term goal is for communities eventually to manage the information centers on their own. As one advisor to the SDNP has commented, "You cannot drop information technology like a bomb and run away. That does not work. You have to train people, show them how to use it in a way that can help them, and that takes time, a lot of time."[a]

Point: It remains to be seen how important the Internet will be in terms of aiding sustainable development, but modest international efforts are underway.

[a]Esther Braun, "Internet: A Tool for Sustainable Development," *UN Chronicle*, No. 2, (1999), p. 77.

A study in contrast: Masai tribesmen in Kenya try out a lap-top computer.

Practicing World Politics

Regional Organizations on Sustainable Development

Regional international organizations play important roles in formulating and implementing strategies on development and the environment. Visit some of their Web sites:

- Andean Group [www.itcilo.it]
- Asia-Pacific Economic Cooperation [www.apec.org]
- Association of Southeast Asian Nations [www.asean.org]
- Caribbean Community and Common Market [www.caricom.org]
- Economic Community of West African States [www.cedeao.org]
- European Union [europa.eu.int and in USA www.eurunion.org]
- Mercosur (Common Market Southern Cone, South America) [www.mercosur.com]
- North American Free Trade Association [www.nafta-sec-alena.org]

UN Regional Economic Commissions

- Africa (Addis Ababa) [www.un.org/Depts/eca]
- Asia and the Pacific (Bangkok) [www.unescap.org]
- Europe (Geneva) [www.unece.org]
- Latin America (Santiago) [www.ecla.org]

Regional Development Banks

- Inter-American Development Bank [www.IADB.org]
- Asian Development Bank [www.adb.org]
- African Development Bank [www.afdb.org]
- North American Development Bank [www.nadb.org]

of trade and paying interest on increasing debt obligations to banks and foreign governments drain capital from Mexico and other Third World countries, block their economic development, and keep them securely in a state of dependency that works to First World advantage.

Population Growth as a Constraint on Third World Economic Development

Economies that grow depend on a continuing investment of capital. Populations that grow too fast consume whatever surplus would have been produced for capital investment. Planners who want to lift the capacities of Third World political economies to provide a better level of living for their peoples seek to reduce birth rates even as improved medical and health conditions also reduce death rates.

Populations have continued to grow at a very rapid rate in Third World countries, although substantial progress has been made, as annual growth rates as high as 3 percent or more in the 1960s have been trimmed substantially in most countries. With a 3 percent growth rate, population doubles in just about a quarter-century, but a 2 percent growth rate only slows this doubling time to about three

A P P L Y I N G   T H E O R Y

MARXIST PERSPECTIVES ON THE PLIGHT OF THE THIRD WORLD

Marxists are not at all surprised by the depressed state of affairs in many Third World countries. In the Marxist view the **bourgeoisie** or capitalist class uses its base in the capital-rich North to reach out to its class allies in the South for new markets in which to sell and new workers and peasants to exploit. In short, the *bourgeoisie* in the North joins with *bourgeois* elements at the top of societies in Third World countries in exploitative joint ventures. In advanced, global capitalism, older colonial forms of imperialism have been replaced by multinational corporations and banks, the present-day agents of the owners of capital who are able to use neocolonial ties and channels to facilitate their efforts.

In this Marxist perspective it is the class structure of dominance that explains the misery of peasants and workers in Third World countries. The prevalence of malnutrition and disease, high infant mortality rates, and low life expectancies constitute a relatively silent but particularly brutal form of **structural violence** against the common peoples. To Marxist revolutionaries this analysis is sufficient motivation for action against an oppressive, worldwide class structure.

Karl Marx (1818–83), born and reared in Trier in present-day Germany, wrote extensively on the political-economic history and practice of capitalism. Much of his research and writing took place during his stay in London where he was able to observe first-hand the kind of labor exploitation in early industrial capitalism that also inspired the literary contributions of Charles Dickens. Marx was both a political-economic theorist and a revolutionary who challenged the capitalist or *bourgeois* interests of his time. Present-day theorists who focus on the South's dependency on the North and the resulting exploitation of peoples in the Third World owe an intellectual debt to Marx even if they do not share all of Marx's premises.

and a half decades. By contrast population is actually declining in some First World countries. The 0.6 percent average growth rate in the First World taken as a whole means that it will take a much longer time—some 120 years—to double their numbers at this relatively slow rate. The final box in this chapter (see p. 401) discusses how population growth can be estimated.

A 1994 United Nation conference held in Cairo on population issues and economic development was part of an international consensus-building process that included governmental representatives of UN member states, UN and other international organization delegates and staff members, and representatives of numerous nongovernmental organizations (NGOs). Significant differences of view on what was to be done were readily apparent. The Chinese policy of one child per family was scrutinized closely by those concerned that enforcement (which for all intents and purposes has lapsed) could easily violate human rights, particularly should violators face punitive sanctions or even forced sterilization. Many delegates preferred an approach focusing on empowering women, educating them in the use of contraceptives, medications, and other birth-control devices. Another objective for many was to make birth-control technologies readily available free of charge or at relatively low cost. A separate NGO forum was also attended by almost 4,000 individuals representing 200 nongovernmental organizations.

Slower-growing (but also better-educated and trained) populations coupled with substantial capital investment are key ingredients in the recipe for economic development and continued growth for any economy. Success in curbing population growth removes a significant obstacle or impediment to economic development. Other impediments to growth include heavy interest payments on loans. Debt-service burdens drain off capital that could be used for domestic investment or for other needs. Excessive military spending, engaged in by many Third World countries, also drains important resources that could be used for more productive economic development purposes.

Relatively unconstrained efforts to achieve rapid economic growth can undermine the continued sustainability of economic development. The sheer size of populations in countries now industrializing magnifies the environmental impact of economic development. The adverse environmental impact of industrialization seen in First World societies with populations in the millions when the industrialization process was well underway in the nineteenth and early twentieth centuries can be expected on an even greater scale of damage if China (with more than 1.2 billion people) and India (with some 900 million people) continue to follow the same approach to industrialization in the first decades of the twenty-first century as they did in the last half of the twentieth century.

In addition to bearing the burden of soaring population, agricultural productivity can be destroyed through erosion and misuse of fertilizers, water supplies can be contaminated, and other forms of pollution can wreak havoc on agricultural and other forms of production. Resource depletion, reduction of wildlife, fishery, and seafood stocks, and other forms of environmental degradation can make continued production unsustainable even at present levels. These issues were at the core of UN-sponsored meetings in Rio de Janeiro in 1992 attended by representatives of governments and international organizations. About 17,000 individuals including 2,400 representatives of NGOs held separate but simultaneous meetings in Rio on these same environmental and sustainable development issues. Events were covered by 10,000 journalists representing print, radio, television, and other telecommunications media.

A GLOBAL PERSPECTIVE

The Global Environment

A case can be made that the greatest environmental threats to global security and the continued viability of the global economy are the reduction of natural resource stocks as well as land, water, and atmospheric pollution—the latter resulting in global warming, acid rain, and ozone-layer depletion in the high atmosphere.

Production and use of chlorofluorocarbons (CFCs) for air conditioners, refrigerators, and spray cans is blamed for ozone-layer depletion in the upper atmosphere. Depleting this ozone layer removes an important filter of the sun's rays and thus exposes human beings and other living things to a greater risk of skin cancer. Given this scientific consensus on cause and effect, negotiations in the late 1980s in Montreal and subsequently have produced international agreements to

A P P L Y I N G   T H E O R Y

UNDERSTANDING ENVIRONMENTAL CHALLENGES

In his study of organizations, J.D. Thompson noted how uncertainties can make decision making difficult. If we apply his insights to environmental problems like global warming we find uncertainty among atmospheric scientists about possible outcomes as well as the relative importance of different causes for global climate change. Given this uncertainty it is extraordinarily difficult to form a global political consensus on what is to be done, particularly since proposed remedies are usually very costly.

By contrast the scientific understanding of ozone-layer depletion caused by chlorofluorocarbon (CFC) emissions has been far clearer, making a political consensus on remedies to be implemented much easier to

achieve in what became the Montreal Protocol and later the Vienna Convention, which eliminate or reduce CFC emissions. Somewhere in between global warming and ozone-layer depletion in terms of degree of uncertainty is the case of increased acidification of precipitation—acid rain.

Thompson's matrix (Figure 12.A) may help us understand these problems analytically as we explore building political consensus nationally and globally on appropriate remedies. In which of the four cells would you place global warming, ozone-layer depletion, and acid rain? Or are you even uncertain about how to categorize them?

Preferences Regarding Possible Outcomes

	Certainty	Uncertainty
Certainty	A	B
Uncertainty	C	D

Beliefs About Cause-Effect Relations

FIGURE 12.A
DECISION-MAKING MATRIX

Source: J.D. Thompson, *Organizations in Action* (New York: McGraw-Hill, 1967), pp. 134–35.

reduce and eventually eliminate CFC production. Even so, CFCs already produced (e.g., freon in old air conditioners, refrigerators, and spray cans—many of which are rusting in garbage dumps) will continue to pollute the upper atmosphere for decades to come.

Industrial societies consume enormous quantities of oil, gas, coal, or wood (so-called *fossil fuels*) in factories, households, and transportation vehicles of all kinds. Burning these hydrocarbon fuels contributes to *acid rain*—production of carbonic, hydrochloric, and sulfuric acids that fall to earth mixed with rain water, thus increasing the acidity of soils, lakes, and streams and killing fish, trees, and other forest plant life. States have taken some steps to reduce the atmospheric pollution that contributes to acid rain (as in reducing sulfur content in industrial smokestack emissions or curbing auto emissions) and have tried to deacidify affected areas by adding calcium carbonate or other bases to lakes and streams. The problem, however, remains an enormous one as scientists try to identify more precisely the causes of undesired effects and suggest possible remedies or approaches to policy makers.

Even more devastating in terms of climatic consequences is the degree to which burning hydrocarbon fuels contributes to global warming. If atmospheric scientists are correct (and there are some who disagree), burning such fuels over many decades increases the overall volume of carbon dioxide in the atmosphere, creating a *greenhouse* effect or thermal blanket that keeps more heat from escaping into space. Clearing rain forests and other forested areas exacerbates the problems by removing an important, natural recycling mechanism—trees and other plant life take carbon dioxide in and release oxygen as part of the photosynthesis process. Even a degree or two in overall global temperature increase can produce seasonal variation, rainfall, and other effects that can reduce or even eliminate agricultural production in some regions, flood some landscapes, create deserts in other areas, and increase sea levels (due to melting polar ice caps) with consequent flooding of coastal and other low-lying areas.

While scholars often have taken the lead in investigating the topic, some political leaders now define security in environmental terms. Such problems obviously cross state boundaries, making it impossible for states acting alone to solve them. If unchecked, environmental degradation threatens to change life on Earth for the worst. But the scientific evidence concerning such processes is still subject to scholarly dispute—and the time horizon so seemingly distant—that ozone-layer depletion, acid rain, global warming, and pollution of the land, oceans, and other bodies of water only occasionally move to the forefront of debates about security aspects of global concern.

The Environment and Security

A key question is whether environmental issues may undermine international security. This requires us to bring politics back into the discussion. The Project on Environmental Change and Acute Conflict, which involved the efforts of thirty researchers from ten countries, asked three specific questions: (1) Do decreasing supplies of resources such as clean water and arable land provoke interstate "resource wars"? (2) Does large-scale migration caused by environmental stress lead to "group-identity" conflicts, particularly ethnic clashes? (3) Does severe environmental scarcity increase economic deprivation, disrupt key institutions, and hence contribute directly to civil strife and crises of authority?[5] All three questions directly deal with war, identity, and crises of authority, major themes of this book.

Conventional wisdom suggests that resource wars are rather prevalent. But scarcity of renewable resources such as forests and cropland rarely cause resource wars between states. It is rather conflict over nonrenewable resources that occurs. Examples include Japan's attempts to secure oil, minerals, and other resources in China and Southeast Asia during World War II, and in part Iraq's invasion of

---

[5]The framework, evidence, and conclusions of this impressive effort are presented in Thomas F. Homer-Dixon, "Environmental Scarcity and Violent Conflict: Evidence from Cases," *International Security*, v. 19, no. 1 (Summer 1994): 5–40.

Kuwait in 1990 to secure disputed oil fields. Oil and minerals are understandably of greater concern to states, as they can more easily be converted into state power than can land, fish, and forests.

The most likely renewable resource to generate conflict among states is fresh water in lakes, rivers, and aquifers shared by two or more states. No society can survive without adequate water supplies. Shared water resources that have caused disputes include the Nile, Jordan, and Euphrates rivers in the Middle East; the Indus, Ganges, and Brahmaputra rivers in south Asia; and the Rio Grande, Colorado, and Parana rivers in the Americas.[6] Since rivers often pass through more than one state they are a constant source of potential tension. States upstream may not only pollute the water, but as a means of coercive diplomacy they may also threaten to dam the river, thus reducing downstream flow. Particularly in those cases in which the state downstream believes it has the military capabilities to rectify the situation, the chances for conflict increase.

In 1986, for example, North Korea announced it would build a hydroelectric dam on a tributary of the Han River, which flows down to South Korea's capital of Seoul. South Korea feared the dam could be used to limit its water supplies, or perhaps as a military weapon if the dam were destroyed and most of Seoul flooded. In the Middle East the Euphrates flows from Turkey through Syria and Iraq and into the Persian Gulf. Syria and Iraq both rely on the Euphrates for drinking water, irrigation, industrial use, and hydroelectric power. In 1974 Iraq threatened to bomb the al-Thawra dam in Syria, claiming the dam had reduced Iraq's share of the water. Then in 1990 Turkey completed the Ataturk dam, the largest of twenty-one proposed dams in a major water supply plan to improve hydroelectric power and irrigation. Both Syria and Iraq protested, viewing the project as a potential source of Turkish coercive diplomacy. The fears were perhaps not unwarranted—in mid-1990 the president of Turkey threatened to restrict

Hauling their buckets, jugs, and jerricans filled at a communal well, these women begin their long trek home.

[6]Peter H. Gleick, "Water and Conflict: Fresh Water Resources and International Security," *International Security*, v. 18, no. 1 (Summer 1993): 80.

TABLE 12.4	FRESH WATER DEPENDENCY		
	PERCENTAGE OF FRESH WATER ORIGINATING OUTSIDE OF BORDER		**PERCENTAGE OF FRESH WATER ORIGINATING OUTSIDE OF BORDER**
Egypt	96%	Lithuania	45%
Hungary	95	Ukraine	40
Botswana	94	Pakistan	36
Cambodia	82	Argentina	30
Syria	76	Jordan	28
Paraguay	70	Israel	21

Source: Percentages calculated from statistics (drawn from multiple sources) in World Resources Institute, *World Resources* (New York: Oxford University Press, 1994), pp. 346–47.

water flow to Syria in the hope of forcing Syria to end support for Kurdish rebels operating in southern Turkey. While Turkey later disavowed the threat, the fact remains that completion of the Turkish projects reduces water to Syria by up to 40 percent and to Iraq by up to 80 percent.[7] Numerous other states also depend on imported surface water (see Table 12.4).

The second question—whether there is a link between "group-identity" conflicts and large-scale migration caused by environmental stress—is supported by substantial empirical evidence. The link in any particular case has to be carefully traced as the environmental factors that may lead people to migrate occur slowly over time, just as the social and political problems that arise in a host country also may take time to develop; there is no sudden explosion of ethnic conflict. In fact ethnic conflict may not even occur as in many cases immigrants simply suffer quietly in isolated misery.

But the situation is quite different in such cases as Bangladesh and northeast India. Over the years large numbers of Bangladeshi have moved to India, causing group-identity conflicts. Degradation of the soil is less problematic than the increasing size of the Bangladeshi population. The United Nations estimates that Bangladesh's current population of more than 120 million will nearly double to some 235 million by the year 2025. Almost all of the arable land is already under cultivation, and land scarcity and poverty are exacerbated by flooding. It is estimated that migrants from Bangladesh have increased the population of neighboring regions of India by 12 to 17 million, with at most 2 million accounted for by migration resulting from the 1971 war between India and Pakistan that created Bangladesh.

This massive influx of peoples has affected land distribution patterns, economic relations, and the balance of political power among ethnic and religious groups. The result has been intergroup conflict and violence. In the state of Assam, for example, members of the Lalung tribe have accused Bengali immigrants of taking the best farmland. In 1983 during an election campaign, nearly

---

[7]*Ibid.*, pp. 88–89.

1,700 Bengali were massacred in the village of Nellie. Similar tensions exist in Tripura where the Bengali influx has reduced the original Buddhist and Christian inhabitants to less than 30 percent of the population. This change in the local balance of power led to an insurgency between 1980 and 1988 that ended only after the central government agreed both to return land to the native Tripuris and work to stop the influx of Bangladeshi.[8]

The third question—whether severe environmental scarcity increases economic deprivation, disrupts key institutions, and hence contributes directly to civil strife and crises of authority—is partially supported by empirical evidence. The first part of the equation—environmental scarcity leading to economic deprivation—is well established. Soil erosion in upland Indonesia costs the agricultural economy about half a billion dollars in loss of income per year. The destruction of the dry land in Burkina Faso in Africa reduces the country's gross domestic product by an estimated 9 percent a year due to fuelwood loss, lower yields of crops, and reduction in numbers of livestock.

China provides an interesting example as it is best known for its booming economy—at least in the coastal regions—over the past twenty years. It is estimated that the combined costs of environmental degradation are about 15 percent of China's gross national product. The cost derives from such factors as lower crop yields because of water, soil, and air pollution; higher death rates from air pollution; lost farmland caused by soil erosion and construction; flooding and loss of soil nutrients from erosion and deforestation; and loss of timber because of poor harvesting practices.[9]

The last part of the equation concerning the political effects of environmental scarcity and economic deprivation apply to the state. Particularly in the Third World, the effect has been to undermine the legitimacy and hence the authority of certain states. Given the precarious finances of many governments, the loss of water, soil, and forests results in demands for new dams, irrigation systems, and reforestation programs. If those living in the countryside do not receive adequate government support, rural poverty increases. This may lead to an exodus to the city in the often vain hope of finding a better livelihood. The demands then take the form of calls for housing, transportation, food, and employment. With the increase in urban population come subsidies that strain financial coffers and misallocate capital. Such state intervention often breeds corruption and tends to concentrate financial and political power in the hands of a small elite.[10]

When the elite is drawn from one ethnic group, urban unrest is possible, if not likely. This is not to suggest that conflict in the Third World is simply a function of environmental scarcity and economic deprivation. The idea that poverty in and of itself leads to political violence has proven simply to be untrue. Other factors such as conceptions of what is economically just, perceptions of economic and political opportunities, the coercive power of the state, and the ability of political elites to exploit and politicize the poverty issue all play a role. But such scarcity certainly exacerbates the myriad of problems faced by people of the Third World and works to undermine the legitimacy of many developing states.

In sum, environmental scarcity will only worsen over the next few decades as population growth leads to a decrease in the quantity and quality of renewable resources with some groups enjoying disproportionate access to them. The

---

[8]Homer-Dixon, "Environmental Scarcity," pp. 21–23.

[9]*Ibid.*, p. 24.

[10]*Ibid.*, p. 25.

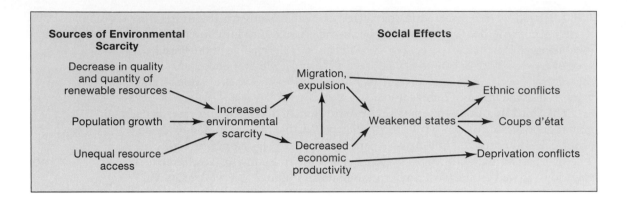

FIGURE 12.5   SOME SOURCES AND CONSEQUENCES
OF ENVIRONMENTAL SCARCITY

Source: Thomas F. Homer-Dixon, "Environmental Scarcities and Violent Conflict: Evidence from
Cases," *International Security,* vol. 19 no. 1 (Summer 1994): 5–40. © 1994 by the President and
Fellows of Harvard College and the Massachusetts Institute of Technology.

population explosion will occur in the developing regions of the world, those
least able to deal with such a development. The political and social effects are
outlined in Figure 12.5.

International Organizations and the Environment

In our discussion of states and national security, we noted that realists claim the
anarchic structure of the international system makes it difficult for states to work
together. National interests and anarchy emphasize what divides states and people
from one another. In the case of the physical environment, however, it is apparent
to even the most obtuse leader that environmental concerns transcend state borders. Industrial pollution in one country can drift downstream or blow across borders; environmental degradation can lead to economic refugees looking for a
better life; the implications of global warming and ozone-layer depletion affect
people around the world. Not surprisingly it is in the area of the environment
that a number of international agreements have been drafted, although the number of signatories varies as does the level of commitment. Nevertheless basic rules
or norms constituting various environmental regimes have been emerging (see
Table 12.5).

Even when the environmental implications of industrial and economic practices are accepted, agreement on what needs to be done can be difficult to achieve.
Many Third World countries, for example, suffer from massive unemployment
and underemployment and resent being told by developed countries that industrialization is bad for the environment, particularly when during their own early
phases of industrialization these latter countries paid little or no heed to the impact of their activities on the environment.

In an attempt to reconcile Third World emphasis on economic development and First World concern for the global environment, the concept of *sustainable development* has gained increasing acceptance. Sustainable development
is based on the premise that there needs to be a balance between consumption

TABLE 12.5	SELECTED INTERNATIONAL ENVIRONMENTAL REGIME AGREEMENTS

Environmental Agreements Relating to Atmospheric Regimes

Air Pollution	Convention on Long-Range Transboundary Air Pollution (1979)
Air Pollution-Nitrogen Oxides	Protocol to the 1979 Convention on Long-Range Transboundary Air Pollution Concerning the Control of Emissions of Nitogen Oxides or Their Transboundary Fluxes
Air Pollution-Sulphur	Protocols to the 1979 Convention on Long-Range Transboundary Air Pollution on the Reduction of Sulphur Emissions or Their Transboundary Fluxes by at least 30 percent (1985); further reductions (1994)
Air Pollution-Volatile Organic Compounds	Protocol to the 1979 Convention on Long-Range Transboundary Air Pollution Concerning the Control of Emissions of Volatile Organic Compounds or Their Transboundary Fluxes
Ozone Layer	Montreal Protocol on Substances That Deplete the Ozone Layer and Vienna Convention for the Protection of the Ozone Layer
Climate Change	UN Framework Convention on Climate Change
Environmental Modification	Convention on the Prohibition of Military or Any Other Hostile Use of Environmental Modification Techniques

Environmental Agreements Relating to Regimes for the High Seas

Law of the Sea	UN Convention on the Law of the Sea (LOS)
Marine Dumping (London Convention)	Convention on the Prevention of Marine Pollution by Dumping Wastes and Other Matter
Marine Life Conservation	Convention on Fishing and Conservation of Living Resources of the High Seas
Ship Pollution	Protocol of 1978 Relating to the International Convention for the Prevention of Pollution from Ships (MARPOL) (1973)
Whaling	International Convention for the Regulation of Whaling

Environmental Agreements Relating to Regimes for Land Areas

Antarctic-Environmental Protocol	Protocol on Environmental Protection to the Antarctic Treaty
Desertification	UN Convention to Combat Desertification in Those Countries Experiencing Serious Drought or Desertification, particularly in Africa
Hazardous Wastes	Basel Convention on the Control of Transboundary Movements of Hazardous Wastes and Their Disposal
Tropical Timber	International Tropical Timber Agreements (1983 and 1994)
Wetlands	Convention on Wetlands of International Importance, especially as Waterfowl Habitat (also known as Ramsar)

(table continues)

TABLE 12.5	SELECTED INTERNATIONAL ENVIRONMENTAL REGIME AGREEMENTS (CONTINUED)
Agreements for Other Environmental Regimes	
Biodiversity	Convention on Biological Diversity
Endangered Species	Convention on the International Trade in Endangered Species of Wild Flora and Fauna (CITES)
Comprehensive Nuclear Test Ban	Bans all nuclear tests in the atmosphere, underground or under water, or in outer space

Sources: UN Environmental Programme and *The World Fact Book* (Washington, D.C.).

and population size within overall limits imposed by nature. Without an improvement in resource and environmental stewardship, development ultimately will be undermined as eventually there will be little or nothing left of nature to be exploited. But without accelerated economic growth in the poorest countries in the near term, environmental policies will fail, as the poor peasants likely will exploit the land to the maximum merely in order to survive. Trying to implement such a balancing act is not a function of the "ignorant" poor failing to understand the implications of their actions; for example, ranchers and farmers in developed countries often also focus on the near term, tending to discount considerations that lie in the future.

As noted previously, UN-sponsored conferences have addressed many of these issues. The United Nations Conference on Environment and Development held in Rio de Janeiro, Brazil, in 1992 is a good example of a forum that brought diverse governmental and nongovernmental actors together. As the formal United Nations members, states controlled most of the action, but parallel meetings by nongovernmental actors also contributed substantially to the consensus reached on a sustainable development approach, assuring a sensitivity to the environmental impacts of economic activities and demographics. The distillation of this consensus was the Rio Declaration later endorsed by the United Nations General Assembly and the creation of the Commission on Sustainable Development, an intergovernmental body of some fifty-two members that serves as a focal point within the United Nations system for coordination of various UN programs.

From the perspective of some environmental activists, however, much of the Rio Conference consisted of world leaders posturing and mouthing platitudes about their concern for the environment. Hundreds of pages of proposals for international and national action were produced, but not

Since Rio, a growing body of actors—governments, nongovernmental organizations, the private sector, civil society, and the scientific and research community—have responded to environmental challenges in a variety of ways . . . Nevertheless, despite progress on several fronts, from a global perspective the environment has continued to degrade during the past decade, and significant environmental problems remain deeply embedded in the socio-economic fabric of nations in all regions. Progress towards a global sustainable future is just too slow. A sense of urgency is lacking. Internationally and nationally, the funds and political will are insufficient to halt further global environmental degradation.

United Nations Environment Programme, *Global Environment Outlook-1*, available at www.unep.org/unep/eia/geo1.

IT'S BEEN SAID...

much has happened. For the poorest countries the problem is not simply lack of will, but lack of resources to implement a program of sustainable development that balances economic and environmental needs at a time when population continues to grow.

Environmental activists note, however, that the sustainable development concept also places developed countries on the hook. These countries, after all, far and away consume more both per capita and in the aggregate than do those in the developing world. Indeed, it is not always certain whether Third World population growth rates or the expanding appetites for the consumption of raw materials on the part of the industrial nations is the greatest danger. (Figure 12.6 illustrates this point.)

A related international effort was undertaken in 1994 at a meeting under UN auspices in Cairo, Egypt, to address global population growth in relation to economic development, the environment, and social concerns. Although a Cairo declaration addressing measures to slow population growth rates eventually passed, conflicting views were not easily reconciled—some Islamic countries even refused to send representatives to the conference. As such some international conferences may well reflect the absence of consensus among the parties. Table 12.6 lists examples of UN conferences that have examined global political economy and society.

Even when an international consensus is worked out such as in the Law of the Sea negotiations in the late 1970s that dealt with navigation rights and economic uses of offshore waters and the seabed, domestic political processes may preclude ratification of treaties and other agreements reached. Treaties may go for decades without ratification when effective domestic opposition is in place.

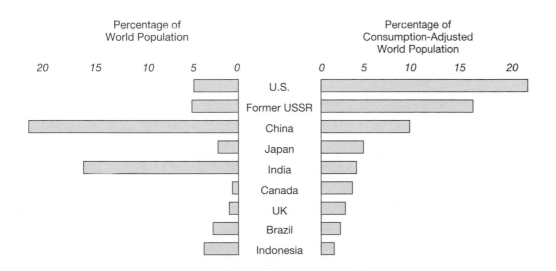

FIGURE 12.6   POPULATION AND CONSUMPTION

Source: The Commission on Global Governance, *Our Global Neighborhood* (Oxford, England: Oxford University Press, 1995), p. 144.

TABLE 12.6	UN CONFERENCE DIPLOMACY ON GLOBAL POLITICAL ECONOMY AND SOCIETY

Conference diplomacy under UN auspices has brought states, nongovernmental organizations (NGOs), and individuals together to address issues of common concern in the global economy and society.

MAJOR CONFERENCES

World Summit for Children, New York, 1990

Survival, protection and development of children, setting goals for children's health, nutrition, education, and access to safe water and sanitation

UN Conference on Environment and Development, Rio de Janeiro, 1992

Continuing work that began in 1972 at the UN Conference on the Human Environment in Stockholm, this Earth Summit addressed sustainable development—global environment and development policy; developed Agenda 21—a global blueprint for sustainable development (dealing with poverty, excess consumption, toxic and other hazardous wastes from production processes, alternative energy sources, greater reliance on public transportation systems, environmental impact of national economic decisions, etc.); drafted a Declaration on Environment and Development; prepared a Statement of Forest Principles; and took up both the UN Framework Convention on Climate Change and the Convention on Biological Diversity

World Conference on Human Rights, Vienna, 1993

Reaffirmed international commitment to human rights, strengthening mechanisms for monitoring and promoting human rights globally; led to the appointment of the first UN High Commissioner for Human Rights; made human rights integral to UN peacekeeping missions; linked democracy, development, and human rights

International Conference on Population and Development, Cairo, 1994

Worked toward consensus on family planning as part of development programs, seeking education and empowerment of women as the most effective way to reduce population growth rates and promote sustainable development, reaffirming that voluntary family planning decisions are a basic human right, and encouraging donor countries to increase funding for population-related activities. Follow-up special session of the UN General Assembly held in June 1999

World Summit for Social Development, Copenhagen, 1995

Committed governments to eradicating poverty "as an ethical, social, political and economic imperative"; raised the negative side of economic globalization—growing gaps between rich and poor, shrinking social safety nets, and increasing insecurity about jobs and social services in both developed and developing countries; formulated a plan for meeting basic human needs, reducing economic and social inequalities, and providing sustainable livelihoods

Fourth World Conference on Women, Beijing, 1995

Addressed advancement and empowerment of women in relation to women's human rights, women and poverty, women and decision making, the girl-child, violence against women and other areas of concern; supported effort to fight violence against women and afford them greater legal protection. Follow-up special session of the UN General Assembly in June 2000

(table continues)

TABLE 12.6   (CONTINUED)

Second UN Conference on Human Settlements (Habitat II), Istanbul, 1996

Adopted a global plan and policy guidelines to improve living conditions in urban and rural settlements and to implement the "full and progressive realization of the right to adequate housing," identifying mayors and other local officials as key players in implementation of the Habitat action plan

The Millennium Assembly of the United Nations, New York, 2000

Set forth "animating" vision "to strengthen the role of the United Nations in meeting the challenges of the twenty-first century" for the United Nations in the new era of "global society"—underscoring the relation between development on the one hand and peace and security on the other, promoting peace and sustainable development; agenda included disarmament and other aspects of peace and security, development and poverty eradication, human rights, and measures to strengthen the United Nations organization to meet new challenges to multilateralism in the era of globalization; separate "Millennium Forum" for NGOs and other individuals

SELECTED LIST OF OTHER UN CONFERENCES ON GLOBAL ECONOMY AND SOCIETY

UN Global Conference on the Sustainable Development of Small Island Developing States, 1994

International Conference on Natural Disaster Reduction, 1994

World Summit on Trade Efficiency, 1994

Ninth UN Congress on the Prevention of Crime and the Treatment of Offenders, 1995

Conference on Highly Migratory Fish Stocks, 1995

World Food Summit, 1996

Ninth UN Conference on Trade and Development (UNCTAD IX), 1996

Earth Summit+5, 1997

UN Conference on the Establishment of an International Criminal Court, Rome, 1998

General Assembly Twentieth Special Session—World Drug Problem, 1998

General Assembly Special Session on Small Island Developing States, 1999

Third United Nations Conference on the Exploration and Peaceful Uses of Outer Space, Vienna, 1999

General Assembly Special Session on the International Conference on Population and Development, New York, 1999

General Assembly Special Session on Social Development and Beyond, Geneva, 2000

UN Workshop on Energy Efficiency, Global Competitiveness, and Deregulation, 2000

Development Finance for the World's Least Developed Countries, 2001

World Conference Against Racism, Racial Discrimination, Xenophobia, and Related Intolerance, South Africa, 2001

Reservations or interpretations appended to international agreements can even alter concessions made by negotiators or change substantial portions of agreements made in the give-and-take of international negotiations. Of course other parties may not accept such changes made by individual countries in unilateral fashion.

A Special Session of the UN General Assembly in 1998 took up the adverse impact on development of the illicit narcotics trade, observing that "drugs destroy lives and communities, undermine sustainable human development and generate crime." The approach urged on member states is to attack the problem comprehensively, focusing not only on curbing the supply of drugs but also attempting demand reduction through social programs and action.

Transnational Organizations and the Environment

The impact of transnational nongovernmental organizations (NGOs) on environmental issues is perhaps more evident than in any other area of global politics. At the three international conferences in Rio, Cairo, and Beijing, private transnational organizations influenced the agenda, actively participated, and pressured states to hold these conferences in the first place. They have also played an important watchdog role in a wide variety of functional areas, ranging from environmental protection of the oceans to forests, Antarctica, and the ozone layer, always reminding political leaders of their public commitments. Such environmental organizations as the World Wildlife Fund, Greenpeace, Conservation International, Friends of the Earth, World Business Council for Sustainable Development, Earth Council, and the International Council for Local Environment Initiatives exemplify the diversity of actors that compose global civil society.

Transnational organizations demonstrate that instruments of power are not solely available to the state. One instrument has been modern communications. Greenpeace, for example, has created wonderful photo opportunities for journalists by climbing aboard whaling ships, parachuting from smokestacks, and floating hot air balloons into nuclear test sites. Greenpeace has its own media facilities, allowing it to produce video spots and photographs for news organizations. Through dramatic actions and publications, Greenpeace and other environmental organizations can change public perceptions of the activities of states as well as nonstate actors. A good example involves Greenpeace's antiwhaling efforts. They have changed whaling's original image of man versus vicious, Moby Dick–like monsters of the deep, substituting the image of rapacious hunters slaughtering peaceful, nurturing mammals.

Utilizing the power of modern communications to alter how people view topics of potential international concern requires money, an obvious source of power in the world. Since the 1970s the budgets of the largest transnational environmental groups are greater than the amount spent by most states on environmental issues. Some of these organizations have budgets equal to—or sometimes close to double—that of the United Nations Environment Programme. In the 1990s, for example, both Greenpeace International and the World Wildlife Fund had annual budgets of some $100 million and $200 million respectively, while UNEP's yearly budget was only about $75 million.

Table 12.7 describes various environmental networks.

TABLE 12.7	SELECTED GLOBAL ENVIRONMENTAL NETWORKS	
NETWORK	**DATE LAUNCHED**	**DESCRIPTION**
Sponsored by NGOs: *Association for Progressive* *Communications (APC)* *<www.apc.org>*	1990	Links NGOs promoting human rights and environmental justice.
OneWorld Online *<www.oneworld.net>*	1995	A "supersite" that links to hundreds of Web sites to provide information on development.
Global Forest Watch *<www.wri.org/gfw>*	1999	Linking to NGOs in five countries to monitor the world's large, intact "frontier forests."
Sponsored by U.N. Agencies: *UNEPNet (UNEP)* *<www.unep.net>*	1997	Links eight UNEP offices and at least nine other partner institutions by satellite to improve the flow of global environmental information.
Global Urban Observatory *(Habitat)* *<www.urbanobservatory.org>*	1998	Links researchers worldwide to compile statistics and examples of best practices in urban management.
HORIZON Solutions Web site *(UNDP, UNEP, UNFPA,* *UNICEF, IDRC, Harvard, Yale)* *<www.solutions-site.org>*	1999	Provides case studies on solutions to problems of water, waste, energy, transportation, toxic chemicals, public health, industry, desertification, biodiversity, air pollution, and agriculture.

Source: Molly O'Meara, "Harnessing Information Technology for the Environment," in Lester Brown et al., *State of the World 2000* (New York: W. W. Norton, 2000), p. 139.

Finally, initial successes of such organizations are often followed by further successes. Greenpeace and the World Wildlife Fund have enrolled over six million members around the globe supported by a well-developed staff and cadre of scientific experts able to contest the arguments and evidence put forward by state bureaucracies and corporations. These experts often provide input into the development of programs such as the Global Environment Outlook, sponsored by the United Nations Environment Programme. Such NGOs illustrate that the state is not the only focus for collective efforts to affect world politics.[11]

Greenpeace activist on a Japanese whaling ship.

[11]Paul Wapner, "Politics Beyond the State: Environmental Activism and World Civic Politics," *World Politics*, 47, no. 3 (April 1995): 315 (footnotes 12 and 13), 320–21.

Practicing World Politics

Development and the Environment

In addition to the U.N.'s main Web page [www.un.org], see the UN Environmental Programme [www.unep.org] and the UN Development Programme [www.undp.org] sites. See also the World Bank [www.worldbank.org] and the UN Conference on Trade and Development [www.unctad.org]. On workers' rights concerning health, safety, working conditions, and child labor, see the International Labor Organization in Geneva [www.ilo.org]. For the U.S. government site on environmental matters, see the Environmental Protection Agency [www.epa.gov]. Nongovernmental organizations on these subjects include Greenpeace [www.greenpeace.org], the World Wildlife Fund [www.worldwildlife.org], World Watch [www.worldwatch.org], Conservation International [www.conservation.org], and Friends of the Earth [www.foe.org in the U.S.; in Canada www.foecanada.org], and other national chapters linked to these sites. A U.S.-focused NGO concerned with the environment is the Sierra Club [www.sierraclub.org].

Governance therefore is not necessarily synonymous with *government*.[12] Transnational environmental organizations contribute to global governance through their influence on how publics, states, and corporations perceive international issues. Such organizations rely not on force but rather on persuasion to help change and define the boundaries and conceptions of what are considered "good" ecological policies. In other words they work to restructure the "environment" within which environmental policies are framed, by politicizing such actions as whaling or pollution, issues that historically have been viewed as simply economic in nature. Most importantly transnational environmental organizations have utilized this noncoercive power in efforts designed to change the behavior of states and corporations.

Global Population

Some demographers project that within three decades or so world population will have passed nine billion persons. Thomas Malthus (1766-1834), a minister and social analyst, published "An Essay on the Principle of Population" on the eve of the nineteenth century in 1798. He published a shorter summary in 1830 for "those who have not had the leisure to read the whole work."[13] Noting the "prodigious power of increase in plants and animals," Malthus observed that human "population, when unchecked, increases in a geometrical progression of such a nature as to double itself every twenty-five years."[14]

---

[12]James N. Rosenau, "Governance, Order and Change in World Politics," in James N. Rosenau and Ernst-Otto Czempiel, eds., *Governance Without Government: Order and Change in World Politics* (Cambridge, England: Cambridge University Press, 1992).

[13]See Thomas Malthus, *An Essay on the Principle of Population and A Summary View of the Principle of Population* (London: Penguin Books, 1982, 1985), p. 221.

[14]*Ibid.*, pp. 223 and 238.

ESTIMATING POPULATION GROWTH

Annual population growth rate (usually expressed as a proportion or percentage) for a given population is calculated by subtracting the number of deaths from the number of births at the end of a given year and dividing that figure by the total population at the beginning of that year.

A convenient way to estimate the impact of population growth rate on total population over time is the "Rule of 72," which is also used by financial analysts as a quick rule of thumb in estimating the effect of compound interest rates on the growth of principal over time. The length of time in years that a population can be expected to double is 72 divided by the growth rate. Thus a 2 percent growth rate means that population can be expected to double in 36 years (72 divided by 2), assuming of course that the 2 percent rate remains constant over the period.

It is easy to overestimate future population size by projecting present growth rates. Reduction in population growth rates will slow the doubling time. Because population growth rates tend to decline as societies industrialize, there is a danger in projecting present population growth rates for Third World countries too far into the future. Unexpected catastrophes due to natural disasters, widespread famine, disease, or warfare will also have a negative impact on population growth rate. On the other hand if assumptions on reduced population growth rates are too optimistic, future population size can just as easily be underestimated.

He worried that food supplies would not keep pace with population growth. How would humanity cope with its tendency "to increase, if unchecked, beyond the possibility of an adequate supply of food?" He foresaw "diseases and epidemics, wars, infanticide, plague, and famine."[15] Malthus acknowledged that technology would contribute to increased food production, but at some point, he believed that human ingenuity would run up against the Earth's limits to produce, resulting in awful consequences for the human condition.

In the almost two centuries since Malthus made these predictions, global population has grown dramatically from the hundreds of millions of his time to more than six billion people today. Through industrialization and modern medicine, population has continued to grow even more significantly. From the 1820s to the 1920s the global population doubled and reached two billion. From 1925 to 1976 it doubled again to four billion. By 1990 the figure was 5.3 billion, increasing by more than 700 million people in the last decade of the twentieth century. Doubling populations when numbers are in the millions is challenging enough; doubling when the base is in billions is potentially catastrophic. Indeed, current estimates for the end of the twenty-first century put the numbers in a

---

[15] *Ibid.*, pp. 268 and 250.

wide range from about 11 billion to more than 15 billion people. Can the Earth sustain so many? Are there limits to growth? Figures 12.7 and 12.8 graphically present data on world population growth.

In the early 1970s a nongovernmental organization known as the Club of Rome sponsored studies and conferences on limits to growth. The push for industrial development that got underway in Europe and North America in the nineteenth-century world of Parson Malthus had enormous impact on the environment as forests were cleared, resources mined, and factories put into operation. Consumption of nonrenewable energy resources and other minerals increased dramatically, reducing stocks and adding to ground, sea, and air pollution levels.

Production of goods and services for increasing numbers of peoples has had adverse environmental impact, but continued development thus far has still been sustainable. The negative environmental impact of the industrial revolution, however, was less than it would have been had population levels been as high as they are today. If the more than 1.2 billion people currently in China and some 900 million now in India (not to mention projected increases in these numbers and additional billions in other less-developed countries) continue to industrialize following the European, American, or Japanese models, the result could be truly devastating, not only for these countries but also for the world as a whole. Resource depletion and environmental degradation on a global scale could undermine any capacity to continue producing at ever-increasing levels. Renewable resources would also suffer from growing scarcity as demand dramatically increases, with obvious implications in terms of arable land, fisheries, and the degradation of aquifers, rivers, and lakes. Development in these circumstances would not be sustainable. The limits predicted by Malthus might finally be reached.

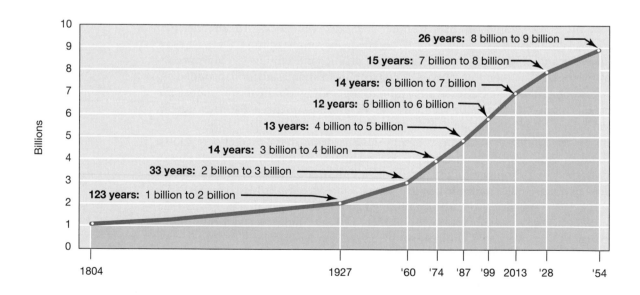

FIGURE 12.7   WORLD POPULATION INCREASE
Source: UN Population Division as cited by *Washington Post*, Feb. 7, 1999, p. A3.

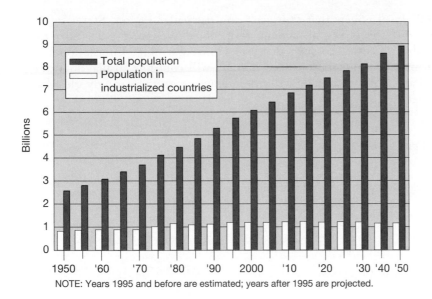

NOTE: Years 1995 and before are estimated; years after 1995 are projected.

FIGURE 12.8   POPULATION GROWTH IN INDUSTRIAL
AND DEVELOPING COUNTRIES
Source: UN Population Division, as cited by *Washington Post,* Feb. 7, 1999, p. A3.

CONCLUSION

Fostering economic growth and sustaining economic development on a global
scale will remain formidable challenges throughout the coming decades. It may
be, as some have suggested, that we will redefine development needs to be more
consistent with quality-of-life criteria rather than a seemingly never ending quest
for economic growth. Whether economic well-being, the environment, social
justice, human rights, the natural environment, and the overall improvement of
the human condition can be served at lower economic growth rates is not altogether clear. It is indeed a tall order!

Realists also recognize that the issues discussed in this chapter can contribute
to international conflict. They tend to doubt, however, that increasing populations, resource scarcity, and environmental degradation are in and of themselves
the major causes of conflict among states. As a result realists also believe that by
dramatically elevating such concerns to the level of national and international security issues, more important causes of conflict such as the basic clash of state interests can become obscured. Furthermore, if such problems are to be mitigated,
then it will be states that will take the lead and be the final arbiters of whatever
global policies are devised.

Those who view the world through pluralist lenses, however, disagree.
They believe that viewing such problems merely from the parochial perspective of individual states is myopic. Not only can these issues be catalysts for international conflict, but resource scarcity and environmental pollution can also

have truly global effects that transcend any particular region. States tend to think in terms of short- and medium-term objectives, lacking a longer time horizon when it comes to such issues as global warming. International and nongovernmental organizations can, do, and will continue to play important roles in dealing transnationally with these issues in an increasingly globalized world society.

KEY TERMS

sustainable development
   p. 368
factors of production
   p. 370

New International
   Economic Order
   (NIEO) *p. 378*

terms of trade   *p. 381*

OTHER CONCEPTS

concessionary rates   *p. 372*
nationalization   *p. 372*
expropriation   *p. 372*
subsidiary   *p. 375*
transfer pricing   *p. 375*

repatriation   *p. 376*
trade preferences   *p. 376*
cartel   *p. 381*
neocolonialism   *p. 382*
dependency   *p. 382*

newly industrializing
   countries (NICs)   *p. 382*
bourgeoisie   *p. 385*
structural violence   *p. 385*

ADDITIONAL READINGS

To understand the roots of global agenda setting on what we now call sustainable development, good sources are the *Brundtland Commission Report* published as World Commission on Environmental and Development, *Our Common Future*

(Oxford, UK: Oxford University Press, 1987) as well as the *Brandt Commission Report* (more formally the *Report of the Independent Commission on International Development Issues*), a document available in libraries and also published as *North-South: A Program for Survival* (Cambridge, Mass.: The MIT Press, 1980). The idea of sustainable development is a response to the more pessimistic view of there being very real limits to growth, a thesis presented in the 1970s by a transnational NGO, the Club of Rome. See Dennis L. Meadows *et al.*, *The Limits to Growth* (New York: Signet Books, 1972). Publications of the United Nations organization, World Bank, the UN Economic Development Program, the UN Environmental Program, and other international organizations are rich sources available in libraries and usually advertised on the organizations' Web sites. For statistical data, see the UN Development Program's *Human Development Report* and the World Bank's *World Development Report.* Both are published annually by Oxford University Press.

For further background reading, see Robert Gilpin's chapters on multinational corporations and the issue of dependency and economic development in *The Political Economy of International Relations* (Princeton, N.J.: Princeton University Press, 1987). On multinational corporations, development, North-South relations, OPEC, and other commodity cartels, see Joan E. Spero and Jeffrey A. Hart, *The Politics of International Economic Relations* (New York: St. Martin's Press, 1996). An anthology of articles on global power and wealth is Jeffry A. Frieden and David A. Lake, eds., *International Political Economy* (New York: St. Martin's Press, 1995). Another anthology that includes diverse readings reflecting liberal, Marxist, rational-choice, and regime-oriented understanding of global political economy is George T. Crane and Abla Amawi, eds., *The Theoretical Evolution of International Political Economy* (New York: Oxford University Press, 1997). On development and related global problems, see David N. Balaam and Michael Veseth, *Introduction to International Political Economy*, 2nd ed. (Upper Saddle River, N.J.: Prentice Hall, 2001), especially parts IV and V.

NATIONALISM
AND
CONFLICTING
IDENTITIES

"The concept of nation requires that all its members should form as it were only one individual."

FRIEDRICH SCHLEGAL,
GERMAN CRITIC AND WRITER,
1772–1829

Migjen Kelmendi is a well-known Kosovo Albanian writer and journalist. In March 1999 Serbian police began to clear out Pristina, the Kosovar capital. Kelmendi, assuming he was marked for execution, borrowed a baby and pretended to be part of a family. On March 31 he began a journey he could never have imagined. The police went from house to house and ordered everyone out. Some three thousand people were herded down the street to the railroad station. "They were driving us like cattle. The children were screaming and the elderly were very slow," he said. They passed down Pristina's main street. "The saddest bit was that along the way I saw bunches of people, Serbs. They looked at us with complete indifference. It was unimaginable." When they got to the train station, there were already 25,000 to 30,000 people there, all waiting for trains to take them to the border with neighboring Macedonia. Just before midnight the crowd heard NATO planes wheeling across the night sky. "People began to clap. They were shouting 'NATO!

NATO!' and saying 'They will help us.' Then we heard shooting very close to us. Everyone fell silent immediately."[1]

What am I? What are you? What are our identities? If we are Americans are we Native Americans, or are we also of some European, Asian, African, or other origin? Are you a Christian, Jew, Muslim, or Buddhist? Does it matter? Should it matter? Do these distinctions that define our identities set us into mutually exclusive, often conflicting, groups, or do we let our common human identity transcend these differences?

As will become clear in this chapter, questions relating to national, ethnic, tribal, clan, or other human identities are universal. Human beings are social creatures, as Aristotle observed, a fact that has both up and down sides. For the most part we live and work together cooperatively, divided only by relatively small differences or conflicts. The great achievements of humankind have depended on our ability to pool talents and resources in social groups of one kind or another. At the same time, however, human beings who are organized into separate, conflicting groups can be the source of mutually destructive activities as has been evident in recent years in the former Yugoslavia.

The world is conventionally divided into single **nation-states**, **multinational states**, and *nations* dispersed in two or more states. Individuals may derive a sense of security or other value from having a particular national or ethnic identity, but this ethnic identification may make others (particularly minority groups) feel insecure. Mutually exclusive communities within, between, or across state boundaries are often the source of conflict based on these national, ethnic, religious, historical and cultural, racial and physical, or other differences. Conflicts may smolder for decades (and even centuries), breaking out as interstate or civil wars, insurgencies, terrorism, or other forms of revolutionary violence.

This chapter begins a discussion concerning one of the most vexing and important issues in world politics at the beginning of the twenty-first century: conflicts relating to state sovereignty, national identity, and human rights. A whole host of questions arise. For example, in the name of upholding the concept of state sovereignty, should the aspirations of a minority ethnic group for an independent country be ignored? On the other hand, if national self-determination is embraced across the board, then will the world witness increasing fragmentation of the international state system? If so, is this such a bad thing in the age of globalization? If in the name of sovereignty a state claims the outside world has no right to interfere in its policies against an indigenous minority, what does this mean in terms of protecting human rights around the globe? Such questions are not part of an abstract academic enterprise. For example Kosovo has long been part of the Republic of Yugoslavia or Serbia (the principal part of what remains of Yugoslavia) and Chechnya an integral part of the former Soviet Union (and now the Russian Federation). Why then did NATO claim that humanitarianism was a reason for going to war against Serbia but stood by when the Russians attempted to quell national separatism in Chechnya?

nations   People with a common identity who have formed a nation-state or usually aspire to do so.

---

[1]Tim Judah, "Inside the KLA," *New York Review of Books*, June 10, 1999, p. 19.

We begin by considering the role of religion in global politics. This is followed by a discussion of nationality and ethnicity as concepts used to describe identities peoples may have within and across the formal boundaries of states. We illustrate the obvious fact that the world is replete with conflicts and controversies related to nationality, ethnicity, and race. We then turn to a discussion of approaches designed to foster peace among differing nationalities. Given the confines of a single chapter, we make no attempt to be exhaustive on this subject but do provide representative examples of these national, ethnic, and racial cleavages that often divide societies and peoples across state and communal boundaries.

RELIGION

One impact of the cold war was to overshadow the role of religion in global politics. Although from the perspective of some in the West, the cold war was a battle between Christianity and other religions against "godless communism," most people saw it in nonreligious terms as a battle between two visions of the appropriate political and economic forms of governance—Western-style democracy and market capitalism versus centrally directed state-socialist or communist economies.

Historically, however, religion has at times played a major role in international politics. The attempt of Christian crusaders to "liberate" the Holy Land in the Middle Ages—and the efforts to repel the "infidels" on the part of the Muslims—is one example. The seventeenth-century Thirty Years' War on the continent and the English civil war also involved significant religious issues involving Protestants versus Catholics. Not confined to Europe, religious conflict spread to the western hemisphere and later to Africa, Asia, and the Pacific with Protestant and Catholic missionaries competing with each other in a quest to save the souls of the indigenous "heathens."

In more recent times the Iranian revolution of 1978–79 and the coming to power of Shiite-Muslim religious leaders were seen as a possible harbinger of things to come. But observers of international relations failed to foresee the significant challenge to modern, secular regimes posed by a global resurgence of religious ideas and movements at the end of the twentieth and continuing as well into the twenty-first centuries. What is fascinating about this global phenomenon is that it is occurring within diverse cultures, different types of political systems, and in countries with varying levels of economic development.[2] Figure 13.1 graphs the relative numbers of people who identify with the religions of the world.

The global rediscovery of religion has some obvious and some contradictory implications. First, transnational organizations such as the Roman Catholic Church, the World Council of Churches, and the Society for the Propagation of Islam assume more important roles. The pronouncements of various religious organizations over the years, of course, have supposedly had universal application, no matter where the flock may reside. But thanks to modern telecommunications technologies, religious organizations have found it even easier to communicate their messages. Their global religious networks reach out across and beyond the more confining borders of states, thus effectively expanding the extent of communications in a still emerging global civil society discussed at length in Chapter Nine.

---

[2]Scott Thomas, "The Global Resurgence of Religion and the Study of World Politics," *Millennium*, v. 24, no. 2 (1995): 289.

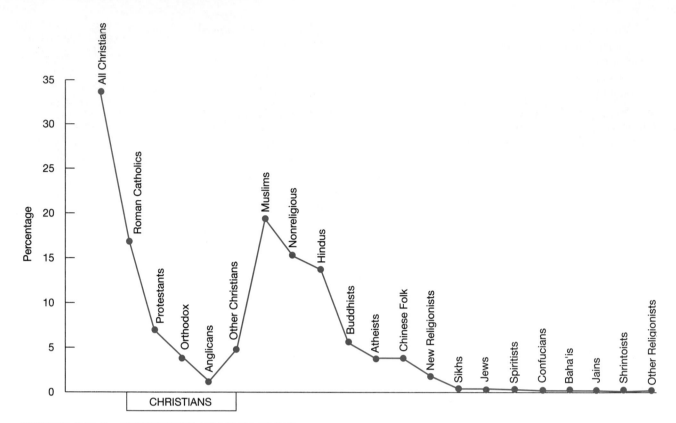

FIGURE 13.1 RELIGIONS OF THE WORLD

Based on data in the *1997 Britannica Book of the Year* (Chicago: 1997), p. 311.

Second, transnational movements and beliefs also strengthen the development of transnational identities not constrained either by state borders or secular nationalism. For some religious identity is more important than any particular national identity. To these people, loyalty to God comes first, the state a more distant second or third.

Third, if such a trend continues, its implications for global conflict are uncertain. On the one hand some religious movements have spearheaded peace movements and crusades for human rights and justice. On the other hand one author suggests that religious identity could be a key component of a broader clash of civilizations[3] with the fault lines of conflict, for example, between civilizations or cultures influenced by Judeo-Christian religious traditions and those influenced by Islam.

Finally we wish to observe that from a realist perspective, religion remains less important than other factors in relations among states. While religious groups will undoubtedly continue to influence government policies around the globe, realists would argue that the governments themselves will continue to operate in the international system on the basis of national interests and security—factors discussed in Chapter Three. Even the Iranian and the Afghani Taliban governments, for all their Islamic pronouncements, have used religion not as the exclusive road map for foreign policy, but rather as a means to guide and facilitate pursuit of basic domestic and foreign policy objectives. Realists argue that very

[3]Samuel P. Huntington, "The Clash of Civilizations," *Foreign Affairs*, v. 72, no. 3 (1993): 22–49.

Muslim men at prayer.

The joy of youth: Malaysian boys studying the Koran.

often secular objectives are cast in religious garb in order to make them more appealing to peoples of various nationalities.

From the pluralist perspective religious diversity is not inevitably associated with conflict. As we will see in the case of national identities, many pluralists hold out the prospect that international organizations, transnational nongovernmental organizations, and increasing globalization may reduce or ameliorate conflict among religious groups professing diverse faiths. Religious diversity in their view is one of the defining elements of an emerging global civil society.

NATIONS, ETHNIC GROUPS, AND STATES

While the role of religion in international politics has only recently been rediscovered, the concepts of *nation* and *state* have been at the forefront of studies of global politics for years. A certain amount of confusion, however, continues to exist over their meanings and the meanings of related terms.

The terms *nation* and *state* are frequently used interchangeably as if they were synonyms. To use the terms this way, however, is to miss important differences in meaning. As noted earlier, the term *state* is a legal concept that refers to a population administered by a government (or other administrative authority) on a given territory with a claim to sovereignty recognized by other sovereign states. When a particular state is composed of a single *nation* or people with a common identity, we call it a *nation-state* because the people who compose the "nation" live on the territory of that "state." Nation and state are coterminous or overlapping, as in the United States where most of the people consider themselves to be American, notwithstanding the diversity of racial, ethnic, and cultural differences among them.

Race refers to identifiable physical differences used to categorize people, whether or not individuals share a common identity. Although race can be a basis for identity, it is also a very problematic basis for establishing unity. Racial distinctions that are used to justify divisiveness, discrimination, or unequal treatment are common enough. In the extreme **racism** can also lead to **genocide**—the mass murder of people because of their race or other identity. Because of this many prefer not to draw racial distinctions among peoples at all; it is better from this perspective to identify only with the *human* race. Focusing on a common humanity avoids the scourge of racism that may come from accentuating separate identities based on physical or other differences.

The distinction between a nation and an ethnic group is often difficult to make. One reason is that the terms are subjective; people themselves are the ones who make the choice when they define their identities in either national or ethnic terms. Adding to the confusion, the two terms are frequently used interchangeably. In the United States people tend to identify nationally as Americans while at the same time holding other *ethnic* identities that define them as individuals or groups within society.

Nationality involves a significant degree of self-definition and refers to a people with a sense of common identity, if not destiny. In other words a nation is whatever a group of people say it is. This common identity may be the result of such diverse

 GENOCIDE IN THE TWENTIETH CENTURY

The twentieth century witnessed many appalling instances of genocide—killing of people based on racial or ethnic differences. Chief among these was the Holocaust, Nazi Germany's persecution, enslavement, and methodical elimination of European Jews. Approximately six million Jews, along with Gypsies, communists, and others deemed by the Nazis to be "undesirables" died under Nazi rule from 1933 to 1945, often in such notorious slave labor and death camps as Treblinka, Auschwitz, and Dachau. Other ethnic groups have suffered from genocide as well. Beginning in 1894 nearly 200,000 Armenians were slain in two years by Turkish soldiers and police. In 1909 the renewed massacre of Armenians began again and ended only because of the intervention of outside powers, including the United States. Armenian support for the Allied cause in World War I led to the estimated elimination of one million Armenians. More recently ethnic conflict in the African state of Rwanda resulted in the massacre of at least 500,000 Tutsi at the hands of the Hutus. Genocide in the former Yugoslavia has also claimed large numbers of Muslims, Croats, Serbs, and Kosovars as victims.

The gates of the Nazi concentration camp at Auschwitz. The sign above them is "Arbeit Macht Frei"—"Work Makes You Free."

factors as race, ethnicity, religion, culture, shared historical experiences, or some combination of these. When this common identity has political consequences and serves as a basis for national mobilization, the result is ***nationalism***.

Nations and Nationalism

The birth of modern nationalism is generally traced back to the eighteenth century. More than a mere change of political regime and authorities, the French Revolution that began in 1789 was a watershed of political ideas and ideologies—some democratic and others authoritarian—that would take root throughout Europe and later spread primarily through colonialism throughout the rest of the world. The mobilization of the masses in politics, which had previously been the exclusive domain of upper classes or elites, was one important legacy; nationalism was another.

Local (and even national) identities were not new to Europe. In the fifteenth century Machiavelli had written in *The Prince* that the ruler of the city of Florence, Lorenzo de Medici, needed to use his resources to unify Italy and thus avoid continual warfare among Italian city-states and invasion or other intrusions by France and Spain. Because they were without unity, Machiavelli observed rather emotionally that Italians had been "more enslaved than the Hebrews, more oppressed than the Persians, and more scattered than the Athenians." They were "without a head, without order, beaten, despoiled, lacerated, and overrun," having "suffered ruin of every kind."[4] Machiavelli is honored in present-day Florence for having been among the first advocates of Italian unity.

In fact, however, unification of Italy would have to wait until the 1880s. It was the French in their revolution and its aftermath who first put to practical use the notion of nationalism to inspire an entire nation of people to act as a unit. This idea dominated much of the nineteenth and twentieth centuries.

In past centuries French and English kings had raised armies to fight one another, but they had relied heavily on professionals or mercenaries in their employ. Departing from this tradition, Oliver Cromwell's "new model army" was raised from the general population during the 1640s to fight the king's forces in the English civil war. This very successful approach was used to fill the ranks of Napoleon's mass armies as they set forth on military campaigns across the European continent. The French employed a draft—conscription for national service (the *levée en masse*)—as an effective means to raise popular armies galvanized in their fervor by nationalism and nationalist appeals. It was a model followed in Europe and elsewhere (often with disastrous consequences) throughout the nineteenth and twentieth centuries.

Nationalism can be a benign force or even make a contribution to peace as when fostering a common national identity within a state and is used to overcome conflicts in an ethnically or racially diverse population. It has also been used to unify a people and lead to the formation of a single nation-state, as was true in Germany and Italy in the 1870s and 1880s and Israel in 1948.

The Italian patriot and revolutionary Giuseppe Mazzini (1805–72) and the Hungarian Jewish newspaper correspondent Theodor Herzl (1860–1904) are representative of writers in the nineteenth-century nationalist genre.[5] Mazzini argued that God had "divided humanity into distinct groups upon the face of our

---

[4]Niccolo Machiavelli, *The Prince*, Ch. xxvi.
[5]Quotes are taken from Mazzini's *The Duties of Man* and Herzl's *The Jewish State* as reprinted in Michael Curtis, ed., *The Great Political Theories*, vol. 2 (New York: Avon Books, 1962, 1981), pp. 237–48.

nationalism Devotion to the interests of one's nation, usually to the exclusion of other competing identities.

globe, and thus planted the seeds of nations." He wrote that Italians were a people "speaking the same language, endowed with the same tendencies, and educated by the same historic tradition" and Italy "the home that God has given us, placing therein a numerous family we love and are loved by, and with which we have a more intimate and quicker communion of feeling and thought than with others."

In a similar line of argumentation, Herzl asserted that Jews throughout the world "are a people—*one* people." He and fellow Jewish nationalists or *Zionists*, referring to ancient biblical lands that were home to the Israelites, called for "restoration of the Jewish State." Observing that "no nation on earth has endured such struggles and sufferings," he saw "the distinctive nationality of the Jews" as best preserved within a Jewish state.

Early nineteenth-century nationalism in Latin America took the form of independence movements that ended Spanish and Portuguese empires there. Nationalist political movements in the 1940s, 1950s, and 1960s also succeeded in ending European colonial rule in most of Africa and Asia.

Nationalism, however, can also serve darker purposes when it is used at the expense of others and contributes to civil strife and warfare. In these circumstances there is a mutual exclusivity or intolerance of differing national and ethnic groups. Extreme nationalism, often expressed by those feeling that their people have been oppressed, usually fosters an intolerance of others, particularly if *they* are seen as the oppressors.

In some cases, as in Germany during the 1930s, the extreme-nationalist appeal may take the illusory form that the oppressed are actually a superior people who have been downtrodden unjustly by so-called inferiors. Adolf Hitler's twentieth-century ultranationalist and racist supremacy arguments went well beyond those of Johann Fichte (1762–1814) and other eighteenth- and nineteenth-century German nationalist writers. Hitler (1889–1945) and his National Socialist movement portrayed Jews, Slavs, Gypsies, and other non-Germanic peoples as racially and culturally inferior. Germans were said to be Aryans—a master "race"—who deserved to be treated as such and given the territory needed to expand and grow. Nationalism pushed to this racist extreme was the rationale used in an attempt to "justify" Germany's aggression against non-German nation-states in World War II and the Holocaust in which more than six million Jews as well as Slavs, Gypsies, and others were murdered or worked to death.

Countries that enjoy a relatively strong sense of unity (as is true for most Americans in the United States) tend to characterize additional identities among peoples as ***ethnic*** distinctions rather than seeing them as differences in nationality. Thus Native Americans, Hispanics, Jews, and other Americans of European, African, or Asian origin are referred to as ethnic groups, not nations. Whatever their differences, they still identify themselves as Americans.

In this usage ethnic groups retain a separate identity within the larger, more ethnically diverse nation. Members of ethnic groups may speak the same language, share cultural values, or even have physical similarities; however, all of these groups still maintain an overarching or common national identity.

Although most French are of European origin, many of African or Asian derivation (often from local elites in nineteenth- and twentieth-century French colonial populations) consider themselves as French nationals despite racial differences with those of European origins. More homogeneous as a nation-state than either the United States or France is Japan. Indeed, with the exception of a

ethnic, ethnicity   A common, often cultural, identity of a group of people who usually also identify themselves with a larger society.

very few people of Korean or other origin, almost all of Japan's population share a common language, history, culture, physical characteristics, and national identity.

Things get more confusing when we talk of a state made up of several "countries," as in the United Kingdom (U.K.), which is composed of England, Scotland, Wales, and Northern Ireland (see Map 13.1). States are countries, but not all

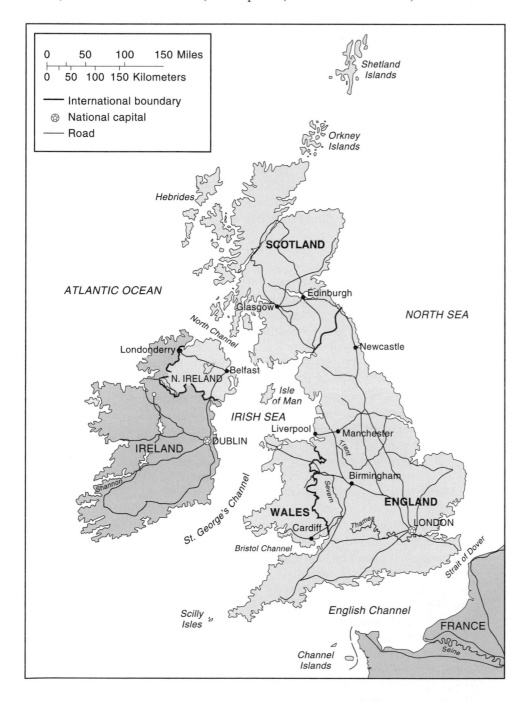

MAP 13.1   THE UNITED KINGDOM AND IRELAND

countries are states. After all, Scotland and England, which already had established dominance in earlier centuries over Wales and Ireland, did not unite as a single state until they finally became a united kingdom in 1707. English and Scottish monarchs were almost always at odds and had often been at war with each other. Although the United Kingdom is a single state, frictions and conflicts among the different national or ethnic groups continue to the present day. Scottish nationalists, a minority within Scotland, certainly see "Scottishness" as much more than a mere ethnic distinction. If they had their way, their country would again become a separate state. It remains to be seen whether the creation of Scottish and Welsh parliaments at the end of the 1990s to handle many regional affairs will satisfy nationalist sentiment or simply spur demands for eventual complete independence.

Binational States

Very often two or more nations exist *within* the borders of a single state. After World War I the victorious allied powers created a single Czechoslovak state from some of the territory that had been part of the just-defeated Austro-Hungarian empire. Physically the same people, Czechs and Slovaks shared the same language and, although there were some Protestants and Jews in the population, most were Catholics.

Of course this focus on physical, linguistic, and religious similarities overlooked significant cultural differences related to their separate development over some 500 years. Among other factors, for example, Czechs were subject more to Austrian and Slovaks more to Hungarian influences. Complicating reconciliation of these Czech-Slovak cultural differences were ethnic (at times "national") differences between Bohemian Czechs in the western part and Moravian Czechs in the eastern part of the present-day Czech Republic.

Separate identities between Czechs and Slovaks proved to be more than just ethnic differences, leading in 1993 to the formal breakup of Czechoslovakia into separate Czech and Slovak states. Czechoslovakia is thus an example of a **binational state** that has become separate Czech and Slovak nation-states.

There are other binational states, by contrast, that thus far have stayed together. One example is Belgium with its separate Flemish- and French-speaking national groups. Some see the Belgian state as being composed of two separate countries or nations—Flanders to the north with its Flemish-speaking Flemings and Wallonia to the south with its French-speaking Walloons. Different language groups in a particular country usually are an indicator of diverse cultures with different histories and, as a result, separate national identities.

Keeping Belgium together as a single state has been a formidable challenge for more than a century and a half. A common religious affiliation (most Belgians are Catholics) has not been enough. Indeed, the Church in Belgium has come to reflect Flemish-Wallonian cultural differences. In such circumstances choosing a common form of governance has proven to be as difficult in the twentieth century as in the nineteenth. In the winter of 1830–31, the great powers meeting in London brought in a king from one of the German states (Leopold of Saxe-Coburg) in an effort to keep the country together. The monarchy of Belgium continues its efforts (as it has for over 170 years) to perform the same national-unity function.

The king of the Belgians—now seen as very much a Belgian himself—is neither a Fleming nor a Walloon. As chief of state, the Belgian king symbolizes Belgian national unity; his role is to take concrete steps to help maintain some degree of

unity among Flemings and Walloons. At the same time, however, the Belgian government has increasingly become fractured into separate sets of institutions servicing the separate Flemish and Wallonian national groups. Even universities have been divided along national lines.

Canada is yet another example of a binational state with its separate English- and French-speaking national groups. Some Canadians say "binational" is inaccurate because it excludes Canada's *Inuit*, the Arctic peoples, or other native Americans referred to by many Canadian ethnologists as "first nations." In any event the extent to which these peoples identify themselves as "Canadians" or choose instead to have separate national identities is a crucial distinction if we are to understand the complexity of the Canadian society. Of course a feeling of national unity as Canadians, notwithstanding considerable national diversity, contributes to keeping the country together. In other words, as the Canadian example demonstrates, it is possible to have different levels of national identity. Thus one can be Canadian first and English- or French-speaking Canadian second. More troublesome for national unity, however, is when French- or English-speakers see themselves as separate (and separable) nations. In 1995, for example, another referendum in Quebec to create an independent state was barely defeated.

Multinational, Multitribal, and Other Multiethnic States

Switzerland is an example of a relatively successful *multinational* state composed of German-, French-, Italian-, and Romansch-speaking Swiss. (Romansch, a language closely related to Latin, the language of the Roman empire, survives among a minority of Swiss, mainly in the very mountainous area in the southeast part of the country.) The Swiss confederation allows a considerable degree of local autonomy, while still allowing broad Swiss identification.

In fact Swiss citizenship is not established by the central government in Bern; it is determined instead by the canton (the state or provincial level) and more specifically by the local *Gemeinde* (to use the German word) or community of one's family at birth. Key to keeping the country together over centuries has been decentralization of as many matters as possible. Over time, however, there has been agreement to collaborate in such matters as establishing a common currency and to cooperate centrally in other ways to promote commerce, maintaining common defenses (although with considerable local authority), and conducting a common foreign policy.

Unsuccessful examples of multinational states include the former Soviet Union and the former Yugoslavia, both of which have broken apart into separate states since 1991. Given a changed international climate and much domestic turmoil after the end of the cold war, national groups in both countries found that most of the obstacles to separatism had been either removed or weakened substantially. Use of coercive means to maintain unity—actions by the police and armed forces—failed in both countries. Both cases are worthy of further comment.

The Disintegration of Yugoslavia   From what was Yugoslavia, separate Slovene and Croat states emerged quickly in the north. Macedonia, north of Greece, followed suit, while Serbia and Montenegro, with their predominantly Serbian populations, stayed together as the residual of what had been Yugoslavia. Fierce fighting broke out in Bosnia-Hercegovina among Muslims, Croats, and Serbs, with Muslims losing most of their territory to the other parties (see Map 13.2).

MAP 13.2   YUGOSLAVIA AND SUCCESSOR STATES

Like Czechoslovakia, Yugoslavia was created after World War I in an attempt to create a common national identity among "south Slavs" (the word "Yugoslavia" itself referring to a land of south Slavs). Beyond linguistic similarities, these Slavic-speaking peoples had little else in common. Serbs and Croats, for example, though in physical appearance the same people speaking a common language (Serbo-Croatian), wrote with different alphabets. Croats were predominantly Catholics (as were Slovenes and the other populations that had been part of the Austro-Hungarian empire). By contrast Serbia and Montenegro had been part of the Ottoman (or Turkish) empire composed of Orthodox Christians and Muslims. It was not easy to set aside cultural cleavages that had developed over centuries when these peoples were subject to such different imperial influences.

Notwithstanding atrocities conducted against each other during World War II by elements of Croat and Serb populations, Josip Broz Tito was able to forge a greater degree of national unity in postwar Yugoslavia than previously had been thought possible. Tito, a nationalist war hero and a Croat, had fostered collaboration with Serbs as fellow "Yugoslavs" in World War II against a common enemy, the Germans, then occupying much of the country. Tito and his Yugoslav Communist Party followers worked after the war until his death in 1980 to build Yugoslav national unity, trying as much as possible to reduce national and cultural differences if they could to mere ethnic distinctions among fellow Yugoslav "workers."

As events in the 1990s demonstrated, however, the idea of Yugoslav nationalism had never really displaced separate Serb, Croat, Slovene, Muslim, or Macedonian national identities. Even in Tito's lifetime, no matter what one was expected or had to say in public, most people in the country considered themselves Serb, Muslim, Macedonian, Croat, or Slovene first, Yugoslav second. Thus when the opportunity for secession emerged, Slovenes, Croats, and later the Macedonians, all withdrew from the Yugoslav federation. Slovenes and Croats received diplomatic or other support for secession from Austria, Hungary, and Germany—a sympathy based no doubt on pre-World War I associations when Croatia and Slovenia had been part of the Austro-Hungarian empire. It is significant that these historically based ties survived the East-West divisions of the cold war and had been maintained, often informally, over many decades.

That fighting became concentrated in Bosnia-Hercegovina is not surprising. Historically by the nineteenth century this area between Serbia and Croatia had become the frontier that divided the Austro-Hungarian and Ottoman empires. In their expansionary phase the Ottoman Turks had reached as far north as Vienna where they were finally turned back in 1683, beginning a gradual retreat southward over several centuries. Although the remains of the Austro-Hungarian and Ottoman empires were dismantled after World War I, the legacy of their separate imperial influences was felt by present-day Balkan peoples, leaving them with separate national identities not easily displaced even now after some eighty or more years.

There are those who argue that nationality, ethnicity, and historically based cultural differences are merely excuses used to justify **irredentism** and aggression. No doubt some leaders *do* know how to manipulate their populations by national and ethnic appeals that mesh nicely with other objectives. On the other hand, even in these cases, that leaders are able to mobilize people on these grounds suggests that national and ethnic difference are, in fact, real to the peoples involved and not just artificial constructions.

The Breakup of the Soviet Union   Comparing the breakup in the early 1990s of Czechoslovakia, Yugoslavia, and the Soviet Union, the most peaceful transition was the establishment of separate Czech and Slovak republics and the most violent was both civil war and war among newly recognized states in the former Yugoslavia. The Soviet case fits between the two.

Violence and the use of force were present in early Soviet efforts to forestall secession by the Baltic and other republics. In the turmoil after an abortive military coup in Moscow in 1991, many of the republics elected to go their separate ways rather than remain in the Soviet Union. Efforts were made to provide only

 CYBER YUGOSLAVIA

The country of Cyber Yugoslavia has been created on the Internet. At this site you can apply for a passport, read the constitution, and vote on issues. The main page provides the following overview of this virtual country [www.juga.com]:

> This is Cyber Yugoslavia. We lost our country in 1991 and became citizens of Atlantis. Since September 9, 1999, this is our home. We don't have a physical land, but we do have nationality, and we are giving citizenship and passports. Because this is Atlantis, we are allowing double and triple citizenship. If you feel Yugoslav, you are welcome to apply for CY citizenship regardless of your current nationality and citizenship, and you will be accepted. Please read our Constitution for the details. If you are just curious, you are welcome to visit as tourists.

> This land will grow as our citizens wish. Neither faster nor slower. Neither more, nor less. So, this site will always be under construction. For a solid country to grow, even a virtual one, it takes some time.

> When we have five million citizens, we plan to apply for UN member status. When this happens, we will ask for 20 square meters of land anywhere on earth to be our country. On this land, we'll keep our server.

Point: While whimsical, Cyber Yugoslavia actually raises the important question of what is meant by the term "nationality"? Is it a physical characteristic or a state of mind?

for a loose association for those republics joining in a Commonwealth of Independent States (CIS).[6] Given their separate, strong national identities and earlier histories of greater independence, the Baltic republics (Estonia, Latvia, and Lithuania) opted out of even this relatively weak association with Russia.

An aim of communist ideology had been to eliminate not only class, but also ethnic and national distinctions that divided workers within and among fellow "socialist" states and eventually throughout the world as a whole. Open talk of separate national identities had been forbidden or discouraged in the Soviet Union and in the socialist states of East-Central Europe and elsewhere. Instead international (and transnational) solidarity of factory workers, peasants, and other "toilers" was the goal.

Reality was quite different, as indicated by the fast pace by which Hungary, Poland, Czechoslovakia, Romania, Bulgaria, and East Germany curtailed their

---

[6]Republics joining the Russian Federation in the commonwealth were Byelarus, Ukraine, Kazakhstan, Turkmenistan, Uzbekistan, Kyrgystan, Tajikistan, Moldova, Armenia, and Azerbaijan.

cold war economic and military ties with the Soviet Union to pursue their separate national agendas. The pace at which these ties were dissolved was to be surpassed only by the speed with which the Soviet Union itself broke apart into separate national republics. National identities suppressed even by the tsars (as in Ukraine, for example) could now find their clear expression in the form of newly independent countries recognized as sovereign states and members of the United Nations.

Dominance by Russians, whether under the tsars or under Marxists-Leninists after the 1917 Bolshevik Revolution, had been the experience of many nationalities. In its most extreme form the pan-Slavic movement that began in Tsarist days attempted to replace separate identities with a common identity among all European Slavs.[7] In fact Slavic peoples had had separate histories for more than a thousand years, their basis for common identity being similarity in language that suggested common historic or tribal origins.

Perceptions by many that pan-Slavism was really a cover for Russian domination of East-Central Europe were reinforced by efforts under Stalin to "Russify" non-Russians within the Soviet Union. Russification—a clear departure from the ideological notion that nationality was to be displaced by worker solidarity— ranged from active promotion to coercive imposition of Russian language and culture upon non-Russians. Later abandoned as a policy, its net effect had been to reinforce national antagonisms within the Soviet Union. A return to policies fostering unity, while acknowledging ethnic, linguistic, and cultural diversity, did not alter the reality that it was the Russians who continued to possess the bulk of political power and authority throughout the Soviet Union.

The important point is that separate national identities had survived all efforts to replace them either with notions of a worker solidarity intended to transcend national and ethnic distinctions or by such national-suppression policies as Russification. It is not surprising, therefore, that East-Central European states broke from Moscow when able to do so and separate nation-states also came to displace what had been a multinational Soviet state.

Multinational and Multiethnic States in the Third World   The boundaries of states in much of Africa, Asia, and Latin America were determined by divisions agreed upon by the former colonial or imperial powers for reasons often having very little to do with respecting national, tribal, ethnic, or other local identities. In fact, containing peoples with diverse identities within the same borders allowed colonial powers to maintain control by capitalizing on these differences, thus making national unity against their rule more difficult to achieve. This was particularly true in Africa where in Nigeria, for example, boundaries of this former British colony include three separate tribal groups (Ibo, Yoruba, and Hausa-Fulani) that outnumber the populations of many countries. After independence and the departure of British administrators and security forces from Nigeria, civil war broke out there with fighting among tribal groups continuing into the 1970s. "Nigerian" as a national identity has proven to be elusive at best. People continue to identify by

---

[7]Slavic countries in East-Central Europe—those identified by Slavic-language group—include Russia, Byelarus, Ukraine, Poland, the Czech and Slovak republics, Bulgaria, and the republics of the former Yugoslavia. Decidedly non-Slavic are Hungary, Romania, and Albania.

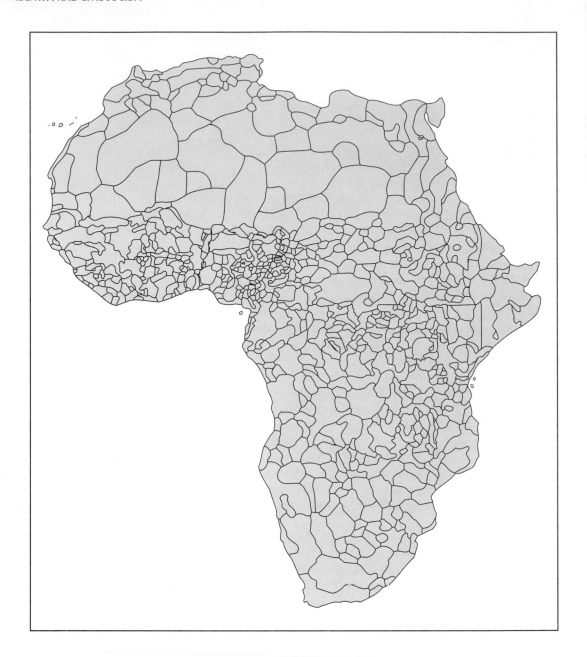

MAP 13.3 AFRICA: TRIBAL BOUNDARIES

Source: George Demko, Agel Jerome, Eugene Boe, *Why in the World: Adventures in Geography*
(New York: Anchor Books, 1992).

tribal group and resent advantages taken by some groups over others. Map 13.3
shows the social complexity of Africa divided by tribal boundaries.

While one could call Nigeria a multinational state, it is referred to more commonly as a *multiethnic* or *multitribal* state. It is interesting to note that in the case
of Africa, it is common to use the terms **tribes** and **tribalism** rather than *nations*

and *nationalism*. For some observers *tribalism* carries negative (if not pejorative) connotations, while *nationalism* has more positive overtones. Hence the massacres that occurred in Rwanda in 1994 were ascribed to tribalism, whereas much of the slaughter occurring in the former Yugoslavia in the 1990s was generally attributed to Serbian or Croatian nationalism. Whether the different use of terms is an accurate reflection of regional or local preferences or instead is indicative of bias or ignorance on the part of the observer is often unclear.

By no means are Nigeria and Rwanda isolated cases in Africa or elsewhere, especially in the Third World. Divisions by tribe or clan in Africa are often much stronger than any pretense to national unity. To avoid civil war and other forms of ethnic strife as have occurred in places as diverse as Nigeria, Rwanda, Burundi, Ethiopia, Somalia, Chad, Liberia, and the Sudan, postcolonial governments have tried with varying degrees of success to build working arrangements to manage this diversity.

While *tribalism* is associated with Africa, group identities in many countries throughout the rest of the Third World are often characterized in terms of ethnicity. Hence civil strife occurs involving Sikh, Tamil, and other ethnic minorities in India and in Sri Lanka (the island state known as Ceylon when it was part of British India). The potential for (or reality of) ethnic strife persists in Indonesia, Malaysia, and other multiethnic societies in South and Southeast Asia, as elsewhere in the Third World. Again, what is characterized as *nationalism* in Europe is often termed *tribalism* or *ethnicity* in other regions.

Neocolonialism refers to foreign influence by the former colonial power that persists despite an end to its physical, controlling presence. Although neocolonialism is sometimes criticized, some unity among elites has been found through their linguistic, cultural, and commercial ties with the former colonial powers, particularly in Africa and Asia. Quite apart from local identities along tribal, familial, or other ethnic affiliation, elites who initially came to power in these countries had developed strong European associations. To varying degrees they acquired either British, French, Belgian, Dutch, or Portuguese linkages that have been retained in the postcolonial period to the present day. As a practical matter it was the European colonial language that had provided a means of communication across tribal and linguistic groups. In addition aspects of European social and political values were either blended with or grafted onto local cultures and customs.

English, for example, is the common language of the political, social, and commercial elites in both Indian and Pakistani societies. After World War II, when the British and local nationalists negotiated independence in India in 1947–48, a decision was made to divide India and Pakistan along Hindu-Muslim lines as separate countries. **Partition** into different states did not prevent war, continuing tensions, and more recently, a nuclear weapons development competition between the two. Moreover partition still left India itself as a very heterogeneous society with many ethnic divisions.

> "The brutality of the conflicts in Kosovo, East Timor, and Rwanda—and the messiness of the international responses to them—obscures the larger shift from confrontation toward accommodation. But the trends are there: a sharp decline in new ethnic wars, the settlement of many old ones, and proactive efforts by states and international organizations to recognize group rights and channel ethnic disputes into conventional politics. In Kosovo and East Timor, intervention was chosen only after other means failed. The fact that the United States, NATO, the United Nations, and Australia intervened was itself a testament to the underlying premise that managing ethnic conflict has become an international responsibility."
>
> **Professor Ted Robert Gurr, "Ethnic Warfare on the Wane," *Foreign Affairs*, 79, no. 3 (May/June 2000): 52–53.**

IT'S BEEN SAID...

Nation-States and Nations Without States

As noted at the outset of this chapter, it is possible for a nation to exist without being associated with a particular state. The Irish were a nation without a state until 1922, when nationalists finally were successful in establishing a separate state after several centuries of British rule. Omitted from the new Irish Republic, however, were six of the nine counties in the northern region known as Ulster. Protestant majorities in Ulster with their historical ties to Scotland and the English crown remained under British protection as part of the United Kingdom.

Although the strife in Northern Ireland is commonly understood as being strife between Catholics and Protestants, the conflict is really not about religion *per se*. Religious difference between the two communities is only a surface-level indicator of much deeper historical, cultural, and political cleavages underlying recurrent **intercommunal** strife.

The aim of some Irish nationalists to drive the British out of Ireland has continued since the 1920s. Known collectively as the Irish Republican Army or IRA, these nationalists are really a collection of diverse nongovernmental factions, some of which have been as hostile to the Irish government in Dublin as to the British government in London. Indeed, the police and military forces of both countries collaborate routinely to curb those IRA factions prone to engage in violent activities. The best known—the Provisional Irish Republican Army or PIRA—has engaged in a terrorist campaign over more than two decades beginning in 1970. Negotiations brought a tenuous peace to Northern Ireland by the end of the 1990s. Efforts have continued to establish home rule in Northern Ireland and the eventual reconciliation of two communities historically divided by fear, suspicion, and hatred.

Until the creation of Israel in 1948, Jews were dispersed in any number of countries (as they still are). The late nineteenth- and twentieth-century Zionist movement sought a state (or at least a homeland) for Jews in the ancient biblical lands. The horror of the Holocaust of the 1930s and 1940s in which some six million Jews died in concentration camps primarily in Germany and occupied Poland contributed to the international decision to create a Jewish state in Israel. Although many ethnic Jews have chosen to retain American or other national identities, those who wish to make their homes in Israel have been able to emigrate there and formally become Israeli nationals.

Palestinians and Kurds are two national groups (many of the latter having distinct tribal identities as well) without single states to call their own. The Kurds were promised a state in the peace settlements after World War I, but have remained dispersed in and near mountainous areas of Iran, Iraq, Syria, Turkey, Azerbaijan and elsewhere in the trans-Caucasus region of the former Soviet Union.

Palestinians, a population with many highly educated people, live in a number of countries including Israel, Jordan, southern Lebanon, Syria, and the Gulf states. Palestinians also remain in the Israeli-occupied territories taken in the June 1967 war, primarily in and around Jerusalem and on territory on the West Bank of the Jordan River, which is referred to by those Israelis laying ancient claim to the area as the biblical lands of Judea and Samaria. One also finds Palestinians in many cities throughout the Middle East where they often hold highly

UNREPRESENTED NATIONS

Nations without states may form various expatriate associations to lobby governments in other countries for the creation of an independent homeland. This certainly was the case with many European colonies following World War II. There is, however, an Unrepresented Nations and Peoples Organization (UNPO) associated with the United Nations. Also known as the United Nations Council for Oppressed Nations (UNCON), it was founded in 1991 to represent and promote the interests of minority groups and occupied territories not officially recognized by the United Nations. Membership is extended to groups with distinct linguistic and cultural heritages who are not UN members and otherwise would not have access to institutions that address the international community. There are currently more than fifty members whose population totals 100 million persons.

The founding charter was signed by representatives of Armenia, Crimea, Estonia, Georgia, Turkestan, and the Volga region in the former Soviet Union; Australian Aborigines, Native Americans, West Irians and West Papuans in Indonesia, Kurds, Cordillera minorities in the Philippines, the Greek minority in Albania, and non-Chinese in Taiwan and Tibet. Several of the original members—Estonians and Latvians—have become member states in the United Nations. The General Assembly of the UNPO meets annually and appoints a Steering Committee. The secretariat is located in The Hague, Netherlands. For further information, see www.unpo.org.

skilled positions as well as providing clerical, information technology, and other commercial services.

Palestinians and Kurds, as minorities in the countries in which they live, have suffered from severe forms of discrimination. Turkish government policy at one time was to deny the very existence of Kurds as a separate national group, referring to them instead as "mountain Turks." Many Palestinians felt dispossessed of their homes and homeland in Palestine when Israel was established as a Jewish state in 1948. Aside from routine forms of discrimination, governments have conducted military campaigns and other attacks against Kurdish and Palestinian groups.

For their part, involvement in insurgent or terrorist activities by Kurds and Palestinians have added to hostilities, promoting further discord and no doubt encouraging further recriminations against them. At least in the Palestinian case, the 1990s witnessed a move toward a degree of political autonomy in the West Bank and Gaza strip. Terrorism was abandoned by mainline groups, although it was continued by Palestinian factions such as Hamas displeased with settlements negotiated with Israel. Most Palestinians hope that the current trend toward self-rule in areas of the West Bank eventually leads to an independent Palestinian state with worldwide recognition of its sovereignty.

APPLYING THEORY

❧ NATIONALISM, WAR, AND ETHNIC CONFLICT ❧

A tremendous amount of literature has been produced on nationalism. Typologies abound, and numerous hypotheses, frameworks, and theories have been advanced to explain the origin of nationalism and the conditions under which it contributes to international conflict. David A. Lake and Donald Rothchild have developed an interesting framework and argument concerning the circumstances under which ethnic conflict arises.

They argue that many popular explanations are incomplete or simply wrong. Ethnic conflict is not caused directly by intergroup differences, ancient hatreds, or the stresses of modern life caused by a global economy. For them intense ethnic conflict is most often caused by collective fears of the future. This occurs when states lose their ability to arbitrate between groups or provide credible guarantees of protection for groups. In other words a crisis of confidence in the state or the actual specter of state failure is the key underlying factor they identify for the rise in ethnic conflict. The effects of international anarchy—fear and a feeling that self-help is the only option—take effect at the societal level of analysis. Groups may arm out of a sense of fear, but the result is to stimulate competition among groups, raising the collective fear factor even higher. Groups become suspicious of the intentions of other ethnic groups—the security dilemma is at work. State weakness, therefore, is a precondition for violent ethnic conflict within states, just as the absence of a superordinate authority

in the international system or world politics is a permissive cause of war (see Chapter Five).

Once groups begin to fear for their safety, other factors come to the fore. Of particular importance is the rise of ethnic activists and political entrepreneurs who build on group fears. Political memories and historical symbols are stirred and utilized to whip up nationalist feeling and gain broader support. Such entrepreneurs cannot achieve their goals on their own. In one sense they are as much a product as a producer of ethnic fears. Yet individuals such as Milosevic in Serbia certainly exacerbate ethnic tensions and contribute to polarization within societies. Once political minorities realize they cannot rely on the state for their protection, they usually look outward to the international community for protection. The international response has been, in the minds of Lake and Rothchild, feeble and unconvincing. With the possible exception of Kosovo, states are reluctant to intervene to end systematic, state-sanctioned ethnic killing. When they do, as in Rwanda, it is often after hundreds of thousands of people have already died.

Stephen Van Evera is particularly interested in the impact of nationalism on the stability of the international system and its contribution to international war. He has suggested that four primary attributes of a nationalist movement determine the potential to produce violence. First is the movement's political status: Is statehood attained or not? If the nationalist movement

APPROACHES TO DEALING WITH NATIONALISM AND ETHNICITY ❧

National Self-Determination

national self-determination
The view that a people with a common identity have the right to be independent from outside control, as in establishing a state.

The principle of **national self-determination**, advocated by American President Woodrow Wilson and other leaders after World War I, was used as a criterion for determining the boundaries of states in their efforts to redraw the map of Europe. The aim was to create nation-states to take the place of the defeated German, Austro-Hungarian, and Turkish empires that had dominated East-Central Europe. Each nation was to have its own state.

A P P L Y I N G   T H E O R Y

does not have a state, he argues this raises the risks of war in the international system. A struggle for national freedom can produce wars of secession, risking the conflict spilling over into the international arena. For example, 15 of the 104 nationalities of the former Soviet Union have achieved statehood, but the other 89 have not. Chechnya is one example. Such stateless nationalities total approximately 25.6 million people, or 10 percent of the former USSR's total population. Furthermore even if a nationalist movement successfully creates a new state, the seeds of future conflict may be planted if other groups are displaced. For example Zionism's displacement of the Palestinian Arabs in 1948 set the stage for later Arab-Israeli wars as well as terrorist activities. Finally successful nationalist leaders may reject the old "rules of the game" of interstate politics, creating regional instability.

The second factor that determines the potential of a national movement producing violence is the movement's stance toward its national diaspora (the dispersion or scattering of persons across different lands): If the movement has a national state, will it try to incorporate its nationals via territorial expansion or by encouraging immigration? The latter policy has been pursued after World War II by both German and Israeli governments. The territorial expansion route was pursued by pre-1914 pan-Germanism and by pan-Serbianism in the 1990s.

The third factor is the movement's attitude toward other independent nationalities: Is it one of tolerance or hegemony? In other words does the nationalist ideology respect the freedom of other nationalities or does it assume a right or duty to rule them? Hegemonic nationalism is the rarest and most dangerous variety. The obvious examples are interwar Nazi nationalism in Germany, fascist nationalism in Mussolini's Italy, and militarist nationalism in imperial Japan.

Fourth is the nationalist movement's treatment of its own minorities: Are the rights of minorities respected or abused? The nationalism of many immigrant nations (such as the United States and Canada) tend to be relatively more minority-respecting. By contrast, nonimmigrant nationalisms tend to discriminate against or even suppress or oppress their minorities, for example, Iraqi and Turkish policy against the Kurds, China's actions in Tibet, and Serbian oppression of Slavic Muslim and Albanian (Kosovar) minorities.

According to Van Evera, these four attributes constitute a "danger-scale," highlighting the level of danger posed by any given nationalism. If all four attributes are positive or benign, such nationalisms may actually dampen the risk of war. Conversely if all four attributes are negative or malign, the nationalism at issue is bound to clash with others, increasing the risk of war.

Sources: David A. Lake and Donald Rothchild, "Containing Fear: The Origins and Management of Ethnic Conflict," *International Security*, vol. 21, no. 2 (Fall 1996): 41–75; Stephen Van Evera, "Hypotheses on Nationalism and War," *International Security*, vol. 18, no. 4 (Spring 1994): 5–39.

However well intentioned, the national-self-determination principle has been abused. Hitler, for example, claimed in 1938 that the Sudetenland—that part of Bohemia in Czechoslovakia in which German-speaking people lived—should be a part of Germany. Hitler got his way at a 1938 summit conference held in Munich. After all, and quite apart from German aggressive designs on the territory of Czechoslovakia, supporters of the Munich concession could point to the arrangement merely as a line-drawing adjustment to post–World War I maps, an exercise consistent with the principle of national self-determination.

In recent years with the seeming explosion of ethnic conflict within some states, the international community is forced to come to terms with two conflicting principles: *respect for territorial sovereignty of the state* and *the right of national self-determination*. During the cold war this was less of a problem. When political independence movements in the Third World struggled to end colonialism, they were not calling for the partition of a state, but rather its complete independence from foreign rule. Leaders in emerging Third World states agreed to respect colonial borders. There were exceptions: Tibetans in China, the Ibos in Nigeria, and Kashmir in India. Still the one major successful break-up of an existing state during the cold war occurred in 1971 when Bangladesh, with India's help, shattered the unity of Pakistan at the cost of tens of thousands of deaths and the flight of ten million refugees to India.

Limiting self-determination was actually endorsed unanimously by the UN General Assembly in the 1970 Declaration of Principles of International Law Concerning Friendly Relations Among States. This resolution sought to sustain the international stability resulting from reaffirmation of the primacy of the sovereign state over people on its own territory. The end of the cold war, however, has seen substantial erosion of this idea. The outbreak of nationalist sentiment, particularly the unraveling of the Soviet Union with the recognition of the independence of the Baltic states and other republics in central Asia, set a different precedent: Self-determination could be achieved even at the expense of the unity of an existing state. What was largely a voluntary and peaceful development in the former Soviet Union, however, played out quite differently as the former Yugoslavia broke apart in the early 1990s, spawning a series of Balkan wars accompanied by widespread civil strife. In the case of sub-Saharan Africa, during the cold war both Moscow and Washington as well as former European colonial powers worked to keep their favorite strongmen in control as the two superpowers engaged in fierce global competition. In the 1960s and 1970s China also competed for favor in Africa and elsewhere in the Third World. With the end of this strategic competition on the African continent, countries such as Zaire or the Congo were no longer strategic battlegrounds and outside powers seemed to lose interest in the fate of many of these ethnically diverse states.[8]

Alternative Approaches to Maintaining Unity in Binational, Multinational, and Multiethnic States

With varying degrees of success or failure, several different strategies or approaches have been adopted to manage two or more nations within a given state. Keeping binational and multinational states together in intercommunal peace and mutual acceptance has proven to be a formidable task wherever it has been tried. What can be done to stem a potential tide of ethno-nationalist conflicts that threaten to undermine regional if not international stability?

Partition   Partition or formal separation can be used to stop or reduce national and ethnic strife, at least for a limited time. Separating national and ethnic groups into distinct, mutually exclusive communities—drawing solid-line boundaries around them—is at best a short-term approach or coping mechanism as long as they remain within a single state. It is not by any means a long-term solution to the problem of national and ethnic or racial strife.

Intercommunal fighting in Lebanon in the 1970s and 1980s, for example, could be stopped only by creating what amounted to strict territorial zones for

---

[8]Richard Falk, "Caught Between National Interests and Nationalism," *Washington Post*, September 19, 1999.

different religious and cultural groups, policed by Syrian and other troops as well as multinational peacekeepers. At best such informal or *de facto* partition could produce only a very fragile peace, which easily could (and did) break down again into inter-communal warfare. Similarly, *de jure* or formal, legal division into separate Pakistani and Indian states in 1948 did not resolve differences between Muslim and Hindu communities either. As already noted, hostilities (actual warfare or continual threat of warfare) have remained a fairly constant condition in Pakistani-Indian relations. These conflictual relations, moreover, have contributed substantially to efforts by both countries to acquire nuclear-weapons capabilities, which now poses a threat to security in South Asia that goes well beyond differences between India and Pakistan.

Similarly, dividing peoples by national and ethnic identity into separate states in the former Yugoslavia did not promote peace. Civil strife became international war as each new state sought to expand or defend its territorial base. Not surprisingly some of the worst fighting occurred in Bosnia, the state that was most ethnically diverse. Again, when faced with such conflicts, a cease-fire with strict divisions among the parties may be necessary to halt bloodshed in the short run, but partition alone (whether within or between states) has not provided a foundation for long-term peace anywhere.

One of the most severe examples of separation policies was racial division of blacks and whites in South Africa. Universally criticized for its injustice, South African **apartheid**, a policy of strict racial segregation, allowed a white minority to maintain a dominant position over the black majority. Moreover, as a white-dominated state, South Africa became isolated from neighboring black African states, giving the latter ample incentive to support antigovernment, black nationalist groups in South Africa. Ending formal apartheid by the early 1990s, of course, did not resolve black-white problems, much less tribal and other differences within the black majority. Efforts were in fact taken in the 1990s to expose abuses by all parties during the apartheid period in an attempt to achieve reconciliation. As elsewhere prospects for a long-term peace in South Africa rest instead on improved economic well-being and greater social tolerance or acceptance across ethnic communities, aspirations always much more easily stated than achieved.

Assimilation Another strategy or approach, sometimes a very oppressive one, is **assimilation** of diverse populations into a single national grouping. This may entail denying that national differences exist at all or, if they do, denying their legitimacy as separate identities. As noted, assimilationist policies, for example, were adopted in the Soviet Union during Stalin's time in an effort to "Russify" non-Russian peoples. The Iraqi government has conducted military campaigns to suppress or maintain control

IT'S BEEN SAID...

Given the mixed blessings nationalism has bestowed on the modern world, it is not surprising that many commentators have critically examined the relation between nationalism and the glorification of the state. All too often, it is suggested, human rights are sacrificed in the name of maintaining state sovereignty. One such critic is Vaclav Havel, president of the Czech Republic. He made the following comments in April 1999 during the NATO air campaign against Serbia and Serbian attempts to "cleanse" ethnically the province of Kosovo by removing Muslims.

There is every indication that the glory of the nation-state as the culmination of every national community's history, and its highest earthly value—the only one, in fact, in the name of which it is permissible to kill, or for which people are expected to die—has already passed its peak.

It would seem that the enlightened efforts of generations of democrats, the terrible experiences of two world wars—which contributed so much to the adoption of the Universal Declaration of Human Rights—and the evolution of civilization have finally brought humanity to the recognition that human beings are more important than the state.

In this new world, people—regardless of borders—are connected in millions of different ways: through trade, finance, property, and information. Such relationships bring with them a wide variety of values and cultural models that have a universal validity. It is a world, moreover, in which a threat to some has an immediate impact on everyone . . . in which all of us—whether we like it or not—must begin to bear responsibility for everything that occurs. In such a world, the idol of state sovereignty must inevitably dissolve.

Clearly, blind love for one's own country—a love that defers to nothing beyond itself, that excuses anything one's own state does only because it is one's own country, yet rejects everything else only because it *is different—has necessarily become a dangerous anachronism, a source of conflict and, in extreme cases, of immense human suffering.*

In the [twenty-first] century I believe that most states will begin to change from cultlike entities charged with emotion into far simpler and more civilized entities, into less powerful and more rational administrative units that will represent only one of the many complex and multilevel ways in which our planetary society is organized.

With this transformation, the idea of noninterference—the notion that it is none of our business what happens in another country and whether human rights are violated in that country—should vanish down the trapdoor of history.

Question: Do you think globalization will make Havel's vision more or less likely to be fulfilled?

Source: Vaclav Havel, President of Czech Republic, address given to the Canadian Senate and House of Commons in Ottawa, Canada, as reprinted in *New York Review of Books*, June 10, 1999, p. 4.

IT'S BEEN SAID...

over the non-Arab Kurdish population in the northern part of the country. Turkish policies mentioned previously that denied Kurds a separate identity, referring to them merely as "mountain Turks," are another example of assimilationist policy.

The United States has also tried to assimilate diverse populations, establishing "American" as a common national identity. Earlier in its history, particularly in the nineteenth century, military campaigns were conducted to gain control over Native American populations, later placing them on reservations. This policy of formal exclusion gradually changed as many Native Americans were encouraged to leave the reservations and become part of the larger American society.

Slavery in the United States lasted until the 1860s and effectively denied African-Americans in slave states any degree of autonomy. Racial segregation policies that formally separated blacks from whites, particularly in the American South, survived into the 1960s. Segregationists did not intend that blacks ever see themselves as a separate nation (as many American Indians did); the goal of segregationist policies was to impose on blacks a separate (and lower) status within American society. Similarly mainstream civil rights reformers opposed the few who advocated separation into different, racially distinct states or societies. The aim instead was racial integration, a view perfectly consistent with assimilationist strategy.

Consistent with the assimilationist idea, Indians are referred to in present-day parlance as Native Americans and blacks as African-Americans, in much the same way as European and Asian populations came to be identified as Polish-Americans, Irish-Americans, Italian-Americans, Norwegian-Americans, Japanese-Americans, Chinese-Americans, and so forth. There are those, of course, who object to any such hyphenation of the American nationality, preferring the complete assimilation or unity implied by the single term *American*. But those who want to retain ethnic identities as part of the American fabric, particularly those living in and identifying as part of ethnic communities, do not object to hyphenation or ethnic labels in which they take pride. Thus from this perspective, to acknowledge explicitly that one is of Japanese, Finnish , Hispanic (or Latino) origin, for example, is still to be very much an American.

Wherever assimilationist policies have been relatively successful, adopting a common national identity has not necessarily meant dropping all other identities. There can still be unity in diversity. Separate ethnic and racial identities have survived, if not flourished, in the United States. The important point, however, is that almost all members of these groups still commonly identify themselves as "Americans." The common bond is a commitment to the idea of being an American or to the democratic ideals expressed in the national Constitution, not to any single or separate ethnic identity.

A commitment to multiculturalism allows for the richness of cultural diversity while still retaining an overarching national identity. It is when cultural diversity is interpreted as separatism that controversy ensues. One sees this in the United States in the debate over national language. Most assimilationists in the United States, for example, acknowledge that different ethnic and cultural groups have a right to speak Spanish, Mandarin or one of the other Chinese dialects, Italian, Vietnamese, or whatever. On the other hand they voice opposition to giving other languages equal status with English. To be bilingual or multilingual is a matter of choice, not a requirement for other Americans who choose to communicate only in English. They refer to English as the traditional, spoken language in the United States that cuts across—and thus contributes to uniting—different ethnic, cultural, or other identities. The controversy is particularly acute in major cities such as New York and Miami or in the American Southwest where large numbers (in some cases approaching a majority) of people speak languages other than English.

Consociationalism in Multinational Unitary States   In *a unitary state*, all political power and authority come to rest in the institutions of a central government. Although almost all countries have at least one or more ethnic minorities in their societies, those coming closest to being single nation-states—states with one common or overarching national identity and lacking deep national and ethnic divisions—may choose to vest central government institutions with significant political power and authority. This is the case in France, Japan, the Scandinavian countries, the Republic of Korea, and most nation-states throughout the world.

On the other hand when unitary states are composed of two or more nations or strong ethnic communities, a **consociational** model may be the means for maintaining peace and keeping the state together. Through agreements and formal rules that share or divide the powers and positions of government among different national and ethnic groups, consociationalism typically allows a maximum of local autonomy for the different communities within binational and multinational states.

Prior to its breakdown into civil war in the 1970s, Lebanon was viewed by many as a model of consociational arrangements among different cultural communities. Strict rules were followed for several decades that allocated positions of political authority and representation among the different Christian and Muslim communities. It proved extraordinarily difficult to renegotiate these arrangements, partly because any such alteration was seen by many Christian Lebanese as undermining their position in favor of increasing the representation of one or another of the Muslim communities. Differences among familial and other factions vying for power in the different communities contributed to the complexity of recasting political relationships. The interests of outside states as diverse as Syria, Iran, and Israel made an already difficult problem next to impossible to resolve. Intercommunal bloodshed, direct and indirect interventions by outside powers, and *de facto*

The Green Line divided Beirut's Christian and Muslim sectors for fifteen years. The sign, showing Pope John Paul II beside a map of Lebanon, reads in both Arabic and French, "Lebanon, more than a country, it's a message," is one of the many that greeted the Holy Father on his visit to Beirut in May 1997.

partition of the different communities ensued. Although consociationalism can contribute to unity and civility among diverse peoples within a state, the Lebanese example underscores how fragile these arrangements can be.

Belgian accommodation of different Flemish and Wallonian interests has required continual attention. Establishing duplicate governmental ministries, political parties, and even universities for the separate Flemish- and French-speaking communities is an approach consistent with the consociational model. A central government has remained in Brussels even as there has been considerable decentralization of political authority to the separate communities.

If diverse communities are to stay together within a single state, considerable efforts are required continually over time to refine, modify, correct, and legitimize these power-sharing and power-dividing arrangements. Political elites must be dedicated to maintaining the system as opposed to exacerbating ethnic tensions.

Federal and Confederal Approaches   As noted, unitary states establish single, centralized governments. By contrast a *federal state* is one composed of separate state or provincial governments that have important functions to perform independently but must coexist with a strong central government that may well take the upper hand on many matters. The United States is an example of a federation, although the reasons for Americans choosing federalism were not related to problems of nationality and ethnicity. The American rationale for establishing a federated state had more to do with distrust of unchallenged centralized power, geographic distances that were significant in the eighteenth century when the U.S. Constitution was written, and a desire to provide for security as well as some degree of local autonomy to states that had developed historically as separate colonies.

In Canada, on the other hand, the rationale for federalism goes beyond such geographic and other concerns to provide a vehicle for managing differences between separate French-speaking and English-speaking communities. Thus francophone Quebec has a separate distinction and some local authority even as it remains part of the Canadian federation. Separatists, thus far still a minority, find present arrangements unsatisfactory. Efforts have been made, however, to accommodate the national and ethnic concerns they represent. Agreements have been made protecting separate language and cultural identities and allocating additional funds and more local authority over issues of importance to the different provinces. These agreements have served a similar function to the consociational arrangements discussed above, which is to keep different peoples together within a single (in this case, federal) state.

The terms perhaps can be best understood as different points on a continuum. The distinction between federation and **confederation** is not always clear-cut. Federations and confederations are both composed of states, republics, provinces, cantons, or other political units with their own separate governments. Confederations, however, have much weaker central governance than federations and put relatively more political authority at local levels. In short confederalism takes a major step further in the direction of greater local autonomy through decentralization.

Decentralized governance, for example, has been a key ingredient in Switzerland's success in keeping its Italian-, French-, German-, and Romansch-speaking peoples together in a single state—a confederation. Cantons the size of American counties retain considerable authority over education, health care, law enforcement, and even the conveying of citizenship. Important functions are entrusted to central authorities—making a common foreign policy, planning for defense against invasion by outside powers, and maintaining the country's economic and monetary systems. Even these are subject to scrutiny by authorities representing local interests.

Rather than having a single president of the Swiss Confederation, for example, there is a seven-person presidency that (similar to consociational arrangements in some unitary states) assures representation in national councils of diverse interests among the different cantons. This is in addition to a national legislature constituted to bring representatives together to deal with issues that cannot be dealt with at the local (or cantonal) level. Important questions are frequently given to the people to vote on directly in a referendum. Such direct democracy is consistent with a "town meeting" tradition still practiced, particularly in smaller Swiss cantons.

The USSR or Union of Soviet Socialist Republics formally had been a federation, even though in practice political authority always had been concentrated within the central leadership of the communist party. Given this experience, breakaway national republics found even confederation too strong a set of ties for their political taste. With the collapse of the Soviet Union, the most that could be worked out was agreement on establishing a **commonwealth**—a very loose association of sovereign states.

SOCIAL AND ECONOMIC APPROACHES
TO INTERCOMMUNAL PEACE

How can intercommunal conflicts be halted? Over a half-century of experience in UN and other multilateral efforts to establish and maintain peace in places as diverse as Cyprus, the Sinai, and the Balkans, three functions have been identified. A first step is to establish peace. Diplomatic efforts to end fighting among the groups is the *peacemaking* function. An alternative or supplement to diplomatic efforts is the function of *peace enforcement*—the threat or actual use of force by local or multilateral authorities (as when actions are taken under United Nations auspices) designed to stop the fighting and halt or at least reduce bloodshed among national or ethnic groups. This may be followed by *peacekeeping*, a maintenance function that typically involves monitoring or enforcing in a neutral fashion a cease-fire or peace already agreed to by the contending parties. The problem with all three, however, is that they are stopgap or short-term measures and do little to address the underlying causes of intercommunal strife.

When the social orientation of human beings takes a turn toward the mutual exclusivity of different national, ethnic, or other group identities, we are usually observing a problem with deep psychological or social-psychological roots. From peace theory we learn that *prospects for peace are greatest if there at least can be an acceptance or tolerance of people with diverse identities*. Some degree of intercommunal tolerance or acceptance is a minimal condition for maintaining peace over time.

Of course, no easy remedy can be found to solve problems of national, ethnic, or racial strife. In the short term we may need to draw lines on maps to partition or separate people just to keep them from fighting. Peace theorists do look, however, to a longer-run transformation of these *solid* lines that divide peoples (dividing them from one another in mutually exclusive categories) into *dotted* or permeable lines that allow for passage across intercommunal boundaries of people, their ideas, and economic resources. This prescription for peace is based on liberal principles. The idea is hardly new.

That there can be tolerance or acceptance of diverse peoples has roots in the seventeenth- and eighteenth-century Enlightenment, in the **cosmopolitan** sense of unity among peoples that prevailed in the Middle Ages, and in the ancient Greco-Roman Stoic idea that whatever our differences, it is common humanity that unites us. Such tolerance or acceptance of cultural diversity and different identities within, between, and across societies is a minimum condition for a durable domestic peace. Difficult as it may be to achieve, this intercommunal peace can be strengthened still further when social relationships go beyond mere tolerance to a higher level of mutual respect for diverse cultures.

A durable peace, of course, cannot rest on mere assertion, however pleasing or enlightened cosmopolitanism may sound. When it has been achieved it is the outcome of policies pursued patiently over time. Although peacemaking, peace enforcement, and peacekeeping provide security in the short term by stopping the violence and bloodshed of intercommunal strife, it is not enough merely to establish law and order through the use of force or otherwise. Two kinds of development—social and economic—are necessary to provide a firm, long-term basis for lasting peace among diverse peoples.

Social development means establishing over time a greater degree of mutual acceptance or tolerance among different peoples. It involves education, cultural exchanges, communications, and other constructive efforts that over decades tend to bring diverse peoples together. Commercial and professional ties, friendships, and marriages that cross intercommunal lines are indicative of a relatively high level of social development. Social development involves values that are usually slow to change. Education of younger generations, reeducation of older generations, and building new human associations across communal lines are core tasks in social-developmental efforts.

Even so measures intended to promote greater tolerance or acceptance proceed at a glacial pace, with progress measured only over decades. Older generations are least likely to change their outlook, particularly if they have experienced the human costs of civil strife or intercommunal warfare.

Such memories often block the best-designed reconciliation efforts. In such circumstances peace practitioners adopt a patient stance, waiting for the eventual passing of older generations, while at the same time fostering cosmopolitan values among younger generations. To a considerable degree this has been the approach followed in Western Europe after World War II. Even though old antagonisms have not been eliminated entirely, there is today a much higher degree of tolerance or mutual acceptance than many would have thought possible among the Germans, French, British, Belgians, Dutch, Danes and other Scandinavians, Spaniards, Italians, Greeks, and others.

This Western European achievement did not just happen; it was the result of a decided effort to change the mutual exclusivity of national and ethnic mind sets. European international organizations were established and expanded into what is now the European Union (EU). In addition to the specific purposes of particular organizations or channels of communication across national borders, the attempt was to go beyond the national and ethnic divisions that had contributed to the bloodshed of two major world wars in the first half of the twentieth century.

Economic development that reduces disparities in levels of living among different communities is also an essential ingredient. It is difficult to have open frontiers when disparate economic levels on different sides of borders result in migration of large numbers of people from poorer countries or areas to richer ones.

Even the better-off economies of advanced industrial countries have limits on how many immigrants they can absorb before suffering real economic costs. This is as true in North America as in Europe. Thus attempts have been made to restrict the flow of labor from Mexico into the United States. In Europe there are limits in place on flows of people from Eastern countries moving to Germany and other highly developed Western countries. Only when levels of economic development have become somewhat less disparate (if not equalized) may it be possible to open borders to unrestricted movements of peoples.

Social and economic development policies pursued with determination over time can result in a freer flow of diverse peoples, their ideas, and economic resources across borders. Even though lines on maps will still be solid, they will in fact have become dotted lines—permeable rather than exclusionary boundaries. If peace theorists are right—and there are empirical grounds for thinking they are—these circumstances are more conducive to maintaining intercommunal peace.

The problem is that we are talking, in some cases, of no less than a long-term international endeavor and commitment to save failed states and their peoples. In this regard, some advocates favor an international "conservatorship" to administer critical government functions until the country can govern itself. But how long might that take if ethnic war has destroyed the social and economic infrastructure? How patient would outside powers be? Even if basic state functions are reestablished, how can the memories of ethnic violence be muted in the case of those who have witnessed atrocities perpetrated on their communities?

Some may think, therefore, that to rely on social and economic development over time to be simply a utopian approach to countries ravaged by ethnic conflict. It may be. On the other hand to proceed as if national and ethnic strife are insoluble problems would be a self-fulfilling prophecy. Although there is no certainty that social and economic development conducted in a physically secure environment will put national and ethnic strife to rest, the degree of civility among nations that has been achieved in Western Europe supports the view that such social and economic development policies can be fruitful.

CONCLUSION

From the perspective of many realists, nationalism, or serving the national interest, is perhaps the single biggest reason the state will continue into the indefinite future. Crises of authority may cause a state to be torn in two, but the result will be the seceding territory joining a neighboring state, or the creation of a newly independent state. Similarly if a state motivated by extreme nationalism and an expansionist ideology successfully conquers a neighbor, the result is simply a larger state. The point is that whether nationalism helps to keep a current state together or tears it apart, the end result is the same—a state. Nationalists are not interested in transferring power and sovereignty upward to an international organization, let alone a world government. They also are suspicious of regional associations among states, which helps to account for the fact that even in the European Union people still tend to call themselves Germans, French, or English first, not "European."

Pluralists also recognize that nationalism is a primary cause of conflict in the world. But they tend to be more optimistic about the possibility of taming nationalism despite the Yugoslavia disaster. This will not happen by either avoiding or somehow transcending politics; it will happen *through* politics. People can learn from the past and from past mistakes. International organizations and regimes can facilitate the more orderly conduct of interstate relations. Nongovernmental organizations and the growing global civil society provide other voices for moderation in the relations among peoples. The state will not wither away, as predicted by orthodox Marxists and idealistic world federalists. The state and the people it encompasses within its borders will continue to be a major focus of identity. But that does not necessarily mean that the state's function is to be the vehicle for expressing national prejudices against other states and peoples.

Nationalism, therefore, is one of the most significant phenomena in world politics. With the end of the cold war, the suppressed nationalisms of Central and Eastern Europe (to include the former Soviet Union) burst forth. On the one hand nationalism can be a force for unity and solidarity and be supportive of democracy as has continued to be the case in the Czech Republic after its peaceful break with Slovakia. On the other hand, it can also tear a society apart, as we have seen in the former Yugoslavia. Nationalism can buttress existing political authority or be the rallying cry of those who wish to overthrow it. It can be a progressive as well as a repressive force, fostering at the same time unity at home and wars of aggression abroad. As we have seen, the constitutive elements of nationalism vary from case to case. Despite its importance and the amount of research and thought conducted on the subject, it remains complex, elusive and often difficult to grasp.

Key Terms

nations *p. 408*
nationalism *p. 413*

ethnic, ethnicity *p. 414*

national self-determination *p. 426*

Other Concepts

nation-states *p. 408*
multinational states *p. 408*
race *p. 412*
racism *p. 412*
genocide *p. 412*
binational state *p. 416*
irredentism *p. 419*

tribe, tribalism *p. 422*
neocolonialism *p. 423*
partition *p. 423*
intercommunal *p. 424*
apartheid *p. 429*
assimilation *p. 429*
consociational *p. 431*

confederation *p. 432*
commonwealth *p. 433*
cosmopolitan *p. 434*
social development *p. 434*
economic development *p. 436*

ADDITIONAL READINGS

The amount of work published on nationalism is daunting. We would recommend Walker Connor, *Ethnonationalism: The Quest for Understanding* (Princeton, N.J.: Princeton University Press, 1994). This is a collection of essays by one of the most perceptive observers of nationalism, who throughout his career has challenged conventional thinking on the subject. See also Elie Kedourie, *Nationalism*, 4th ed. (Oxford, England: Blackwell, 1993); E. J. Hobsbawn, *Nations and Nationalism Since 1780: Programme, Myth, and Reality* (Cambridge, England: Cambridge University Press, 1990); and Ernst B. Haas, "Nationalism: An Instrumental Social Construction," *Millennium* (January 1994): 505–45 and *Nationalism, Liberalism, and Progress* (Ithaca, N.Y.: Cornell University Press, 1997). While taking account of the downside, work by Haas on this subject also underscores the positive impact and potential of nationalism and national identity as social constructs that serve the welfare of a nation's people.

HUMANITARIANISM: HUMAN RIGHTS AND REFUGEES

To establish conditions under which justice and respect for the obligations arising from treaties and other sources of international law can be maintained.

FROM THE *PREAMBLE TO THE CHARTER OF THE UNITED NATIONS*

ung San Suu Kyi is one of the most famous political activists in the world today. Due to her defense of human rights and nonviolent opposition to the military regime in Myanmar (formerly known as Burma), she was awarded the Nobel Peace Prize in 1991. Viewed as a threat to state security, she was held under house arrest from July 1989 to July 1995. The daughter of the revered father of Burmese independence, Suu Kyi returned to Burma in 1988 to take care of her dying mother. She became actively involved in the democracy movement, helping to form the National League for Democracy (NLD). The NLD is the largest legally recognized political party. The military, however, which came to power in a bloody military coup in September 1988, reigns supreme.

Nonviolent resistance to martial law led to a series of arrests in 1989. In July of that year Suu Kyi and her colleagues had planned a Martyrs' Day March but called it off when extensive military preparations were evident. Returning home she found eleven truckloads of troops waiting for her. During most of her six years of house arrest, she was denied access to the outside world. In April 1995 she was finally allowed two visits from her husband and sons, the first in over two years. Her husband, terminally ill with cancer and living in London, applied for a visa in 1999 to pay a farewell visit to his wife in Myanmar, his first in three years. The junta refused, hoping Suu Kyi would go to Britain instead. Suu Kyi's husband died in March 1999, but she has continued to work for democracy and human rights in Myanmar. Many states, international organizations, and nongovernmental organizations have supported her efforts. Indeed, her international stature is the best protection she has from government reprisals. Lesser-known human rights activists, however, are not similarly protected. This is as true in Myanmar as it is in numerous other countries.

We live in a world of some six billion people, a large proportion of whom suffer from political oppression, social discrimination, poverty, starvation or malnutrition, disease, and early death. Freedom from want is an elusive goal in much of the world where poverty is the norm, life expectancy is much lower than in high-income countries, and infant mortality is still very high. Insecurity reigns supreme and there is relatively little prospect of eliminating either the fact or fear of political and other abuses. Many human rights advocates lament how President Franklin Roosevelt's "four freedoms" enumerated in his 1941 State of the Union address—freedom of speech and expression, freedom of religion, freedom from want, and freedom from fear—seem so unattainable for most of the world's population.

We approach the subject of human rights in this chapter by examining how rights or values can be considered universal and not just representations of particular cultural or national preferences. In this regard it is important for Americans (or the nationals of any country, for that matter) to understand the lack of universal agreement on *which* rights or *whose* rights ought to be protected. We also examine the problem of refugees, not simply in terms of human rights, but also as a potentially destabilizing element in international relations and world politics.

We deal explicitly with human rights as part of the human condition and in relation to concepts of justice and state sovereignty. After an overview of historical and contemporary human rights abuses, we examine how human rights can be understood not only from the U.S. perspective, but also from the perspective of different cultures. Lists of human rights have been made in universal declarations, covenants, and other documents of the United Nations and regional organizations such as the Council of Europe, the European Union (EU), the Organization of American States (OAS), and the Organization of African Unity (OAU). We close by returning to the issue of how the evolving doctrine of internationally protected human rights poses a challenge to traditional conceptions of sovereignty, and we examine the role of transnational organizations in globalizing the issue of human rights.

HUMAN RIGHTS AND THE HUMAN CONDITION

A belief in certain inalienable human rights is at the core of our understanding of the human condition. Yet the human condition is beset by widespread abuses related to intercommunal strife, politically oppressive regimes, and deeply set prejudices within and across different societies and cultures. We focus in this section on some of these circumstances that produce widespread human rights violations.

Racial and ethnic discrimination is a global problem. South African apartheid or racial-separation policies were implemented by white-minority governments against the black majority population until the 1990s. Suppression of a majority by a small, powerful minority made the South African case particularly egregious.

Much more common in various countries, however, are racial, national, and ethnic prejudices that result in oppression of minority populations. These are not just Third World issues. Europe, Japan, and North America also offer considerable evidence of discriminatory practices on racial or ethnic lines.

For its part legalized, racially based slavery in the United States lasted until President Lincoln's Emancipation Proclamation of 1863 and Amendment 13 to the U.S. Constitution, passed in 1865, prohibited the practice. Outlawing slavery, of course, did not eliminate racial discrimination. Legalized, racial segregation continued until Supreme Court rulings beginning in 1954 and passage of the Civil Rights Act of 1965. Notwithstanding considerable progress toward equal rights, there is still substantial evidence of continuing racial discrimination in various forms.

Some societies value free expression and religious choice, but others do not. Brutality directed against other human beings, by no means a new phenomenon, seemed nevertheless to intensify during the 1980s and 1990s, as evidenced by the 1989 massacre of demonstrators at Tiananmen Square in the Chinese capital of Beijing; the slaying of peasant villagers in the southern Mexican state of Chiapas and in El Salvador, Honduras, Nicaragua, Haiti, and other parts of Central America and the Caribbean; the breakup of Yugoslavia and the intercommunal violence among Croat, Serb, and Muslim populations that followed; and intertribal atrocities committed in the Sudan, Ethiopia, Rwanda, and elsewhere in Africa. These incidents gained worldwide attention not just as localized atrocities, but also because they are indicative of a pattern of intercommunal violence throughout the world.

Massive numbers of migrant populations—especially economic refugees seeking work and a place to live for themselves and their families—have swelled the ranks of other refugees, most of whom are seeking asylum or protection from various forms of political oppression throughout the world. These growing numbers challenge even those countries historically sympathetic to their plight. Widespread national and ethnic strife in Africa, the Balkans, the Gulf, the Transcaucasus, South and Southeast Asia, and the Caribbean have produced literally millions of displaced persons who have been forced, or who have fled, from their home areas, often across national borders. In sub-Saharan Africa alone the United Nations High Commission for Refugees (UNHCR) has counted more than six million displaced persons—greater than 10 percent of the region's population.[1]

Not all countries share a deep commitment to admitting immigrants seeking asylum or refugee status, but even those that do face practical limits to their population-absorption capacities; large-scale immigration pressures typically are balanced by governments that also are concerned about the impact of immigration on the welfare of their own citizens. The United States certainly has grappled with this issue, given pressures from populations fleeing regimes in Cuba, Haiti, and other locations in Central America and the Caribbean. In addition there are large numbers of employment-driven migrations from Mexico, many of them illegal.

Widespread gender discrimination also denies equal rights to women. The term "gender discrimination" hardly captures the nature of existence for the vast majority of women in the Third World, where a combination of culture, laws, and religion not only deprive women of basic human rights, but relegate them in some places to almost subhuman status. In parts of Latin America, Asia,

CASE & Point

WOMEN IN THE THIRD WORLD

- An estimated 500,000 women die of pregnancy-related causes each year, more than 90 percent of them in the Third World.
- 100,000 women die each year from unsafe abortions, almost all in the Third World.
- The World Health Organization estimates that seventy million women, most of them Africans, have undergone some form of female circumcision.
- In 1991 bridal dowry disputes led husbands and in-laws to kill more than 5,000 wives in India.
- Approximately 855 million people in the world are illiterate (almost one-sixth of humanity); two-thirds of them are women.
- Of the 1.3 billion persons living in absolute poverty, 70 percent are women.

In South Asia

- One of every eighteen women dies of a pregnancy-related cause.
- More than one of every ten babies dies during delivery.

In Nepal and Bangladesh

- One in every five girls dies before age five.

In India

- Approximately 25 percent of the twelve million girls born each year die by age fifteen.

Point: As difficult as life may be for the vast majority of humanity, it is even more trying for females.

Source: UNICEF, *The State of the World's Children 2000,* Fact Sheets [www.unicef.org/sowc99/facts] and press reports.

---

[1]For the most recent data on refugees, see the UNHCR Web site [www.unhcr.ch].

or Africa, women suffer from endless discrimination that begins even before birth with forced abortions in some countries. Infanticide, the practice of killing newborn girls, is a common rural phenomenon in India and China. Although data are hard to come by, one survey conducted by the Community Services Guild of Madras, India, questioned 1,250 women, and more than half apparently had killed baby daughters. For cultural as well as economic reasons, boys are preferred.[2] Government policies that limit overall family size have had the unintended consequence of encouraging resort to female abortion and infanticide in these circumstances.

Even if a baby girl survives the first few years, life continues to be precarious. As children, girls are fed less than their brothers, often only table scraps. Genital mutilation, a severely damaging ritual often referred to as female circumcision, is widely practiced in parts of Africa. The largest obstacle to advancement of women is lack of educational opportunities. Throughout the Third World, even if girls are allowed to attend school, they are withdrawn sooner than boys so they can carry water, work in the fields, raise younger siblings, and do other domestic chores. In Pakistan where schools are segregated by sex, only one-third are for women, and one-third of those have no building. Almost 90 percent of women over age 25 in Pakistan are illiterate. Women also are provided with less medical care. A 1990 study showed that at the Islamabad Children's Hospital in Pakistan, for example, 71 percent of the babies admitted under the age of two were boys.[3]

Deeply rooted cultural values or prejudices are, of course, not easily changed even when laws are passed to condemn such practices. In some cases, however, laws have been passed that actively discriminate against women. In some African countries there are laws that prohibit women from owning houses. In old age these trials and indignities often become worse. In India a women's identity is so intertwined with that of her husband that if she should outlive him, she is often treated as a nonentity. In some parts of the country women are forced to marry the dead husband's brother so that property stays in the family. Small wonder that one study states that in India half the women age 60 and older are widows, and their mortality rate is three times that of married women the same age.[4]

Such conditions and extreme practices are not commonplace in advanced industrial societies. Yet women still have not achieved equality of opportunity or position in the work place or in other aspects of social life in these countries. Progress has been made on these issues, but only at a very slow pace. One international effort to publicize the problems facing women around the globe has been through UN-sponsored conferences. One held in Beijing, China, in September 1995 aimed to develop a worldwide strategy to advance the situation of women. Parallel to this official conference was a Non-Governmental Organizations Forum on Women that attracted some 35,000 participants, 2,000 organizations, and 4,000 journalists. This gave the forum perhaps even more press coverage than the official conference received.

---

[2]"Born Oppressed," *Washington Post*, February 14, 1993, p. A48.
[3]*Ibid.*
[4]*Ibid.*

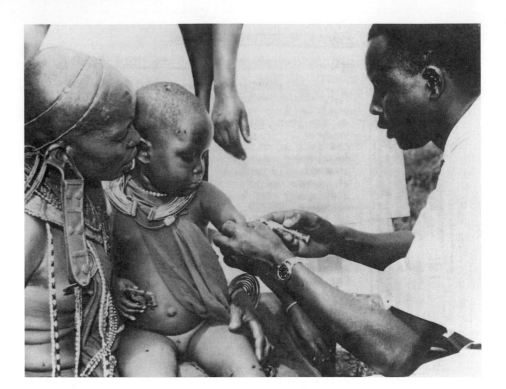

A doctor from UNICEF inoculates a Sudanese child in the arms of her mother.

JUSTICE: THE UNIVERSALITY OF HUMAN RIGHTS VERSUS STATE SOVEREIGNTY

Quite apart from how we may feel about human rights abuses, do we have any obligation to act or any right to do so, particularly if actions conflict with the prerogatives of sovereign states? Indeed, international or transnational actions in support of human rights often directly challenge or violate state sovereignty. For example NATO's war against Serbia over Serbian actions in Kosovo clearly violated state sovereignty since Kosovo was recognized by most all states as being a province of the Yugoslav Republic. Still, injustices offend the human conscience and cry out for corrective action. If justice is understood universally as fairness,[5] is there agreed or common cause for external action on behalf of human rights? Or does their sovereignty (affirmed by Article 2, Section 7 of the United Nations Charter) legally preclude intervention in the domestic affairs of states, however just a cause might be?

To what extent, then, need we be concerned with the **welfare** of other human beings in different cultural, socioeconomic, and geographic settings? Are there grounds for such concerns that go beyond the bounds of a given state or society? Is it enough to be concerned about justice and human rights within one's own country? Should we seek application of universal norms of justice and human rights? Is the human condition properly a global or **supranational** concern?

---

[5] See John Rawls, *A Theory of Justice* (Cambridge, Mass.: Harvard University Press, 1971).

It is an understatement to say that there is no consensus on the answers to these questions. A traditional response is that sovereign states have an exclusive right to address such questions within their own jurisdictions. Others would argue that universal norms (some of which now are part of international law) apply across national borders. The existence of human rights from this perspective concerns international or global society as a whole, not just an internal matter for particular states to manage or handle.

We may be more likely to address human rights or questions of justice in global terms if we see the world as composed of individuals (or tribes, classes, or other groups of people) rather than of states. By contrast if we adopt a more abstract, state-centric view, we may see demands for justice and respect for human rights in other countries as unwarranted intrusions into their domestic affairs.

A further significant complication is the absence of agreement on what human rights *are* (much less on what constitutes justice, either within a particular society or across national boundaries). Efforts have been made to define human rights in formal terms, as in the UN Declaration of Human Rights and in the documents of such regional organizations as the Council of Europe, the Organization for Security and Cooperation in Europe, the European Union, the Organization of American States, and the Organization of African Unity.

Human Rights and the Liberal Tradition

The degree of emphasis on human rights in United States foreign policy has varied from one governmental administration to another and even within administrations. Regardless of the degree of emphasis, the U.S. approach has been criticized because of its distinctly American point of view. The American focus on *individual* rights, a concern deeply embedded in its liberal tradition, tends to overlook **communitarian**, group, or class rights that occupy a more prominent place in other political cultures.

Americans also tend to place more weight on liberty and its relation to order than on the egalitarian and socioeconomic issues emphasized in other countries. Notwithstanding what may be the best of intentions, American foreign policy pronouncements on human rights that project an individually oriented, *libertarian* focus are sometimes taken as yet another imposition of American values on others. The severest critics call it quite simply cultural imperialism. As such, U.S. and other national efforts in the human rights field have often been interpreted as intrusions on the sovereign prerogatives of states not sharing the same perspectives on these issues.

The American understanding of human rights stems in large part from the ideas of seventeenth- and eighteenth-century Enlightenment thinkers and the American historical experience itself. One of the best summations of this thesis is Louis Hartz's now-classic book, *The Liberal Tradition in America*.[6] Hartz notes that the United States, unlike Europe, lacked any direct experience with feudalism and its hierarchic authority structure. European medieval society was dominated by an aristocracy with antidemocratic values. By contrast the new American political culture had embedded within it what Hartz calls "the

---

[6]See Louis Hartz, *The Liberal Tradition in America: An Interpretation of American Political Thought Since the Revolution* (New York: Harcourt, Brace & World, 1955).

libertarian A philosophical position emphasizing individual rights, often preferring specific limits or restraints on government.

liberal idea."[7] What then is the nature of "liberal society" from the American point of view?

The term *liberal* as used by Hartz in its classic meaning should not be confused with contemporary American political usage that places "liberals" and "conservatives" into opposing categories. Although modern-day American social liberals and conservatives differ on many political issues, they are all "liberals" in the classical meaning of the term used by Hartz; that is, they share a belief in **individualism**, a commitment to individuals as human beings worthy of regard in themselves, and not just as part of larger groups or classes.

Individualism built further on notions of equality among individuals; however, this egalitarianism would not readily support a redistribution of property or other socialist design. Alexis de Tocqueville, an early nineteenth-century French observer of the American scene, commented how the egalitarian spirit in the United States existed among individuals who were part of a very individualistic society.

Because the United States had not experienced feudalism in its national history, the country lacked even the vestiges of aristocratic titles and deference to authorities that, by contrast, were integral parts of European societies. Feudalism, of course, had long since given way to preindustrial market capitalism in Europe, but many of the class inequalities of feudalism had survived into the modern era.[8] Notwithstanding actual differences among individuals in wealth and opportunity in the United States, its society and culture exhibited a stronger spirit of equality than in most early nineteenth-century European societies.

To many Americans of Tocqueville's time, government was a necessary evil at best. As he noted, "Whenever the political laws of the United States are to be discussed, it is with the doctrine of sovereignty of the people that we must begin."[9] The best way for people as equal individuals to remain sovereign was to constrain the authority and power of government. In the America that Tocqueville observed, it was the "people"—understood not in some abstract way as society as a whole but rather as individual "citizens" (or groups of them)—who were "the real directing power."[10]

The framers of the U.S. Constitution, educated in the Greek and Roman classics, also drew heavily from the writings of such Enlightenment thinkers as Montesquieu and Locke. Following the late Greek historian Polybius (ca. 203–120 B.C.), Montesquieu developed the idea of *separation of powers* in his *Spirit of the Laws*. This idea would be adopted in the U.S. Constitution as a means of keeping central government from growing too strong at the expense of the governed. Human rights were to be conserved by restricting government's size and involvement in the private affairs of individual citizens.

---

iberalism   A political philosophy with origins in the seventeenth and eighteenth centuries that emphasizes individual liberty, which originally was to be achieved through a minimal state.

[7]That "the absence of feudalism and the presence of the liberal idea" are key factors in "an analysis of American history and politics" is a core thesis in the entire book, first discussed by Hartz on pp. 20–23. It is incorrect to identify the plantation system (with its reliance on slavery as the principal source of labor) merely as a form of feudalism; democratic structures and values, though obviously denied to slaves, were nevertheless characteristic of the rest of society. It was, of course, a contradiction that was understood by many of the men who drafted the U.S. Constitution and Bill of Rights. Slaveholders included such notables as George Washington and Thomas Jefferson.

[8]See Alexis de Tocqueville, *Democracy in America*, Henry Reeve, trans. (New York: Schocken Books, 1961). The first English translations were published in 1835 and 1840, accompanied by introductions written by the English liberal and political philosopher John Stuart Mill. In developing his thesis Louis Hartz draws directly from Tocqueville's observations of early American society.

[9]*Ibid.*, p. 48.

[10]*Ibid.*, pp. 193–94.

Locke advocated an important but relatively minimal role for government at the service of individuals, primarily the protection of their lives, liberties, and property. Consistent with Locke, the U.S. Constitution explicitly prohibits government infringing on individual rights; citizens grant their consent to be governed and do not delegate all their rights to government. Isaiah Berlin and other political writers have called this a "negative" construction of libertarian rights. Liberties are *negatively* maintained by constraining government rather than by empowering it in some *positive* way to serve individual rights. The government role was thus to be as small as possible. The framers of the U.S. Constitution understood that this liberal philosophy of governmental *laissez faire* offered the most consistent and effective means of protecting individual liberty.

In the course of its history, American government in practice would depart from this strict *laissez-faire* philosophy, particularly in the twentieth century. Even the meaning of the term "liberal" in its American context took on a more positive orientation toward governmental action for social and economic purposes. By contrast American **conservatives** have articulated greater skepticism toward governmental activism, preferring to underscore their preference for governmental *laissez faire*.

The key point is that what survived alongside new and expanded governmental attention to social and economic issues was a tendency for Americans to see and deal with human rights in individualist terms. American liberals and conservatives have differed on the *means* by which individuals are to be served and the role government is to play in this regard, but both groups have retained their classical liberal focus on *individuals*. Thus laws passed since the 1930s have government do such things for *individuals* as guarantee a minimum wage, provide for a safer work place, give unemployment and disability compensation, establish retirement pensions, offer job training, make higher-education loans and grants, and provide medical care.

Even advocacy of civil rights in the United States has been based primarily on the Constitutional view that individuals as citizens are entitled to **equal protection** under the law. With few exceptions (e.g., group rights for Native Americans or the right of organized labor to bargain collectively), Americans have been much less comfortable with recognizing rights on a group or class basis. Even collective bargaining by labor unions was understood as a tactical means for representing individual worker interests; groups of individuals were understood in this context as being more effective than individuals standing alone in disputes with managers or owners of firms.

Arguments in favor of *socioeconomic* rights for large groups, classes, or society as a whole have enjoyed far less support in American thinking and practice than claims in favor of individual *political* rights and liberties. Even though the doctrine of **eminent domain** allows public need to supersede individual property rights (e.g., when government takes private property in order to build a highway or school), the law upholds individual rights at the same time by specific provisions to assure just compensation. Such property is also to be taken in a nondiscriminatory way; no individuals are supposed to receive either more favorable or unfair treatment compared to any one else.

Human Rights Across Cultures

It should not be surprising, therefore, that Americans (whether social liberals or conservatives) tend to view human rights through these same individualist and liberal lenses, focusing more on individual rather than collective rights and liberties. Not everyone agrees with this decidedly American perspective. In fact when we examine the issue as it is addressed in different cultures, we find a lack of consensus on *whose* rights and *what* rights are bases for legitimate claims.[11]

Some cultures perceive rights less in relation to individuals than to tribes, classes, or other groups. The state and society as a whole also may claim to have rights. States thus claim to be sovereign with *rights* to exercise complete jurisdiction over their domestic affairs and to be independent or autonomous in the conduct of their foreign affairs. The existence of rights belonging to the world's population taken as a whole—human civilization or humankind (to include generations not yet born)—is a claim quite different from the liberal idea that rights are primarily an individual matter.

Does a tribe, for example, have rights as a tribe that supersede rights claimed by individuals, whether or not they are members of the tribe? Can the same be said of society as a whole in relation to the individuals, tribes, classes, or other groups of which it is composed? For human civilization as a whole? Unfortunately there is no consensus across societies and cultures on this question of *whose* rights are to take priority when they conflict.

Cross-cultural disagreement also exists even on *what* rights are to be considered human rights. Consistent with their focus on individual, civil or political, and legal rights, Americans often fault foreign governments for failure to provide adequate **due process** or equal protection of the laws. This is particularly troublesome for Americans who are arrested while traveling abroad who may not have the same rights to a fair and speedy trial as at home and may suffer mistreatment or what they consider to be cruel and unusual punishments.

A celebrated case in which Singapore administered severe corporal punishment by caning an American youth who was found guilty of vandalism is by no means unique. In any given year more than 2,500 Americans are incarcerated abroad for crimes or alleged crimes, often involving drug use or trade. Complaints concerning abuses of rights claimed by these American citizens in custody abroad are commonplace. The U.S. State Department's Bureau of Consular Affairs monitors the issue, but U.S. consular officials stationed abroad must rely for the most part on persuasion to extricate Americans unjustly implicated or mistreated. The host government and local authorities claim complete jurisdiction or sovereign authority over the acts of individuals committed on their own territory, regardless of the citizenship of these alleged offenders or convicted felons.

This American focus on legal and political rights (especially relating to life, liberty, and property), which puts much less emphasis on claims to social, cultural, and economic rights, is by no means universally shared. For citizens merely to be equal before the law is considered in many other cultures to be too narrow and a rather abstract construction of human rights. If they have human rights sensitivity at all, human welfare or social security in its fullest sense may be more highly valued.

Do people have sufficient food, clothing, shelter, medical care, and other necessities? From this perspective, ignoring or doing little about conditions that promote disease, hunger, and high mortality rates are understood as human rights violations of greater consequence than the more abstract legal and political rights concerning liberty or property. This priority stands quite apart from whether rights are understood in individual terms or as applying to tribes, classes, or other groups in a given society.

---

[11]See Ernst B. Haas, *Global Evangelism Rides Again: How to Protect Human Rights Without Really Trying* (Berkeley, Calif.: University of California Institute of International Studies, 1978).

Culturally Specific Rights and Values

It is sometimes tempting to adopt a moral or **cultural relativism** and assert that rights or any other values can be understood only within their separate cultural contexts. Cultural relativists reject claims to human rights as universal, arguing that such universal claims are artificial constructions. To a relativist values cannot be separated from the cultural context. Who is to say which culture's values should supersede another's?

It is not hard to show that different cultures (and subcultures within a given society) have different ways of thinking about and doing things. For example the time of day and the size and content of different meals considered appropriate varies across cultures and subcultures. How one eats—with one's hands, with chopsticks, or with fork, knife, and spoon—is also quite variable. We refer to such practices as customs or manners. Even though there may be a correct way to act in a particular cultural context, we usually do not understand the values associated with manners or customs as having *moral* content.

Other values in a particular cultural context may be part of its moral code. Thus respecting the elderly as a group or as individuals may be seen as a moral obligation in some cultures but not in others, at least not to the same degree. The same is true for children (see Map 14.1 and Table 14.1). Providing for some minimum level of living may be understood in moral terms as social responsibility in some cultures, whereas others prefer to hold individuals primarily responsible to provide for themselves.

CHILDREN AND HUMAN RIGHTS

The worldwide population of children under the age of fourteen who work full time is estimated to exceed 200 million. Pakistan illustrates the gap between a government's declared commitment to protecting the welfare of its children and its actual policies. According to the Human Rights Commission of Pakistan, some eleven to twelve million children work full time, about half under the age of ten. They are found in virtually every factory, workshop, and field in situations best characterized as indentured servitude. The carpet-making industry is a good example. According to UNICEF, between 500,000 and one million Pakistani children between the ages of four and fourteen work long hours as full-time carpet weavers, accounting for up to 90 percent of the workforce.

A carpet master in the Punjab village of Wasan Pura states that he aggressively pursues boys from poverty-stricken families who are between the ages of seven and ten: "They make ideal employees. Boys at this stage of development are at the peak of their dexterity and endurance, and they're wonderfully obedient—they'd work around the clock if I asked them. I hire them first and foremost because they're economical. For what I'd pay one second-class adult weaver I can get three boys, sometimes four, who can produce first-class rugs in no time." The low cost of child labor allows Pakistan to undersell its foreign competitors that prohibit child labor.

A Pakistani human rights nongovernmental organization known as the Bonded Labor Liberation Front (BLLF) has worked hard since its founding in 1988 against bonded and child labor, liberating some 30,000 adults and children from brick kilns, carpet factories, and farms. It has won some 25,000 court cases against unscrupulous employers.

Point: The plight of children in the Third World at times fails to receive the amount of publicity that other human rights cases receive.

Source: Jonathan Silvers, "Child Labor in Pakistan," *Atlantic Monthly,* February 1996, pp. 79–92.

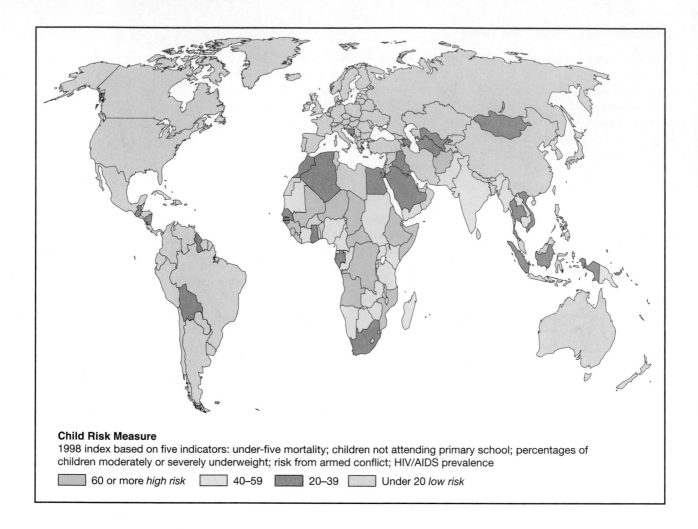

Child Risk Measure

1998 index based on five indicators: under-five mortality; children not attending primary school; percentages of children moderately or severely underweight; risk from armed conflict; HIV/AIDS prevalence

| | 60 or more *high risk* | | 40–59 | | 20–39 | | Under 20 *low risk* |

MAP 14.1   CHILDREN AND ADOLESCENTS AT SPECIAL RISK.

Source: UNICEF, *The State of the World's Children 2000* [www.unicef.org/sowc00/map4.htm].

Thus many societies hold governments, whether democratic or authoritarian in character, responsible for assuring at least a basic level of living and welfare for their people, but this is not a universally held view. In American society, for example, there may be a higher value placed on equality of opportunity rather than on fairness of socioeconomic outcomes. Although Americans disagree among themselves on such matters, many who are well off may not feel there is any individual or societal obligation to assist those who are not. This perspective views charity as properly a voluntary effort undertaken primarily by individuals, not by governments. Value is often placed on the marketplace as the best mechanism for allocating goods and services, a view challenged, of course, by Americans with greater **social-liberal** (or social-democratic) commitments.

TABLE 14.1 AIDS ORPHANS, 1997	
COUNTRY	NUMBER OF ORPHANS[a]
Côte d'Ivoire	240,000
Malawi	270,000
Dem. Rep. of Congo	310,000
Nigeria	350,000
Kenya	350,000
Zimbabwe	360,000
Zambia	360,000
Tanzania	520,000
Ethiopia	700,000
Uganda	1,100,000

[a]Children under fifteen who lost their mother or both parents to AIDS.
Source: UNAIDS/WHO

The American approach to such matters not only differs from most other advanced industrial countries, which expect a larger government role in assuring a greater degree of socioeconomic welfare, but also from many less-developed countries, which have social security systems based on tribal or clan loyalties. The more *laissez-faire* perspective still prevalent in the United States is not in any way typical of the rest of the world.

TOWARD GLOBAL SOCIETY AND VALUES THAT TRANSCEND DIVERSE CULTURES

Although some values do vary across cultures from one society to another, does this mean that *all* values are dependent on certain societal or cultural contexts? Do any values apply to human beings or humanity as a whole independently of cultural context?

Students of philosophy observe that if we really believe in a strict cultural relativism—that values and rights are only to be defined by separate cultures and can have no independent standing of their own—then we are saying in effect that there is no such thing as morality or ethics. Can morality, ethical principles, and human rights really be said to exist if they can be changed so readily within and across cultures and subcultures? Is there no basis independent of a given society or culture for moral or ethical standards of behavior?

One significant problem with moral or cultural relativism is that it gives us no universal basis for condemning atrocities and such human tragedies as the Holocaust. Just because eliminating the Jews as a people may have been considered legitimate within a Nazi political subculture, this belief did not make it right. Even if we have difficulty agreeing on many other values, *genocide* is so offensive to the human spirit that it is condemned as mass murder on universal, not just on cultural grounds. Any rational human being, regardless of cultural origin, would understand the immorality of such atrocities.

What about a religious basis for universal human rights? Islam, Christianity, Judaism, Hinduism, Buddhism, and other religions do not just limit themselves to their followers but frequently also make universally applicable moral claims. As a practical matter rejection of religion by some and the absence of theological consensus even among the followers of various religious groups prevent us from using particular religions as the solitary bases for common, world wide acceptance of human rights and other moral claims.

Instead many writers have tried to identify secular bases for their universalist positions. The eighteenth-century German philosopher Immanuel Kant identified what he called **categorical imperatives** or absolute obligations that he argued had applicability to all reasoning human beings, regardless of religious or other cultural differences. Thus according to Kant we should follow only those maxims that we would be willing to make into universal laws. This "categorical imperative" binds all human beings. Regardless of cultural or religious identity, rational human beings would not want to legitimize murder, lying, stealing, or other forms of dishonesty by making them into universal "laws." Even though human beings engage in such activities, they cannot be considered right by rational human beings in any cultural context.

genocide   Mass murder of a people typically because of their racial, ethnic, religious or other, particular identity.

Children behind a barbed wire fence at the Nazi concentration camp in Auschwitz.

In short a difference is recognized between how human beings *should* act and how they *do* act. Kant also understood as universal the obligation to treat human beings as ends worthy in themselves, not just as means to other ends. From the Kantian perspective this categorical imperative is also universally binding as a moral or ethical guide to behavior, even though it too is often violated. Again, even though the actual conduct of human beings deviates from these norms or maxims, they are not any less morally binding. According to Kant human beings have a duty to follow those ethical principles that are discoverable through their rational faculties.

Kant was not the only writer to provide a secular basis for universal norms of right conduct. The nineteenth-century English **utilitarians** Jeremy Bentham and John Stuart Mill argued that we should act in accordance with the maxim of assuring the greatest good (or greatest happiness) for the greatest number. Utilitarians take this abstract principle and apply it to a wide range of human circumstances, including a defense of liberty and other human rights as representing the greatest good for the greatest number.

The seventeenth-century English writer John Locke reasoned that human beings have certain **natural rights** to life, liberty, and property, which they surrender only as part of a **social contract**. The notion among social-contract theorists that, quite apart from cultural context, human beings have rights as part of their nature obviously provides another secular ground for making universalist moral claims. To Locke (and to Thomas Jefferson who followed Locke's lead), human rights are thus part of human nature. The citizenry or people who empower governments in the first place must therefore strictly limit the authority of governments to abridge them. In fact governments are created in part to guarantee certain **civil rights**, which are those rights that individuals have as members of the societies to which they belong.

Locke and Jefferson clearly put particular emphasis on individual liberties, although another social-contract theorist, the eighteenth-century French-Swiss writer Jean-Jacques Rousseau, placed relatively greater emphasis on equality and on the obligations to one's community. In his "Discourse on the Origin of Inequality," Rousseau found fault with the division of property among individuals, believing it to be the source of much that is wrong in society. That "the fruits of the earth belong to all and the earth to no one" is at once egalitarian and communitarian, a universalist moral.

At the same time, in his *Social Contract* Rousseau argues in favor of liberty, lamenting that "man is born free" but that "everywhere he is in chains." Rousseau's thoughts on such matters are more complex, of course, than merely providing an endorsement of liberty and equality. He sees human beings as part of a larger community or society in which decisions are to serve the "general will" or interest of society as a whole, rather than the particular wills or interests of certain individuals.

The important point for this discussion, however, is that some human rights advocates in Europe and elsewhere have been influenced by this mode of thought. They have tended to offer a vision of a just world society based more on egalitarian and communitarian values than is present in the more individualist, Lockean mode of thought. John Rawls, a present-day theorist in the social-contract tradition, comes closer to Rousseau in his focus on the equity or fairness we would expect in a just society. If human beings did not know in advance how they would fare, what rules would they establish to assure fair or just outcomes?[12]

The lack of intellectual agreement among social-contract theorists, utilitarians, Kantians, and others who think about values in universal terms is part of the global confusion on such matters. This lack of consensus on human rights—how we are to understand rights and values and what we are to do about them—underlies the global debate on what commitments and obligations we have to fellow human beings throughout the world. Disagreement on what and whose human rights ought to be recognized hinders the construction of a just world society.

From Theory to Fact

English, French, and American theories of rights, developed in the seventeenth and eighteenth centuries as part of liberal revolutions then underway in these societies, remain important as philosophical underpinnings of present-day, global concerns about justice and human rights. The idea of agreeing on principles of human rights and then declaring them as binding obligations is also consistent with a *positivist* view. From this perspective, whether or not rights exist as part of human nature, their existence as *civil rights* can be declared as a positive act. Indeed, when states ratify treaties to this effect, human rights become binding as part of international law.

The idea of constraining government authority by the positive assertion of rights is contained in the English *Magna Carta* (1215), by which the English nobility set limits on their own monarch. The English civil war of the 1640s was followed by a period of turmoil that finally resulted in Parliament's restoration of a constitutional (or limited) monarchy in 1688, proclaiming an English Bill of Rights in 1689. The American understanding of rights was profoundly influenced by the British experience in general and English and Scottish writers in particular. The Declaration of Independence (1776) and the addition of a Bill of Rights to those rights specified in the original draft of the U.S. Constitution underscored an American commitment to the civil rights and liberties of individuals.

Following in this liberal tradition, a Universal Declaration of the Rights of Man was proclaimed in 1789 by the French revolutionary National Assembly. The eighteenth-century English writer Thomas Paine, who was widely read by Americans at the time, provided an eloquent defense of the French position on human rights.[13] In doing so he directly contradicted the conservative Edmund Burke, then a member of Parliament, who saw the French Revolution as dangerous in the extreme. Paine justified French claims by expounding a theory of natural human rights. Going beyond individual rights and liberties, Paine also provided justification for egalitarian and communitarian claims.

The Universal Declaration of Human Rights (1948) included in this chapter and subsequent efforts to codify human rights as treaty obligations owe much to an historical legacy of constitutional liberalism in which governments were

positivism   The concept that law is what lawmakers, following constitutional procedures, define it to be.

---

[12]See Rawls, *A Theory of Justice.*

[13]Thomas Paine published *Rights of Man* in two parts in 1791 and 1792.

◇ MAGNA CARTA (1215) ◇

His barons and members of clergy in revolt over costly, unsuccessful military ventures and other grievances, England's King John finally agreed to grant them certain rights in a formal document written in Latin and known as *Magna Carta,* which he signed in the year 1215. Most of its sixty-three articles deal with issues important at the time—for example, provision for "standard measures of wine, ale, and corn" or prohibition against taking "wood for our castle, or for any other purpose, without the consent of the owner."

Included among the clauses in this selection, however, are a few that have had lasting significance as part of the foundation of rights and liberties that have been reaffirmed in succeeding centuries and in other countries around the world. Rights to trial, due process of law, and equitable punishment for offenses are among those addressed. Importantly, these rights were not just reserved to a few, but were extended to subjects throughout the kingdom.

John, by the grace of God King of England, Lord of Ireland, Duke of Normandy and Aquitaine, and Count of Anjou, to his archbishops, abbots, earls, barons, justices, foresters, sheriffs, stewards, servants, and to all his officials and loyal subjects, Greeting.

Know that before God . . .

(1) We have granted . . . that the English Church shall be free, and shall have its rights undiminished, and its liberties unimpaired. . . .

(2) The city of London shall enjoy all its ancient liberties and free customs, both by land and water. We also will and grant that all other cities, boroughs, towns, and ports shall enjoy all their liberties and free customs. . . .

(3) Ordinary lawsuits shall not follow the royal court around, but shall be held in a fixed place. . . .

(4) For a trivial offense, a free man shall be fined only in proportion to the degree of his offense, and for a serious offense correspondingly. . . .

(5) Earls and barons shall be fined only by their equals, and in proportion to the gravity of their offense. . . .

(6) If a free man dies intestate [that is, without a will], his movable goods are to be distributed by his next-of-kin and friends, under the supervision of the Church. The rights of his debtors are to be preserved. . . .

(7) In future no official shall place a man on trial upon his own unsupported statement, without producing credible witnesses to the truth of it. . . .

(8) No free man shall be seized or imprisoned, or stripped of his rights or possessions, or outlawed or exiled, or deprived of his standing in any other way, nor will we proceed with force against him, or send others to do so, except by the lawful judgment of his equals or by the law of the land.

(9) To no one will we sell, to no one deny or delay right or justice. . . .

(10) We will appoint as justices, constables, sheriffs, or other officials, only men that know the law of the realm and are minded to keep it well. . . .

(11) To any man whom we have deprived or dispossessed of lands, castles, liberties, or rights, without the lawful judgments of his equals, we will at once restore these. . . .

(12) All fines that have been given to us unjustly and against the law of the land, and all fines that we have exacted unjustly, shall be entirely remitted. . . .

(13) All these customs and liberties that we have granted shall be observed in our kingdom in so far as concerns our own relations with our subjects. Let all men of our kingdom, whether clergy or laymen, observe them similarly in their relations with their own men. . . .

(14) It is accordingly our wish and command that the English Church shall be free, and that men in our kingdom shall have and keep all these liberties, rights, and concessions, well and peaceably in their fullness and entirety for them and their heirs, of us and our heirs, in all things and all places forever. . . .

Given by our hand in the meadow that is called Runnymede, between Windsor and Staines, on the fifteenth day of June in the seventeenth year of our reign [that is, 1215 A.D.].

DECLARATION OF THE RIGHTS OF MAN AND OF CITIZENS (1789)

The liberal character of the French Revolution at its outset is captured in this document. Reflecting a continental European tradition, the list of rights goes beyond individual liberties to focus on equality, adding a communal dimension. Thomas Paine's *Rights of Man* (1791), written in opposition to Edmund Burke's criticisms of the French Revolution, actively promoted these ideas in the United States as well as in England.

. . . The National Assembly doth recognise and declare . . . the following sacred rights of men and of citizens:

(1) Men are born, and always continue, free and equal in respect of their rights. Civil distinctions, therefore, can be founded only on public utility.

(2) The end of all political associations is the preservation of the natural and imprescriptable rights of man; and these rights are liberty, property, security, and resistance of oppression.

(3) The nation is essentially the source of all sovereignty; nor can any individual, or any body of men, be entitled to any authority which is not expressly derived from it.

(4) Political liberty consists in the power of doing whatever does not injure another. The exercise of the natural rights of every man, has no other limits than those which are necessary to secure to every other man the free exercise of the same rights; and these rights are determinable only by the law.

(5) The law ought to prohibit only actions hurtful to society. What is not prohibited by the law should not be hindered; nor should anyone be compelled to that which the law does not require.

(6) The law is an expression of the will of the community. All citizens have a right to concur, either personally or by their representatives, in its formation. It should be the same to all, whether it protects or punishes; and all being equal in its sight, are equally eligible to all honours, places, and employments, according to their different abilities, without any other distinction than that created by their virtue and talents.

(7) No man should be accused, arrested, or held in confinement, except in cases determined by the law, and according to the forms which it has prescribed. All who promote, solicit, execute, or cause to be executed, arbitrary orders, ought to be punished, and every citizen called upon, or apprehended by virtue of the law, ought immediately to obey, and renders himself culpable by resistance.

(8) The law ought to impose no other penalties but such as are absolutely and evidently necessary; and no one ought to be punished, but in virtue of a law promulgated before the offence, and legally applied.

(9) Every man being presumed innocent till he has been convicted, whenever his detention becomes indispensable, all rigour to him, more than is necessary to secure his person, ought to be provided against by the law.

(10) No man ought to be molested on account of his opinions, not even on account of his religious opinions, provided his avowal of them does not disturb the public order established by the law.

(11) The unrestrained communication of thoughts and opinions being one of the most precious rights of man, every citizen may speak, write, and publish freely, provided he is responsible for the abuse of this liberty, in cases determined by the law.

(12) A public force being necessary to give security to the rights of men and of citizens, that force is instituted for the benefit of the community and not for the particular benefit of the persons to whom it is intrusted.

(13) A common contribution being necessary for the support of the public force, and for defraying the other expenses of government, it ought to be divided equally among the members of the community, according to their abilities.

(14) Every citizen has a right, either by himself or his representative, to a free voice in determining the necessity of public contributions, the appropriation of them, and their amount, mode of assessment, and duration.

(15) Every community has a right to demand of all its agents an account of their conduct.

(16) Every community in which a separation of powers and a security of rights is not provided for, wants a constitution.

(17) The right to property being inviolable and sacred, no one ought to be deprived of it, except in cases of evident public necessity, legally ascertained, and on condition of a previous just indemnity.

 ## THE U.S. BILL OF RIGHTS (1791)

The English Bill of Rights was composed in 1689, a year after William and Mary assumed the crown upon Parliament's invitation in what is commonly referred to as the Glorious (and bloodless) Revolution. The monarchy, however, was subject to certain limitations set down by Parliament, which had at last established its supremacy. Moreover, the civil and political rights of Englishmen that had evolved since Magna Carta were reaffirmed in this document. As British subjects prior to the revolution of 1776–83, the American constitutional framers brought this liberal English civil and political rights tradition to their deliberations, incorporating constitutional limitations on governing authority.

Thomas Jefferson and others lobbied for the addition of a Bill of Rights to the U.S. Constitution, which was ratified and went into effect in 1789. In addition to these first ten amendments are excerpts of three others ratified after the U.S. Civil War and three more ratified in the twentieth century as a more inclusive statement of civil rights and liberties to which American citizens as individuals are constitutionally entitled.

(1) Congress shall make no law respecting an establishment of religion, or prohibiting the free exercise thereof; or abridging the freedom of speech, or of the press; or the right of the people peaceably to assemble, and to petition the Government for a redress of grievances.

(2) A well regulated Militia, being necessary to the security of a free State, the right of the people to keep and bear Arms, shall not be infringed.

(3) No Soldier shall, in time of peace be quartered in any house, without the consent of the Owner, nor in time of war, but in a manner to be prescribed by law.

(4) The right of the people to be secure in their persons, houses, papers, and effects, against unreasonable searches and seizures, shall not be violated, and no Warrants shall issue, but upon probable cause, supported by Oath or affirmation, and particularly describing the place to be searched, and the persons or things to be seized.

continued

(5) No person shall be held to answer for a capital, or otherwise infamous crime, unless on a presentment or indictment of a Grand Jury, except in cases arising in the land or naval forces, or in the Militia, when in actual service in time of War or public danger; nor shall any person be subject for the same offence to be twice put in jeopardy of life or limb; nor shall be compelled in a criminal case to be a witness against himself, nor be deprived of life, liberty, or property, without due process of law; nor shall private property be taken for public use, without just compensation.

(6) In all criminal prosecutions, the accused shall enjoy the right to a speedy and public trial, by an impartial jury of the State and district wherein the crime shall have been committed, which district shall have been previously ascertained by law, and to be informed of the nature and cause of the accusation; to be confronted with the witnesses against him; to have compulsory process for obtaining witnesses in his favor, and to have the assistance of Counsel for his defence.

(7) In Suits at common law, where the value in controversy shall exceed twenty dollars, the right of trial by jury shall be preserved, and no fact tried by jury, shall be otherwise re-examined in any Court of the United States, than according to the rules of the common law.

(8) Excessive bail shall not be required, nor excessive fines imposed, nor cruel and unusual punishments inflicted.

(9) The enumeration in the Constitution, of certain rights, shall not be construed to deny or disparage others retained by the people.

(10) The powers not delegated to the United States by the Constitution, nor prohibited by it to the States, are reserved to the States respectively, or to the people.

* * *

(13) [1865] . . . Neither slavery nor involuntary servitude, except as a punishment for crime whereof the party shall have been duly convicted, shall exist within the United States, or any place subject to their jurisdiction. . . .

(14) [1868] . . . All persons born or naturalized in the United States, and subject to the jurisdiction thereof, are citizens of the United States and of the State wherein they reside. No State shall make or enforce any law which shall abridge the privileges or immunities of citizens of the United States; nor shall any State deprive any person of life, liberty, or property, without due process of law; nor deny to any person within its jurisdiction the equal protection of the laws. . . .

(15) [1870] . . . The right of citizens of the United States to vote shall not be denied or abridged by the United States or by any State on account of race, color, or previous condition of servitude. . . .

(19) [1920] . . . The right of citizens of the United States to vote shall not be denied or abridged by the United States or by any State on account of sex. . . .

(24) [1964] . . . The right of citizens of the United States to vote . . . shall not be denied or abridged by the United States, or any State by reason of failure to pay any poll tax or other tax.

(26) [1971] . . . The right of citizens of the United States, who are eighteen years of age or older, to vote shall not be denied or abridged by the United States or by any State on account of age.

constrained and citizen rights were declared. On this and following pages a few of these are presented. Because of their global influence in the nineteenth and twentieth centuries, this bedrock of predominantly Anglo-American and French ideas has provided the foundation for the universal declaration and international conventions on human rights promulgated since 1945.

Whether or not we are satisfied with one or another of the intellectual justifications that have been offered for the universality of human rights in Kantian, natural, utilitarian, religious or other terms, we should take note of several positivist constructions since the end of World War II. These are part of a growing body of human rights principles, some of which have the binding character of international law. Consistent with its preamble, Articles 1 and 55 of the United Nations Charter (1945) established the principle of "universal respect for, and observance of human rights and fundamental freedoms for all without distinction as to race, sex, language, or religion." Many of these rights were also specified in the Universal Declaration on Human Rights, passed by the United Nations General Assembly in 1948.

The declaration did not establish these specified rights in international law with the binding force of a treaty. Some have argued, however, that the declaration did give formal recognition to rights as they have come to be accepted in practice and thus have become in effect part of **customary international law**. Whatever the outcome of this argument among international lawyers, what is most important for our purposes in this chapter is that by vote of the UN General Assembly, sovereign states formally acknowledged the legitimacy of human rights as *universal* rights.

Former American Ambassador to the UN Eleanor Roosevelt, a principal architect and advocate of the universal declaration, joined with others in seeking to legitimize the idea that rights exist independently of particular sovereign states and their respective societies. Not surprisingly, given the dominant position of the United States in world politics at the time, the declaration conformed more to American and other Western preferences for individual, political rights in the liberal tradition and gave relatively less emphasis to communitarian and socioeconomic interpretations of human rights.

Nevertheless six of the thirty articles in the universal declaration did address such socioeconomic and cultural rights, but even these were cast largely in individual rather than collective terms.[14] Further specification of these rights was contained in two 1966 covenants that entered into force in 1976—one for civil and political rights and the other for economic, social, and cultural rights. Reference in these later documents to "peoples" indicated some acceptance that rights could be understood in terms of collectivities, not just individuals.

In any event these two covenants, built as they are on the foundation of the United Nations Charter and the Universal Declaration of Human Rights, are the main pillars of the UN's human rights "structure." Other documents include the International Covenant on the Elimination of All Forms of Racial Discrimination (1966), the Convention on the Elimination of All Forms of Discrimination Against Women (1979), Convention Against Torture and other Cruel, Inhuman or Degrading Treatment or Punishment (1984), and a Convention on the Rights of a Child (1989). Documents produced by the United Nations Educational, Scientific, and Cultural Organization (UNESCO), the International

---

[14]Articles 22–27 specifically address social security, rights to work and leisure, adequate standard of living, education, and participation in cultural life. Geoffrey Best, "Human Rights as Universal and/or International Norms," paper presented to the London School of Economics, April 29, 1994.

UNIVERSAL DECLARATION OF HUMAN RIGHTS

Adopted by the UN General Assembly Resolution 217A (III) of 10 December 1948

Preamble

Whereas recognition of the inherent dignity and of the equal and inalienable rights of all members of the human family is the foundation of freedom, justice and peace in the world,

Whereas disregard and contempt for human rights have resulted in barbarous acts which have outraged the conscience of mankind, and the advent of a world in which human beings shall enjoy freedom of speech and belief and freedom from fear and want has been proclaimed as the highest aspiration of the common people,

Whereas it is essential, if man is not to be compelled to have recourse, as a last resort, to rebellion against tyranny and oppression, that human rights should be protected by the rule of law,

Whereas it is essential to promote the development of friendly relations between nations,

Whereas the peoples of the United Nations have in the Charter reaffirmed their faith in fundamental human rights, in the dignity and worth of the human person and in the equal rights of men and women and have determined to promote social progress and better standards of life in larger freedom,

Whereas Member States have pledged themselves to achieve, in cooperation with the United Nations, the promotion of universal respect for and observance of human rights and fundamental freedoms,

Whereas a common understanding of these rights and freedoms is of the greatest importance for the full realization of this pledge,

Now, therefore,

The General Assembly,

Proclaims this Universal Declaration of Human Rights as a common standard of achievement for all peoples and all nations, to the end that every individual and every organ of society, keeping this Declaration constantly in mind, shall strive by teaching and education to promote respect for these rights and freedoms and by progressive measures, national and international, to secure their universal and effective recognition and observance, both among the peoples of Member States themselves and among the peoples of territories under their jurisdiction.

Article 1

All human beings are born free and equal in dignity and rights. They are endowed with reason and conscience and should act towards one another in a spirit of brotherhood.

Article 2

Everyone is entitled to all the rights and freedoms set forth in this Declaration, without distinction of any kind, such as race, colour, sex, language, religion, political or other opinion, national or social origin, property, birth or other status.

Furthermore, no distinction shall be made on the basis of the political, jurisdictional or international status of the country or territory to which a person belongs, whether it be independent, trust, non-self-governing or under any other limitation of sovereignty.

Article 3

Everyone has the right to life, liberty and security of person.

Article 4

No one shall be held in slavery or servitude; slavery and the slave trade shall be prohibited in all their forms.

Article 5

No one shall be subjected to torture or to cruel, inhuman or degrading treatment or punishment.

Article 6

Everyone has the right to recognition everywhere as a person before the law.

Article 7

All are equal before the law and are entitled without any discrimination to equal protection of the law. All are entitled to equal protection against any discrimination in violation of this Declaration and against any incitement to such discrimination.

Article 8

Everyone has the right to an effective remedy by the competent national tribunals for acts violating the fundamental rights granted him by the constitution or by law.

Article 9

No one shall be subjected to arbitrary arrest, detention or exile.

Article 10

Everyone is entitled in full equality to a fair and public hearing by an independent and impartial tribunal, in the determination of his rights and obligations and of any criminal charge against him.

Article 11

1. Everyone charged with a penal offence has the right to be presumed innocent until proved guilty according to law in a public trial at which he has had all the guarantees necessary for his defence.

2. No one shall be held guilty of any penal offence on account of any act or omission which did not constitute a penal offence, under national or international law, at the time when it was committed. Nor shall a heavier penalty be imposed than the one that was applicable at the time the penal offence was committed.

Article 12

No one shall be subjected to arbitrary interference with his privacy, family, home or correspondence, nor to attacks upon his honour and reputation. Everyone has the right to the protection of the law against such interference or attacks.

Article 13

1. Everyone has the right to freedom of movement and residence within the borders of each State.

2. Everyone has the right to leave any country, including his own, and to return to his country.

Article 14

1. Everyone has the right to seek and to enjoy in other countries asylum from persecution.

2. This right may not be invoked in the case of prosecutions genuinely arising from non-political crimes or from acts contrary to the purposes and principles of the United Nations.

Article 15

1. Everyone has the right to a nationality.

2. No one shall be arbitrarily deprived of his nationality nor denied the right to change his nationality.

continued

Article 16

1. Men and women of full age, without any limitations due to race, nationality or religion, have the right to marry and to found a family. They are entitled to equal rights as to marriage, during marriage and at its dissolution.
2. Marriage shall be entered into only with the free and full consent of the intending spouses.
3. The family is the natural and fundamental group of society and is entitled to protection by society and the State.

Article 17

1. Everyone has the right to own property alone as well as in association with others.
2. No one shall be arbitrarily deprived of his property.

Article 18

Everyone has the right to freedom of thought, conscience and religion; this right includes freedom to change his religion or belief, and freedom, either alone or in community with others and in public or private, to manifest his religion or belief in teaching, practice, worship and observance.

Article 19

Everyone has the right to freedom of opinion and expression; this right includes freedom to hold opinions without interference and to seek, receive and impart information and ideas through any media and regardless of frontiers.

Article 20

1. Everyone has the right to freedom of peaceful assembly and association.
2. No one may be compelled to belong to an association.

Article 21

1. Everyone has the right to take part in the government of his country, directly or through freely chosen representatives.
2. Everyone has the right to equal access to public service in his country.
3. The will of the people shall be the basis of the authority of government; this will shall be expressed in periodic and genuine elections which shall be by universal suffrage and shall be held by secret vote or by equivalent free voting procedures.

Article 22

Everyone, as a member of society, has the right to social security and is entitled to realization, through national effort and international co-operation and in accordance with the organization and resources of each State, of the economic, social and cultural rights indispensable for his dignity and the free development of his personality.

Article 23

1. Everyone has the right to work, to free choice of employment, to just and favourable conditions of work and to protection against unemployment.
2. Everyone, without any discrimination, has the right to equal pay for equal work.
3. Everyone who works has the right to just and favourable remuneration ensuring for himself and his family an existence worthy of human dignity, and supplemented, if necessary, by other means of social protection.
4. Everyone has the right to form and to join trade unions for the protection of his interests.

Article 24

Everyone has the right to rest and leisure, including reasonable limitation of working hours and periodic holidays with pay.

Article 25

1. Everyone has the right to a standard of living adequate for the health and well-being of himself and of his family, including food, clothing, housing and medical care and necessary social services, and the right to security in the event of unemployment, sickness, disability, widowhood, old age or other lack of livelihood in circumstances beyond his control.

2. Motherhood and childhood are entitled to special care and assistance. All children, whether born in or out of wedlock, shall enjoy the same social protection.

Article 26

1. Everyone has the right to education. Education shall be free, at least in the elementary and fundamental stages. Elementary education shall be compulsory. Technical and professional education shall be made generally available and higher education shall be equally accessible to all on the basis of merit.

2. Education shall be directed to the full development of the human personality and to the strengthening of respect for human rights and fundamental freedoms. It shall promote understanding, tolerance and friendship among all nations, racial or religious groups, and shall further the activities of the United Nations for the maintenance of peace.

3. Parents have a prior right to choose the kind of education that shall be given to their children.

Article 27

1. Everyone has the right freely to participate in the cultural life of his community, to enjoy the arts and to share in scientific advancement and its benefits.

2. Everyone has the right to the protection of the moral and material interests resulting from any scientific, literary or artistic production of which he is the author.

Article 28

Everyone is entitled to a social and international order in which the rights and freedoms set forth in this Declaration can be fully realized.

Article 29

1. Everyone has duties to the community in which alone the free and full development of his personality is possible.

2. In the exercise of his rights and freedoms, everyone shall be subject only to such limitations as are determined by law solely for the purpose of securing due recognition and respect for the rights and freedoms of others and of meeting the just requirements of morality, public order and the general welfare in a democratic society.

3. These rights and freedoms may in no case be exercised contrary to the purposes and principles of the United Nations.

Article 30

Nothing in this Declaration may be interpreted as implying for any State, group or person any right to engage in any activity or to perform any act aimed at the destruction of any of the rights and freedoms set forth herein.

Labor Organization (ILO), the World Health Organization (WHO), and other specialized agencies have contributed directly and indirectly to the corpus of this emergent UN human rights regime. See Table 14.2 for a list of documentary sources that specify human rights.

TABLE 14.2	SELECTED DOCUMENTS DEFINING A GLOBAL HUMAN RIGHTS REGIME
1948	Universal Declaration of Human Rights
1948	Convention on the Prevention and Punishment of the Crime of Genocide

1949	Geneva Conventions for
	    Amelioration of the Condition of the Wounded and Sick Members of
	        Armed Forces in the Field
	    Amelioration of the Condition of Wounded, Sick and Shipwrecked
	        Members of Armed Forces at Sea
	    Treatment of Prisoners of War
	    Protection of Civilian Persons in Time of War

1951	Convention Relating to the Status of Refugees
1966	International Convention of Civil and Political Rights
1966	International Convention on Social and Cultural Rights
1966	International Convention on the Elimination of All Forms of Racial Discrimination

1977	Protocols to the Geneva Conventions (see 1949 above)
	    Protection of Victims of International Armed Conflicts
	    Non-International Armed Conflicts

1979	Convention on the Elimination of All Forms of Discrimination Against Women
1984	Convention Against Torture and Other Cruel, Inhuman or Degrading Treatment or Punishment
1989	Convention on the Rights of the Child

Machinery for Human Rights Issues and Cases

Sovereign states have jealously guarded their legal jurisdiction and have been very reluctant to surrender such authority to international institutions on all types of cases including human rights. A Permanent Court of International Justice (PCIJ) was established under the League of Nations in 1922 at The Hague in the Netherlands. Its jurisdiction was limited to cases involving states. Legal accountability of individuals was left to the courts of individual states. Germany's invasion of Poland in 1939 marked the *de facto* end of the PCIJ, which was officially disbanded in 1946.

Following World War II a new International Court of Justice (ICJ) or World Court was established at The Hague in the Netherlands as a principal organ of the United Nations organization and successor to the earlier PCIJ. The ICJ also meets to hear only those cases brought voluntarily by states agreeing to submit to its jurisdiction. Moreover the ICJ does not have jurisdiction in cases involving individuals; the ICJ's jurisdiction thus fully respects the sovereignty of states.

Even the Universal Declaration of Human Rights has been viewed with a certain degree of skepticism. It was easy to agree on high principles when the matter

Practicing World Politics

The Internet: Checking Out Some Web Sites on International Jurisprudence

A principal organ of the United Nations organization, the International Court of Justice at The Hague in the Netherlands [www.icj-cij.org] contains basic documents, the current docket, and decisions of the Court. The United Nations main page [www.un.org] provides access to human rights and international criminal tribunal reports. In particular, see the UN High Commissioner on Human Rights [www.unhchr.org].

Founded in 1952, the International Commission of Jurists in Geneva [www.ICJ.org] is a nongovernmental organization site that advocates the rule of law, promotes protection of human rights, and has consultative status with the United Nations Economic and Social Council, the UN Educational, Scientific, and Cultural Organization (UNESCO), the Organization of African Unity, and the Council of Europe. For reports of progress on human rights in regional contexts, see also the Council of Europe [www.coe.fr] and more specifically its human rights pages [www.dhdirhr.coe.fr], the European Union [europa.eu.int], the Organization for Security and Cooperation in Europe [www.osce.org], the Organization of American States in Washington, D.C. [www.oas.org], and the Organization of African Unity in Addis Ababa, Ethiopia [www.oau.oua.org].

of enforcement was left unresolved. Nowhere in the Declaration was it mandated that a member state had the right to intervene in another country's affairs to stop human rights abuses; state sovereignty still ruled.

Individual accountability for such crimes against the law of nations as piracy on the high seas was established in international legal practice centuries ago. It was left, however, to the domestic courts of states to try pirates and other alleged offenders of the law of nations. War crimes trials of individuals following World War II under the International Military Tribunal at Nuremberg, Germany, set an enormously important precedent for the assertion of international jurisdiction over such cases. The Nuremberg Tribunal was given its authority in 1945 by the victorious "Big Four" Allied powers or "united nations" of World War II—the United States, Soviet Union, the United Kingdom, and France—which had just defeated the German Reich and its allies. War crimes trials were also conducted in Tokyo under U.S. occupation authority over Japan.

The Nuremberg Tribunal not only dealt with war crimes ("violations of the laws or customs of war") but also with two new crimes under international law—crimes against peace ("planning, preparation, initiation or waging of a war of aggression"), and crimes against humanity ("murder, extermination, enslavement, deportation, and other inhumane acts committed against any civilian population"). The concept of crimes against humanity was affirmed further when the General Assembly adopted the Convention on the Prevention and Punishment of the Crime of Genocide in December 1948. The

> The most striking development of the last year [of the twentieth century] was the decline of sovereignty as an obstacle to international action in the face of crimes against humanity. Governmental leaders faced a much greater chance of prosecution for these crimes, and in two cases—East Timor and Kosovo—the international community was actually willing to deploy troops, or peacekeepers, to stop these crimes in action.
>
> **Kenneth Roth,**
> *executive director of Human Rights Watch*

IT'S BEEN SAID...

Shown on November 15, 1945, in the dock at the courtroom at Nuremberg during the early months of the year-long trial of the Nazi war criminals, are, from left to right: Herman Goering, Rudolf Hess, Joachim von Ribbentrop, Wilhelm Keitel, and Alfred Rosenberg.

Human rights has become the major article of faith of a secular culture that fears it believes in nothing else. The military campaign in Kosovo depended on the legitimacy of what fifty years of human rights has done to our moral instincts, weakening the presumption of sovereignty, strengthening the presumption in favor of intervention when massacre and deportation become state policy. Do we intervene everywhere or only somewhere? And if we don't intervene everywhere, does that make us hypocrites? And then what price are we prepared to pay?

Michael Ignatieff,
author and professor
Source: New York Review of Books,
May 20, 1999, p. 58.

IT'S BEEN SAID...

convention declared genocide to be a crime under international law and stated that persons charged with genocide shall be tried "by a competent tribunal." After adjournment of the Nuremberg Tribunal, states reassumed first jurisdiction in such matters, but a precedent for international hearing of criminal cases involving individuals had been set.

Calls for new international war crimes trials have occurred from time to time. A number of issues that need to be resolved include the following: How broad should the scope of the court's jurisdiction be? Should the court be established on a regional or global basis? How should the judges be selected? What should be the rules of evidence?[15]

Global horror over atrocities in Bosnia and elsewhere in the former Yugoslavia finally produced enough pressure for war crimes trials to be organized, the first since Nuremberg after World War II. The statute establishing the International Criminal Tribunal for the Former Yugoslavia (ICTY) was adopted by the U.N. Security Council in May 1993. The tribunal was mandated to prosecute persons responsible for serious violations of basic international humanitarian laws (war crimes, crimes against humanity, and genocide). The Tribunal is an independent body consisting of fourteen judges, an Office of the Prosecutor, and staff of more than 850 persons from sixty-nine countries.

---

[15]John F. Murphy, "International Crimes," in Christopher Joyner, ed., *The United Nations and International Law* (Cambridge, England: Cambridge University Press, 1997), p. 380.

A United Nations investigative commission reported to the Security Council in 1994 its findings of "crimes against humanity" that "constitute genocide" in Bosnia.[16] Human rights violations were committed by all sides, but the principal victims were Bosnian Muslims. The report indicated that among the tactics used was rape of women "for the purpose of terrorizing and humiliating them often as part of the policy of 'ethnic cleansing.'" Beyond regrouping and forcing movements of peoples based on their ethnic identities, humiliation of women apparently was part of "a systematic rape" campaign designed to break up Muslim families and communities because of the shame rape victims would carry, particularly in these more traditional Muslim communal settings. Further victimization of innocent rape victims by shunning, ostracizing, or holding them somehow responsible or guilty is common enough in many societies. To use this vulnerability as a calculated tactic in the destruction of a people, however, is what makes mass rape part of an overall program of genocide. In March 1998 the Tribunal's Office of the Prosecutor announced the extension of its jurisdiction over events also occurring during the armed conflict in Kosovo. Trials began two years later.

A major weakness of the Tribunal has been the fact that it has no constabulary to enforce its indictments. It must rely on the voluntary cooperation of states, including the very governments whose officials it seeks to prosecute. In effect the Tribunal has had to rely on NATO forces to enforce its rulings. In the case of Bosnia, NATO forces were given the authorization, but not the responsibility, for apprehending indicted war criminals. Significantly the June 1999 peace plan to end the war in Kosovo did not give NATO forces a mandate to arrest Milosevic, the president of Serbia and an indicted war criminal.

Nevertheless the Tribunal has gained the grudging respect even of its critics. Since the ICTY's inception more than ninety individuals were indicted with some thirty-five actually involved in legal proceedings. Those found guilty of crimes against humanity received sentences ranging between five and forty years of imprisonment.[17]

Similarly an International Criminal Tribunal for Rwanda (ICTR) was established in Tanzania to prosecute those suspected of committing genocide and other serious human rights violations during Hutu-Tutsi tribal warfare in 1994. Specifically listed offenses include widespread murder of civilians, torture, and mass rape. More than twenty-five indictments have been issued. The first-ever sentencing for the crime of genocide by an international court occurred in 1998. Two individuals, including the former prime minister of Rwanda, were given life sentences.[18]

An international conference in Rome did take a major step forward in 1998 when it formulated as a treaty for signature and ratification a new Statute for an International Criminal Court with global jurisdiction, complementary to national courts, for genocide, war crimes, and crimes against humanity. Gains in criminal accountability before international courts have not been matched, however, by expansion of international jurisdiction for civil cases (as when individuals or corporations sue each other for violations of contracts, torts, and other offenses, or

---

[16]See Paul Lewis, "Word for Word: The Balkan War-Crimes Report," *New York Times,* June 12, 1994.

[17]From www.un.org/icty/glance/fact.htm (dated 22 December 1999).

[18]*Ibid.*

when allowed by domestic law, try to sue or petition governments for redress of grievances). For the most part civil law remains the domain of states exercising jurisdiction within their territorial boundaries.

Regional Human Rights Efforts in Europe

Efforts to build upon the base established by the Universal Declaration have continued within the United Nations, expanding the scope of rights to include social, economic, and cultural concerns that retain—but go well beyond—the liberal, individual commitments embodied in the original declaration. Further specification of rights by treaty (and thus with a firmer basis in international law) has been achieved by states participating on regional bases in the Council of Europe, the Organization for Security and Cooperation in Europe (OSCE), the European Union, and the Organization of American States.

Some of these regional efforts have made substantial progress in the human rights field. Members of the Council of Europe (an international organization formed in 1949 and located in Strasbourg, France) are democratically oriented European states seeking to expand civil society and the rule of law. In 1950 the Council adopted the European Convention for the Protection of Human Rights and Fundamental Freedoms. As an international organization composed of European democracies, the Council oversees the work of an executive agency (the European Commission on Human Rights) and a judicial arm (the European Court of Human Rights), both of which are located in Strasbourg. Only member states or the Commission may actually bring cases before this court. Europeans as individuals, however, may petition the European Commission on Human Rights after exhausting domestic legal remedies. In turn the Commission (or states) may refer such matters to the European Court of Human Rights. Although individuals thus do not have *direct* access to this court, individual cases deemed worthy by the Commission or states belonging to the Council of Europe may be heard. Moreover the European Court of Human Rights not only may award compensation to individuals for damages but also may exercise limited judicial review by requiring states to change domestic laws found in violation of the Convention.

Not to be confused with the Council of Europe and its European Court of Human Rights is the European Union's European Court of Justice (ECJ) located in Luxembourg. In the European Union's legal system, ECJ rulings supersede domestic laws of EU members when these laws are in conflict with EU law. Significantly the ECJ not only hears cases brought by states and EU institutions but also cases brought by or against individuals or corporations (so-called natural or legal persons, respectively). Thus in addition to states and EU institutions, individuals and corporations may take cases directly to the European Court of Justice without having secured the consent of their national authorities. Indeed, its caseload has grown substantially in recent years, ruling on thousands of cases involving contract and other economic issues, some of which have had human rights aspects. International courts in Europe have thus acquired some jurisdiction for certain civil and criminal cases involving persons.

Relying on regional courts and asserting legal arguments and decisions that overrule national courts is mainly a European development. In addition to the Council of Europe and the European Union, the human rights obligations assumed by OSCE member states have been invoked many times since the Act of Helsinki (1975) that specified these rights in the first Conference on Security and

Cooperation in Europe (CSCE). With more than fifty members, the OSCE also includes the United States and Canada and almost all countries in Europe from the Atlantic to the Urals. Review conferences allow an opportunity for the airing of human rights violations and the application of public and private pressures for their correction. During the 1980s, for example, the United States and other Western states used various CSCE review conferences to criticize the USSR and other East European states for human rights violations.

More recently, however, human rights questions are dealt with as part of the OSCE's commitment to the "human dimension." This refers to commitments made by OSCE participating states to ensure full respect for human rights and fundamental freedoms. Since 1990 the OSCE has developed institutions and mechanisms to promote respect for these commitments such as the Office for Democratic Institutions and Human Rights. The current approach of the OSCE is to assist states in living up to their obligations rather than isolating them.

Whether within the OSCE, other international organizational settings, or in bilateral diplomacy, public airing of human rights violations usually contributes very little to correcting these violations. In fact such publicity often contributes to a hardening of the offending state's position lest it lose face in submitting to such public rebuke. China, for example, has been reluctant to change its policies despite foreign criticism. It is true that accusing states may use human rights to score propaganda points against alleged offenders, but this is use of the human rights issue for other purposes.

States and governments genuinely committed to rectifying perceived human rights abuses usually find confidential, behind-the-scenes diplomacy—however forceful—more effective in achieving these ends. Positive incentives for compliance may be offered in these quiet, diplomatic efforts on behalf of human rights. Of course accusing states may also choose to use the threat of public exposure as a negative tactic. It may become necessary to act on the threat, however, when quiet efforts have failed.

In the final analysis the OSCE and its human rights charter can claim at least some degree of credit for changes since the fall of the Berlin Wall in 1989 and the subsequent demise of the Soviet bloc and the Soviet Union itself. Indeed, democratic reforms and human rights assurances offered by the new governments in many of these countries have enabled them to join the Council of Europe with its more developed legal structure for human rights cases. These are modest but still very positive developments that seemed unthinkable just a few years earlier.

Other Regional Human Rights Efforts

Efforts in Latin America and Africa, in contrast to Europe, have been far more modest. Human rights obligations were specified in 1948 as part of inter-American law in the OAS Charter and the American Declaration of the Rights and Duties of Man. The Inter-American Commission on Human Rights was created in 1960, and in 1969 the American Convention on Human Rights established an Inter-American Court of Human Rights.

OAS Charter revision in 1970 gave the Inter-American Commission a greater role in human rights matters, which was underscored by OAS approval in 1979 of a revised statute for the Commission. The Commission engages in human rights education and awareness efforts and receives petitions and complaints, even from private persons; it may publicize human rights violations, but it has no real enforcement authority. For its part the Inter-American Court of Human Rights located in Costa Rica has heard a small number of cases but has not played the decisive role of its European counterparts in carving out authority over member states on human rights matters. Its opinions have tended to be advisory in nature.

The human rights structure of the Organization of African Unity is even less developed. Nevertheless the 1981 African Charter on Human and People's Rights (the "Banjul Declaration") did enter into force in 1986. In addition to individual and collective rights, a list of duties to humanity and to state and society also was prescribed. The mandate to the newly created African Commission on Human and Peoples' Rights was explicitly limited to interpretation, promotion, and protection of human rights; however, no judicial arrangements or enforcement authorities were provided.

Practicing World Politics

The Internet: Checking Out Some Web Sites on Human Rights

In addition to the UN's main page [www.un.org], see the UN's High Commissioners for Human Rights [www.unhchr.ch] and Refugees [www.unhcr.ch], the UN Development Program [www.undp.org], and the United Nations International Children's Emergency Fund [www.unicef.org]. On workers' rights concerning health, safety, working conditions, and child labor, see the International Labor Organization in Geneva [www.ilo.org]. Nongovernmental organizations involved with these subjects include Amnesty International [www.amnesty.org], Human Rights Watch [www.hrw.org], and the American Civil Liberties Union [www.aclu.org]. You might also want to take a look at the journal *Human Rights Review*.

NGOs and Human Rights

Particularly in the post–World War II era, states, international organizations, and nongovernmental organizations have all contributed to raising the international profile of human rights. For some states pointing out human rights violations in another state may be a matter of principle, or it may simply be a way to embarrass a government. At times a state may issue a condemnatory statement due to the efforts of NGOs such as Amnesty International, which relies heavily on global letter-writing campaigns, press releases, and publications to shame governments into releasing political prisoners or shame other states into making good their publicly stated support for human rights.

The origins of Amnesty International date to 1961 when a London lawyer, Peter Benenson, read about a group of students in Portugal who had been arrested for toasting freedom in a restaurant. This event prompted him to launch an "Appeal for Amnesty," calling for the release of all people imprisoned because of their peaceful expression of beliefs, politics, race, religion, or national origin. The campaign caught on and spread to other countries. By the end of 1961 Amnesty International had been formed. Amnesty's initial activities involved letter-writing campaigns on behalf of prisoners of conscience. Groups of volunteers were assigned to a particular prisoner whose fate was closely monitored. Unfortunately few of these letters were ever answered, so in the late 1960s adoption groups were formed at the local level. These groups adopted a particular prisoner, country, or issue and helped with publicity, education, and fund-raising at the grassroots level. Outreach activity included churches, schools, businesses, professional organizations, and labor unions. New members and more financial contributions aided Amnesty's growth. In the early 1980s the number of college campus groups expanded. Today Amnesty International has more than one million members, subscribers, and regular donors in more than 160 countries and territories.

LAND MINES

In Ottawa, Canada, in December 1997, 122 governments signed a treaty banning antipersonnel land mines. Much of the credit for this achievement was due to an alliance of NGOs and sympathetic governments. A major media campaign highlighted the role of land mines in contributing to humanitarian crises. It is estimated that there are 250 million antipersonnel land mines in the arsenals of 108 countries. The major arsenals are in China (110 million), Russia (60–70 million), Byelarus (estimated tens of millions), the United States (11 million), the Ukraine (10 million), Italy (7 million), and India (4–5 million). Some 115 million land mines are currently laid in sixty-eight countries. The cost of buying one land mine is between $3 and $10; the cost of removing one land mine is between $300 and $1,000. It is estimated that 8,000 to 10,000 children are killed or maimed by land mines each year.

Subsequent to the signing of the agreement, the International Campaign to Ban Land Mines (ICBL) was awarded the Nobel Peace Prize. The ICBL is a global network of more than 1,000 NGOs active in more than seventy-five countries. The goal is to prevent the further manufacturing, deployment, and selling of land mines, and eventually removing them from state arsenals. The United States has not signed the treaty, but it also has not produced any land mines since 1997 and has banned exports of these weapons.

Point: The ICBL is a prime example of the persuasiveness if not the power of NGOs.

Source: ICBL, *Land Mine Monitor Report 1999: Toward a Mine-Free World*, available at www.hrw.org/reports/1999; and UNICEF, *The State of the World's Children 2000*, available at www.unicef.org/sowc00/map6.

The largest human rights organization in the United States is Human Rights Watch. The organization was founded in 1978 as Helsinki Watch. Local human rights groups in Moscow, Warsaw, and Prague had been established in the mid-1970s to monitor their governments' compliance with the Helsinki accords. Not surprisingly, they came under pressure from the communist governments and Helsinki Watch was created to provide support for these embattled groups. A few years later Americas Watch was created to monitor human rights abuses in North and South America. The strategy of Human Rights Watch is straightforward—painstaking documentation of abuses and vigorous advocacy in the media and halls of governments and international organizations. As the organization notes: "Our goal is to make governments pay a heavy price in reputation and legitimacy if they violate the rights of their people."[19]

---

[19]From www.hrw.org/about/info/gna.html

Amnesty International is only the best-known NGO working for human rights. Indeed, recent years have seen a veritable explosion in such organizations: 38 in 1950, 72 in 1960, 103 in 1970, 138 in 1980, and 275 in 1990. Not only is the number of groups significant, but also the fact that these NGOs form coalitions and communication networks to link them together continuing from the twentieth into the twenty-first century. The growth of the Internet has certainly facilitated this networking by providing data and information on Web sites. Now anyone can easily access information about the latest advocacy campaigns or learn how to become directly involved in supporting human rights around the globe. These human rights organizations are in turn linked to domestic movements and organizations in countries suffering from human rights abuses.

REFUGEES

Migration and *refugee* issues are no longer the sole concern of midlevel bureaucrats and advocates of human rights; they have become a topic of conversation and negotiation among heads of state. This is because these issues have generated conflict both within and between states, no matter what the underlying cause for an outflow of migrants might happen to be. International migration has implications for sovereignty, stability, and security for a growing number of states. In fact the issue promises to become even more salient due to three political, economic, and environmental trends that cause international migration.

First, with the end of the cold war, barriers to movement were lifted for many people living in former communist states. As the Soviet empire collapsed and independent states came into existence, new minorities were created within these borders who now feel less secure. One option is for minorities to create secessionist movements and demand their own states; another option is to migrate. This scenario is all too familiar to many people living in Africa and South Asia, areas that have been plagued by civil wars.

Second, the huge gap in income and employment opportunities among countries motivates thousands of persons to become economic migrants. Western Europe has been particularly concerned in recent years over the immigration issue. In the 1970s and early 1980s, about 100,000 people left the Warsaw Pact countries for the West for essentially political reasons, and they were welcomed there. But as communism began to collapse, the number of migrants rose dramatically as their motivation became economic as well as political. In 1989 alone 1.2 million people left the former Warsaw Pact states. The economic restructuring and privatization process in the former Soviet Union and Eastern Europe may also increase the number of those who want to migrate. While many people may seek to move to Western Europe, other countries such as Poland may see their own economic reform efforts hampered by a dramatic influx of immigrants.[20] In the developing world there are similar concerns among the so-called economic "Little Tigers" or NICs—newly industrializing countries—in Asia and among the oil producing countries of the Middle East.

migration   The movement of peoples from one country or area to others; *immigration* involves arrivals, *emigration*, departures.

refugees   Persons displaced because of war (usually) or other political or economic causes. Refugees may flee or be forced to leave a country, or they may be internally displaced persons within their own state.

[20]F. Stephen Larrabee, "Down and Out in Warsaw and Budapest: Eastern Europe and East-West Migration," *International Security*, v. 16, no. 4 (Spring 1992): 5–6.

Finally drought, floods, and famines may also stimulate migration. According to one estimate, two million Africans were displaced in the mid-1980s due to drought alone. This does not even take into account refugees created by conflict in such places as Somalia, Rwanda, and Burundi. One can begin to sense the magnitude of the problem.[21]

Most movement is from one developing country to another, however, with the largest refugee flows being in Africa and Asia. Table 14.3 shows numbers of refugees, asylum-seekers, returned refugees (those not yet resettled in their homeland), and internally displaced persons.

In this section we focus on refugees, who can be viewed as one type of immigrant. While a true immigrant is influenced by both push and pull factors such as better options in another country, refugees are unwillingly forced from their homes. The most generally accepted definition of a refugee comes from the United Nations: A refugee is a person who "owing to a well-founded fear of being persecuted for reasons of race, religion, nationality, membership of a particular social group or political opinion, is outside the country of his nationality and is unable, or unwilling to avail himself of the protection of that country."[22]

TABLE 14.3	REFUGEES AND OTHERS OF CONCERN BY REGION, 1998
Asia/Middle East	7,475,000
Africa	6,285,000
Europe	4,222,000[a]
Former Soviet Union/ Eastern Europe	1,477,000
North America	1,305,000
Latin America	102,000
Oceania	80,000
Australia/New Zealand	71,000
TOTAL	21,017,000

[a]Bosnia-Hercegovina accounts for 1,206,700 of the total.

Source: UNHCR, Statistics [www.unhcr.ch].

---

[21]Myron Weiner, "Security, Stability, and International Migration," *International Security*, v. 17, no. 3 (Winter 1992/93): footnote 5.

[22]The definition comes from the 1951 United Nations Convention Relating to the Status of Refugees.

The human cost of civil strife, and the constructive role of the United Nations High Commissioner for Refugees (UNHCR), in Bosnia-Hercegovina.

Thanks to the wonders of modern global communications, refugees trek across our television screens on a regular basis. The report may come from Africa, Asia, Latin America, or Europe, but the image is always the same—men, women, and children trudging down dusty roads, their few possessions on their backs or in horse-drawn carts or dilapidated automobiles and trucks. No matter who the unfortunate inhabitants may be, refugee camps share similar characteristics—smoky cooking fires, endless rows of tents, skinny children with saucer-sized eyes, and long lines of the ill and infirm waiting patiently to see a specialist from organizations like Doctors Without Borders. Most reports include the obligatory thirty-second interview with the representative from the United Nations High Commissioner for Refugees (UNHCR), who once again emphasizes the need for a sustained global response to the latest humanitarian crisis. Other refugees are not so lucky. Some refugees are separated from their families and subjected to armed attacks and exploitation.

The humanitarian response to refugee crises is in part a moral argument. How can the comparatively wealthy of the world sit idly by and watch fellow human beings exist in unspeakable conditions and subject to extreme deprivations? But watching the endless replay of refugee crises and scenes of famine sometimes induces **compassion fatigue**. Eventually television viewers may feel that investing emotion and money in what seems to be an inalterable fact of life on this planet is pointless.

Some refugees are victims of natural disasters such as drought, floods, or typhoons. The fact of the matter is, however, that most refugee crises are not a function of acts of God or weather but of politics. Political turmoil is most often the root cause of the crisis, dictating the type and level of international response. In 1971, for example, ten million East Pakistani refugees fled to India, most not returning until the creation of an independent Bangladesh. The disintegration of the former Yugoslavia displaced some four million people within the former communist state and scattered another half million across Europe. Throughout many other areas of the world men, women, and children flee their homelands because of armed conflict, intimidation, and repression.

Particularly when the political conflict has racial, religious, and ethnic overtones, those who have been expelled from their homeland will find it increasingly difficult to integrate into neighboring host nations or be resettled in distant countries. But thanks to modern means of travel, those refugees with the financial wherewithal have the ability to travel by sea or air to more distant lands. For those who manage to reach their destination, they are often viewed with fear and resentment. Others are kept in a legal limbo.

REFUGEE LIMBO LAND

Ba is a young law student from Abidjan University in the Côte d'Ivoire. In 1994 he arrived at Heathrow Airport in London via Paris, where he immediately applied for political asylum. Ba claimed that he suffered repeated harassment from the police in his country because he belonged to an opposition political party and a student trade union. The British initially kept him in the transit zone at Heathrow and then expelled him to France, the former colonial master of the Côte d'Ivoire. When Ba arrived at Roissy Airport in Paris, he was arrested and taken to another transit area. He was eventually sent back to London where he was once again taken into custody by the British and three weeks later was released after an interview with a customs official who issued him a six-month residence permit—he was one of the lucky ones.

Point: Making it to a country of asylum does not guarantee one will be allowed to stay, despite the justification for fleeing one's homeland.

Source: UNHCR, *Refugees*, No. 101 (1995): 22.

The exodus of refugees is as old as repression. It was not until 1951, however, that the Office of the United Nations High Commissioner for Refugees was established, principally in response to the large number of refugees fleeing the oppression of Eastern European communist regimes. These refugees were resettled and generally integrated into Western states, aided by sympathy for their plight as well as cultural and ethnic affinities. As a result of this experience, international standards concerning the treatment of refugees were adopted and are reflected in the 1951 United Nations Convention Relating to the Status of Refugees.

This convention states that the international community will treat refugees as a distinct category of human rights victims and hence should be accorded special protection. As noted, refugees are defined as people who have been forced for political, racial, or ideological reasons to flee their home countries. The host nation should not compel refugees to return to their homes if doing so would place them in danger of persecution. Furthermore refugees have the right to apply for asylum and be given a chance to plead the political nature of their plight. While their appeal is in process, refugees are to be granted adequate assistance. The convention was essentially written with the European case in mind, but since the United Nations was involved, nods were made toward universalizing these norms.

In the 1960s, however, the focus of international efforts began to shift to the Third World, which had been undergoing the pains of decolonization and wars of national liberation. Compared to later years the reaction of African states and the international community to the displacement of hundreds of thousands of people went relatively smoothly, in part because many African states shared a common colonial experience. Regional norms for the treatment of refugees were embodied in a 1969 Organization of African Unity agreement, and the 1951 Convention added a protocol in 1967.

In the 1970s, however, the size and complexity of the problem dramatically increased in a manner the signatories of the 1951 Convention could not have foreseen. In terms of sheer numbers, little can match the ten million refugees from East Pakistan in 1971. But with the era of decolonization almost over, political conflicts now involved independent Third World states. Developed countries increasingly looked askance at asylum seekers from countries that had achieved independence years before as well as countries with no historical ties to a European state. What did the developed world owe to these people? Were these refugees seeking **political asylum** or were they actually economic refugees or, less charitably, fortune seekers?[23] Could they contribute economically, socially, and culturally to the host nation, or would they simply be a drain on resources?

Such questions and attitudes are found in Europe, which has had to absorb the brunt of refugees resulting from the end-of-cold war fall of communism, but they also resonate in immigration debates in the United States and Canada. Downturns in the business cycle marked by sluggish economic growth rates particularly tend to heighten public awareness of the numbers of refugees and legal or illegal immigrants competing with citizens for employment and other opportunities.

An International Regime for Refugees

As noted, the 1951 Convention was the first international and transnational response to the refugee problem. Since that time basic norms concerning the treatment of refugees have been institutionalized in refugee-receiving nations and also in the complex structure of international and private transnational organizations that attempt to deal with the problem. In other words we can speak of an *international regime* or agreed set of rules for dealing with refugees. As with all such regimes, it requires the support of the major powers that dominate world politics. As such, the norms and programs of the regime effectively cannot run counter to the interests of these key states. The United States, for example, was initially quite suspicious of yielding authority to UNHCR. Over time, however, it has become apparent to most states that the network of international agencies and voluntary organizations is critical if the refugee problem is not going to spin out of control. Unilateral *ad hoc* responses to crisis conditions are deemed unsatisfactory.[24]

Nevertheless the treatment of refugee groups under this international regime varies widely. A number of factors come into play, all of them involving politics:

- Domestic support for certain refugees in the receiving country
- The publicity the refugees receive
- The financial cost incurred by accepting them
- Foreign policy concerns of the receiving country in terms of the country of origin or other interested countries

During the cold war, for example, local conflicts drew in outside powers. These conflicts generated large numbers of refugees in the Horn of Africa, southern Africa, and Central America. The United States and other donor countries responded out of humanitarian concern but also for reasons of national interest and broader foreign policy objectives. As the former U.S. Coordinator for Refugee Affairs stated in 1982, refugee policy helped to counter Soviet expansionism because it could be used to "wean away client states from Soviet domination."[25] Similarly Western Europe welcomed refugees from the Eastern bloc

---

[23]Jean-Pierre Hocke, "Beyond Humanitarianism," in Gil Loescher and Laila Monahan, eds., *Refugees and International Relations* (Oxford, England: Clarendon Press, 1990), pp. 39–40.

[24]Gil Loescher, "Introduction: Refugee Issues in International Relations," in Loescher and Monahan, eds., *Refugees and International Relations*, p. 9.

[25]*Ibid.*, p. 12.

who, by voting with their feet, symbolically demonstrated the bankruptcy of communist regimes in the East. In some cases such as in Central America, support for refugees went beyond humanitarian assistance and a desire to score propaganda points; refugees were armed and sent back to fight their oppressors. In general, therefore, states will be more positively disposed toward involvement in refugee crises if they believe interests and foreign policy objectives are at stake—no surprise to a realist.

The interests of the major donors to UN programs—the United States, Western Europe, Japan, Australia, and Canada—in particular ultimately decide the nature and extent of the international refugee regime. The UNHCR and voluntary transnational organizations therefore are constrained in what they can do given limited resources.[26] Voluntary organizations in an age of instantaneous global communication, however, can help sway domestic public opinion. This was evident in the case of the conflict and resultant creation in 1995 of refugee camps in Rwanda, Africa. Based upon a cold, hard calculation of U.S. national security interests, there was little reason to expect U.S. relief and logistical support to such a country. The American public and leadership, however, were willing to help, in part due to humanitarian concerns and worldwide appeals on the part of international and transnational refugee-relief organizations.

It is not only foreign policy considerations that influence the attitude of potential host and donor countries. Refugees can also be created by regimes that want to rid themselves of political dissidents or other undesirables. This was the case in Vietnam's expulsion of hundreds of thousands of Vietnamese of Chinese origin in the early 1980s as well as Fidel Castro's expulsion of criminals and mentally ill people in 1980 during the Mariel boatlift. Once such an action occurs, states may attempt to score political points such as anticommunist states did by accepting the Vietnamese boat people in the 1980s.[27]

The international refugee regime essentially deals with the appropriate responses expected of states, IOs, and NGOs *after* a crisis has occurred. Indeed, the UNHCR's mandate prohibits it from protesting against the *cause* of refugee outflows, allowing it to respond once refugee flight has happened. Little headway has been made in dealing with the roots of refugee crises, although doing so might help the international community extricate itself from a reactive mode. The problem is evident: To prevent refugee crises may require outside powers to intervene *before* people flee or are expelled from their country; however, any such interference violates the sovereignty of such states.

Quite apart from legal considerations, in the post–cold war era the advanced industrial states have relatively little appetite for intervention. This is the case in particular with the Third World, where the West sees few if any vital interests. Yet it is in the Third World that refugee crises will most likely continue to occur. Not just plagued with drought and famine, the Third World is the primary setting for armed conflict. From 1945 to 1990, for example, there were over 100 internal and interstate wars in the Third World. Since 1945 nearly twenty million people have died in wars or as a result of civil strife and the use of force. Out of this total some 200,000 or about 10 percent occurred in Europe in conflicts such as the Greek civil war in the late 1940s and Soviet military intervention in Hungary in 1956. The rest

---

[26]*Ibid.*, pp. 9–10.
[27]*Ibid.*, p. 13.

died from wars in the Third World.[28] Even taking into account the deaths caused by conflicts in the former Yugoslavia and Chechnya in the Russian Federation, interstate wars are primarily a Third World phenomenon, and this is where refugee crises will most likely continue to occur.

It has also been in the Third World where outside interventions have challenged the concept of *sovereignty* held by political leaders and many analysts of the international state system. In 1991 the UN Security Council passed Resolution 688, demanding that the Government of Iraq "allow immediate access by international humanitarian organizations to all those in need of assistance." Subsequent UN resolutions and state actions regarding Haiti, Rwanda, and Somalia overrode the principle of noninterference in the domestic affairs of states on the legal ground that these conflicts also endangered international peace and security, a condition allowing UN-authorized actions consistent with Article 42 of the UN Charter. Compared to the cold war and given their humanitarian concerns, the major powers are now much more willing to acknowledge that events that take place within a country can constitute a threat to regional and international peace and security, although it may be difficult to identify a threat to a particular state's "national security." Notwithstanding difficulties encountered during the UN peacekeeping effort in Somalia and the international consensus that the UN peacekeeping effort failed to halt the war in the former Yugoslavia, the West still was willing to introduce NATO troops into Bosnia in December 1995 and go to war with Serbia over Kosovo in 1999.[29]

 **CASE & Point   THE RWANDESE REFUGEE CRISIS**

The fastest and largest refugee exodus in modern times occurred in July 1994 when one million Rwandese fled across the border into neighboring Zaire. Almost immediately many began to die from dysentery, dehydration, cholera, and other diseases. Almost 200 humanitarian relief organizations arrived on the scene to provide food, water, shelter, and medical care. With UNHCR and other international and transnational relief organizations already stretched thin due to humanitarian efforts elsewhere, it was decided that only large-scale military support could reduce the high mortality rates. By mid-August several countries, including the United States, provided key logistical support. Particularly important was the U.S. role in establishing a purified water link to more than 200,000 refugees at the Kimbumba camp. The French military helped by handling air traffic control duty, cargo handling, runway repairs, the transportation and distribution of food, and the task of collecting and burying bodies. Within two months of the arrival of military support, the cholera epidemic was brought under control. UNHCR and the states that provided the military units realized that lines of communication needed to be established to avoid the sorts of confusion and delays experienced in the Rwandan case.

Point: All parties involved assumed that military participation will occur again in similar exceptional circumstances.

Source: UNHCR, *The State of the World's Refugees* (Oxford, England: Oxford University Press, 1995), p. 122.

---

[28]Steven R. David, "Why the Third World Still Matters," *International Security*, v. 17, no. 3 (Winter 1992/93): 131. See also Guy Arnold, *Wars in the Third World Since 1945* (London: Cassell Publishers, 1991).

[29]UNHCR, *The State of the World's Refugees 1995: In Search of Solutions* (Oxford, England: Oxford University Press, 1995), pp. 39–40.

For international and transnational organizations dealing with refugee problems, such concerns over sovereignty issues pale in comparison to the sorts of challenges they face in the post–cold war international environment. First refugee crises have increased in number and severity, leading to the understandable perception that the situation is out of control.[30]

Second traditional solutions and procedures appear to be inadequate in the current environment. For example voluntary repatriation of refugees to their homes is virtually impossible when the country is plagued by continual war and economic devastation. At the same time few host countries are willing to allow refugees to take up permanent residence in their countries. In fact even UN officials are now beginning to recognize that the very success of resettling Vietnamese boat people in the 1980s as well as the expensive long-term assistance programs for refugees in Africa have actually made the global situation *worse*, as states that create refugees believe they have no responsibility for finding viable solutions. For example what will happen to displaced Muslims and Croats whose land was seized by Serbs, or the Azeris of Nagorno-Karabakh whose territory in the trans-Caucasus region north of Iran and Iraq was seized by neighboring Armenia?

Third donor states are grumbling over the increasing costs of these humanitarian missions. In 1994, for example, UNHCR received $1.3 billion in contributions, and this does not include the large sums of money provided to other international organizations such as World Food Programme and the International Committee of the Red Cross, nor the money spent by nongovernmental organizations or bilateral state programs.

Finally the conventional categories used since the early 1950s have proved inadequate to deal with the refugee crises of the current era. Traditionally humanitarian organizations made fairly rigid distinctions between refugees, returnees, internally displaced persons, and the resident population. But in the border areas of a number of African countries such as Sierra Leone, Ethiopia, and Somalia, people from all four categories live side by side in similarly appalling circumstances. The same situation exists in parts of Bosnia-Hercegovina. In this case the UNHCR, which has always seen itself as an organization concerned with refugees, has provided food and shelter to persons besieged in their own communities. Little has been done to resolve the legal status of displaced persons, some of whom may be able to return to their homes, but thousands of others cannot or will not return.

Conclusion

Perhaps international human rights efforts and attempts to deal with refugee crises in recent years need to be assessed not so much for what they have accomplished in concrete terms, but rather in terms of the contribution to developing a universal consensus on human rights and proper responses in what is still an anarchic world society. On the other hand it may be, as some Islamic diplomats have implied, that universality in human rights amounts to "no more than a plurality of mutually tolerant national and regional variants."[31] The United Nations–sponsored World

---

[30]This and following points are made in UNHCR, *The State of the World's Refugees 1995*, pp. 35–39.
[31]Best, "Human Rights."

Conference on Human Rights held in Vienna in 1993 illustrated the different interpretations of human rights concepts. In particular there was an obvious gap between Western norms and those of many developing countries.

The difficulty in pursuing international human rights is particularly evident when it is discussed in the context of some of the other themes addressed in this book. By definition a concern for human rights raises the basic issue of what the term *sovereignty* means today. If, as we have noted, the internal aspect of sovereignty traditionally has meant that how a state treats its own citizens is a matter of domestic jurisdiction, then criticizing a state on the grounds of human rights violations undermines the concept of sovereignty. Although some states such as China or Myanmar may continue to claim that no state, international organization, or transnational organization has the *right* to criticize how it treats its dissidents, the reality of the world today is that they do.

The violation of a person's rights due to his or her political beliefs and activities is relatively easy to condemn. In other cases it is not quite as easy. Consider, for example, how the AIDS epidemic in Africa has begun to change the international debate about human rights. AIDS can not only devastate a country's workforce and worsen its economic prospects, it can also weaken its military forces. How far should a state go to prevent the spread of AIDS? In the case of Cuba, for example, mandatory testing, immigration controls, and quarantine were implemented, testing Western human rights precepts about an individual's dignity and privacy. How should a state balance the rights of AIDS or other victims with its concurrent responsibilities for economic and national security? Do foreigners have the right to criticize a state's decision and demand an end to discriminatory policies and proclaim that access to health care and treatment should be a basic human right?

Reconciling diverse interpretations of human rights is not an easy task. Nevertheless we can expect to see continuing efforts to cast human rights and human rights enforcement in global terms. This quest is pursued not just by diplomats but also by such NGOs as Asia Watch, Americas Watch, Human Rights Watch, Amnesty International, and other similarly motivated transnational and domestic interest groups. Even if states are reluctant to act, such NGOs and movements continue to give human rights issues a high profile, contributing to an emerging global civil society. Assuming such trends continue, the idea that basic human rights of individuals are not the exclusive domain of a state but also are a legitimate concern of the larger international community will continue to be strengthened.

KEY TERMS

libertarian *p. 445*	genocide *p. 452*	migration *p. 462*
liberal *p. 446*	positivism *p. 454*	refugees *p. 462*

OTHER CONCEPTS

welfare   *p. 444*
supranational   *p. 444*
communitarian   *p. 445*
individualism   *p. 446*
conservative   *p. 447*
equal protection   *p. 447*
eminent domain   *p. 447*

due process   *p. 448*
cultural relativism   *p. 448*
social liberal   *p. 450*
categorical imperatives
   p. 452
utilitarian   *p. 453*
natural rights   *p. 453*

social contract   *p. 153*
civil rights   *p. 453*
customary international law
   p. 459
compassion fatigue   *p. 474*
political asylum   *p. 476*

ADDITIONAL READINGS

On the United Nations and human rights, see Philip Alston, ed., *The United Nations and Human Rights* (New York: Oxford University Press, 1992) and Johannes Morsink, *The Universal Declaration of Human Rights: Origins, Drafting and Intent* (Philadelphia: University of Pennsylvania Press, 1999). Political essays, speeches, and documents on human rights may be found in Micheline R. Ishay (ed.), *The Human Rights Reader* (London and New York: Routledge, 1997). For a discussion of the evolution of human rights regimes, see Jack Donnelly, *Universal Human Rights in Theory and Practice* (Ithaca, N.Y.: Cornell University Press, 1989) as well as his *International Human Rights* (Boulder, Colo: Westview Press, 1993). See also Paul Gordon Lauren, *The Evolution of International Human Rights: Visions Seen* (Philadelphia: University of Pennsylvania Press, 1998). For a world view that sees human rights as a core element of global politics, see Richard Falk, *On Humane Governance* (University Park: Pennsylvania State University Press, 1995). A quick overview of international law on human rights is Thomas Buergenthal, *International Human Rights in a Nutshell* (St. Paul, MN: West Publishing Co., 1995). On NGOs see William Korey, *NGOs and the Universal Declaration of Human Rights: A Curious Grapevine* (New York: St. Martin's, 1998). Lectures delivered at Oxford University on human rights related to religion, cross-cultural and comparative perspectives, gender, and other topics are in Olwen Hufton (ed.), *Historical Change and Human Rights* (New York: Basic Books, 1995). A classic treatment of the subject rooted in political philosophy that deals with the public and private realms, work, dignity, and various human activities is Hannah Arendt, *The Human Condition* (Chicago: University of Chicago Press, 1958). On refugees the UNHCR Web site [www.unhcr.ch] provides up-to-date information, statistics, and the magazine *Refugees*. On human rights, see also the UNHCHR Web site [www.unhchr.ch].

CONCLUSION: SOME TWENTY-FIRST CENTURY VIEWS OF GLOBAL POLITICS

"Globalization is bringing us new choices and opportunities. It is making us more familiar with global diversity. Yet, millions of people experience it not as an agent of progress, but as a disruptive force that can destroy lives, jobs and traditions. Faced with the potential good of globalization as well as its risks, faced with the persistence of deadly conflicts in which civilians are the primary targets, faced with the pervasiveness of poverty and injustice, we must be able to identify the areas where collective action is needed to safeguard global interests."

KOFI ANNAN, UNITED NATIONS SECRETARY GENERAL

- Economic and Technological Optimists

- Social and Environmental Pessimists

- Realists and Pluralists

- Final Words

We end where we began. When the communist hammer-and-sickle flag was lowered from the Kremlin on December 25, 1991, there was a dramatic increase in speculation on the future of international relations and world politics. Such efforts included newspaper pundits and political leaders as well as scholars. Given the failure of seasoned observers to foresee the end of the cold war, one would have thought that humility might have kept these same crystal-ball gazers from prognosticating about world politics in the twenty-first century. History has a way of confounding our best efforts to divine what lies ahead.

After World War I, for example, optimists thought that interstate war could be banished through such mechanisms as collective security. They were tragically wrong. Pessimists thought that the cold war would end in a hot war—a catastrophic nuclear exchange between the United States and the Soviet Union. Fortunately they too were wrong. In fact in most cases straight-line extrapolations of current trends are generally incorrect, as adherents of chaos and complexity theory are eager to point out.[1]

More generally nineteenth-century techno-optimists, looking toward the twentieth century, anticipated the marvels that applied science and technology would achieve. These marvels turned out to be a mixed blessing. Mobilizing the machinery of industrial capitalism certainly has brought great rewards, empowering individuals and groups and providing higher standards of living for many. On the other hand economic development has had

---

[1]M. Mitchell Waldrop, *Complexity: The Emerging Science at the Edge of Order and Chaos* (New York: Touchstone, 1992).

heavy environmental and social costs as well. Industrialization and new technologies also have produced armed forces ever more destructive, raising the human costs of warfare to an unprecedented, terribly high level, making the twentieth century (especially during the two world wars in the first half) the bloodiest and most destructive period in human history.

In this concluding chapter we resist the temptation to make specific predictions about the twenty-first century. Instead we provide optimistic and pessimistic scenarios of the future that summarize much recent work. We conclude with some observations of how realists and pluralists tend to look at the future of international relations and world politics.

ECONOMIC AND TECHNOLOGICAL OPTIMISTS

Late twentieth-century optimists can be compared to their counterparts 100 years ago who heralded the coming age of economic growth and social transformation. Advanced telecommunications, transportation, and production technologies are creating new domains of interaction that do not respect the lines that otherwise separate states and their societies. Megacities and areas that cross state boundaries link societies regionally as peoples interact, exchange ideas, and engage in economic transactions. Specialists in technical fields and others who share common interests communicate directly and establish bonds that constitute global communities. Evidence of globalization is pervasive.

Although technology has not yet created a global society, advances in telecommunications and transportation have created a large number of overlapping domains of interaction among peoples throughout the world, not conforming at all to the neat lines on maps that currently define the conventional understanding of international relations. From this new technological perspective, it is a world of the Internet in which Web sites double every fifty days and a new home page comes online every four seconds. Information superhighways and virtual reality provide a basis for a complex array of interdependent and interconnected linkages. Indeed, of the major trends we have emphasized in this book, current optimists on the subject of global politics tend to emphasize the benefits of increasing global interdependence and interconnectedness.

Life spans may well be enhanced by new genetic and biological discoveries. Optimists look to new energy technologies like cold fusion (which relies on a virtually endless supply of hydrogen from sea water) or its equivalent as a basic, relatively inexpensive, and nonpolluting source of energy that would transform present-day economies as we have known them. A few optimists even turn their eyes toward space, seeking external remedies to compensate for resource depletion and environmental constraints of Earth-bound populations. The future is bright, and even those without the appropriate skills can at least be carried along on the tides of rapid global change, benefiting indirectly.

One View of the Future of the Nation-State

Like a mothball, which goes from solid to gas directly, I expect the nation-state to evaporate without first going into a gooey, inoperative mess, before some global cyberstate commands the political ether. Without question, the role of the nation-state will change dramatically and there will be no more room for nationalism than there is for smallpox. Nations today are the wrong size. They are not small enough to be local and they are not large enough to be global.

Nicholas Negroponte,
Professor of Media Technology at the Massachusetts Institute of Technology (MIT)
Source: Being Digital (New York: Random House, 1995), p. 238.

IT'S BEEN SAID...

SOCIAL AND ENVIRONMENTAL PESSIMISTS

Many other observers of global politics, however, take a dim view of the future. We have already discussed in Chapter Twelve, for example, some of the implications of an ever-expanding global population. The best that can be said on this front is that in recent years overall fertility rates are declining in many areas of the world. Many demographers expect that even in countries with the fastest growing populations, average family sizes will decline in the future and numbers will stabilize. Still the numbers are daunting and the implications even more so.

To make matters worse many atmospheric scientists predict climatic change due to global warming caused by industrial and other pollutants. It is now the consensus of the world scientific community that a hole in the ozone layer in the upper atmosphere exists above Antarctica. Rainfall and temperature patterns are expected to change, with negative effect on agricultural output. What was once marginal farmland may become a desert. Severe food production shortfalls will in turn lead to a strain on food production in more hospitable areas of the world. According to this scenario widespread famines that decimate populations will occur even in parts of the world that have successfully avoided this fate in the twentieth and earlier centuries. This is a cruel way to manage the global population problem.

 DEMOGRAPHIC NIGHTMARE?

In 1973 a Frenchman, Jean Raspail, published a futuristic and highly controversial novel entitled *Camp of the Saints*. In the novel the Belgian government responds compassionately to accounts of a widespread famine in India, brought into homes around the world due to the marvels of modern global communications, by adopting a number of poor young children. When thousands of desperate mothers descend on the Belgian consul general's residence, begging him to take their children to a better life, a startled Belgian government reverses its decision. As a result a charismatic "untouchable" calls on the poor to make their way to the Western paradise: "The nations are rising from the four corners of the earth," he says, "and their number is like the sand of the sea. They will march up over the broad earth and surround the camp of the saints and the beloved city."

Commandeering every seaworthy ship available, the hordes of the poor make a horrific voyage around Africa and into the Mediterranean. French sailors are unable to bring themselves to sink this decrepit armada, and the destitute pour ashore as the French flee the south of France and soldiers desert their army units. The novel points to two global realities—an imbalance in resources between the haves and the have-nots and similarly unbalanced demographic trends. If these trends continue, the author makes clear that mass migration such as he describes will eventually overwhelm the West or force it into responding in a brutal and morally questionable fashion.

Densely populated countries and areas are also more susceptible to pestilence and diseases of one kind or another, particularly when hygienic standards also are low. Biologists note how densely populated areas offer more hosts to rats, insects, and other pests as well as to microbes, encouraging more and newer forms of bacterial and viral diseases to spread. Throughout history plagues have wiped out large numbers of human beings. An unfortunate consequence of interdependence and globalization is that bacteria, viruses, and pests are much more easily spread from one part of the globe to another thanks to modern air travel and transport. Regionally refugees may bring with them certain diseases or may be exposed to new ones in overcrowded camps. In addition people continue to make inroads into ecosystems such as in the Amazon area in Latin America and in tropical rain forests in Africa, where they encounter heretofore unknown organisms. Microorganisms also may migrate to newly hospitable environments as temperatures and rainfall levels change. Finally microorganisms can mutate and be difficult to eradicate or control.

CASE & Point

PANDEMICS

The influenza epidemic of 1918 to 1919 killed approximately twenty-five million people, far more than the number of battlefield deaths of World War I—7.7 million.

Point: The battle against diseases can be viewed as an international security issue.

The AIDS virus is the obvious example. Some two dozen countries, most in Africa, are suffering the devastating social and economic impact of the AIDS plague. For example, AIDS affects one out of five young adults in the African state of Uganda, leading to a generation of orphans to be raised by grandparents. While hope is held out for a cure, AIDS shares a sobering similarity with bacterial diseases—even if a drug is 99 percent effective, the minuscule portion that survives may mutate over many generations to the point that it is resistant to a drug cure.[2]

Unconstrained, the net effect of famine, pestilence, disease, and warfare will be to reduce human populations, imposing a "natural" ceiling on their growth. The spread of AIDS and other epidemics may decimate populations and significantly alter population growth rates in certain regions of the world. Even the eighteenth-century pessimist Thomas Malthus hoped for more than this rather dismal, barbaric scenario offers. He looked beyond what he called "creating habits of prudence" to limit population growth, underscoring the need for actions taken by "just and enlightened government" that is necessary to avert this human crisis.[3] But government is not the only hope. As we have argued in earlier chapters, the expansion of global civil society has meant an increasingly important role for local and transnational organizations, which can alter the thinking and behavior of people.

[2]Dennis Pirages, "Microsecurity: Disease Organisms and Human Well-Being," *Washington Quarterly*, v. 18, no. 4 (1995): 6, 10.
[3]Thomas Malthus, *An Essay on the Principle of Population and a Summary View of the Principle of Population* (London: Penguin Books, 1982, 1985), p. 251.

REALISTS AND PLURALISTS

Despite their differences realists and pluralists both take a more optimistic view than the social and environmental pessimists and a more pessimistic view than the economic and technological optimists. Realists and pluralists would argue that what is missing in many scenarios is *politics*—the processes that determine who gets what, when, how, and why. Both the optimistic and pessimistic scenarios outlined in this chapter imply a purely *laissez-faire* approach by states, international organizations, and nongovernmental organizations to social, economic, and technological issues, extrapolating current conditions into the future. This is the very danger we warned against in Chapter One.

Human beings have the cognitive capacity to analyze situations, plan ahead, and take action. The surest way to reduce the chances of something terrible happening on the world stage is to predict it will occur and make sure your prediction receives wide publicity. If you are lucky, those with the power to do so will take action and (one hopes) make your prediction wrong. In other words it is likely that a *laissez-faire* approach to world problems will not gain ground and efforts in fact will be made to tackle these difficult problems. This may result in part from guilt and moral qualms induced by telecasts of people starving to death or dying of disease, or it may be a more calculated decision based on concerns for human security in an increasingly globalized world.

Assuming that world actors will realize the need to take action of some kind, existing political institutions at state and interstate levels may not be adequate. World federalists certainly do not think so. They contend that managing life on the planet as a whole requires empowering central authorities or creating world government to deal with these and other issues on a global scale. But such a solution threatens to create as many problems as it purports to resolve: Abuse of power as well as bureaucratic inefficiencies often accompany centralization.

But as we have noted elsewhere, global *governance* is not necessarily the same thing as global *government*. A somewhat more modest approach offered by pluralists is the construction and maintenance of a greater number of functionally specific international regimes and associated institutions that can in turn forge links among themselves to deal with policy issues that cross their separate domains. For example global and regional international organizations tasked with agricultural production and distribution might well establish cooperative or collaborative links with institutions in regimes performing trade, monetary, and climate-management tasks. Such tasks may be performed in areas of high economic activity as in central Europe, the southern cone of South America, or the transborder area of Mexico and the United States.

Taken as a whole the apparent architecture or structure of world politics would be one of multiple overlapping regimes with global and regional responsibilities. The responsibilities, norms, and values inherent in these regimes would be influenced by transnational organizations and movements that are part of a growing global civil society. Such NGOs would also play an important role in monitoring and highlighting the successes and failures of such international regimes. At the same time that many tasks become more collective and integrated, decentralization would also be possible, devolving state authority to local administrations for certain tasks better performed at those levels.

A P P L Y I N G   T H E O R Y

❧ ALTERNATIVE PERSPECTIVES ❧

This book has focused primarily on the practice of international relations and world politics in war and in peace, involving diverse aspects of security, economy, and identity. Using different conceptual lenses or images, realists and pluralists often have different understandings of what they observe, which we have noted in various places throughout the text. The terms *international relations* and *world politics* are often used interchangeably; however, the title of this book does take into account realist and pluralist worldviews: international (or interstate) relations are more the focus of realists, while world politics with its multiplicity of actors and diverse channels of interaction is more the focus of pluralists (or liberals as they are sometimes called). We focus primarily on realist and pluralist perspectives, although we also take account of Marxist understandings, particularly in our treatment of global political economy.

Although this book is not primarily about theory—a topic the authors undertake in another volume,[a] we have included in this book a number of boxes such as this one on applying theory to the world around us. Indeed nothing is more practical than good theory that makes the world more intelligible, contributing to better understanding, explanation, or prediction of international relations and world politics as we cope with life in an increasingly globalized world.

Beyond *empirical theory*, which focuses on factual and causal considerations, **normative theory** also provides moral or ethical guidelines that can be used by policy makers and other actors engaged in international relations and world politics. Applying normative theory to practice thus crosses a wide diversity of global issues now confronting humankind—enhanced concern with economic equity or justice in the face of massive poverty, human rights violations, poor health conditions, environmental degradation, and intercommunal strife and interstate war. When (if ever, some would say) is it legitimate to use force? How are we to apply just-war criteria to the question of right conduct in warfare as well as humanitarian intervention?

[a]Paul R. Viotti and Mark V. Kauppi, *International Relations Theory: Realism, Pluralism, Globalism* (Upper Saddle River, NJ: Prentice Hall, 1999).

Critical and Postmodern Challenges to Positivist Science

Most of the theoretical work that relies on realist and pluralist images of international relations and world politics embraces *positivism*. **Positivism** involves a commitment to a unified view of science, meaning a belief that it is possible to adopt the methodologies of the natural sciences to explain the social world, which includes international relations and world politics. Positivists believe that objective knowledge of the world is possible and, hence, have a faith in and a commitment to the Enlightenment's rationalist tradition that underlies science or what some refer to as *modernism*.

Positivism has been under assault by critical and postmodern theorists for its attempts in international relations and other social sciences to separate facts from values, to define and operationalize concepts into precisely and accurately measurable variables, and to test truth claims in the form of hypotheses drawn from theories. Whether using quantitative or statistical methods, or such nonquantitative (or qualitative) methods as case and comparative-case studies, those who have tried to be scientific have been criticized for ignoring or taking insufficient account of the personal or human dimension of scholarship. What we observe in either the natural or social sciences is heavily influenced by the interpretive understanding we have of the concepts we employ. The same holds for the causal relations we infer when we specify the relations among variables, theories, hypotheses, and the observed behavior of states and nonstate actors in the political and social milieu in which they are immersed.

If the central question of **epistemology** is how we know what we think we know, critical and postmodernist theorists set aside the abstract universalist, scientific claims. They focus instead on the human perception and understandings that give diverse meanings to the concepts and theories we formulate and the behavior we observe.

That facts, concepts, and theories may not be separated from values stems from their observation and construction by human agency. To postmodernists, what we see, what we choose to see or measure, and the mechanisms or methods we employ are all of human construction that essentially rely on perception

A P P L Y I N G   T H E O R Y

and cognitive processes influenced as well by prior understandings and meanings. Even the language we use constitutes an embedded set of values that are an integral part of any culture.

Some critical theorists argue that beliefs held by theorists necessarily bias their truth claims and may well be part of global ideological schemes to legitimate particular world orders. In supporting an alleged agenda of domination, it may be convenient to advance ideologies often masquerading as scientifically based theories. One of the tasks of critical theorists is to unmask such deceptions, probe for deeper understandings or meanings, and expose the class or other interests these ideologies or alleged theories are designed to serve. Power is a core concept for critical theorists, particularly in relation to those who wield it.

Critical theory may be viewed separately from postmodernism since most critical theorists retain strict methodological criteria to guide their work. Nevertheless, some critical theory does overlap with, or can be understood more broadly as, part of a postmodernist understanding. In this regard postmodernist **ontology** is prone to find the subtexts and to deconstruct—unpack and take apart—the meanings embedded in what we say or write and even in the ways we act. Human beings are essentially subjective creatures; to postmodernists, claims made to empirically based, objective truth are necessarily hollow. Our understandings and meanings are, after all, humanly constructed. In the extreme no knowledge or truth is possible apart from the motivations and purposes people put into their construction. From this perspective, truth is entirely relative.

Feminist Challenges

Although some feminists are critical theorists or postmodernists, others remain positivists. Accordingly we place feminism as another, separate critique of conventional international relations theory that offers an alternative perspective and starting point for both theory and practice.

Feminist understandings concerning human rights to equal treatment and the empowerment of women, allowing them the same opportunities that traditionally and historically have been reserved in most cultures to men, have had and likely will continue to have substantial impact on a global scale. Some feminists note that empowering women will also give them the means to limit family size voluntarily, thus reducing population growth rates to economically sustainable levels. Women are also seen by many feminists as more prone to constructive, peaceful approaches to the many conflictual issues on the global agenda. They are underrepresented in these efforts.

At the risk of pushing gender stereotypes too far, we can summarize a feminist perspective in international relations as being more prone to see human beings coming together constructively and collaboratively in various organizational forms. Human relationships matter. Rather than adopt a cold, abstract analysis of the interaction of states and nonstate actors as, for example, structural realists or neorealists often do, the feminist perspective underscores the constructivist potential of people. Multilateral rather than unilateral or hegemonic models enhance this human potential for building peaceful relationships and positive, interdependent linkages across national borders. Pluralist liberal institutionalism and international regime construction are consistent with this perspective.

It is not as if men are incapable of such thoughts or that women cannot be hard-headed realists or any more or less aggressive than men. Indeed it may be that many women have adopted what some feminist theorists have labeled "masculine" understandings, perhaps in order to be taken seriously in a seemingly male-dominated world that extends to academic communities.

Advocates of the feminist perspective in international relations theory, however, identify a feminist perspective not tied by gender to particular individuals, but rather generally associated with women across cultures resulting from both genetic and environmental factors. Although not all would agree, a few point to traditional family and community-building roles that women have historically played as informing the feminist perspective. Having said that, however, feminist perspectives are not in any way restricted to women. Indeed, many men engaged in theorizing are quite capable (and often have adopted) what are labeled feminist perspectives.

Assessing the Challenges

These are, to say the least, significant challenges to "modernist" science more generally and to international

continued

relations theory in particular. It is difficult, however, so quickly to deny or dismiss scientific methodologies that have produced so much accumulated knowledge in so many diverse fields of human inquiry. Defenders of positivism see critical and postmodernist thinkers as misrepresenting science, which, after all, retains an inherently skeptical orientation to truth claims and demands continued and unending empirical tests of such propositions. Just as it historically has accommodated empirical, theoretical, and philosophical critiques by modifying its methods and understandings, science remains open to critical, postmodernist, and other challenges.

What critical, postmodernist, and feminist perspectives do contribute to theorizing about international relations and world politics is an ever-increased epistemological sensitivity to, and caution concerning, the fragility of what we think to be true. The values we hold and normative theories we apply may also influence the interpretive understanding that leads us to formulate the concepts we adopt. Interpretive understanding thus has its place in international relations theorizing by aiding in the ongoing search for new syntheses in human understandings of our political world.

The actors discussed in this book all have their limitations when it comes to tackling global challenges. *International organizations* remain weak as global governing structures and are often viewed with skepticism—if not suspicion—by states concerned with maintaining their sovereignty and sovereign prerogatives. For their part *states* and their governments claim the right to address global problems, but they are less qualified for this task than collective, concerted action on a global scale would be. Transnational *nongovernmental organizations* are playing an increasingly important role in an expanding global civil society, but it is arguable how representative they are. Developing consensus on what is to be done is no easy task, especially since there is no scientific agreement, except on the most general level, on remedies or ways to reduce these problems effectively. Even if wealthy countries could develop a consensus and then tried to impose solutions on the rest of the world in the name of "humanity," such measures would undoubtedly fail both morally and practically.

From the *pluralist* perspective the state continues to exist well into the future, but it does so in functionally truncated or reduced form. In the *economic* realm global interdependence makes for a borderless world, and crises of authority affect states to varying degrees. In this more complex future architecture, states and their governments operate alongside other international, transnational, and local actors. States still retain substantial authority, albeit for fewer tasks, relegating others to more central or local institutions. States also serve as an important go-between as they coordinate global, regional, and local efforts. State-as-coordinator is a very important future role, although quite different from the position of states as they first emerged in the late Middle Ages and have remained for several centuries—functionally diffuse actors, claiming exclusive authority, sovereignty, and performing a wide array of tasks for their societies.

From the *realist* perspectives, all of this is quite speculative. A safer bet is that the state most likely will remain pretty much as it is without either surrendering to world government or passing much more of its authority to other regimes or institutions. The state has proven to be a very durable and attractive set of institutions for people of all political persuasions for several reasons.

First, with the exception of anarchists, most revolutionaries of the left and right do not aim for the abolition of the state, but rather the overthrow of its current rulers. They share a strong belief that there is nothing wrong in principle with the state that *they* could not fix if they were in charge.

Second the nation-state has been able to provide something no other entity has been able to match—a sense of political and social *identity*. One might admire an international organization or an NGO, but they cannot compete with the emotional power of nationalism, and they are certainly hard to love.

Finally the state seems to be able to provide people with one other valuable commodity—a sense of *security*. While increasing global interdependence has reduced the ability of states to limit or negate external economic, social, and political influences, states still overwhelmingly control the use of force. From the realist perspective, therefore, if the state is becoming increasingly obsolete, one would certainly not know it by the sheer number of new states that have been created in the more than half-century since the end of World War II.

FINAL WORDS

At the risk of ending this book on a cliché, we must repeat that whatever the nature of twenty-first century world politics becomes, the problems that confront humankind do not lend themselves to easy solutions. Unquestioned faith in growing economic and technological interdependence that will somehow lead us to a better world politically and socially is naive. Similarly to believe that world politics and the state will remain essentially unchanged is reminiscent of the confidence of feudal lords who were blind to the rise of the then-new sovereign state. We hope this book has helped the reader to begin thinking about what the nature of international relations and world politics will be as the twenty-first century unfolds and to realize how much of the past may be prologue.

CONCEPTS

normative theory   *p. 488*   epistemology   *p. 488*   ontology   *p. 489*
positivism   *p. 488*

ADDITIONAL READING

On critical theory and postmodernism, we suggest Hayward R. Alker, ed., *Rediscoveries and Reformations: Humanistic Methodologies for International Studies* (New York: Cambridge University Press, 1996) and James Der Derian, ed., *International Theory: Critical Investigations* (New York: New York University Press, 1995). On feminism, see Cynthia Enloe, *Bananas, Beaches, and Bases: Making Feminist Sense of International Relations* (Berkeley: University of California Press, 1990); V. Spike Peterson, ed., *Gendered States: Feminist (Re)Visions of International Relations Theory* (Boulder, CO: Lynne Rienner, 1992); and Sue Ellen Charlton, Jana Everett, and Kathleen Staudt, eds., *Women, the State, and Development* (Albany, NY: SUNY Press, 1989). For a more positive take on the role of states, albeit from a pluralist perspective, see Ernst B. Haas, *Nationalism, Liberalism, and Progress* (Ithaca, NY: Cornell University Press, 1997).

GLOSSARY

actor A participant or player. In international relations or world politics, actors include states, international organizations, multinational corporations and banks, and other nongovernmental (or nonstate, transnational) organizations.

alliance A formal agreement between two (bilateral) or more (multilateral) states to cooperate in security matters; a formal security coalition of states with specified commitments.

ambassador (*See* mission.)

anarchists People who believe there should be no centralized political authority, as such authority abuses the rights of individuals. Historically, anarchists have been against the governments of states. Many anarchists are nonviolent; however, the nineteenth-century People's Will in Russia is an example of an anarchist terrorist group.

anarchy The absence of political authority. International politics or the international system is said to be anarchic because there is no world government—no central or superordinate authority over states, which retain their sovereign rights. (*See also* sovereignty.)

ancien regime The ruling order in prerevolutionary (1789) France. More generally the term refers to the old order or former constitutional regime in an earlier time by which a state was previously governed.

Andean Group International organization established in 1969 to promote economic integration. Members now include Bolivia, Colombia, Ecuador, Peru, and Venezuela.

apartheid A policy of discrimination and strict racial segregation or separateness in society. The term is associated primarily with the former white-dominated state of South Africa.

APEC (Asia-Pacific Economic Cooperation) Established in 1989, inclusive Asia and Pacific rim association of states with periodic summit meetings on economic and other policy issues. Members include Japan, China, Russia, Taiwan, and South Korea in Northeast Asia; Australia, Brunei, Indonesia, Malaysia, New Zealand, Papua New Guinea, the Philippines, Singapore, Thailand, and Vietnam in Southeast Asia and the western Pacific; and the United States, Canada, Mexico, Peru, and Chile in the Americas along the eastern Pacific rim.

appreciate, appreciation Increase in value over time of currency or other asset. (*See also* depreciate, depreciation.)

Arab League Founded in 1945, this pan-Arab international organization facilitates cooperation among its Arab-state members and advances Arab causes in relation to Palestine and other issues. Original members were Egypt, Iraq, Lebanon, Saudi Arabia, Syria, Yemen, Palestine (representatives of Palestinian Arabs), and Jordan. Members now also include Morocco, Mauritania, Algeria, Tunisia, Libya, Sudan, Somalia, Djibouti, Oman, United Arab Emirates (UAE), Qatar, Bahrain, Comoros and Kuwait.

armed conflict A struggle involving the use of weapons and force.

armed intervention (*See* intervention.)

arms control Negotiations designed to reduce the quantity or quality of certain types or classes of weapons or the geographical area or circumstances under which they may be possessed or used; more broadly, arms control may also include confidence- and security-building measures intended to reduce the likely use of weaponry by lowering the risk of war. Reasons for pursuing arms control include (1) curbing arms race competition, (2) saving money, (3) reducing the risk of war, (4) reducing the damage done by war, and (5) securing either some mutual advantage or other advantage over an opponent. (*See also* functional approaches.)

arms transfers The sale or giving away of weapons from one political entity (usually a state) to another.

Article 51 (of the UN Charter) If attacked, states have the inherent right of individual or collective self-defense.

artificial intelligence Generally associated with advanced computers that are able to conduct computations in a manner similar to that of the human brain.

ASEAN (Association of Southeast Asian Nations) Formed in 1967, this international organization tries to advance regional peace and security, especially through economic cooperation. Regional security has also been added to the ASEAN agenda. Original members were Indonesia, Malaysia, the Philippines, Singapore, and Thailand. Membership now also includes Brunei, Vietnam, Laos, Myanmar (Burma), and Cambodia.

assimilation A strategy to create a single national identity out of diverse populations. It may be repressive (as were the efforts under Stalin's communist Soviet Union) or noncoercive.

asylum Allowing a refugee to stay in a country to which he or she has fled out of fear of political repression or fear for his or her life in the home country. (*See also* extraterritoriality.)

asymmetry, asymmetric Lacking precise correspondence or relation—that is, symmetry—between or among components. An interdependent relation is said to be asymmetric if Party A is more dependent on Party B than Party B is on Party A.

autarky An independent posture of self-sufficiency without dependence on other actors. Autarky occurs when as a matter of policy a state attempts to exist in economic isolation from other states.

authority A legitimate right to direct or command and to make, decide, and enforce rules. The term *authority* has a moral or legal quality and, as such, can be distinguished from control by brute force or by coercion. (*See also* power and crisis of authority.)

balance of payments Accounting concept by which the international economic transactions (inflows and outflows) of states and their corporate and private elements are tracked. Balance of payments includes export and import of merchandise goods and services (balance of trade), capital investment and other "invisible" or financial flows, and official reserve transactions [gold, certain national currencies acceptable as reserves, and Special Drawing Rights (SDRs) in the International Monetary Fund]. "Balance" is achieved when reserves flow in or out to cover differences in other accounts, as when a country exporting more than it imports receives foreign currency that it can hold as a financial reserve.

balance of power   A key concept among realists that refers to a condition of, or tendency toward, equilibrium among states. Realists differ on whether the equilibrium or balance is created by diplomats (that is, by influencing balance of power as a policy); is useful as a rational basis for justifying policies; and occurs as a natural outcome of international politics, whether or not diplomats intend such an outcome. A dynamic equilibrium refers to an inherent systemic tendency to return to equilibrium each and every time the balance is upset. Because of its multiple definitions, some critics question the utility of the concept—if balance of power means so many different things, then does it mean anything at all? (*See also* equilibrium.)

balance of trade   One account in the balance of payments, it is the difference between a country's *exports* (what is sold abroad) and its *imports* (what is purchased from abroad). A negative balance of trade exists when imports of goods and services exceed exports; a positive balance of trade exists when exports exceed imports.

ballistic missiles   Missiles that when launched follow a trajectory to the ground subject to gravitational forces; depending upon its range, a ballistic missile may hit targets nearby or in a neighboring or distant country.

banks   Organizations that perform various financial services, including lending money at interest for purchases or capital investment. International (or multinational) banks are key players in the global political economy.

barter   (*See* money.)

bellicism   A term constructed from the Latin word *bellum* (war), sometimes used to refer to the belief in the value or utility of force or war as a preferred instrument of policy.

bilateral diplomacy   (*See* diplomacy.)

binational state   (*See* state.)

bipolar, bipolarity   (*See* structure.)

blockade   (*See* economic leverage.)

bourgeoisie   The capitalist (and, at the time of its emergence, the "middle") class. The bourgeoisie is the class defined in Marxian terms by its relation to the means of production—its ownership of capital, including factories and other machinery of production in a capitalist mode of production. (*See also* class struggle.)

boycott   (*See* economic leverage.)

capabilities   Resources or power any international actor can bring to bear to achieve its goals and defend its interests.

capital   Savings that can be used for investment in the means for producing goods and services, typically expenditures for plants and equipment.

capital controls   Restrictions placed by a state on the export of money or wealth. (*See* capital goods.)

capital formation   New and continuing investment in capital goods for production and consumption.

capital goods   Goods used in the production of other goods or services, for example, the machinery and tools in a factory.

capitalism   An economic system, form of political economy, or mode of production that emphasizes money, market-oriented trade, and capital investment for further production. Capitalism is also associated with a set of values or culture that sustains it. Commonly the term refers to private ownership of the means of production and a free market; however, as presented here, capitalism may be understood in global terms, taking different forms in different societies at different times. Capitalism is often further subdivided into the different forms it has taken over some 500 years—*early, industrial,* and *post-industrial. State* capitalism refers to collective ownership of capital or other property by "the people" or by the state or government as opposed to being privately owned. *Free-market* capitalism refers either to the absence or, more accurately, the minimization of government intervention or regulation of merchandise, service, capital, or other financial exchange transactions. In Marxist usage, a *mode of production.* (*See* mode of production.)

Caribbean Community and Common Market (CARICOM)   Formed as a free-trade association in 1965, it assumed its present title in 1973. Participants include British dependency Montserrat and a number of British Commonwealth members—the Bahamas, Antigua and Barbuda, Barbados, St. Kitts and Nevis, Dominica, St. Lucia, St. Vincent, Grenada, Trinidad and Tobago, Jamaica, Guyana, and Belize—plus the Dominican Republic, Haiti, and Surinam as observers.

cartel   An association among financial, commodity-producing, or industrial interests, including states, for establishing a national or international market control, setting production levels and increasing or stabilizing the prices of such diverse products as oil, tin, and coffee.

categorical imperative   Concept associated with the work of the East Prussian philosopher and ethicist Immanuel Kant, that one ought to act "according to the maxim that you can at the same time will [such conduct] to be a universal law" and that one should treat others "as an end as well as a means, never merely as a means."

causes, causality, causal   Factors that occur prior to and appear to produce certain outcomes or effects. Some causes may be *necessary* but not *sufficient* to produce a given effect; some are *efficient*—the proximate, immediate, or direct cause(s), while others are *permissive* underlying cause(s) that allow certain outcomes or effects to occur, as when international *anarchy* or the absence of central authority over states is said to pose no obstacle to the onset of war between or among them. What is to be explained causally (for example, war) is referred to as the *dependent variable* and the factors that account for or causally explain a phenomenon such as war are referred to as the *independent variables.*

Central American Common Market (CACM)   Formed in 1960 to liberalize trade, its members are Costa Rica, El Salvador, Guatemala, Honduras, and Nicaragua.

Chargé d'Affaires   (*See* mission.)

Chief of Mission   (*See* mission.)

city-state   (*See* state.)

civil liberties   Freedoms guaranteed to citizens typically by the constitution and laws of a state and society. (*See also* civil rights.)

civil rights   Claims typically made by or on behalf of individuals concerning their equal status and role as citizens. (*See also* civil liberties.)

civil war   (*See* war.)

class   A stratum of society with an identifiable characteristic or set of characteristics that differentiate it from another stratum. In Marxist usage, the term is defined by relations to the means of production—in capitalism the *bourgeoisie* by its ownership of capital and workers or the *proletariat* by its labor; in feudalism the *aristocracy* by its ownership of land and the *peasantry* by its labor.

class conflict, class struggle   A concept associated with Marxism that emphasizes the inevitable clash of interests between classes, which are defined in terms of their relations to the means (how goods, services, and value are produced) in a particular mode of production or form of political economy such as feudalism or capitalism. Marx, for example, analyzed the class struggle between the *bourgeoisie* (owners of capital, especially factories) and the *proletariat* or working class (defined by its labor).

classical economics, political economy, economists   Although they understood the importance of finance capital and capital goods in early capitalism, Adam Smith, David Ricardo, and other 18th- and 19th-century classical writers saw value in goods and services produced as the result of labor put into the production process, a labor theory of value. Specialization and division of labor that enhances efficiency in domestic production, free trade, and specialization in production for export based on comparative advantage are among the concepts developed by the classical economists. (*See also* neoclassical economics.)

coalition   A formal or informal grouping of actors that share some common purpose or purposes. Alliances and some international organizations (particularly those that are exclusive or less inclusive) are examples of *formal* coalitions; however, *ad hoc* coalitions among states or other actors that also form from time to time both *outside of* and *within* alliances and international organizations are often more transient or less durable than formal coalitions. (*See also* alliance.)

coercion   (*See* power.)

coercive diplomacy   (*See* diplomacy.)

cognition, cognitive   The process by which human beings acquire knowledge through perception, reasoning, and (some would say) intuition.

collateral death and destruction   Damage to human beings and property coincident to or following the intentional destruction of military targets; the damage is not confined to the intended targets but spills over to harm other victims and property.

collective defense   A function performed by alliances that pool power or capabilities of state members to balance or countervail the power of other states, alliances, or other coalitions. The right to individual and collective defense is legally recognized by Article 51 of the UN Charter. (*See also* Article 51; collective security.)

collective goods   Goods (or services) to which others (including other states) cannot be excluded even though they have not contributed to paying for them. For example, the security produced by an alliance can be understood as a collective good. This security benefits nonalliance members, referred to as *free riders*, because they have not made direct payments or other contributions to the collective alliance effort. Sometimes referred to as *public goods*, provision of collective goods is often done by state or governmental authorities.

collective security   The term is used commonly as if it were synonymous with *collective defense;* however, such usage overlooks the important distinction that, in principle, collective security is based on international law-enforcement obligations whereas collective defense is merely a form of balance-of-power politics. Under collective security, states agree to enforce international law by confronting any aggressor with the preponderant power that comes from pooling their collective efforts. A variety of diplomatic, economic, and other measures including the use of force may be employed. Unlike *collective defense* or *balance-of-power* policies, collective security is understood as a law-enforcement or police activity. Unlike an *alliance* that is directed against adversaries, the goal in collective security is to encourage international law-abiding behavior by states, dissuading them from committing aggression or other illegal actions taken against other states. As an all-inclusive or "universal" organization open to membership by all states, the League of Nations in the period between World War I and World War II was organized around this concept of collective security through collective law enforcement. Its successor, the United Nations, learned from League failures to stop aggression and provides not only a collective-security framework under Security Council jurisdiction, but also to allow states to enter balance-of-power–based alliances or other collective-defense arrangements, particularly if collective security fails to prevent aggression or other breaches of international law. (*See also* collective defense.)

collectivization   Refers typically to expropriation of private property as has occurred particularly in present-day and former Marxist-Leninist regimes. In the agricultural sector, not only was land taken from its owners, but the labor of farm workers or peasants was aggregated or put together on so-called collective farms.

colonialism   (*See* imperialism.)

command economy   (*See* markets.)

commodity   Broadly, any article bought or sold; agricultural products, metals, and other minerals are often referred to as commodities and are traded in bulk on commodities exchanges.

common market   Level of economic integration that in addition to the free trade of goods and services among members (as in a free-trade area) and common external tariffs on imports from nonmember countries (as in a customs union), there is also free movement across the borders of member states by all three factors of production—land, labor, and capital. (*See* integration.)

commonwealth   A loose association of sovereign states that, notwithstanding their differences and desire for independence or autonomy, have some overarching identity that makes the association meaningful. Examples include the British Commonwealth of Nations, made up of former colonies and dominions, as well as the Commonwealth of Independent States, made up of former Soviet republics.

communism   A mode of production in Marxist theory or the ultimate form of political economy in a classless society in which the state withers away as each person works maximally according to ability, receiving the fruits of collective labors in accordance with need. (*See also* mode of production.)

communitarian   While compatible in principle with an orientation toward individual or libertarian concerns, the communitarian focus is more on collective or group service obligations of individuals to one another in society.

comparative advantage   Economic free-trade principle associated with David Ricardo's work in classical economics. Ricardian economics holds that countries tend to specialize in producing those goods and services for export for which they are most efficient or have a comparative advantage, importing from other countries those goods and services for which their production is relatively less efficient. In a free-trade environment there would be, according to theory, a global specialization or division of labor with aggregate productivity maximized.

compassion fatigue   As a result of recurrent crises over time, scenes of famine and refugee camps tend to lose their impact on audiences.

compellence   Term coined by Thomas Schelling to refer to diplomatic efforts often using force (or threats of force) to compel other states to do what they would not otherwise do. By contrast, *deterrence* is directed more passively to keep other states from doing something or from undertaking an undesirable action through threat of punishment if such action were undertaken. (*See also* coercive diplomacy; deterrence.)

competitive devaluation   (*See* devalue.)

compliance   (*See* verification.)

concentration of forces   (*See* principles of war.)

concept   A construct or idea of a general or abstract nature that may, for example, refer to a particular phenomenon such as *war, power,* or *authority.*

Concert of Europe   Nineteenth-century association of states that devised the rules of great-power competition following the Napoleonic Wars and settlement at the Congress of Vienna (1815). (*See also* collective security.)

concessionary, concessionary rate   Often a form of *foreign aid,* an interest rate below market rates that allows the recipient of loan proceeds to take a portion of the loan for reinvestment at market rates, compounding the gains from higher interest and applying the proceeds toward amortization of principal.

confederation, confederalism   A loose federation or association of component states or provinces; the confederal concept can be used to integrate societies often divided by regional, national-ethnic, or other cleavages.

Conference on Security and Cooperation in Europe (CSCE)   (*See* Organization for Security and Cooperation in Europe.)

confidence- and security-building measures (CSBMs)   Agreed-upon mechanisms among states aimed at improving security over time by building trust. Notice of military exercises, allowing adversaries and others to observe them, providing for scheduled and surprise inspections of military installations on a reciprocal basis, and an open information environment are among the CSBMs that have been established, particularly in Europe. (*See also* transparency.)

conflict   Disagreement; the opposition or clash of units. Conflicts may be nonviolent or at varying degrees or levels of violence. Some theorists see the management of conflicts that cannot be resolved as being central to establishing and maintaining peace. Conflicts in international relations or world politics exist between or among states, national or ethnic communities, tribes, and so on.

conservative   In Edmund Burke's definition, conservatives distrust change, particularly any radical transformation of existing arrangements in society. Reliance is on traditional, established ways of doing things. Incremental or reformist rather than revolutionary activities are preferred if any changes are needed. Many present-day social conservatives doubt the efficacy of social engineering or other governmental programs that would effect substantial changes in the status quo, preferring instead to rely more on private, nongovernmental efforts.

consociational   Refers to formal arrangements for sharing power in society among diverse national, ethnic, or other groups that lack a common identity.

constructivist   (*See* social constructivism.)

consul, consul general   (*See* mission.)

consulate   (*See* mission.)

consumption   In economics, the use of goods or services that have been produced. Some of what is produced is not consumed, but rather is set aside or saved for investment in future production efforts. There is thus an inverse relation between consumption and savings or investment: the more that is consumed, the less will be left for saving and investment.

containment   The grand strategy of the United States designed to deal with the Soviet Union during the cold war. Through support to democratic states and forces, the building up of robust military forces, the creation of military alliances, and the support of capitalist economic development, it was hoped the Soviet Union specifically and communism in general could be "contained" or confined within existing borders.

convertible currency   Readily accepted in exchange for other currencies; originally meant a "hard" currency readily exchangeable for gold and thus other currencies.

cosmopolitan, cosmopolitanism Outward or worldly in orientation, avoiding local and ethnocentric prejudices; the "citizen of the world" with human associations across the frontiers of states and other jurisdictions.

cost A loss as opposed to a benefit; something paid as opposed to something received.

Council of Europe International organization that promotes democracy in the European area.

counterforce targets (*See* targeting.)

counter-offensive (*See* offensive.)

countervalue targets (*See* targeting.)

country team (*See* mission.)

credibility (*See* deterrence.)

crisis A situation characterized by surprise, high threat to values or interests, and short decision time.

crisis of authority A loss of legitimacy on the part of a government or other actor. A result may be the breakdown of order as people refuse to follow the orders of those who claim to be in positions of authority. (*See also* authority.)

crisis diplomacy (*See* diplomacy.)

crusades Efforts in the eleventh, twelfth, and thirteenth centuries by European Christians that included the use of force in the Middle East to regain the Holy Land and religious shrines that had fallen under Islamic influence and control.

cujus regio ejus religio Latin phrase referring to the peace settlement at Westphalia (1648) that ended the Thirty Years' War among German and other states by establishing the principle by which the religion of the inhabitants of a state would be determined by the prince to whom they were subject. Such authority was indicative of the growing strength of states and the evolving concept of sovereignty. (*See also* sovereignty.)

cultural imperialism (*See* imperialism.)

cultural relativism (*See* relativism.)

cultures of violence Refers to values in societies or subgroups that accept or even legitimize the use of violent means to attain social and political ends.

customary international law Established practice over time by states that provides a base for international law. Thus centuries of practice had established diplomatic immunity and other diplomatic rights.

customs union Level of economic integration in which states not only have agreed to eliminate tariffs on imports and other barriers to trade among themselves, but have also established a common external tariff imposed on imports from nonmembers of the customs union. (*See also* integration.)

cyberterrorism Computer-based attacks on information systems designed to destroy or manipulate data banks or cause the system to crash with the goal of furthering a political agenda.

decision Choosing among often competing alternatives or options; making a judgment or drawing a conclusion. A *rational* decision-making process is one in which alternative means to achieve certain objectives are evaluated and the best (or at least satisfactory) option or options for attaining these objectives are selected. (*See also* policy.)

defense Security against attack or threat of attack. In *strategic defense* against attack by nuclear or other weapons of mass destruction, defenses include both active and passive measures. *Active defense* includes actual *warfighting* capabilities such as fighter-interceptor aircraft, surface-to-air missiles (SAM), and anti-aircraft artillery (AAA) against invading bombers; antiballistic missiles (ABM) against incoming missiles as in national missile defense; and surface ships and attack submarines in antisubmarine warfare (ASW). An even more offensive form of active defense is construed to include intercontinental (ICBM), submarine-launched (SLBM), or other ballistic missiles directed preemptively against an enemy's own offensive ballistic missiles or launch-control system before launching has occurred. Although related to a country's overall warfighting posture, *passive defense* does not include warfighting activities per se. Such passive measures include deploying radar and other means to detect and thus provide warning of attack. *Civil defense*, such as notifying populations to take cover or moving them to blast or other fall-out shelters, is an additional passive defense measure. *Strategic defense* can be designed to protect specific targets an enemy might attack (sometimes called *point defenses*) or large expanses of territory (sometimes called *area defenses*).

delegation (*See* mission.)

demand In economics, the desire for a good or service and the ability to pay for some quantity of it at a certain price or range of prices. (*See also* elasticity.)

démarche A diplomatic representation, request, or protest from one government to another.

democratic centralism An organizing principle in Leninist or communist parties that allows participation by party members on issues under discussion but requires party members to adhere to decisions once they are made by higher party authorities. The *politburo* is usually the highest level of party decision making and thus retains central authority over subordinate levels of party organization and membership.

demographics, demography Measures relating to population, including overall numbers; life, death, and social statistics; categorization (such as national, ethnic, tribal, racial, or cultural affiliations); and, more broadly, implications of such variables for human beings for political economy or political regime, war or domestic strife, and climate change or other environmental factors.

dependency The concept that low-income countries (sometimes referred to as Third World or South) are economically subordinated to serve primarily the interests or advantage of high-income countries (sometimes referred to as First World or North). In class-analytical terms, workers and peasants on a worldwide scale are subordinated and exploited to varying degrees by capital-owning classes or *bourgeoisie* in their own and/or in First World countries.

dependent variable (*See* causes, causality, causal.)

depreciate, depreciation Decrease in value over time of a currency or other asset. (*See also* appreciate, appreciation.)

Deputy Chief of Mission (DCM) (*See* mission.)

détente   An easing or relaxing of tensions between states, as in the late 1960s and 1970s between the United States and the Soviet Union and their respective allies.

deterrence   Threat of the use of force aimed at persuading another actor not to do what it intends or may like to do; a psychological effect on an opponent that results in a rational decision to desist because of the expected consequences of attacking or starting a war. Deterrence usually involves threat of *punishment;* however, in some usages it refers to *denial*—that other states are deterred because they expect an effective military response to their actions, know they cannot achieve their objectives through the use of force, and thus rationally do not try to do so. To be effective, deterrence threats must be *credible* or believed by policy makers in the threatened country as being real (and not just bluffs)—that is, that they would be carried out. *Extended deterrence* refers to deterrence threats designed to protect other countries in addition to the country making the deterrence threats, as when a great power makes deterrence commitments to its allies, thus effectively putting them under its security "umbrella." In *strategic* or *nuclear deterrence, minimum* or *finite* deterrence refers to a country maintaining a relatively small number of nuclear or other weapons of mass destruction for use in making deterrence threats. Critics of minimum deterrence usually argue that the small numbers of such weapons may make them vulnerable to preemptive destruction or that threats from such countries may not be credible.

devalue   To reduce the exchange value of a country's currency, as when one unit of a country's currency that could buy ten units of another currency yesterday can buy only eight units today, representing a 20 percent devaluation. Because devaluation effectively reduces the export price of goods and services produced domestically and sold to other countries, some countries may choose to devalue merely to gain a competitive advantage (e.g., a good selling for one currency unit cost foreign importers ten units of their currency yesterday, but today only eight units—a 20 percent discount that may undercut the price foreign producers can offer). *Competitive devaluations* occur when foreign countries match a devaluation in one country with devaluations of their own to even the score or gain an advantage of their own. Experience with competitive devaluations in the 1930s, for example, had the net effect of substantially reducing the overall volume of world trade. (*See also* exchange rate.)

development   The process associated with economic growth or the industrialization of societies. As used in this text, a distinction is drawn between economic and social development. (*See also* economic development; social development; sustainable development.)

diplomacy, diplomat   The management of international relations by negotiations; the method by which these relations are adjusted and managed by ambassadors and envoys; the business or art of the *diplomat,* who is the official representative of states and international organizations who defends state or organizational interests through negotiation. To do their job, diplomats require

diplomatic immunity, a reciprocal privilege among states by which diplomats are not subject to arrest, prosecution, or penalty in the foreign state to which they are assigned. Such *reciprocity* among states is essential if countries are to maintain and conduct business with one another. To expel a diplomat, the state must declare him or her *persona non grata* (person not welcome); in such cases the person is forced to leave the country and is removed from the *diplomatic list* maintained by the host country. *Bilateral diplomacy* involves two states, whereas *multilateral diplomacy* involves three or more states. *Preventive diplomacy* refers to efforts taken to address international problems with constructive approaches, avoiding if possible the deterioration of relations that could lead to armed conflict. *Good offices* can be offered by a third-party state whose diplomats assist in getting two disputant states to communicate, cease hostilities, work toward conflict resolution, or keep the peace. *Crisis diplomacy* involves negotiation between actors often characterized by surprise, high threat to values or interests, and short decision time, as occurred, for example, in the October 1962 Cuban missile crisis when the United States and Soviet Union came to the brink of nuclear war. *Coercive diplomacy* refers to veiled or explicit threats of economic sanctions or military actions designed to influence diplomats or policy makers in other states to do something they would not otherwise do. (*See also* compellence *and, by contrast, see also* deterrence; *see also* asylum; extraterritoriality.)

diplomatic immunity   (*See* diplomacy.)

disarmament   The reduction of armaments or weapons of war, ultimately to zero in *general and complete disarmament.*

dissuade, dissuasion   To persuade other states from a position of strength not to do something they might otherwise do; dissuasion is usually seen as using both positive and negative measures, but falling short of *deterrence* (that is, making threats to punish another state or states if they commit aggression or pursue some other undesirable policy). (*See also* compellence; coercive diplomacy; deterrence.)

division of labor   In international trade, the specialization in production of goods and services in which some countries as more efficient producers have a *comparative advantage* that may result in what amounts to a division of labor among countries in world markets, with some countries producing some things for export while importing other goods and services from foreign producers. The concept is drawn from production efficiencies in domestic economies achieved through specialization and the resulting division of labor and is associated with Ricardian free-trade theory. (*See also* comparative advantage.)

division of powers   As between a central government and the governments of constituent parts such as provinces or states. (*See also* state.)

dual or double-effect principle   (*See* just-war theory.)

due process   The citizen's expectation of or right to fairness, especially in relation to government, often operationalized in the form of procedures that, if followed, have a higher likelihood of assuring a fair or just outcome.

East   During the cold war years, *East* referred to the Soviet Union and other Marxist-Leninist countries, mainly those in Eastern Europe, that were part of an *East-West* struggle or conflict. A more traditional meaning is the Orient or countries of Asia. (*See also* West.)

East African Community (EAC)   Formed in 1967 in an effort to strengthen economic ties in the region; members are Kenya, Uganda, and Tanzania. An East African Development Bank also serves these three countries.

East-West   (*See* East; West.)

economic and monetary union   Economic integration to a high degree that includes not only a customs union and common market, but also centralized monetary policy making, as in a single central bank and coordination of fiscal (tax and government expenditure) policy decision making.

Economic Community of West African States (ECOWAS)   Formed in 1975 in an effort to liberalize regional trade. Members include Benin, Burkina Faso, Cape Verde, Côte d'Ivoire, the Gambia, Ghana, Guinea, Guinea-Bissau, Ivory Coast, Liberia, Mali, Mauritania, Niger, Nigeria, Senegal, Sierra Leone, and Togo.

economic development   The sustained expansion of production in an economy that raises the standard of living for the citizenry. (*See also* development.)

economic infrastructure   Production-support factors such as roads, seaports, airports, public transportation, and telecommunications that enhance a country's ability to sustain production and develop economically.

economic leverage   Carrots and sticks used to influence, persuade, or coerce another state to do something or to stop doing something. *Foreign aid* includes grants, loans, trade preferences, or military assistance provided by one country to another, often with the hope of the provider gaining something in return, such as political support for its foreign policy agenda. *Economic sanctions* include such coercive means to influence a state's behavior as a *boycott* (not purchasing the other country's exports) or going one step further with an *embargo* (prohibiting not only a government's agencies, but nongovernment or private firms as well from dealing with the country being embargoed). Although they may have value symbolically, boycotts and embargoes are often ineffective unless all states that have major economic dealings with the country collaborate. A *blockade* is the physical imposition of ships, troops, or air power to prevent goods from entering or leaving the country.

economic liberalism   (*See* liberalism.)

economic and monetary union   The deepest form of economic integration short of full political union; in addition to free trade, a common external tariff, and free movement of factors of production, an economic and monetary union integrates (or at least coordinates) fiscal and monetary policy, usually establishing a common currency and central bank to manage it. (*See also* integration.)

economic sanctions   (*See* economic leverage.)

economies of scale   Efficiencies that come from larger quantities or mass production resulting in lower costs.

economy   The production, distribution, and consumption of goods and services. Discussions of the economy generally focus on a particular state and society, but the growth of an international or global economy has expanded the focus to regional and global economies and the interdependency and interconnectedness of economies and economic actors such as multinational corporations and banks that cross national boundaries. Economic concerns can also be viewed from the perspective of individuals or groups.

economy of forces   (*See* principles of war.)

egalitarian   A democratic focus on rights to *equality* either in terms of opportunity or outcome for individuals, groups, tribes, classes, and so on. (*See also* equal protection.)

effect   Outcome of some cause or causes. (*See also* causes.)

elasticity   Ratio of the change in quantity of demand (or supply) caused by a change in price or income, the former referred to as price elasticity and latter income elasticity of demand (or supply).

elite   The upper stratum or strata of a society.

embargo   (*See* economic leverage.)

embassy   (*See* mission.)

eminent domain   A government's right to take private property for public use, usually with compensation for the owner.

emissary   One who officially represents a state; he or she may be an ambassador, or someone specially designated to convey a government's wishes, concerns, or demands.

empires   (*See* imperial system.)

empirical, empirical theory   Factual or known through observation; theories are interrelated propositions that explain or predict what is observed. Empirical theories are differentiated from value-oriented, prescriptive, or normative theories. (*See also* normative theory, cause.)

epistemic community   Associations typically across national borders among knowledgeable persons or experts in particular (often very technical) fields; these are networks of personal contacts established and maintained over time in various settings—international meetings and conferences, joint research projects, contacts in international and nongovernmental organizations, and direct communications facilitated by the Internet.

epistemology   Refers to a theory of knowledge: how we come to know what we think we know about the world and what we observe in it, a pursuit that leads us to adopt various methods and methodologies for testing and expanding our knowledge. (*See also* ontology.)

equal protection   Refers to a civil right claimed by citizens (as in the United States) to equal protection of the laws—the equality of treatment citizens have a right to demand or expect before the law. (*See also* egalitarian.)

equilibrium   When various elements of a system are in balance, as in a *balance of power among states*. (*See also* balance of power.)

espionage   The act of spying on others, as in efforts to obtain secret intelligence. *Sabotage* is destruction of property, sometimes including loss of lives, or disruption of normal operations, typically by an agent or others working for a foreign government or cause. (*See also* intelligence collection.)

ethnic, ethnicity A common, often cultural, identity of a group of people who usually also identify themselves with a larger society that includes other groups within the nation as a whole; ethnic ties can cross the formal boundaries of states. In common usage, ethnicity is usually differentiated from nationality, that is, an over-arching identity that includes diverse ethnic and other groups in society and is often associated with a particular state, as in *a nation-state*.

European Community, European Communities (EC) (*See* European Union, EU.)

European Free Trade Area (EFTA) Composed of non-European Union members, the organization originally formed as an alternative to what is now the European Union.

European Union (EU) A collaborative association of European states previously known as the European Communities (EC)—the European Coal and Steel Community (ECSC), the European Economic Community (EEC), and the European Atomic Energy Community (EURATOM). Since agreeing at a summit meeting in December 1991 in the city of Maastricht in the Netherlands to move beyond a customs union and common market toward a full economic and monetary union, the association of states is now referred to as the European Union. Members include the original six France, Germany, Italy, Belgium, the Netherlands, and Luxembourg—and nine later additions—Austria, Denmark, Finland, Greece, Ireland, Portugal, Spain, Sweden, and the United Kingdom. (*On security matters, see* Western European Union, functions to be absorbed by the EU itself.)

exchange controls Limits placed on the amounts of domestic currency that can be exchanged for other currencies, as in placing constraints on purchases of imports or the amount of domestic currency that can be taken out of the country.

exchange rate The value of one currency in terms of another currency, as when one unit of a given currency can be exchanged for ten units of another.

executive agreement Agreements made between the leaders of two or more countries that do not have the more formal characteristics of treaties. Leaders of democratic states often find such agreements preferable to treaties that, in the case of the United States, require the consent of two-thirds of the Senate before the treaty comes into force.

exports (*See* balance of trade.)

expropriation When a state nationalizes or takes private property, the state is obligated under international law to give just compensation for any property seized; however, states do not always choose to comply with this requirement. (*See also* nationalization.)

extended deterrence (*See* deterrence.)

externality When a state or other actor takes an action that has an intended or unintended impact (positive or negative) on another actor. For example, a negative external-ity occurs when Country A devalues its currency (making it less in value compared to other currencies), hence making the price of foreign imports higher and less likely to be purchased from abroad by importers in Country A.

extradition Governments often have agreements or otherwise request another government to transfer and release persons to its own custody when, for example, persons accused of crimes have sought refuge in another country.

extraterritoriality The legal fiction that an embassy or consulate and the ground it stands on are part of the sovereign territory and property of the foreign country. As a result, the host government is not supposed to enter the grounds, for example, in pursuit of dissidents. Embassies and consulates, therefore, may serve as places of *asylum* or refuge for host-country citizens seeking protection. (*See also* asylum; diplomacy.)

factor endowments (*See* factors of production.)

factors of production Land (including natural resources), labor, and capital are the *factors* essential to the production of goods and services. Countries vary significantly in the amounts of these different factors they possess. These different *factor endowments* may make some countries more efficient than others in the production of certain goods or services, which may result in specialization in accordance with the principle of *comparative advantage*. (*See also* comparative advantage.)

federal, federalism, federation (*See* state.)

feudalism, feudal system Diverse group of governmental units in ninth- to fourteenth-century Europe, including trading associations, merchant banks, local feudal barons, emperor of the Holy Roman Empire, and the Christian Church. A prime example of a *pluralist* era. In Marxist usage, a mode of production. (*See also* mode of production.)

finite, minimum deterrence (*See* deterrence.)

first-, second-strike capability In nuclear strategy, first-strike capability does not mean simply an ability to strike first. Only if a country's strategic arsenal has robust defenses in addition to substantial offenses will it be in a position to launch an attack against another nuclear-weapons state, nullifying or reducing to a tolerable level the damage that would be sustained by a retaliatory counterattack. As such, it is said to have a *first-strike capability*. Put another way, it is the military ability to blunt or withstand counterattack and to win or prevail in any such nuclear confrontation that is the acid test of whether a country has a first-strike capability, which, in turn, could be used as leverage against other states. A *second-strike capability* refers merely to being able to absorb a nuclear first strike with sufficient retaliatory forces surviving to launch a counterattack. A country without second-strike capability faces the problem that its retaliatory forces could be destroyed before they were launched, thus giving an incentive to launch a retaliatory strike on earliest warning of an attack, even before the attack is confirmed. By contrast, nuclear deterrence relations are generally more stable if the parties have a second-strike capability, because no country would have to launch its retaliatory forces until confirming that it had, in fact, been attacked. (*See also* deterrence.)

First World (*See* Third World.)

fiscal policy   National budget decisions and actions on taxing and spending. (*See also* macroeconomics; monetary policy.)

float   Nonintervention by governments in currency markets, allowing currency exchange rates to move flexibly in response to market forces (supply and demand).

fog of war   (*See* friction.)

force   Military measures intended to coerce other states against their will.

force posture   Numbers, types, locations, and other qualitative factors concerning a state's military forces.

foreign aid   (*See* economic leverage.)

foreign policy   (*See* policy.)

free markets   (*See* capitalism.)

free rider   (*See* collective goods.)

free trade, free-trade area   In the purest sense, free trade is commerce unobstructed by tariffs, quotas, or other barriers to trade, particularly the absence of government interference in market transactions. A free-trade area includes states that have eliminated (or are in the process of eliminating) tariffs, quotas, or other barriers to trade. (*See also* integration.)

friction   Clausewitz observed that when implemented, war plans in practice may not work as expected because of a number of real-world, often unexpected factors he referred to collectively as *friction*.

functional approaches   Approaches to controlling or managing conflicts that include (1) maintaining effective communications between adversaries, (2) establishing confidence- and security-building measures, and (3) conducting peacekeeping operations.

functionalism, functionalist   Functionalist theories posit that international organizations form when functions need to be performed; for example, postal exchange led in the nineteenth century to creation of the Universal Postal Union; maintenance of international liquidity led to creation of an International Monetary Fund (IMF); management of telecommunications on a global scale led to construction of the International Telecommunications Union, and so forth. *Neofunctionalism*, by contrast, looks beyond functions that need to be performed and puts more emphasis on politics, especially within and across elites, as essential to understanding how international regimes and organizations are constructed and maintained.

game theory   A decision-making approach based on the assumption of actor rationality in a competitive situation, in which each party tries to maximize gains or minimize losses. Some games are zero-sum while others are variable- or positive-sum. (*See also* zero-sum.)

genocide   Mass murder of a people typically because of their racial, ethnic, or particular identity. No other example compares in magnitude or brutality to the *Holocaust* of the 1930s and 1940s in Germany and other countries in central Europe, which was responsible for the deaths of some 6 million Jews as well as Slavs, Gypsies, homosexuals, and others considered undesirable by National Socialist (Nazi) authorities in Germany. More recent examples in the 1990s have occurred in the Balkan republics of the former Yugoslavia and among Hutu and Tutsi tribes in Rwanda and Burundi in sub-Saharan Africa.

global civil society   The gradual emergence worldwide of the rule of law and networks of relationships among people around the world composed of both state and nonstate actors to include nongovernmental organizations (NGOs) that aggregate individual interests within states, operating across the border of any single state. The explosion in the number of NGOs in recent years exemplifies this trend, as does the ability of individuals to communicate with one another through such technological means as satellite links and the Internet. The concept of global civil society captures the idea that global politics is much more than just the interactions of states; people are not just the subjects of state authorities, but as parts of worldwide organizations and as individuals able to move and communicate globally, they also influence both governmental and nongovernmental decisions and actions.

globalization   The continual increase in transnational and worldwide economic, social, and cultural interactions that transcend the boundaries of states, aided by advances in technology.

global politics   (*See* world politics.)

global warming   An increase in the volume of carbon dioxide in the atmosphere, contributing to a "greenhouse" or insulating effect that traps heat from the sun's rays and raises the average temperature around the world. Changes of only a degree or two can have substantial or even catastrophic climatic effects with changes in rainfall patterns affecting agriculture and polar ice cap meltings raising sea levels, threatening lower-lying coastal areas. Burning of hydrocarbon fuels and destruction of rain forests are among the causes usually cited for global warming.

good offices   (*See* diplomacy.)

government   Administrative unit or units that exercise authority in a political unit, making decisions and taking actions. A *puppet government* is one installed by an outside or occupying power, usually involving indigenous collaborators; the Vichy regime in France during World War II, for example, was subject to daily influence and ultimate control by the National Socialist (Nazi) regime in Germany. When a state has been invaded and occupied, a *government in exile* may be set up in a foreign country; during the Nazi occupation of World War II, General Charles de Gaulle located the French government in exile in London.

government in exile   (*See* government.)

gross domestic product (GDP)   The total value or sum of goods and services produced *domestically* usually within a given year. It amounts to GNP minus return on foreign investment, since the latter is a measure of foreign, rather than domestic, production. (*See also* gross national product.)

gross national product (GNP)   The total value or sum of a country's output of goods and services. Usually calculated on an annual basis, it is the sum of consumption, investment, government spending, and exports minus imports.

Group of Eight (G-8)   (*See* Group of Seven.)

Group of Seven (G-7)   States having the world's largest market economies—the United States, Japan, Germany,

France, the United Kingdom, Italy, and Canada. The Russian Federation is now included in the group, now often referred to as the G-8. Leaders of these countries hold periodic summit meetings at which macroeconomic and other policy issues are discussed.

groupthink A mode of thinking that people engage in when they are deeply involved in a cohesive in-group, when the members' strivings for unanimity override their motivation to appraise realistically alternative courses of actions. (The social psychologist Irving Janis is credited with important work on this subject as well as with coining the term.) Indicators of groupthink include social pressure to enforce conformity, limiting discussion to a few alternatives, failing to examine initial decisions, and making little effort to seek information from outside experts. It is assumed that groupthink enhances the possibility of poor foreign policy decisions. By contrast, measures taken to avoid groupthink—bringing alternative views and perspectives legitimately into consideration—can have an opposite, positive effect on foreign policy making.

guerrilla warfare War conducted by irregulars or *guerrillas*, usually against regular, uniformed forces, employing hit-and-run, ambush, and other tactics that allow smaller numbers of guerrillas to win battles against numerically superior, often heavily armed regular forces. Guerrilla warfare can be particularly successful if the guerrillas can rely on popular support from the people. (*See also* war.)

Gulf Cooperation Council (GCC) Formed in 1981, this international organization addresses economic and security issues of concern to Arab Gulf member states—Bahrain, Kuwait, Oman, Qatar, Saudi Arabia, and the United Arab Emirates. Iraq and non-Arab Iran are not members.

hard currencies Money preferred for use in settling obligations among countries because it is readily convertible from one currency to another and can be kept by national treasuries as monetary reserves. The U.S. dollar is a key hard currency as is the European Euro and the Japanese yen. (*See also* soft currencies.)

Heckscher-Ohlin theorem Holds that because different countries have diverse factor endowments (different amounts of land, labor, and capital), they likely will export those goods or services in which the combination of these production factors gives them a comparative advantage.

hegemonic state system (*See* state.)

hegemony, hegemonic Relations of dominance as when a major power exercises authority over countries within its sphere of influence. A state exercising hegemony is sometimes called a *hegemon*.

humanitarian intervention (*See* intervention.)

hypothesis A proposition subject to empirical test for its veracity. (*See* causes, causality, causal.)

idealism A tradition of political thought that emphasizes what unites (as opposed to divides) peoples. Traced back to the philosophical school of thought known as Stoicism, it is also associated with the writers Hugo Grotius and Immanuel Kant, who searched for such universal, uniting concepts as international law or moral

principles. A high value orientation in idealism has led many writers to present it as different from, even the opposite of, realism in foreign policy, which focuses primarily on national interest and power considerations. This rigid idealist-realist dichotomy can be misleading, however, since many realists also incorporate value considerations in their analyses and prescriptions.

ideal (or pure) type A concept developed by the German sociologist Max Weber to describe an extreme, or pure, case that is not found in this form anywhere but that serves as an analytical benchmark useful in comparing real-world cases.

identity Consists of the answer to the question "Who am I and with whom do I identify?" In international relations the answer is usually in terms of identification with a nation that may or may not be associated with an existing state. Identity, however, can be transnational, such as religious or gender identification.

imperial (suzerain) system Separate societal units associated by regular interaction, but with one among them asserting political supremacy and the others formally or tacitly accepting this claim as, for example, in the Roman empire under the Caesars. In feudal Europe and after, when a state or ruler had some authority or control over other countries or lesser political entities, these political units were said to be under the *suzerainty* of that state or ruler.

imperialism In its classic meaning, a position or policy of preeminence or dominance with respect to foreign elements, as in the Roman or British empires. Imperialism in earlier centuries involved the establishment of colonies staffed by personnel (administrators, military troops, missionaries) from the imperial country or *metropole*, which reflected what is known as *colonialism*. Although most of these former colonies have formally become independent states, the relations of economic, social, cultural, and even political dominance by the former colonial power remain, a phenomenon often called *neo-colonialism*. Influence or dominance by a former colonial or other great power by virtue of the capabilities it has over less powerful states is sometimes referred to by critics as economic, social, or cultural imperialism.

imports (*See* balance of trade.)

independent state system (*See* state.)

independent variable (*See* causes, causality, causal.)

individualism Associated with *liberalism*, the belief that individuals have particular value in themselves and for what they can do; people as individuals have more importance than the groups, tribes, communities, or societies to which they may belong. (*See also* liberalism.)

infant industry As a country develops economically, new industries may form that in the early stages are not competitive in global markets with well-established industries of the same type from other countries. As such, governments may choose to protect these infant industries from foreign competition by imposing tariffs or quotas against imports or seeking trade preferences by other countries that allow infant-industry firms to export on favorable terms to these foreign countries.

influence   (*See* power.)

insurgency   (*See* war.)

insurgent warfare   (*See* war.)

integration   The process by which political units such as states come together in varying degrees of unity, often to serve specific functions or purposes. Thus economic integration may range from defining a free trade area or customs union to agreeing on terms for a common market or economic and monetary union. (*See also* common market; customs union; economic and monetary union; free trade area.)

intelligence, intelligence collection   The overt or covert gathering of information by intelligence operatives from human sources or photography, electronic emissions, intercepted communications, and other transmissions gathered by *national technical means* (NTM) in ground stations and on ships at sea, aircraft, or earth satellites. *Strategic intelligence* supports the formulation of strategy, policy, plans, and operations at the national level, providing intelligence of use to policy makers and senior military commanders and their staffs. *Operational intelligence* supports planning and conducting military campaigns to accomplish objectives in a particular contingency or within a particular region. (*See also* espionage.)

intercommunal   Relations between communities with separate identities often within the same society. These can be friendly relations or, conversely, can involve strife including violent acts by members of one community against the other, as between Protestants and Catholics in Ireland; Hutu and Tutsi tribes in Rwanda; or Croats, Muslims, and Serbs in Bosnia.

interdependence   A situation whereby actions and events in one state, society, or part of the world affect peoples elsewhere. For interdependence to exist, there must be some degree of mutual dependence or reciprocal ties and effects among the parties involved. In most cases interdependence is *asymmetric*, meaning one party is more affected than the other. Interdependence relations can exist among states or involve other actors, such as transnational organizations or individuals, with channels of interaction or links that transcend the boundaries of states and their respective societies.

interest section   (*See* mission.)

interests   Security and welfare considerations constitute the interests often expressed as goals or objectives that any actor in world politics (whether a state, an international organization, multinational corporation, or some other nongovernmental organization) may seek to pursue. The term *national interests* is associated with states, and all states at a minimum typically seek not only to survive, but also to achieve economic vitality (or at least viability) and the protection of what they deem to be their core values. Given the general nature of interests, *objectives* are more specific goals that any international actor may choose to pursue. For example, a concern for the security and welfare of a state with a long coastline that depends on foreign trade would likely lead its policy makers to view protection of sea lanes as an important national objective.

International Atomic Energy Agency (IAEA)   International organization located in Vienna and established in 1956 with responsibilities for peaceful uses of nuclear energy while, at the same time, precluding use of these technologies or otherwise acquiring nuclear weapons by countries not now possessing them. (*See also* Nuclear Non-Proliferation Treaty.)

international commerce   Trade of goods and services between and among states and their societies.

international governmental or intergovernmental organizations (IGOs)   (*See* international organizations.)

internationalization   Increasing trade, communication, investment, and other interactions between or among *states* and their societies. When we refer to internationalization, we think in terms of national identities, a view that can be contrasted with *globalization*, which transcends or goes beyond states and their respective corporations or other organizations, taking a broad or global view of such matters. (*See also* globalization.)

international law   Law that transcends borders and applies to states as well as to individuals (natural persons) and organizations or corporations (legal persons). Sources of international law are *treaties* or *conventions* that bind states to these formal agreements even when their existing governments change, *customary practice* that has been established by states over time, the *writings of jurists* (justices or judges) such as those on the International Court of Justice, and *general principles* such as those to be discovered through reason or found in the *jus naturale*—laws of nature that some writers see as superseding those laws of individual states that contradict these general principles. The idea of a *jus gentium*—laws applicable to all of humanity, nations, and individuals—dates at least from the time of the Roman Empire and is to be found in Stoic thought.

international law of war, international law of armed conflicts   International law governing warfare and the use of force in international relations that requires legitimate reasons for using force and places specific limitations on the actual use of force. (*See also* just-war theory, doctrine.)

international liquidity   (*See* liquidity, international.)

international monetary regime   The rules on how money is exchanged and international liquidity is maintained as well as associated multilateral institutions (such as the International Monetary Fund and Bank for International Settlements).

international organizations   The multilateral institutions created by states in order to pursue common objectives that usually cannot be achieved as easily (or as well, if at all) by states acting unilaterally; for example, the European Union and its component institutions and the United Nations and its associated agencies, including the World Health Organization, World Bank, International Monetary Fund, International Civil Aviation and Maritime Organizations, and so forth. Sometimes called international governmental or intergovernmental organizations (IGOs), members of international organizations are states, which differentiates them from transnational or nongovernmental organizations (NGOs). (*See also* nongovernmental organization, NGO.)

international politics   The *political* focus is on choices made by actors with authority to do so on issues external to states or that cross the frontiers or boundaries of state jurisdiction. (*See also* international relations; world politics.)

international regime   The set of rules and associated institutions or international organizations, if any, that have been constructed by states to coordinate, manage, or regulate their relations in a particular issue area. Some regime rules have the binding character of international law, but others are followed by states because they simplify international relations by routinizing many recurring transactions or are seen as generally being in the state's enlightened self-interest. States may enforce regime rules on nonstate actors. An *international monetary regime*, for example, specifies the rules for exchanging currency among states, making provision for maintaining international liquidity through credit arrangements by which some states or institutions such as the International Monetary Fund in Washington lend currencies to states in balance-of-trade or balance-of-payments deficit. Other institutions associated with this regime include the Bank for International Settlements in Basel, Switzerland, as well as central banks and treasuries of states participating in the international regime. (*See also* international security regime.)

international relations   Generally refers to relations among states—the total of political, social, economic, cultural, and other interactions. Realists tend to feel most comfortable with this state-centric definition of the term because they customarily view states as far more important or significant than nonstate actors. (*See also* international politics; world politics.)

international security   In its narrowest construction, the term refers to defense matters among states and their respective societies. In its broadest sense, it encompasses a wide range of issues that affect the welfare of human beings—not just defense, but also economics, health, environment, human rights, and other social questions that cross national boundaries. Critics of broad definitions argue that if *security* as a concept can be construed to mean so many things, then as a practical matter it means nothing. They prefer to retain the more traditional distinction between *security* (and related defense issues) and *welfare* issues.

international security regime   A particular type of international regime with rules and associated institutions, if any, concerning some defense-related or other security concern of member states. For example, a nuclear nonproliferation international security regime exists in an effort to curb the spread of nuclear weapons and weapons-related technologies to nonnuclear states while, at the same time, it is committed in principle to working toward nuclear disarmament by those states already possessing such arms. The International Atomic Energy Agency (IAEA) in Vienna is a key institution associated with this regime. (*See also* international regime; Nuclear Non-Proliferation Treaty.)

international systems   An aggregation of similar or diverse entities united by regular interaction that sets them apart from other systems; for example, the *interstate* or *international* system of states or *world politics* understood as a system composed of both state and nonstate actors.

international terrorism   (*See* terrorism.)

interstate war   (*See* war.)

intervention   Interference in the domestic affairs of another state by diplomatic, economic, military, or other means. *Armed* or *military intervention* is a particular kind of intervention. Even though it has often occurred under one pretext or another, intervention in civil wars—understood as unresolved domestic affairs—is prohibited by international law. By contrast, intervention in a war between states in defense of the side suffering from aggression is allowable under the UN Charter, Article 51, that acknowledges the right of states to individual or collective self-defense. Some interventions are for humanitarian purposes, concerning welfare, rights, justice, or other factors relating to the condition of human beings.

investment   In business terms, the input of money or saved resources to maintain or expand productive capacity and, in turn, to generate a profit or return on investment for the investor.

invisible hand   The idea drawn from Book IV of Adam Smith's *Wealth of Nations* that competitive markets are self-regulating; that the allocation of factors of production for bringing goods and services to market can be efficiently achieved without government intervention or other actions that would affect these market transactions.

irredentism, irredentist   Seeking to acquire neighboring or other territories in another state, particularly if it is populated by peoples with a common national or ethnic heritage. (*See also* revanchism.)

irregulars   (*See* war.)

jus ad bellum   (*See* just-war theory.)

jus gentium **(law or laws of nations)**   (*See* international law.)

jus in bello   (*See* just-war theory.)

jus naturale **(natural law, law or laws of nature)**   (*See* international law.)

just-war theory, doctrine   Relying on Platonic thought, Cicero developed one of the earliest formulations of just-war theory: just wars ought to be fought justly. This idea would be developed over the centuries into a Christian doctrine by Augustine, Aquinas, Suarez, Gentilis, Vitoria, and others. Grotius adapted this thinking to an international law of war, which would become more formalized in succeeding centuries. The Hague and Geneva Conventions, for example, are based on or rely very heavily on earlier just-war theory. *Jus ad bellum* refers to the right to use force or go to war in the first place, which must satisfy all of the following conditions: (1) *just or legitimate cause* for using force, (2) that waging war is a *proportionate* response to the provocation or cause for war, (3) that the decisions for war are made by *legitimate authority*, (4) that *peaceful remedies have been exhausted*, and (5) because warfare results in destruction of lives and property that it will not be undertaken unless there is at least some *chance of success*—that using force or waging war is at best a legitimate *means* to redress a grievance; it is not a legitimate *end* in itself. *Jus in bello* refers to limitations on actual conduct in warfare, including obligations: (1) to *spare noncombatants* (sometimes referred to as innocents), (2) to exercise restraint so that the means used in war are *proportionate* to the ends sought and do not produce needless death and destruction, (3) to use only those *weapons that are not immoral in themselves* (that is, indiscriminate weapons or those that cause needless suffering), and (4) to see *military necessity as a limiting rather than expansive principle.* Sometimes the same actions in warfare can have both positive, morally legitimate effects (as in destroying a military target without any unnecessary loss of life or property) and morally negative or evil effects, as when there is also *collateral damage*—loss of life or destruction of property. According to the *principle of dual or double-effect*, such actions are legitimate only if the positive or legitimate purpose is intended, efforts have been taken to minimize collateral damage, the collateral damage caused is not disproportionate, and it occurs at the same time or after the positive effect (a provision to assure that positive or morally legitimate ends do not rely on evil means, but that evil consequences are merely another effect). To be effective, both the *jus ad bellum* and *jus in bello* rely heavily on the *right intention* of policy makers who try to follow these guidelines. In practice these principles, contrary to the requirement for *right intention*, have frequently been violated or manipulated in such a way as to justify or rationalize all forms of misconduct. Defenders of just-war theory acknowledge this criticism but argue that if war cannot be avoided altogether, these principles at least offer a means for reducing the barbarity of war, as long as policy makers choose to follow them.

kiloton   (*See* targeting.)

laissez-faire   The classical liberal idea that governments should not intervene in markets because competitive markets are understood to be self-regulating. (*See also* invisible hand.)

law of war   (*See* just-war theory; international law; international law of war.)

legitimacy   In terms of *domestic politics*, the right to rule or be obeyed based on legal grounds or, more commonly, in the eyes of the citizenry based on custom or consent. Legitimacy may apply to a form of government or regime (e.g., a particular constitution has legitimacy) or to the authorities currently in power. Lacking legitimacy, rulers often have to rely on coercion to enforce obedience, finding it difficult to carry out domestic policies, and perhaps foreign policies as well. In international politics *legitimacy* often refers to whether a government, particularly a new government of a state, is recognized by other governments of foreign states as the proper representative or agent of the state in question. After a revolution or *coup d'état*, the governments of other states may choose to withhold recognition in an effort to deny legitimacy to the new government or regime.

levels of analysis   A way to organize thinking about and analysis of world politics. Individuals, groups, states and their societies, or the overall international system are separate points of focus, each illuminating some aspect of international relations. Such levels of analysis help scholars to be systematic in their approach to understanding world politics. In examining a phenomenon such as war, for example, the observer may identify possible causes as a characteristic of the international system, states and their societies, or groups or individuals.

liberal (*See* liberalism.)

liberalism   Political philosophy with origins in the seventeenth and eighteenth centuries that emphasizes individual liberty to be achieved through a minimal state. A *laissez-faire* government—one that provides for law and order but is otherwise relatively more constrained or restricted, particularly from intervention in markets—is said to be politically and economically liberal. In both domestic and international economy, liberalism implies commitment to free-market principles generally without government intervention, including advocacy of international free-trade policies. In more recent times, liberalism has taken on a more social meaning, particularly in the United States, with reference to enhancing individual rights and well-being, typically through government action or programs.

liberalization   In the economic realm, a reduction of barriers making it easier for the import and export of goods and services, investment, and commerce in general.

libertarian   A philosophical position emphasizing individual rights, often preferring specific limits or restraints on government.

liquidity (international)   In monetary affairs, the ease with which foreign currencies are available for countries so they can settle their accounts with other countries.

long-cycle theory   An explanation of international system change in which it is argued that the global political system goes through distinct and identifiable historical cycles or recurrent patterns of behavior. The dominance of any particular state corresponds to a "long cycle," with war tending to mark the end of one cycle and the beginning of another.

macroeconomics   Focus is on how the economy as a whole works in relation to such aggregates as gross national product (GNP), gross domestic product (GDP), and so on. How government fiscal and monetary policy affects these aggregates, levels of employment, and inflation are also macroeconomic concerns. (*See also* fiscal policy; microeconomics; monetary policy.)

managed trade   Rather than leave trade to free markets, states choose to intervene, establishing understandings or making trade arrangements with other states, often to serve economic development, employment, or other domestic considerations.

market prices   The monetary value at which exchange takes place freely in accordance with supply of goods and services offered to market and demand for them.

market rates   Usually refers to interest or discount rates, rates of return on investment, currency exchange rates, or other financial rates set freely in markets in accordance with supply and demand for securities (e.g., stocks and bonds), deposits in financial institutions, foreign currencies, and other financial instruments.

markets   Refers to the exchange of goods, services, money, and other financial instruments between buyers and sellers. Governments play a role in markets through the policies they pursue concerning fiscal (taxing and spending) and monetary (managing the money supply and affecting interest rates) matters. "Free" markets refer to those left to the private or nongovernmental actors, eliminating (or at least minimizing) government interference. In practice, the degree and kind of government actions in markets vary widely. (By contrast, in "command" economies, such as Marxist-Leninist regimes, government plays a strong directive or controlling role by allocating human and natural resources and capital, setting production targets, overseeing production and distribution, and regulating prices.) Facilitated by liberalization as well as technological improvements in telecommunications and transportation, markets have become increasingly globalized. (*See also* global civil society; liberalization.)

Marxism-Leninism A body of thought inspired by the German Karl Marx and the Russian revolutionary Vladimir Lenin. Marx stressed the importance of economic and material forces and class analysis. He emphasized the dialectical and clashing unfolding of history. He predicted that contradictions in each historical epoch eventually led to the rise of a new dominant class. Lenin, building on Marx's work, argued that contradictions in capitalist societies made *imperialism* inevitable, leading to war among capitalist states as they fought over colonial resources and territory throughout the world.

mass (*See* principles of war.)

means of production The combination of land, labor, and capital used to produce goods and services. In Marxist understanding, classes are defined by their relations to the means of production; for example, in feudalism the aristocracy is identifiable by its ownership of land and the peasantry by its labor; in capitalism, the bourgeoisie owns capital (factories, machinery, and financial assets related to production), the workers contributing labor. (*See also* factors of production; mode of production.)

megaton (*See* targeting.)

mercantilism, mercantile A theory of early capitalism that saw the wealth of a nation as a function of the amount of gold and other treasure that it could accumulate. Accordingly, running trade surpluses (more exports than imports), while finding new gold in mines or accepting it in payment for goods or services became national economic policy. In his *Wealth of Nations* (1776), Adam Smith challenged this view, arguing that the true wealth of a nation was to be found in its productive capacity, not its treasure. Present-day *neomercantilist* policies pursued by some states try to maximize trade surpluses, accumulating large monetary-reserve balances.

MERCOSUR (Mercado Comun del Sur) Formed in 1991, this international organization promotes economic integration among Argentina, Brazil, Chile, Paraguay, and Uruguay.

methodology The approach one takes to an academic study; modes of research and analysis, as in the use of historical and comparative case studies, or the use of statistics as in formal hypothesis testing or causal modeling of variables.

microeconomics Focuses on how markets work, how supply and demand relate, and how prices are set. Sometimes referred to as *price theory*. On the supply side, for example, the number of firms matters in explanations of behavior in particular markets with notable variation as to whether the market in question is an oligopoly (several dominant firms), duopoly (two dominant firms), monopoly (one dominant firm), pure competition (no dominant firms), and so on. Structural realism (or neorealism) draws explicitly from these microeconomic insights in developing what is referred to as microtheory on behavior in international systems in which the number of dominant states (multipolar, bipolar, unipolar) is similar in concept to the number of dominant firms in particular markets. (*See also* macroeconomics; structural realism.)

migration The movement of peoples from one country or area to others. Some *immigration* (arrivals) and *emigration* (departures) occur routinely; however, in the absence of obstacles, political refugees and economically deprived peoples are likely to move in large numbers.

military (force-employment) doctrines The approaches developed over time by military or other security experts to the effective use of armed forces for specified purposes; for example, doctrine may hold that full-scale use of tactical air forces against military targets in another country be preceded by attacks against that country's air-defense capabilities in order to establish air superiority or command of the air, which, when established, will allow the full-scale attack to proceed without effective opposition.

military necessity Principle in warfare that battlefield success depends on destroying or weakening an adversary's warfighting capabilities. A narrow construction of military necessity restricts actions in war to only those required for destruction or weakening of an enemy's warmaking capability; however, some have used (or abused) the principle to justify or rationalize any number of actions in war, including atrocities committed against civilian populations.

minimum deterrence (*See* deterrence.)

Missile Technology Control Regime (MTCR) An international security regime with rules that restrain transfer of missiles and missile-related technologies. (*See also* international regime; international security regime.)

mission A country's official foreign representation to another country or an international organization. A *delegation* is an official government representation to an international organization or conference. The *ambassador* is a state's highest ranking representative, assigned to the country's *embassy* in another state or its *mission* to an international organization. The ambassador is also the personal representative of a state's president or prime minister. The *Chief of Mission* is the highest ranking diplomat at a mission, usually the ambassador. The *Deputy Chief of Mission* (DCM) is the second highest ranking diplomat at a mission. *Chargé d'Affaires* is a French term that usually refers to the DCM or number-two ranking diplomat at a mission when the Chief of Mission is not present or has left the capital or country.

Country team is an American management concept that aids in coordinating the work of the many agencies represented at a U.S. mission. In principle country-team meetings allow for discussion of issues, enhancing the overall effectiveness of the mission. *Consul general* is the title of the official in charge of a *consulate*, which is a mission (usually subordinate to the country's embassy in the capital of the host country, but in a different city) that deals with citizen services whether for their own country, the host country, or those of other foreign countries (e.g., issuance of visas to foreign nationals desiring rights to enter the home country for tourist, student, or business purposes or to emigrate and acquire citizenship; visitation to citizens in foreign jails and prisons; or promotion of commerce such as trade and investment). *Consular sections* also perform similar functions within the embassy in the capital city. When diplomatic relations are first established or are being *normalized* after a period in which they have been broken, a consulate may be the first mission established, later upgrading the level of representation to an embassy with exchange of ambassadors, when *normalization* of relations is complete. When two countries have severed diplomatic relations and closed their respective missions, an *interest section* is often established in a mutually friendly or disinterested country's embassy to maintain an avenue for some minimal contact (e.g., the United States relies on its interest section in the Swiss embassy in Havana as a point of contact for dealing with the Cuban government, should it be necessary).

mode of production   The form of political economy associated with the production of goods and services at different historical periods—a term used in Marxist understanding of ancient slavery, feudalism, and capitalism as different modes of production. (*See also* means of production.)

monetarists   Those putting emphasis on understanding how money supply (volume of money in circulation, the "velocity" of money exchange or transaction flows, interest rates, currency exchange rates, etc.) affect the economy as a whole and markets in particular. As between monetary and fiscal policy, greater emphasis is placed on the former. (*See also* exchange rate; macroeconomics; microeconomics; monetary policy.)

monetary policy   National decisions and actions that affect the money supply, interest rates, and exchange rates. (*See also* exchange rate; fiscal policy; macroeconomics; monetarists.)

money   An instrument that provides a store of value and serves as a medium to facilitate exchange in market transactions. In the absence of money, exchange of goods and services is by trading one for another, referred to as barter.

multi-ethnic state   (*See* state.)

multilateral diplomacy   (*See* diplomacy.)

multilateralism   Working international issues jointly rather than unilaterally by a single state; a means to achieve mutual gains as in developing mutually acceptable norms and institutions. Associated with international relations as well as the idea of an emerging *global civil society*.

multinational banks   (*See* banks.)

multinational corporation (MNC)   A corporate firm based or headquartered in one country but producing goods or services and conducting other operations in two or more countries.

multinational state   (*See* state.)

multipolar, multipolarity   (*See* structure.)

multi-tribal state   (*See* state.)

mutually assured destruction (MAD)   (also referred to as **mutual assured destruction**) The nuclear deterrence doctrine that avoids resort to war by reciprocal threat of punishment through an unacceptable level of (or mass) destruction, should either party commit aggression or take other hostile action against the other that would provoke such a response.

nation, nationality   People with a common identity who have formed a nation-state or aspire to do so. (*See* ethnic, ethnicity; nation-state.)

nationalization   The taking by governments of private property for public ownership or use. Owners suffering such loss of assets may or may not be compensated; however, consistent with international law such takings are supposed to be accompanied by fair compensation as well as being nondiscriminatory (e.g., not singling out or targeting a particular firm or a particular foreign country's nationals). (*See also* expropriation.)

nation-state   (*See* state.)

national interest   (*See* interest.)

national self-determination   The view that a people with a common identity have the right to be independent from outside control, as in establishing a state for such a national group.

national technical means   (*See* verification.)

nationalism   Promoting national identity, usually to the exclusion of other, competing identities and legitimizing actions of states taken for national purposes. Nations without states often solidify movements to establish a nation-state around nationalist themes.

natural law   A philosophical view that claims there are laws inherent in nature that transcend any laws made by mere mortals. Such thinking is closely tied to the writings of Augustine, Aquinas, and other Christian writers of the late Roman empire and Middle Ages.

natural rights   Reference to the theory that human rights in nature can be discovered through reason. Social-contract theorists such as Locke and Rousseau saw rights in this naturalist understanding; however, utilitarians such as Bentham and Mill argued that human rights rested on other grounds also discoverable through reason, that human rights constitute the greatest good or happiness for the greatest number. (*See* utilitarian.)

neoclassical economics, political economy, economists   Late nineteenth- and early twentieth-century developments in economic thought departed from the labor theory of value held by classical economists, seeing value in a market context with price as the outcome of demand for and supply of particular products (goods or services). Utility and marginal utility (the value to be found in each additional unit of a good or service), marginal cost in relation to marginal revenue, and elasticity of supply and demand are examples of concepts in market analysis developed by neoclassical economists. The English writer Alfred Marshall and the French writer Leon Walras were among the most prominent early neoclassical contributors. (*See also* classical economics.)

neocolonial, neocolonialism (*See* imperialism.)

neofunctionalism, neofunctionalist (*See* functionalism.)

neomercantilist (*See* mercantilism, mercantile.)

netwar Conflicts in which the combatant is organized along networked lines or employs networks for operational control and other communications. Such networks provide lucrative targets to an adversary.

neutrality, neutral Neutral states do not take sides in an international dispute or war or join an alliance. Some, such as Switzerland, claim *permanent* neutrality. Others choose to be neutral, or perhaps more accurately, *nonaligned* as a tactical choice that serves their interests at a particular time.

New International Economic Order (NIEO) Project developed under UN auspices, particularly in the 1960s, 1970s, and 1980s, that called for trade preferences, concessionary loans, capital investment and other measures by economically advanced countries, thus contributing to Third World development.

newly industrializing country (NIC) Country such as Brazil, Taiwan, Singapore, South Korea, or Malaysia whose rapid economic growth over the past thirty years made the label *Third World* inappropriate. These countries exhibit strong *market* orientations, develop industrially, and heavily emphasize *exports*.

Nonaligned Movement (NAM) Composed of those Third World states wishing to avoid cold war alliances with the United States, the Soviet Union or other major powers, the NAM originated formally in the 1955 Bandung (Indonesia) Conference. Early leaders included India's Nehru, Yugoslavia's Tito, and Indonesia's Sukarno.

nongovernmental organization (NGO) Transnational organizations with a standing independent of governments, often with diversified membership, that work to fulfill specific political, social, or economic objectives that may benefit or have some positive or negative impact on a wide range of persons. Examples include Amnesty International (human rights) and Doctors Without Borders (medical support for health care crises in the Third World). Because of their nongovernmental character, NGOs may refer to multinational corporations and banks; labor unions; privately owned telecommunications, newspaper, and other print media firms; churches and other religious organizations; and others. (*See also* international organizations.)

normative theory Value-oriented or philosophical theory that focuses on what ought to be. As such it is usually different from *empirical* theories, which try to explain the way things are or predict what they will be. (*See also* empirical, empirical theory.)

norms Values that states or peoples over time take seriously and by which they are influenced, for instance, a belief in universal human rights. Norms may also erode over time, for example, the prohibition against intervention in the internal affairs of a state.

North, South North refers to advanced industrial and post industrial, high-income, First World countries and societies generally in northern parts of the northern hemisphere (with such notable exceptions as Australia and New Zealand); the South is composed of the less industrially developed, lower income, Third World countries that tend to be located farther south, including most countries in the southern hemisphere.

North American Free Trade Agreement (NAFTA) Free-trade area or association among the United States, Canada, and Mexico. (*See also* free-trade area.)

North Atlantic Treaty Organization (NATO) Formed in 1949 during the cold war, NATO is an alliance or collective-defense organization now headquartered in Brussels, Belgium. Its members include Belgium, Canada, Czech Republic, Denmark, France, Germany, Greece, Hungary, Iceland, Italy, Luxembourg, Norway, the Netherlands, Poland, Portugal, Turkey, Spain, the United Kingdom, and the United States. Since the end of the cold war, other nonmember Central and Eastern European states have established formal links or association with NATO in a Partnership for Peace. In addition to its UN Charter Article 51 collective-defense status, NATO also performs collective-security, peacekeeping, and other tasks under UN auspices. (*See also* Article 51; collective defense; collective security.)

Nuclear Non-Proliferation Treaty (NPT) Convention that prohibits transfer of nuclear weapons and nuclear-weapons technologies to nonnuclear countries, pledging nuclear countries to work constructively toward nuclear disarmament.

objectives (*See* interests.)

offense, offensive, counter-offensive To initiate actions that threaten or attack another state or to posture military forces to take such actions. A credible offensive posture requires robust defenses as well. If attacked, a state may choose to take defensive measures first as it prepares to launch a *counteroffensive*.

ontology Refers to one's worldview: the essence of things and the properties of existence in the world as we understand them. As human beings, we often bring to the study different assumptions and presuppositions about the way things are and how they relate. (*See also* epistemology.)

opportunity cost When a decision is made to do one thing, the cost of not pursuing some alternative course of action; for example, in national budgets, money spent for one program is no longer available for spending on some other program, the latter being an opportunity cost.

Organization for Security and Cooperation in Europe (OSCE) Growing out of a series of conferences (CSCE) that began in the 1970s, the OSCE is a widely inclusive international organization that includes most European countries in the Atlantic-to-Urals area as well as the United States and Canada. Confidence- and security-building as well as cultural, commercial, and human rights issues have been core concerns on its agenda.

Organization for the Prohibition of Chemical Weapons Designed to verify that state signatories of various chemical weapons conventions are abiding by the agreements.

Organization of African Unity (OAU) Pan-African international organization that includes both Saharan and sub-Saharan states.

Organization of American States (OAS) Pan-American international organization that includes North, Central (and Caribbean), and South American states.

Organization of Arab Petroleum Exporting Countries (OAPEC) Formed in 1968, this international organization includes Arab OPEC members Algeria, Bahrain, Egypt, Iraq, Kuwait, Libya, Qatar, Saudi Arabia, Syria, Tunisia and the United Arab Emirates.

Organization of Petroleum Exporting Countries (OPEC) Formed in 1960, this international organization performs like a *cartel*, setting production limits in an attempt to regulate supply and prices on the global market. Member states now include Algeria, Libya, Nigeria, Indonesia, Iran, Iraq, Kuwait, Qatar, Saudi Arabia, United Arab Emirates, and Venezuela. (*See also* cartel.)

overvalued currency Overvalued currencies are those in which a country's currency exchange rate is too high because it stimulates imports by making the price of imports below market (relatively inexpensive to domestic consumers) and, by contrast, discourages or dampens exports by making the price of exports relatively expensive to would-be buyers from abroad. (*See also* undervalued currency.)

pacta sunt servanda (*See* treaty.)

pacifism The rejection of the use of force, war, and other forms of violence against other human beings.

parliamentary government A form of government in which the head of the government (the prime minister) and those in the cabinet are also members of the legislature. In the United Kingdom, for example, there is a fusion of powers between the executive and legislative branches. (*See also* presidential government.)

partition Division and separation of peoples, particularly those with a propensity or demonstrated record of engaging in intercommunal violence; there is, for example, partition between Greek- and Turkish-speaking inhabitants of Cyprus. De facto partition (partition as a matter of fact) occurs when peoples divide and separate themselves into separate areas; de jure partition (partition as a matter of law) is a more formal set of legally binding division and separation arrangements.

peace Definitions include the absence of war; a situation of security, order, or stability; and harmonious relations among states and other actors.

peacekeeping Task performed by UN or other multilateral forces in an effort to keep conflicting parties from resorting (or returning) to armed hostilities. Related functions are *peace monitoring* and *peace enforcement* of terms between the conflicting parties. *Peace making* refers to measures, including the use of armed force, to establish a ceasefire and basis for a more durable peace.

per capita income (PCI) The mean or average income for each person. Calculated on an annualized national basis,

it is the gross national product or gross domestic product divided by the total population.

persona non grata (*See* diplomat.)

pluralism, pluralists An image of world politics that emphasizes the multiplicity of international actors—states, international organizations, and transnational organizations—challenging the realist preoccupation with the state. Pluralists do not view the state as a unitary, rational actor, but rather as a battleground for conflicting bureaucratic and other interests, subject to the pressures of both domestic and transnational interest groups.

polarity (*See* structure.)

policy Decisions and actions taken by governments or other authoritative actors. Some policies of states deal with domestic and societal matters; externally oriented decisions and actions are the domain of foreign policy. (*See also* decision.)

political asylum Protection granted to individuals who face persecution, violation of human rights, or other denial of civil rights and liberties in their home and other countries.

political culture The norms, values, and orientations of a society's culture that are politically relevant; for instance, many societies traditionally defer to political authorities in making domestic and foreign policies. Other, more participatory political cultures reflect a public interest in political matters with individuals, groups, and organizations attempting to influence political decisions.

political economy The intersection of politics (or authoritative choice) with economics, which is concerned with seemingly unlimited wants in a world of relative scarcity of resources.

political exception rule Used by states to justify their refusal to extradite a suspected terrorist to another country when they believe the act was done for political (not criminal) reasons.

political liberalism (*See* liberalism.)

positive sum (*See* game theory; zero-sum.)

positivism The concept that law is what law makers, following constitutional procedures, define it to be. In international law, treaties and conventions are a key source of this human-constructed law. A positive law tradition, as in Anglo-American law, differs from the natural law tradition in some continental European countries and their former colonies, which see legal principles as discoverable through reason in relation to natural law. Positivism may also refer to a modern or scientific methodology by which truth claims are formalized and hypotheses are subject to rigorous empirical test.

power The actual or potential influence or coercion a state (or other actor) can assert relative to other states and nonstate actors because of the political, geographic, economic and financial, technological, military, social, cultural, or other capabilities it possesses. *Influence* is the ability to get a state or other unit to do something it would otherwise not do through its deference to the relative capabilities or status of the requesting party, by explicit promises or provision of rewards, or by threats or actual punishment. *Coercion* is the ability to force another state or other unit to do something it would not otherwise do through the threat or use of force or other sanctions. Particularly from a realist perspective, power is the currency of world politics. (*See also* authority.)

power transition theory An explanation of change in the international system that can be traced back to Thucydides. It is argued that there is a tendency for the powers of member states to change at different rates because of political, economic, and technological developments. In time, the differential growth of power of the various states causes a fundamental redistribution of power in the system, usually as a result of a war when an ascending power challenges the hegemony of the dominant power.

predict (*See* theory.)

presidential government Strong powers reside in the office of the president as chief executive separate from legislative authority; presidential governments include the United States and France. (*See also* parliamentary government; separation of powers.)

preventive diplomacy (*See* diplomacy.)

price elasticity (*See* elasticity.)

principles of war Associated with the Prussian Clausewitz, the Frenchman Jomini, and others, such warfighting criteria or principles have been specified as guides for planners and commanders. These include principles of the *objective* (what is the goal, clearly stated and understood), *offensive* (aimed at destroying or substantially weakening an enemy's war-making capability), *mass or concentration of forces* (avoiding weak fronts through excessive dispersion of forces), *economy of forces* (not wasting finite military resources), *maneuver* (to include mobility), *surprise* (gaining an offensive advantage), *security* (including defense of one's forces from surprise or other decisive attack), *simplicity* (avoiding excessive, unnecessary complexity), and *unity of command* (with the locus or loci of authority clearly specified and understood).

privateering, privateer As when privately owned, armed ships have governmental authority to attack enemy shipping, typically in wartime.

privatization vs. socialization The former is an effort or program to shift ownership to nongovernmental or private hands, and the latter, by contrast, to publicly or state-owned means of production. (*See also* factors of production; markets; means of production.)

profit Net revenues, derived from subtracting outlays or costs from gross revenues or income. (*See also* surplus value.)

proletariat (*See* class struggle.)

protectionism Policies intended to favor the market position of a country's industries and other producers by imposing tariffs or quotas on imports, subsidizing production, and other measures. (*See also* free trade; markets.)

public goods (*See* collective goods.)

public opinion The views of the citizenry on issues of public interest and concern. When public opinion supports a government's domestic and foreign policies, the political capabilities of the state are enhanced. Loss of public support may undermine the legitimacy of policies and the political authorities responsible for them.

puppet government (*See* government.)

race, racial, racism Distinctions based primarily on physical similarities and differences such as skin color, although cultural and other factors may also be significant. Racism usually refers to assertions of alleged superiority by one racial group over another.

raison d'état, Staatsräson French and German terms, respectively, that indicate the realist justification for policies pursued by state authorities. First and foremost of these justifications or criteria is security, followed by other interests and associated objectives.

rational choice To act rationally requires a rank ordering of preferred goals, consideration of all feasible alternatives to attain these goals in the light of existing capabilities, and consideration of the costs and benefits associated with using particular methods to attain particular goals. The assumption is often made in international relations research that actors do indeed act rationally. This assumption is made in order to develop hypotheses and to produce insights, theoretical explanation, and prediction.

real terms Since the value or purchasing power of a currency changes over time, particularly because of inflation, statistics expressed in *real terms* are those that factor inflation out of calculations. For example, for comparative purposes GNP or GDP statistics over a ten-year period may be expressed in constant or uninflated dollars, converting each year's actual totals to the same value expressed in the value of dollars in a particular, specified year. Thus one can refer to 2001 dollars or 1991 dollars, using one or the other as the benchmark for comparison.

realism, realists An image of international relations or world politics that can be traced back more than two thousand years. Realists tend to hold a rather pessimistic view, emphasizing the struggle for power and influence among political units acting in a rational, unitary manner in pursuit of objectives grounded in their separate, often divergent interests.

realpolitik A German term referring to foreign policy ordered or motivated by power politics. As Thucydides commented on the conflict between ancient Athens and Melos, the strong (Athens) do what they will and the weak (Melos) do what they must.

reciprocity (*See* diplomat.)

refugee Persons displaced because of war or other political or economic causes. (*See also* political asylum.)

regime Domestically, another term for government or a particular form of government, as in a *democratic regime* or *authoritarian regime*. (*See also* international regime.)

relativism (moral or cultural) The belief that moral or ethical principles are not universal, but rather are tied to particular situational or cultural contexts.

repatriation In economics, a multinational corporation taking its profits out of a country in which it has invested and sending them back to the home country.

reserves (monetary) Cash or assets easily converted into cash held out of use by a bank, company, or state to meet expected or unexpected demands.

revanchism   A militaristic movement or philosophy aimed at reclaiming lost lands. (*See also* irredentism.)

sabotage   (*See* espionage.)

savings   Production minus consumption is surplus that can be saved or invested. (*See also* surplus value.)

second-strike capability   (*See* first-, second-strike capability.)

Second World   (*See* Third World.)

security   For realists, the basic survival and protection of the state. Pluralists have a more expansive definition, also applying the concept to individuals and groups of people. In fact, the state may be not a provider of security, but rather a threat to the security of many people.

security dilemma   As states spend more on defense, even if only for defensive purposes, their opponents may feel threatened and increase their own defense spending. An increasing spiral of defense spending does not in fact increase security, as each party feels more and more threatened.

separation of powers   A form of government in which power is divided among two or more branches of government, for example, the United States, with executive, legislative, and judicial branches. (*See also* state, federal, presidential government.)

slavery   A social system or form of political economy based on involuntary servitude. In Marxist usage, reference is to ancient *slavery* as a *mode of production*. (*See also* mode of production.)

social constructivism   A theoretical perspective on international relations and world politics that claims that values and ideas or concepts (such as balance of power or multilateralism) are constituted or constructed over time such that they acquire legitimacy or acceptance as the way international relations are (or ought to be) conducted. Ideas and concepts about international relations do not exist somehow in nature; they are not "givens" or essential attributes but are rather of human origin and humanly constructed. The world is what states (and others) choose to make of it.

social contract   The idea that human beings, acting in their own enlightened self-interest, would agree to bind themselves to one or another political or governing arrangement.

social democratic   A political perspective that, while favoring liberty, puts greater emphasis than libertarianism does on equality and community as values to be realized in social policy. Social democrats also tend to rely on government programmatic approaches to social questions. (*See also* libertarian.)

social development   Concept used in this text for dealing with intercommunal conflict that refers first to building an acceptance of people in other communities, states, or societies as fellow human beings, expanding from this base to developing relations based on mutual respect, trust, and other higher values. (*See also* development.)

social liberalism, social liberal   A political perspective that, while sharing the commitment to individualism, puts emphasis on government programs or other social actions as means to improve the position or conditions of individuals. By contrast, classical liberalism is *laissez-faire*, minimizing the role of government.

socialism   Public (as in state or governmental) ownership of the means of production, particularly major industries or utilities. In Marxist usage, a *mode of production*. (*See also* mode of production.)

society of states   The view of some realists that at certain times in history states have agreed upon basic rules, norms, and international laws to govern their relations. The nineteenth-century Concert of Europe is one example.

soft currencies   Money not readily convertible from one currency to another and, as a result, may or may not be accepted as payment for international obligations. Although small amounts may be kept on hand, soft currencies normally are not counted as monetary reserves. (*See also* hard currencies.)

South   (*See* North, South.)

Southern Cone   (*See* MERCOSUR.)

sovereign, sovereignty   A claim to political authority based on territory and autonomy, historically associated with the modern state. Internally it is the right claimed by states to exercise exclusive political authority over a defined geographic space or territory; it also includes the claim to a right to autonomy. No external actor such as another state enjoys authority within the borders of the state. A sovereign state claims a right to exercise *internal* sovereignty over its territory and *external* sovereignty in terms of relations with other states—no one has the right to tell a state how to conduct its domestic or foreign relations. States differ in power, but as sovereign entities they are, in principle, legal equals.

Special Drawing Rights (SDRs)   Once dubbed by journalists as "paper gold," SDRs are an IMF line of credit that member countries can draw on for getting foreign currencies needed for making international payments; as such, SDRs can be counted as part of the country's monetary reserves.

Staaträson   (*See* raison d'état.)

stability, destabilizing   Some theorists compare unipolar, bipolar, and multipolar international systems in terms of which is more or less stable. Stable deterrence relations are said to depend on maintaining second-strike capabilities that would allow either party to absorb a first strike prior to choosing whether and how to retaliate. By contrast, when one party fears it has lost (or will lose) its second-strike capability, this may be *destabilizing*, because it may be prone in a crisis to launch first or to launch on warning of an attack, even before it has confirmed that an attack has actually taken place.

stake holder   Denotes an ownership stake in a given firm. Because it is a broader, more inclusive term, *stake holder* is often preferred to *stock holder*.

state   Consists of a territory with defined boundaries, a population (with or without a common identity), a government or administration, and recognition as a sovereign state by other sovereign states. The state is viewed as the key actor in international or world politics. A *nation-state* is a single people with a common identity (nation) who live in a given state (such as Japan or Germany). *Nonstate nations* such as the Kurds have aspired to the creation of a Kurdish nation-state; Kurdish peoples are to be found in Turkey, Syria,

Iraq, Iran, and in former Soviet republics in the trans-Caucasus region. A *binational state* includes a society with two nations or national identities (such as the Flemish-speaking and French-speaking "nations" in Belgian society); an example of a *multinational* or *multiethnic state* is the Russian Federation with its Russian majority and non-Russian minorities; and a *multitribal state* such as Nigeria that includes Yoruba, Ibo, and Hausa-Fulani tribal identities. A *city-state*, as suggested by the term itself, refers to a city that has many of the attributes of a modern state, including a government, armed forces, and foreign and domestic policies. Historic city-states include Sparta and Athens in ancient Greece and Venice and Florence in Renaissance Italy. A *unitary state* has only one government with all significant executive, legislative, and judicial power concentrated at the national level (e.g., Japan, France, and the United Kingdom). By contrast, a *federal state* or *federation* is one in which there is a *division of power* between the central government and constituent governments in states or provinces (e.g., the United States, Canada, and the Federal Republic of Germany). A *welfare state* is one in which extensive government programs exist to provide for the well-being or welfare of the population. The term *hegemonic state system* refers to a condition in which one or more states enjoy a position of dominance over other states in the international or interstate system (such as Athens and Sparta in the fifth century B.C. or, quite apart from their own rivalries, the collective hegemony of five European powers for several decades following the Congress of Vienna in 1815). By contrast, the term *independent state system* refers to political entities that claim and can retain the ultimate authority and ability to make both foreign and domestic policies without external interference.

state capitalism (*See* capitalism.)

state of nature A philosophical construct referring to a time prior to the creation of civil society—a world without governmental authority, also an analogy to the *anarchic* structure of the international system. An important concept, particularly for realists who follow the thinking of Hobbes, as it raises the issue of how order and stability can be achieved in an international system of states competing for power and prestige.

strategic defense (*See* defense.)

strategy, tactics Strategy usually refers to an overall plan for the use of various capabilities to accomplish objectives, whereas tactics are usually specific or particular measures for accomplishing tasks consistent with these strategic purposes.

structural adjustment The use of fiscal and monetary policies (cutting spending, increasing taxes, raising interest rates, etc.) to curb or dampen an economy deemed to be "overheated"; such policies often have adverse effects in the short run on businesses, employment, and return on investment, although the objective of such austerity policies is to provide a foundation for sustained economic growth over the longer term. (*See also* fiscal policy; macroeconomics; monetary policy.)

structural violence Refers, particularly in contemporary Marxist thought, to the oppression and poor living conditions of victims of class domination that result in lower life expectancy, sustained poverty, malnutrition, and disease.

structure (systemic), structural realism (neorealism) In realist thought about international systems, particularly structural or "neorealist" theorizing, *structure* refers to the distribution of power among states. Thus a world subject to the influence of one great power is *unipolar*; to two principal great powers is *bipolar*; and to three or more is *multipolar*. (*See also the discussion in* microeconomics.)

suboptimal Less than the best choice or outcome, although it may be deemed good enough.

subsidiary A subordinate firm or unit of a larger corporation.

supply What is available for purchase (brought to market) at a given price or range of possible prices, whether currency (such as U.S. dollars), commodity (such as oil), manufactured goods (such as automobiles and computers), or a service (such as airline transportation, education, or banking). (*See also* elasticity.)

supranational Beyond or above the level of a state. If one were created, a world government would be a supranational authority, governing the relations among states and other actors in world politics.

surplus value In Marxist usage, the value of goods and services produced comes from the labor put into their production. After paying wages (which tend toward subsistence or minimum levels) and other costs, the remainder is *surplus* that can be pocketed or invested by the owners of land or capital. (*See* profit.)

surprise (*See* principles of war.)

survivability In nuclear deterrence theory, a second-strike capability depends upon the ability of some proportion of retaliatory forces to avoid destruction and thus survive a first strike, particularly a surprise attack. Survivability can be enhanced by increased numbers of dispersed forces, hardening or shielding weaponry against attack, putting weapons underground or underwater, and making at least some weapons mobile.

sustainable development Increased economic production puts increasing pressure on resources and adds pollution, which can undermine continued development. Rapid population growth adds further strain. For economic development to continue or be sustained over the long term, attention must be paid to these resource, environmental, and demographic constraints.

system (*See* international systems.)

tactics (*See* strategy.)

targeting Process of selecting certain objects or *targets* against which military force is directed. Selecting military targets (such as tank and troop concentrations, railroad junctions, air fields, command posts) is referred to as *counterforce* targeting, while selecting industrial targets and population centers is referred to as *countervalue* targeting. When particular targets are struck, some damage may spill over to kill people and destroy property—so-called *collateral damage*. Different targets require different weaponry and modes of attack. Nuclear weapons are measured in terms of yield or explosive force as *kilotons* (equivalent to thousands of tons of TNT) or *megatons* (millions of tons of TNT).

tariffs Taxes placed by a government on imported goods from other countries.

telemetry (*See* verification.)

terms of trade The value or prices of a country's exports compared to the value or prices of imports. Third World or low-income countries, for example, often have adverse terms of trade. The agricultural or mineral commodities they produce for export tend to have relatively static or declining prices, whereas the manufactures and other products they import tend to be rising in price.

terrorism Politically motivated violence, designed to influence an audience beyond the immediate victim and perpetrated by clandestine state agents or by subnational or transnational groups. *Domestic* terrorism involves a domestic terrorist group attacking against a domestic target. By contrast, *international* terrorism goes beyond the borders of any one state with respect to the terrorist group, target attacked, or territory on which the incident is planned or takes place. Thus, if Jihad terrorists attack an Egyptian government building in Cairo, it is domestic terrorism. But if the same group attacks foreign tourists in Cairo, it is an act of international terrorism.

theory (*See* empirical theory; normative theory.)

Third World A term devised during the cold war era referring to less-developed countries, many being part of the so-called "nonaligned movement," meaning they did not wish to choose sides between the capitalist West or *First World* and the socialist or communist *Second World*. The term *Third World* also had the positive meaning among French socialists in the 1960s that, like the *third estate* of common people at the time of the French Revolution, the bulk of the world's population in the Third World need not remain at the bottom of the heap. The First World—sometimes referred to as the "West" or the "North"—includes North America, much of Europe, and Japan. With the collapse of communism in many countries at the end of the cold war, the terms *First* and *Second World* are used less frequently.

trade (*See* balance of trade; comparative advantage; Hekscher-Ohlin theorem; trade barriers; trade preferences.)

trade barriers Restrictions placed on the import of foreign goods or services. The barrier may be a tariff (tax) or quota (quantitative limitation) on imports or a nontariff barrier, such as health standards on imported meats that effectively exclude them from the domestic market.

trade preference A special arrangement that allows easy access on a cost-competitive basis by a foreign producer to a country's domestic market; for example, European Union members have granted trade preferences to Third World countries, particularly to their former colonies.

transfer pricing Scheme by which a corporation with subsidiaries or divisions in different countries can price components manufactured or exchanged between one division or subsidiary and another *within* the same corporation to minimize tax exposure, maximize profits, or repatriate earnings to the corporate home country. Transfer-pricing schemes are sometimes contrary to the interests of the governments and states in which an MNC operates.

transgovernmental Relations involving links, ties, or even coalitions among bureaucratic or other official actors of different states.

transnational (*See* transnational organizations and movements.)

transnational criminal organizations (TCOs) (*See* transnational organizations and movements.)

transnational organizations and movements Nonstate actors that cross state borders, including (1) institutions pursuing their own economic goals such as international banks and multinational corporations (MNCs); (2) nongovernmental organizations (NGOs) with a strictly humanitarian agenda (e.g., Doctors Without Borders) or organizations with broader political, social, or environmental agendas and constituencies (such as Amnesty International or Greenpeace); and (3) terrorist groups that operate across borders as well as transnational criminal organizations (TCOs).

transparency Refers to an open-information environment even among adversaries so that each state can know what the others are doing through exchange of information, intelligence, and other means. (*See* confidence- and security-building measures.)

treaty A written agreement or contract between two or more states pledging adherence to any number of commitments, including arms reduction, trade arrangements, the pursuit of collective security via an alliance, health standards, protection of the environment, and so forth. In international law, treaties are binding (*pacta sunt servanda*) even though there is no global or international enforcing authority per se.

trend A recurrent pattern observable over time that may differ from what was typical or expected in an earlier period.

tribe, tribalism Tribes are social or societal units with an authority structure and shared or common identity in a society (e.g., Tutsis and Hutus are competing tribes in Rwanda and Burundi; Ibo, Yoruba, and Hausa-Fulani are tribal groupings in Nigeria). Tribalism refers to the culture of tribal life, particularly a commitment to it.

ultimatum A statement issued from one state to another demanding compliance, specifying that certain actions be taken or halted, usually within a specified time period.

undervalued currency Undervalued currencies are those in which a country's currency exchange rate is too low because it discourages or dampens imports by making the price of imports above market (relatively expensive to domestic consumers) and, by contrast, stimulates exports by making them relatively inexpensive to would-be buyers from abroad. (*See also* exchange rates; overvalued currency.)

uneven development The gains from economic growth tend to be asymmetric with some countries or parts of countries gaining more than others.

UNHCR   (*See* United Nations.)

unipolar, unipolarity   (*See* structure.)

unit of analysis   What is being studied, for example, a state or a decision-making unit.

unitary state   (*See* state.)

United Nations (UN)   Formed in 1945, an international organization that includes almost all (some 193) of the world's states as members. Principal organs include the General Assembly, Security Council, Secretariat, Economic and Social Council, Trusteeship Council, and International Court of Justice. *Specialized agencies* affiliated with the UN through the Economic and Social Council include the following international organizations: World Bank (or IBRD, International Bank for Reconstruction and Development), International Monetary Fund (IMF), International Labor Organization (ILO), Food and Agricultural Organization (FAO), Educational, Scientific, and Cultural Organization (UNESCO), International Civil Aviation Organization (ICAO), Universal Postal Union (UPU), International Telecommunications Union (ITU), World Meteorological Organization (WMO), International Maritime Organization (IMO), World Trade Organization (WTO), the Industrial Development Organization (UNIDO), and others. *Organizational units tied to the UN General Assembly* include the United Nations High Commissioner for Refugees (UNHCR), the High Commissioner for Human Rights (UNHCHR), the Conference on Trade and Development (UNCTAD), International Children's Emergency Fund (UNICEF), Development Programme (UNDP), Environment Program (UNEP), World Food Program (WFP), Population Fund (UNFPA), and others.

utilitarian   A philosophical school associated with Jeremy Bentham and John Stuart Mill based on the principle of the greatest good or happiness for the greatest number.

variable-sum   (*See* game theory; zero-sum.)

verification   Finding out whether another party to a treaty or other agreement is living up to its obligations. Arms control treaties and agreements have relied when possible on onsite inspections, but also on *national technical means* (NTM) of verification (such as high-technology ground stations, ships, aircraft, and satellites). For example, intercepting *telemetry*—communications sent to ground stations by missiles in flight—can yield important information or intelligence about operational characteristics of the missile. Verification is typically the first step; negotiating to assure *compliance* when violations have been discovered is the next step.

voluntarist, voluntarism   A philosophical position that reality is created by human will; that humans can affect, if not control, their destinies. In international relations, it generally means that decision makers have effective choice and are able to influence outcomes. *Social constructivism*, for example, can be understood as a voluntarist formulation to the extent that knowingly or otherwise it is human beings and their ideas that shape the institutions and processes that constitute international or world politics. (*See also* social constructivism.)

war, warfare, warfighting   War is organized armed conflict between or among states (*interstate war*) or within a given state or society (*civil war*). *Guerrilla warfare* is a type of war involving *irregular,* usually nonuniformed fighters; *guerrillas* may be associated with either civil or interstate wars. *Insurgency* is armed resistance to a government's authority.

weapons proliferation   The sale, transfer, or indigenous production of various types and classes of weapons. An example would be nuclear weapons. When states acquire larger and larger stockpiles of weapons, we refer to vertical proliferation; when weapons or weapons technologies (whether nuclear, biological, chemical, or "conventional") are transferred laterally to other countries, we refer to horizontal proliferation.

welfare issues   Socioeconomic, human rights, and other issues associated with improving the human condition.

welfare state   (*See* state.)

West   Generally the countries of North America, Western Europe and, paradoxically, Japan, because of its level of industrial development and its links to other advanced capitalist states. (*See also* East.)

Western European Union (WEU)   Security organization formed by European states in the 1948 Brussels pact. For security matters the WEU acts as agent for the European Union, the latter having decided gradually to absorb WEU defense functions in its own right.

world federalism   The goal of individuals favoring a world government that would have authority over constituent states. Some world federalists posit more modest goals such as achieving greater criminal and civil accountability before international courts, matters historically reserved to states.

world government   (*See* world federalism.)

world (or global) politics   The term favored by those who emphasize the multidimensional or pluralist nature of international relations today, which includes not simply states, but also a wide diversity of international and nongovernmental, transnational organizations, other groups, and individuals; not simply the physical security of the state, but also environmental, human rights, and demographic issues. (*See also* international politics; international relations.)

world system   Term associated with the work of Immanuel Wallerstein and his colleagues, focusing on capitalism as a world system, a perspective influenced by Marxist understandings of capitalism as a global system.

zero-sum   Concept in game theory that one side's gain amounts to the other's loss. *Variable sum* games allow both parties to gain or both to lose asymmetrically (by differing amounts); in *positive-sum* games, both parties win. One approach to conflicts is to transform them such that both (or all) parties see them as *positive-sum* games in which all may win. (*See also* game theory.)

PHOTO CREDITS

INDEX

Universal Postal Union (UPU), 201
Unrepresented Nations and Peoples Organization (UNPO), 425
Urbanization, world profile of, 317, 319
Ury, William, 134*n*
Usability paradox, 234
Utilitarianism, 453
Utility, 338

V

Value(s)
  capitalism and social, 301–3
  core, 75
  culturally specific, 449–51
  differences in commercial and political, 309–11
  labor theory of, 305
  in neoclassical economic theory, 338
  transcending diverse cultures, 451–72
    machinery for human rights issues and cases, 464–68
    NGOs and human rights, 470–72, 480
    regional human rights efforts, 468–70
    from theory to fact, 454–64
    in universal terms, 452–54
Value systems, economic capabilities and, 93
van Creveld, Martin, 151
Van Evera, Stephen, 426
Variables
  dependent, 13–14
  independent, 13
Vattel, Emmerich de, 56
Venice Declaration (1980), 137
Verification of compliance, 222–24
  national technical means (NTM) of, 223
Versailles Treaty, 114
Vichy regime in France, 116
Vienna Conventions on Diplomatic and Consular Relations (1961, 1963), 114, 289
Vietnam War, 111, 117, 163–64
Violence. *See also* Military force; Terrorism; War(s)
  attributes determining potential to produce, 426–27
  cultures of, 255
  structural, 385
Viotti, Paul R., 21*n*, 37*n*, 40*n*, 48*n*, 488*n*
Volatility of money, 343–45
Voltaire, 49
Voluntarist perspective on balance of power, 36
von Hardenberg of Prussia, Prince, 104

W

Waldrop, M. Mitchell, 483*n*
Wallenstein, Albrecht von, 30
Wallerstein, Immanuel, 296, 316–17
Walloons in Belgium, 416–17, 432
Walras, Leon, 338
Waltz, Kenneth N., 36, 144*n*
Waltzer, Michael, 167*n*
Wandrey, June, 141
Wang Qishan, 4
Wapner, Paul, 399*n*
War(s). *See also* Civil war; Military force
  in bipolar vs. multipolar system, 36
  casualties of, 142
  causes of, 144–49
    individual and group levels of analysis of, 146–47
    international system level of analysis of, 144–46
    state and societal levels of analysis of, 147–49
  Clausewitz on, 149–54
  diplomacy and prevention of, 106
  fog of, 154

gap between conception and execution of, 154
high tech vs. low tech future of, 151–52
Hobbes on, 55
IMF lending authorities for countries in, 357
interstate, 142–47, 163
legal approach to, 289–90
military necessity in, 149–50, 158
in modern European history, 61
nationalism and, 426–27
principles of, 150
as rational choice, 143–44
resource, 388–90
restraining, 154–62
  conduct during war, 157, 158–59
  just-war theory, 156–62
  noncombatants, 159–62
  pacifism and bellicism, 154–56
Thucydides on, 43
as zero-sum phenomenon, 154
War crimes trials, 292, 465–68
Warfare, 143
Warfighting, 232–33
  as active use of force for defense, 227
War of 1812, 77
War of the Spanish Succession (1701–14), 61
War on drugs, U.S., 274–77
War Prayer, The (Twain), 155–56
Warsaw Pact, 4, 185, 186
  NATO-Warsaw Pact force reduction talks (1973–1989), 133–34
Washington, George, 93
Wassenaar Arrangement (1996–97), 219, 244–46
  participation in, 245–46
Water, resource wars over, 389–90
Watson, Adam, 34*n*, 39*n*, 42*n*, 59*n*, 285
Watt, James, 311
Wealth of nation, productive capacity and, 302, 304
Wealth of Nations, The (Smith), 304–5
Weapons. *See also* Arms control; Nuclear weapons
  biological and chemical, 161, 217, 238–40
  high technology, 151
  immoral, 161
Weapons of mass destruction (WMD) terrorism, 258–60
Weapons production and stockpiling treaties, 217
Weapons proliferation, 234–46
  ballistic missiles, 240
  chemical and biological weapons, 238–40
  conventional weapons, 240–46
  defined, 234
  nuclear weapons and material, 235–38
Weber, Max, 301–3, 309
Web sites
  on arms control, 215
  on development and environment, 400
  on diplomacy, 124
  on disarmament, 215
  on economically oriented international organizations, 291
  on extremist groups and terrorism, 264
  on human rights, 470
  on international jurisprudence, 465
  on international organizations, 361
  for job and position information, 27
  on media, 23
  on membership organizations, 27
  of regional international organizations, 189
  on security and use of force, 169
  on world federalism, 289
Weekly news magazines, Web sites for, 23
Weiner, Myron, 473*n*
Welfare states, 309
Wendt, Alexander, 182, 288
Western European Union (WEU), 174, 177, 180, 186
White, Harry Dexter, 350
Wight, Martin, 37*n*, 285
Williams, Phil, 237*n*, 270*n*

Wilson, Woodrow, 145, 147, 190, 426
Win-win outcomes, guidelines for, 134–37
Wireless technology, 282
Woessner, Paul N., 237*n*
Wolfers, Arnold, 359
Women
  discrimination against, 442–43
  rape of, as war crime, 467
  trafficking in, 271
Woods, Ngaire, 321*n*
Working Peace System, A (Mitrany), 201
World Affairs Councils, 27
World Bank, 291, 313, 314, 351
  as source of capital, 372–78
World Conference on Human Rights (Vienna, 1993), 396, 479–80
World Court, 163, 192, 193, 464, 465
World federalism, 148–49, 183, 289, 487
World Federalist Association (WFAA), 289
World Order Models Project (WOMP), 293
World politics, international relations and, 26–28
World profile, global political, economic, and social indicators in, 315–19
World Summit for Children (New York, 1990), 396
World Summit for Social Development (Copenhagen, 1995), 396
World-system theory, 316–17
World Trade Center bombing, 253, 261
World Trade Organization (WTO), 291, 312
  protest against (1999), 10, 279–80, 358
World War I, 61, 64
  cause of, 145–46
  international monetary regime after, 349–50
  Versailles Treaty following, 114
World War II, 61, 64. *See also* Holocaust
  cataclysmic finale of, 114
  Germany's violations of sovereign rights to neutrality in, 115
  obliteration bombing of cities and population centers in, 158
World Wildlife Fund, 398

X

Xerxes, King, 41

Y

Yalta Conference, 65
Yeltsin, Boris, 233, 235
Yousef, Ramzi, 261
Yugoslavia. *See also* Bosnia; Kosovo, Serbian assault on
  Cyber Yugoslavia on Internet, 420
  diplomacy in, 108
  disintegration of, 417–19, 429
  distinction between civil war and interstate war in, 164
  NATO military action against, 18, 164, 444
  successor states to, 418

Z

Zapatista National Liberation Army (EZLN), 262
Zealots, 251
Zero-sum games
  getting-to-yes negotiations as, 134
  war as zero-sum phenomenon, 154
"Zero-zero option" in U.S.-Soviet arms negotiations, 133
Zionist movement, 414, 424, 427